Jewish Law from Jesus to the Mishnah

E. P. SANDERS

Jewish Law from Jesus to the Mishnah

Five Studies

SCM PRESS
London

TRINITY PRESS INTERNATIONAL
Philadelphia

First published 1990

SCM Press
26–30 Tottenham Road
London N1 4BZ

Trinity Press International
1725 Chestnut Street
Philadelphia, Pa. 19104

British Library Cataloguing in Publication data

Sanders, E. P. (Ed Parish) *1937–*
    Jewish law from Jesus to the Mishnah.
    1. Jewish law, history
    I. Title
    296.18

    ISBN 0–334–02455–2
    ISBN 0–334–02102–2 pbk

Library of Congress Cataloging-in-Publication Data

Sanders. E. P.
    Jewish law from Jesus to the Mishnah: five studies/E. P.
Sanders
        p.   cm.
    Includes bibliographical references.
        ISBN 0–334–02455–2. — ISBN 0–334–02102–2 (pbk.)
        1. Jewish law—History. 2. Judaism—History—Talmudic
period, 10–425. 3. Jesus Christ—Views on Jewish law.
4. Pharisees.
I. Title.
BM520.5.S25   1990
296.1'8'09015—dc20   90–33392

Typeset at The Spartan Press Ltd, Lymington, Hants
and printed in Great Britain by
The Camelot Press Ltd, Southampton

Contents

Preface

Three of the studies collected here were written on the way to completing what I hope will be a fairly short book on Jewish practice and belief – with the emphasis on practice – in the early Roman period (63 BCE to CE 66). Some topics – pharisaic oral traditions (ch. II), pharisaic purity laws (ch. III), and various aspects of Diaspora *praxis* (ch. IV) – required extended presentation of the primary evidence, since my views diverge rather sharply from those which currently prevail. I argue that the special pharisaic traditions did not have the same status as the written law, that the Pharisees did not eat ordinary food in priestly purity, and that in the Diaspora Jews went their own way with regard to food, purity and donations to the temple, rather than basing their behaviour on Palestinian rules. Their food laws were their own, their purity practices were distinctive, and their gifts to the temple were determined by their own reading of the scriptures in Greek.

The first study, 'The Synoptic Jesus and the Law', serves two functions. It surveys the passage on the Jewish law in the synoptic gospels which I did not discuss in detail in *Jesus and Judaism* (1985) and demonstrates that my earlier conclusions stand even if one accepts many more passages as 'authentic'. I have expanded the essay so that it will also serve as a primary introduction to numerous legal topics, many of which are taken up in greater detail in chs II–IV.

Chapters II and III deal extensively with two aspects of the work of Jacob Neusner. Chapter V, on his view of the 'philosophy' of the Mishnah, rounds off an assessment of his major proposals of the 1970s and early 1980s. Critical evaluation of Neusner's work is not abundant, for perfectly understandable reasons, among which are the volume and scope of his publications. It has taken me some years to decide just what to make of his work on the Pharisees and the Mishnah, and I hope that my assessment, though belated, will be of interest to other scholars. The importance of the topics demands careful study of his methods and conclusions.

The nature of the volume has required more repetitions than are aesthetically pleasing. Some of these arise from the overlap of ch. I with more detailed analyses in later chapters. In other cases, I have thought it useful to repeat explanations so that the studies need not be read in the order in which they are presented. I have given what I hope are adequate cross-references to indicate where the most thorough discussion of a given point may be found. The Index of Subjects can be used to supplement the cross-references.

None of these studies has been previously published. The original, much shorter version of 'The Synoptic Jesus and the Law' was given as the Manson Memorial Lecture at Manchester University in November 1987. It also served as the basis for papers or lectures at Cambridge University, Sheffield University, and Saint David's University College, Lampeter. Parts of chs III and V were read as a paper at an Oxford seminar sponsored by Geza Vermes. An earlier version of ch. IV.B (purity in the Diaspora) was presented at a seminar at the University of London which was sponsored by Judith Lieu and John North, and also at the Oxford Seminar on Religion in the Graeco-Roman World. Chapter IV.D (offerings to the Jerusalem temple from the Greek-speaking Diaspora) was given as a lecture at the Hebrew University in Jerusalem, at the invitation of Moshe David Herr. I am very grateful to those who made these opportunities available, and also to the numerous scholars who offered suggestions, most of which I have incorporated in some way or other. Several scholars did research on my behalf. I am especially indebted to Angus Bowie (Greek sacrifice), W. E. H. Cockle and Peter Parsons (offerings from the Diaspora), and Chaim Milikowsky (tithes).

In April 1989, I examined the remains of several synagogues and many more immersion pools in Israel. For advice on what to see and with whom, I am grateful to Lee I. Levine, and for on-site explanations to Meir Ben-Dov, Hanan Eshel, Tzvi Ma'oz, Mary June Nestler and Ronny Reich. Their generosity went far beyond the normal bounds of scholarly assistance.

My thanks also go to Therese Lysaught for the initial work on the index of names and passages, and to Margaret Davies and Rebecca Gray for assistance in their final preparation.

During the period in which I wrote these studies, I had the honour and support of a Fellowship from the John Simon Memorial Foundation. The British Academy provided a travel grant. I am very grateful to both institutions, and also to the University of Oxford for sabbatical leave.

Abbreviations

AB	Anchor Bible, New York
Albeck	Editor of Mishnah; see Bibliography 1.
ANRW	Aufstieg und Niedergang der römischen Welt, Berlin
Antiq.	Josephus, *Biblical Antiquities*
Apion	Josephus, *Against Apion*
Arist.	*Letter of Aristeas*
ARN	Aboth d'Rabbi Nathan
ARNA	Aboth d'Rabbi Nathan, recension A
BA	*Biblical Archaeologist*, Philadelphia
BASOR	*Bulletin of the American Schools of Oriental Research*
BCE	Before the Common Era (= BC)
BJS	Brown Judaic Studies, Chico, California, Atlanta, etc.
CD	*Covenant of Damascus* or *Zadokite Documents*; see Rabin, Bibliography 1.
CE	Common Era (= AD)
CRINT	Compendia Rerum Iudaicarum ad Novum Testamentum, Assen and Philadelphia
Danby	Translator of Mishnah; see Bibliography 1.
DJD	*Discoveries in the Judaean Desert*; see Bibliography 1.
Enc. Jud.	*Encyclopaedia Judaica*; see Bibliography 2.
ET	English translation
Heb.	Hebrew
HJP	*History of the Jewish People in the Age of Jesus Christ*; see Schürer, Bibliography 3.
IDB	*Interpreter's Dictionary of the Bible*; see Bibliography 2.
IEJ	*Israel Exploration Journal*
JAAR	*Journal of the American Academy of Religion*
JAOS	*Journal of the American Oriental Society*
J & J	*Jesus and Judaism*; see Sanders, Bibliography 3.
Jastrow	See Bibliography 2.
JB	Jerusalem Bible

JSJ	*Journal for the Study of Judaism*
Jub.	Jubilees
LCL	Loeb Classical Library, London and Cambridge, Massachusetts
Liddell and Scott	See Bibliography 2.
Life	Josephus, *The Life*
LXX	The Septuagint
NEB	New English Bible
OTP	*Old Testament Pseudepigrapha*, ed. Charlesworth; see Bibliography 1.
p.	Palestinian Talmud (Talmud Yerushalmi)
1QH	Hodayot: the Thanksgiving Hymns from Qumran
1QS	Serekh: the Community Rule from Qumran
1QSa	Serekh appendix A: the Messianic Rule from Qumran
4QMMT	Scroll of 'Some of the Precepts of the Torah' from Qumran
4Q503	Scroll of prayers from Qumran
11QTemple	The Temple Scroll from Qumran
Rabb. Trads.	*Rabbinic Traditions*; see Neusner, Bibliography 3.
RSR	*Religious Studies Review*, Waterloo, Ontario
RSV	Revised Standard Version
SJLA	Studies in Judaism in Late Antiquity, Leiden
S.P.-B	Studia Post-Biblica, Leiden
Sib. Or.	*Sibylline Oracles*
Spec. Laws	Philo, *Special Laws*
T.	Tosefta
TDNT	*Theological Dictionary of the New Testament*, Grand Rapids
War	Josephus, *The Jewish War*

Transliterations

There are three systems of transliterating Hebrew in the present work.

1. A fairly precise or scientific system for technical terms or portions of the Hebrew text of an ancient document. So, for example *t'rûmah, 'êrûb*; see the Glossary.

2. A simplified system used when Hebrew words are anglicized: terumah, eruv. The same system is used for the titles of tractates in the Tosefta and the Talmuds.

3. Danby's spelling is used when citing the Mishnah. The intention is to assist the reader in distinguishing the Mishnah from the Babylonian Talmud. The principal distinction is that the Mishnah is cited by chapter and mishnah, the Babylonian Talmud by folio and side:

Shabbath 1.2 = Mishnah tractate Shabbath chapter 1 mishnah 2

Shabbat 13a = Babylonian Talmud tractate Shabbat, folio 13 side a.

Glossary

'Amme ha—'arets	The ordinary people, neither Pharisees nor priests.
B^ekôrôt	Firstlings; see pp. 290; 365 n. 19.
Bikkûrîm	First produce; see pp. 290; 365 n. 19.
'êrûb, eruv	'Fusion' of houses; see pp. 8f.; 106f.
First fruits	An offering to the temple; see pp. 44f. and n. 3 (p. 336); 289f.; 365 n. 19.
Ḥaber, haver (pl. –im)	Associate(s) see p. 152.
Halakah, halakah	A rule governing behaviour; see pp. 32; 117.
Hasmoneans	Members of the family which led the Jewish revolt against the Seleucid kingdom in Syria, and their descendants.
Heave offering	See *t^erûmah* below.
K^elî, keli (pl. –im)	Vessel or utensil; see pp. 203; 353 n. 2.
Mezuzah (pl. *–ot*)	Container of biblical passages which is attached to a doorpost; see pp. 71f.
Miqveh, miqva'ot	Immersion pool(s); see pp. 214–217.
'Ôtsar	'Treasury'; storage pool beside miqveh; see p. 218.
Rē'shît	First fruits; see pp. 290; 365 n. 19.
Septuagint (abbrev. LXX)	Greek translation of the Hebrew Bible ('Old Testament').
S^etam, stam	Anonymous opinion; see p. 167.
Sh^ema'	'Hear [O Israel]': Deut. 6.4–9; see p. 68.
T^ebûl yôm, tevul yom	A person who has immersed, but upon whom the sun has not set, considered by the Pharisees to be half-pure; see pp. 149f.; 251 (*n*).
Tefillin	Containers of biblical passages which are attached to the head and arm; pp. 71f.
T^erûmah	Heave offering; see pp. 290; 299; 365 n. 19.
Zab, Zabah, zav, zavah	A man or woman with a genital discharge; see p. 138.
Zibah	The state of having such a discharge; see pp. 210f.

The Synoptic Jesus and the Law

Conflicts and agreements in comparison with other
contemporary debates

A. INTRODUCTION

§1. In the pages that follow I shall discuss the points of Jewish law which appear in the synoptic gospels. In most of the passages Jesus is in conflict with others, though in some instances he is in agreement. The aim of this study is to describe the range of opinion in first-century Judaism about the law in question, and especially to note debates about it, so that we shall have grounds for saying, 'this was a very serious conflict' or 'this disagreement is relatively insubstantial'.

For the purpose of this study I shall for the most part work on the basis of two assumptions which I do not actually hold: that all the material which is attributed to Jesus in fact goes back to him, and that he was a Rabbi who studied the law and intended to stake out his own position on numerous aspects of it.

In *Jesus and Judaism* I brushed aside the disputes about sabbath, purity and food as being probably inauthentic, and I have not changed my mind. Some of the sayings within the passages may well be authentic, but the settings are contrived: Pharisees following Jesus and his disciples through grain fields on the sabbath, or making a special trip from Jerusalem to Galilee to check on whether or not his disciples washed their hands (Mark 2.23–24; 7.1–2). Scholars seem still not to see how determinative of meaning the setting is; but once the setting is seen to be 'ideal' – that is, in Bultmann's terms, both symbolic and imaginary – our ability to establish the meaning of the saying with precision vanishes.[1] Further, sabbath and food were major points of debate in the early church, which makes it unlikely that Jesus had directly opposed observance of these laws. In the minds of many, however, the argument of smoke and fire remains compelling: since sabbath is mentioned so frequently as a point of debate, Jesus must have had some sort of dispute with the Pharisees over it. Without being persuaded by this argument, I feel its force, and I see why it does persuade some. They then, however, proceed to what I consider a worse historical judgment: they think that these conflicts led to Jesus' death, or at least played an important role in the growth of animosity which resulted in it. That judgment is based in part on the assumption that the Pharisees rigidly controlled first-century Palestine and could enforce compliance with their interpretation of the law, and in part on lack of knowledge of the range of legal debate. I shall not discuss in this chapter the question of pharisaic control,[2] but shall attempt to make a contribution only on the last point: the range of disagreement over various aspects of the law. I shall ask, *Even* on the assumption that this debate is authentic, is it a substantial one, or relatively trivial?

At various points I shall drop the pretence that the passages are verbatim records of disputes from the lifetime of Jesus, and in one or two cases I offer a sketch of a historical reconstruction. These instances are intended to encourage the reader to consider various possibilities with regard to the historical Jesus and to serve as a reminder of the difference between synoptic exegesis and historical assessment.

In surveying each point, I shall deal almost exclusively with primary material. Scholarship has long been divided between the view that conflict with the Pharisees over the law was a cardinal element in the hostility which led to Jesus' death, and the opposite: that such conflicts were minor and would not have been seriously regarded. It is noteworthy that Christian scholars have become increasingly confident of the first view, while Jewish scholars for several generations have held the opposite view. Eduard Schweizer, for example, proposed that

> there can be no doubt that Jesus, through his entire conduct, again and again ostentatiously transgressed the Old Testament commandment to observe the Sabbath and had little concern for the Old Testament laws relating to ritual purity.[3]

Many other scholars, such as Geza Vermes, have found no instances in which Jesus broke a biblical commandment, though he clashed with others over 'customs'.[4] It is not difficult to judge between these positions: Schweizer's is without foundation, Vermes' is hard to fault. A major biblical purity law which figures in the synoptics is that governing leprosy, and here Jesus acts in general conformity with the law (Mark 1.40–44). One suspects that Schweizer shares the common failing of not knowing what the biblical purity laws are, much less how they were developed and modified in various parts of first-century Judaism.

My concern, however, is not to referee between contending scholars, but to get to the nitty-gritty of first-century debates about individual points of law. What sorts of things did others argue about, and what range of disagreement was tolerated? When we turn to the synoptic passages, one may imagine a range of scholarly opinion, some holding that the conflict led to mortal enmity, some that it was not very serious, some that it was serious but not fatal.

The primary evidence surveyed often includes the Greek-speaking Diaspora, though I have canvassed Diaspora material less thoroughly than Palestinian. There are two reasons for including the Diaspora in a discussion of the synoptic Jesus and the law. One is simply that I wish this study to provide a survey of numerous points of law and to serve as an introduction to the more detailed treatment of difficult aspects in chapters II–IV. The second is that some or all of the gospels were written in the Diaspora. The pretence that the synoptic debates are 'authentic' is not so thorough that I wish to ignore information which may be relevant to the context in which the gospels were written.

The discussion of a series of legal points may make it sound as if Jesus was a teacher of the law. It has often been proposed that we should think of him as a 'Rabbi', one who studied the law, considered the parties' positions on it, gathered disciples, and taught them his own view on the points then under debate. This, it seems to me, leads us astray. For one thing, 'Rabbi' was an occupation which, as such, did not lead to death in first-century Judaism. Yes, I know that some ideas are perceived as dangerous to society, but the entirety of our evidence for first-century Palestine indicates that ideas led to death only if they inspired someone to hostile action in public or aroused 'the crowds' too much. The probably pharisaic teachers, Matthias and Judas, who, about 4 BCE, taught the young that death in defence of the law was noble, were executed only because finally they inspired their students to tear down the golden eagle which Herod had put up over the entrance to the temple (Josephus, *War* 1.648–655; *Antiq.* 17.149–167).[5] Teaching them not to divorce would not have had the same result – revolutionary though that idea is (see further pp. 84–89 below).

Jesus is better seen as a charismatic – either (with Vermes) a charismatic healer like Hanina ben Dosa and Honi the Circle-Drawer or (with Hengel, Theissen and others) a charismatic prophet.[6] I incline to the second view,[7] but in either case the important point is that a charismatic does not set out to take a stance on a series of legal questions, though he may bump up against them now and then. It is in theory possible that a charismatic might stumble into serious questions about the law, and into quite serious offences against it, though I know of no evidence that this happened in Jesus' case. I do not, however, wish to anticipate the discussion which follows, but at this point only to warn the reader that the present discussion, in which one legal point after another is taken up, may make it sound as if Jesus worked his way through the law in just this way, which I would regard as being a misleading depiction of him.

In addition to these caveats, I should point out a substantial limitation of the present study. Although the gospels agree in presenting Jesus as in fairly active and serious conflict with his contemporaries, especially with the Pharisees, over the law, each gospel has its own way of both highlighting and nuancing these conflicts, and a full account would have to treat each gospel separately. I shall not attempt a redactional study of the role of the disputes in each gospel, but rather I shall deal with individual passages as posing actual or possible disputes between the historical Jesus and Jewish legal experts of his day. Those which appear in the triple tradition I shall usually consider in their Markan form.

§2. I do not wish to presuppose that the reader of this essay has read my book *Jesus and Judaism*, but I also do not wish to repeat at length what I wrote there. I shall here very briefly summarize the main points with regard to the law, and also include them in the conclusion. A more detailed discussion of Divorce, Burying the Dead and Associating with Sinners will be found in *J & J*.

We noted above that many scholars regard the disputes over the law as serious and important, while a few hold that they were relatively minor. I joined the minority and argued that most of the conflicts are historically dubious and that, even if authentic, they would not have been serious. Thus they fell out of consideration, since two of the main points of the book were to deal only with 'bedrock' and to search for serious conflicts.

Three points, however, I did take to be part of the bedrock information about Jesus: the prohibition of divorce, the accusation of associating with sinners, and the command to one would-be disciple to 'let the dead bury the dead' in order to follow the master.

(*a*) I proposed that the association with sinners (e.g. Matt. 11.19) was fairly (not very) serious, provided that the conflict is correctly understood: Jesus offered the kingdom to those who were outside the law, even though they remained outside, rather than repenting and becoming observant (*J & J*, ch. 6). In this context, by 'repenting' I meant 'repenting in the prescribed way', and by 'becoming observant' I meant 'becoming observant of the law' (esp. pp. 203, 206).

(*b*) The command to the prospective disciple to leave his dead father (Matt. 8.21f. and par.) was in direct conflict with the commandment to honour father and mother, but it seems to have been a one-time-only requirement, at least as a specific demand. There is other anti-family material in the synoptics (Matt. 10.35–37 and par.; Mark 3.31–35 and parr.; Mark 13.12

and parr.), but it does not give the impression that Jesus studied the laws on family relationships (e.g. Deut. 21.18–21) and decided to oppose them. The passage on the burial of the father shows, rather, that he was prepared in one instance to put following him above observance of one of the ten commandments (pp. 252–255).

(*c*) The prohibition of divorce, especially the long form (Matt. 19.3–9// Mark 10.2–9) is radical in a way similar to the *Covenant of Damascus*, where divorce is also prohibited (a parallel which has often been noted), but it is not against the law, since staying married is not a transgression: the person who remains married will never transgress Deut. 24.1–4. Jesus' prohibition implies that the Mosaic code is not strict enough, and thus that it is not wholly adequate, at least for the time which he envisaged (pp. 256–260). That time was 'the eschatological period', which he seems to have conceived vaguely as 'other-worldly' in that God would bring it to pass miraculously, but 'this-worldly' in that it would have a recognizable social order. (On this form of future expectation, see *J & J*, pp. 228–237.)

§3. Only one other preliminary point needs to be made: In this discussion I shall consider as pharisaic the rabbinic passages which Jacob Neusner assigned to the Pharisees in *The Rabbinic Traditions about the Pharisees before 70* (1971), and for the most part I shall cite only those which are in the Mishnah. The majority of these passages are discussions between the 'Schools' or 'Houses' of Hillel and Shammai: not Hillel and Shammai themselves, but their followers, one or even two generations later. That is, some of the Houses passages are post-70, but probably from the generation of scholars born before 70, and presumably representative of pre-70 discussions. The dating and use of these are discussed in ch. III below, as is the question of whether or not the earliest rabbinic passages represent the Pharisees rather than some nameless group.[8] I shall make no effort to date the passages more precisely. The ones used here have been culled from Neusner's *Rabbinic Traditions*, but I have compared the discussions in his later *History of the Mishnaic Law*. It is possible that we should include more passages or fewer, but at present this restriction of material is the best available. When post-pharisaic rabbinic passages are cited, the purpose is either to ask what they reveal about earlier practice or to show continuity with earlier evidence.

We turn now to successive points of law, beginning with legal practices which were of most importance within first-century Judaism in general. All the laws were in theory on the same plane of importance, since they were all given by God,[9] but it is nevertheless possible to single some out as standing at the head of the list. Since keeping or transgressing the law is mostly a question of action or inaction, those laws are in some sense most important which cover frequent activities. Further, some laws cover behaviour which is readily observable, and these serve as identity markers: acting in a certain way shows that one is pious and sometimes points to a sub-category of piety, such as Pharisaism. The definition of importance will of course vary from time to time and group to group, and I do not want to make too much of the sequence in which topics are discussed. I have tried, however, to give most attention to the most contentious issues and those which would stand high if one wished to evaluate Jesus' overall obedience or disobedience.

To repeat the point of the exercise: I wish to compare the synoptic passages which involve the law (except for those mentioned in §2) with discussions of the same legal point in more-or-less contemporary literature, and I shall focus especially on disputes either between other Jewish groups or within them. This should allow us to test the question of whether the synoptic debates are trivial or substantial, an issue on which people have often taken sides without the advantage of a detailed comparison with other disputes.

B. SABBATH

§1. In the post-biblical period, both insiders and outsiders singled out observance of the sabbath as one of the most striking aspects of standard Jewish practice. It figures large in pagan and Christian comments on the Jews,[1] and it is a major topic in Jewish literature. The general requirement to keep the sabbath as a day of rest is one of the ten commandments (Ex. 20.8–11; Deut. 5.12–15). Both lists apply the commandment not only to Israelites (adult males and, in this case, females) but also to children, servants, foreigners and animals. Short forms of the sabbath requirement appear in Ex. 34.21 and Lev. 19.3. There is a lengthy reiteration in Ex. 31.12–17, which stipulates execution and 'cutting off' as the penalty for transgression. Numbers 15.32–36 introduces as a law previously unknown the penalty of stoning for deliberate transgression.

Most passages in the Pentateuch simply prohibit 'work' but there are some specifications. Exodus 34.21 explicitly requires that the day of rest be kept during plowing time and harvest, thus ruling out the appeal to the pressure of work to justify non-observance. Gathering food, cooking and making a fire are prohibited in Ex. 16; 35.2f. On the other hand, one form of work is required: the sabbath offerings (Num. 28.9). Jeremiah opposed bearing a burden through the gates of Jerusalem or even carrying it out of one's own house on the sabbath (Jer. 17.19–27).

'Work' requires a good deal more definition. One could imagine a society of stock brokers in which reading the paper was considered work (since it might contain news relevant to investments), but digging up dandelions was not. Or the reverse, in a society of gardeners. Ancient society did not pose as many such problems as would modern society, but there were some. The need of definition is clear in Nehemiah, where there are several new restrictions. According to Neh. 10.31 [Heb. v.32] the Israelites pledged themselves not to buy things from Gentiles on the sabbath, as well as to let the land lie fallow and not to claim debts in the seventh year. Nehemiah 13.15–22 narrates the governor's strong measures to prevent trading on the sabbath, both by Jews and Gentiles. To do this he shut the gates of Jerusalem and posted Levites as guards.

Later in the second temple period there are further signs of a tendency – possibly sporadic – to heighten the sabbath law by extending the domain of 'work'. The most famous story comes from the early days of the Maccabaean revolt. Many of the pious were killed because they would not defend themselves when attacked on the sabbath. This comes as a surprise, since the sabbath seems not to have interfered with Jewish warfare during the pre-exilic period. The story probably reflects how the sabbath law had grown in force and scope during the peaceful years of the Persian period and the Hellenistic monarchies – peaceful, that is, for the Jews. The result of this superb display of obedience to the sabbath, and its tragic consequence, was a resolution to fight in self-defence, but not otherwise (I Macc. 2.29–41).

Josephus' stories about keeping the sabbath seem to be less well known. They show that both during the years of independence and in the Roman period the sabbath was generally observed very strictly and that the resolution to fight only in self-defence characterized not only the specially pious, but most Jews.

An early Hasmonean, John Hyrcanus (135–104 BCE), broke off an important siege because of the coming of the sabbath year (*War* 1.157–160). In 63 BCE, when the Roman general Pompey had hemmed up the Jewish defenders in Jerusalem, he took advantage of Jewish adherence to the law by raising earthworks on the sabbath, while refraining from firing missiles. The Jews could have responded to missiles, a direct attack, but not to the building of earthworks. Josephus explains that 'the Jews fight only in self-defence', which they interpreted to mean only when directly attacked. The consequence was that the Roman battering rams could be brought into service in perfect safety (*War* 1.145–147). During the siege the temple area was controlled by the followers of Aristobulus II, while his brother Hyrcanus II and his supporters occupied the rest of the city. Both Jewish factions seem to have kept the same sabbath law. We cannot consider that they were all super pious. Aristobulus II, for example, was a friend of 'the eminent', not of the Pharisees (*Antiq.* 13.411). When his supporters refused to attack the Romans on the sabbath they were simply following standard Jewish law.

That strict observance of the sabbath was the rule is, finally, proved by the fact that Rome recognized that sabbath law kept Jews from serving in the imperial armies (*Antiq.* 14.237; earlier see *Antiq.* 13.252). It accords with this that Julius Caesar exempted Judaea from tribute in the seventh year (*Antiq.* 14.202). All the laws governing days, years and seasons seem to have been faithfully kept. The prosbul, which is attributed to Hillel, also presupposes that the sabbath years were kept.[2]

§2. Although standard Jewish observance of the sabbath was very high, pious groups elaborated the sabbath laws and made them stricter yet. According to Josephus the Essenes would not light a fire, remove a vessel 'or even go to stool' (*War* 2.147).[3] The *Covenant of Damascus*, which speaks for a group of town-dwelling and non-celibate Essenes, contains a long list of sabbath laws (CD 10.14–11.18), which are neatly summarized by Vermes: the sectarian sabbath began early, 'when the sun's orb is distant by its own fullness from the gate' behind which it would set. Not only was the conduct of business forbidden, so was speaking about work. One should not walk more than 1,000 cubits from home (approx. 500 yards or 450 metres), edible fruit and other food could not be picked up, water could not be carried, a beast could not be struck, servants could not carry children, perfume could not be worn – and so on. Perhaps most striking, CD stipulates that if an animal gave birth in such a way that the offspring dropped into a cistern or pit, it could not be lifted out.[4] In view of pharisaic debates (see below), it is instructive to note that the *Covenant of Damascus* prohibits any sacrifice on the sabbath except the sabbath offering (CD 11.17–18). That is, when a festival fell on the sabbath, only the sabbath offerings were to be sacrificed, not the festival offerings as well.

We can seldom comment directly on Sadducean practice, but in the present case there is some evidence. We noted above that Aristobulus II was the friend of the 'eminent'; these probably included Sadducees, and we must assume that they shared the common view that fighting on the sabbath must be limited to defence against direct assault. A passage in the Mishnah points towards Sadducean strictness in observing the sabbath law. One of the pharisaic 'traditions' got around some of the anti-social consequences of a strict application of the law. Jeremiah, we noted above, forbade vessels to be carried out of one's house on the sabbath. The Pharisees decided that the construction of doorposts and lintels at the entrances to alleys or courtyards allowed all the houses in the alley or court to become one house, and thus vessels could be carried within the entire area.[5] This 'fusion' or 'interweaving' ('êrûb) of houses permitted communal dining on the sabbath (Erubin 6.6). The Mishnah relates a story by Rabban Gammaliel II about his father, Simeon b. Gamaliel, who was active in the middle of the first century. A Sadducee lived in the same alley, and Simeon b. Gamaliel told his family to put their vessels into the alley before the Sadducee put his there, which would prevent their using it. That is, Sadducees did not agree with the pharisaic tradition about 'eruv, and they could prevent Pharisees from making use of it in alleys which they shared (see the general rule to this effect in Erubin 6.1). There are reasons to think that the story has been misattributed,[6] but there is no reason to doubt the substantial point. Sadducees believed in upholding the written law, they opposed pharisaic traditions which got around it, and they must have regarded most Pharisees as transgressors of the sabbath law.

In other ways the Pharisees elaborated sabbath observance. The Mishnah tractate Shabbath contains numerous prohibitions which are extra-biblical, such as giving Gentiles work which they cannot finish before the sabbath begins (since the Jew would then be encouraging work on the sabbath) (Shabbath 1.8, the House of Shammai). There were debates between the House of Shammai and the House of Hillel over whether or not work which had been set in train before the sabbath could proceed if no further human effort was required:

> The House of Shammai say: Bundles of flax may not be put in an oven unless there is time for them to steam off the same day; nor may wool be put into a [dyer's] cauldron unless there is time for it to absorb the colour the same day. And the House of Hillel permit it. The House of Shammai say: Nets may not be spread for wild animals, birds, or fishes unless there is time for them to be caught the same day. And the House of Hillel permit it. (Shabbath 1.6)

The Mishnah does not attribute to Pharisees or to the Houses of Hillel and Shammai many passages on the sabbath itself, but light is thrown on our question – the range of disagreement – by consideration of the numerous surviving discussions of 'festival days', which were in part governed by sabbath law. During the festivals and the public fast, the Day of Atonement, there are six days which, according to the Bible, are to be treated like sabbaths, with one exception: work involved in the preparation of food to be eaten that day is permitted (Lev. 23; Ex. 12.16). The dual nature of the festival days made them the subject of numerous legal rulings. Thus, for example, it was debated whether or not one could move a ladder in order to bring down a dove from the dovecote when the menu called for fowl (Betzah 1.3). The work involved in carrying, slaughtering, plucking and cutting up the dove was accepted without comment as being obviously required, but moving the ladder was a contentious issue. It could have been done the day before. According to T. Yom Tov 1.8 the Houses agreed that the ladder could be moved to the dovecote, but disagreed over whether it could be returned to its original place. The question was, What work is strictly required for the day's food?

The debate on which there are more surviving pharisaic opinions than on any other also concerns a festival day: whether or not one could lay one's hands on the head of a sacrificial animal on such a day (Hagigah 2.2–3; Betzah 2.4; important variants in Betzah 19a–b).

These discussions may sound nit-picking, but in fact they are quite important. Observing the sabbath day is one of the ten commandments, and faithful Jews naturally wanted to know just what could and could not be done. This was also the case with regard to festival days, since the Bible itself extends to them the prohibition of most forms of work (e.g. Lev. 23.23–25). The issue of laying hands on the head of a sacrificial animal was also important. The Bible, again, requires it (e.g. for the whole-burnt offering, Lev. 1.14; for the peace offering, Lev. 3.2,8,13). Further, this was a problem which actually arose. Most Jews came to Jerusalem only occasionally, and most trips fell during one of the three pilgrimage festivals (Passover, Weeks and Tabernacles, Deut. 16.16). Two of the festival days fall in Passover (Ex. 12.16; Lev. 23.7–8), one during Weeks (Lev. 23.21) and two during Tabernacles (Lev. 23.35–36). (The sixth 'festival day', in this case better called a 'fast day', is the Day of Atonement: Lev. 23.28–32). Pilgrims who came to Jerusalem for one of the festivals naturally wanted to make one trip serve many purposes. Each family might wish to offer several sacrifices: for childbirth, for other purifications, for transgression, or for celebration (the peace offering). They therefore needed to know whether or not they could offer one or more of their sacrifices on a festival day. Sacrifices involved 'work', since the animal's head was pushed down, and one had to know whether or not such work broke the law.

In the case of the Pharisees and sacrifices on festival days, the House of Shammai ruled that peace offerings could be brought, but without the laying on of hands, while whole-burnt offerings could not be brought. The House of Hillel accepted both offerings and allowed hands to be laid on in both cases (Hag. 2.3; Betzah 2.4).[7] These two sacrifices were singled out for discussion because on a festival day the work which is permitted is that which supplies food for that day. Peace offerings are called 'communion sacrifices' in the Jerusalem Bible and 'shared offerings' in the New English Bible, quite appropriately, since the basic idea was that offerer, priest and altar all participated in consuming the sacrifice. The blood and the fat went to the altar, the breast and one thigh to the priest, and the rest of the meat could be taken out of the temple by the person who brought the sacrifice, who could feast on it along with family and friends. In most of the sub-categories of the peace offering, however, the food was allowed to be eaten over a two-day period (Lev. 7.12–36). Private whole-burnt offerings, on the other hand, were brought to atone for transgression (Lev. 1.4), and none of the animal served as food.

Both the Shammaites and the Hillelites wished to keep the letter and the spirit of the biblical law. The law expects that sacrifices be brought, requires them in some cases, and specifies that hands be laid on the head of the animal. The law also prohibits work on the sabbath and on festival days (except for the preparation of food). It appears that the Shammaites thought that the law prohibiting work should prevail in case of conflict. The Tosefta assigns a series of analogical arguments to the Houses. The Hillelites' preferred analogy is with the sabbath day itself. Since on the sabbath, when one cannot prepare food for a human, one can nevertheless prepare food for God (the official sabbath sacrifices), then surely on a festival day, when one can prepare food for a human (if it is eaten that day), one can also prepare food for God (T. Hagigah 2.10). This seems not entirely to prove the case for laying hands on peace offerings, but it is a good example of arguments from legal analogies. At stake throughout is the question of which law should prevail in case of conflict. We cannot know whether non-exegetical, humane reasons lie behind the arguments from scripture. Possibly the Hillelites had in mind the fact that for some pilgrims it was a case of sacrificing on a festival day or not at all.

Since the Houses debated offerings on festival days, they must have agreed that on the sabbath individuals could not bring sacrifices. This is presupposed in a discussion between Rabbis Joshua and Eliezer in Pesahim 6.5 (cf. 6.3), but in rabbinic literature it is never debated and (as far as I have noted) seldom mentioned. The absence of debates reveals consensus: sacrificing is work, therefore one does not sacrifice on the sabbath, except for the priests, who are specifically required to sacrifice the daily whole-burnt offerings and the additional sabbath offerings.[8] It is noteworthy that in Matt. 12.5 Jesus' defence of plucking grain on the sabbath is that priests work on the sabbath, not individuals who bring offerings. Because CD and rabbinic literature alike simply assume that individuals did not present sacrifices on the sabbath, and the same inference is derived from Matthew, I would guess that no one disagreed.

Pharisees probably, however, disagreed with the Damascus covenanters about what happened when festivals and the sabbath overlapped, since the Bible requires the priests to offer sacrifices on both occasions. CD, we saw above (p. 8), would forbid festival sacrifices on the sabbath. The Rabbis later would argue that required festival sacrifices 'override' the sabbath, and that both should be offered when the days overlapped;[9] probably the Pharisees thought the same.

In both of our pharisaic examples (passively allowing work to be completed on the sabbath; sacrificing on festival days), one wing of the pharisaic party must have thought that the others were breaking one of the laws requiring rest. The Hillelites may well have thought that some of the Shammaites' peace offerings – those offered on a festival day – were invalid, since hands were not laid on the animals' heads as the Bible requires, or were not laid on at the time of the sacrifice, which is what Lev. 3.2 seems to require. The Shammaites presumably thought that some of the Hillelites' offerings for atonement were invalid, since they permitted themselves to bring these sacrifices on days when, in the Shammaites' view, they were prohibited. In short, the two parties could have accused each other of malpractice (offering invalid sacrifices), and the Shammaites could accuse the Hillelites of transgression (working on festival days).

One of the questions which is important for our study is whether or not the pietist groups tried to force others to follow their rules when they were stricter than those of the Bible. The *Covenant of Damascus*, in prohibiting any sacrifices on the sabbath except those specifically required as sabbath offerings by the Bible, might be addressing the priests: you should not offer festival sacrifices on the sabbath. The pharisaic debates about festival offerings clearly have the more modest goal of instructing members. Neither House pretends to tell the priests what to do; they are debating among themselves what sacrifices are correct for their own constituents and what may be done on festival days. We should not imagine the Pharisees banding together across the steps leading up to the temple every festival day, intent on turning back people who wished to offer private sacrifices. As we shall see below (p. 87), some Shammaites are said to have glared menacingly at Hillel because he was sacrificing on a festival day, but there is no indication that the Pharisees tried to impose their own rules on others – especially since there were serious internal disputes about numerous important issues.

The average Jew, of course, would bring sacrifices according to family tradition, and if there was a question of legality the natural step would be to look around: if the priests were accepting sacrifices, presumably they were legal! One of the points of being an Essene or a Pharisee, however, was to have one's own set of interpretations.

In view of the synoptic disputes, we should consider the questions of eating in the field and healing minor ailments. The normal supposition about food on the sabbath was that it was prepared the day before and eaten on the sabbath without further preparation. The work involved in picking up dishes, moving the food to one's mouth etc. was accepted. CD explicitly prohibits eating what had not been previously prepared, including what was found lying in the field (CD 10.22f.). At some unspecified date 'the sages' rebuked the people of Jericho who picked up fruit on the sabbath (Pesahim 4.8). We may infer that many Jews would be willing to pick up and eat raw fruit. The sabbath rules in CD are formulated precisely to be stricter than those which prevailed generally; the practice of the people of Jericho may have been common. 'Picking up', of course, is not the same as 'plucking'. CD does not prohibit 'plucking', probably because it was generally recognized to be forbidden work.

There is, however, a rule which could cut the other way: one should not fast on the sabbath. This was the view of all. Josephus describes a very important meeting in the prayer house in Tiberias, held to discuss who their leaders in the revolt should be, which broke up at the sixth hour (*c.* 12.00 or 1.00 p.m.) because it was the time of the sabbath meal (*Life* 279). Judith, who fasted 'all the days of her widowhood', did not fast on Friday or Saturday (Judith 8.6). Even direst necessity would not move the Rabbis to fast on the sabbath (Taanith 1.6; see I.K below).

Both CD and the Mishnah and Tosefta generally oppose minor cures on the sabbath (CD 11.10; Shabbath 14.3f.; T. Shabbat 12.8–14). So many particulars are debated in rabbinic literature that we may assume that the understanding 'no minor cures' is early, probably pharisaic. The discussions pay some attention to ways of getting around the general ban. One may not put water on a sponge and then place the sponge on a wound, but one may wash one's feet with the sponge under them, and so allow it to become moist, and then place it on the wound (T. Shabbat 12.14). Similarly one may not suck vinegar through one's teeth to cure toothache, but one may take vinegar on one's food and hope for the best (Shabbath 14.4).

The implied definition, 'practising medicine is work', and the implied rule, 'no minor cures on the sabbath', are tough, but the application is more humane. We should recall that these are the discussions of the strict, and we may suppose that most people would be more tolerant of minor cures.

A threat to life, of course, was another matter entirely. If one could shed blood on the sabbath in self-defence, one could certainly bind up a serious wound. The discussions of wearing medication in CD and of minor cures in rabbinic literature imply that work in case of more serious danger or illness would not be challenged. The explicit rule, 'whenever there is doubt whether life is in danger this overrides the Sabbath' is attributed to R. Mattithiah b. Heresh (early second century) in Yoma 8.6, but from the days of the Hasmonean wars this would have been the common understanding.

Interlude: assessing importance

Above I wrote that we would consider legal issues in the order of their importance in first-century Judaism. Now that we have seen some examples of debates about sabbath and festival law, especially in the two principal pietist groups, the Essenes and the Pharisees, we should return to the question of how one knows what was most important. Neusner has considered this question with regard to the Pharisees and has responded: Count and measure. The most important things are those which appear most frequently and which get the most space. Following this logic, he counted the presumably pharisaic passages in rabbinic literature, found that 67% had to do with the 'sect's' own food laws, and concluded that the pre-70 Pharisees were basically a 'pure food club', a group of laymen who were principally concerned to handle and eat ordinary food in a priestly state of purity.

We shall take up this issue below (ch. III), and I shall show elaborately that Neusner misdescribed the passages which he collected and, consequently, miscounted them. We shall also consider more fully the problems of counting to determine importance. With regard to sabbath law, however, something must be said about counting.

The first point is that, if one correctly described and then recounted Neusner's passages, the largest number of traditions would be seen to be on Work – on the sabbath, during the sabbatical year, and on festival days.

The second point is that counting can be misleading, though I am not entirely against it. The count is sometimes interesting, and in any case it makes one seek explanations. There are, for example, very few pharisaic disputes in the entire order Nezikin, which means that the large part of the Mishnah which deals with civil and family law (almost one-sixth) contains very little pharisaic material. Neusner interprets this as showing that the Pharisees neither controlled nor wanted to control the apparatus of civil law. I agree that they did not control it, but I take the small number of passages to show that they did not feel called upon to make rulings for themselves which required a standard of conduct which was appreciably different from the one normally expected. I would not infer from the small number of debates that the Pharisees did not care about society (as does Neusner[10]), but rather that they did not need a sub-set of civil laws. They may have agreed whole-heartedly with the common civil law of the day, and praised it morning and night.

Let us apply this reasoning to the topic of the sabbath. Although in the present Mishnah the tractate Shabbath is very large, the topic of the seventh day itself occupies very few of the pharisaic debates. My reckoning of the Mishnah's pharisaic passages on Work is this:

Shabbath (the seventh day)	7
Shebiith (the seventh year)	7
Erubin (sabbath limits for carrying etc.)	2
Betzah (festival days)	21

It is not reasonable to think that, since festival days have three times the number of discussions as does the sabbath day itself, festival days were much more important to the Pharisees. The topic, rather, is more intricate (since festival days are partly like the sabbath and partly not), and there was probably less agreement about practice on festival days than on the sabbath. The sabbath day comes once a week, and observing it is routine. The Pharisees (as Neusner sometimes says) must have had a complete repertoire of habitual observances which were not in dispute.[11] The most basic and obvious points are not in the Mishnah, such as 'do not perform your usual job on the sabbath'. Since such points were not controverted, they did not make it into the Mishnah, because the Mishnah is a collection of legal and semi-legal debates. As I show fully in the final chapter of this volume, mistaking the Mishnah to be a work of systematic philosophy, which says, with each emphasis nicely judged, precisely what the authors thought to be important (or, rather, says it in code), is fundamental to Neusner's misinterpretation of the Pharisees and the Rabbis.

The point can be made even more starkly by comparing the *Covenant of Damascus* (CD) and the Qumran *Community Rule* (1QS). We saw above that the group represented by CD was extremely strict about the sabbath – far stricter than the Pharisees appear to have been – and that there are numerous sabbath rules in the document. CD represents a branch of the Essene party, a branch which permitted marriage, taking sacrifices to the temple, and having private property. The Qumran sect proper appears to have been monastic, to have shunned the temple entirely (because an incorrectly designed building was being used by a false and wicked priesthood to present invalid sacrifices according to an erroneous calendar), and to have practised a form of communism. Both CD and 1QS are law codes or manuals, and the group behind 1QS was much stricter than that behind CD. We would, then, expect there to be extremely strict sabbath rules in 1QS. It turns out, however, that there are none at all.

What can it mean? On the basis of Neusner's assumptions, one would say that the Qumran sectarians, or at least the authors of 1QS, cared nothing at all for the sabbath, and that their most important statement about it was that it does not deserve a single line: they neither kept it nor thought about it.[12] But this cannot be correct. We may reason *qal vaḥomer* (*a fortiori*): if the CD community, the less fanatical, multiplied sabbath laws, all the more did the

1QS community, the more fanatical. Then why are they not mentioned? 1QS presupposes the entirety of the biblical law. One finds in it neither the commandment not to kill nor the prohibition of pork. Further, it seems even to presuppose many of the 'hidden' laws of the sectarians. It deals with extremely fine points and their punishments – what if one sneezes or snorts while reading the scripture? Compliance with a whole library of laws, some common Jewish, some common Essene, some Qumran sectarian, is simply taken for granted.

Thus, though Work is the most frequent topic of pharisaic debate in the Mishnah, I do not conclude simply from that fact that it was important. On the contrary, it owes its high profile entirely to festival days, which we must regard as less central and important to the Pharisees than the sabbath day and the sabbath year (to the degree that those who believe that God gave the law can be viewed as making comparative value judgments about parts of it).

How, then, do we know that the sabbath (and related parts of the law) was a very important part of ordinary first-century Judaism in Jesus' day? On the most general and basic grounds. (1) It is one of the ten commandments. (2) It is one of the two which require positive action (the other is honour of father and mother). (3) Non-observance of it is, in a Jewish community, highly visible. (4) It thus serves as a principal identity-marker, establishing one not only as Jewish, but also indicating publicly one's party affiliation (if any).

The degree to which sabbath law is not debated in the earliest layer of the Mishnah probably shows not only that there were fairly few intra-pharisaic disagreements, but also that a wide consensus governed the practice of most of the inhabitants of Jewish Palestine. Not doing one's regular work, not lighting a fire, not starting on a journey – all these must have been standard. The Pharisees do not berate the 'amme ha-'arets (the ordinary people) for tending their fields on the sabbath, which doubtless means that they did not do it. Thus if Jesus and his followers transgressed the sabbath substantially, they would have done something serious indeed.

§3. The seriousness of transgressing the sabbath raises the issue of punishment, which requires brief consideration. Exodus 31.14–15 prescribes both 'death' and 'cutting off' as punishment for transgression. ('Cutting off', or 'extirpation', seems to be the most grievous punishment in the early biblical books. It apparently implies not only the death penalty, but also that one will have no progeny, or else that they will not be counted within Israel.) Numbers 15.32–36, we noted above, specifies stoning. Inadvertent transgression which was later discovered, however, required only a sin offering (Lev. 4.27–35). What a sin offering was depended on one's financial circumstances. It could be either a goat, a lamb, two birds or a small amount of flour (Lev. 4.28,32; 5.7,11).

We cannot here deal very fully with the question of whether or not any Jewish court during the Roman period had the right to inflict the death penalty. This is usually discussed with regard to the final trial of Jesus in Jerusalem. Without discussion I shall simply indicate that I think that a court convened by the high priest could not inflict the death penalty without permission from the Roman prefect or procurator, except in the case of a Gentile who entered the temple farther than was allowed. It may be, however, that a Roman official would have turned a blind eye to local Jewish justice if no harm (such as an uprising or complaints to Rome) came of it. In any case Jesus lived in Galilee, not Judaea, and there the situation was entirely different. Despite the views of scholars who refer to the Roman 'occupation' of Palestine,[13] Roman troops never occupied it substantially (except during the war), and they seem not to have been garrisoned at all in the principalities of client rulers. Antipas did not command Roman troops (his own army was put to rout by Aretas *c.* CE 37; *Antiq.* 18.114), and he probably also did not govern according to Roman law – unless, of course, it conflicted with local law and needed to be enforced for the peace of the realm.

What law did he enforce? Some would have us believe that Rome had bypassed Antipas and given Galilee into the hands of the Pharisees, or, alternatively, that the Pharisees controlled Antipas because they governed the masses, whom he greatly feared. I shall not pause over these fanciful creations. Antipas did not enforce pharisaic law: it was not they who asked for the head of John the Baptist. He would have enforced some obvious points of Jewish law, especially where they coincided with common law (theft, murder and the like). Antipas, like most of the other Herodians, did not have a human image put on his coins, and so we should not rule out specifically Jewish content. On the other hand, he built his capital, Tiberias, on the site of a graveyard, thus rendering impure everyone who lived there.[14] He did not care overly much about the fine points of the law, and presumably he did not enforce them. It is difficult to imagine him having someone executed for gathering kindling on the sabbath (the crime in Num. 15).

Like most other rulers Antipas probably left local law enforcement to local authorities. This would put it into the hands of the leading townsmen or villagers. These, in turn, were probably either priests and Levites (who were literate and who knew the biblical law) or 'elders', heads of families, especially important and prosperous ones. Some of these people may have been fanatics of one kind or another, though the general tendency of local civic leadership is not towards fanaticism. These elders and leading citizens presumably bore (at least in Greek) the title 'magistrate' (*archōn*), and around them were probably small courts or councils. Josephus' (idealized) description of his own efforts to administer Galilee would lead us to think that a seven man judicial body would have been the norm for a small town or a sizable village. Such men were probably not empowered to inflict the death penalty, but would be expected to refer difficult or dangerous cases to Tiberias (cf. Josephus, *War* 2.571). Nevertheless, it is conceivable that occasionally justice was done in a wave of popular enthusiasm. I think that it would have been just possible to get stoned to death in a town or village of Galilee if one really persisted.[15]

Thus the locals may have been quite keen to enforce the biblical law to the fullest, but not have been able to do so. To the degree that the local leaders were priests – and I think that this probability has been sadly neglected – they would have had a vested interest in insisting on sin or guilt offerings, which are required in the case of inadvertent transgression, and which supported the priesthood by providing the serving priests with meat (Lev. 7.7).

Now we come to what I regard as in some ways the most interesting point. The two main pietist parties – which in many ways made the sabbath law more difficult to fulfil – seem to have been intent on reducing the penalty for transgression. This is the regulation in CD:

> But everyone who goes astray so as to profane the Sabbath and the appointed times shall not be put to death, for it falls to men to guard him; and if he is healed from it, they shall guard him for a period of seven years, and afterwards he shall come into the assembly. (CD 12.3–6)[16]

As Rabin points out (p. 60), the passage does not appear to mean 'inadvertently' or 'unintentionally': it apparently means that even intentional transgression is punished by imprisonment rather than by death. The person to be punished is, obviously, a member of the group ('afterwards he shall come into the assembly'); the authors do not propose to apply their special punishment to others. This may mean that the penalty applies only to the special, non-biblical parts of CD's sabbath rules, and that they expected general justice to take care of transgression of the biblical law. In any case, they presumably did not have to reckon seriously with the possibility that one of their members would do something so heinous as to violate the written law.

There are no rabbinic passages which can directly show what pre-70 Pharisees thought about punishment for transgression of the sabbath. We can say with some confidence what the Rabbis subsequently thought. It is well known that the Mishnah tractate Sanhedrin makes the death penalty virtually impossible. With others, I think that most of the unique parts of the tractate were never enforced anywhere (some parts are common Jewish or common Near Eastern law). But, just for the record, Sanhedrin 7.8 rules thus: one who was first warned (by two witnesses, that they would testify against him), and who then intentionally transgressed the sabbath, and did so in such a way as to incur the biblical punishment of 'cutting off' (that is, did some real work on it, like gathering wood), was liable to death by stoning. If he acted unwittingly, the penalty was a sin offering. The tractate, that is, agrees with Numbers (stoning for deliberate and substantial transgression) and Leviticus (a sin offering for unwitting transgression), except that in the first case it adds the condition that witnesses must have warned the transgressor *in advance* of the action.

Even more interesting is Shabbath 7.1:

A great general rule have they laid down concerning the Sabbath: whosoever, forgetful of the principle of the Sabbath, committed many acts of work on many Sabbaths, is liable only to one Sin-offering; but if, mindful of the principle of the Sabbath, he yet committed many acts of work on many Sabbaths, he is liable for every Sabbath [which he profaned]. If he knew that it was the Sabbath and he yet* committed many acts of work on many Sabbaths, he is liable for every main class of work [which he performed]; if he committed many acts of work of one main class, he is liable only to one Sin-offering.

At yet* Danby explains (following the Babylonian Talmud, Shabbat 67b–70a) that unintentional transgressions are meant: the person knew that it was the sabbath, yet was unaware that a certain category of actions constituted transgression.

Were we able to attribute Sanhedrin 7.8 and Shabbath 7.1 to pre-70 Pharisees – which we are not – we would conclude that intentional transgression of the sort that would incur the death penalty was impossible; that the most unlikely excuses by an offender would be accepted as showing that he or she was 'unwitting' ('I knew about the sabbath, but did not know not to cook'); and that the minimal number of sin offerings would be required. Josephus says that the Pharisees inclined to leniency (*Antiq.* 13.294), and perhaps we can see that tendency being continued in the work of their successors.

In any case, there is no reason to think that Pharisees sought the death penalty for minor transgressions of the sabbath. We shall return to the question of the seriousness of their own internal disputes at a later point.

§4. We turn now to 'the synoptic Jesus and the sabbath'. The two principal passages in the synoptics are Plucking Grain on the Sabbath (Mark 2.23–28 and parr.) and the Man with the Withered Hand (Mark 3.1–6 and parr.) In the case of the grain, the disciples (not Jesus himself) pluck grain on the sabbath in order to eat it. 'Plucking' is considered work by their opponents, identified as Pharisees.

In the Markan passage about the man with a withered hand, Jesus heals him by a simple command, 'Stretch out your hand'.

There are two further passages about healing on the sabbath in Luke, 13.10–17 and 14.1–6. These seem to be dependent on Mark 3.1–6 – or, more precisely, they are variants of the sort of tradition which resulted in the Markan passage. In Luke 14.1–6 there is no specification of how the healing was performed, though there is in 13.10–17: Jesus laid his hands on the woman who was ill. I somewhat doubt that Luke was aware of this fine legal distinction – that the laying on of hands was work – though in an actual debate in Palestine it would have been an important issue. There is a distinction among these healing passages with regard to the outcome. According to Mark 3.6 the Pharisees and Herodians were motivated by the healing of the man with a withered hand to seek Jesus' death. According to the further passages in Luke, Jesus defended the healings by citing the treatment of animals. In 13.15 he points out that animals which need to be watered are untied and led to water on the sabbath, while in 14.5 he reminds the audience that a son or an ox that falls into a well is pulled out on the sabbath. Both answers confound his opponents and leave them speechless. They do not plot execution.

The Lukan passages have more verisimilitude than the Markan, but I do not suppose that this makes them more probably 'authentic'. I doubt that we can find out just what Jesus did on each occasion that he healed, or just who said what to him about it. An assessment of the synoptic conflicts ideally requires us to know things which we cannot know, such as precisely what happened and precisely what the circumstances were. To take the story about grain as an example: Why did Jesus' disciples pluck and eat the grain? Why could they not enter a town or village and request food? One assumes that at the time they were within a few hundred yards of a town or village, or otherwise Pharisees could not have seen them. (The Pharisees probably accepted a limit on travel of 2,000 cubits, c. 1,000 yards/915 metres, double that of CD; see Erubin 4.5.) Why did they not return to their previous base? If it was too far, why were they not charged with exceeding the limit on travel? The question is why they were hungry enough to break the sabbath by plucking grain and why there was no other way to get something to eat. As we saw, Jews were not expected to fast on the sabbath; on the contrary, it was a day to be enjoyed, and those who fasted did not do so on the sabbath. The defence which Mark attributes to Jesus – that David, when hungry, ate the showbread (Mark 2.25f.) – though it does not relate to the sabbath, is a pretty fair defence: it is a precedent for allowing hunger to override the law. If the disciples were hungry with good cause, rather than as a result of laziness the previous day, when food should have been prepared, few would have thought them guilty of a grievous offence. We shall see in the next section that there are stories about priests going hungry rather than transgressing the law, but the manner in which the stories are told shows that this was not a general expectation.

Matthew adds an argument: on the sabbath the priests work in the temple, and 'something greater than the temple is here' (Matt. 12.5f.). This is an interesting defence. We saw above that the Hillelites appealed to the priests' work on the sabbath to justify sacrificing on a festival day. The problem with the argument in Matthew, however, is that the Bible explicitly prohibits gathering food on the sabbath (Ex. 16.26). The temple analogy, as it is presented in Matthew, would mean either that all forms of work are permitted on the sabbath – an argument which no one would accept – or that Jesus and his followers (greater than the temple) need not obey the sabbath – which, if understood, would be very offensive.

The problem, then, is that, even if we accept the story as a verbatim report of an eye-witness, we still have a hard time evaluating it, since none of the pertinent circumstances are given. As the Markan story runs, the Pharisees ask why the disciples are plucking grain, and Jesus defends them, apparently successfully: no more is heard of the critics. If we overlook the general improbability of the story – Jesus and his disciples were more than a sabbath day's walk from food, and there were Pharisees in the same grainfield inspecting them – the actual exchange is not unreasonable. The Pharisees ask why the disciples are working, and Jesus says, in effect, because they are extremely hungry. He adds that the sabbath is for humans, not humans for the sabbath, a principle with which most would have agreed. The matter was then dropped. The additional argument in Matthew adds little (though the self-claim, 'greater than the temple' would be offensive if taken to apply to Jesus' disciples in particular rather than to hungry people in general).

In the second story, the healing of a man with a withered hand (Mark 3.1–5 and parr.), Jesus heals a man by telling him to stretch out his hand. Talking is not regarded as work in any Jewish tradition, and so no work was performed. What is remarkable is Mark 3.6, which states that the Pharisees then took counsel with the Herodians, 'how to destroy him'. The story itself, in 3.1–5, is not impossible. People looked at Jesus to see what he would do, he enunciated a principle with which they would have agreed but which did not apply to the present case – saving life overrides the sabbath – and he then performed a minor healing without doing any work. Matthew, again, alters the defence: anyone will pull a sheep out of a pit on the sabbath, and so it is lawful to do good on the sabbath. The argument from analogy is not a very good one: the conclusion, 'lawful to do good' is too vague and might mean anything.

The plot in Mark 3.6, as most scholars recognize, is editorial, put here by the person who collected the sequence of conflict narratives in Mark 2.1–3.5. The story itself reveals no actual conflict over the sabbath.

According to Luke 13.10–17, Jesus healed a deformed woman by laying his hands on her. This was in a synagogue on the sabbath. The ruler of the synagogue (not said to be a Pharisee) rebuked him for working on the sabbath. He replied that people routinely lead their animals to water on the sabbath, and that it was all the more justifiable to heal the woman. 'As he said this, all his adversaries were put to shame.' This is a reasonable debate. Jesus performed work, by laying his hands on the woman. The work was not strictly required for the saving of life, but it cured the woman's discomfort one day earlier than if he had declined to heal her on the sabbath. The ruler of the synagogue recommended that he heal on the six days when work is allowed; Jesus replied by pointing out that compassion for an animal's discomfort justifies minor work. The ruler, embarrassed, backed down. Had a well-trained Pharisee been head of the synagogue, he and Jesus probably could have had a lively debate over small amounts of work which ease human discomfort. The Pharisees, we noted above, were probably stricter on this point than were most people; but no Pharisees seem to have been present.

Luke 14.1–6 requires only a brief glance: we are not told whether the healing involved work; a legal analogy provides justification; Jesus' critics retire in confusion.

Let us take it, however, that the passages all depict a group of Jews as being very concerned about the observance of the sabbath, so much so that they queried possible breaches of it which were either almost necessary (plucking in order to eat) or beneficial (healing), and that a protest was lodged even when no work was actually done. I can well believe that there were in Galilee radicals who questioned any unusual activity on the sabbath, though I would guess that such people had surely thought about biblical precedents and legal analogies and would have been able to debate them.

In any case – and here is the point of the discussion – these incidents on the sabbath, even if taken as literally true in all their aspects, were extremely minor in the context of the period. CD, we recall, forbade carrying a child, wearing perfume or assisting animals in distress (11.10–17). The Pharisees disagreed with the Sadducees (and presumably other non-Pharisees) about carrying vessels in a courtyard in which the houses were linked by doorposts and cross-beams. This issue is approximately as serious as plucking grain, but it seems never to have led to a legal charge: the Pharisees were permitted to live according to their traditions. Within the party, leading factions disagreed with each other about the work involved in bringing sacrifices. Yet they all remained Pharisees, and neither the Shammaites nor the Hillelites attempted to have the other group prosecuted.

We do not, in fact, know that either Essenes or Pharisees tried to get others to keep their sabbath rules when they were more stringent than the Bible requires. It seems pretty clear from the discussion above that they did not.[17] But let us take a maximum case. Let us suppose that Jesus' disciples really plucked grain on the sabbath and that Jesus actually laid his hands on someone for the purpose of healing. Let us further suppose that a village was dominated by the Essenes of CD or by the Pharisees of the mishnaic debates. Finally, let us suppose that these Essenes or Pharisees actively sought to enforce on others their own sabbath rules. It is reasonable to think that they would have proposed as a penalty imprisonment (in the case of the Essenes) or a sin offering (in the case of the Pharisees), since the trangressions were 'inadvertent'. That is, since Jesus was prepared to argue that what he or his disciples did was lawful, he had not known in advance that the action was transgression, that it belonged to the category of forbidden activity. Neither Essenes nor Pharisees could have enforced either penalty, but the evidence indicates that they would have proposed no worse. (There is more doubt about the Essenes than about the Pharisees, since we are not sure that we have their comments on transgression of the written law.)

I conclude, then, that the synoptic Jesus behaved on the sabbath in a way which fell inside the range of current debate about it, and well inside the range of permitted behaviour. He is depicted as being queried about some of his actions, and about permitting his disciples to pluck grain when they were hungry; but he defended every case by some sort of legal argument (sometimes not a very good one), and there is no indication that his justifications were not accepted or that those who scrutinized him laid charges with the local magistrate. Other Jews disagreed about equally substantial issues. The synoptic stories show that any possible transgression on the part of Jesus or his followers was minor and would have been seen as such by even the strictest groups.

C. FOOD

§1. Food and purity laws may be placed alongside the sabbath as being especially important. The reason, again, is that they define Jews as being distinct from others. Food laws, like sabbath laws, are also subject to public scrutiny. The basic food laws are found in Lev. 11 and Deut. 14, which forbid principally the following: (1) all four-footed animals except sheep, goats, cattle and some species of deer; (2) shellfish and molluscs; (3) birds of prey; (4) most insects and other things which crawl and creep, except locusts, crickets and grasshoppers. In addition, Jews are forbidden to eat (5) all blood and fat, from whatever source (Lev. 3.17 and often). In practice, this allows mutton, goat, beef, pigeon, dove and fish (with fins and scales). Not explicitly forbidden by the Bible, but accepted as prohibited by most Jews, was also Gentile wine, on the ground that some of it would have been poured as a libation to an idol. These restrictions are seen in Dan. 1.12–16; Daniel and his friends lived on vegetables and water. Gentile meat and wine were, pious Jews often assumed, unfit for their consumption. The food laws, especially the prohibition of pork, stood out, and they attracted a good deal of comment by pagans (see ch. IV below).

The food laws may be considered to be purity laws, since forbidden food is called 'impure' (e.g. Lev. 11.4). They deserve separate treatment, however, because impure foods are strictly prohibited; they are not only 'impure', they are 'abominable' (e.g. Lev. 11.10), and there is no rite of purification in the Bible, either for impure food or for the person who eats it. In the case of other purity laws, an impure person is prohibited from doing certain things, but becoming impure is not forbidden: semen-impurity may not be conveyed to the sanctuary, but contracting it is a good thing, since fulfilling the commandment to be fruitful and multiply requires contact with semen.

§2. In general, food laws did not develop in the way sabbath laws did. The biblical exclusions are perfectly clear, much clearer than the definition of 'Work'. In the Diaspora new animals were encountered and had to be classified (ch. IV), but no new categories of meat were excluded even by pietist groups.[1] There were, however, some extensions, and food restrictions were rigorously observed.

This means that there were some food extremists in first-century Palestine. I shall present here instances of food restrictions practised by Palestinian Jews, over and above keeping the biblical dietary laws. The first four are from Josephus:

1. and 2. On two different occasions Josephus relates that the tithes on which the priests depended were stolen, with the result that some starved to death (*Antiq.* 20.181, 206–207).

3. Some priests who were imprisoned in Rome lived on figs and nuts (*Life* 13–14).

4. Some Essenes who were expelled from the order starved to death because they would not eat food which was impure by the standard which they had sworn to accept (*War* 2.143–144).

5. The House of Shammai held that a fowl could be served on the same table as cheese, but that the two could not be eaten together; while the

House of Hillel said that they could be neither eaten nor served together (Hullin 8.1; Eduyoth 5.2).

The first three examples concern the priesthood, and we may add a passage in which Josephus depicts the priests as keeping the biblical law even under duress. Once when Passover came in the midst of a drought, the priests would not eat leavened bread even though it was the only bread available (*Antiq.* 3.320). The prohibition of leavened bread during Passover is biblical (e.g. Ex. 12.8), but it is still noteworthy that the priests observed it during a famine. Most Jewish groups most of the time took the attitude that one should live by the law, not die by it; and physical danger, or even severe distress, was usually held to override the observance of most laws (cf. Mark 2.23–28 in the previous section). It is noteworthy that Josephus does not say that the populace went hungry, but rather the priesthood.

The two stories about priests starving to death are a bit puzzling. It is not clear why they should have starved when the tithes were stolen. The stories presuppose some development of the biblical law governing the priesthood: in the Bible there is no direct statement to the effect that priests must never eat anything except the food which is set aside for them or offered in sacrifice. It appears that Deut. 18.1–4 was read in an exclusivist sense. The priests and Levites have 'no portion or inheritance with Israel; they shall eat the offerings by fire to the Lord, and his rightful dues'. 'No portion' presumably means 'no land', and 'they shall eat' does not have 'only' attached to it. The passage could have been construed as permitting priests and Levites to eat ordinary food: that is, it could have been interpreted as meaning that they should eat the offerings and dues when available, and other food when necessary. The passages in Josephus apparently mean that this was not the priests' understanding in the first century; they, or at least some of them, would eat *only* the offerings and dues.

There are still problems with the two passages about priests starving. Tithes went to the Levites, who in turn tithed to the priests.[2] It appears from other passages that the priests could go out and collect tithes (*Life* 63); the stories about stealing and starving assume that the only food available to the priests was stored in a central place. First fruits also served the priests as food, but perhaps Josephus here intends 'tithes' to cover all forms of priestly food stored in the temple.[3] Following the story, let us assume that all the temple's food stores were stolen and that the priests could not collect food; perhaps it was the wrong season and the farmers had no more to give. Nevertheless, there were still the sacrifices, most of which provided the priesthood with some food. To eat it, the priests would have had to come to the temple, since most sacrificial food had to be eaten in 'a most holy place' (Num. 18.9–10). The sacrifices would not have fed all 18,000 (or so)[4] priests every day, but with good organization and appeals for more sacrifices to be brought, and for freewill offerings to be made, one would think that starvation could have been avoided.

While there are difficulties in understanding precisely what happened, we can probably take it to be the case that some priests took to an extreme the biblical laws that they should live on the proceeds of the temple and eat holy food. The mere telling of these stories seems to presuppose that priests did not have access to secular food. (I leave aside here the probability that at least some priests, in contravention of the biblical law, owned land. Those who starved obviously did not belong to this category.)

The priests who lived on figs and nuts while captives in Rome (3 on the list above) were not just avoiding 'meat offered to idols', as Thackeray proposed,[5] but rather all cooked food, even vegetables, which were acceptable in Daniel. Josephus takes this to be an obvious way of observing the ancestral laws (the priests 'had not forgotten the pious practices of religion'), but the reasoning is by no means evident. I can only offer a guess about how they had extended the law. Possibly they were avoiding all food which had been cooked because the cooking vessels had previously been used to cook non-kosher and possibly idolatrous food. Whatever their interpretation of the law, Josephus regards their behaviour as noteworthy only because they maintained their ancestral customs so devoutly.

Josephus's statement that expelled Essenes starved to death (4) throws interesting light on the *Community Rule* from Qumran. One of its main topics is 'the Purity', which appears to refer to food and drink. Those who are admitted to the sect are admitted to 'the Purity' (*taharah*), and they are forbidden to mix with 'the men of falsehood', which includes eating and drinking 'anything of theirs' (1QS 5.13–16). From Josephus it appears that members of the community regarded their own vows not to eat other food as binding even if they were expelled. The group represented by CD, on the other hand, accepted some relations with outsiders, even Gentiles, though it put limits on selling food to them (CD 12.8–10). One supposes that the authors of CD would have forbidden eating any Gentile food, but not necessarily food supplied by other Israelites. In this instance Josephus's statement reflects the practice of the Qumran community, not that of the Damascus Document.

The passage from the Mishnah which is no. 5 above has as an introduction a more general rule:

No flesh may be cooked in milk excepting the flesh of fish and locusts; and no flesh may be served up on the table together with cheese excepting the flesh of fish and locusts. A fowl may be served . . . together with cheese . . .

So the School of Shammai . . . Neither served nor eaten with it . . . So the School of Hillel. (Hullin 8.1)

It is not clear whether we are to understand the ruling of the House of Shammai as beginning with 'A fowl may be served . . . together with cheese' or with the opening sentence, 'No flesh may be cooked in milk'. The parallel in Eduyoth 5.2 attributes to the House of Shammai only the rule about serving fowl and cheese, not the general statement about meat and milk. In either case, the debate between the Houses presupposes that some laws about meat and dairy products were already accepted by both. The reason for concern with meat and dairy products is that the Bible warns three times against 'cooking a kid in its mother's milk' (Ex. 23.19; 34.26; Deut. 14.21). The repetition was taken to show that one should go beyond the strict requirement of the law itself. The Pharisees seem to have accepted this as a general principle and to have debated only the question of fowl and cheese served together. This assumes that no meat will be cooked in milk and that meat from milk-giving animals will not be served with any dairy product.

Thus we see that the three most identifiable groups in first-century Palestine (priests, Essenes and Pharisees) had elaborated or at least emphasized the food laws and were diligent to keep them.

We should now observe that Jews in the Diaspora were very conscious of having special food laws and seem generally to have observed them. Without going into detail, I shall simply mention the fact that, after Julius Caesar showed various favours towards the Jews, their rights were extended throughout the Mediterranean. The decrees of the city of Sardis and of the governor of Asia, Dolabella, show the concern of Greek-speaking Jews to obtain 'native food' (*Antiq*. 14.226,261).[6] Later the issue of food was important to the churches of the Diaspora (Gal. 2.12; Rom. 14.6). We shall see in the chapter on the Diaspora that one of the most frequent pagan criticisms of Jews was that they had peculiar food laws.

If we bring together the facts that pious groups in Palestine had some special food laws and interpreted all the laws strictly, and that the food laws of Lev. 11 were observed in the Diaspora, where it was more difficult to keep them than in Palestine, we must conclude that the biblical food laws were in general kept very strictly throughout Jewish Palestine. In terms of day-in and day-out Jewish practice, both in Palestine and in the Diaspora, the food laws stood out, along with observance of the sabbath, as being a central and defining aspect of Judaism. In a Jewish community, transgression of the food laws would be almost as obvious as transgression of the sabbath, and thus keeping them was an important way of identifying oneself as an observant Jew. In Palestine, except in the partially Gentile cities, non-kosher food would be difficult to obtain, and non-observance of the basic laws would be almost impossible.

§3. The most obvious meaning of Mark 7.15 ('there is nothing outside a person which by going in can defile; but the things which come out are what defile') is that 'all foods are clean', as the author comments (7.19). In this case the saying attributed to Jesus – it is not what goes in that defiles – appears to me to be too revolutionary to have been said by Jesus himself. The significance for the Christian movement of denying the Jewish dietary code was immense, and this saying makes Jesus the direct source of a rupture with ordinary Judaism. The Christian circles which broke with the dietary code surely broke at that very moment with Judaism as it was generally known. As we just noted, it is hard to imagine the circumstances in which Jews living in Jewish communities in Palestine could have started breaking the dietary laws, and I continue to think that the issue actually arose either in the Diaspora (e.g. in Paul's churches) or in connection with the conversion of Gentiles in Palestine (as in Acts 10; see pp. 1, 96). But whatever the origin of the saying that what goes into a person does not defile, this statement, if it really means what it appears to mean, nullifies the food laws and falls completely outside the limits of debate about the law in first-century Judaism. In this instance I cannot maintain the assumption which I have made for the sake of the argument: that all the material really goes back to Jesus.

If, of course, we provide a new context for the saying, it can be saved as an authentic logion.[7] Its meaning could be understood to be, 'What matters morally is what comes out' or 'What comes out is much more important'. The 'not . . . but' contrast can mean 'not this only, but much more that', as some examples will make clear. When Moses told the Israelites that their murmurings were *not* against Aaron and himself, *but* against the Lord, they had just been complaining to *him* (Ex. 16.2–8). The sentence means, 'Your murmurings directed against us are in reality against the Lord, since we do his will'. When the author of the *Letter of Aristeas* wrote that Jews 'honour God', '*not* with gifts or sacrifices, *but* with purity of heart and of devout disposition' (*Arist.* 234), he did not mean that sacrifices were not brought, nor that he was against them (see e.g. 170–171), but rather that what really matters is what they symbolize. Similarly Mark 9.37, 'Whoever receives me, receives *not* me *but* the one who sent me', means 'receiving me is tantamount to receiving God'.[8] '*Not* what goes in *but* what comes out' in Mark 7.15, then, could well mean, 'What comes out – the wickedness of a person's heart – is what really matters', leaving the food laws as such untouched. In this case there is no conflict with the law. This interpretation of the saying, however, grants the point that as it is intended in Mark 7 it is inauthentic.

D. PURITY

§1. The biblical purity laws are treated in detail in section B of ch. III. Two types of impurity – of corpses and dead swarming things – will be explained when we come to pharisaic developments in §2 immediately below. Here we shall fix just on the question of bathing and handwashing. The Bible required bathing the body and washing the clothes – one or the other or both – to remove impurities which were caused by: touching the carcass of an impure creature; eating an animal which died of itself; touching the carcass of a pure animal which died of itself; contact with semen; indirect contact with menstruation or with certain other bodily discharges. In the first century it was probably also accepted that women bathed after the menstrual period and after childbirth, though this is not required by Lev. 15 and 12. Sexual intercourse during a woman's menstrual period, or during stage one of childbirth-impurity, was strictly forbidden. Purity laws also limit what foods can be eaten[1] and, in some cases, what vessels can be used. Otherwise impurities principally affect entry to the temple, and failing to remove them did not interfere with most aspects of ordinary life.

Handwashing figures only once: a man with a discharge from his penis should rinse his hands before touching anyone else; if not, the person whom he touches becomes impure (Lev. 15.11).

§2. Purity laws, like sabbath laws, were subject to considerable elaboration. For example, by the first century Jews in Palestine generally thought that the biblical requirement to 'bathe' meant to immerse in a special pool. The person who reads ch. III below will find quite a lot of developments of the biblical law.

Of greater interest for understanding the gospels is the fact that substitutes for bathing were developed and were applied to cases not covered by biblical law. Let me first mention developments in the Diaspora (more fully, see ch. IV). According to Philo a couple, after intercourse, could not touch anything until they had 'made their ablutions and purged themselves with water' (*Spec. Laws* 3.63). This looks like a compensation for a temple law. The Bible prohibits entering the temple if impure from contact with semen (Lev. 15.16–18,31); and Philo (as well as other Diaspora Jews[2]), living apart from the temple, seems to have substituted 'anything' for 'the holy precincts'. He also seems to have had an extra-biblical purification, valid for life in the Disapora, for those who contracted corpse-impurity. This, the greatest of all impurities, required special water kept at the temple, and by biblical law all

Jews in the Diaspora had, or were assumed to have, corpse-impurity until they made a pilgrimage. Yet Philo reflects a domestic rite of sprinkling and washing which removed corpse-impurity (ch. IV). Such new prohibitions as 'do not touch anything after intercourse until you have washed' show a tendency to develop purity laws.

Handwashing belongs to this category, and it is attested in the Diaspora earlier than in Palestine.[3] According to *Arist.* 305–306 it was the custom of Jews to wash their hands in the sea while praying. The explanation is that the act shows that they have done no evil (as in 'pure hands and pure heart'). The practice of washing while praying is also attested in *Sib. Or.* 3.591–593, 'at dawn they lift up holy arms towards heaven, from their beds, always sanctifying their flesh with water'. Some manuscripts have 'hands' instead of 'flesh'. To this literary evidence may be added the fact that some Diaspora synagogues were built near the sea (details in IV.B).

None of these ablutions, especially the requirement to wash in the sea, has any biblical base. We have here either an extension of purity laws or a substitution or compensation. That is, handwashing before or while praying, or before touching the scripture, may have developed as a simple addition to washing after intercourse and menstruation. Since in the Diaspora private prayer and worship at the synagogue substituted for going to the temple, and since the priests washed their hands and feet before sacrificing (e.g. Ex. 30.18–21), it is possible that handwashing is a conscious though partial imitation of worship in the temple. We shall see in ch. IV, however, that it is more likely to have been borrowed from pagan practice.

In Palestine there were various developments of purity practices beyond the requirements of the Pentateuch. One point may be briefly exemplified: biblical law does not require priests' food to be specially handled before it reaches them, though they have to eat it in purity. Yet Isa. 66.20 refers to bringing the cereal offering in 'pure vessels', and according to Judith 11.13 it was considered to be against the law for impure people to touch the priests' food. Both passages are a bit uncertain as regards date. We may take it that even the latest passages in Isaiah are earlier than the rise of the Pharisees, and Judith is also probably pre-pharisaic.[4] It is in any case non-pharisaic.

The Pharisees' purity rules and debates are the subject of ch. III, and here I shall offer just enough explanation to allow New Testament passages to be clarified. We shall discuss first washing and bathing and then a few special pharisaic concerns (the food laws of Lev. 11.32–38, corpse-impurity, and the relationship between purity and the setting of the sun). In the course of this discussion we shall note disagreements between the Pharisees and others and also disputes among themselves.

The rabbinic passages which are assigned to the earliest, presumably pharisaic, layer discuss handwashing in three contexts: handling food which would go to the priesthood; the Pharisees' own sabbath and festival meals; handling scripture.[5] The evidence is that handwashing before separating the priests' food from the rest of the harvest was introduced at the time of Hillel and Shammai, fairly late in the history of Pharisaism. This seems to have been the last step in the development of rules about handling the priests' food. Below I argue that handwashing then began to be practised at the Pharisees' own sabbath and festival meals since they were 'holy convocations', and it seemed appropriate to observe a special rite. There is no evidence from rabbinic literature that Pharisees washed hands before eating ordinary meals.

First-century Palestinian Jews seem all to have agreed that the biblical requirement to bathe after certain impurities should be fulfilled by immersing in a special pool (III.E§8). The Pharisees had their own views about what water was valid for removing impurities. They held that water should have collected naturally, and that drawing or carrying it rendered it invalid. In cities it was very difficult to keep pools which were large enough for immersion full of water which collected naturally. Shammai, Hillel and other Pharisees disagreed about the issue of how much drawn water could be used in an immersion pool; but all agreed that only a very small quantity of drawn water was permitted (below, pp. 219f). Those who had stricter limits logically should have suspected others of being always impure.

It is not surprising that the Pharisees (and probably other pietists) came up with a more radical solution. They decided that invalid water could be rendered acceptable if it was in contact with valid water. They achieved this by building a second pool, kept always full of pure water, beside the pool which was actually used for immersion. The two were connected at the top by a pipe, and when the immersion pool was filled with drawn water, the pipe could be briefly opened. The resulting contact between the pools served to make the immersion pool valid. Several such pools have been found: in Jerusalem, in both the Hasmonean and Herodian palaces at Jericho, at Matsada, and elsewhere. Those just listed were built before CE 70 (or 74).[6]

While Pharisees disagreed among themselves about immersion pools, they disagreed more with others, especially the post-Hasmonean priesthood (a Hasmonean pool at Jericho is 'pharisaic'). There were many pools in Jerusalem and elsewhere which were not built according to the pharisaic standard, but which consisted of only one large pool.[7] They are too numerous to have been kept full naturally. Many of these were in private houses in West Jerusalem, the upper city, where the aristocrats lived. Several others were built near the temple, in sight of the gates.[8] It seems that the priesthood, which was responsible for the public pools near the temple, allowed more drawn water to be used to top up the pools than would even the most lenient Pharisees, or possibly that they did not observe the distinction between drawn water and water which collected naturally.

Since they disagreed about immersion pools, one might expect the Pharisees and the priesthood to regard each other as being always impure. Yet this appears not to have been the case, and tolerance of each others' views prevailed. The priests obviously allowed the Pharisees to use the temple. The Pharisees, for their part, accepted the temple service and considered that its sacrifices atoned for their sins. A clue which probably indicates how they thought is found in Parah 11.5. According to this mishnah those who were impure according to 'the words of the Scribes', but not according to the Bible, could enter the temple. This mishnah is anonymous, and it cannot be attributed to pre-70 Pharisees, but it probably indicates their attitude. They knew perfectly well that they had extended the law beyond what the Bible requires, and they thought that they were right to do so; but they did not think that those who observed only the biblical law actually transgressed.[9] We see here a degree of mutual tolerance which allowed the Pharisees to live in Jerusalem, side-by-side with a priesthood which had a partially different *halakah* (set of rules). The priesthood was from time to time attacked by the pious for not following the correct purity laws (see the end of this section). We must imagine the Pharisees as criticizing them on this ground, yet still bringing to the temple their sacrifices, tithes and offerings.

We can assign to Pharisees two highly developed purity concerns: to avoid the impurity imparted to wet foodstuff by a dead 'swarming thing'; to extend the sphere of corpse-impurity and then to avoid contracting it from the new sources. Both these are explained in considerable detail in ch. III, but I shall mention two aspects which had bearing on common public life.

Leviticus 11.31–38 discusses the carcass of a dead 'swarming thing' and what it renders impure. 'Swarming things' are mostly insects; but rodents, weasels, crocodiles and other creeping and crawling creatures are included (Lev. 11.20–23,29f.). Leviticus 11.34 says that drink or moist food which is in a vessel into which fell the carcass of a swarming thing is impure; 11.38 that seed on which water has been put is impure if it is touched by such a carcass. It will be seen that these impurities are extremely difficult to avoid. Rain or dew can easily moisten food and seed, and where insects fall when they die is beyond human control.

The Pharisees moderated the biblical law in two ways. First, they eliminated the smallest of the swarming things (gnats, midges, mites and the like) by specifying that bits of carcass smaller than a lentil did not render foodstuff impure. Because of this decision, I shall use the term 'fly-impurity' to describe the pharisaic interpretation of the law on dead swarming things. The second and more important decision was that moisture did not count unless a human *intended* the foodstuff to be wet. This step was supported by exegesis. According to Lev. 11.37f. a seed becomes impure when a forbidden carcass falls on it only if water *was put* on the seed. The verb *yutan* clearly implies 'put by human intention'. They then applied this verb not only to seeds, but to all foodstuff. Thus the law became much easier to observe, since its application was determined by human intention.

This interesting bit of biblical law, slightly watered down by the Pharisees, explains one of the mishnaic passages which is usually taken to prove that the Pharisees despised ordinary people and held themselves aloof from them. The passage is Demai 6.6:

> The School of Shammai say: A man may sell his olives only to an Associate [*ḥabēr*]. The School of Hillel say: Even to one that [only] pays Tithes. Yet the more scrupulous of the School of Hillel used to observe the words of the School of Shammai.

The reason olives are being debated is that their owner wants them to become moist, so that they will be ready to be pressed for oil. Since the moisture is desired, olives become susceptible to fly-impurity after they secrete it. In selling olives to someone who is not as scrupulous as one might wish, one may be leading him into transgression. He might let the olives grow moist, and then allow a dead fly to fall on them, and yet still turn them into oil – contaminated oil. In a similar way, we recall, some Pharisees restricted giving work to Gentiles which might carry over to the sabbath. The other person should be passively prevented from transgression. The Pharisees did not patrol the countryside, seeing whose olives were moist, but they at least would not contribute to possible transgression.

Here we have an interesting case in which the Pharisees did not expand the biblical law or make it stricter, but rather made it easier; nevertheless they worked quite hard at defining it precisely and deciding how to apply it. This category of law is not, I should add, an instance in which laypeople apply priestly laws to themselves (though Neusner and others treat it as if it were). The laws of Lev. 11 apply to all Israelites equally.

The second purity rule which it will be useful to explain here is corpse-impurity. According to biblical law (Num. 19), corpses render impure those who touch them or who are under the same roof (in terms of Num. 19, supposedly given in the wilderness, the impurity was contracted by those in the same 'tent' as a corpse). For the ordinary person, contracting corpse-impurity was not wrong; rather, piety required the care of the dead. The only transgression was to enter the temple while impure. Priests, on the other hand, are enjoined in the Bible not to contract corpse-impurity except for their closest relatives (Lev. 21.1–3).

In the pharisaic corpus we encounter a development in defining how corpse-impurity spreads. Not only people and objects in the same room as the corpse become impure, but also anyone or anything which 'overshadows' the corpse or which it 'overshadows'. Thus, when a corpse is being carried down the street, if an oven has a vent which projects into the street the corpse will render the oven impure by overshadowing the vent. Similarly a person becomes impure by overshadowing the corpse; for example, by leaning out of a window when the corpse is being carried past. Walking on graves also results in corpse-impurity.

The Pharisees tried to avoid overshadowing and being overshadowed, and they fretted about food and vessels in the upper room: the corpse certainly rendered impure everything in the room where it lay, but what about the room above? The corpse-impurity which they were avoiding, however, was not that of the Bible, but only the extension of it. Pharisees did not refuse to tend the dead, nor to mourn beside the grave. We are not told that, when someone died – and people died at home, since there were no hospitals – the Pharisees moved out of the house and refused to touch anyone who had tended the corpse. Such domestic disruptions would have led to a different set of legal debates from those that we have, which have to do with the question, 'How far does corpse-impurity spread?', not 'which members of the family stay at home and which leave?' There is not a word in the Mishnah to the effect that Pharisees should avoid *biblical* corpse-impurity, contracted by tending and mourning the dead. In the middle of the second century R. Judah proposed that Associates should not contract corpse-impurity, but he was overruled (Demai 2.3). Avoiding it could not have been of the essence of Pharisaism; but, on the other hand, it does seem that they had a special concern with it.

Other pietists also thought that people who walk over graves contract corpse-impurity: there is a similar rule in CD 12.15–17. There is evidence that substantial portions of the populace agreed. That is why Antipas had a hard time populating Tiberias, part of which was built over a graveyard (*Antiq.* 18.36–38). Here we see the idea of 'overshadowing'. It is quite possible that this conception was generally accepted.

One could say that this proves how influential the Pharisees were: they got a lot of people to worry about overshadowing corpses. I think that it is more likely that they shared some interpretations with others, and that the spread of corpse-impurity by overshadowing was generally accepted. Other Jews probably shared the pharisaic definition of immersion pools. The 'pharisaic' construction of the immersion pool on Matsada may prove not that Pharisees were prominent among those who were besieged there, but rather that they and other pietists had similar views. One's judgment on this topic obviously rests on the larger issues of the sources of Pharisaism, agreements among different pietist groups, and the number and influence of the Pharisees. For my own part, I am for several reasons inclined to a moderate view of pharisaic influence, especially on these points. One of the reasons is the striking fact that Josephus does not mention purity among their special concerns, though he makes a great deal of the purity laws of the Essenes. The extensions of biblical law which we now find paralleled in pharisaic sources, such as reluctance to live over a graveyard, are treated by Josephus as *common* views, and I think it likely that they were more widespread than would have been the case if they were sponsored by Pharisees alone. Similarly the extension of the law which is paralleled in Judith 11.13 – handling the priests' food in purity – was accepted by others besides the Pharisees, and some aspects were accepted even by the ordinary people.[10] Some of these points are pre-pharisaic, and we see here not control of the populace by the Pharisees, but rather the common development of purity laws.

Pharisees disagreed among themselves about purity rules. We saw above that the Hillelites and Shammaites disagreed about how much drawn water could be used in an immersion pool. Hillel and Shammai (not the Houses) differed on at least one important issue of purity. According to Shammai, women were impure only from the time when they actually noticed a mentrual flow, while according to Hillel they were considered to be impure from the time of the previous examination to the examination which showed blood (Eduyoth 1.1; Niddah 1.1). This means that, according to Hillel, intercourse on a day which fell between a negative and a positive examination transgressed the law (Lev. 18.19; 20.18) and both the man and woman were required to bring sin offerings for unintentional transgression (cf. Niddah 2.2). Hillelites should have regarded Shammaites as regularly transgressing the law which prohibits intercourse with a menstruant.

Let us now ask about coercion of others to obey their special rules. In discussing the sabbath laws, I said that I doubted that Pharisees tried to impose their own extensions on the populace in general. We can draw the same conclusion, and do so quite firmly, with regard to purity. They may have wanted to avoid the new sources of corpse-impurity, but they did not expect others to do so (see below, pp. 188–90), similarly they had their own rules about building immersion pools, but they accepted that others used pools of different construction. Tolerance of disagreement is most striking in the debate about intercourse with a possible menstruant. Since intercourse with a menstruant is strictly forbidden by the Bible (e.g. Lev. 18.19), it would seem from the dispute mentioned above that the Hillelites would not have allowed intermarriage with Shammaites. At some point one of the contributors to the Mishnah noticed a similar point. The two Houses disagreed completely about several laws of marriage,

> yet the [men of] the House of Shammai did not refrain from marrying women from [the families of] the House of Hillel, nor the [men of] the House of Hillel from marrying women from [the families of] the House of Shammai. Despite all the disputes about what is clean and unclean wherein these declare clean what the others declare unclean, neither scrupled to use aught that pertained to the others in matters concerned with cleanness. (Yebamoth 1.4)

We shall later note that everything was not always sweetness and light, but generally this comment is correct. Further, the Pharisees had a good deal of tolerance for others as well. They did not (despite Jeremias & co.) consider ordinary people, priests, Essenes and others as 'excluded' from 'Israel' (see III.F below). They could not have enforced social and religious exclusion had they tried, but on the whole they seem not to have tried.[11]

One mishnaic passage may give an instance in which Pharisees tried to force others to obey their purity laws. For many impurities the Bible says that the person is pure after he or she has bathed *and* the sun has set (e.g. Lev. 15.21). The Rabbis, and probably the Pharisees before them, decided that a person who had immersed, but upon whom the sun had not yet set, was in an intermediate state of purity and could do many of the things for which purity is required. Here they doubtless disagreed with the Sadducees, who, following the biblical text, found no degrees of purity. According to the Mishnah, 'the elders' once rendered impure the priest who was to burn the red heifer, so that the Sadducees 'should not be able to say, "It must be performed only by them on whom the sun has set"' (Parah 3.7). The red heifer was burned and its ashes were used in order to remove corpse-impurity. The Bible explicitly says that the priest who burns the heifer should have bathed and that the sun should have set (Num. 19.8). The 'elders', presumably Pharisees, wanted to force the Sadducees to accept their view that a priest who had immersed the same day was pure enough to burn the heifer, and to do this they defiled him while *en route* to his task. The mishnah explains that there was a place of immersion where the Heifer was burned; the priest could immerse there and, by the Pharisees' rules, complete the ceremony the same day. We are not told the outcome. Did the Sadducean priesthood send a completely pure priest and a guard to see that he was not defiled as well? We do not know, but there is no reason to think that this incident succeeded in forcing the Sadducees to accept the pharisaic view.

This passage is not in Neusner's canon of pharisaic passages, since no Pharisees are named. We can be certain, however, that the substance of the dispute is pre-70, since a halakic letter found at Qumran (4QMMT) takes the same view as the Sadducees, apparently against the Jerusalem authorities, who must, at that time, have accepted the pharisaic rule.[12] If we accept the mishnaic passage as representing a dispute between the Pharisees and the Sadducees, we see that it was serious. *No matter whose views prevailed*, however, both continued to use the mixture of water and ashes and to worship in the same temple.

The Essenes greatly developed purity laws. According to Josephus' description they did not anoint themselves with oil; dressed in white; worked not in their robes, but in a loincloth; bathed before eating; and bathed after contact with anyone outside their own circle – including members in other ranks of the order (*War* 2.124, 129, 131, 150). Josephus does not explicitly point it out, but the priestly origins of the group here are clear. In Jerusalem only priests wore white (Levites were allowed white robes in CE 65: *Antiq.* 20.216–218). The Essenes bathed and put on their robes before eating, just as in Jerusalem priests bathed and donned their white robes before entering the temple – where, among other things, they ate from what was sacrificed. (For the requirement that priests bathe before eating 'holy things' see Lev. 22.1–7.) The Essenes, that is, treated the community as if it were the temple and the common table as if it were the altar. This is what people say about the Pharisees; it appears to have been true of the Essenes, or at least some of them. Though Josephus may not have known that these practices originated among priests, the Zadokite founders of the sect, he did see the analogy to the priesthood. He wrote of the Essenes: 'pure now themselves, they repair to the refectory, as to some sacred shrine' (2.129). About their stripping for work, he appropriately noted that they laid aside their garments 'as holy vestments' (2.131). The Essenes observed the priestly analogy so strictly that they bathed after touching anyone who might be less pure. The Jerusalem priesthood may have observed this or a similar precaution, since priests (and their dependants) were to eat in ritual purity (on eating first fruits in purity, see Num. 18.13).

Turning to direct evidence for the Qumran sect, we note that purity is prominent in 1QS, and it especially attached to food and drink. We recall that the common meal is routinely called 'the Purity'. Before partaking of it the members 'entered the water' (1QS 5.13). The Scrolls do not mention the white robes, nor their reservation for eating, studying and worshipping, but it is likely that on these points Josephus's information was sound.

Looking forward to the messianic era, 1QSa states that 'no man smitten with any human uncleanness shall enter the assembly of God' and that those with blemishes would not be able to hold offices (2.1–6). These are temple or priestly purity rules, applied to the wider community of the endtime. There are a lot of special purity laws for the future Jerusalem in 11QTemple. A few examples will be given in III.C below.

Excavations at Qumran have revealed pools in which water was collected. It rains but seldom near the Dead Sea; but when it does rain, water pours down the wadis in great abundance. The sect built channels to bring the water into deep pits within the community area. Some of these pits were used for 'ritual' bathing. It is noteworthy that in some instances the steps are quite wide, wider than necessary for carrying water up for cooking or drinking. Vermes believes that at least two of these pits were immersion pools.[13] My own count is appreciably higher, though the matter is complicated, since not all the immersion pools were in use at the same time.[14]

The concern for purity is seen in CD, for example in the prohibition of sexual relations in Jerusalem (12.1–2). According to biblical law, as we noted, one must bathe after emission and before entering the temple. The Zadokite Document extends the holy area to cover the entire city, at least with regard to sexual relations, and the same extension is also known from the Temple Scroll.[15]

CD also requires washing before attending meetings of the group to worship (11.22). When the groups from various cities met together, they were concerned 'to distinguish between the unclean and the clean, and to make known the distinction between the holy and the profane' (12.19–20). As did other first-century Jews, those of CD thought that purificatory bathing must be done in a pool large enough to allow full immersion (CD 10.11–13).

§3. With regard to Jesus and purity, we should first take up three points from Matt. 23 which attribute to Pharisees purity concerns which are close to those seen in the earliest stratum of rabbinic literature.

Jesus accuses the Pharisees, among other things, of 'straining out a gnat and swallowing a camel' (23.24). According to Lev. 11, both gnats and camels are impure and may not be eaten, and we recall that the Pharisees were especially concerned to keep all of the laws in that chapter, not just the large and most obvious ones, such as abstaining from donkeys and camels, but also the more difficult ones, such as not consuming anything wet on to or into which a dead swarming thing had fallen. We saw that pharisaic law as we have it from the Houses debates was that a swarming thing smaller than a lentil would not render wet food and drink impure. I do not for one moment doubt that if a fly fell into a Pharisee's cup, he would have tried to strain it out before it died and contaminated the drink. It is not unreasonable to think that the Pharisee would also have removed a gnat before it drowned, even though it was smaller than a lentil.

The second point is that tombs were whitewashed (Matt. 23.27). This passage does not connect whitewashing directly with Pharisees, but rather sounds more general, as if tombs were commonly whitewashed. There are no definitely pharisaic passages on marking graves with white, though the practice is assumed in the anonymous statement which opens Maaser Sheni 5.1. The first commentator is Rabban Simeon b. Gamaliel II, mid-second century. Despite the lack of early evidence from rabbinic sources, it is probable that marking tombs was common, and this supports the evidence from CD and Josephus that others besides Pharisees wished to avoid overshadowing a corpse.

We may be able to shed light on the difficult passage Matt. 23.25–26, which implies that Pharisees purified the outside of dishes but not the inside. Vessels can be rendered impure in several different ways (see III.E§1, §3, §4, §7). Some Pharisees seem to have thought that, at sabbath and festival meals, the outside of the cup should be kept free of fly-impurity, and that this could be accomplished by handwashing. The passage is this:

> The House of Shammai say, 'They wash their hands and then mix the cup [of wine with water] – lest liquids on the outer surface of the cup become impure through contact with hands and in turn render the cup impure. The House of Hillel say, 'The outer surface of the cup is always deemed impure'. (T. Berakot 5.26)

As will be explained below (III.E §3.d), the concern here is fly-impurity. The hands may have touched a dead insect, and if there is liquid on the outside of the cup, the impurity would be mediated to the cup via the liquid. The Hillelites were not worried about the outside of the cup, but the Shammaites were. It may follow that they would have washed the outside of the cups before using them. We should note that, if a fly fell into a cup and died, the cup should be broken (if earthenware) or washed (if of wood; Lev. 11.32f.). Some were worried about conveying impurity to an otherwise pure cup.

The major purity passage in the synoptics is Mark 7.1–4, where we are told that Jesus' disciples did not wash their hands, though the Pharisees, and indeed all the Jews, wash before eating (Mark 7.1–4). The remark about 'the Jews' shows, of course, that the redactor or author of the passage is addressing the explanation to an audience of Gentile Christians, and the point is that Jews keep purity laws which are not kept in Gentile Christian circles. The purity practice which has been singled out is a very easy one to know about and to explain, and the passage does not necessarily show very extensive knowledge of Judaism – as would, for example, a dispute over the construction of immersion pools. Further, the passage could reflect Diaspora practice more easily than Palestinian. Diaspora Jews seem to have washed their hands while praying, as did many pagans, and since they probably prayed in the morning and evening[16] they may have washed their hands more than once a day. Handwashing in connection with prayer is not known from early rabbinic sources, though it is found in a later period.[17] We noted that Pharisees seem to have washed hands only before handling the priests' food, before eating their own sabbath and festival meals, and after handling the scripture. The depiction of handwashing in Mark 7.1–4 is closer to probable Diaspora practice than to pharisaic.

How serious was it not to wash one's hands? Not serious in the least. Besides the fact that Pharisees themselves probably did not regard it as obligatory to wash their hands before every meal, the evidence is that they did not try to coerce others to follow their extensions of the biblical law. But, for the sake of the argument, let us say that some group of Pharisees *did* practise handwashing before each meal and *had* decided to campaign in favour of their own special purity laws. I would think that there were many more serious breaches for which purity enthusiasts could have criticized Jesus and his followers. Perhaps they had eaten food cooked in an oven whose vent had been overshadowed by a corpse. Such an accusation would have been more serious than that the disciples ate with unwashed hands, since the impurity is greater. The Essenes could have jumped on Jesus' followers for anointing themselves with oil, especially when they fasted (see Matt. 6.17).

In assessing the possible affront which Jesus might have given the pious because he was not sufficiently strict with regard to purity, we might note what is not in the gospels: there is no reference to Jesus' going to Tiberias. From the point of view of social history, the absence of the three Galilean cities (Sepphoris, Tiberias and Scythopolis) from the gospels is striking and important. With regard to purity, however, Tiberias is especially significant. Everyone there, as we saw, had a permanent case of corpse-impurity. I have a private suspicion as to why Antipas built his new capital there. His first capital was Sepphoris, and it was the northern centre in which there was a strong contingent of the aristocracy, probably including some of the priestly aristocrats.[18] Antipas may very well simply have wanted to escape their interference. Building a new capital on a graveyard doubtless kept the leading Jews away from his court, and in Tiberias he would have been perfectly safe from priestly meddling. In any case, there was, quite near to Capernaum, a large group of impure people, and had Jesus wanted seriously to challenge the purity laws he could have gone there and told them that they were fine just as they were, that they need think no more about the ashes of the Red Heifer, and that they should enter the temple unpurified to prove the point. As a further aside, I shall mention that Tiberias was probably also the home of Antipas' main tax collectors.[19]

One must always hesitate before making too much of what someone did not do: perhaps Jesus just did not think of going to Tiberias but naturally went to his own kind – villagers. Nevertheless, this observation, coupled with the fact that handwashing was to most Jews a relatively unimportant matter, leads to the conclusion that Jesus was not in serious dispute with his contemporaries over laws of purity.[20]

Within Judaism, then, there were extensive disagreements about purity, and there were many issues which were more important to pietist groups than handwashing. Menstrual impurity and the water used in immersion pools both fall into the category of serious purity issues. Yet even on such important points the Pharisees tolerated variety of practice and interpretation, without seeking the punishment of those who disagreed with them. Further, handwashing was not necessarily a hallmark of Pharisaism, since other Jews practised it as well. Finally, not all Jews practised it, and extremists doubtless could have found many other people to criticize besides Jesus' disciples.

There are two further passages in the synoptics which involve purity. One had to do with leprosy. The laws on identification and purification are lengthy and complex (Lev. 13–14). 'Show yourself to the priest, and offer for cleansing what Moses commanded' (Mark 2.44) reflects knowledge of Lev. 13.49 ('show the priest'), the physical examination required in Lev. 14.1–2, and the sacrifices detailed in 14.3–32. This is the clearest reference to biblical purity laws in the synoptics, and they are accepted.

Under this heading may also be mentioned the criticism of a priest and a Levite in the Parable of the Good Samaritan (Luke 10.30–37). According to biblical law, 'The priests, the sons of Aaron' are strictly forbidden to contract corpse-impurity except for very close relatives. A son of Aaron is to come into proximity with a corpse only in order to tend and bury his mother, father, son, daughter, brother, or virgin sister (Lev. 21.1–3). This was, as far as we know, strictly kept but not developed further.

In the parable, Jesus criticizes a priest and a Levite for not being willing to risk coming into contact with a corpse. The point seems to be that they did not know whether or not the man by the side of the road was dead, and they were unwilling to risk incurring corpse-impurity simply on the chance that they might have been able to help. This is surely the motive which we must offer for the priest in the story. The Bible, however, does not explicitly forbid Levites to contract corpse-impurity, and Lev. 21.1–3 specifies *ha-Kohanim*, priests. It may nevertheless have been the case that Levites extended the priestly law to themselves. According to Num. 18.2–4 the Levites (in biblical theory, descendants of Aaron's father Levi, not of Aaron himself) were to 'join' (*yillavû*) the priests, and this may have led them to accept some of the restrictions laid on the priesthood. Or, possibly, they avoided corpse-impurity simply as a practical matter, since they would have to be purified of it before taking their turn in the temple service. This, however, is simply speculation, and I shall concentrate only on the legal issue faced by the parabolic priest.

Jesus' implied criticism is serious, since in effect it asks priests to risk transgression when there is a chance – only a chance, not a certainty – of helping an injured person. In this case, in order to see the issue in context we need to consider other pietist criticisms of the priesthood. The pietists who wrote the *Psalms of Solomon* (*c.* 63 BCE) accused the priests of bringing menstrual blood into the temple and thus defiling the sacrifices (8.14), and those of the CD accused them of lying with a woman who sees 'the blood of her flux' (5.6–8). These are much worse criticisms, since they accuse the priests of breaking a biblical law, rather than being too careful in observing one – the point of Jesus' parable. In the overall context of often bitter attacks, Jesus' parable is fairly mild. We should note that the priesthood seems to have shrugged off much more severe criticism. They did not, as far as we know, contrive to have their pietist critics executed.

E. OFFERINGS

Only one point of biblical law on sacrifices and offerings is needed to illuminate Matt. 5.23–24. According to Lev. 6.1–7 [Heb. 5.20–26] a person who wrongs another should (1) restore what was wrongfully acquired; (2) add a fifth and give it to the person; (3) bring a guilt offering. This leads to atonement and forgiveness. The prophets would develop at length the point that sacrifices are useless or worse than useless unless accompanied by mercy and just behaviour. 'I will have mercy and not sacrifice' (Hosea 6.6), which is quoted in Matt. 9.13 and 12.7, is the most famous of many passages.

In the period of the second temple this theme was emphasized. I shall cite only two authors, Ben Sira and Philo. Ben Sira urges.

> Do not offer him [God] a bribe, for he will not accept it;
>   and do not trust to an unrighteous sacrifice;
> for the Lord is the judge,
>   and with him is no partiality. (35.12).

Philo comments that 'if the worshipper is without kindly feeling or justice, the sacrifices are no sacrifices . . . But, if [the offerer] is pure of heart and just [*hosios* and *dikaios*], the sacrifice stands firm' (*Moses* 2.107f.). *Hosios*, usually translated 'pious', means 'towards God', while 'just' or 'righteous' means 'towards other people'. Piety and justice require, among other things, that an offender, *before* bringing the sacrifice, must have made full compensation plus one-fifth (*Spec. Laws* 1.234).[1]

Thus when Jesus said that the one who presents an offering, and who remembers that another person has been wronged (implying that it was a guilt offering), should first reconcile the brother (Matt. 5.23f.), he was in agreement with a long line of people who had made the same point about the relationship between justice and the laws of sacrifice.

F. TITHES

§1. Deuteronomy requires tithes – 10% of farm produce, including wine and oil, but apparently not animals – every year except the seventh (sabbatical) year, when the land lies fallow.[1] Most years, however, the people who separated the tithe of their produce enjoyed its benefit: they ate it. The food was to be taken to Jerusalem and consumed there – or, which was the usual practice, converted into money which was to be spent in Jerusalem as the one who tithed wished: 'spend the money for whatever you desire, oxen, or sheep, or wine or strong drink . . .' (Deut. 14.22–27). The purpose of the provision was to support Jerusalem financially. Every third year the tithe was to be given to support the Levites and the needy (Deut. 14.27–29; 26.12–13). Whether 'every third year' originally meant once in the seven year cycle or twice (the third and sixth years) is not entirely clear. Deut. 26.12 speaks of 'the third year, which is the year of tithing', which on its own could be interpreted to mean 'the third year of the seven year cycle'. The more generous interpretation – every third and sixth year of the seven year cycle – is presupposed in later literature, and I shall assume it throughout.

By contrast, Lev. 27.30–32 requires that one-tenth of the crops and one of every ten animals owned – apparently not just one-tenth of the animals born that year – should be given to 'the Lord'. The simplest explanation of this is that the tithe should be given to the priesthood.

The tithing law of Numbers is different again. The tithes were for the Levites, who in turn paid a tithe of the tithes to the priests. The Levitical tithe provided food for the Levites and their families: it was not eaten in the temple (Num. 18.21–32). No mention is made of the poor, nor of the consumption of the tithe by those who produce it. The situation is the same in Nehemiah: the Levites receive the tithes, pay a tithe to the priests, and keep the rest (Neh. 10.37b–39 [Heb. vv. 38b–40]). Subsequently the other temple employees are named as being supported by the tithes: 'the Levites, singers and gatekeepers' (Neh. 13.5) (unless 'singers and gatekeepers' simply specify the duties of the Levites).

The historical relationship among these tithing laws is disputed, and fortunately we do not have to decide it. The laws of Leviticus and Numbers may go back to a monarchical tax in the pre-exilic period, in which case they represent a 'take-over' of taxation by the temple castes. I Samuel 8.17 warns that if the people have a king he will require one-tenth of everything. The Chronicler depicts Hezekiah as re-establishing tithes for the priests and Levites (II Chron. 31.4–5), but the actual relationship between the rulers' taxes and the support of the priesthood during the monarchical period is not clear, nor is the relationship of the Deuteronomic law to the 10% tax.[2]

A reader who had only Deuteronomy would have a light law of tithing: 10% of one's crops to be consumed in Jerusalem, except for the third and sixth years, when the tithe would support the Levites and the poor. There would be no tithe in the seventh year. The reader of Numbers, Leviticus and Nehemiah would have a more expensive law: 10% of the year's produce, plus 10% of the animals, would be given to the priests or to the Levites, who in turn would tithe to the priests. But the first-century reader, who had all these books, and who did not separate them, assigning some to one period and some to another, found that scripture required tithes to support the Levites (and via them the priests), the city of Jerusalem, and the poor.

§2. Ancient literature offers two different ways of sorting out these requirements, and the differences are most instructive. According to Josephus, there were three tithes. The first tithe, given each year (except, presumably, the seventh), went to the Levites, who in turn tithed to the priests (*Antiq.* 4.69). This is the tithe of Numbers and Nehemiah, and it is evident that Leviticus has been read in light of the other two books. Its one-tenth 'to the Lord' is understood to mean 'to the Levites, who themselves give some to the priests'. Each year, Josephus continues, a second tithe was to be sold and the money spent in Jerusalem for 'repasts' and sacrifices (*Antiq.* 4.205). Finally, in the third and sixth years there was a third tithe, to support widows and orphans (*Antiq.* 4.240). Tobit 1.6–8 also refers to the third tithe (though not limiting it to specific years); and Jubilees 32.10–14, which requires that a tithe be eaten in Jerusalem every year, implies that in some years a third tithe was given to the poor.

The cruelest tithe, that of Lev. 27.32, was ignored. That verse requires 'every tenth animal of all that pass under the herdsman's staff', which amounts to a tax on capital. Josephus, however, is quite clear. In detailing the priestly revenues, he mentions their tithe of the Levites' tithe and also 'first fruits'. This offering, required by Num. 18.12–18, includes both crops (an unspecified amount) and animals (the first-born male of each pure animal, cash compensation for the first-born of impure animals).[3] Josephus also points out that the priests received meat from the sacrifices, as well as portions of animals which were slaughtered at home;[4] but animals are not otherwise mentioned in his list of the priests' income (*Antiq.* 4.69–75). He could not have forgotten a tax of 10% of all animals, and we may be sure that it was not collected.

The Mishnah (Maaseroth and Maaser Sheni) agrees that the first tithe should be given to the Levites and that they should tithe to the priests. The Deuteronomic tithe (called 'Second Tithe') should be spent in Jerusalem in years 1, 2, 4, and 5 of each seven year cycle, while in years 3 and 6 it should be given to the poor. In these years the second tithe was called 'Poor Tithe'. The Mishnah treats the requirement of a tenth of the animals (Lev. 27.32) as Second Tithe or as a peace offering, eaten in any part of Jerusalem by the family that produced it (and guests).[5] If the tithe of animals was treated as second tithe, it would not often have been a tithe of all the animals owned; it would be reasonable to eat in Jerusalem no more than one animal at each of the three pilgrimage festivals.[6]

Thus the Mishnah and Josephus agree in not taking Lev. 27.32 to be a priestly or Levitical tax on animals, and they accept the three requirements which come from combining the biblical books; but these they handle differently. Still assuming that Josephus did not think that there was a tithe in the seventh year, though he does not explicitly exclude it,[7] we see that according to his system the farmers had to give a total of fourteen tithes in each seven year cycle. The Mishnah requires a total of twelve. The difference is that the Mishnah requires that four tithes in the seven year cycle be spent in Jerusalem, while Josephus requires six. Both allow the poor two tithes in the cycle.

In comparison with the Mishnah, then, Josephus is harder on the farmers and herdsmen and more generous to Jerusalem. There seems to me little doubt that the mishnaic law is in this instance based on Pharisaic opinion, and that here we have a disagreement between the more 'populist' Pharisees and the aristocratic priesthood (represented by Josephus).

So, who actually tithed what? Tobit indicates that his accepting the three-tithe rule marked him as especially pious, and doubtless most people would want to avoid it. But could tithing laws in any case be enforced? Here we must distinguish the second tithe (Deuteronomy) from the first (Leviticus, Numbers and Nehemiah).

Since second tithe money could be spent in Jerusalem on anything – including sacrifices – many Palestinian Jews brought their second tithe money to the big city, with its famous and fascinating temple worship, and spent it. It would be out of place here to describe the pilgrimage festivals and how they were celebrated, but there is no doubt that throngs came to Jerusalem at Passover especially, and that the Festival of Booths or Tabernacles (Sukkot) was almost equally popular. As we noted above (p. 10), people would want to sacrifice, whether for purification (e.g. after childbirth), from a knowledge that a sin or guilt offering was required of them, or for feasting: the 'peace offering' was mostly consumed by the person who brought it, who could share it with family and friends, and it was the occasion of private celebrations and enjoyment in a world where red meat was a rarity. Thus, added to the requirement to spend second tithe money in Jerusalem, there was the attraction that it was an entertaining and highly enjoyable thing to do. I think that most people observed the Deuteronomic tithe (or some approximation thereof). There could be no enforcement – except for God's command – but it was doubtless a command which was usually cheerfully obeyed.[8]

The Levitical or first tithe was enforced by local pressure, especially from the Levites and priests. Many Levites lived outside Jerusalem, in the towns and villages, and Neh. 10.37b [Heb. v.38b] is explicit about their role: 'It is the Levites who collect our tithes in all our rural towns'. They were accompanied by priests (Neh. 10.38 [Heb. v. 39]). The priests' portion of the tithes was to be brought to the temple for distribution (Neh. 10.38 [Heb. v. 39]; cf. Neh. 13.5; II Chron. 31.11).[9] There is no reason to think that this practice was dropped in later years. The fact that priests accompanied the Levites when gathering the tithes means that the full moral authority of God's ordained clergy was put behind the collection. Philo made a theological point about the central deposit and redistribution of the priests' food: they could then receive the offerings as having come to them from God, and thus accept them with no sense of shame (*Spec. Laws* 1.152).

That tithes and offerings actually reached the temple is readily proved: we saw above two stories about the theft of the priests' portions of the tithes. That the collection system functioned in the first century can also be shown. When, at the start of the revolt against Rome, Josephus first went to Galilee to assess the situation there, he was accompanied by two other priests (*Life* 29). They collected tithes and returned with them to Jerusalem (*Life* 63). Secondly, there is a passage in the Tosefta which represents priests and Levites as standing by the threshing floor waiting to collect (T. Peah 4.3). This passage is probably post-70; payment of tithes did not cease with the destruction of the temple, and so the question of collection was still a live one. The evidence from Nehemiah, Josephus and the Tosefta shows continuity of practice.

A third passage may be of relevance. At the time of crisis just before the revolt actually started, the chief priests and the *bouletai* (council members) went into the villages of Judaea and Galilee to collect tribute money for the Romans (*War* 2.405). Presumably these were the men who generally arranged for the payment of tribute. (The Romans did not station their own tax collectors around the country, but held local leaders responsible for collecting tax and tribute.) If these people, headed by the chief priesthood, could collect Roman tribute, presumably they could also collect tithes.

Thus far, it would appear that, during Jesus' day, the laws of tithing were kept, either because people believed that divine law should be obeyed, or because the collection system for first tithe was effective – or both. We know from rabbinic literature, however, that the Pharisees, and after them the Rabbis, developed the category called *demai*, 'produce not certainly tithed' or 'produce which may or may not have been tithed'. If someone strict about the law acquired produce from someone who was not strict, the buyer was expected to tithe it again. The existence of this category shows that evasion of first tithe was possible.

Below we shall have occasion to study in detail the attitudes of Pharisees towards the various sources of income of the priests and the Levites. We shall see that they trusted the ordinary people to pay 'first fruits' and 'heave offering', as well as to spend second tithe money in Jerusalem, but that they were dubious that the common person could be counted on to tithe fully. Even some Pharisees, however, regarded the Levites' portion as not requiring the utmost strictness. To mention only one passage: the House of Hillel took the view that a strict observer of the law, when he came into possession of demai-produce, need separate only the priests' portion of first tithe – one-hundredth of the total rather than one-tenth ('I'. Maaser Sheni 3.15). Some, however, to be sure that the Levites were supported, paid the full one-tenth of demai-produce, and we may suppose that all Pharisees thought that the entire tithe should be paid.[10] It was apparently the Levites' portion of the tithe, their only legal source of support, which was in jeopardy.

Now we return to the difference between the three-tithe law of Josephus and the two-tithe law of the Mishnah, and the question of who paid what. The third tithe (Poor Tithe) was probably also collected by the Levites, though other 'almoners' may also have existed. Let us now suppose that a Levite and a priest approached to demand the first and third tithes in year three or six, and that they reminded the farmer that in that year he also was to take a third tithe to Jerusalem and consume it there. Most Palestinian Israelites wished to obey God's law. If a Levite or priest came up and said: 'God has commanded you to pay this tithe, hand it over', no one, except the full apostate, would say: 'I choose not to obey God's law'. But some might be happy to say: 'I am an ignorant man, and I know that you are an expert in the law. But there is another group of experts, the Pharisees, and they say that we do not owe three tithes during this, the third year. I give you two tithes, one for yourself and the priests, one for the poor, but I am exempt from the requirement to spend another tithe in Jerusalem.' That is, the farmer or herdsman would be reluctant as an individual to challenge the authority of a priest or Levite, but it may have been very useful to be able to say that another group of experts interpreted the law differently. This could be done by the pious Israelite with a clear conscience, not with the feeling of wilfully disobeying the law of God.

We cannot know how many people followed each interpretation, nor how thoroughly the Levitical collectors canvassed the countryside. It appears, however, that there was a problem about full payment of first tithe. To meet the problem of non-payment, we saw, some Pharisees were willing to pay the tithe on produce which they purchased from someone whom they did not fully trust.

There were a few disagreements about what should be tithed. The general principle obviously was that foodstuff should be tithed, but there is room for disagreement about what counts as 'food'. According to the House of Hillel, black cummin is susceptible to impurity and also should be tithed, while the House of Shammai disagreed (Uktzin 3.6). The seeds of black cummin (Latin *nigella sativa*; Hebrew *qetsah*; Greek *melanthion*) could be used in very small quantities as a spice. Apparently the Shammaites did not consider it to be a food.

§3. Now we may understand the criticism of the Pharisees for tithing mint, dill and cummin, but neglecting the weightier matters (Matt. 23.23). Jesus' accusation is simply that they spent too much time making sure that the tithing laws were kept and that the Levites and priests were fully supported. Jesus (or the part of the early church which remembered or created this saying) does not disagree with this aim in the least. There is no actual conflict over the law. The lengthy explanation above serves simply to explain the context in which tithing minor herbs was an issue. Some were suspected of trying to escape all or part of first tithe. Some went to considerable lengths to tithe all that was required and even more.

What would Pharisees have replied if Jesus had actually said this to them? My guess would be that they would have answered in the spirit of these lines from Aboth:

Ben Azzai said: Run to fulfil the lightest duty even as the weightiest, and flee from transgression; for one duty draws another duty in its train, and one transgression draws another transgression in its train. (Aboth 4.2)

That is, once you start disobeying, where will it end? We do not intend to stress trivia over love, justice and mercy; but we are certainly not going to disobey God in the small matters which we can control.

G. TEMPLE TAX

§1. If one were thinking of Jews outside Palestine, whether in the rest of the Roman Empire or in Mesopotamia, the temple tax, along with observance of sabbath and food laws, would be a major sign of Jewish identity. Paying it marked one as a Jew; not paying it would lead others to think that one had apostatized. Refusal to pay it in Palestine would have the same effect, but only in some cities was there an alternative community – Gentile paganism – to belong to. We may safely say that all Jews who wished to be counted as such paid the tax.

The basic facts about it are very simple. According to Exodus the Lord commanded Moses that

> each who is numbered in the census shall give this: half a shekel according to the shekel of the sanctuary (the shekel is twenty gerahs), half a shekel as an offering to the Lord. Every one who is numbered in the census, from twenty years old and upward, shall give the Lord's offering. The rich shall not give more, and the poor shall not give less, than the half shekel, when you give the Lord's offering to make atonement for yourselves. And you shall take the atonement money from the people of Israel, and shall appoint it for the service of the tent of meeting [the temple]; that it may bring the people of Israel to remembrance before the Lord, so as to make atonement for yourselves. (Ex. 30.13–16).

This is an extremely clear law: a census and a specified per capita tax, in a specified coinage, for a specified purpose – atonement (30.15, *l'kappēr*, *exilasasthai*; in v.12 the Greek word is *lutra*, 'ransom'). The census and tax in Exodus, however, are not presented as recurring annually. The income went for the construction of the tabernacle. Nehemiah 10.32 [Heb. v. 33] requires an annual tax of one-third shekel, which would pay for the community offerings, such as the daily whole-burnt offerings, and also for the general upkeep of the sanctuary (10.33 [34]).[1]

§2. In the first century there was an annual temple tax (as in Nehemiah) of a half-shekel (as in Exodus), and it was paid by Jews all over the world. The sums collected were quite large. Pseudo-Aristeas refers to a contribution from Egypt of 'one hundred talents of silver for sacrifices and the other requirements' (as well as 'first fruits'; *Arist.* 40),[2] and Philo mentions the envoys who took money from every city to the temple (*Spec. Laws* 1.77–78). Josephus says that two drachmas (=one-half shekel) were collected from each Jew in Mesopotamia (as well as other offerings; *Antiq.* 18.312). There is even better proof that the tax was paid and that it served to identify Jews as Jews: after each of the two revolts (66–73/74; 132–135) Rome ordered that the money still be paid, but for other purposes (*War* 7.218; Dio Cassius 66.7 and elsewhere).[3]

It is quite difficult to convert ancient sums of money into modern terms. It is even hard to convert (say) 1930 pounds, dollars, marks etc. into their equivalents in the 1980s or '90s. In the parable of the labourers in the vineyard, a day's wage for casual labour is a denarius (Matt. 20.2). A denarius was approximately equivalent to a drachma, and thus the tax of one-half shekel or two drachmas was the equivalent of two days' pay for those at the very bottom of the economic scale.[4] The one hundred talents of *Arist.* 40 was a very large sum of money: one talent was 6,000 denarii. A talent is basically a weight, approximately 40 kg or 88 lbs. Thus the text in *Aristeas* refers to 4000 kg or 8800 lbs of silver. One may assume exaggeration, but certainly the total revenue brought in by this tax was very large.[5]

§3. There is an extremely curious story of the temple tax in Matt. 17.24–27. The collectors asked Peter whether or not his teacher paid the two drachmas. Peter confirmed that he did. Privately, though, Jesus asked Peter, 'What do you think, Simon? From whom do kings of the earth take toll or tribute? From their sons or from others?' Peter acknowledged that it was from others. Jesus replied, 'Then the sons are free'. In order not to cause offence 'to them', however, he told Peter to catch a fish and that in its mouth he would find a stater (approximately four drachmas), which would pay the tax for the two of them. Jesus' saying, 'then the sons are free' is extraordinarily striking (if he said it), since the point of the tax was (1) to atone for the sins of Israel and (2) to identify oneself as a loyal Jew. Jesus seems to be saying that 'the sons' are not Jews. He and Peter, *true* sons, should have been exempt. This is reminiscent of the statement by John the Baptist that Jews should not appeal to descent from Abraham, since 'God is able from these stones to raise up children to Abraham' (Matt. 3.9). (We may ignore the difference between 'sons of Abraham' and 'sons of God', since both refer to membership in the people of God.) John did not *deny* that Jews were 'sons', but rather warned them not to rely on the fact. The passage about the temple tax seems to presuppose that only Jesus and Peter (and presumably Jesus' other followers) were truly sons of God.

David Daube has recently proposed that Jesus was here applying to himself a prerogative which the priesthood claimed, that they should be free of the tax (so Shekalim 1.3).[6] He marshalls other evidence that Jesus assigned to himself priestly prerogatives. It is beyond my purpose here to try to evaluate this; for in fact I would attribute the passage to a branch of the early church which felt ambivalent towards the temple and, moreover, about their being 'sons' by virtue of being Jewish. That Jews as such were 'sons' is challenged directly by Paul in Gal. 3; and other Christian communities may have had their own doubts about it – though less radical doubts than Paul's. Nowhere else in Jesus' teaching is there a saying which indicates that he intended to distinguish 'sons of the kingdom' from those of Jewish descent. (See e.g. the harsh statement of Matt. 8.12: the cast out Jews are nevertheless 'sons of the kingdom').

But, following our hypothetical position that all the material really goes back to Jesus, and thus that Jesus really said to Peter that 'the sons' should not have to pay the very tax which stamped them as Jewish, I must say that Daube has made a brilliant suggestion. In this passage 'the synoptic Jesus' claims that he and his followers *should* have the prerogative of priests, though in fact he paid the tax.

H. OATHS AND VOWS

§1. Biblical law, and consequently law in first-century Judaism, included what we now consider 'civil law': laws concerning property, damages and the like. Oaths were important for society because they guaranteed a word or action by appealing to God and calling down his curse if it was broken. A man might say on oath that he had not committed a crime, and he had a good chance of being believed, since a false oath meant that the curse would befall him. Or a man might say, for example, 'I swear by God that, if you let me have your ox today, I shall pay you for it tomorrow'. If both parties believed in God and his justice – his reliability to punish transgressors – the oath would be good security.

While the full form of an oath includes a curse, most of the biblical examples do not give it explicitly, probably because of the awe-fulness of the words.[1] An example of an oath which clearly implies the curse is Solomon's oath to kill his brother Adonijah:

God do so to me and more also if this word does not cost Adonijah his life! Now therefore as the Lord lives, who has established me, and placed me on the throne of David my father, and who has made me a house, as he promised, Adonijah shall be put to death this day (I Kings 2.23–24).

This says, in effect, 'May God strike me dead if I do not . . .'. These are awesome words, which few would utter lightly.

In the ten commandments there are no distinctions within the category of oath. The only oath that is envisaged is swearing by the name of God, and transgressing it is said to be unforgivable: 'The Lord will not hold him guiltless who takes his name in vain' (Ex. 20.7; Deut. 5.11). This extreme rigour is probably due to the fact that the legislators supposed that taking the Lord's name falsely – not fulfilling an oath sworn 'by God' – must be intentional. It is a deliberate profanation of the holiness of God himself.

In Leviticus the prohibition is repeated: one should not swear falsely 'and so profane the name of your God: I am the Lord' (Lev. 19.11–12). The legislation of Leviticus, however, reckoned with the possibility of a 'rash oath'. If someone swears an oath inadvertently, and later realizes that he has done so, he should bring a guilt offering and thus find forgiveness (Lev. 5.4–6). The rigour of Exodus and Deuteronomy is thus moderated.

A vow is essentially a promise, with a guarantee of divine sanction if it is not fulfilled. An ancient, and horrific, example is that of Jephthat, who vowed that he would sacrifice the next person who walked through his door. He kept the vow even though it meant the sacrifice of his daughter (Judg. 11.29–40). This was a vow of a sacrifice to God. In later times vows to the temple were common. People and property which have been 'sanctified' or 'devoted' – vowed to God – are discussed in Lev. 27.1–29. The best known biblical vow is that of the Nazirite, who undertook not to eat or drink anything which came from grapes, not to cut his or her hair, and not to incur corpse-impurity (Num. 6.1–21). Here the vow involves abstinence or avoidance. These two types of vow – to give something to God, or to give something up – were the most common. They could of course be combined: one gave up what one gave to God.

Vows promise future action; and, since oaths could also cover future behaviour, the difference between vow and oath is sometimes only technical. 'In the vow the person prohibits the thing to himself by declaring, "I take upon myself"; in the oath he prohibits himself to the thing by saying, "I swear to do this, or not to do this."'[2]

The biblical discussion of the binding character of vows (Num. 30) allows some vows to be cancelled: the father of a woman not yet married, if he disapproves of her vow 'on the day he hears of it', may cancel it (v. 5); a woman's husband may cancel her vow in the same circumstances (vv. 8–12). Otherwise all vows stand, as do all oaths; they must be fulfilled.

§2. In the post-biblical period the binding character of oaths and vows was accepted. This is exemplified by the story in Matthew and Mark of Antipas' decision to execute John the Baptist. Antipas was pleased with Salome's dancing and promised her whatever she wished. When she asked for the head of the Baptist, he was compelled to grant the request because he had made the promise with an oath (Mark 6.26//Matt. 14.7,9). This shows that rash oaths, or oaths taken in passion, could be a problem. Vows too continued to be made and observed. A biblical word for 'offering', *qorban*, came to be used in a technical sense to refer to what was specially vowed to the temple. This usage is known both from rabbinic literature and inscriptions.[3] Some authors who wrote in Greek retained the Hebrew word (Mark 7.11; Josephus, *Antiq.* 4.73). Thus *korbanas* is used in Greek for the temple treasury in both Matt. 27.6 and *War* 2.175. In describing the Nazirite vow, Josephus used *korban* and then translated it as *dōron*, 'gift' (*Antiq.* 4.73).[4]

The Essenes and the Pharisees, who sometimes elaborated and intensified biblical law in the same direction, went in opposite ways with regard to oaths. According to Josephus the Essenes, after the solemn oaths taken on admission,[5] refused to swear at all. They held that 'one who is not believed without an appeal to God stands condemned already' (*War* 2.135–139). This may explain why Herod dispensed them from the requirement to swear an oath of loyalty (*Antiq.* 15.371).[6] The Pharisees, on the other hand, accepted the usefulness and validity of oaths. When they refused to give Herod the oath of allegiance he fined them (*Antiq.* 17.42). They could not claim, as could the Essenes, that they were against oaths in principle.

There is, however, conflicting evidence on the Essenes. In the Covenant of Damascus oaths on topics other than joining the group are accepted (CD 9.9–12; 15.3–5; 16.7–12). There was more than one branch of the Essene party, as is clear both from Josephus (*War* 2.160–161) and from the differences between the *Covenant of Damascus* and the *Community Rule* of Qumran. Thus, for example, sacrifices at the Jerusalem temple are permitted in the former but not in the latter (CD 11.17–21; 16.13; 1QS 9.4f.). I am inclined to accept Josephus's statement that the Essenes would not take oaths as applying to one group, especially since it makes such good sense of Herod's treatment of them when they refused the oath of loyalty.

Pharisaic scholars did a lot of legal work on oaths, especially formulating rules about valid and invalid oath-forms. People in general seem to have sworn a lot – as they still do – and to have sworn not only by God but by people ('by my mother'), themselves ('by my head') and things ('by the temple'); and the practice was not limited just to the unlearned. R. Tarfon (mid-second century) is said to have emphasized some remarks by the oath, 'May I bury my sons if . . . not . . .' (e.g. T. Ahilot 15.12). The social situation has been described by Lieberman: Jews, like their Gentile contemporaries, used vows and oaths indiscriminately for all sorts of circumstances. There was a tendency to develop new terms in a way that devalued the coinage of binding words. Lieberman proposed that the masses avoided the 'valid and binding terms' and sought substitutes, such as 'by Jerusalem'. Then this was avoided, and they went on to 'absurd oaths like "by the fish-nets"'. 'No sooner did the absurd expression become a fixed oath-term, than the people tended to use a substitute for it, thus progressing from the stupid to the ridiculous'.[7] Lieberman's view was that the people regarded all oaths (and vows) as equally binding. The sages (the Pharisees and later the Rabbis) attempted to stop abuses of the solemn oath or vow, and they did this in part by 'ruling' that certain oaths or vows did not count.[8]

One may suspect that there was also a tendency to seek lesser oaths than those in the name of God, reduced formulations which were serious but not absolutely binding. Many oaths, moreover, were doubtless just words, with no serious intent. We need not give details of the Pharisees' efforts to sort out oath-forms, nor – fortunately – try to disentangle them from later rabbinic discussions. We may also leave undiscussed post-biblical views about release from oaths, especially oaths sworn in passion.[9] We do need, however, to pay some attention to the analogous problem with regard to vows: When were vows, especially the vow *qorban*, binding?

Before turning to the Pharisees, we may note Philo's strict view of vows: a vow in the name of God, even if it were 'a chance verbal promise', was still binding (*Hypothetica* 7.3). He continues, 'If a man had devoted his wife's substance to a sacred purpose he must refrain from giving her that sustenance; so with a father's gifts to his son or a ruler's to his subjects' (7.5). This stringency is moderated by allowing two forms of release: the best is for the priest to refuse the dedicated property. A second mode of release is difficult to decipher: 'those who have the higher authority may lawfully declare that God is propitiated so that there is no necessity to accept the dedication' (ibid.). Colson, the Loeb translator, notes that the Greek is not entirely clear. The reference to 'higher authority', however, possibly means that the high priest or king, rather than the priest to whom the property is actually offered, can release the vow.

Discussions of vows are attributed to the Schools of Shammai and Hillel.

> If a man saw others eating [his] figs and said, 'May they be *Korban* to you!' and they were found to be his father and brothers and others with them, the School of Shammai say: For them the vow is not binding, but for the others with them it is binding. And the School of Hillel say: the vow is binding for neither of them. (Nedarim 3.2)

In this mishnah the declaration *qorban* may be used literally, meaning that his figs are vowed or dedicated to the temple and consequently cannot be used for secular purposes. When irritated that others were eating his figs, the man dedicated the fruit to the temple. A second possibility, however, is that the man meant that the figs were *like qorban*, meaning that the others had to treat the figs *as if* they were dedicated to the temple: they could then not be eaten by anyone. In either case, the Houses thought that the vow should be disallowed in whole (the Hillelites) or in part (the Shammaites).

Baumgarten has shown that the second use of *qorban*, to mean simply 'forbidden to you', existed. An ossuary has on it this inscription: 'Everything which a man will find to his profit in this ossuary is an offering (*qorban*) to God from the one within it'.[10] The contents of an ossuary could not be given to the temple, since anything which had corpse-impurity could not enter it. The inscription, therefore, must mean simply that the finder was to treat the contents as if they were *qorban*. Whether or not this is the meaning of the declaration *qorban* in the Houses dispute just above, we see that they accepted the declaration and attempted to define when it was valid, just as they accepted oaths and attempted to define binding oath-forms.

In later rabbinic literature, reasons for the release of vows are multiplied. As Baumgarten has pointed out, however, this is not the case in the earliest layer of rabbinic literature, where few justifications for release are proposed, and they are subject to dispute. This is so, he notes, whether one accepts Neusner's or Epstein's analysis of which passages are early.[11]

§3. In Matt. 23.16–22 Jesus criticizes the Pharisees for distinguishing between an oath 'by the temple', which is invalid, and an oath 'by the gold of the temple', which is valid; and between an oath 'by the altar', invalid, and an oath 'by the gift on the altar', valid. He takes the position that all these oaths are of equal seriousness, and that they are actually oaths taken in the name of God himself. While we cannot attribute these precise distinctions to Pharisees on the basis of rabbinic literature, for the present purposes we may accept them.[12] Jesus rejects the pharisaic attempt to distinguish binding from non-binding oath-forms. This stance might have agreed with that of the Sadducees, who favoured observing the letter of the law and not developing new traditions. Jesus takes the position that the new formulations are really oaths 'by God', which is one of the possible choices on the basis of Sadducean principles. The other would be that non-biblical oath-forms are all equally invalid.

It is striking that the Jesus of Matt. 5.34–37, like some of the Essenes, forbade swearing oaths entirely: 'Let what you say be simply "Yes" or "No".' This position on oaths is analogous to that of the Essenes and Jesus on divorce (above, p.5): it is not against the biblical law, since the person who does not swear obviously would not transgress the law which forbids swearing falsely. The position that oaths should not be taken at all implicitly criticizes the law, however, for catering to human weakness. In a better world or time it would be unnecessary for there to be oaths, just as it would be unnecessary for people to divorce.

If applied in the present, the rejection of oaths would create social problems: a person who would not swear could not do business, except within the confines of a small group. It is probable that we should understand the rejection of oaths by the synoptic Jesus and some of the Essenes in just this way: members of the group dealt only with one another. It is noteworthy that in Matt. 5.42 Jesus urges his followers, 'give to him who begs from you, and do not refuse him who would borrow from you'. Ordinarily, a loan has to be secured, and an oath might be required. In a small community of like-minded, equally pious people, other financial relationships could obtain, and one of the civil reasons for oaths could be dispensed with.

It is not in the least impossible for the same person to have criticized the Pharisees for making distinctions among oaths and to have commanded his followers not to swear. Oaths if sworn are all by God and are binding, but it is better not to swear at all. In this case Jesus would be seen as opposing one pharisaic device for controlling the popular tendency to swear, but agreeing with their concern: the proliferation of oaths for minor issues should be checked, and checked drastically; they should not be used at all. For our present purposes, the most important point to note is that in both passages – Matt. 23 and Matt. 5 – Jesus is depicted as taking a stance which falls well within the parameters of debate about the law in the first century.

We turn now to the New Testament passage on *korban*, Mark 7.9 –13// Matt. 15.3–6. Jesus, being accused of transgressing 'the tradition (*paradosis*) of the elders' by not requiring his disciples to wash their hands (Mark 7.5), responds by saying that the 'tradition' of the scribes and Pharisees allows transgression of the written law: the Bible commands honour of father and mother, but their tradition allows a son to tell his parents that money or property which they could expect of him is *korban*. This would mean that it was owed to the temple, or that the parents had to treat it as if it were. In neither case could anyone make use of it. The declaration *korban*, as in the case of people eating figs above, would be based on spite or malice: the man did not profit by declaring his goods *korban*, he just kept his parents from using them.

Baumgarten has proposed that this criticism corresponds to probable pharisaic practice. He reconstructs the issue thus: Jesus rules out the man's vow as 'inherently invalid', while the Pharisees accept the vow as binding. They have not yet, however, developed rules of release which would cover the case, and so they have to support the man against his parents. The vow is binding unless there are grounds for invalidating it.

This discussion counts in favour of those who have held that Jesus did not attack the law, but only pharisaic interpretation. Clearly he makes no criticism of the written law. I would just add, however, that Jesus' criticism could be much more specifically applied to Philo's interpretation of vows and their release than to the Pharisees'. Philo explicitly allows a man to forbid his wife from making use of her property by dedicating it, and he extends the point to include a man's gift to his son. The case in Mark 7 is simply the reverse: property which parents expected from their son. It is somewhat doubtful that Pharisees held that *qorban* could function as a weapon in intra-family animosity, since in Nedarim 3.2 both Houses rule that the man's declaration *qorban* over the figs does not apply to members of his family. There are not enough Houses disputes on *qorban* to allow us to be confident about what Pharisees would or would not allow, but such evidence as there is indicates that their leaders would not have been guilty of permitting a vow made in malice to distort natural justice. We know, however, that at least one Alexandrian Jew thought that vows could be used in this way. It is doubtful that this is Philo's private rule, and it may well have been accepted throughout Egyptian Judaism – and possibly beyond. We saw above that the first issue of Mark 7, handwashing, also makes good sense in the Diaspora.

I. BLASPHEMY

§1. In Lev. 24.10–23 the person is condemned to stoning who 'curses (*qillel*) the name' of God (see 24.11). The phrase 'specify (*naqab*) the name' in 24.16 would lead later readers to say that blasphemy requires the explicit use of the Proper Name of God, which modern scholars reconstruct as Yahweh. By the first century it was no longer pronounced (except by the high priest on the Day of Atonement), and thus there is no unbroken tradition to tell us how it was said. What are certain are the four consonants YHWH.

In Isa. 37.6, however, an Assyrian is said to have 'reviled' or 'blasphemed' (*giddēp*) God merely by saying that He would not deliver Israel. Here God is not cursed, but rather spoken of denigratingly. Since there is no single word for 'blasphemy' in the Hebrew Bible, there could be no single definition of it. There was, rather, a range of derogatory statements which may best be called 'blasphemy', and there was a variety of Hebrew terms for the general conception. In the few verses just referred to, we see 'curse' and 'revile' in Hebrew, which are translated appropriately in Greek (*katarasthai*, 'curse'; *oneidizein*, 'reproach' or 'revile').[1] In Ex. 22.28 [Heb. v. 27] the people are commanded not to curse (*t'qallēl*) God nor to curse (*ta'ōr*, from *'arar*) their ruler. This invites applying the same penalty in both cases.

Neither *blasphēmein* nor *blasphēmia* occurs in the Pentateuchal books in the Greek translation (the Septuagint, abbreviated LXX), but the root *blasphēm –* appears several times in other books.[2] The LXX uses 'blasphemy' for cursing, speaking ill of, belittling or defaming God (so II Kings [IV Bas.] 19.4, 6, 22).* Activities which are entirely antithetical to Israelite religion are termed 'blasphemy' in I Macc. 2.6 (referring especially to the defilement of the temple by Antiochus IV) and II Macc. 8.4 (referring to the activities of the Syrians in general). Especially interesting is LXX Ezek. 35.12. Where the Hebrew refers to 'the revilings which you [Edom] uttered *against* ('*al*) the mountains of Israel', the LXX reads, 'your blasphemies, *in that* (*hoti*) you said, "the desert mountains of Israel are given to us as food"'. The passage continues by accusing Edom of 'speaking exaggerated words (*emegalorremonēsas*) against me' (35.13). The blasphemy here is presumption, specifically the presumption that a gentile nation can take for itself what God gave to Israel.

In the LXX we see that blasphemy need not involve an explicit curse or reviling of God. Destruction of what he has ordained can be called blasphemy (I and II Maccabees), as can presumptuously supposing that humans can set his word at nought (Ezekiel). This does not count as hard evidence for views in Palestine, though it is not unreasonable to think that the understanding of blasphemy in the LXX reflects opinions which were current in post-biblical Judaism generally, not just in the Greek-speaking Diaspora.

§2. Josephus inserted the root *blasphēm-* at several points when recounting biblical passages. Sometimes he used *blasphēmein* where the Hebrew and the LXX have 'curse': thus the summary of Lev. 24.10–16 (*Antiq.* 4.202); the narration of the accusation of Naboth (*Antiq.* 8.358f.; Heb. I Kings 21.13 and LXX 20.13 have the euphemism 'bless'). According to Josephus, Moses forbade anyone to 'blaspheme' local rulers (*Antiq.* 4.215; cf. Deut. 16.18). This is an insertion into Deuteronomy, but it is probably influenced by Ex. 22.28 [27], cited above, where the Hebrew has 'curse' and the Greek 'speak ill of'. Occasionally blasphemy is simply added to the story: David accused Goliath of blaspheming God (*Antiq.* 6.183).

Some cases appear to be exegetical in a way that goes beyond translating 'curse' or the euphemistic 'blessing' as 'blasphemy'. Josephus wrote that Belshazzar was 'drinking and blaspheming God' when he saw a hand write on the wall (*Antiq.* 10.233; Dan. 5). The meaning of 'blasphemy' here becomes clear in 10.242: Belshazzar 'had grievously blasphemed the Deity and had allowed himself with his concubines to be served from His vessels'. The

*I shall cite the books of the LXX by their Hebrew/English titles: thus LXX II Kings rather than IV Basileiōn or IV Kingdoms.

blasphemy was not just what Belshazzar said, but also what he did; Josephus inferred blasphemy from Dan. 5.2, where Belshazzar decides to make use of the temple vessels. Similarly he wrote that a prophet rebuked King Ahab for allowing Ben-hadad, the Syrian king, to blaspheme God' (*Antiq.* 8.391). Josephus here was probably interpreting I Kings 20.28, where the Syrians say that '"The Lord is a god of the hills but he is not a god of the valleys"'. Josephus construed this denigrating speech as 'blasphemy'.

Finally, we note the story of a Roman soldier who uncovered his genitals and exhibited them publicly while he was standing on a portico of the temple, watching the crowd for unrest at Passover. The onlookers considered this blasphemy against God (*Antiq.* 20.108), presumably because of the location and the occasion.

Josephus used the root *blasphēm-* to mean all sorts of verbal abuse. Thus far I have attempted to select just the instances in which he translates 'curse' as *blasphēm-* and those in which he clearly means blasphemy against God in the full religious sense. There are interesting borderline passages, and one of them merits consideration. When a Pharisee said that he had heard that the mother of Hyrcanus I had been a captive (implying that the high priest may have been illegitimate), Josephus characterizes the statement as *blasphēmia* (*Antiq.* 13.293–295). Is this ordinary human slander or, since it is against the high priest, blasphemy? The Pharisees recommended that the man be flogged – thus indicating that in their view it was not a case of blasphemy – while Hyrcanus wanted execution. He probably applied Ex. 22.28 [27], which links denigration of the ruler with that of God, and thus expected the man to be stoned.

Philo's interpretation of Lev. 24.10–16 deserves rescuing from obscurity. It is not mentioned at all by Beyer (n. 2 above), and, quite remarkably, even Wolfson seems to miss it. Philo fixed not only on Lev. 24.16 (as Wolfson thought);[3] rather, he found a contrast between 24.11 and 24.16. The former verse, with the phrase 'curse god', he took to be a relatively light offence: it refers to 'the gods of the different cities who are falsely so called'. Thus he read it in light of the LXX of Ex. 22.28 [27], which he and other Greek readers understood to prohibit speaking ill of pagan gods, since the LXX retains the Hebrew plural.[4] It is only Lev. 24.16 which requires the death sentence: 'the one who names the name of the Lord, let him die'. Philo moderates this a bit by saying that the death penalty is merited when God's name is uttered 'unseasonably', *akairos*. 'Naming the name of the Lord' doubtless means using his proper name, which Philo refers to elsewhere as the 'tetragrammaton' (YHWH).[5] He notes that this is not actually 'blasphemy'; but, though a lighter offence, it nevertheless deserves death (*Moses* 2.203–206). Thus there is a hierarchy: cursing other gods is wrong; using the proper Name of God 'unseasonably' requires death; blaspheming is worse yet.

I have discovered no rabbinic passages attributed to Pharisees which deal with blasphemy. The Mishnah tractate Sanhedrin, which is marked by extreme leniency, requires for conviction that 'the one who curses' (*ha-m‘gaddēp*), to be guilty, must explicitly pronounce the Proper Name of God. This is based on straight exegesis of Lev. 24.10–16.[6] As in other capital cases, conviction of blasphemy ('cursing God') also requires two witnesses (Sanhedrin 7.5). Here the definition of the offence is strict, and vague denigrations do not count.

The biblical words for 'revile' and the like occur in the Dead Sea Scrolls, but they are ordinarily said to be directed against God's elect, not God (e.g. 1QpHab 10.13). The opponents of the Essenes – the Jews who controlled the temple, CD 5.6 – are accused of having a 'cursing tongue' (*lishôn giddûpîm*), in that they speak 'against the ordinances of the covenant of God' (CD 5.11f.), and the same phrase is used of people who walk in the way of 'the spirit of falsehood' in 1QS 4.11. The first of these passages probably means that the 'cursing tongues' are directed against the sectarian laws, but the second is more general and might include cursing God. In CD 12.8 the members of the group are urged not to steal from the Gentiles, so that they will not blaspheme (*giddēp*), that is, curse God on account of the behaviour of his people. So far were the Qumran sectarians from thinking that any of their own number might actually blaspheme that they required expulsion for one who slanders the community (1QS 7.16f.). 'Cursing' inadvertently while reading the Book or praying also resulted in permanent expulsion (1QS 7.1–2). Here presumably 'cursing the Name' is not meant, but rather utterly any kind of profanity because of an unpleasant surprise (e.g. being stung by a wasp while praying).

§3. Blasphemy is obviously a most grievous sin, and I have put it this low on the list for two reasons. One is that, because of the connection with using the Name of God, it is best taken together with the discussion of Oaths. The second is that the synoptic passages on blasphemy do not depict Jesus as actually transgressing the law.

There are two passages, Mark 2.1–12 and parr.; Mark 14.61–64// Matt. 26.65 (omitted from Luke). According to the first, Jesus said to the paralytic, 'Your sins are forgiven', which led the scribes to say 'in their hearts' that he was blaspheming, since only God can forgive sins. According to the second, the high priest asked Jesus if he was the Son of God. In Mark's version, he answers, 'I am; and you will see the Son of man . . . coming with the clouds of heaven'. In Matthew, however, he only replies, 'You have said so. But I tell you . . . you will see the Son of man . . .' (Matt.

26.64). In both cases the result is the same: The high priest tears his robes and pronounces blasphemy.

Two points about the verses on forgiveness of sins (Mark 2.5–7) should be emphasized: (1) Jesus speaks in the passive voice, 'Your sins are forgiven', which must mean not by himself but by God, whose forgiveness he declares;[7] (2) the scribes say only 'in their hearts' that Jesus blasphemed. Often in New Testament scholarship, one or both of these points are overlooked but the rest of the passage is accepted. Bornkamm noted neither the divine passive nor that the complaint was unspoken, but otherwise accepted the passage as historically accurate: the opponents were 'enraged' because Jesus did what was God's prerogative. Bornkamm then quoted the scribes' thoughts as if they had been spoken aloud.[8] Schweizer understood Jesus to have 'offered forgiveness as though he stood in the place of God'.[9] Jeremias, though recognizing that Jesus did not forgive in his own name, nevertheless thought it to be historically true that 'Pharisaic circles' accused him of blasphemy for 'encroaching on the area reserved for God alone'.[10] Perrin, despite accepting Bultmann's view that the scene is 'ideal', nevertheless held that it corresponds essentially to historical reality. Opponents really did accuse Jesus of blasphemy for forgiving sins.[11] Other scholars have been more reasonable. Taylor, for example, noted that the charge was 'not actually made'. With regard to what Jesus claimed, he quoted with approval a suggestion that Jesus went 'beyond that of delegated or prophetic "authority" to speak in God's name the Divine forgiveness of the man's sins'.[12] That is, Taylor recognized that claiming to speak on behalf of God is not a claim to put oneself in his place, though he supposed that the narrator really knew what was in the scribes' hearts. Their thoughts are in the text of the New Testament, and so they must be thoughts which Jesus' enemies really held: so all these scholars and many more.

The wisest course, here as elsewhere, is to use literary-historical methods and analyse the passage as something other than a transcript of people's thoughts. As Bultmann said, the scene is 'ideal' – both imaginary and intended to make a general point, the point in this case presumably being that forgiveness of sins was available in the (post-resurrection) Christian church.[13] Further, the passage as it now stands shows the workmanship of Mark (or possibly, in part, a pre-Markan redactor). It is the first conflict story in the gospel, and it includes the term 'blasphemy', as does the last (Mark 14.61–64); this is the work of an author.[14] The interior thoughts of the scribes are also a narrative device, intended to get a sequence of conflict passages started: at first enemies only 'questioned in their hearts' (Mark 2.7); next they complained to Jesus' disciples (2.16); then they complained directly to him (2.24); finally they plotted his death (3.6). In order to arrange the drama, the narrator must start by reading thoughts. If an important group had really thought that Jesus committed blasphemy in Galilee, they should have laid a charge.

But following our goal of taking the passages at face value, let us enquire what 'your sins are forgiven' would have meant in first-century Palestine, and how the statement might be construed as blasphemy. The standard view was of course that sins were forgiven by God. If any human pronounced God's forgiveness, it would have been a priest. A transgressor should bring a sacrifice and make a confession (as well as making restitution and adding a fifth if someone else had been wronged). The priest had to know what kind of sacrifice it was, and so the offerer had to designate it – 'this is a guilt offering'. Numbers 5.7 specifies that guilt offerings require confession, and presumably the confession over the sacrifice, with the offerer's hand on its head, was heard by the priest. The priestly code does not provide a formula of forgiveness for the priest to say. The standard statement in Leviticus is that the priest 'makes atonement' and the person 'is forgiven' (e.g. Lev. 5.16), and it is possible that forgiveness was understood rather than pronounced. Thus while it is reasonable that priests had the prerogative of pronouncing God's forgiveness, we cannot know that such pronouncements were actually made sacrifice by sacrifice. There is also no indication that they considered pronouncing forgiveness to be their exclusive right.

They could not have defended such a right had they claimed it. Jews believed not only in sacrifice, confession and forgiveness, but also in simple repentance and forgiveness. Otherwise no one would have accepted John's baptism, which was for forgiveness of sins (so Mark 1.4). In former days prophets had freely discussed forgiveness (e.g. Isa. 40.2), and the Psalms offered numerous examples of pleas for pardon (e.g. Ps. 25.11). Jews would have agreed that, if they had committed a transgression which required a sacrifice, the sacrifice should be presented. In all Jewish sources prayer plays such an important part, however, that we may be sure that confession and forgiveness figured in prayer, and were not mechanically linked to sacrifices, even though the biblical requirement of sacrifice was accepted. Thus, though Jesus' pronouncement might conceivably have been seen as challenging the priestly prerogative, there is no evidence that anyone understood it to do so, nor that the priests thought that only they could discuss God's forgiveness.

It might, however, have come as a surprise to an individual to be told 'your sins are forgiven' with no preparation, when confession had not been made nor forgiveness sought. This would be striking, audacious, bold, possibly arrogant. That is, in this passage Jesus 'knows' that God forgives the man's sins without knowing what is in the man's heart (unless there is an implied claim to know that too). Arrogance and great presumption before God can be considered blasphemy, as we saw above (LXX Ezek. 35.13). The presumption in the Greek translation of Ezekiel, however, is much worse than in Mark 2.5–7; in LXX Ezek. 35.13, God is virtually taunted, and Jesus' statement is not presumptuous in that sense. The claim to speak for God, and to be supported by him, were it made by a wicked person, might be considered blasphemy: denigrating God by association. But there is no sign that Jesus was himself openly wicked – despite some of the company he kept. A claim to speak for God which was simply disbelieved would not be considered blasphemy by those who did not believe, unless the nature of the claim demanded it. In the first century numerous would-be prophets arose, who were followed by some but not by others (*Antiq.* 20.97–99, 168–172; *War* 2.259–263). The Romans sometimes intervened, but there is no indication that these 'false' prophets (as most would have deemed them) were considered to be blasphemers. False prophecy, after all, is a separate charge (Deut. 18.20).

As far as I can see, the best case that can be made for connecting Jesus' statement 'your sins are forgiven' with blasphemy is presumption – not the presumption of forgiving sins in place of God (the text does not say that), nor the presumption of discussing forgiveness even though not accredited (the priesthood did not exercise that kind of control). One might find blasphemous presumption in Jesus' saying that God forgave a man who was not known to have confessed and made restitution. The case for blasphemy, however, is extremely weak (even if one were to have no doubts at all about the pericope).

The second case, Jesus' statement before the Sanhedrin, is more difficult. We require to know Jesus' precise words and also their nuance; but the gospels disagree about what he said, and we must guess about nuance. For the present purposes, I shall reduce our difficulties by looking only at the text of Mark. In Matthew's trial scene (26.59–68) Jesus is more circumspect than in Mark's (compare Matthew's 'you have said so, but I tell you' with Mark's 'I am, and I tell you'), and thus blasphemy is harder to find: by taking Mark I take the stronger case.

Luke 22.66–71 poses different problems. One is that the word 'blasphemy' does not appear, though one supposes that it is implied. The next is the separation of one question and answer from another. 'Are you the Christ?' comes in 22.67; 'Are you the son of God?' in 22.70, whereas in Mark and Matthew the titles occur together. Third, Jesus' answers are evasive. To 'Are you the Christ?' he replies, 'If I tell you, you will not believe . . .' To 'Are you the son of God?' he responds, 'You say that I am'. David Catchpole, who maintains that Luke's account is earlier than Mark's, has argued that the first title (Christ) is evaded, but that 'son of God' is accepted: 'you say that I am' is 'affirmative in content, and reluctant or circumlocutory in formulation'.[15] He then further proposes that this confession of divine sonship was the cause of Jesus' death. Since divine sonship comes up in Mark, where the term blasphemy also appears, I shall not take these interesting proposals into account.[16] Thus we turn to Mark.

The high priest asked, 'Are you the Messiah, the son of the Blessed One?', and Jesus responded that he was. He continued, 'And you will see the Son of man seated at the right hand of Power, and coming with the clouds of heaven'. The high priest rent his garments and pronounced 'Blasphemy' (Mark 14.61–64). The blasphemy is not obvious, and this has led to diligent investigation of each phrase; each one has been found blasphemous by at least a few scholars.

The first term, 'Christ' or 'messiah', has gained least support, and now it may have none. There was no one messianic dogma in Judaism, and no views of a messiah which are known to us would lead to a charge of blasphemy against a false claimant. A self-designated messiah might be regarded as arrogant (as well as deluded, and so forth), but there is nothing in the title which would make claiming it highly presumptuous vis à vis God.[17]

A claim to be 'son of God' also need not be blasphemy. Here, however, the matter depends entirely on nuance and context. 'The son of God' (literally, 'of the Blessed') was not a standing title for a divine or semi-divine figure. That is, if someone said 'I am the son of God' hearers would not be able to say immediately what he meant. At one level, this was a claim which any Jew might make ('sons' was used generically to include women).[18] For it to be blasphemous, the hearers would have to understand that Jesus claimed more than the normal degree of sonship. Conceivably this could be seen as blasphemy, since it might mean that God was being reduced to Jesus' own level; if Jesus claimed to be God's *special* son, and if Jesus was regarded as a false spokesman, God would be implicitly denigrated. This depends, however, on some further definition of the term.

The combination 'messiah, son of God' is no more blasphemous than each term separately – except, of course, in Christianity. The two favourite Christian titles for Jesus came to be 'messiah' (in Greek, 'christos') and 'Son of God', and Jesus was thought to be the Messiah and *the* Son of God in some very special way. Thus *Christians* might have been accused by Jews of blasphemy. These facts stand behind the scepticism which many feel about the exchange between the high priest and Jesus: the combination 'messiah' and 'Son of God' is Christian, and the accusation 'blasphemy' is a reasonable Jewish response to Christian thought about Jesus. I fully share the view that we have here a Christian composition. But if it is not a Christian composition, it is very difficult to find blasphemy in these two titles.

One scholar took the blasphemy to be Jesus' first two words, 'I am'.[19] Translated into Hebrew, this is *'anî hû'*, 'I [am] he'. According to Stauffer, this was a divine word of self-revelation in the Hebrew Bible, used by God of himself. There are two principal problems with this proposal. One is that 'I am he' could be said by anyone in response to the right question (a woman would say 'I am she', *'anî hî'*). Taking 'I am' or (as Hebrew would phrase it) 'I am he' with a full stop, and understanding it as if it answered the question, 'Who are you?', rather than 'Are you the Messiah?', constitute a revision of the passage. Stauffer does not hesitate to revise it: the high priest rent his garments when Jesus said 'I am he', before he finished his response about the Son of man.[20] As rewritings go, this is not very probable. Stauffer simply ignores the context in Mark, in which 'I am' answers a specific question and means 'I am who *you* say'.

The second problem is that most of the biblical formulas for 'I am he' which Stauffer cites do not have the required words. Psalm 46.11, for example, is *'anokî 'elohîm*, 'I am God'. Going through the Bible and marking places where God uses the first person pronoun hardly establishes Stauffer's case that, as soon as the high priest heard a different verbal formulation, he recognized in it a claim to be God.

'And you will see the Son of man seated at the right hand of Power, and coming with the clouds of heaven', the concluding part of Jesus' answer, would be a nice bit of blasphemy had Jesus said, '*I* will sit at the right hand of Power . . .', or if the apparent reference to the Son of man as another person were understood by the high priest to mean 'I'. In some contexts, 'son of man' can mean 'a person' or 'I'. Thus blasphemy is a conceivable response to the Son of man saying.[21] One must say, however, that it is not obvious from reading the passage, since the referent of Son of man is not clear.

The last observation brings us back to the point of departure. There is no obvious or straightforward instance of blasphemy in the Markan trial scene. One can find possible or potential blasphemy in several aspects of Jesus' answer. Each requires a fairly definite interpretation: if the high priest understood Jesus to mean . . .

If we apply ourselves now to the question of 'Jesus and the law regarding blasphemy', we must say that there is no evidence at all that he studied biblical passages on cursing God (it is to be remembered that Jesus did not read the Bible in Greek, and so did not have the word *blasphēmia* to guide him) and then decided to transgress them. Conceivably he said something which could be *construed* as *denigrating* God by elevating himself, but it is impossible to find a conscious attack on the law.

My doubts about the historicity of the exchange with the high priest were made clear above. For those who do not already know it,[22] I shall briefly give my view of the actual reason for Jesus' condemnation. It is necessary first to back up chronologically. Before Jesus was tried, he was arrested. Why was he arrested? It was not because he had gone around Jerusalem giving himself titles (messiah, son of man, son of God). If a title would have led to his arrest, one would have done so a few days earlier, when others had called out 'Blessed is he who comes in the name of the Lord! Blessed is the kingdom of our father David that is coming!' (so Mark 11.9f.). 'He who comes in the name of the Lord', taken from Ps. 118.26, is not precisely a title, but if followed by reference to the coming Davidic kingdom it would be clear enough. According to the synoptics, that is, some people thought that Jesus was the son of David who would re-establish Israel as an independent state. If this title, with its overtone of military and political independence, did not lead to his arrest, what would?

The synoptics offer us as the immediate cause not another title, but an action, turning over tables of money-changers in the temple (Mark 11.15–18). This was apparently the last public deed which Jesus performed before his arrest, and his physical demonstration is probably what immediately moved the high priest to take him into custody. Then we note that, according to Matthew and Mark, the first charge against him was that he threatened the temple (Mark 14.58 and par.). Mark wants the reader not to believe that he did this, but to believe that Jesus unthreateningly predicted that the temple would sometime be destroyed (13.2). With regard to the trial, the evangelist wants Jesus to have been condemned for making a Christian confession: he was Christ and Son of God. These, especially 'Son of God', are Mark's own preferred titles for Jesus (Mark 1.1; 15.39). In accord with the general principles of critical study of tendentious documents, I think it likely that the charge which Mark assures us was false was true, and that his preferred charge is unhistorical.[23]

Thus, in a historical reconstruction, I would move from the demonstration against the temple, to the charge that Jesus threatened it, to some sort of condemnation by the high priest and his advisers, and finally to an accusation laid before Pilate. Apparently Jesus was crucified for claiming to be 'king of the Jews' (Mark 15.26 and parr.). This more reasonably goes back to the triumphal entry (Mark 11.9f.), or to Jesus' preaching about 'the kingdom', than to 'son of God' in the trial scene. The high priest, of course, could have condemned Jesus for one reason and put another one to Pilate. Still, the better historical connections (physical violence in the temple – arrest – kingdom of David or simply kingdom – king of the Jews) bypass the exchange between the high priest and Jesus in Mark 14.61–64.

I do not doubt that Jesus died for his self-claim, particularly the implied claim that he had the right to make the demonstration against the temple (Mark 11.15). Attacking the temple, even by a minor symbolic gesture, might have been seen as denigrating and thus blaspheming God. Emphasis on the temple threat does not require us to reject the charge of blasphemy.[24] If a group of Jewish jurists actually concluded that he committed blasphemy, it was probably because of the substance of his behaviour – which was highly presumptuous – rather than because of titles to which he may have admitted. In any case, what got him hauled before the high priest in the first place was almost certainly his action in the temple, not the titles which he gave himself – if any.

My historical assessment, in summary, is this: (1) It is conceivable, but not probable, that Jesus replied to the question, 'Are you the Christ, the son of the Blessed?' in such a way as to lead the high priest and others to think that he denigrated God by claiming a special relationship with him. (2) It is almost certain that the action which led to his arrest and interrogation was the overthrow of one or more tables in the area where doves were sold and money exchanged. (3) This itself might have been considered an affront to God and thus blasphemous. (4) The action in the temple showed that Jesus might do something which would lead to bloodshed (a point not discussed just now, but one which the high priest would have put uppermost).

J. WORSHIP AT HOME AND SYNAGOGUE

With this topic we begin a transition to semi-legal issues, customs which some or many Jews regarded as obligatory, but which are not in fact required by biblical law. The practices connected with worship outside the temple, we shall see, were partly required by the Bible and partly not. Fasting (the next section) was greatly developed beyond what the Bible demands. The customs here in view were widely observed; they are not the extra-biblical 'traditions' which distinguished the Pharisees from others (ch. II). They were not only widespread but also very important, and this is especially true of the least biblical of them, daily and weekly worship. The binding character of custom can hardly be overemphasized. To this day most Christians and Jews regard regular attendance at church or synagogue as obligatory. People who do not regularly attend services usually regard themselves and are regarded by others as being 'not very good' Christians or Jews. Yet this, one of the most basic acts of self-identification, is not a biblical requirement.[1]

For the study of Jewish worship, we begin with the foundational biblical passage and then proceed to examine *tefillin* and *mezuzot*, daily prayers and attendance at the synagogue.

The Shema´ and the core of the law

This passage, which is named after its first word, was fundamental to Jewish life and worship. It begins 'Hear [*sh^ema´*], O Israel, the Lord our God, the Lord is one; and you shall love the Lord your God with all your heart, and with all your soul, and with all your might' (Deut. 6.4–5). It continues: the commandments are to be 'upon the heart', taught to children, spoken of at home and abroad, and remembered before sleep and upon waking. They are to be bound upon the hand, placed 'as frontlets' between the eyes, and put on the doorpost of the house and on the gate (vv. 6–9). Most of Deut. 6.4–9 is paralleled in 11.13–21.

The plain meaning of the text is that one is to remember in these ways all of the commandments, especially those which immediately precede the Shema´ – the ten commandments of Deut. 5. In the first century this was generally understood and widely observed. Various biblical passages – such as the opening verses of the Shema´ ('hear . . . love'), the ten commandments, the list of what the Lord requires in Deut. 10.12–20, and the parallel to the Shema´ in Deut. 11.18–21 – were written and posted in the doorway and bound between the eyes and on the hand. The Shema´ was recited (or, perhaps, recalled) morning and evening. The Shema´ and the ten commandments sometimes served as a kind of core of the law. They appear together on the Nash Papyrus, a single sheet of the second or first century BCE emanating from Egypt. The importance of its being a single sheet, not part of a scroll, is that this makes it likely that it was used for devotional or educational purposes.

According to the Mishnah, the priests recited the Shema´, along with the ten commandments and a few other passages, after the sacrifice of the whole-burnt offering each morning and afternoon (Tamid 4.3; 5.1; Taanith 4.3).[2] Further, the mishnaic Rabbis simply took it for granted, as something which did not require debate or proof, that every Jew said the Shema´ (along with prayers) twice a day, morning and evening (Berakoth 1.1–3). Since the Houses of Hillel and Shammai debated posture when saying the Shema´ (lying or standing), we may attribute the custom to the Pharisees.

Recalling the Shema´ morning and evening seems also to be referred to in the Dead Sea Scrolls. One author wrote that 'With the coming of day and night I will enter the Covenant of God' (1QS 10.10). In rabbinic literature the phrase 'to take upon oneself the yoke of the kingdom of heaven' refers to reciting the Shema' (e.g. Berakoth 2.2), and it is quite likely that 'entering the covenant' morning and night in 1QS also refers to saying the Shema' twice daily. Pseudo-Aristeas also mentions the command to 'meditate on the ordinances of God' both when lying down and when rising up (*Arist.* 160). Saying or recalling the Shema' seems to have been very widespread.

Since the biblical passages mention 'when you lie down' and 'when you rise up', many people probably said the evening Shema' at bedtime, whenever that might be. 1QS 10.10, 'with the *coming* of day and night', points to sunrise and sunset. The rabbinic discussions allow for considerable variation. According to R. Eliezer, the evening Shema' could be said as early as the time when the priests enter their houses to eat heave offering (Berakoth 1.1), that is, just after sunset.[3] Various Rabbis had different views about how late the evening Shema' could be said. It seems that the time at which individuals said the Shema' was not coordinated with the time it was said in the temple (assuming that Tamid 4.3–5.1 reflects temple practice), which was before sunset.

We can never be sure how many individuals followed any given religious practice. I think, however, that Jews generally thought that they *should*, both morning and night, say the Shema' or recall the commandments in some other way. I shall venture the opinion that most actually did what they thought they should do. Part of the evidence for this – use of *mezuzot* and *tefillin* – will be given below. Here I shall offer more general considerations. The Bible itself commands that some of its major aspects be recalled morning and night; ancient Jews, along with the rest of ancient humanity, were religious. They believed in God, and they tried to do what he said. Moderns are often sceptical about such generalizations as 'Jews in general said the Shema' or otherwise recalled the commandments', I think, because being non-religious or only nominally religious is now common. It was otherwise in the first century. The literary evidence is that Jews in general understood Deut. 6.4–9 to require reflection morning and night; if they so understood it, they probably obeyed it and recalled the commandments twice a day.

Thus few would have found surprising Jesus' quotation of Deut. 6.4–5 when he was asked about the greatest commandment. It is noteworthy that, according to Mark 12.28–34, a scribe agreed with him.

Jesus' selection of Lev. 19.18 – 'love your neighbour as yourself' – as a second 'core' commandment is equally unsurprising. Leviticus 19 contains the priestly author's version of the ten commandments. The prohibition of idolatry is in v. 4, of theft in v. 11, of swearing falsely in the name of God in v. 12, and so on. There are also important commandments dealing with the treatment of others, such as leaving part of agricultural produce for the poor (vv. 9–10). Leviticus 19.18 summarizes the particulars of loving the neighbour which are given in the preceding verses. Subsequently there are commandments on the treatment of aliens, summarized by the admonition to love the stranger as one's self (vv. 33–34). Thus the 'love commandments' are presented in Leviticus as summaries, and it was obvious to quote them, or one of them, as such.

While Deut. 6.4–5 summarizes or speaks for the commandments which govern relations between humans and God, Lev. 19.18 gives the gist of the 'second table' of commandments, those which govern relations among humans. Jews in general were aware of the two categories.[4] Thus Philo commented that 'sins are sometimes committed against humans, sometimes against things sacred and holy' (*Spec. Laws* 1.234; similarly 2.63). He relied on the two biblical passages chosen by Jesus to summarize the laws in each category. 'God asks nothing from thee that is heavy or complicated or difficult, but only something quite simple and easy. And this is just to love Him . . ., to serve Him . . . with thy whole soul . . . and to cling to His commandments . . .' (*Spec. Laws* 1.299–300). Here he relies on the Shema´. Subsequently comes another summary: 'the law stands pre-eminent in enjoining fellowship and humanity' (*Spec. Laws* 1.324), a statement which is in the spirit of Lev. 19.18,34.

Jesus' choice of the two commandments as 'greatest', then, was very much with the grain of the Bible itself, which presents them as summaries, and other Jews who thought about and studied the law would have approved the selection.

Most people who sought an epitome of the law, however, seem to have wanted a one–line statement, and they chose an epigram based on Lev. 19.18,34. 'What you hate, do not do to any one' (Tobit 4.15; cf. Hillel according to Shabbat 31a); 'What a man would hate to suffer he must not do to others' (Philo, *Hypothetica* 7.6). Jesus too could summarize the entire Bible by offering an epigram which actually summarizes only the 'second table': 'Whatever you wish that people would do to you, so do to them; for this is the law and the prophets' (Matt. 7.12). The reason for saying that these epigrams are based on both Lev. 19.18 and 19.34 is that 19.18 requires 'love of neighbour' – that is, other Jews – while 19.34 requires love of 'strangers' – non-Jews. The epigram includes both: 'do not do to *any one*' or 'whatever you wish that *people* would do'.

Jesus' positive epigram, 'do to them' is often contrasted favourably with the negative form known from other literature, 'do not do'. The negative version follows naturally from Lev. 19, where, 'love your neighbour' summarizes prohibitions, such as: do not deal fraudulently with your neighbour, do not rob him, do not curse the dumb, do not be partial in judgment, do not bear hatred for your brother in your heart. Even the commandment to be charitable to the poor is mostly phrased negatively: 'do not reap your field to its very border', etc. (19.9–10a). The negatives serve to make the positive admonition ('you shall leave them for the poor and for the sojourner', v. 10b) specific and to define how it should be obeyed. Negative commandments are stronger in Jewish law (and in law generally) than are positive command-ments: transgression of a prohibition is more serious than is failure to give effect to a positive commandment.[5] Thus the epigrams which revise Lev. 19.18 to a negative form ('do not do to others what you would not like') make it a stronger and more specific commandment.

The negative form, however, does not mean that no more is expected than the avoidance of serious transgression. Authors who quoted epigrammatic epitomes may have had positive commandments as well as prohibitions in mind. This is certainly the case with Philo. After the 'negative golden rule', he states that one must give fire to one who needs it, that one must give alms to the poor, and so on (*Hypothetica* 7.6–8). Similarly when Paul wrote that 'love does no wrong to a neighbour' (Rom. 13.10), apparently showing knowledge of the negative epitome, it should not be thought that he wished to exclude positive good deeds. Later rabbinic literature, however, does offer a positive epitome of the law: 'Charity (*tsedaqah*) and deeds of loving-kindness (*gemilut hasadim*) are equal to all the commandments (*mitsvot*) in the Torah' (T. Peah 4.19).[6]

Jesus' positive epitome is open-ended, and it fits its context in the Sermon on the Mount very well. It requires more than an individual can fulfil, and in this way it agrees with the commandments not to lust in one's heart (Matt. 5.28) and not to be angry (5.22), and with the general admonition to be better than the scribes and Pharisees (5.20): in short, to be perfect (5.48).

Mezuzot and Tefillin

The Shema´ requires that the commandments be placed on the hand, on the forehead and on the doorposts (Deut. 6.8f.; cf. 11.18; Ex. 13.9,16), and there is good evidence that this was obeyed by the use of *mezuzot* and *tefillin*. *M⁽e⁾zûzah* (plural – *ôt*) means 'doorpost', and it is the word used in Deut. 6.9 (// 11.20). By extension it came to refer to containers with biblical passages in them which are attached to the doorpost. *T⁽e⁾pillîn* is a post-biblical Semitic word for the containers which are tied to the arm and head.[7] The latter are often called 'phylacteries' in English, because of the Greek word *phylaktēria* in Matt. 23.5 and elsewhere. 'Phylactery', in turn, often means 'amulet', referring to a magical or semi-magical good luck charm against demonic forces. While both mezuzot and tefillin may have had, for many Jews, the virtues of warding off demons, that is a secondary or derived function; and using 'phylacteries' can be misleading. For this reason I shall use the Aramaic/Hebrew tefillin, which may be connected to the word for 'prayer'.[8]

The practice of putting key portions of the Bible into small containers, and fixing them to the doorpost (mezuzot), on the arm and on the brow (tefillin), is well attested for the ancient world. According to Pseudo-Aristeas, Jews kept the commandments to put the 'words' on their gates and doors, as well as on their hands (*Arist.* 158–159). Josephus refers to inscribing the blessings of God on the doors and displaying them on the arms. All who wished to show the power of God and his goodwill towards his followers should 'bear a record thereof written on the head and on the arm' (*Antiq.* 4.213). The observance was also kept at Qumran, where texts from tefillin and mezuzot have been found.[9]

According to Matt. 23.5 Jesus criticized the Pharisees for making their tefillin (*phylaktēria*) too broad, but not for wearing them, which shows that others wore them as well. We note that the criticism has to do with a matter of degree, not the practice itself. Consequently, the commandment is not challenged.

Daily prayers

It should be said at the outset that private and spontaneous prayer was well known in first-century Judaism. Individual prayers and references to them are frequent in the Pseudepigrapha, the Apocrypha, Philo, Josephus and the Dead Sea Scrolls. In rabbinic literature, where the Eighteen Benedictions[10] are emphasized, spontaneity is also urged: 'R. Eliezer says: He that makes his prayer a fixed task, his prayer is no supplication' (Berakoth 4.4).[11]

Our present concern, however, is with prayers which were regarded as obligatory or at least customary. There are three closely related questions: Were there set texts? Were there set places where people prayed communally? Were there set times for prayer?

We do not know to what degree there were standard texts. According to Berakoth 4.3, Rabban Gamaliel II and R. Joshua, both of whom were born before 70, debated whether one should pray the Eighteen Benedictions or 'their substance'. The distinction implies that something close to a set text was known in their circles, but we can say no more. Even if these two Rabbis agreed on the contents of a series of petitions, and even if agreement extended to actual wording, we should still not think of a set text in the modern sense – one published and circulated. We do not know how widespread the idea of Eighteen Benedictions was, nor how commonly accepted were the main themes. The rabbinic discussions may reflect only pharisaic practice. On the other hand, they probably do reflect that. I think it likely that the Pharisees had worked out set themes for daily prayers. The question of how many people followed their lead is more difficult. We shall consider below the issue of communal prayers.

There is better evidence that the Essenes had fixed texts. Josephus reported that each morning they offered to the sun 'certain prayers which [had] been handed down from their forefathers' (*War* 2.128). A badly fragmented text containing morning and evening prayers for each day of a month was found in Qumran cave 4 (4Q503). The editor, Maurice Baillet, dates the text *c.* 100–75 BCE.[12]

The natural assumption would be that set texts imply communal prayers and that communal prayers require set texts. The Essenes, at least those at Qumran, prayed communally, as did the Therapeutae described by Philo (*Contemplative Life* 27). It is noteworthy that the discussions in the Mishnah and Tosefta of saying the Shema᾽ and praying for the most part presuppose that these are *individual* activities. There are few references to the synagogue or to any other setting for group prayers, and no such references which can be attributed to Pharisees or the Houses of Hillel and Shammai.[13] Levine proposes that the term *proseuchē* ('prayer' or 'house of prayer'), usually used for synagogues in the Diaspora, implies communal prayer there, but states that the evidence for such a practice in Palestine is limited to the Essenes and the temple (Tamid 5.1). He grants, on the evidence of Matt. 6.5, that there may have been organized prayer in Palestinian synagogues outside Jerusalem.[14] The almost unanimous assumption in early rabbinic literature that prayers were said individually is so impressive that we must think communal prayer to have been the exception rather than the rule.[15] This point constitutes a further argument against the standardization of the Eighteen Benedictions.

There is, however, one passage to put into the other side of the scales. Quite a lot of interesting things happened in the synagogue (*proseuchē*) in Tiberias, according to Josephus's account of his efforts in Galilee to organize the revolt. One day, he and others had agreed to meet in the synagogue first thing in the morning (*Life* 290, cf. 280). 'We were proceeding with the ordinary service (*ta nomima*, 'the regulations') and engaged in prayer (*pros euchas trapomenōn*), when Jesus rose and began to question me . . .' (295). This was on Monday, not the sabbath (279f., 290, 293). We are not to think that this proves that people routinely went to the synagogue at 7.00 each morning. Josephus and others met there by agreement. On the other hand, once there, there were 'regulations' to follow, which included prayer. Even so, everyone who came for the meeting may not have said the same prayers in unison. Christians now say the Lord's prayer that way, and in some churches a lot of the service is said in unison; yet this is not the case in many synagogues today. Even though all the members of the congregation have the same prayer book, they do not necessarily recite in unison. We cannot know just what Josephus and his companions did. His prayer was interrupted by Jesus' question, and Jesus may already have prayed. The prayers in question may have been those which ordinarily were said at home, together with the Shema´. Perhaps Josephus prayed at the synagogue only because he came there so early.

The casual, incidental reference, 'we were following standard procedure' (to translate *nomima* in another way), shows that in Josephus's mind there was a regular form, followed either at home or at the synagogue. Yet we do not know that everyone agreed. The problem with well-established customs is that people do not bother to describe them.

My current opinion on set texts prayed in unison is that probably the Qumran community, or the Essene movement in general, was unusual. Josephus, after all, comments on the Essenes' use of inherited prayers, which surely proves that this was not the rule. Further, I think that we should agree with Levine that full worship services in synagogues become more likely as distance from the temple increases. Nevertheless, customary patterns of worship developed, and many people had a regular routine. How uniform the various customs were is completely unknown.

Praying at set times was probably more widespread than standard texts or even themes, but even so not everyone followed the same practice. Some sources mention only morning prayers: *Sib. Or.* 3.591–593 seems to show that some Diaspora Jews prayed before rising each morning: 'at dawn they lift up holy arms towards heaven, from their beds'. This does not, to be sure, rule out evening prayers; it may be that there was no occasion to mention them. According to *Arist.* 305–306, Jews customarily prayed each morning while washing their hands in the sea. Possibly regular evening prayers are implied by *Arist.* 184–185: before dinner in Alexandria, which was arranged 'in accordance with the customs practiced by all [the king's] visitors from Judaea', one of the Jewish priests was asked to offer a prayer. We cannot be sure whether this indicates a special occasion or a standard Jewish daily practice.

There is a good deal of evidence for prayer twice a day. Two different religious practices encouraged prayer both early and late: the saying of the Shema´ (when you lie down and when you rise up) and the beginning and close of the temple service. The temple service began as soon as the sun was up, and it ended just before sunset. The last acts were the sacrifice of the evening whole-burnt offering, the saying of the Shema´ and blessings, and the burning of incense. Pesahim 5.1 puts the slaughter of the last lamb at the eighth and a half hour of the day (*c.* 3.30) and its offering an hour later. Scriptures, prayers and incense then followed.[16]

The Book of Judith describes the heroine as going outside the tent to pray as soon as she rose. Each evening she bathed and prayed for deliverance (Judith 12.5–9). The time of the second prayer is not clear in this passage, which first says that she bathed (and prayed) each *night* (*kata nukta*, 12.7), but that she then remained in her tent until she ate *towards evening* (*pros hespēran*, 12.9). According to 9.1, on one occasion at least she prayed 'at the very time when that evening's incense was being offered' at the temple. The incense was burned after the last sacrifice (Ex. 30.8), therefore in the late afternoon. The net impression given by Judith is that the evening prayer was said before sunset. It is connected not with 'lying down', but rather with the last part of the daily temple service. Philo interpreted the whole-burnt offerings as thank offerings (*Special Laws* 1.169),[17] and he saw prayer primarily as thanksgiving,[18] but he makes no explicit connection between the offering of sacrifices and the time of prayer.

The Qumran *Community Rule* prescribes prayer ('blessing God') 'at the times ordained by Him', which include 'the beginning of the dominion of light' and 'its end when it retires to its appointed place' (1QS 9.26–10.1); that is, at sunrise and sunset. The Qumran text mentioned above (4Q503; see n. 12) refers to morning and evening prayer, and the scanty remains imply that the latter comes when night is about to fall.[19] The time of the evening prayer was probably determined by the conclusion of the temple service, as in Judith 9. We recall that the Shemaʿ was said at Qumran at sunset; evening prayer and evening Shemaʿ were apparently said at the same time.

Josephus thought that Moses himself required prayers of thanksgiving at rising up and going to bed (*Antiq.* 4.212). Daily prayers are not required in the law; Josephus's putting them in that category probably shows that they were a standard part of Jewish practice and were generally considered obligatory. Not only does he put the evening prayer at bedtime, he follows the statement on prayers with the requirement to post mezuzot and to wear tefillin. Thus in his view the second prayer was connected with saying the Shemaʿ. This paragraph in Josephus's summary of the law, which makes morning and evening worship at home a commandment of Moses, supports the suggestion above that the *nomima* which Josephus followed in Tiberias were his own regular practices, usually carried out at home.

In the Mishnah tractate Berakoth there are somewhat diverse traditions about both the right posture and the correct times for prayers. The Houses of Hillel and Shammai accepted that prayers accompanied the Shemaʿ and thus were said morning and evening, but they debated posture. According to the House of Shammai, the evening prayers should be said lying down, while the morning prayers were to be said while standing, and they cite as proof the phrases 'when you lie down and when you rise up'. The House of Hillel were of the view that each person could decide in what posture to say the prayers, since Deut. 6.7 says 'and when you walk by the way'. 'When you lie down and when you rise up', they held, gives only the time for prayers, not the correct posture (Berakoth 1.4). According to Berakoth 1.4, three of the Eighteen Benedictions were said in connection with the morning Shema´, four at the time of the evening Shema´. Another passage in the Mishnah, however, prescribes saying the Eighteen Benedictions three times a day – morning, afternoon and evening (Berakoth 4.1). If this was an early practice, we can guess at the origin of the three-a-day rule. It may be that afternoon prayers were said at the time of the last part of the temple service (as in Judith),[20] and evening prayers at bedtime, in connection with the evening Shema´.[21]

Most of the early evidence – Judith, the Dead Sea Scrolls, Josephus, the debate between the House of Hillel and the House of Shammai – points towards prayer twice a day, morning and either afternoon or evening.[22] It appears, however, that in the first century some people already followed the three-a-day rule which the Rabbis eventually adopted.

The best early evidence for praying in the afternoon is the condemnation of praying in public in Matt. 6.5–6 (cf. Dan. 6.10; Acts 3.1). These verses criticize 'hypocrites' for standing and praying both in synagogues and on street corners. Some scholars have taken this to prove that the Pharisees generally prayed in the synagogues,[23] but this quite evidently was not the case with regard to the morning and evening prayers. Mid-day prayers, however, are another matter, and those who said them may well have gone to a synagogue if they could, and otherwise simply prayed in public. A probably second-century passage depicts someone saying the Shema´ in the afternoon while walking (T. Berakot 2.17). The passage in Matthew points towards a similar practice in the first century, but criticizes it as ostentatious.

In Matt. 6.9–13 and Luke 11.2–4, Jesus teaches his disciples a prayer, and the use of the first person plural ('give us this day') shows this to be a communal prayer. This, we noted above, was the exception, and within Palestine we can securely attribute regular communal prayers only to the Essenes. Little of the contents of the prayers in 4Q503 can be recovered, but it is clear that there were at least slightly different prayers each day. This is appropriate, of course, for a monastic community. The Eighteen Benedictions, the themes of which the Pharisees and others may have said each day in private prayer, cover many more topics than Jesus' prayer. In comparison with them, his short prayer lacks many themes, especially prayers for corporate well-being – such as for Jerusalem and the people of Israel. There is, of course, no reason to think that Jesus meant the disciples to pray only the prayer which he taught them. It is presented more as a model than as a prayer to be recited (especially in Matthew, 'pray like this'), and the differences between the Matthaean and the Lukan versions show that it was not recited without variation.

Home and synagogue

The home was the most frequent place of worship; it was there that people prayed and observed the sabbath and many other holy occasions. There was, however, a public place of worship besides the temple: the synagogue.[24] It appears that there was one for each major residential area.[25] Even Tiberias, which was permanently impure, had a synagogue (*proseuchē*, 'house of prayer') large enough to contain not only the city council (600 men), but also a general assembly of the populace (*Life* 277–279, 280, 284, 293). The same passages show that synagogues were not reserved for worship, and they fulfilled many public functions. On the other hand, both the name 'house of prayer' and other clues show that there were special buildings for study and worship. A decree of Halicarnassus granted local Jews the right to worship near the sea 'in accord with ancestral custom', and this permission comes immediately after a reference to their 'sacred rites' (*Antiq.* 14.258). Presumably they used a building for the purpose.[26] Josephus discusses synagogues in Caesarea (*War* 2.285–289), Dora in Syria (*Antiq.* 19.300–305; from the context obviously used for worship), and in Antioch (*War* 7.44). He quotes Apion as saying that Moses erected houses of prayer 'in the various precincts of the city, all facing eastwards' (*Apion* 2.10); this obviously refers to their imitation of the temple and indicates that they were primarily places of worship. It is not, however, entirely correct: not all synagogues faced east.

Archaeology has not thus far revealed many first-century synagogues in Palestine. One has been found in Gamla (in the Golan Heights, northeast of the Sea of Galilee), one on Matsada, and one on the Herodium (the last two were built during the time of the revolt, CE 66–73).[27] A pre-70 Greek inscription found in Jerusalem refers to a synagogue which was at least three generations old; it had recently been expanded by a priest, Theodotus, who was head of the synagogue and whose father and grandfather had also been heads of the synagogue.[28] Two explanations probably account for the small number of identifiable early Palestinian synagogues: most likely sites are inhabited and cannot be excavated (the revolt ended habitation at the three sites just mentioned); later synagogues were probably built on top of earlier ones, and the early remains were completely destroyed or rendered unidentifiable. As Margaret Davies has remarked to me, the difficulty of finding Saxon churches in England tells us about the building habits of the Normans and does not prove that the Saxons did not build churches. We may take it that most Jewish communities, both in Palestine and in the Diaspora, had synagogues – special buildings used primarily for study and worship, but also for other assemblies.[29]

It is striking that three ancient authors regarded assembly on the sabbath as a Mosaic decree (Philo, *Hypothetica* 7.12–13; cf. *Creation of the World* 128; Josephus, *Apion* 2.175; Pseudo-Philo, *Bibilical Antiq.* 11.8, who makes it part of the ten commandments).[30] This assumption, like Josephus's view that Moses required twice-daily prayers, shows how common the practice of sabbath assembly was. The Bible (Deut. 31.10) requires the public reading of the law once every seven years, at the Feast of Booths, but by the first century it was read and studied weekly, and many people regarded this custom as being obligatory. That on the sabbath Jews assembled at the local synagogue is assumed in *War* 2.289 and in several passages in Philo (see below).

Reading and study of the Bible is the principal and best attested use of synagogues. As Philo put it, on the seventh day Jews gave 'their time to the one sole object of philosophy with a view to the improvement of character and submission to the scrutiny of conscience' (*Creation of the World* 128). This study was carried out in a regular location. The teacher was a priest or elder, and the sessions lasted until late afternoon (*Hypothetica* 7.12–13; cf. *Embassy* 157; *Dreams* 2.127). Elsewhere he wrote of 'thousands of schools of good sense . . . and the other virtues' which are open on the seventh day in every city. Teaching fell under two main heads: duty to God and duty to humans, phrases which point towards the 'two tables' of biblical law (*Spec. Laws* 2.62f.). According to *Every Good Man* 81, on the sabbath Jews went to 'sacred spots (*hierous topous*), which they call synagogues' (*synagōgai*), where they were instructed in the ethical part of 'philosophy'. According to Josephus, Moses had decreed that once every week people should 'assemble to listen to the Law and to obtain a thorough and accurate knowledge of it' (*Apion* 2.175). The Jerusalem synagogue expanded by Theodotus was 'for reading the law and teaching the commandments'. Early rabbinic literature assumes that the Bible was read in the synagogues (Berakoth 7.3; Rosh ha-Shanah 3.7).

We should not suppose that all synagogues functioned in the same way. It is intrinsically probable that Diaspora synagogues had a wider range of functions than those in Palestine, and it is noteworthy that there are references to meals and 'rites' in the Diaspora (*Antiq.* 14.214–216, 260 ['sacrifices']).[31] In Palestine, the pilgrimage festivals, when family and friends could share a peace offering, provided the occasion for communal banquets. We noted above that other forms of worship, such as prayer and hymns, may also have figured more in synagogues far removed from the temple than in those nearby. Paul refers to hymns and lessons during gatherings of the church (I Cor. 14.26–33). This probably reflects synagogal practice as he knew it. There is no reason to think that customs were uniform; Philo emphasizes study, Pseudo-Philo 'praise [of] the Lord'. In any case, most Jews seem to have accepted synagogue attendance as a basic mark of being an observant Jew.

The numerous references in the gospels to Jesus' attending the synagogue reveal no criticism of it as an institution.

Although the question of who, as a general rule, was in charge of the synagogues is not an issue of law, it is important enough for New Testament studies and Jewish history to merit a few paragraphs. In the biblical period public reading of the law was assigned to priests – who could, among other things, read. Ezra, priest and scribe, read the law publicly, being assisted in interpretation by the Levites (Neh. 8.4–8). Scholars often think that synagogues were uniformly run by laymen, and sometimes even that they gave expression to the desire to escape priestly control.[32] It is likely, however, that in the first century priests retained their traditional role as teachers, especially in Palestine, and they doubtless were often leaders of synagogues. We know of one concrete case: Theodotus, his father and grandfather, all priests, were heads of a synagogue. We also noted above Philo's statement that the synagogue service was led by a priest or by an elder (*Hypothetica* 7.13).[33] 'Elders' are the other candidates for the role of 'head of the synagogue'. They were the heads of prominent lay families; and they, with the priests who were local residents, had always served as magistrates and rulers in towns and villages (see e.g. Ezra 10.14, 'elders and judges from each town').

The prosperous – or, preferably, the wealthy – constituted the ruling class throughout the ancient Mediterranean world, and in Judaism there was a centuries-old tradition that the leaders were the aristocratic priests, who were joined by the prosperous laity. It is quite evident in Josephus' accounts of his own career in Galilee that he had no difficulty identifying the 'leading men' in each locality (e.g. *Life* 64, 69).[34] He explicitly comments on the fact that the only two ordinary Pharisees who appear in his work, though they were *dēmotikoi* (laymen 'of the lower ranks'), were nevertheless educated in the Bible (*Life* 197). This simply shows how strong was the assumption that priests and men of property knew things and ran things; the two went together, and not everyone was well educated. It then comes as no surprise that a majority of the generals appointed by the first revolutionary council were aristocratic priests (*War* 2.566–568) and that the council was led by two members of the same group. And so on, as long as one wishes. Martin Goodman has now shown decisively that in second-century Galilee the 'prominent' remained in place even after the Rabbis began to settle there following the second revolt.[35] I might also add that, by the time the leading Rabbi was officially recognized by Rome as spokesman for the Jews, he had become extremely wealthy.

In Palestine Judaism was the national religion, almost everyone partici-pated, and there was no separation of 'church' and 'state'. Thus the leaders in one sphere were likely to be the leaders in another. Above all, the synagogue leadership needed to be able to read. This makes it likely that most leaders of synagogues were men who were otherwise prominent.

This view does not mean that a Pharisee could not be leader of a synagogue. A few Pharisees counted as 'eminent': one, Simeon b. Gamaliel, was a leader of the revolutionary council along with the priestly aristocrats (*Life* 190–196). Others, though they were for the most part non-aristocratic laymen, studied the law and could read and teach. Conceivably a learned pharisaic layman of moderate means might assume the leading role in a given synagogue. We should, however, doubt the impression given by Matt. 23.2 that synagogues were generally dominated by Pharisees. Apart from the evidence that the aristocrats, especially including the priestly aristocrats, controlled public activities, there is the problem of arithmetic. The Pharisees, said by Josephus to number about 6,000 at the time of Herod (*Antiq.* 17.42), could not possibly have fulfilled all the functions which scholars now assign to them: running almost all the synagogues, controlling and teaching in the schools, serving as scribes, going on missions to instruct Diaspora Jews, being magistrates, telling the priests how to sacrifice, regulating tithes and the other sources of the temple's revenue, advising all and sundry on the law – while working at a regular job, often running a small farm, all day, six days a week.[36] The only large source of underemployed manpower which could meet the need for scribes, magistrates and teachers was the priesthood, including the 'lesser clergy', the Levites. Some 20,000 strong, they were forbidden to earn their livings by farming, and they had to be on duty in the temple only one week in twenty-four. Thus they had both the time and the education to serve as synagogue leaders.[37]

It should be added that, apart from Matt. 23.2, the synoptics do not depict Pharisees as being in charge of synagogues. According to Mark 3.6, some Pharisees were present at the synagogue, but not necessarily as the leaders; Jairus, a head of a synagogue, is not said to have been a Pharisee (Mark 5.21–24, 35–43), nor is the ruler of the synagogue in Luke 13.14.[38]

The New Testament is probably accurate in giving the impression that, at meetings in the synagogue, anyone with something important to say would be allowed to speak (e.g. Mark 1.14–15; 6.1–5; Acts 13.15: 'Brethren, if you have any word of exhortation for the people, say it.'). We note also that Paul gives instructions about prophesying and exhorting in the Christian worship services, and that he supposes that first one then another participant would speak. His assumption of active participation by many probably reflects synagogue practice as he knew it. Philo, however, indicates that the synagogue services which he attended were less informal and spontaneous. While the priest or elder who led the service read and offered an exposition, most sat in silence, 'except when it is the practice to add something to signify approval of what is read' (*Hypothetica* 7.13).

We cannot say to what degree meetings of the synagogue were influenced by the temple service.[39] There were at least some overlaps. Several of the activities which we have listed – reading the scripture, praying and singing – had already been introduced into temple worship.[40] At home too the commandments were recalled and prayer was offered. Domestication and democratization of worship were extremely significant steps towards making all of life responsive to the will of God. The Bible itself requires that Jews daily remind themselves that God is one, and that he is to be loved and obeyed. But the law as interpreted in the first century went still further in inculcating in its followers the consciousness of serving God: it was understood to require daily prayers and weekly study. This is a very important semi-legal or para-legal aspect of Jewish life, and Jesus is reported to have criticized only a few minor aspects of it.

K. FASTING

§1. The Bible prescribes only one fast: the Day of Atonement (Lev. 16.29,31; 23.27,32; Num. 29.7). 'Anyone who fails to fast that day shall be outlawed from his people' (Lev. 23.29). Individuals could take a vow or oath to fast for particular reasons (Num. 30.14 [RSV v. 13]). In the above cases the Hebrew is 'afflict oneself' (*'innah nepesh*), which may imply more than just going without food. Abstinence from other pleasures and comforts will be detailed below, in discussing the Mishnah. The signs of self-abasement which frequently accompany fasting in the Bible are rending garments, wearing sackcloth and putting earth or ashes on the head (e.g. I Kings 21.27, rent garments and sackcloth; Neh. 9.1, sackcloth and earth on the head; Isa. 58.5, sackcloth and ashes; Esther 4.3, weeping, lamenting, sackcloth and ashes).

There are in addition numerous biblical examples of fasting (abstaining from food, in Hebrew often *tsûm*) to 'avert or terminate a calamity by eliciting God's compassion'.[1] David, for example, fasted in the hope that his ill son would be spared (II Sam. 12.16f.). By the time of Zechariah it appears that there were fixed fast days, at least one of which, that of the fifth month, Ab, had to do with remembering the first destruction of the temple (Zech. 7.3,5; *hinnazēr* and *tsûm*, abstain from food). Zechariah, speaking for the Lord, commanded that 'the fast (*tsôm*, abstinence from food) of the fourth month, the fast of the fifth, the fast of the seventh and the fast of the tenth are to become gladness and happiness and days of joyful feasting for the House of Judah' (8.19).[2] Nevertheless, some may have continued to observe these fasts. Though not sanctioned by the Pentateuch, fasts in addition to that on the Day of Atonement may have been regarded as obligatory in the later biblical period.

Besides fasts to mourn and to obtain some special favour, there were fasts to show contrition (I Sam. 7.6, *tsûm*).

§2. In the post-biblical period numerous individuals fasted for various reasons: Judith, for example, because of the death of her husband (Judith 8.1–6). It is noteworthy that she did not fast on Friday, Saturday or feast days. Some fasted to atone for individual sins (*Ps. Sol.* 3.8), a practice which probably developed from the community fast on the Day of Atonement. There were also community fasts in time of need. During the hard decision-making period in Tiberias which was described in the previous section (pp.73f.), a fast was proposed. Apparently it involved abstaining from regular activities as well as from food, since the community gathered at the synagogue early in the morning (*Life* 290). In the face of serious trouble, even children might be forced to fast (Judith 4.9–11; Pseudo-Philo, *Bibl. Antiq.* 30.4–5). In later periods fasts were especially employed in times of drought. There are lots of stories about fasting for rain in rabbinic literature, which here probably shows continuity with pre-70 Jewish practice. Geza Vermes has made famous Honi the Circle Drawer and Hanina b. Dosa, who fasted for rain (see e.g. Taanith 3.8).[3] Much of the Mishnah tractate Taanith ('affliction') is taken up with discussions of fasting for rain. Other examples are given by Martin Goodman.[4]

According to the *Didache*, an early Christian work, 'the hypocrites' fasted on Mondays and Thursdays, whereas one should fast on Wednesdays and Fridays (8.1). Since Jews would not fast on Fridays (Judith above, the Mishnah below), we see here the Christian community being urged to distance itself from its parent. I doubt that this means that both Jews and Christians fasted two days of every week. More likely, the discussion is about which two days should be chosen when an individual or the community did decide to fast.

The practice of fasting twice a week is mentioned by the Pharisee of Luke 18.9–14. Whether this was a regular or occasional practice is not clear. Rabbinic literature refers to public fasts on Mondays and Thursdays during droughts (Taanith 1.3–7; 2.9). These passages prescribe an escalating series of steps if rain did not fall: first, prayer only, then fasting by some individuals (though they could work, wash, anoint themselves, wear sandals and have sexual intercourse). Next would come public fasting, when the things listed in the previous sentence were forbidden and the bathhouses were closed. Finally even shops were shut, and there were further abstentions. Here we have, at least in rabbinic theory, an obligatory community fast. There is no reason to doubt that a community which was hard-pressed would require fasting of all its members.

According to Taanith 4.7, during the week which included the 9th of Ab (the anniversary of the two destructions of the temple, which were thought to have happened on the same day) men neither cut their hair nor washed their clothes. It appears that people did not abstain from food entirely, though the Rabbis debated the degree of abstention.

In view of the general inclination of people to fast in time of need or to mourn, the passages on fasting in Zechariah, and the post-biblical literature, it is certain that in Jesus' day there were occasional fasts (e.g. for rain), and there may have been one or more regular fasts in addition to the one on the Day of Atonement. The likeliest candidate is the 9th of Ab.

The overall impression is that fasting mostly consisted of abstinence from food and drink, either entire or partial, but it might also include further signs of self-abasement, such as wearing sackcloth, putting ashes on the head, not washing, not anointing and not engaging in sexual relations. The Hebrew term 'afflict oneself' for the Day of Atonement makes it likely that in the first century Jews went beyond mere abstinence from food and drink on this day, and this may well have been true on the 9th of Ab as well (assuming that this was a well-established fast day before the second destruction of the temple).

§3. According to Mark 2.18–22 and parr. Jesus would not allow his disciples to fast on some occasion when the Pharisees and the disciples of John the Baptist were fasting. The accusation implies that these two groups regarded this particular fast as obligatory. Naming the disciples of John and the Pharisees, however, seems to indicate that the entire community was not fasting. In this case the behaviour of Jesus' disciples would not have been generally offensive; we would learn only that they did not follow the lead of two pious groups.

In explaining why his followers were not fasting, Jesus said that after 'the bridegroom' was taken away they would fast (Mark 2.20). This points forward to the post-resurrection church, and it also leads us to the next pericope. Matthew 6.16–18 gives rules for fasts among Jesus' followers, presumably when he was no longer with them: they are to anoint their heads and wash their faces. This would cause offence only at a time when the rest of the community was going without washing and anointing. It is likely that in these passages we see the transition from the lifetime of Jesus (his followers did not fast) to the early church (after he was gone they did fast but did not otherwise 'afflict themselves'). If, however, we take Matt. 6.16–18 as coming from Jesus' lifetime, how serious was it to anoint and wash during a fast? Anointing and washing were not against biblical law, since refraining from them is not explicitly prescribed for the Day of Atonement. The Jewish community, however, may have regarded this degree of self-affliction as obligatory on the Day of Atonement and at some other times of fasting as well. Breaking an established community custom would cause serious offence; but, without knowing the circumstances, no more can be said.

L. CONFLICT OVER THE LAW

The story of conflict within Judaism is a complex one, far too complex to explore here very fully. In many cases it is impossible to attribute internal conflict to any one factor, such as the law, and to distinguish legal disagreements from power struggles. Granted all this, it is still worthwhile to say a few words about conflict, and in fact it is necessary to do so if we are to draw conclusions about the possible level of conflict between Jesus and his contemporaries over legal questions. We shall consider first the Essenes and then the Pharisees.

The Essenes

The existence of the Essenes[1] immediately reveals how legal disputes and a power struggle can be interwoven. The party separated from the Jerusalem leadership after the success of the Hasmonean revolt. It was led, possibly from its very origins, by the Zadokites – the high priestly family which had governed Judaea since the return from exile. Members of this family took different attitudes towards Hellenization and relations with the kingdom of Syria. When it came to open revolt, however, the fight was led by an ordinary priestly family, the Hasmoneans. In the end the revolt was successful and, in 140 BCE, Simon of that family was declared 'leader and high priest for ever, until a trustworthy prophet should arise' (I Macc. 14.41). The Zadokites were out. It is easily possible that the break between part of the old high-priestly family and the Hasmonean upstarts came earlier than the installation of Simon as high priest 'for ever', since leadership had already passed to the Hasmonean family. The solemn declaration quoted in I Maccabees, however, could have left no doubt. Its negative implication for the Zadokites is as clear as its affirmation of the Hasmoneans.

It is too simple to say that the strife between the Essenes and the Hasmoneans probably arose 'from far-reaching differences of opinion in

Jewish law, particularly over the Jewish calendar',[2] and it is more likely that the sect adopted a different calendar as a *sign* of its separate identity.[3] We cannot, however, chart the history of the break between the Essenes and the prevailing authorities in Jerusalem. We know that there was some strife. One year, on the Day of Atonement according to the Essene calendar (not according to the Jerusalem calendar), the 'Wicked Priest' attacked the Essene 'Teacher of Righteousness' (1QpHab 11.2–8). The text is allusive, and we cannot tell precisely what happened, nor can the two opposing leaders be identified with certainty. It is likely that the Wicked Priest was Jonathan – the Hasmonean brother who preceded Simon as leader and high priest – but the identity of the Teacher of Righteousness is completely unknown.[4] It is probable, however, that the attack came in the early years of the sect.

Thereafter the Hasmoneans did not carry on a war of extirpation against the Essenes, who lived in peace. Relations between the Qumran sect and the Jerusalem high priesthood were amicable enough to allow them to debate legal issues. After a delay of almost forty years, some information has finally been published about a 'halakic' letter found in Qumran cave 4. It is believed to be an early sectarian document, a copy of a letter actually sent to the Jerusalem high priest. It states the sectarian position on about twenty points of law. On the basis of a partial description and two published fragments, one can say that the tone is curt but civil. If there is raging and ranting, the editors have not disclosed it.[5] We know from other documents that the sectarians did rant and rave about the 'men of the pit' or 'the sons of darkness', as they called other Jews. Nevertheless, it appears that they could also debate points of law with them and that neither side engaged in violence against the other. When the revolt came, Essenes joined the Jerusalemites and others in fighting the Romans (*War* 2.567, 152).

We may conclude that after the earliest period of the new sect things settled down. The sectarians and the Jerusalem leadership lived, if not precisely side by side, nevertheless in the same country, disagreeing quite substantially about the law, but not at each other's throats.[6]

The Pharisees

I have at several points observed that the Pharisees were fairly tolerant, that they knew when their own rules went beyond the biblical law, and that they did not try to coerce others to accept their extra-biblical traditions. This is, I am sure, the correct view to take of their attitude towards non-pharisaic Jews at the time of Jesus. There are, however, two points to note which do not contradict this but which set boundaries to their policy of toleration.

In the first place, it had not always been thus: they were prepared to engage in strife with the Hasmoneans longer than were the Essenes. Perhaps they had more support. Pharisees apparently led an insurrection against John Hyrancus (135–104 BCE). At the time of Alexander Jannaeus (103–76 BCE), pietists, probably Pharisees, led a very serious revolt. When Salome Alexandra (76–67 BCE) succeeded Jannaeus, she gave the Pharisees their head, and they turned on 'the eminent' ruthlessly, executing some and forcing others into exile. These three sentences summarize conclusions drawn from study of Josephus' complex and sometimes obscure accounts of the three Hasmoneans in question (*War* 1.67, 88, 96–98, 110–114; *Antiq.* 13.288–299, 372–383, 401–418). General histories of the period often do not explain why the opponents of Janneaus, who are not named, are to be regarded as Pharisees, but the identification is fairly secure.[7] For our present purpose, what is noteworthy is that, after the death of Salome Alexandra, reports of internecine strife which involve the Pharisees disappear. Thirteen years after her death Pompey conquered Jerusalem, and soon Herod came to the fore. The Pharisees do not entirely disappear from the history, and there is some evidence that they opposed Herod, though with enough caution not to be executed *en masse* (*Antiq.* 15.370; 17.41–45). Their prudence increased, and strife with the Sadducees or 'the eminent' seems to have disappeared. At least no more is heard of it. This is so to such a degree that Neusner could propose that, from the time of Herod and Hillel, the Pharisees withdrew from public life.[8] I am not persuaded that this is true, but it is true that there are no more signs of bloodshed among Jewish factions until the outbreak of the great revolt.

During their time of prudence, Pharisees risked death only for major causes: Herod's eagle over the entrance to the temple, and then only when they thought that he was too sick to act against them (*c.* 4 BCE), and Rome's census (CE 6).[9] They did not make obedience to their view of the law a matter of life or death.

These two exceptions to the rule of pharisaic quietism between Herod and the outbreak of the revolt in 66 deserve a closer look. The second, the uprising at the time of the Roman census of Judaea, was not a conflict over the Jewish law, but against full submission to direct Roman rule; the census had been ordered when Rome deposed Archelaus and decided to create the Province of Judaea and govern it directly.

The earlier event is more to our purpose. Teachers, probably Pharisees, inspired young men to pull down the eagle which Herod had placed above the temple gate. They urged that 'it was a noble deed to die for the law of one's country' (*War* 2.650). The law in view was presumably that against graven images, which strictly requires that no image should be made, neither of what is in heaven, nor of what is on earth, nor of what is in the sea (Deut. 5.8; Ex.

20.4). Yet the young men did not rush into the court of the priests and tear down the curtain on which was portrayed 'a panorama of the heavens', nor did they destroy the golden grapevine 'from which depended grape-clusters as tall as a man' (*War* 5.210,214). They selectively applied the law about images to exclude the eagle – the symbol of Rome.

Mostly, from the time of Herod on, the Pharisees and others in Jerusalem lived at peace with one another. The Pharisees accepted – to repeat a point from above – the temple service, though the chief priests did not follow their views. The attacks on the Sadducees in rabbinic literature are vigorous, but not beyond the bounds of brisk debate. We noted above that once some Pharisees rendered impure a priest who was going to burn the Red Heifer, but there is no indication in any source of physical violence between the parties, or between the Pharisees and any other group, over a purely legal question.

We should note, secondly, a few reports of intra-pharisaic strife. Rabbinic literature, by its very nature, is not given to narrative history, but it contains what appear to be echoes of serious disagreements between the Houses of Hillel and Shammai, some of which involve Hillel and Shammai themselves.

(*a*) According to T. Hagigah 2.11, once on a festival day Hillel laid his hands on a sacrificial animal, and he was 'ganged up on' by disciples of Shammai. We recall that Shammai did not approve of laying hands on a sacrifice on a festival day, while Hillel allowed it (I.B). In the case of a peace offering, Shammai ruled that hands could be laid on the animal the day before and the animal offered on the festival day. He excluded private whole-burnt sacrifices on festival days entirely. In the present case, the disciples of Shammai thought that Hillel was about to sacrifice a whole-burnt offering, laying his hands on it, and thus committing a double offence – both bringing a sacrifice prohibited by their master and laying his hands on its head. When Hillel was criticized he turned Shammai's disciples aside by saying that the animal was female and that it would be a peace offering. This was, in the Shammaite view, a lesser offence. Hillel is depicted as yielding to pressure.

(*b*) According to Berakoth 1.3 Tarfon once said that he recited the Shema' according to the rule of Shammai (reclining in the evening, standing in the morning). He was rebuked: 'They said to him: Thou hadst deserved aught that befell thee in that thou didst transgress the words of the School of Hillel.' 'Aught that befell thee' might include even death, but this is hyperbolic. Non-Shammaites did not actually think that Shammai and Shammaites should all die because of such disagreements. Tarfon survived.

(*c*) There is a faint and curious tradition of conflict between the two schools on the day when the Shammaites forced through eighteen restrictive decrees.[10]

A sword was planted in the Beth Hamidrash and it was proclaimed, 'He who would enter, let him enter, but he who would depart, let him not depart!' And on that day Hillel sat submissive before Shammai, like one of the disciples . . . (Shabbat 17a)

This seems to mean that when the Shammaites had a majority they were willing to use force to maintain it. The story of conflict between the two schools occurs in even more violent forms. According to p. Shabbat 1.4 (3c), 'the disciples of the House of Shammai took up positions for themselves downstairs and would slay the disciples of the House of Hillel'.[11]

It is hard to know just what to make of these stories, but Neusner's proposal seems to me the best available: Before 70 the Shammaites in fact predominated. This is occasionally reflected in the literature: thus according to R. Meir in Mikwaoth 4.1, the Shammaites outvoted the Hillelites. Though Meir says that 'one day' this happened, Neusner proposes that this was generally the case. In the Yavnean period (after 70), when competition between the Houses was most severe, and when the Hillelites came to dominate the movement, they had to recognize that many Shammaite practices were in fact generally followed. They could not imagine that Hillel and his party had often been outvoted, nor that Hillel had not been nasi ('prince': head of the academy). Thus they attributed the numerous Shammaite practices which stemmed from before 70 to coercion and force. As this tradition rolled on, various ways of describing the coercion developed – finally including the threat of slaughter.[12] The Shammaites and Hillelites did not actually kill one another.

Jews did, however, kill one another, and sometimes legal disagreements were involved. This is such an important point, and the contrast between the Hasmonean period and the time of Shammai, Hillel and Jesus is so important, that I shall return to the earlier period. According to Josephus, the first revolt against Alexander Jannaeus started during Tabernacles:

. . . as he stood beside the altar and was about to sacrifice, they pelted him with citrons, it being a custom among the Jews that at the festival of Tabernacles everyone holds wands made of palm branches and citrons . . . ; and they added insult to injury by saying that he was descended from captives and was unfit to hold office and to sacrifice; and being enraged at this, he killed some six thousand of them . . . (*Antiq.* 13.372f.)

One might construe this as meaning that the populace objected to Jannaeus's sacrificial procedure and then decided both to slander and injure him. We may be sure, however, that there was more to it than that. As Josephus says in briefly narrating this revolt in *War* 2.88f., it was at festivals 'that sedition is most apt to break out'. That is probably what happened: sedition erupted during but was not caused by Jannaeus's priestly method. We do not know just what the objections to Jannaeus were, but there was further and substantial revolt against him later. Legal disagreements with the Pharisees were almost certainly involved (the implication of *Antiq.* 13.401). *But legal interpretation in the period of the priest-kings was inseparable from political control.* The claim that he was descended from captives, which echoed a pharisaic complaint against his father (*Antiq.* 13.291), meant that he should resign as high priest and thus lose much of his authority. The role was not purely ceremonial. That is why first Herod and then Rome reserved to themselves the power to appoint and dismiss high priests, and even took control of the official robe (*Antiq.* 15.403–405; 18.90–95; 20.6–16). The connection between 'interpretation' and 'power' is seen immediately after Jannaeus's reign. When his successor, Salome Alexandra, accepted the Pharisees' regulations, she also accepted their decisions on execution and exile. Party strife in the Hasmonean period had to do with actual power.

Many scholars use the period of Jannaeus as the model for understanding first-century Judaism, but the differences are enormous. In between came Rome and Herod, and the conditions changed. There was no longer a single priest-king, sovereign in all areas. Under either Herod or Rome, warfare among groups was pointless, both because militarily a partial insurgency was not viable (as 4 BCE and CE 6 showed), and also because power now lay in the hands of outsiders. Members of the competing factions stopped killing one another. In Jesus' day the fierce internal strife which was a feature of the Hasmonean period was a thing of the past. To assess the relationship between legal disagreement and bloodshed in the 30s CE, we have to study the period from CE 6 to 40 (the imposition of direct Roman rule in Judaea; the threat of Gaius's statue). There we shall find no indication that people killed one another over party differences. Civil bloodshed would return, and return with a vengeance, when the revolt with Rome broke out, and there was again the possibility of contesting for control of Jerusalem and Judaea. Jews killed one another when government was at stake, not over legal disagreements which had no overtones of civil or governmental control. To explain bloodshed we must have something other than *purely* legal disagreements. There were a lot of those among first-century Jews, and for the most part they tolerated one another.

M. CONCLUSIONS

The synoptic Jesus lived as a law-abiding Jew. He accepted Deut. 6.5 and Lev. 19.18 as the 'two greatest' commandments, and his epigram, 'Do unto others', is based on Lev. 19.18 + 19.34. These verses are presented in the law itself as summaries or epitomes of the two aspects of the law – relations between humans and God and relations among humans – and in choosing them Jesus fixed on the passages which others of his time also saw as central. He attended the synagogue, he did not eat pork, he did not work on the sabbath in any obvious way. He accepted the sacrificial system both as atoning (Matt. 5.23f.) and purifying (Mark 1.40–44). In common with other teachers, he cautioned his followers not to sacrifice until wrongdoing had been rectified and grievances assuaged. He also paid the temple tax – by a very curious means.[1]

On the sabbath there are two minor infringements: his disciples pick grain, he puts his hand on a sick woman to heal her (Luke 13.10–17). In both cases there is a legal defence: hunger overrides the law, and the sabbath is made for people, not people for the sabbath; everyone unties and leads animals to water on the sabbath. Offering a defence shows respect for the law. Lawbreaking is *heinous* when it constitutes the denial that God was right to give the law and the assertion that one knows better. This is sinning with the full intent to sin: sinning 'with a high hand'. Justifying minor transgression on the grounds of a larger good, or arguing by legal analogy that an action is not an offence, is quite a different matter. Had a magistrate heard the accusation and the defence, it would have been hard for him to come to a harsher judgment than 'ill-judged and therefore inadvertent transgression; two doves as a sin offering when you are next in Jerusalem'.

The points of disagreement over the sabbath are not more substantial than those which separated group from group, and even one sub-group from another. The Shammaites thought that the Hillelites routinely worked on festival days, when most of the sabbath law applied, by laying their hands on sacrificial animals. The Hillelites argued from the analogy of priests, who sacrificed on the sabbath, but the argument was rejected by the Shammaites on the grounds of other biblical analogies. Did the Shammaites impose sin offerings on the Hillelites? Perhaps, had they been in positions of authority, they would have done just that.

Failure to wash hands before eating would not have been much of an issue. Handwashing is not a biblical requirement, and it is probable that even the Pharisees washed hands only before sabbath and festival meals. They could have accused most of the populace of not following their extra-biblical practices. In many ways the setting of the discussion of handwashing (Mark 7.1f.) is more 'ideal' (imaginary) than the setting of the incident in the grainfield (Mark 2.23f.). The entire handwashing pericope – the trip of scribes and Pharisees from Jerusalem, their appearance where Jesus and his disciples were eating, and their accusation that his disciples had not previously washed their hands – has the primary purpose of leading up to Jesus' criticism of them for their rules about vows. There is no saying by Jesus about handwashing around which this introduction developed, and I am inclined to think that it was custom-made to lead up to the *korban* accusation – especially since handwashing has a firmer setting in the Diaspora than in Palestine. The link between handwashing and *korban* is the word 'tradition'. Still, even if we take the scene as beyond question, it is an extremely minor issue.

A second purity topic is the criticism of the priesthood which is implied in the Parable of the Good Samaritan. It is less severe than that of the *Psalms of Solomon* or the *Covenant of Damascus*, and it did not mean rejection of the temple service. Further, Jesus accepted the biblical laws relating to leprosy, including sacrifice for purification (that is, *ritual* purity).

On the question of food the Jesus of Mark 7 takes a position which is radically at variance with all known first-century Jewish thought and practice. The saying that what goes in does not defile – unless an instance of antithetic hyperbole – is a strong contravention of the law, and the circles in which such a saying resulted in disobedience of the food laws had clearly broken with Judaism. This is the significance which it has in Mark, where it is interpreted by 7.19, 'he declared all foods clean'. If we make a historical judgment, we must conclude that Jesus said nothing this unambiguously negative about the food laws.

On oaths the synoptic Jesus is well within the parameters of first-century Jewish debate. The admonition not to take oaths is paralleled among one group of the Essenes, who also refused to swear, except when joining the sect (so Josephus). According to Matt. 23 Jesus criticized the Pharisees for making non-biblical distinctions among oaths. The Sadducees might well have made the same criticism, though they probably would have concluded that the new forms were all invalid, rather than that they were tantamount to oaths sworn by God.

On the question of divorce, which I have not discussed here,[2] Jesus took a position which is more stringent than the law requires. Not divorcing at all would keep one from ever disobeying the Mosaic demand to write one's wife a bill of divorce before 'putting her away'. The prohibition of divorce is paralleled in CD 4.20–5.6.

An accusation of blasphemy was of course an extremely serious charge. There are two points which keep us from saying that here the synoptic Jesus is depicted as taking a stand which is contrary to the law or which constitutes a serious point of dispute with his contemporaries: (1) The words which are attributed to Jesus in the passages where the charge 'blasphemy' occurs (The Healing of the Paralytic; Mark's Trial Scene) are extremely hard to construe as blasphemy. The passive verb in 'your sins are forgiven' means 'by God', and saying that God forgives is not blasphemous. There is nothing obviously blasphemous about the titles 'messiah' and 'son of God'. (2) Even taking the Trial narrative at face value, one would have to conclude that the opponents *already* had something against him, and that it was not his words at the trial which got him into trouble. If we accept Mark's account as it stands, we must note that Jesus was not arrested for giving himself titles and that he was at first accused of threatening the temple. When this charge failed (since the witnesses did not agree), the high priest was forced to find a cause for execution in Jesus' own words. He got him to confess that two titles, each of which had a very wide range of meaning, applied to him. The high priest decided to take them at their most extreme and cried, 'Blasphemy'.

It seems to me that the only reasonable construal of the account as it lies on the page is that the high priest was looking for an excuse to execute Jesus. When one effort failed, he tried another. He then had to interpret the answer in a certain way in order to find an offence. Since he was convinced on other grounds that Jesus should die, he decided to take 'messiah' and 'son of God' as titles which elevated Jesus too much, and so implicitly denigrated God. I cannot see in the titles anything which is obviously blasphemous or which – given first-century views of blasphemy – would reasonably be construed as such. Thus I conclude that even taking the passages as they stand, one finds in them no actual transgression of the law. The real offence had already been committed, and the high priest had already decided that Jesus should die.

I do not, however, think that in a historical reconstruction the Trial passage should be accepted as it stands. The exchange between the high priest and Jesus (messiah, Son of God, blasphemy) is probably a Christian composition which has Jesus die for holding the church's christology.

I am not arguing that the historical Jesus did nothing to offend his Jewish contemporaries. On the contrary, I have maintained, against many, that he did so, and that the offence led to his death. That is one of the main arguments of *Jesus and Judaism*, developed over several chapters. I think that his position on the inclusion of 'sinners' (in Semitic terms, probably 'the wicked') was offensive, and that the conflict over the temple was sufficient to lead to his execution.[3] Common to both is explicit or implicit *self-claim*, and the implicit self-claim is evident in the command to a would-be follower to 'let the dead bury the dead'. With regard to an explicit claim, however, the reticence of the synoptic Jesus to claim or accept such a title as 'messiah' (Mark 8.27–30) probably reflects the reticence of the historical Jesus. In looking at self-claim, whether in the trial scene, the healing stories or elsewhere, we are best advised to look for implicit assertions: he felt empowered by God to do what he did and say what he said, and this was conveyed to others in one way or another. Some of them took offence.

Some have thought that Jesus' self-claim is asserted vis-à-vis the law in the so-called antitheses of the Sermon on the Mount (Matt. 5.21–48), where 'but I say to you' is set over against 'you have heard that it was said', which is followed by a quotation, usually from the Bible. Does Jesus set his own authority directly against the law? As Daube and Davies have argued, he does not.[4] The first 'antithesis' is this:

> You have heard that it was said to the men of old, 'You shall not kill; and whoever kills shall be liable to judgment'. But I say to you that every one who is angry with his brother shall be liable to judgment.

'You have heard that it was said to the men of old' is not the same as 'Moses wrote' (see Mark 10.3–5) or 'Moses commanded' (Matt. 8.4), which we should expect if Jesus were to discuss the written law as such. 'Heard that it was said' points towards interpretation.[5] The interpretation is not itself discussed, but what Jesus presents as his own view is interpretation, not a new law. 'Do not kill' means also 'do not be angry'; 'do not commit adultery' means also 'do not look with lust'.

The rest of the terminology also points towards interpretation. 'But I say to you' is similar to 'and concerning [this] we say' (v^c-'al [zeh] 'anahnû 'ôm^crîm) in 4QMMT[6], or to 'R. X says' in rabbinic literature. The verb 'to say' in legal debate means 'to interpret'. The use of the first person depends on the literary genre; in and of itself it does not imply any special claim, except that the speaker is a worthy interpreter. The Greek conjunction *de* in 'but I say' may mean either 'and' or 'but'. If a translation, it probably does not represent a strongly adversative 'but' (such as 'ella'), but the simple Hebrew *vav* ('and' or 'but'). (This sort of legal discussion might well have been held in Hebrew.) If one imagines that 'but I say to you' was translated from Aramaic, there would have been no conjunction at all. In sum: the vocabulary is that of debate over interpretation and does not point towards 'antithesis' to the law.

As Daube said, 'You shall not be angry' is 'the revelation of a fuller meaning [of the commandment] for a new age. The second member unfolds rather than sweeps away the first'.[7] Jesus here appears as interpreter of the law, not its opponent. This was certainly the understanding of the earliest known student of these sayings, the person who put together the Sermon on the Mount, where the 'antitheses' are not antithetical to the law, but rather exemplify the preceding passage: 'I have not come to abolish [the law and the prophets] but to fulfil them' (5.17) – fulfil them by going beyond them in some instances.

Going beyond the law may imply a kind of criticism of it: it is not rigorous enough, or it is not adequate for the new age. We have already noted this point in discussing the pericope on divorce, one of the versions of which occurs in the 'antitheses' (5.31f.)

Thus the synoptic Jesus makes a substantial self-claim, and he makes a perfectionist critique of the law. Since at least the divorce pericope is authentic, both points are true of the historical Jesus as well. These do not, however, amount to opposition to the law.

With regard to the actual cause of Jesus' death, I remain impressed by the fact that he was not executed until after the demonstration in the temple, but that then he was executed immediately. Words could get one killed, as the case of John the Baptist shows. On the other hand, the stories of Jesus son of Ananias, who cried Woe! on Jerusalem and the temple, and of the teachers who inspired their students to pull down Herod's eagle from the entrance to the temple, indicate that one could say rather a lot and live through it, while *doing* something, especially something which affected the temple, was more certain to be fatal.[8] Jesus' deed, like the words and the healings, was based on self-claim. Further, one of the words was 'kingdom'. Hopes for the restoration of a Jewish kingdom, of no matter what type, were potentially dangerous, since they might inspire rioting or insurrection. The Entry to Jerusalem, if it came to the attention of the high priest, would have warned him that this danger existed. The term 'kingdom', especially 'coming kingdom', together with the saying about the destruction of the temple and the overthrow of tables, provided all the evidence that was needed for Jesus' execution.

The point of this study has been to focus on how serious the legal disagreements were *if* Jesus is viewed as a teacher of the law. Yet formulating the conflict in terms of legal disputes seems to me to be misleading. It supposes that Jesus was a legal student and teacher, who sat down, worked out positions, and challenged people who held different views. Most of these challenges, it turns out, would have been extremely minor. Viewing Jesus as primarily Rabbi then means seeing others as preferring their own slightly different views so much that they would kill in their defence. This, I think, is wrong, both with regard to Jesus and with regard to others.

We should recall from the discussion of conflict that, in life-and-death struggles, legal questions might be involved, but more would be at stake. Different legal practices might be the symbol of opposition. I agree with others that this was the case at Qumran. What the Zadokite priests *really* wanted was to take over Jerusalem and the temple. Since they had this desire, they probably had a complete set of the rules by which they would govern. The mere fact of their having their own laws and interpretations was not the cause of persecution; they held on to their laws for over two hundred years, but harassment of them seems to have been limited to the earliest period. One branch of the party withdrew from Jerusalem, and one lived in the broader community. Both observed their own rules, and they were not exterminated.

I do not think that Jesus actually wanted to govern Jerusalem, and so I doubt that he had a full repertoire of distinctive legal positions. If one compares the very minor disputes between Jesus and others with the major disagreements which separated Qumran from Jerusalem, one will see the point. He was much less likely than an Essene to get into trouble because of variations in legal practice and interpretation. What he wanted, what he said and what he did, finally led to his execution, but to think of the conflict as being determined by differences over various points of the law is to misconceive it.

Of the material which depicts legal conflict, what actually goes back to the historical Jesus? I continue to think that relatively little does. I remain persuaded by the classical form-critical analysis of the principal conflict passages: in most cases the settings are 'ideal', and without the original context we cannot reconstruct the original meaning. The story of Pharisees in the grainfield sets two ambiguous sayings in the context of sabbath-breaking. Outside the Markan context they are not against the sabbath. Mark 7 offers an even better illustration. As the chapter now stands, Jesus rejects Pharisaism (handwashing and *korban*) and the law itself (food). Let us say that each of its three elements has an authentic core. Jesus' disciples really did not wash their hands; Jesus criticized the Pharisees for their rules on vows; he said 'not what goes in defiles, but what comes out'. From the first point we would learn only that Jesus' disciples were neither Pharisees nor Diaspora Jews. From the second we would learn that Jesus *criticized* the Pharisees. The party either already had or shortly would correct their view of which vows were binding, and this implies the acceptance of either external or internal criticism. We do not know the meaning of the saying 'what goes in', and cannot know it without a context: if said while eating shellfish it would mean one thing, if said while discussing which laws are most important it would mean something else. In the latter case it would be antithetical hyperbole for 'what comes out is much more important'.

Deprived of the Markan context, the three elements provide us with evidence that Jesus' disciples were not Pharisees, that he criticized pharisaic interpretation of a difficult point of law, and that he said something ambiguous about 'going in and coming out'. The settings of the conflict passages are 'ideal', and without the present settings we have very little conflict.

Other passages which depict fierce opposition are clearly editorial, such as knowledge of what scribes said 'in their hearts' (Mark 2.6f.) or what Pharisees and Herodians said when in private consultation with one another (Mark 3.6). An author's hand is responsible for the sequence of disputes in Mark 2.1–3.6, and though they may contain authentic bits little more can be said. Historical reconstruction cannot rest on their details.

Even if each conflict narrative were literally true, however, it would be seen that Jesus did not seriously challenge the law as it was practised in his day, not even by the strict rules of observance of pietist groups – except on the issue of food. The subsequent debate on that issue in the early church, however (Gal. 2; Rom. 14; Acts 10; 15), makes this the point which may be denied to the historical Jesus with most confidence. He may have been in minor disagreement with one group or another about some legal observances, but prior to the attack on the Temple I cannot find a single issue which would have been the occasion of a serious charge.

II

Did the Pharisees Have Oral Law?

A. INTRODUCTION

The answer to the question has almost always been Yes, and asking it means 'I doubt it'. This much the reader knows in advance, because of the conventions which govern the titles of essays.

We must start by agreeing on what the topic is. It is not the much discussed question of what 'oral' means – whether word-for-word memorization of non-written texts, memorization of catchwords and themes, memorization supported by notes, and so on.[1] For this essay, I shall be happy for 'oral' to mean almost anything at all, including 'written in notebooks but not published'. I wish to ask instead about the *status* of the Pharisees' non-biblical traditions. In what sense, if any, were they 'laws'?

Every first-century Jew lived by 'oral law', if oral law means 'the law as interpreted'. Laws then as now were believed to contain things which are not explicitly there. In the USA of my youth it was believed that the Constitution prohibits the teaching of religion in tax-supported institutions. The First Amendment forbids the establishment of an official religion of the state, but it was commonly spoken of as requiring 'separation of church and state'; 'separation' was understood to mean 'no relationship between taxes and anything having to do with religion'; this understanding was called a 'doctrine'. The supposed law had binding force because of the common perception of it. The question has now been examined and tested in court, and the Constitution has been interpreted to allow instruction about religion, though not propaganda for it, to be supported by taxpayers' money. In my generation, the 'doctrine of separation of church and state' was (at least on the part of non-lawyers) an unconscious interpretation of the Constitution. When this 'doctrine' was examined, we became aware that the old, unconscious interpretation, which we had equated with the Constitution itself, was just that: interpretation.

The Bible requires a lot of interpretation. At virtually no point is it precise and detailed enough to dictate concrete practice, and it does not cover numerous areas at all. Moshe David Herr notes that there is only passing reference to a law of sale and acquisition, that marriage is not regulated, that the basic divorce law is mentioned 'only incidentally in connection with the injunction that a man may not remarry his divorced wife after she has married and become divorced again', that often crimes and punishments are not correlated (flogging is discussed, but not which crimes it punished) – and so on.[2] We may not doubt that in the first century Jews lived by some laws which are not to be found in the law of Moses, nor that there were customs which were generally followed and which came to be more-or-less as binding as laws. We shall also see that it cannot be doubted that Pharisees had special 'traditions' which they observed. I wish to ask whether or not the Pharisees had *traditions* which they *knew* were non-biblical, but which they regarded as being *equal in age and authority* to the written law. Most scholars would say 'yes' to the question, but this has recently been challenged by Jacob Neusner (see below). I think that the topic is more difficult than it is usually thought to be, and I wish first to explore it generally and then to look at some rabbinic evidence in detail.

Since the term 'oral law' is used differently by different scholars, and since I wish to grant that there are some senses in which not only Pharisees but others must be said to have had oral law, I shall lay out a bit more fully meanings which I do not wish to challenge. The second of these in particular will reveal how complicated the topic of oral law is, and we shall see that the Sadducees' position is as difficult to understand as the Pharisees'.

1. The Hebrew word *tôrah* had a wide meaning in the Bible. Scholars often propose 'instruction' as a better translation than 'law'. In the post-biblical period 'torah' could be used for the entire contents of the Bible and consequently for a broad range of subjects.[3] Recently Shmuel Safrai has discussed oral torah in light of this broad definition of torah, retaining the Hebrew word so as not to have to choose between the various translations (such as 'law' and 'tradition').[4] He defines oral torah as including everything which eventually ended up as rabbinic literature, plus the Aramaic Targums. Qumran had its own literature, and so did the Sadducees, though theirs is now lost. The Sages (first the Pharisees and then the Rabbis) were responsible for everything else, and everything else is oral torah: legal rulings (halakot), stories, sermons and other edifying material (haggadot) and biblical paraphrases (targumim). Josephus attributes some things to Moses which are not in the Bible[5]; according to Safrai, he took these from the pharisaic oral torah. Philo's interpretations have the same source: 'these authors used, consciously or not, elements from the oral tradition of the Sages'.[6] The justification for attributing almost everything to the Pharisees is

the supposition that second temple Judaism, apparently including the Diaspora, was *divided* among the three parties. Those who were not Sadducees or Essenes were Pharisees.[7]

Safrai's view, that in the period of the second temple Pharisees ran everything,[8] is widely held, as is the opinion that they generated virtually all interpretations and applications of the law. He seems even to push their activity back to the time of Nehemiah,[9] and this gives pharisaic oral torah enormous scope.

I do not wish to quibble over definitions. I think that it is not useful to define oral torah this broadly, but Safrai's definition does have in its favour the wide meaning of the Hebrew word 'torah'. In the current essay, however, 'oral law' is meant in the narrow sense: *laws* which are not found in the Bible. The more serious points of disagreement are those concerning the composition of Jewish society and the role of the Pharisees. I shall return to this immediately below, and here only note that I cannot accept the view that the Pharisees generated all non-written traditions and interpretations. Some they shared with others, some preceded them, and some were simply different.[10] We shall see examples below.

2. Moshe David Herr (n. 2 above) understands oral law to be interpretation of the written law. On the basis of this definition he points out that everyone, including the Sadducees, had oral law, which served to supplement and apply the written law. Since Herr's point cannot be contested, we must ask why it is that Josephus makes acceptance or rejection of tradition one of the main points of difference between Pharisees and Sadducees.

> The Pharisees handed down [*paredosan*] to the populace certain regulations [*nomima*] from [*their*] forebears [*ek paterōn diadochēs*], which are not written in the laws of Moses, and which on this account are rejected by the Sadducean group, who hold that only those regulations should be considered valid which are written down, and that those which are from the tradition of the fathers (*ek paradoseōs tōn paterōn*) do not need to be kept. (*Antiq.* 13.297).

Since anyone who applies the law must interpret and supplement it, wherein did the two parties differ?

There are two answers to this question from the traditional point of view. One is that the Sadducees had supplementary laws but wrote them down; the Pharisees were alone in having *oral* law.[11] This proposal is based on separating the two halves of Josephus's statement and taking only the second half to describe the Sadducees' view: they accepted regulations which were written down anywhere, not just in the Bible, but also in their own Book of Decrees.[12] Peter Schäfer favours this interpretation: the real contrast, he proposes, is between 'written' and the implied, not stated, 'oral', rather than between 'in the law of Moses' and 'not in the law'.[13] This, however, is against Josephus's plain meaning. He first puts it this way: the Pharisees accept

1. *nomima* handed down (*paredosan*) from the fathers	2. which are not written (*anagegraptai*) in the laws of Moses

He then offers a contrast:

4. the Pharisees accept *nomima* from the tradition (*ek paradoseōs*) of the fathers	3. the Sadducees accept only *nomima* which are written (*ta gegrammena*)

I have reversed the order of the contrast in order to line up the columns. Doing this allows us to see clearly that (2) is the negative form of (3): the Sadducees accept only the *nomima* which are *written*, i.e., they reject the Pharisaic traditions which are not *written in the laws of Moses*. It seems to me simply impossible to suppose that the second 'written' means something other than the first, and that Josephus first contrasts ancestral traditions with the written law of Moses, and then the same traditions with *anything* written. He simply avoided the repetition of 'in the law'; the second 'written' refers back to the first. Thus Josephus states – whether correctly or not – that the Sadducees rejected pharisaic traditions because they were not in the Bible (see also *Antiq.* 18.16).

The second traditional answer is that the Sadducean view did not matter. It is all right to talk about oral law being required and also to limit it to the Pharisees, since they governed society. The Sadducees were a 'dissenting sect outside normative Judaism'. They 'belonged to the fringes of Judaism, and it was not they who determined the *halakhah*'.[14] Thus Herr argues, in effect, that, to govern, one must have oral law, and that those who governed, the Pharisees, had it. This becomes a problem when we realize that during the periods of direct Roman rule, CE 6–41 and 44–66, the chief priesthood effectively governed Judaea, and that from 41–44, Agrippa II was king. There is no reason to think that either Agrippa or the chief priests governed in accord with pharisaic 'oral law'. What did they use? Josephus's distinction between the Pharisees and Sadducees still has not been explained.

Most discussions of law and government in the post-biblical period have an air of timelessness. 'The Sages decided that . . .', or 'the Rabbis laid it down that . . .', and so it was done. In the revision of Schürer's history, we read that there were three categories of oral law, all binding: halakot which go back to Moses, further halakot, and 'words of the scribes'. 'Towards the end of the period under discussion' – that is, presumably, after the beginning of the common era – these rules were 'in the main transmitted only orally'. This sounds as if these rabbinic categories existed throughout the period of Schürer's history (175 BCE – CE 135) and as if Pharisees governed all the time.[15] We must in fact take the chronology of the post-biblical period very seriously.

The questions of the composition of Jewish society and of the role of the Pharisees are large and fundamental, and they must be approached from many different directions. As I have indicated more than once, I hope to publish in the near future a study which will have as one of its main themes the question 'Who ran what?' In the present volume we shall see some reasons for doubting the long-standing consensus that the Pharisees governed Palestine, a consensus which was first seriously challenged by Morton Smith.[16] While I cannot treat this matter fully here, the present topic requires a summary of my views.

(1) The parties arose out of the Hasmonean revolt against Seleucid rule. By that time (c. 167–164 BCE for the opening phase) the written law had been subject to centuries of interpretation both in Palestine and in the Diaspora. Numerous practices and decisions had assumed the force of law. We cannot attribute this vast activity to Pharisees. (2) In the period from John Hyrcanus to the first revolt, c. 135 BCE – CE 66, most Jews did not belong to any party. The parties were quite small. (3) The Pharisees were predominant only when Josephus says they were: at the outset of the reign of John Hyrcanus and during the reign of Salome Alexandra (76–67 BCE).[17] Possibly they were dominant earlier (e.g. the high priesthood of Simon, c. 142–135)[18] and in the councils of Hyrcanus II (63–40),[19] but this would not have amounted to much, since he never had full authority.[20] The Pharisees had only nuisance value during the reign of Herod (37–4 BCE),[21] and after Judaea became a Roman province (CE 6) the chief priesthood played the major role in Jerusalem. Possibly not all high priests were Sadducees, but it is doubtful that any were Pharisees. (4) The Pharisees did not have the manpower to control every aspect of life behind the scenes. Since all of life was to be lived by the law, and since all aspects of the law require interpretation, the traditional view requires – as Safrai explicitly states – that Pharisees controlled all public activities.[22] Apart from being against the evidence, this is simply impossible.

The traditional view relies heavily on a passage in Josephus:

> There are but few men to whom this doctrine [Sadduceeism] has been made known, but these are the men of the highest standing. They accomplish practically nothing, however. For whenever they assume some office, though they submit unwillingly and perforce, yet submit they do to the formulas of the Pharisees, since otherwise the masses would not tolerate them. (*Antiq.* 18.17)[23]

Most scholars take this to be true beyond question, to the letter and all the time; and they simply ignore the statements in which Josephus assigns authority to the high priests (*Antiq.* 20.251; *Apion* 2.187), as well as his detailed narratives. In these, from the death of Salome Alexandra to the formation of a coalition government when the first revolt broke out – that is, from 67 BCE to CE 66 – the Pharisees play virtually no role in Josephus's history. This is probably a bit misleading, but nevertheless reading incident after incident gives the overwhelming impression that, except during the reign of Herod, the aristocratic priesthood had control and did not follow the orders of the Pharisees.[24]

Let us now return to post-exilic chronology, which will help us put the question of oral law and the Pharisees in context. Since the return from Babylon, the problem of law had been coped with daily. The Pentateuch is supplemented and modified in Nehemiah, and legal developments can be perceived in Chronicles. Decision-making was going on all the time, and whole sets of observances were established. Some new laws were added to the Pentateuch, and some made it into the post-exilic biblical books or other literature. Yet all of Leviticus and Numbers, including the probably post-exilic parts, requires interpretation and supplement. Legal development did not stop with the last word added to Leviticus. In order to have dates to work with, let us say that the last bits were added to the Pentateuch by 400 BCE, 115 years after the rebuilding of the temple, and that Nehemiah was written by the same date. Let us date the origins of the 'parties' early, choosing for convenience 164 BCE, the year Judas Maccabeus purified the temple. In this case, between the completion of the biblical laws and the rise of the parties, custom and precedent had determined innumerable points of practice for 236 years. While it is unlikely that this period saw as much legal development in Judaea as did the period 1754–1990 in the modern West, we must nevertheless grant that, when the revolt against the Seleucids broke out, many aspects of life were governed by non-biblical laws. In addition, custom would have dictated how all the biblical laws were applied.

While the Hasmoneans inherited a lot of laws, doubtless they created some of their own. The parties arose, and they went to work on laws, probably making a point of developing differences from one another. They all started, however, from a large common base, and some points of practice seem never to have been questioned, even though they are not in the written law. Shall we call these 'oral law'? That is just the question.

To get at it, I wish to make further distinctions: (1) between conscious and unconscious interpretation of the written law; (2) between interpretation and consciously formulated supplements, alterations or additions which are known not to be in the law at all. These distinctions are easier to state than to demonstrate, since exegesis can be fanciful and produce results which are now thought to be remote from the text, and since we have no direct access to what was 'conscious' and 'unconscious'. Nevertheless, if we bear these distinctions in mind and consider some examples, we shall improve our understanding of the problem.

1. The calendar was the most comprehensive common law. From the Bible come clues which show that both months and seasons are to be observed. The festivals fall on specified days of certain months, yet they are seasonal and have to correspond to the agricultural year (e.g. Lev. 23.9–21). The phases of the moon, which produce months, do not, however, correspond to a seasonal pattern. Three lunar months will always fall short of a seasonal quarter year, and twelve lunar months are about eleven days short of a seasonal year. The consequence is that each month falls earlier in each successive year. Soon the month in which the autumn harvest is celebrated falls in early summer. From the time when the first seasonal offerings were brought to the temple, there had to be *a* calendar which reconciled the lunar year with the seasonal or solar year. We may take it that there was such a calendar before the Maccabean revolt, and that it was continued by the Hasmoneans. The Qumran sect, we know, had a different calendar, and this ensured full separation from common religious life. 'Common religious life' implies 'common calendar', and this aspect of common law was not written, or if so the document did not survive.

Yet it was accepted by Pharisees, Sadducees and others – all but the Qumran sect (and possibly a few other dissenters). Therefore, it was not a 'tradition' or 'oral law' which separated Pharisee from Sadducee. Why not? Did each party think that it was interpretation of the written text? Were they not conscious that their calendrical arrangement was only one of numerous possibilities?

The Qumran dispute guarantees consciousness. Everyone who knew about it also knew that there was more than one way to make a calendar. Possibly exegetical arguments were advanced, but nevertheless there was full consciousness of accepting something which was not in the Bible in so many words. Then how could the Pharisees and Sadducees both have accepted the same non-biblical calendar?

I propose that they accepted it because it was common and inherited, and neither party had any reason to change it. Then how did they think of it? The traditional answer would be that the Pharisees thought it up and that it was part of their oral law; the Sadducees accepted it because they had to do so: the masses would have tossed them out had they not gone along with the Pharisees. But once we grant that the Sadducees did not run in terror of the Pharisees, and that they sometimes had a free hand, the question is more difficult. Further, the calendar is doubtless pre-pharisaic.

A possible solution is that it was not regarded as 'law' at all, but as 'practice', what would be called in rabbinic literature 'halakah', 'walking', that is, 'behaviour'. Did anyone think that halakah was divine and as binding as the biblical law? I think not, and the evidence for this will be given below. Here, however, we need to note a distinction. Assuming that this possibility is correct, that the calendar was understood as agreed practice rather than divine fiat, it is nevertheless the case that, in terms of what people did, it was *at least* as binding as the written law. A jurist might grant that there was some other way of arranging the year and that in theory Passover could fall on some other day, but in practice it fell only when the temple said so. Thus when Schürer[25] states that 'a large number of legal decisions' had 'authority equal to that of the written law', one must agree in terms of practice. A practice, however, can be changed, and changed consciously. To revert to the analogy with the United States Constitution: The country is governed by ceaselessly changing legislation, all of it under the Constitution, which itself is very difficult to alter. Possibly the calendar was agreed practice which was absolutely binding, but which nevertheless was not regarded as divine law.

The other – I think more likely – possibility is that the Jerusalem calendar was defended by exegesis and was regarded as being the right interpretation of the law. The solemn wording of the Bible ('and it shall be a statute to you for ever that in the seventh month, on the tenth day of the month', Lev. 16.29) implies that the right day matters; and people who observed a holy occasion (in this case, the Day of Atonement) wanted to think that they were observing the correct day. Thus they probably defended their calendar as being ordained by God.

2. The Bible does not require the temple to have a Court of the Women or a Court of the Gentiles, but both were prominent in Herod's temple. I shall be very brief. Herod was not under the thumb of the Pharisees; if anything, he disliked and distrusted them.[26] Everyone in common Judaism – Pharisees, Sadducees, some Essenes,[27] and the mass of Jewry both at home and abroad – accepted Herod's temple. It is most probable that careful students of the law – priests and Pharisees – knew that aspects of the temple had no biblical basis. Yet they all worshipped in it, and they regarded the distinctions among the courts as absolutely binding. Some of this may be considered common inheritance: According to Neh. 8.1–3 Ezra read the law in the presence of men and women alike (contrast Ex. 19.15),[28] and the temple of the Qumran Temple Scroll was to have three courts; the outer court may have been for women, children and some Gentiles.[29] The Temple Scroll is apparently an early document, and it may reveal that in the Hasmonean period the idea of providing for women and Gentiles was already current.[30] We do not know how, by Herod's day, agreement was

achieved among the non-Qumranian Jews, but the priests who advised him seem to have worked on the basis of a consensus; the system of temple courts was not contested.

Similarly the view that only priests could enter the *area* of the Court of the Priests was understood by Herod (that is, by his advisers) to mean that priests had to be trained as masons (*Antiq.* 15.390). According to Ezra 3.10, builders worked on the temple and the priests blew trumpets, but by Herod's time a different purity law was accepted, and the priests built the most sacred areas themselves.

These views of the temple, like those of the calendar, seem not to have been controversial (leaving aside the Qumran sect). The consensus on the temple differs from the earlier example in an important respect. The definition of temple courts was not inherited from pre-Hasmonean Judaism, since then there had been no Court of the Gentiles (see *Antiq.* 12.145); and, as we noted above, in Ezra's time the priests did not build the inner sanctum. Nevertheless, the new rules which distinguished court from court seem tto have been very fiercely held, and they may have been regarded as divine 'law',

Thus here we have a commonly accepted law which did not depend on practice inherited from the Persian and Greek periods. This counts as 'oral law', held probably in full consciousness that it was not supported by the Bible.

3. In first-century Palestine there was wide agreement that the biblical requirements to 'wash' (e.g. Lev. 15) were to be fulfilled by immersing. Here again we can see that this was not a pharisaic view forced on others. The Pharisees stood apart from others on two points. They had their own definitions of valid immersion pools, and they also made a very important distinction between two parts of biblical purification law: washing (=immersing) and the setting of the sun (I.D above; see further III.E below). There was *common* (possibly not universal; the evidence is not conclusive) agreement on immersing; disagreement about which pools were valid and the importance of sunset.

It is probable that immersion was regarded as a law, at least by the priesthood, and that it was imposed on anyone who wanted to enter the temple. The Hebrew verb *raḥats* seem to have been *interpreted* as *ṭabal*: 'wash' meant 'immerse'. The Pharisees, however (as we shall see), did not think that their own definitions of valid pools and water were 'law'; those who did not follow them did not transgress the law. In this case we have both a commonly accepted interpretation of 'wash' and evidence of pharisaic traditions which others did not accept, and which the Pharisees themselves did not regard as law.

4. The Bible requires that priests and their families eat holy food in purity Num. 18.11). The Pentateuch does not state that the food be handled in purity before it reaches the priests. Late in the biblical period one can find the

beginnings of the view that the food should be carried to the priests in pure vessels (Isa. 66.20), and by the time of Judith it was regarded as being against the law for an impure person to handle the priests' food (see on this more fully III.B below). This was accepted, according to rabbinic literature, by the ordinary people, the *'amme ha-'arets* (p. 238 below). This rule is too early to be pharisaic. As in the previous example, there is evidence for a pharisaic modification of the 'law' of handling priestly food in purity, a modification which others did not accept: the Pharisees 'decreed' handwashing in connection with the priests' food (p. 229 below). We cannot say whether handling the priests' food in purity was a conscious or an unconscious development, nor whether its origins lay in exegesis. It is possible that the practice was unconscious interpretation of the passages requiring the priests to *eat* in purity. In any case it was commonly accepted.

5. We also know of conscious, exegetical interpretations. In I.F I sketched two different interpretations of the biblical tithing laws. The laws of Deuteronomy, Leviticus, Numbers and Nehemiah are not identical, and first-century Jews conflated them. They conflated them, however, in at least two different and competing ways. I assume that each group thought that its interpretation was correct. The existence of competing views guarantees that interpretation was conscious.

6. We saw in I.B above the best example of both unconscious interpretation and conscious re-interpretation in the Judaism of the Pharisees' day. As early as the first years of the Hasmonean revolt we find the assumption that the prohibition of work on the sabbath included the prohibition of fighting. This is an 'interpretation' of the law of the most persuasive kind: an unconscious one, and one which everyone shared. The subsequent decision to fight in self-defence was a conscious re-interpretation. As far as we know, there were no exegetical arguments in its favour; rather, it was decreed and then agreed on by all.

Neither interpretation is pharisaic; both are common. 'Fighting is work', I propose, seemed self-evident. 'Fighting in direct defence of one's life is allowed' was both conscious and independent of the text. Further, it seems to have had the force of law. In one place Josephus calls both the prohibition of fighting and the exception in case of direct attack 'the law' (*Antiq.* 14.63), and here we see a consciously formulated legal tradition creeping into the realm of law itself. This is, then, an 'oral' law (even though Josephus and the author of I Maccabees wrote it down), but not a pharisaic one. Our question is precisely whether or not Pharisees saw their own non-biblical traditions in this way.

The Pharisees had at least one distinctive view about work on the sabbath: the practice which is indicated by the word *'êrub*, anglicized eruv, 'the fusion of sabbath limits' (Danby).[31] By the erection of cross-beams, for example, all the houses in a courtyard or along an alley could be 'fused' into one house, and then vessels containing food could be carried from one part of the fused house to another, thus permitting communal dining on the sabbath. The Sadducees did not agree with this, and the Pharisees did not pretend that the Bible allows the 'fusion of sabbath limits'. This development counts as 'tradition', not 'interpretation'.

In the sphere of sabbath rules, then, we see unconscious interpretation which has become law, a conscious addition to it which was also law, and a peculiarly pharisaic practice which others did not accept.

Could we give details of civil and criminal law, we should doubtless see that numerous other non-biblical laws had become standard in post-exilic Judaism. The above examples, however, serve to show that non-biblical practices could be binding. Some of these were consciously known not to be based on Bible; some were unconscious, some conscious interpretations of the biblical text. We have also come upon pharisaic traditions which were not accepted by others, but we have not fully explored the question of whether or not the Pharisees regarded them as 'law', equal to the Bible.

Before taking up the Pharisees' view of their distinctive traditions, let us ask about the Sadducees. Josephus's statement (above, p. 99), if strictly true, implies that they found biblical authority for all the non-biblical practices which they accepted. We simply cannot know how clever they were in exegesis. In the discussion above I proposed that in some cases (e.g. the division of temple courts) they may have known that they followed a non-biblical custom, but I must concede that possibly they managed to find some sort of textual support. The alternative is that Josephus oversimplified their position. Possibly they accepted some 'traditions of the fathers', such as the calendar, but rejected others – those held by the Pharisees alone.

There is no way to solve this problem decisively, but I shall propose a tentative solution. I am inclined to think that the Sadducees rejected only the Pharisees' traditions; that is, the non-biblical traditions which everyone, including the Pharisees, *granted* were not supported by exegesis. The Sadducees (the tentative proposal continues) employed the rhetoric of living only by the written law (though examination of the customs which they accepted shows that this was not strictly true, or is not true by *our* standards of exegesis), while the Pharisees admitted that some of their practices were not biblical. The distinction, then, would be that the Pharisees were *conscious* of having *non-interpretative traditions*, while the Sadducees claimed that their traditions were based on interpretation. In some cases the interpretation was conscious, in others unconscious; some interpretations must have been very forced. We shall return to this point in the conclusion.

Neither of the traditional solutions of our problem works. It explains nothing to say that the Sadducees rejected purely oral traditions but accepted what they themselves wrote down, since then we would have to ask why they wrote down x but not y; that is, they could have written down the Pharisees' traditions, making them their own. This proposal also, we noted, goes against Josephus's description, according to which they rejected what is not written *in the Bible*.[32] Similarly it is not possible that the Sadducees were forced to accept the Pharisees' customs. Were this the case, they would have been forced to accept them all, but it can be demonstrated that this did not happen. Josephus's point is that the Sadducees *rejected* the Pharisees' non-biblical traditions, and there is ample evidence to support his statement. We saw several instances in the six examples of non-biblical customs immediately above (e.g. 'eruv).

My proposal, then, is this: the Sadducees found biblical support for customs of which they approved, or at least asserted that they had it; they rejected traditions which they did not wish to accept; they attacked these as non-biblical; in some cases the Pharisees cheerfully admitted the charge, but kept the traditions anyway. The Pharisees defended their peculiar traditions not by appeal to the Bible, but to antiquity. They claimed that they observed the 'traditions of the elders' or 'fathers'. This was important in a world in which novelty was scorned.[33]

This explanation of the difference between Sadducee and Pharisee on 'tradition' does not explain *why* various views were or were not accepted. The Sadducees, we know, rejected the idea of an afterlife.[34] Had they wished to accept it, they could have found biblical texts which support the view; later the Rabbis came up with a lot of them. We do not explain the inner workings of Sadduceeism when we say that they rejected what is not biblical, since it lay with them to decide what was biblical and what not. Similarly we do not know why the Pharisees accepted some admittedly non-biblical traditions. Our study can deal only with the phenomena, not with underlying motives.

B. PHARISAIC TRADITIONS AND ORAL LAW

We now begin our investigation of the Pharisees' admittedly non-biblical traditions. We have seen the most substantial passage in which Josephus states that the Pharisees had such traditions (*Antiq.* 13.297). Elsewhere he refers to 'regulations [*nomima*] introduced by the Pharisees in accordance with the tradition [*paradosis*] of their fathers' (*Antiq.* 13.408). The verb *paredōken* and respect for seniors also figure in the description of the

Pharisees in *Antiq.* 18.12. Paul speaks of having been 'zealous for the traditions of [his] fathers' when a Pharisee (Gal. 1.14). From the New Testament there is some evidence as to the content of ancestral tradition: Mark 7.9 indicates that the vow '*korban*' was a 'tradition'. In Mark 7.5 the Pharisees and scribes ask why the disciples do not keep 'the tradition of the elders' by washing their hands. The evangelist extends handwashing to all Jews (7.3), and in fact it was practised by many in the Diaspora, but 7.5 connects it especially with the Pharisees. Neither handwashing nor korban is derived from the Bible. It is, then, beyond dispute that the Pharisees were distinguished by having non-biblical traditions, and we have some idea of what two of them were.

The discussion below will be facilitated if we add a third example to accompany handwashing and korban: eruv, 'the fusion of sabbath day limits'. In the Mishnah there is one dispute between the Houses of Hillel and Shammai which presupposes the practice of fusing houses (Erubin 1.2), and there is a story which claims that a Sadducee at the time of Simeon b. Gamaliel opposed the practice (Erubin 6.2). This I judge adequate to prove its pharisaic origin. Eruv is a prime case of a tradition which has no biblical support, and it serves us very well as an example.

I do not intend to try to determine what all the pharisaic traditions were, since the immediate purpose is to ask what status they had, and this will lead us to a terminological study of categories ('halakah', 'tradition' and the like). We shall discover the surprising fact that these terms in rabbinic literature do not point us towards the major traditions of Pharisaism. The way to discover the latter would be to study the presuppositions of earliest rabbinic literature (see further ch. III), to consider which of these constitute legal topics or decisions, and to determine which are without biblical support. Discovering the topics, however, would not tell us how the Pharisees evaluated them, whether as only in-house rules or as parts of the Mosaic law which all Israelites should observe.

To show that the Pharisees regarded a tradition as *law*, equal in age and authority to the biblical law, we require the following evidence: that the rule or practice was (1) pharisaic rather than common; that it was (2) consciously held to be (3) independent of the written law, not an interpretation of it; and (4) that it was considered as equal to the written law. The four key words for our quest, then, are *pharisaic, conscious, independent* and *equal*. Eruv meets the first three requirements. The question is, whether or not it and similar traditions meet the fourth.

To find answers, we must turn to rabbinic literature, since neither Josephus nor the gospels shed any light on the question. 'Oral torah' does not appear in the earliest rabbinic compilations (the Mishnah and Tosefta), and both by supplying this term and by tracing numerous rabbinic halakot back to Moses, the later strata of rabbinic literature, almost everyone will grant, expand and develop the idea of binding non-biblical rules.[1] Thus we shall concentrate on the earliest collections and ask whether or not they *presuppose* that non-biblical rules have the same status as the Mosaic law. We shall find no instances in which a known Pharisee (e.g. Hillel) comments directly on this issue, and the best we can do is to ask what the Pharisees' immediate successors assumed. If they thought that their rules were as binding as the written law, we shall have evidence in favour of pharisaic oral law in the strict sense. If not, we shall be justified in doubting the theory.

Until very recently the general view has been that rabbinic literature shows that the Pharisees had oral law. According to Ephraim E. Urbach, 'in the Rabbinic world up to the time of the destruction of the Temple' the Sages thought that 'the tradition of the fathers, the enactments, and the decrees' were 'Torah alongside the Written Torah'.[2] This view has been based on three foundations. (1) In Aboth 1.1–2.8 there is a chain of transmission of torah which runs from Moses to Hillel and Shammai, and which then branches, being continued both by Hillel's physical descendants and by his disciple, Johnanan b. Zakkai, and his students. 'Torah' in this passage has been interpreted as including the pharisaic traditions, which are then seen to be called 'law'. (2) The second important piece of evidence is the statement which is ascribed to Hillel in Shabbat 31a (//ARNA 15) that there are two torot, one the oral law (*tôrah she-be'al peh*). (3) The Rabbis sometimes refer to a halakah which was originally given to Moses.

The work of scholars other than Neusner shows that this view is subject to challenge. W. D. Davies recognized that the term 'oral law' is neither early nor widespread, and he did not take the single ascription to Hillel to prove that Pharisees accepted a 'two-fold law', written and oral.[3] Other scholars have also pointed out that the term for non-biblical rules, according to Josephus, the New Testament and early rabbinic literature, was not 'oral law' but 'tradition'.[4] Further, Ellis Rivkin maintained that Pharisees held only other Pharisees responsible for observing their special rules.[5] Observing them made one a Pharisee, but to be an obedient Jew one need only observe biblical law. Rivkin nevertheless used the term 'two-fold law' to describe the pharisaic legal corpus.[6]

Neusner has often maintained that the Rabbis thought of the Mishnah (or the materials of which it is composed) as 'the oral law'.[7] He was sharply criticized for this by Hyam Maccoby, on the grounds that the Mishnah was never *equated* with the oral law.[8] In other publications Neusner has reversed his position and argued that the entire theory of an oral law, coeval with the written law and equal in authority, is a late creation. The story about Hillel in

Shabbat 31a is a retrojection from the time of the Babylonian Talmud.[9] In the earliest rabbinic document, the Mishnah, no passage 'demands the meaning "not-written-down-Torah"', and the implication of the regular distinction between 'words of Torah' and 'teachings of scribes' 'precludes the conception of two Torahs of *equal* standing and authority, both deriving from God's revelation to Moses at Mount Sinai' (*Torah*, p. 26).

We cannot say, however, that this reversal has now become 'Neusner's view', since he also continues to write about rabbinic literature as 'oral law'. As far as I have noted, the first full denial of the traditional view comes in two essays published in 1983. Yet in the same volume another essay both affirms and denies that the mishnaic Rabbis thought of their work as 'oral law'. He states that the conception of 'Moses our Rabbi' 'comes after the completion and promulgation of Mishnah', and also that 'the conception of two Torahs, one written, the other oral', was held by 'the authorities of Mishnah-Tosefta'.[10] In 1985 appeared the full-dress study which I cited just above, in which 'oral law' is said to be a late retrojection. In a book published in 1987, however, Neusner again wrote about the Mishnah as the 'Oral Torah'.[11] Some of this confusion is the result of endlessly republishing, under different titles, things first published years ago. That by no means, however, accounts for all of Neusner's self-contradictions. The affirmation that rabbinic literature is 'oral Torah' is the theme of two books published in 1986 and 1987, which are not, as far as I can tell, republications. Having proposed, in 1983–1985, that the idea of 'oral law' first occurs in the talmuds, in 1986 and 1987 he wrote not only that the Rabbis thought that their words were oral law, but that they really were:

> It is easy to become confused, and think that the written Torah goes back to Sinai, while the oral Torah derives from a much later period in the early centuries C.E. In fact the Torah, God's revelation to Moses at Sinai, is one. Viewed from the perspective of Judaic faith, the teachings of the named sages of late antiquity . . . preserve principles, teachings handed on by tradition from Sinai. These teachings of Sinai in concrete detail become associated only later on with the names of particular authorities . . .

He proposes that the Jewish religion falls if he fails to make his point stick, namely that

> the writings of the ancient sages present, in written form, the oral part of that cogent and one whole Torah of Sinai that defines the way of life and worldview of Israel . . . , the people of the God who revealed the Torah to Moses at Sinai.

In the Acknowledgments, one finds the statement that the book presents, 'in a single sustained account, the results of [his] work on most of the principal documents of the canon of Judaism'. That is, all his work has been aimed at establishing that rabbinic literature was given to Moses. Many pages later there is just the whiff of critical doubt. After discussing several possibilities for relating the Mishnah to scripture or to revelation, he writes, '*Or* matters are otherwise. I hardly need to make them explicit.'[12]

If this represents a critical reservation, it is otherwise repressed. In the companion volume, an anthology of 'oral Torah', he writes,

> When Moses received the Torah at Mount Sinai, God gave that torah, or revelation in two media, the one in writing, the other formulated and transmitted only orally . . . The oral Torah . . . is that half of the one Torah revealed by God to Moses . . .[13]

He adds that this oral Torah 'reached written form' in the second to the seventh centuries and that it is attributed to sages of the first to the seventh centuries. That is, it includes all rabbinic literature, and he says this explicitly on pp. 5f.: rabbinic material is 'the oral Torah, as it had reached writing by the end of late antiquity'. The phrases 'reached written form' and 'reached writing' show the underlying fundamentalist assumption: God really did reveal all of rabbinic literature to Moses. At no point in this volume does Neusner hesitate or retract. Thus on p. 39, just before the anthology of 'oral scripture' begins, he says a few words about how 'the oral Torah relates to the written Torah so that the two form that one whole Torah of Moses, our rabbi'.

It is possible that one of these completely contradictory stances is Neusner's real position, and that the other is adopted simply for tactical purposes, perhaps to sell books to a different audience. The reader, however, cannot tell that one view is a real position and the other not; possibly neither is.

The reason for illustrating the fact that Neusner publishes both hypercritical and completely uncritical work is to point out that one cannot simply say, 'Neusner has shown that . . .', as do so many scholars, especially New Testament scholars. For example, in reviewing Neusner's *Judaism in the Beginning of Christianity*, which was published in 1984, Leslie Houlden wrote that 'more than anyone else' he has applied to rabbinic literature 'the methods of historical criticism, so long and so meticulously used in relation to the Christian scriptures'. Houlden comments approvingly that Neusner shows that the Hillel material 'is so overlaid with the concerns of the post-70 AD period that the authentic voice of Hillel is quite beyond recovery'.[14] Had the reviewer taken account of the rest of the book, he would have reported on the chapter on another first-century Pharisee, Johanan b. Zakkai, in which Neusner wrote that a passage in the Mekilta 'epitomizes Yohanan's viewpoint' (to which Neusner presumably had independent and sure access), and that in Avot de R. Nathan A 'we see [Yohanan's] thought'.[15] In the same year, 1984, Neusner accepted the end of the fourth century as the date of the Mekilta and the third century for Avot de R. Nathan.[16] Thus, in publishing on Johanan b. Zakkai, he was perfectly happy to accept as completely accurate material which is two hundred or three hundred years later than the events. No matter what topic one looks at, it will almost always turn out that Neusner has adopted stance X here and stance anti-X there, quite often in the same year and not infrequently in the same publication. A stance that is fleetingly held and then contradicted is not a 'position' which is laid out, thought through, defended and supported by a series of studies; and consequently it is impossible for the non-Judaica scholar to say 'I accept Neusner's overall position': it does not exist. New Testament scholars in particular think that Neusner has proved rabbinic material to be late and not very reliable. This is the impression which he has given in works which he has intended for that particular audience. It is not what many of his most detailed works show, as we shall see in III.D§1 below.

In any case, the present point is that one cannot simply pick up a book by Neusner and find out his 'position' on a topic. I think, however, that the stance taken on the oral law in *Torah* merits closer attention. The matter is actually not as straightforward as he makes it, since his view includes deleting Aboth from the Mishnah. He proposes that it dates entirely from the time of the latest names in it, which puts it fifty years later than the completion of the Mishnah (*Torah*, pp. 6, 32). It is better to follow the practice of assuming that the document grew and that it contains late additions, rather than that it was written as a pseudepigraphical work in the middle of the third century. When Aboth is returned to the Mishnah, the matter changes a bit. 'Torah' in Aboth 1.1 cannot be the written law, since it is never maintained that the Pharisees and Rabbis had a monopoly on that. It is, thus, non-written. But what does it include? The tractate contains maxims but no legal discussions. Is torah used in its broad meaning, 'teaching'? Or, if it refers to law, does it include the peculiarly pharisaic *traditions* or only their *interpretations* of the written law? We cannot be sure. It is quite possible that Aboth shows the breadth of meaning of the word 'torah', which can include not only rules but also haggadah, and does not demonstrate that the Pharisees put eruv on a par with the biblical sabbath laws. Even if the chain of transmission in Aboth is taken to be very early, it does not give a definitive answer to our question.

The saying ascribed to Hillel on two torahs, written and oral (Shabbat 31a; ARNA 15), is even weaker evidence. It seems to Neusner, and to me, that this is a retrojection of the phrase 'oral torah'. Although rabbinic literature cannot be suspected of wholesale retrojection of legal opinions (see the fuller discussion in III.D§1), the story about Hillel and the oral law is not a rule, but a *tale* which sounds very much like a *legend*. Yet, for the sake of argument, let us drop critical doubts and accept the tale. What does it show? Not that '"the tradition of the fathers" was regarded as Torah' alongside the written law,[17] but rather that written laws require interpretation and application. The story is this: a heathen asked Hillel how many laws there were, and he replied, Two – one oral and one written. In response to a request he proceeded to teach the enquirer Hebrew. First he taught the alphabet, *aleph*, *bet*, *gimmel*, *dalet*. The next day he taught the letters in the reverse order, and when the student objected Hillel remarked that he was dependent on his teacher to understand what is written. The oral torah interprets the written. Even if these are the authentic words of Hillel, we still do not have proof that eruv (for example) was considered on a par with the written law, since the story deals only with interpretation.

A third passage containing the word 'torah' may be briefly mentioned. According to Sanhedrin 11.2, the torah went forth to all Israel from 'the Great Court that was in the Chamber of Hewn Stone'. Does this mean that the rulings of this court were equal to the written law? We deal here, of course, with rabbinic imagination. In the real pre-70 temple (the location of the Chamber of Hewn Stone) there was no court composed entirely of pharisaic sages which dictated law to Israel. The real-life court, wherever it met, was headed by the high priest, who is barely mentioned in Mishnah Sanhedrin (2.1). But, leaving historical reality aside, we ask whether or not the Rabbis thought that a pharisaic court should have had the right to pass decrees which were as binding as the written law. They did think that the decrees of the court should have been binding in terms of practice. An elder did not have to agree with them, but he should not render a decision which was contrary to them (so the sequel; see further on 11.3, below, p. 117). This implicitly makes the rules of the court less important than the written law; the Rabbis would not say that a person need not agree with the Bible. 'Torah' in San. 11.2, then, includes concrete non-biblical rules which should be kept but which were not considered equal to the written law.

Consideration of these three passages, which are usually important in discussions of pharisaic oral law, shows that Neusner's challenge must be taken seriously, though when he excluded Aboth he made the case too easy. His second point is more important: the Mishnah distinguishes between the words of the scribes and those of torah in such a way as to 'preclude' the view that the words of the scribes were torah. Neusner's evidence is not, however, complete.[18] He intended to consider passages in which 'torah' and 'words of the scribes' appear together, but some were omitted,[19] and other passages on the words of the scribes are also relevant. Secondly, the meaning of the word halakah must be taken into account. Thirdly, and most important of all, it is necessary to study the passages which trace a rule to Moses. These have always given substance to the view that the Pharisees thought of their own rules as 'the law of Moses'.

We shall now extend the study begun by Neusner. I shall examine all the instances of 'words of the scribes', 'halakah', 'receive a tradition', and 'halakah given to Moses on Sinai' which occur in the Mishnah and Tosefta. My assumption is that, if these phrases in the Mishnah and Tosefta do not indicate 'oral law' as defined above, the Pharisees did not regard their own traditions as equal to the law of Moses. The reasoning is that the Rabbis would not have downgraded the status of traditional rules which the Pharisees had regarded as equal to the written law. In the case of traditions ascribed to Moses, I shall also take account of some of the more interesting passages in the Talmuds.

C. RABBINIC PASSAGES

§1. Words of the scribes. We saw above that, according to Schürer, this phrase indicates binding rules which were equal to those of Moses, but nevertheless of a lower category than halakot. A study of all the appearances of this phrase in the Mishnah yields these results: Twice it refers to rulings which are supplementary to the written law, but not evaluated as either equal or inferior to it (Yebamoth 2.4; Yadaim 3.2). In the other five passages, the words of the scribes are definitely inferior to the law (a-d, k below). Similarly in several passages in the Tosefta the relative weight of the phrase cannot be determined (T. Tevul Yom 1.10; T. Eduyot 1.1; T. Kelim B.B. 7.7). In some instances the 'words of the scribes' are inferior to 'the words of Torah' (e-h), but there are two passages which might be taken as pointing to a higher status for scribal rulings (i and j).

(a) In Orlah 3.9 there is a descending triad of torah, halakah and words of the scribes: (1) New produce may not be eaten even outside Israel until first fruits have been given. This rule is said to be from the torah, apparently with Lev. 23.14 in mind, though the interpretation is a bit strained. (2) Fruit grown outside Israel may not be eaten until the fifth year. The Bible stipulates this treatment for fruit grown 'in the land' (Lev. 19.23–25). The extension of the rule to other lands, which is not only without scriptural support but contrary to its plain meaning, is called halakah, not torah. (3) Two different kinds of seed cannot be sown among the vines of a vineyard even outside Israel. The application of Deut. 22.9 to other lands is *dibrê sôphrîm*, 'the words of the scribes'. The Rabbis, of course, had no power to control harvesting of fruit and sowing of seeds in the Diaspora. The change of terminology, however, seems not to reflect their assessment of their own authority, but rather the status of the rule itself as they saw it. 'Torah' is reserved for a ruling which can be based on a biblical passage. The evidence from Orlah 3.9 is that torah includes interpretation of scripture, not rules passed with no relationship to it or against its plain intent.

(*b*) In Parah 11.4–5 purity laws are distinguished. People who are impure according to the 'words of torah' are guilty if they enter the temple, while those who are impure according to the 'words of the scribes' are not. Failure to observe the words of the scribes is not transgression.

(*c*) and (*d*) According to Tohoroth 4.7,11 those who are doubtful-if-pure according to the purity laws of the scribes (as distinct from those of the Bible) are considered pure.

(*e*) and (*f*) In T. Niddah 9.14 there are two rulings similar to (*c*) and (*d*): Those who are impure only according to the words of the scribes do not render the sanctuary and the holy things in it impure. A person who carries the corpse of a Gentile does not convey corpse-impurity to others, since the view that Gentile corpses render those who touch them impure is only the 'words of the scribes'.[1]

(*g*) The words of the scribes require more 'hedging' or support than do the words of the Bible (T. Taaniyot 2.6; T. Yevamot 2.4).

(*h*) According to T. Eduyot 1.5 the words of the Bible are to be applied strictly, the words of the scribes leniently.

(*i*) In one case, a person who is impure only according to scribal rule is said to convey impurity: he or she renders impure the water and ashes used to remove corpse-impurity, as well as the priest who sprinkles them (T. Parah 11.5). In the pharisaic/rabbinic view, everything which had to do with removing corpse-impurity belonged to the very highest purity category, higher than the sacrificial food eaten in the temple (see Hagigah 2.7). To protect this highest category they were willing to invoke the requirement of purity according to scribal rules as well as according to the Bible.

This simultaneously shows that they did not regard scribal purity rules as governing other things – a point which is also clear in (*c–f*). Thus in one case they thought the scribal rule should be binding, but even so we see that the category is lower than that of the law.

(*j*) If a scribal purity rule merely supplements the written law, it does govern impurity (T. Miqva'ot 5.4). The example given is a case in which the quantity of an impure substance is determined by scribal rule, while its impurity is a biblical law. In III.E we shall see that the Pharisees thought that a dead 'swarming thing', to render impure, had to be as large as a lentil. We shall also see that these sorts of rules – minimum size requirements – are attributed to Moses in the Babylonian Talmud. These are somewhere between 'interpretation' and 'tradition': they are 'riders' or 'glosses' attached to the biblical law in order to specify when it does or does not apply. We shall return to these below (pp. 124, 127).

(*k*) In Sanhedrin 11.3 it is said that the 'words of the scribes' are 'heavier' than 'the words of torah'. This does not mean, however, that scribal innovations are more important than the written law. Sanhedrin 11.3 continues the discussion of 11.2 (above, p. 114), and in context the statement means that if a person reports the ruling of the court incorrectly, he is culpable if it is a scribal ruling, but innocent if it is part of the written law. The rationale presumably is that misrepresentations of the written law could be identified as such. The mishnah gives an example: 'If a man said, "There is no obligation to wear tefillin"', those who hear the report should not believe it, since the requirement is in the Bible,[2] and the person who gave the report is not guilty if one who heard it transgresses. Incorrectly reporting a scribal rule, however, makes the informant culpable if someone acts on his words. In view here are scribal rules just handed down by the imaginary court of Sanhedrin 11.2, not pharisaic traditions in general, and in any case the words of the scribes are not presented here as equal to the law. Rather, the need to report them accurately is greater, since they are otherwise unknown.

(*l*) In Zuckermandel's text of T. Qiddushin 5.21, we find that Abraham kept the torah before it was given, which is proved by citing Gen. 26.5: '"Abraham . . . kept my charge, my commandments, my statutes and my laws [*tôrôt*]". This teaches us that words of torah and words of scribes were revealed to him.' Here 'words of scribes' are included in *tôrôt* and traced back to Abraham. In Lieberman's text, however, the passage concludes, 'this teaches us that the wisdom of the torah and of the details of its interpretation were revealed'. Here evidence in favour of the standard view is eliminated by textual criticism, though we see that a later copyist held the orthodox view.

§2. Halakah. This term (literally, 'walking') is often used to refer to the manner of observing a commandment which is preferred by the editor of the Mishnah (or other rabbinic collection), usually when deciding which of two competing positions is to be accepted; one position is 'the halakah'. Examples may be seen in Menahoth 4.3 and Niddah 1.3. In a similar vein, 'the halakah' may be what is decided by a majority of Rabbis (Eduyoth 1.5). These and several other passages do not bear on the question of the relative importance of rabbinic rulings and the written law, and so they are omitted from discussion. The situation is the same in the Tosefta. Most instances of the word refer to a rabbinic ruling, often that of the majority. A good example of the use of 'halakah' is this:

> R. Jose and R. Simeon say: We prefer the words of R. Eliezer to the words of R. Joshua, and the words of R. Akiba to those of both of them; but the halakah is according to the words of R. Eliezer. (T. Niddah 9.13)

Here, 'the halakah' is not at the level of the written law, since two Rabbis prefer the opinion of R. Akiba.

With regard to the present issue, we may begin by noting that halakah is held to be valid if it has been 'received as tradition' (usually $m^c q\hat{u}bbal$ `$an\hat{i}$). Three passages which combine 'I received as tradition' and halakah are said to go back to Moses and will be given in §4. The other occurrences of halakah and 'received as tradition' are these:

(a) Yebamoth 8.3: 'If this is halakah [which you received] we receive it; but if it is your own argument, there is a reply to it.'

(b) According to Nazir 7.4 R. Akiba argued a case before R. Eliezer unsuccessfully; but when he proposed it to R. Joshua, the latter told him that he had not needed the argument which he presented, since 'thus they said [as a] halakah'. Here the past tense of the verb functions as does $meq\hat{u}bbal$ `$an\hat{i}$ in other passages and indicates that what is designated halakah is a 'tradition' and is therefore to be accepted.

(c) In Gittin 6.7 a halakah is said to have been 'received as tradition' ($m^c q\hat{u}bbal$ `$an\hat{i}$). It is countered by a conflicting statement (not explicitly called a halakah) which 'we have received as a tradition' (`$an\hat{u}$ $m^c q\hat{u}bbal\hat{i}n$).

(d) Kerithoth 3.9 is a very interesting case. The anonymous 'they' say that they have 'not heard [anything]' on a given topic. R. Joshua states that he has 'heard [something]' ($shama$ '$t\hat{i}$). 'Rabbi Akiba said, "If it is halakah, we accept it [as tradition, $neqabb\bar{e}l$], but if it is your own argument there is a reply to it"' (as in (a) above). In this case, however, the rebuttal is requested and given. It is noteworthy that the claim was to 'have heard', not to 'have received a tradition'. The challenge was, in effect, 'Was what you "heard" a halakah which enjoys the status of "tradition"?' The answer was, in effect, 'No', and what had been only 'heard' was then refuted. 'I have heard', $shama$ '$t\hat{i}$, does not ordinarily refer to a binding rule, but rather to anecdotes or theoretical possibilities (e.g. Eduyoth 8.6).

(e) In Oholoth 16.1 there is a discussion of a halakah which one Rabbi thinks had been heard incorrectly.

These passages are interesting enough to merit some preliminary remarks on the way to conclusions. We note, first, that these 'received-as-tradition halakot' were generally unknown. These are not the famous *traditions* which all Pharisees observed, such as eruv. The claim that one had 'received a halakah as a tradition' is intended to be conclusive, but in each of these cases the halakah thus produced is a bit like a rabbit out of a hat. All the stories indicate that *some one Rabbi* knew a tradition, not that these had been collected and were generally taught. Secondly, we learn that even a halakah received as tradition may be doubted. In Gittin 6.7 (*c*) a halakah-rabbit is produced to prove a case and is promptly countered by tradition-rabbit. Or it may be proposed that the halakah was incorrectly transmitted (*e*). These passages must make us doubt that halakot which were 'received as traditions' were equal to the law of Moses.

We return now to the survey of the word halakah.

In two important cases halakah is distinguished from *miqra'*, 'what is written', that is, scripture; but in one striking case it is superior to a form of scriptural exegesis:

(*f*) In Nedarim 4.3 midrash (exegesis), halakot (non-exegetical rules) and haggadot (non-legal discussions) are all distinguished from scripture, as inferior to it.

(*g*) When taking evidence at a trial, if two speakers say something, and one gives a halakah and one a midrash – exegesis of scripture – the judges 'attend' (*nizqaqîn*) to the one with the halakah. If midrash competes with haggadah, they attend to the midrash – and so on (T. Sanhedrin 7.7). Subsequently a midrash is placed below an argument *qal va-ḥômer* (from the less to the greater or *a fortiori*). The explanation of this seems to be that here 'midrash' does not refer to the obvious meaning of scripture, but to an argument which makes ingenious use of a scriptural passage. Qal va-homer arguments also make use of scriptural passages in most instances, but this form of argument is preferred to 'midrash'. This probably means that 'midrash', in the present instance, is a somewhat tortuous or controversial interpretation of scripture, and a plain rabbinic halakah is to be preferred.

(*h*) Hagigah 1.8 distinguishes halakot on some points from those on others, stating that in some cases the halakot are 'as mountains hanging by a hair', since there is little scripture (*miqra'*) but there are many halakot. In other cases, however, the halakot are well supported by scripture, 'and it is they that are the essentials of the Law (torah)'. In the parallels in the Tosefta (T. Eruvin 8.24; T. Hagigah 1.9), midrash is added: in some cases there are many scriptural passages, much midrash and many halakot.

In these passages halakot are part of the essentials of torah *provided that* they are supported by what is written – i.e., provided that they are well-founded 'interpretations', not additional 'traditions'.

There are passages in which halakah is the correct interpretation of torah:

(*i*) Someone who reveals meanings in the torah which are not according to halakah has no share in the world to come (Aboth 3.11 [ET 3.12.]).

(*j*) Similarly Aboth 5.8 claims that the sword 'comes upon the world' because of those who teach things about the torah which are not according to halakah.

In those two passages halakah is not 'tradition' (as it is in most of the other cases), but rather 'interpretation' (as in (*h*)).

Finally we come to a passage which equates a collection of halakot with 'torah'.

(*k*) In Lieberman's text of T. Hagigah 2.9 (largely paralleled in T. Sanhedrin 7.1; the crucial phrase is not in Zuckermandel), it is said that from the court on the temple mount the halakah goes forth.[3] There came to be many disciples of Shammai and Hillel who did not properly serve their masters, and contentions multiplied, so that there came to be two torahs (on the last clause, see Lieberman's apparatus).

The assumption behind the statement that there came to be two torahs is that ordinarily differences over halakot did not constitute different torahs. Further, in terms of social history we know that the Shammaites and Hillelites did not regard one another as schismatics, following the wrong torah or a different torah. They stayed in contention and argued about their views. Thus the passage is hyperbolic, and it actually reinforces the view that the question of actual practice, halakah, on given issues was not on the same level as the biblical law itself. The Houses, for example, disagreed about some of the rules concerning menstruation and sex, but they did not disagree with the basic biblical principle, that sexual relations with a menstruant were forbidden.

We noted above that, after 70, the Hillelites prevailed,[4] and to this fact we owe such statements as that 'the halakah is always according to the words of the House of Hillel' (T. Yevamot 1.13). The Rabbis then had to reckon, however, with the fact that many people followed the House of Shammai. The same passage adds that what one must not do is to take the lenient rulings of the House of Hillel and the lenient rulings of the House of Shammai; if one wishes to follow the Shammaites, one should be consistent. Thus 'the halakah' may always have been in accord with the Hillelites, but social reality was different. Many Shammaite halakot prevailed. Similarly, there were not really two torahs. This passage emphasizes, rather, that within Pharisaism there were significant differences of practice. We still have not found 'oral law' equal to the written law.

§3. Receive as tradition (without halakah). If halakah without the verb 'receive' may be refuted by argument (see §2a), what is the case with regard to something which is 'received' but not termed a halakah?

(*a*) In reply to the question, Why record views of individuals which are rejected by the majority? this answer is given: So that if one said, 'I have

received a tradition' (*'anî m^eqûbbal*), another may reply, 'You only *heard
(shama'ta)* the saying of an individual' (Eduyoth 1.6). As in 2.d above, we see
the distinction between 'receive as tradition' and 'hear'.

(*b*) According to Zebahim 1.3//Yadaim 4.2, R. Simeon b. Azzai received a
tradition from seventy-two elders on the day when R. Eleazar b. Azariah was
made head of the academy. The tradition seems to be accepted, and when the
tradent proposes an amendment it is rejected.

(*c*)The same formula (tradition from seventy-two elders etc.) appears in
Yadaim 3.5, with slightly different results. The tradition is that the Song of
Songs and Ecclesiastes 'render the hands impure' – that is, they count as
scripture.[5] R. Akiba protests that the tradition cannot be correct – the
tradition, not the conclusion – since no one could ever have doubted the Song
of Songs. The final word, however, is given by R. Johanan b. Joshua, who
upholds the reported tradition.

(*d*) In Yebamoth 16.7 there is a legendary story which is of considerable
interest to our question. R. Akiba reports that he went to Nehardea (in
Babylonia), where he met a man who said that he had heard that, in Israel,
only R. Judah b. Baba allowed a woman to remarry on the evidence of one
witness to the death of her previous husband. Akiba confirmed this. The
Babylonian then said that he had received a tradition (*m^eqûbbelanî*) from
Gamaliel the Elder (no less!) that one witness sufficed. Akiba returned and
told this to Rabban Gamaliel II (grandson of the Elder), who then
remembered that his grandfather had once made this ruling. This did not,
however, settle the case, and there was further discussion.

(*e*) T. Sanhedrin 6.2 contains a 'tradition' about seating or not seating
contestants in a legal case (they must both either sit or stand). The tradition
seems to be accepted.

(*f*) In the very interesting passage T. Pisha 4.12–13 (Zuckermandel 4.2),
Hillel is depicted as arguing that Passover 'overrides' the sabbath, and that
therefore the Passover lambs should be slaughtered when the day of
slaughtering coincides with a sabbath. The scene is the temple, and Hillel
argues against the populace, who have come without their knives. He first of
all argues that since the daily whole-burnt offering overrides the sabbath, so
should the Passover offering. The two offerings are alike in two respects, and
so should be treated the same; while in one respect the daily offering is less
important than the Passover offering, and thus the latter should override the
sabbath all the more than the former. Finally, he adds that he had received a
tradition (*m^eqûbbelanî*) from his teachers that Passover overrides the sabbath.
At this the populace bring out their knives from hiding, prepare to sacrifice
the animals, and elect Hillel *nasî*, 'president' or 'patriarch'. In this story
'tradition' persuades the populace when exegetical arguments failed. The

story, of course, is legendary. It is not really true that Hillel was elected the official teacher of Passover laws by the populace. In any case the story claims that a 'tradition' outweighs an argument qal va-homer and settles a question of how to relate one biblical law (not to work on the sabbath) to another (to slaughter lambs at Passover).

We see in these cases further evidence of respect for tradition. The last passage makes the strongest claim: tradition decides how to interpret the biblical law. Needless to say, here tradition is 'interpretation', not an independent practice. The story about Akiba and the Babylonian (*d*) shows that a tradition might be forgotten by almost everyone. As in the case of several halakot (§2.a–e above), this tradition is not a major pharisaic/rabbinic practice, nor one taught to all Pharisees/Rabbis. We also see that it was subject to debate.

§4. A halakah is a tradition 'given to Moses by God on Mount Sinai'.[6] Three times in the Mishnah (one of which is paralleled in the Tosefta) a rule is said to go back to Moses on Mount Sinai. In all three cases (Peah 2.6; Eduyot 8.7; Yadaim 4:3//T. Yadaim 2.16) there is the same three-fold formula – receive a tradition, halakah, Moses on Mount Sinai. It is to be noted that what goes back to Moses is halakah, not torah. It is these halakot which, above all others, are held to prove the theory of pharisaic oral law.

(*a*) The first instance is this: 'Nahum the Scrivener said: "I have received a tradition (*meqûbbel 'anî*) from R. Measha, who received it from his father, who received it from the Pairs,[7] who received it from the Prophets as a halakah given to Moses from Sinai . . .' (Peah 2.6). This tradition, which concerns how many corners of the field to leave for gleaners, is said not to have been known to Rabban Gamaliel, who had to enquire of a rabbinical court to discover it, and even then we are told that it was known by only one sage.

(*b*) In Yadaim 4.3 (//T. Yadaim 2.15–16), the 'Mosaic' tradition is known only to R. Eliezer, and it comes as a postscript after the story of a lengthy debate conducted in ignorance of it.

(*c*) Eduyoth 8.7 is not a rule at all, but a prediction about what Elijah will do when he returns.

§5. Other traditions attributed to Moses (without the full formula):

(*a*) In T. Peah 3.2 a debate between the Houses of Hillel and Shammai is reported to R. Eleazar b. Azariah, who remarked that 'these things were said to Moses at Sinai'.

(*b*) In T. Sukkah 3.1 the question is raised whether or not the preparation of the *lûlab* and the willow-branch, which are used in the Feast of Booths (Sukkot), overrides the sabbath. We are told that once the Boethusians tried to prevent the cutting of the willow branch for the festival when the appropriate day coincided with the sabbath, by piling boulders against the stand of willows. The ordinary people ('amme ha–'arets) moved the rocks and cut the branches. The justification is that the halakah concerning the willow-branches goes back to Moses on Sinai – though Abba Saul proceeds to establish the point by exegesis.

The passsages in §4 and §5, which should prove the case that the Pharisees or Rabbis considered their distinctive traditions 'law' and traced them back to Moses, thus making them of equal age and standing with the written Mosaic law, fail to do so. §5.b is the only passage which may be read in this light, though it is significant that Abba Saul was not satisfied with this view and wished to base the rule on scripture.

The passages cited in §4.a,b and 5.a, like many of the other rules which were 'received as tradition' (§2.a,b,c.; §3.d), were known to only one individual. We are not here dealing with the great 'traditions' which distinguished the Pharisees as a party and on which they agreed. The pharisaic/rabbinic traditions which are discussed as 'received traditions' or 'traditional halakot' could be lost, or known only to a man in Babylonia, and in any case sometimes they were not considered authoritative. The few minor traditions or halakot which are traced back to Moses serve to refute the idea that the Pharisees ascribed their major distinguishing practices to him. There are two aspects to this. On the one hand, the Rabbis carried on their debates about things which only later someone said had been handed down from Moses, thus showing that rules in this category were not generally taught and were not on a par with the law. On the other hand, the major traditions which we know distinguished them, such as eruv, are not ascribed to Moses.

It is often said that the halakot which are attributed to Moses are those which cannot be derived from the written law: the designation gives 'the authentication of immemorial prescription and divine origin to traditional laws for which no biblical support could be adduced'.[8] These halakot certainly cannot be derived from the Bible, but describing them in this way is fundamentally misleading. It sounds as if the Pharisees or Rabbis generally attributed to Moses their non-biblical practices, or at least the rules which are especially remote from scripture. But this, we have seen, is not true. Eruv and handwashing were defended neither by interpretation nor by the theory of oral commandments from Moses. Items in the second category are noteworthy because they are so minor and were known to only one Rabbi. These are neither the major nor the difficult cases of extra-biblical rules.

Another way of stating the matter is this: the theory of halakot given to Moses is not put forward as 'legitimation' of the Pharisees' peculiar rules, as most scholars seem to think. The only rationale for pharisaic additions to the law which justifies them before critics is their general ascription to previous generations ('traditions of the fathers')[9] Far from being the pharisaic defence of their major non-biblical practices, attribution to Moses is rabbinic one-up-manship, a game played only among Rabbis, not used by Pharisees against Sadducees. We might paraphrase rabbinic claims to Mosaic traditions thus: 'You guys had to argue about it. You could have asked me. I already knew the answer: it's as old as Moses.'

A wider collection of halakot ascribed to Moses would not noticeably affect these conclusions.[10] Some slightly conflicting views about tefillin and mezuzot are attributed to Moses in the Talmuds: according to p. Megillah 75c (4.9), the rule that tefillin had four corners and were black goes back to Moses; according to R. Isaac in Menahot 35a Moses decreed that their straps must be black. Others, however, argued that they could be green, black or white, and stories were told of Rabbis who used blue or purple. For debates about such matters, see also Shabbat 108a; 79b//Menahot 32a. These and other matters – minor and disputed – are attributed to Moses.

One should also mention the theory that some halakot given to Moses were forgotten and had to be rediscovered. In Yoma 80a, this is said to be the case for 'minima required for penalties'. In view here are the minimal quantities which the Rabbis required before decreeing impurity. What is striking is that the statement that these were decreed by Moses follows long exegetical arguments trying to establish the minimum quantity of food which could be regarded as impure. As elsewhere, the Rabbis seem mostly to have been ignorant of halakot given to Moses. I do not doubt that Pharisees had some rules about minimum quantities (e.g. a piece of a carcass or a 'swarming thing' must be at least the size of a lentil to defile). We noted T. Miqva'ot 5.4 in §1.j above, where scribal rules which determine the size required for impurity are accepted as binding. We must note, however, that what are 'words of the scribes' in the Tosefta are 'halakot given to Moses' in the Talmud, and that the Talmud also offers exegetical arguments to support these halakot. Thus we do not have proof that pre-70 Pharisees regarded minimal sizes as equal to the law of Moses, though I believe that they accepted rules on minima in practice. Such 'riders' attached to the law, I proposed above, are somewhere between interpretations of the law (which are equal to the law itself) and independent traditions.

Menahoth 89a ascribes to Moses the rule that after the conclusion of a menstrual period, there were eleven days when blood was not held to be menstrual blood. Here again, I am convinced that this was a pharisaic rule (see below, p. 210), but equally I find no grounds for saying that it was on a par with the basic law which forbids intercourse with a menstruant. It seems to have been, rather, a rule of thumb, and later in the rabbinic movement it was rejected in favour of a more stringent practice (Niddah 66a).

In the nature of the case, passages in the Talmuds (fourth–sixth centuries) cannot prove that Pharisees held their traditions to be equal to the law of Moses. The talmudic passages on Mosaic halakot do show some awareness of old customs and practices, and in some cases these can be shown to be pharisaic. We do not, however, learn from the Talmuds what the Pharisees thought of such rules.

In fairness to the Amoraim (the post-mishnaic Rabbis), we should note that they did not take their ascriptions of minor rules to Moses to be overly serious. They argued about them quite freely. One suspects that some of the talmudic passages were written tongue-in-cheek. There is the famous story of Moses listening to R. Akiba but not being able to follow the discussion. When Akiba was asked how he knew a certain opinion, he replied that it had been given to Moses. Moses went away comforted, glad to know that the law was in such good hands (Menahot 29b). The Rabbis knew perfectly well that Akiba was simply clever and that there was no tradition going back to Moses.

D. CONCLUSIONS AND SUMMARY

This view of pharisaic tradition places the party in the mainstream of thought in the Hellenistic period, which venerated tradition but did not consider it the equivalent of law. In a passage which may be indebted to Aristotle,[1] Philo distinguishes between 'customs' (*ethē*), which are 'unwritten laws', and the written laws. The one who obeys only the latter 'acts under the admonition of restraint and the fear of punishment', while the one who obeys the unwritten laws displays voluntary virtue (*Spec. Laws* 4.149f.; cf. *Embassy* 115). The Pharisees intentionally went beyond the letter of the law, and they seem to have considered themselves to be doing so voluntarily, rather than because they 'knew' more laws than did others and thought that obedience to these further laws was strictly required.

Expanding the investigation to include all occurrences of 'words of the scribes', the use of the word halakah, the term 'receive as a tradition', and the expression 'Moses on Mount Sinai', we have come to a view proposed by Neusner on the basis of a partially different body of evidence: in the legal tractates of the Mishnah and the Tosefta rabbinic rulings are held to be on a lower level of authority than the words of the Bible itself, and this includes rabbinic traditions which are said to go back to Moses.

Our perspective on the status of the pharisaic traditions will be improved if we consider the Essene position on the equivalent point. The *Covenant of Damascus* speaks for a group of Essenes who were not fully sectarian (since they brought sacrifices, see CD 6.20; 9.13–14; 11.17–18; cf. 12.1–2) but who had a large number of special laws; above we noted many of their sabbath rules (p. 8). Although most of the sabbath regulations are not justified exegetically, one is: 'Let no one offer on the altar on the Sabbath [any offering] except the burnt-offering of the Sabbath; for thus it is written: "apart from your Sabbath-offerings"' (CD 11.17–18, tr. Rabin). The last phrase is from Lev. 23.38, but the context is ignored to a degree rare even in ancient exegesis. The passage in Leviticus deals with festivals, which were special days 'apart from' the sabbaths, in the sense of 'in addition to' them. The simple meaning would be that if a festival fell on the sabbath, both the festival offerings and the ordinary sabbath offerings would be presented. CD takes just the two Hebrew words translated 'apart from sabbath offerings' (literally, 'apart from sabbaths'), prefaces them with a negative, 'let no one offer any . . . but . . .', and thus reverses the obvious meaning. In case of overlap, only the sabbath sacrifices are offered.

CD's other sabbath rules, however, are not justified exegetically. Their rationale is apparently given in CD 6.18–19; those who enter the covenant are 'to keep the Sabbath day according to its exact rules and the appointed days and the fast-day according to the finding of the members of the *new* covenant in the land of Damascus'. 'New covenant' here may be syntactically related only to the appointed (festival) days and the fast (the Day of Atonement), but in principle the sect was willing to say that its covenant was at least partially 'new' and therefore different. This new covenant contained 'hidden things' not previously known (CD 3.14).

Similarly the *Community Rule*, which represents the monastic community at Qumran, requires a new member to take an oath to 'return' to the 'law of Moses' according to 'all that was revealed of it to the sons of Zadok' (1QS 5.8–9). In this information the 'law of Moses' includes the traditional Scriptures plus new revelations to the Zadokite priests, and the door is left open for there to be more: 'all that was revealed of it' (*mimmennah*) implies that more yet may be revealed.

The Temple Scroll (11Q Temple) takes this position to its logical conclusion: it attributes an Essene revision of substantial parts of the Hebrew Bible directly to God by use of the first person.

Thus both of the known branches of the Essenes (represented by CD and 1QS respectively) had it both ways: they accepted 'the law of Moses' as their guide; they introduced new laws and claimed that they were new revelations *from the same source* and *of the same authority*. Their handling of and claims for the new sectarian rules contrast sharply with the Pharisees' position on their peculiar traditions.

This leads us to a brief reconsideration of the Sadducean position. We know that on some points they agreed with the Essenes against the Pharisees,[2] but the Essenes broke with them as well. The Pharisees had extra-biblical traditions which they *admitted did not go back to Moses*. The Essenes had *new revelations* which in their view were equivalent to the commonly accepted scripture. The Sadducees *justified all their practices by exegesis*. The discussion of 'apart from your sabbath [offerings]', in CD 11.17f. may give us a good idea of how the Sadducees went about it. Like all good fundamentalists, they could lift any combination of words from any part of the text and prove anything at all.

Josephus wrote of the Pharisees not only that they had traditions which the Sadducees rejected, but also that they were the 'most precise' or 'acute' (*akribēs*) interpreters or exegetes of the law (*War* 1.110; 2.162; *Life* 191; cf. *Antiq.* 18.15, 'exegesis'). We also noted above that the Rabbis sometimes ranked 'midrash', probably fanciful exegesis, quite low (C§2.g). This shows that they knew that some interpretations were flimsy and debatable. Unlike the Sadducees, the Pharisees did not have to base everything on the law, and so they could interpret it in a relatively straightforward manner and avoid the most fanciful midrash and excessively forced exegesis. Unlike the Essenes, they did not appeal to secret parts of the divine revelation. They probably deserved the title, 'the most accurate interpreters of the law'.

I should repeat here that the Pharisees too considered their *interpretations* of the law to be the law itself. In rabbinic terms, the law should be interpreted according to the halakah (C§2.h,i,j). Doubtless in some such cases the Pharisees engaged in exegesis of which we would now disapprove. It is a question of degree and of *their* perceptions of what was interpretation and what was additional tradition.

We now return to the case in which 'words of the scribes' supplement the law and are regarded as binding (C§1.j). This and some of the talmudic halakot attributed to Moses concern minimal quantities necessary for the law to apply. These riders relax the law. Saying that a dead insect, to render foodstuff impure, must be the size of a lentil results in applying the purity laws less stringently than would be the case if the minimum was not set. People who did not use the Pharisees' minima would not, in their view, transgress the biblical law. Thus even if the Pharisees regarded such riders or glosses as part of the law, they would not conclude that people who rejected their minima transgressed it.

The question of transgression is important in studying the Pharisees' views of their own interpretations and traditions. Since the Sadducees often controlled the temple, and since the Pharisees continued to worship there, we know in general terms that the latter did not consider the former to be sinners in such a way as to render the sacrifices invalid. They brought their offerings to the temple, side by side with people who did not observe their rules, and gave them to the priests, most of whom were not Pharisees. This degree of tolerance is confirmed by rabbinic literature, which does not specify atonement for transgression of rabbinic rules. This point is the one which explains how I came to study the issue and to do the preceding word studies. I had long been struck by the curious fact – noticed by many – that the Mishnah often does not give 'the halakah', the result of a debate, but ends a topic with competing views still on the floor. This is especially true of the Houses disputes (House of Hillel versus House of Shammai). These disputes, which are very important for understanding Pharisaism, are often unresolved. When they are resolved it does not seem to matter: the party which loses is not thereby branded a group of sinners and outcasts. In discussing purity, we saw several substantial disputes – Pharisees *versus* Sadducees and Hillelites *versus* Shammaites – which did not lead to a full rupture (I.D. pp.35–37).

Pressing on from this point, I observed that the same is true when the two sides are not the two Houses, but rather the Pharisees, Rabbis or haverim against the ordinary people. The learned and pious seem not to have considered that those who did not follow their own rules were 'sinners' – provided that they observed the major biblical laws (see especially III.F). These considerations fit Neusner's study of torah and 'words of the scribes' like a glove the hand, and they led me to flesh out his study. It confirms that the early Rabbis did not equate their own rules with the Law which had been decreed by God.

If this view is correct and can be applied to the pre-70 Pharisees, as appears to be the case, it means that they were self-conscious when they introduced innovations. They did not think of their own customs, though hallowed by usage, as law, but rather kept them separate. Despite their willingness to introduce new traditions consciously, they were also deeply conservative and intended not to change the biblical law. They interpreted it and they also followed rules in addition to it. Their interpretations – when they agreed on them – they regarded as correct, and doubtless they tried to have them enforced in society as a whole. Their traditions were their own: they made them Pharisees.

When under Salome Alexandra the Pharisees were 'in power', they may well have required observance not only of their biblical interpretations, but also of their separate traditions (*Antiq.* 13.408: *nomima* and *paradosis*). During the Herodian and Roman periods, however, they clearly had to decide whether, when obeying (for example) one of Herod's high priests, or seeing the sacrifices performed in accordance with Sadducean interpretation, they were involved in *transgression*. It is evident that they concluded that they were not. Probably the conscious distinction between interpretation of the written law and their own rules and regulations was of some help.

Summary

The results of the terminological study may be briefly outlined.

1. The words of the scribes are lower in importance than the words of the Bible (torah), and transgression of scribal rulings is not considered to be real transgression (C§1.b,c,d,e,f).

2. Other passages indicate in different ways that 'words of the scribes' are lower in rank than the words of the written law (1.g,h).

3. A scribal ruling which supplements the written law, however, is considered binding (1.j).

4. Scribal purity rules should be invoked in order to protect what is of the highest purity (1.i).

5. The term halakah is often equivalent to 'words of the scribes'. In Orlah 3.9 (1.a) halakah seems to be one grade closer to torah than are the words of the scribes, but in other instances the meaning is the same: traditional rulings which do not need to be proved by argument in order to be accepted within the group (2.b). They are, however, lower in status than the torah (esp. 2.f,h).

6. In several passages halakah is used together with the phrase 'received [as a tradition]'. In these cases the traditional halakah is regarded as correct (2.a; by implication 2.d; 2.e (If heard correctly)), but it is not equated with torah.

7. Halakah is torah only when it is interpretation of *miqra`* or of torah (2.h,i,j).

8. Rulings which are 'received as tradition' are often authoritative (3.b,e).

9. Tradition (by whatever name) may be rejected. Grounds for possible rejection are citation of an authority who was outvoted at the time (3.a), or simple doubt that the report is true (2.e; 3.c), or a conflicting tradition (2.c). Possibly the Rabbis will go ahead and debate the issue anyway (3.d).

10. Tradition sometimes supplements exegesis (3.f), or exegesis may be appended (5.b).

11. A special sub-group of traditional halakot consists of rulings which go back to Moses on Mount Sinai. These last are never said to be 'oral law': they are rather halakot, and presumably like other halakot which are not *interpretations* of the written law, they are inferior to the torah.

12. None of the major pharisaic traditions (e.g. eruv) is proved by any of the terms studied here.

13. In every case of a rule which was 'received as tradition', it was not known to most of the Rabbis (e.g. 5.a), and therefore it was not part of regular

rabbinic instruction. This counts very strongly against the view that these terms indicate 'Mosaic law'.

14. The rabbinic/pharisaic traditions do not have the status of the new laws of the Essenes, which are attributed to revelation.

III

Did the Pharisees Eat Ordinary Food
in Purity?

A. INTRODUCTION

Scholars are almost unanimously of the opinion that the Pharisees ate ordinary food at their own tables as if they were priests in the temple. One may name in favour Louis Finkelstein, Joachim Jeremias, Gedalyahu Alon, Emil Schürer/Geza Vermes and Jacob Neusner. Ellis Rivkin disputed the view, on the grounds that the Pharisees were not *haberîm* ('associates', anglicized as haverim), though he has not objected to depicting the haverim as lay people who treated their food as if they were priests. In previous work I have taken basically the same line as Rivkin, though noting that rabbinic literature does not depict the haverim as accepting all the priestly laws of purity and that not all the post-70 Rabbis were haverim.[1]

The principal intention here is to review the arguments of Jacob Neusner. The evidence on the basis of which Finkelstein, Jeremias and Alon came to this view of the Pharisees is quite different from the evidence used by Neusner. My conclusion, to anticipate, is that Neusner's standards for collecting evidence mark a distinct advance, but that he misinterpreted his own material. Use of his analytical work leads to other conclusions about the Pharisees than the ones which he drew.

The topic posed by the title of this essay is the crucial one of the group's definition: did they pretend to live like priests? Is that what Pharisaism was basically all about? In Neusner's work, this topic and the more general one, 'Pharisaic rules and debates about purity', merge, since he claimed that their purity rules focused almost exclusively on their own food. Once it is shown that this claim is not true, we shall see a broader range of purity issues than 'ordinary food in purity'. The first aim of the essay is to answer the question of definition, but this will lead to a discussion of virtually all the pharisaic purity debates, whether dealing with ordinary food or not.

It will take a bit of time to get to Neusner and the rabbinic evidence for Pharisaism. To understand the Pharisees' practice, we must know what is and what is not in the Bible: it is helpful to know that they followed the Bible when they did so, but crucial to know when they ignored it, got around it by clever exegesis, moderated it or went beyond it. On the present topic, they are said to have *extended* priestly laws to the laity. It follows that we must know what they were. Which laws in the Bible apply only to the priests and the temple? Which were to govern all Israel? Which, of those important later, are not in the Bible at all? Can they be construed as adaptations of priestly practice?

Answers to these questions are harder to obtain than one would expect. We cannot, for example, simply open the *Interpreter's Dictionary of the Bible* to 'Clean and unclean' or the *Encyclopaedia Judaica* to 'Purity and Impurity, Ritual' and find out what we want to know. Neither article even mentions the distinction of the priesthood from the laity in terms of purity. Priestly purity is covered under 'Priests and Priesthood' in *Enc. Jud.*, but not under 'Priests and Levites' in *IDB*; and the *Enc. Jud.* does not deal with food laws in its section 'Holiness of the Priesthood'. The *IDB* article on 'Clean and unclean' does not mention the very important laws of Lev. 11.32–38, and the *Enc. Jud.* article on 'Purity' mentions only one of their aspects (vol. 13, col. 1406). There is a partial survey of biblical purity laws in ch. 1 of Neusner's *The Idea of Purity in Ancient Judaism* (1973), but it deals with only a few of the necessary topics.

It will turn out that Alon's argument founders in part because he took Lev. 11.32–38 to be a priestly law. Neusner made the same mistake, and elaborated on it. Similarly Alon discussed the topic of handling (as distinct from eating) secular food in purity as an innovation[2] (which it would have been, had it been practised), but he did not note that handling the *priests'* food in purity was itself a major innovation. This quick and partial review shows that we must attend to the biblical laws first. I do not wish to propose that the information could not be dredged out of secondary literature if one cast one's net widely enough, but since it is not readily available I have decided to present the biblical material in enough detail to allow the discussion of pharisaic debates to be related to it.

Our procedure will be to take up biblical purity laws (B); to review briefly scholarly arguments prior to Neusner, especially Alon's, but paying some attention also to Rivkin (C); then to analyse Neusner's evidence and argument (D). This will lead us to a new summary of pharisaic purity laws (E). (F) and (G) will draw consequences and offer a summary.

Three preliminary explanations need to be given.

1. In discussing biblical law, I shall try to read it as it was read in the first century: all of a piece, almost all to be observed – 'almost', since some laws were reinterpreted and some became 'dead letters', as we shall see. For the most part first-century Jews took the entire Bible to be applicable to their own existence,

and the Pharisees are noteworthy in this respect. I shall not discuss the reasons for which biblical books disagree with one another, and especially not the chronological stratification of the Pentateuch, since first-century Jews were unaware of it. One clearly sees divergent views, some intentionally reversing others (thus tithes in Deuteronomy versus tithes in Numbers, Leviticus and Nehemiah – or the other way around). First-century practice either ignored one of the competing laws or conflated them.

2. I shall use 'purity' and cognates rather than 'cleanness' and cognates for *t-h-r*, and 'impurity' for *t-m-'* – except where quoting the Mishnah or the Hebrew Bible ('Old Testament'), when the translations of Danby and the RSV will be followed, unless noted otherwise. The application of purity language to moral behaviour[3] does not here come into question, and the discussion is about 'ritual' purity – a term which I shall comment on below.

3. Throughout this essay I shall speak about 'the Pharisees', in accord with the Neusner of *Rabbinic Traditions about the Pharisees Before 70* (1971). He has become increasingly reluctant to use that designation for the people pointed to in these traditions. Thus in *A History of the Mishnaic Law of Purities* XXII (1977), he wrote that 'referring to the earliest stages of Mishnah as pharisaic is for convenience' sake only', and that 'only with grave reservations have we alluded to the Pharisees as the point of origination or even as the sect which principally stands behind the system transmitted through successive generations to the authorities of 70 and afterward' (p. 108). In *Judaism: The Evidence of the Mishnah* (1981), he was more reluctant yet: the earliest group in the Mishnah was centred on its own food and purity, but 'much which is written about the Pharisees [by ancient authors] does not appear to describe a holiness sect or an eating club at all.' '. . . we are not even sure we can call the group by any name more specific and definitive than *group*, for instance a *sect*' (pp. 70–71). Despite this, he called the group a sect over and over in the same work.

The point of his hesitation about the name of the group behind the earliest layer of rabbinic material is that his description of that group does not coincide with the description of the Pharisees in other ancient sources. The problem, however, is not the title of the group behind early rabbinic passages, but his description of it. My own view is that there is no conflict between the earliest stratum of the Mishnah (as Neusner defines it) and the descriptions of the Pharisees in Josephus. It is certainly true that Josephus does not discuss them as a pure food club; but that is not what is implied by the earliest rabbinic evidence, as this essay intends to show.

B. BIBLICAL PURITY LAWS

§1. Biblical law requires that some food be *eaten* in purity. The priests and their families were required to eat some or most of their food in purity. This food can be divided into two categories: (1) individual offerings of sacrificial animals (which were sometimes accompanied by cakes, e.g. Lev. 7.12f.), of birds, or of flour alone; (2) community dues. It is not necessary here to explain in detail the sacrificial system and the food which it produced. As a rule, individual offerings were eaten by the priests inside the temple itself. In the case of sin and guilt offerings, an animal was brought, and the blood, fat and some of the viscera went to the altar. The priest got the hide and the rest of the meat. If two birds were substituted, the priest got one of them (the other being burnt). If flour was substituted, the priest ate most of it (see Lev. 5.1–13; 7.1–10). All of this food was eaten 'in a holy place' (7.6; cf. 6.16 [Heb. 6.9]; 6.26 [Heb. 6.19]), that is, in the temple and in a state of purity. This would mean that the priest must not recently have had contact with menstrual blood or with a corpse, and must not have had an ejaculation after sunset the previous evening.[1] What 'purity' means will be explained more fully below.

The priests also received a portion of peace offerings – 'the breast that is waved' (the 'wave offering') and the right thigh (Lev. 7.28–34). This meat was taken outside the temple and shared by the priest's family. They had to eat in a pure place (Lev. 10.14) and in a state of purity (Num. 18.11): the women could not be menstruants, no one could have had recent contact with semen or with the dead; the house could not be 'leprous', nor could it recently have contained a corpse.

Of the community dues, first fruits were to be eaten in a pure place and in a state of purity, just like the priest's share of the peace offering (Num. 18.12–13).

The second main component of the temple dues was the tithe. What would later be called 'first tithe', ten per cent of produce, was given to the Levites, who in turn tithed to the priests. The Levites could eat their share 'in any place' (Num. 18.31), which means that they were not required to eat it in purity. The priests, however, probably were expected to eat their tithe of the tithe in purity, since it is called 'hallowed' and is compared to first fruits (Num. 18.26–29). Leviticus 22.1–16 requires that priests must be pure when eating 'holy things', which in this passage means any of the priests' special food, not just what was eaten in the temple. This passage, however, does not say that members of the priests' families had to be pure when they ate 'holy things'.

I shall leave aside here 'heave offering', which is not a clearly distinct offering in Leviticus and Numbers. Later, we shall see, it became such. The Pharisees thought that it should be *handled* in purity (see E§2 below), and it is probable that it was generally expected that priests and their families should eat it in purity.[2]

Thus far we have seen food which the priests could eat in a state of purity within the temple and food which they and their families could eat in purity outside the temple. Priests could not always be pure, and the women of priests' families would have been impure at least one-fourth of the time (see below, on semen-impurity and menstrual impurity). We do not know what the women did if they were impure when the priest brought home his share of a peace offering, nor what the couple did about intercourse in relation to eating the peace offerings and first fruits. Did they have sex, wash, wait until sunset and only then eat – which is what biblical law strictly requires? The principle is clear, though some of the details of practice are not. Priests were underemployed, and it is possible that they managed to have sexual relations shortly before sunset, which would solve the problem; they could wash, the sun would set, and then they would be pure. It is also possible that they winked at the rules. They may have had access to ordinary food, at least for their wives. Whatever the realities of their domestic lives, as far as we can tell from the Bible the general rule was that they ate holy food, and they ate it in a pure place and when pure. Passages in Josephus indicate that first-century priests took the rules seriously,[3] and this is confirmed by the number of immersion pools in the Upper City (E§8 below).

Ordinary people sometimes ate holy food – always outside the temple. (Unlike pagan shrines, in the Jerusalem temple there was no drinking, eating and dalliance on the part of the laity, and only eating, no drinking or dalliance, on the part of the priests.) The peace offering (or communion sacrifice[4]) was shared among the altar (the blood, the fat and some of the viscera), the priest and his family (the breast and the right thigh) and the one who brought the sacrifice. He, his family and friends got the rest of the meat. They had to eat it in purity, just as did the priests and their families (Lev. 7.19–21). Similarly the Deuteronomic tithe (later 'second tithe'), which was eaten by those who produced it, the laity, was to be eaten in a state of purity.[5] Passover was to be eaten in purity, or more precisely without corpse-impurity (Num. 9.9–11).

§2. With two exceptions, the legal books do not require that any of the holy food which has just been listed be *handled* in purity on its way to consumption. First fruits (of produce)[6] are discussed several times, but nothing is said about harvesting and carrying the food in purity (Lev. 23.9–14; Num. 18.12–13; Deut. 16.10; 18.4; 26.2–11; cf. the offering of the first of the meal in Num. 15.20). The firstlings of animals are discussed in Num.

18.17–18, but there is no requirement for the person who brings them to do so in a state of purity. We noted that the Levites' share of first tithe can be eaten 'in any place' (Num. 18.31), which doubtless meant that it did not have to be handled in purity.

The exceptional cases, in which holy food should be handled in purity, are these: (1) The Deuteronomic tithe ('second tithe') is to be 'removed' from the rest of the produce in a state of purity (Deut. 26.14). This would seem not to require that it be harvested in purity. (2) A woman with childbirth-impurity cannot touch 'anything holy' (Lev. 12.4).

In some ways the biblical laws regarding food and purity almost cry out for extension and clarification, simply for the sake of symmetry and complete-ness. Precisely which of the holy things was a woman forbidden to touch after childbirth? Should not freedom from all forms of impurity be required for Passover, as it is for second tithe and the peace offering? If priests are to eat food when pure, should not the food be pure when it reaches them? Therefore should not first fruits be harvested and handled in purity, and should not tithe be treated in the same way (since the priests receive a tithe of the Levites' tithe)? In particular, should not corpse-impurity, which priests were to avoid when possible, be prevented from ever coming into contact with food destined for the temple and the priests' families? If a woman after childbirth cannot touch holy things, does it not follow that she should also avoid handling them during menstruation?

Before the days of the Pharisees some people had already said 'yes' to at least some of these questions (cf. I.D above). According to Isa. 66.20 'Israelites bring their cereal offering in a clean vessel to the house of the Lord'. This might mean that many things were expected to be conveyed to the temple in a state of purity, probably especially the food eaten by the priests inside the sacred precincts (as was the cereal offering, Lev. 6.16 [Heb. 6.9]). According to Judith 11.13 (c. 150–125 BCE; see I.D, n. 4), 'it is not lawful' for ordinary people to touch the first fruits. People were generally impure (as will become clear below), and here the assumption is that all forms of impurity should be kept away from food for the priests and their families *after* it had been separated.[7] We shall see that the Pharisees took up the problem of keeping the priests' food pure while it was *en route* to them, and even when it was harvested, though it is striking that they pressed no further the law limiting what a woman with childbirth-impurity could touch. On the contrary, the Rabbis distinguished among holy foods and allowed her to touch all but the most holy (Niddah 10.6–7).

Thus, according to the Bible, ordinary people were required to be pure when consuming sanctified food (at most a few occasions each year). At some time or other in the biblical period (depending on the date of Isa. 66.20), it was concluded that the food eaten within the temple should be carried there in pure vessels. Early in the Hasmonean period some inferred that they should be pure when handling first fruits, after harvesting and setting them aside.

§3. We now ask the meaning of *purity* in biblical law. This much-abused word deserves to be used with some respect. Scholars, especially New Testament scholars, often use 'ritual purity' pejoratively to describe the requirements of any group to which they are hostile. When the Pharisee in Luke 18.11 thanks God that he is not like those who are 'extortioners, unjust, or adulterers', the commentator in the *New Oxford Annotated Bible*, by scholarly reflex, says that the Pharisee thought that he was acceptable to God because of 'ritual observance'. Why is avoiding extortion and adultery 'ritual'? Because we 'know' that Pharisees were interested only in externals and trivia, and 'ritual' is a code word which expresses disapproval of these. The only righteousness that a Pharisee could have would be 'ritual'. 'Purity' is used in about the same way: the Pharisees were greatly interested in it, and this proves their lack of inward, truly moral religion.[8] The nail has been hammered into their coffin when they are said to have been interested in 'ritual purity'.

The Pharisees *were* interested in ritual purity – as was the entirety of ancient religion. But let us say what it is. It is called 'ritual' (or Levitical, cultic or priestly) because it is especially connected with the temple and the priesthood. The adjectives are unnecessary, and they do not appear in the ancient languages. On the whole, I shall drop them. Yet, since our question is whether or not Pharisees applied to lay people when eating ordinary food the laws which governed priests and others when eating sanctified food, and since the priests regularly ate sanctified food, the term 'priestly purity' will sometimes be useful. It should be borne in mind that, when they ate peace offerings and second tithe, laypeople observed the same purity laws as did the priests routinely. 'Peace-offering purity' is a bit cumbersome, but it is just as accurate as 'priestly purity'. The question is, Did Pharisees ordinarily eat in this state of purity?

I shall not attempt a positive definition of 'purity'. It is simpler to define 'impurity', and so we shall proceed by the *via negativa*: purity is the absence of impurity.

According to the Bible, people and things become impure in one of these ways:

List 1 (a table is given on p. 151)

1a. A person is impure who touches a corpse or is in the same room with one (Num. 19.11–15).

1b. The furnishings of a room which contains a corpse, especially open vessels, are impure (Num. 19.15,18).

2. A woman is impure after childbirth (Lev. 12).

3. A menstruant is impure, and anyone who has intercourse with her is also impure. It is probable that any physical contact with menstrual blood conveyed the same degree of impurity (Lev. 15.19–24). (On intercourse with a menstruant, see further below.)

4. A person is impure who has a bodily 'flux' or 'discharge' (Lev. 15.2, 25). The position of these laws, before and after the rules on semen and menstruation, points towards discharge from the genitals, and in the case of the woman a discharge of blood is specified. The most common cause of female 'flux' was probably miscarriage. In the case of a male, gonorrhoea would cause discharge, though there are other forms of spermatorrhoea (non-ejaculatory emission of semen). A male with a discharge is termed a *zab*, a female a *zabah*, anglicized zav and zavah.

5. Contact with semen makes one impure, and semen from a nocturnal emission makes whatever it directly touches impure (Lev.15.16–18).

6a. Things on which sat, lay or leaned a zav, a zavah or a menstruant are impure and convey secondary impurity.

6b. This secondary impurity is incurred by coming into contact with the items in 6a (Lev. 15.5; 15.21–23; 15.26–27), and also by touching a zav (15.7), contacting his spittle (15.8), being touched by a zav who has not rinsed his hands (15.11), or touching a menstruant (15.19).

6c. Vessels which are touched by a zav must be broken (if pottery) or rinsed (if wood) (15.12).

7a. Touching the carcass of a forbidden creature makes one impure (Lev. 5.2; 11.24–25, 27–28, 31, 36). These are the creatures classified as 'impure' or 'abominable' in Lev. 11 and Deut. 14.

7b. Ovens and stoves on to which fell the carcass of a forbidden 'swarming thing', and vessels *into* which fell such a carcass are impure (Lev. 11.33–35). 'Swarming things' are principally insects, but the term includes other creatures which crawl or creep (11.29–30).

7c. Drink, wet food and wet seeds which came into contact with the carcass of a swarming thing are impure (11.34, 38).

8a. 'Leprosy'[9] renders one impure (Lev. 13.8, 14, 46). Presumably coming into contact with leprosy also made one impure (the leper is expelled from the inhabited area, Lev. 13.46; Num 5.2; cf. the impurity of living in a leprous house, Lev. 14.36, 46).

8b. Garments and houses could become leprous (Lev. 13.47–59; 14.33–53).

9. Touching human impurity makes one impure (Lev. 5.3). The wording, 'of whatever sort the impurity may be with which one becomes impure', may simply point forward to the impurities listed here as 6b. For the purpose of this exercise, I shall keep this as a separate item, and suppose that it includes excrement.[10] It will in any case drop out when we turn to pharisaic debates.

10. Impurity is incurred by eating anything, including a permitted animal, which dies of itself or which is killed by wild animals (Lev. 17.15; cf. 11.40; Deut. 14.21).

11. Touching the carcass of a permitted animal which dies of itself also makes one impure (Lev. 11.39–40).

This list excludes, for different reasons, several items which one might expect. There are, in the first place, several impurities which are incurred by disobedience of major prohibitions. Adultery, child sacrifice, homosexuality and bestiality make one impure (Lev. 18.19–24). The same passage includes intercourse with a menstruant, which we shall keep in our list, since it may be accidental. The others are excluded not because they are not impurities, which they are, but because they are much worse: they require capital punishment rather than rites which we would now call 'purifications'. This principle has also led to the omission of murder, which makes the land impure. Here purification is possible: the execution of the murderer (Num. 36.33); but our discussion of food and purity need not take this into account. For the same reason I have not put into this list the intentional consumption of forbidden creatures (e.g., shellfish, pork or mosquitos). Although the word 'impure' is used of them (Lev. 11.1–8), and although these prohibitions are thus technically purity laws, they are such major prohibitions, and so well accepted throughout all of Judaism, that they do not affect our present study (cf. I.C§1 above). I have left in the list, however, some of the other points from Lev. 11, especially 7a–c, which are very important for understanding the Pharisees, and generally misinterpreted by scholars. One could say of these what is said of pork, except for their being major, well-known and generally observed. Thus we need to keep track of them.

Another exclusion is the impurity of touching a living forbidden creature (Lev. 11.26). This rule, which would render impure a person who harnessed his donkey to a plow, seems to have been ignored. In any case no purification is prescribed. The verse may have been understood as referring to the carcass of an impure animal: that is, read in light of 11.27.

Finally, I have not included the prohibition of 'mixed kinds': sowing a field with two kinds of seeds, sowing two kinds of seeds in a vineyard, wearing a garment made of two kinds of material, allowing an animal to breed with a different kind, plowing with an ox and an ass together (Lev. 19.19; Deut. 22.9–11). These are not called 'impurities' in the Bible, and they are not said to make a person impure; they are simple prohibitions.

It is important to know which of the impurities in our list are *prohibited*. We may divide the list into four parts, distinguishing impurities (*a*) which the individual is *forbidden to contract*, (*b*) those which one is *powerless to avoid, but which are regrettable*, (*c*) those which *may be avoided*, and so presumably *should be*, and (*d*) those which are *necessary and proper to incur*. We shall also see some uncertain cases (*e*). These distinctions are my own, not the Bible's, and what I take to be the implication in the discussion of (*c*) may not be correct. I think, however, that we shall better understand purity if we pursue this question for a moment.

(*a*) Impurities which are prohibited: We have excluded from consideration some of the major prohibitions, such as eating pork. Of the impurities listed above, it is forbidden to incur only a few of them. It is forbidden for a man to acquire menstrual impurity by intercourse (3). Touching the carcass of an animal prohibited as food (7a) is forbidden (Lev. 11.8), as is eating what dies of itself (10).

We shall consider purification for 3 below. The purification for 7a is waiting until evening (for touching a forbidden carcass) or washing the clothes and waiting until evening (for carrying) (11.24–28). The ease of purification may reflect recognition that the prohibition could not always be obeyed. An ass that died while bearing a load in the city would have to be removed. In another way, however, the prohibition was seriously meant. If one did not know that one had touched the forbidden creature, and only later learned, a guilt-offering was required (Lev. 5.2–6). Purification for 10 is similar: washing the clothes, bathing[11] and waiting until sunset. One who fails to do this 'bears his or her iniquity' (Lev. 17.15–16) – which may mean, owes a guilt offering.

(*b*) Regrettable but unavoidable, with consequent prohibitions: 'Leprosy', bodily discharges and contamination by dead swarming things fall into this category (nos 8, 4, 6c, 7b, 7c). It would be better if people, garments, houses and the like did not become leprous, better if women did not miscarry or men suffer from spermatorrhoea, better if dead insects did not fall into vessels or on to ovens. In the nature of the case, these things are not prohibited. After these impurities appear, however, and until they are removed, some forms of contact with them are prohibited. Thus, for example, a leper is expelled; leprous spots must be torn out of garments, and the garments must be washed and, if the disease reappears, burnt (Lev. 13.56–58). For our task it is not necessary to detail the other prohibitions and purifications connected with leprosy, which occupy Lev. 13–14.

A bodily discharge also results in exclusion (at least according to Num. 5.2–3[12]), and this implies a prohibition against contact. Vessels which are touched by a zav are to be broken or rinsed, and thus use of vessels with zav-impurity is forbidden (6c). For purification, a zav waits seven days after the discharge stops, washes his clothes, bathes in running ('living') water and offers two doves or pigeons (Lev. 15.13–14). A zavah waits seven days and offers two birds; bathing is not required. Other rules about emissions from the body (6a and 6b) will be taken up in category e.

The requirement to break an oven or stove on to which the carcass of a swarming thing falls (7b) implies the prohibition, Do not use a defiled oven or stove. With regard to 7c, we find this: 'any food in it [a contaminated vessel] . . . , upon which water may come, shall be unclean' (11.34). This identifies impurity; does it forbid the food? Let us first note that the vessel which contains the impure food is to be broken (if earthenware) or washed (if of other material) (Lev. 11.32f.). This implies that the food or drink should not be consumed. We also find the phrase 'impure *to you*', referring to contaminated ovens and stoves (11.35) and seed (11.38). The phrase earlier in the chapter expresses prohibition (e.g. vv. 8, 29).

Impurities 7b and 7c, contamination by dead swarming things, are important for understanding Pharisaism, and they are very significant in studying the topic of *priestly* food laws kept by the laity. I wish to give them prominence here by two simple devices: naming and repetition. In discussing these laws in Leviticus, I shall use as a shorthand term 'gnat-impurity' (because of Matt. 23.24, 'straining out a gnat'). We have already seen that the Pharisees did not count the smallest creatures, and when speaking of pharisaic rules I shall use 'fly-impurity'. The present question is whether or not Lev. 11.32–38 implies a set of prohibitions. The words, 'you shall not' do not appear in these verses. I have proposed, however, that the simple reading of this passage – that is, what it would convey to first-century readers and listeners – is that eating and drinking what had been contaminated by gnat-impurity was prohibited, but that the only sanction was knowledge of impurity. This is not itself unusual: for many biblical laws no penalty for transgression is explicitly prescribed. I shall take these laws as prohibitions, while noting that the wording is not nearly so fierce as that governing the consumption of forbidden creatures itself.

(*c*) Preferable to avoid: I think that the implication is that one should *avoid if possible* the impurities numbered 9 and 11 (if 9 is excrement, rather than the indirect impurities listed under 6b). Unlike those under b, they may usually be avoided and by implication should be whenever possible. It would be better not to touch human excrement, and better not to have to remove the carcass of a sheep killed by wolves. While one should avoid these things, incurring such impurities may be necessary. In the case of illness, contact with human waste may be required. Carrion sometimes must be moved.

The difference between 7a (touching the carcass of an impure animal, such as a dog, cat or donkey) and 11 (touching the carcass of a pure animal which died of itself) deserves notice. The purification is the same: the arrival of sunset for touching (11.24, 39), washing the clothes and sunset for carrying (11.25, 40). No. 11, touching the carcass of a permitted animal, creates impurity but is not forbidden. Yet 7a, touching the impure creature, is *forbidden*; and touching its carcass, if one only later discovers it, requires a guilt offering (Lev. 5.2–6). The prohibition cannot always be observed; in this respect all carrion is the same. The prohibition of touching the carcasses of forbidden creatures drives it home that they are impure.

No rite of purification is prescribed for 9, touching human impurity. If the touching was 'hidden', and only later becomes known, a guilt offering is required (5.3, 6). It may well be that, by a bit of editorial clumsiness, the first-line purification, probably bathing, was omitted.

(*d*) Necessary and proper impurities: Incurring impurities 1, 2, 3 (if one is the menstruant) and 5 is, on the whole, *positively good*, or at least so much a part of nature as to raise no possible objection. On one point we have a clear distinction between ordinary people and the priesthood. Priests were forbidden to contract corpse-impurity (no. 1) except for the next-of-kin (Lev. 21.1–3), and for the high priest there were no exceptions (Lev. 21.11). For others, however, it was a duty; people are required to tend the dead. Childbearing is a positive commandment, as is contact with semen ('be fruitful and multiply') (2 and 5). Menstruation is natural (3). Connected with menstruation, however, there is a strict prohibition: intercourse (Lev. 18.19; 20.18). The last passage specifies 'cutting off', 'extirpation', as the penalty, but this applies only to intentional intercourse. Inadvertent transgression requires a sin offering (Lev. 4.27–35).

The purifications for impurities under this head range from the simple to the complex: for semen-impurity after sexual relations, bathing and waiting until sunset (Lev. 15.18); for semen-impurity after any other emission of semen, bathing, washing garments and sunset (15.16f.); for corpse-impurity, a seven-day rite, including two sprinklings with a mixture of water and the ashes of a burnt red heifer (Num. 19.12). Prior to purification, a person with corpse-impurity was supposed to be excluded from 'the camp' (settled communities, Num. 5.2–3). I shall show below that this rule was not in effect in the first century, and so fulfilling the positive expectation to tend the dead did not result in the severe inconvenience required by Num. 5.[13]

Childbirth-impurity varies in duration according to whether the child is male or female. In either case, the purification proceeds in two stages. During stage one, which is a week for a son and two weeks for a daughter, the woman is impure as during menstruation (and therefore cannot have sexual relations). During stage two, thirty-three more days (for a son) or sixty-six (for a daughter), the woman cannot touch holy things or enter the temple, but she can have intercourse. This period ends with sacrifices (Lev. 12).

Curiously, Lev. 12 and 15 mention no *rite* of purification after menstruation or after stage one of childbirth-impurity, but only the passage of time (one week for menstruation, Lev. 15.19). We recall that bathing is explicitly required for the zav but not the zavah. Bathing is, however, required for certain contacts with a woman in one of these impure conditions, and these laws use the masculine participle: the male who touches something made impure by a woman is required to bathe (e.g. Lev. 15.22). The probable explanation is that the laws of Lev. 15 are intended to keep impurity away from the temple (so 15.31), and at the time of Leviticus women did not actually enter the temple. During stage one of childbirth-impurity the woman is impure as during menstruation (Lev. 12.2), and at the end she is not required to bathe or to purify herself in any way. At the end of stage two, however, she takes a sacrifice, but she gives it to the priest 'at the door of the tent of meeting', that is, at the gate to the temple (12.6). The idea that the temple had a Court of the Women had not yet arisen. If this explanation is correct, the curiosity is not that the menstruant, the zavah and the woman after stage one of childbirth-impurity were *not* ordered to bathe, but rather that women were required to do so after contact with semen (Lev. 15.18).

It is probable that, in the first century, when there was a Court of the Women, it was assumed that women bathed after impurity, as did men. Josephus, unfortunately, provides no proof, for he does not mention bathing after menstruation (see *Antiq.* 3.261; *Apion.* 2.103–104, 198, three places where female purification might have been mentioned). The Mishnah assumes without debate that women immerse after menstruation (e.g. Mikwaoth 8.1, 5; cf. the opinion attributed to R. Akiba in Shabbat 64b). I am inclined to think that here the Mishnah is not peculiarly pharisaic, and that bathing was generally expected after all the impurities of Lev. 15 and after stage one of childbirth-impurity.

(*e*) Uncertain: There are minor uncertainties in the categories which we have just considered, but I am more dubious about how to assign no. 6a–b.

No. 6a covers things upon which impure people sit, lie or ride, and 6b covers other people who come into contact with those things. For example: menstrual impurity (3) is conveyed to the menstruant's bed (6a) and then to anyone who touches the bed (6b). The question is whether or not the Bible expects this chain of impurity to be avoided. Should a menstruant stay off the bed? or, if she lies on it, should her husband avoid it? Do 6a–b fit into b (regrettable but unavoidable), or c (possible and preferable to avoid)? It will be useful to have the full details before us.

> The male with a discharge (a zav): one who touches either him, what he sits on or what he lies on, bathes himself (only the male is specified), usually his clothing as well, and remains impure until sunset. This also applies to one who contacts the zav's spittle, or who is touched by the zav, unless the zav had rinsed his hands. Earthenware vessels touched by the zav are to be broken, wooden vessels rinsed (Lev. 15.1–12).

> The menstruant: she makes impure what she lies on and sits on. Anyone who touches her or one of these items (bed, chair, saddle etc.) contracts impurity, which is removed by bathing and the setting of the sun (Lev. 15.19–24).

> The woman with a discharge (zavah): she makes impure what she lies on and sits on, as well as people who touch them. Touching her is not specified, perhaps by oversight. Those who are made indirectly impure bathe and wash their clothes and are impure until sunset.

What seems to me uncertain is whether it was *expected* that the indirect impurities would be incurred, or *hoped* that they would be avoided. Both categories exist, as we have seen. This question is in a way one of *economic assumptions*. It becomes very important in assessing pharisaic purity, especially menstrual rules, and I wish to give it adequate emphasis here.

Numbers, we saw, requires that a zav (possibly also a zavah?) and a person with corpse-impurity would join the leper outside the 'camp' (Num. 5.2–3; the laws in Numbers are given in the desert, thus 'camp' is used for 'town' etc., 'tent' for 'house'). It is important to be aware of the existence of this little-known law, which is not mentioned in the Mishnah. We shall return to Josephus's use of it below. Just now it is useful for our question. The author of Numbers *did* expect people to avoid contact with the zav (and zavah?) as well as with the leper and the person with corpse-impurity: they are expelled from society. (Even Numbers does not put menstruants outside the camp – a point to which we shall return.)

What about Leviticus, which was usually the more important set of laws in the eyes of first-century Jews?[14] The priestly authors did not imagine that the zav and the zavah were kept outside settled communities. The expulsion of the leper is mentioned (13.46), but Leviticus does not require the expulsion of the others in the list in Numbers (the zav and a person with corpse impurity). On the contrary, Lev. 15 assumes that the zav, zavah and menstruant are all in the house: that is why touching their beds, chairs and persons is discussed. But did the priestly authors *expect* that a man with an unnatural emission from the penis would have his own separate bed and chair, and that no one would touch him, his bed or his chair? This seems to me most unlikely. Houses were on the whole not that large, and furniture not that plentiful. Similarly I doubt whether Leviticus assumes that people would try to avoid a menstruant's bed or chair, which would require all families to have duplicate sets. We hear nothing of extra sets of furniture. It is to be noted that, in terms of purification requirements, all that is demanded is washing – just as in the case of semen-impurity, which was not avoided.

It is my view that the authors of Leviticus did not expect people to avoid the secondary impurities of Lev. 15 (e.g. touching the bed of a menstruant) – any more than to avoid the primary ones (e.g. menstruating). I doubt that in the first century it was regarded as either compulsory or practicable to avoid the secondary impurities, and I offer the suggestion that they were all treated in the same way. Touching the bed of a menstruant was no worse than emitting semen. When the source of the impurity was at an end, everyone (or at least the men) bathed, and until then no one entered the temple.[15] I am inclined to move these secondary impurities to b: impossible to avoid though regrettable. The only consequence of the impurity is non-access to the temple.

We have not quite finished with biblical purity rules, but, having defined them, we may now comment on their number and complexity. The reader of the lists above, and the slightly varying rules about purification, may well become exasperated and find it impossible to keep it all in mind. As a reader's aid, I shall give a chart below. Here, however, I wish to point out that, if one will re-read the list of eleven sources of impurity, one will see that they would not be at all difficult to remember. Many people wince at having to pick up a dead animal; most people (except two-year olds) try to avoid touching defecation; corpses inspire a natural feeling of awe, and we hestitate to touch them; washing off semen and blood is almost natural, and certainly not hard to remember. Even gnat-impurity, which sounds picky, is not hard to understand. Who wants a fly in one's soup? I have a firm rule about beer: if a bee flies into the beer I remove it and drink the beer; if it is a fly (whether dead or alive) I throw the beer away. I have never sat outside on a hot summer day drinking beer with my daughter. But if she and I had done this, she would probably have learned the rules about bees and flies, and she might have gone through life thinking that the distinction is religiously significant. What is peculiar about Leviticus, and biblical law in general, is that such 'rules' are neither personal and idiosyncratic, nor based on modern notions of hygiene, but public and sanctioned by divine authority. To some degree they can be shown to be based on principles, but the principles are not stated.[16] In the case of beer, bees and flies, what matters in Lev. 11.32–38 is whether or not the creature was *a dead swarming thing*, which requires one to know whether or not it has legs above its feet (Lev. 11.21) and whether or not it is still breathing, not what it had dined on (which is the ground of my own rule). The biblical law is a bit different from my own instinctive laws (slightly informed by knowledge of flies' feeding habits), but not in the least difficult to remember.

§4. Although many of the above impurities are not only not wrong, but rather positively desirable, it is a transgression to bring any impurity into the presence of what is holy. Several of the above impurities (1, 2, 3, 5, and aspects of 6) are connected with *passage* in the sense of *rites de passage*, the basic moments of change in a person's life. The longest-lasting impurities are those which have directly to do with life and death. Corpse-impurity lasts for a week, and stage one of childbirth-impurity lasts for one week (if the child is a boy) or two weeks (if a girl). Menstrual impurity lasts for seven days. Semen-impurity, however, requires only bathing, washing and the setting of the sun. Human change is to be kept away from the holy – though in and of itself *passage* is not wicked.

In discussing holy food (§1), we saw that, whether the impurities were 'good' (childbirth) or 'bad' (touching the carcass of a pig), they must not be brought into the temple, and that impure people could not eat certain holy food. Sometimes the *only* restriction with regard to impurity was that it should be kept apart from the holy. The prohibition of entering the temple if impure is not, however, as explicit in the Pentateuch as one would expect. Numbers 19.13, 20 require people to be purified of corpse-impurity so as not to defile the temple ('tabernacle' or 'sanctuary'). The only general statement is Lev. 15.31:

> Thus you shall keep the people of Israel separate from their uncleanness, lest they die in their uncleanness by defiling my tabernacle that is in their midst.

Exegesis might have limited this statement to the forms of impurity discussed in Lev. 15 (discharge, semen and menstruation), but it seems to have been understood – from what date I do not know – quite generally. All impurities were to be kept out of the temple.

It is not the case, however, that the purity laws of the Bible affect *only* the temple and the priesthood. Some scholars (e.g. Gedalyahu Alon; see below) mistakenly think that 'the settled halakah' of purity had to do only with these, but that is not so even in biblical law. I shall present the list of impurities again, this time noting what is forbidden *to the lay person*. Priests, we recall, were forbidden to eat any food dedicated to the Lord if they were impure in any way (Lev. 22.1–9), and this prohibition is not noted in the following list. We continue to deal only with biblical law. The phrase 'only the temple and holy food' is shorthand for 'only entering the temple and *consuming* food which the Bible requires laypeople to eat in purity (second tithe and peace offerings)'.

List 2: What is affected by Impurity? (table, p. 151)

1. Touching a corpse or being in the same room with one: only the temple and holy food, including the Passover meal.
2. Bearing a child: during stage one, sexual contact as well as the temple and holy food. (The prohibition of sexual contact is implied by the clause 'as at the time of her menstruation, she shall be unclean', Lev. 12.2.) During stage two a woman cannot *touch* 'anything holy' (with no further definition).
3. Menstruation: sexual contact as well as the temple and holy food.
4. Having a bodily discharge (other than menstruation and ejaculated semen): The temple and holy food; further, since a woman with a discharge is treated as a menstruant in some respects, *presumably* it was understood that sexual relations were forbidden. Numbers, we recall, requires the isolation of the zav or zavah. Vessels touched by a zav were to be broken or rinsed.
5. Coming into contact with semen: only the temple and holy food.
6. Coming into certain kinds of direct or indirect contact with some of the above sources of impurity: especially touching the bed or chair of someone with a bodily discharge, including menstruation but not the emission of semen: only the temple and holy food, except for vessels touched by a zav, which are washed or broken.
7. Touching the carcass of a forbidden creature: only the temple and holy food. Wet food or seeds on to which a dead swarming thing fell were rendered impure and, I have argued, *unusable for all purposes* (Lev. 11.34, 38). Earthenware vessels, ovens and stoves made impure by the carcass of a swarming thing were to be *broken*.

8. Coming into contact with leprosy: leprosy itself requires isolation outside the community (Lev. 13.46). A leprous garment was to be burned, or the leprous part cut out (13.47–58). The leprous parts of a house must be removed; if the disease spread the house was to be destroyed (14.13–46). A person who ate or slept in a leprous house must wash his clothes (14.46–47) and until then could not enter the temple.
9. Touching human impurity (Lev.5.3): only the temple and holy food.
10. Eating an animal which died of itself: only the temple and holy food.
11. Touching the carcass of a permitted animal which died of itself: only the temple and holy food.

It is seen that biblical law does indeed primarily protect the temple and what was associated with it. But, over and above that, it requires purity of laypeople when eating second tithe and peace offerings, and freedom from corpse-impurity when eating Passover. Purity laws impose some prohibitions on laypeople all the time: sexual contact in the case of menstruation, childbirth and possibly bodily discharge; consuming wet food or using wet seeds which had been contaminated by the corpse of a swarming thing. The Bible further requires that earthenware vessels etc. on which a dead swarming thing fell be broken. Vessels touched by a zav are to be broken or rinsed. Leprous garments and houses are not to be used, and people with some impurities are excluded not only from the temple but also from the city. Thus it is not true to say that biblical purity laws affect only the temple and the priesthood.

The *only purity law governing ordinary food* – apart from the major prohibitions of 'abominations' – is that of wet food on which fell the carcass of a swarming thing. Since vessels, ovens and stoves were subject to the same impurity, the laws of Lev. 11.32–38 have a further indirect impact on domestic eating. There is one more interesting twist with regard to meat. According to Lev. 17.3–5, ordinary people ate *no* ordinary meat: there was to be none. If a person wished to slaughter an animal, he was to bring it to the temple and present it as a peace offering – which, in turn, had to be eaten in purity (Lev. 7.19–21). Deuteronomy, however, has an emphatic rule to the contrary. Because Israelite land was enlarged (Deut. 12.20), people were allowed to slaughter animals in their own towns and villages and eat them in a state of purity or not (12.22). Even firstlings, if blemished, could be eaten in one's own residence in impurity (Deut. 15.21–22). The law of Lev. 17.3–5 was obviously not observable, or not for long, and in the first century it was a dead letter. It is dismissed in the Mishnah (Zebahim 14.1–2).[17]

§5. Still under the heading 'Biblical Law', let us ask what it would mean, in practical terms, to apply to ordinary food the purity laws which governed the priests and the temple – as, we are told, the Pharisees did. Everyone was to observe rules 7a–c in any case. Accepting the priestly purity laws (or peace-offering purity laws) would mean, in the first place, ignoring the permission to eat meat in impurity in Deut. 12.22. It would further mean not eating ordinary food if one had the impurities which we have numbered 1–6 and 8–11: One could not eat if one had corpse-impurity, and one could not eat from vessels which were in a room which housed a corpse. The following also could not eat: women after childbirth; menstruants; people with a discharge; people who had come into contact with semen; someone who touched the chair or bed of a menstruant, a woman after childbirth or someone with a discharge; those who had leprosy, a leprous garment or a leprous house; someone who touched the carcass of any forbidden creature; someone who touched human impurity; or someone who touched a permitted animal which died of itself. All of these restrictions are in addition to those of Lev. 11, which are enjoined on all Israel.

The onerous aspects of the extension of biblical law – which would make ordinary life impossible – would be keeping ordinary food away from men and women with semen-impurity, menstruants, women after childbirth, those who touched the bed or chair of a menstruant or a woman after childbirth, and people and vessels which had been in the same room as a corpse. (I assume that 'discharge' was not a frequent condition.)

Literally observing such supposed laws would require prolonged fasting. In day-to-day life people would have to choose between sexual relations and food in the daytime – unless they could have sex and bathe before sunset. Let us suppose, however, that impure people were allowed to eat something, but not to eat *with* those who were pure. Who would these be? In the case of married couples, on many or most days they would both be impure until sundown because of semen-impurity. Parents could eat with their children only after sunset. If Pharisees lived like priests, we could expect statements to the effect that they ate once a day, or that only the children could have breakfast together, while the parents had to eat impure food apart. We shall not find them. Put another way, the expected pharisaic rules would have to make provision for a 'second supper', eaten by those not eligible to eat 'first supper'. We know what such rules would look like, since Numbers gives a rule for Second Passover, eaten by those who had corpse-impurity at First Passover. But we find no such rules for ordinary meals, nor any which would have the same effect.

One basic position of the Pharisees, however, would greatly ease these problems. The Pharisees, as we noted above, thought that a person who had immersed, but upon whom the sun had not yet set, was partially pure. A person in this category was called a tevul yom, 'one who had immersed that day'. There are a few Houses debates which discuss the tevul yom (Tebul Yom 1.1; T. Tev. Yom 2.3), and we saw above evidence which proves that the idea is an early one (I.D, p.37). If we moderate the above paragraph to take account of this view, we would conclude that Pharisees who lived like priests had to immerse more-or-less every morning. In this case, we should find references to the rite of morning immersion, but there are none. On the contrary, the Pharisees were not morning immersers.[18]

Let us continue to look forward to the rules of a lay group which lived like priests. We would anticipate pharisaic laws which applied the rules of impurity *to food*. A law (for example) which simply forbade a man to lie in bed with a menstruant would not do: it might be that it was intended only to prevent intercourse.

Treating all food as holy and lay people as priests would mean that those who had any impurity could not touch it, since the priests when impure could not *come near* dedicated food (Lev. 22.3). The Pharisees, and possibly others (see above on Judith 11.13), did extend the biblical law in an important way: they thought that the priests' food had to be *handled* in purity. If, however, they then applied this rule to their own food, it would mean that food could not be harvested or cooked by people who were impure. This was not a problem for priests in terms of harvesting, since they were not supposed to work the land. But if ordinary people accepted priestly purity, they could work the land as little as the priests.

The modern reader may say, let us not be ridiculous, let us suppose that semen-impurity was ignored so that people could have sex and harvest, cook and eat in the same day. In this case, we should have legal arguments proving that it should be ignored, but they do not exist. But let us waive the point and press on. Next on the list of impurities which cannot be kept away from ordinary food is menstruation: one week in each month the males would have to handle all the food and the woman would have to have a separate bed and chair, or a separate residence. This requirement would have produced all kinds of regulations: could the two beds touch each other? did the men have one week a month off work? (Preparing food in the days before the food-processor and microwave oven required hours.) The death of a member of the family, a neighbour or a friend would produce a great crisis: people died not in hospitals but at home. Until the special mixture of water and the ashes of a burnt red heifer could be sprinkled on the room and furnishings, twice over a seven day period, the room would be off limits, and its furnishings could not be used. In a four-room house, this would be extremely difficult. Those who attended the funeral could not handle food until they had procured the special water and spent a week in the rite of purification.

Offhand, one judges all this to be impossible. It is now time to consider scholarly views about the Pharisees in more detail, and then to consider pharisaic law on purity, especially as it affects ordinary food.

Table of Biblical Impurities

Impurity	Prohib-ited?*	Means of Purification	What affected**
1a corpse-imp.: pple.	d	7 days, red heifer, sprinking	temple
1b corpse-imp.: things	d	same	temple
2 childbirth	d	I: 7/14 days, no rite in Bible prob. bathing in 1st C	sex
		II: 33/66 days, sacrifices	temple
3 menstruation	d	7 days; prob. bathing in 1st C	sex
4 discharge (if male)	b	7 days; bathing; sacrifices	temple
(if female)	b	7 days; sacrifices; bathing 1st C?	temple; sex?
5 semen	d	bathing and sunset	temple
6a certain things in contact with 3,4,5:		impure but no prescriptions	
6b contact with 2:I,3,4,5 prob.	b	bathing, washing and sunset	temple
6c vessels in contact w. 4	b	prohibited to use: break/wash	domestic
7a carcass of imp. creature	a	sunset/washing & sunset	temple
7b vessels so contaminated	b	break or wash	dmstc. vessels
7c food & seeds so contaminated	b	non-use implied	dmstc. food
8 Leprosy: people, garments & houses	b	long and complicated	inhabited areas
9 Human impurity	c	if unknown, guilt off.	temple
10 eating what dies of itself	a	bathing, washing/sunset	temple
11 touching carcass of pure animal which dies of itself	c	sunset/washing & sunset	temple

*a = prohibited; b = impossible to avoid but regrettable; consequent prohibitions; c = possible to avoid, presumably should; d = right and proper to incur.
** 'Temple' = 'temple and holy food'.

C. SECONDARY LITERATURE: THE STATE OF THE QUESTION

§1. Before 1970, the prevailing wisdom was this: The Pharisees were a major political force in Palestine, and thus they had laws on all aspects of life. Not all, however, accepted their special laws on tithing, food and purity, and these separated them from the rest of Israel. They formed their own association. According to Louis Finkelstein, for example, membership requirements in Pharisaism included agreement not to prepare food together with an ʿam ha-ʾarets (an ordinary person) and always to eat one's own food 'in Levitical purity'.[1] According to Joachim Jeremias, the Pharisees, on joining the community, had to take a strict oath about tithing and purity. They 'drew a hard line between themselves and the masses, the ʿamme haʾarets, who did not observe as they did the rules . . . on tithes and purity'.[2] This view was based on an equation of the Pharisees with the haverim, Associates, who are said in rabbinic literature to have eaten ordinary food in ritual purity. Gedalyahu Alon proposed that 'the sages' (Pharisees, later Rabbis) obliged all Israel to eat only pure food, and to eat it in purity. They realized, however, that this was difficult, and so they formed an association in which the members observed the purity laws as did priests. This practice, he argued, went back to the early (pharisaic) sages, 'who also kept aloof from the ʿAm ha-ʾArets'.[3] *Basically the same view is accepted in the revision of Schürer's History of the Jewish People* by Geza Vermes and others.[4]

§2. The prevailing wisdom was challenged by Ellis Rivkin, who analysed the use of the word *pᵉrûshîm* in rabbinic literature, noting especially what it is opposite.[5] He showed that many passages, especially in late literature, use this Hebrew word to refer to ascetics and other eccentrics of their own time, not the historical Pharisees. This excludes from the evidence for pre-70 Pharisaism many passages beloved by anti-Jewish Christian scholars. In his five and one-fourth page appendix on the Pharisees, Billerbeck used three pages of fine print to quote 'unfavourable opinions about the Pharisees'[6] from rabbinic literature. He made use of such passages as Sotah 22b, which lists seven kinds of *pᵉrûshîm*, all bad. This passage has often been gleefully pointed to as proving that the Pharisees were awful and had to admit it themselves. In fact it comes from a period so late that *pᵉrûshîm* no longer meant the historical party of the Pharisees, but separatists in the sense of deviants from the norm of Judaism in Babylonia. Rivkin's elimination of such irrelevant passages was a substantial achievement.

He also argued that the Pharisees were not haverim. Rather they made laws concerning the obligations of those who, voluntarily, became haverim. He employed the analogy of the Nazirite vow: Pharisees as such were not Nazirites, but they made rulings on what people had to do once they had taken the vow. Similarly, Rivkin proposed, they passed rules about haverim but were not themselves necessarily members of the association.

Positively, the Pharisees were champions of the two-fold law (the written and the oral), whose occupation was making such concrete rules as were needed on any and every point. They were makers of halakot and set themselves against the other group which claimed the same responsibility, the Sadducees.

§3. Rivkin's denial that the Pharisees were haverim, however, proved not to be very influential, since a larger work, which on this point agreed with the old consensus, immediately appeared. At more or less the same time as Rivkin was writing his article on 'Defining the Pharisees', Jacob Neusner was completing *The Rabbinic Traditions about the Pharisees before 70* (3 vols, 1971). He studied not passages containing the word *pᵉrûshîm* but rather those which include either the name of someone known to have been a Pharisee (e.g. Abtalion, usually thought to be the 'Pollion' of Josephus) or the 'Houses' (Schools) of Hillel and Shammai. At the conclusion of his study he defined the Pharisees as being essentially a pure food club, concerned above all with table-fellowship and eating ordinary food in priestly purity. Hillel (*c.* 50 BCE to CE 10), he proposed, converted the group from a 'political party into a table-fellowship-sect' (*Rabb. Trads.* III, pp. 305f.). From then on

The primary mark of Pharisaic commitment was the observance of the laws of ritual purity outside of the Temple, where everyone kept them. Eating one's secular, that is, unconsecrated, food in a state of ritual purity as if one were a Temple priest in the cult was one of the two significations of party membership [the other being special tithing laws]. (ibid., p. 288)[7]

Neusner then proceeded to an analysis of the Mishnaic laws (except for the first order, Zeraim, which has been done by his students). His part of the study required 43 volumes. He was concerned throughout to stratify the material chronologically, specifying whether it was pre-70, between 70 and the 130s (the second revolt), or between 140 and the completion of the Mishnah, *c.* 200 (before the wars, between the wars or after the wars). In 1981 he published a volume summarizing his results: *Judaism: the Evidence of the Mishnah*. With regard to the pre-70 stratum, he stated that 'if someone had set out to organize a "Mishnah" before 70, his single operative category would have been making meals' (*Judaism*, p. 59). That is, the summary of the

History of the Mishnaic Law attributed to the earliest layer of the Mishnah the same concern which he had previously attributed to the Pharisees.

It will be seen that, whereas Rivkin's definition of the Pharisees is contrary to the consensus before his time, Neusner supports a major aspect of it. He departed from the former consensus in maintaining that, from the time of Hillel on, the Pharisees withdrew from public life. They neither governed Palestine nor tried to do so. Pharisaic law became *exclusively* concerned with the 'sect's' own table-fellowship. We saw at the end of section A that in later work Neusner's definition of 'pharisaic law' led him to doubt that it was pharisaic. He has clung, however, to his description of the earliest layer of rabbinic literature as dealing almost exclusively with ordinary food in purity.

I shall very briefly evaluate the positions of Rivkin and traditional talmudics (especially as represented by Alon) before turning to our major task, the consideration of Neusner's material.

§4. Rivkin's first point, that the word *pᵉrûshîm* does not always refer to the pre-70 Pharisees, is to be confirmed. Once one sees the point and pays attention to the dates of the people named in each passage which mentions the *pᵉrûshîm*, Rivkin's conclusion becomes self-evident.[8] I shall not here go through the passages which he discussed, but merely state that anyone who does go through them will agree with him. The ascetics of the period of the Babylonian Talmud were called *pᵉrûshîm*, but the word had lost its original connection with the pre-70 party called by the same word in Hebrew.

With regard to his second principal point, I have previously argued in support of the view that Pharisees were not necessarily haverim.[9] I think, however, that a closer connection can be made than Rivkin allows. If one analyses all the passages about the ʿamme ha-ʾarets, one will see that they are often distinguished from the anonymous 'they' who are to follow the mishnaic law. Since the haverim are also often contrasted with the ordinary people, there seems to be some connection between the followers of rabbinic law and the haverim. A third step, showing that some of the main rabbinic views were inherited from the Pharisees, would result in a contrast between the Pharisees and the ʿamme ha-ʾarets, and a significant parallel between the Pharisees and the haverim.[10] We shall also see that the Houses (of Hillel and Shammai) are sometimes contrasted with the ʿamme ha-ʾarets. The distinction of the Pharisees from the haverim, while correct in many ways, cannot be seen as total. Further, it is necessary to try to date the passages, a task which Rivkin did not pursue.

Rivkin's more general positive point, that the Pharisees ruled on a large range of subjects, in opposition to the Sadducees, is generally correct, though some areas seem not to have been covered. We shall turn up evidence as we consider Neusner's work, modifying both their views of the topics of pharisaic law.

§5. We return now to assess, very briefly, pre-1969 scholarship. Finkelstein, Jeremias and others fixed on a few related proof-texts in the Mishnah and Tosefta tractates on Demai (produce which one was not certain had been tithed). Demai 2.2 forbids one who 'undertakes to be trustworthy' (*ne'eman*) to be a guest of an 'am ha-'arets, although that position is disputed by R. Judah. One who undertakes to be an 'associate' (haver) may not sell an 'am ha-'arets foodstuff which is wet or dry, or buy from him foodstuff that is wet; nor may he receive the 'am ha-'arets as a guest if the latter wears his own clothes. R. Judah was of the view that a haver could not incur corpse-impurity, but here he stood alone (Demai 2.3). A haver undertakes to eat ordinary food in purity, and he will not prepare food which requires purity for (or near; there is a variant reading) an 'am ha-'arets (T. Demai 2.2).

Those who assumed that, at the time of R. Judah (b. Ilai, mid-second century), all Rabbis were haverim and that they continued the views of pre-70 Pharisees – and most people did assume such identity and continuity – had all the evidence they needed. They were not even made to pause by the fact that the majority refused R. Judah's proposal that haverim not incur corpse-impurity. That is, according to the key proof text, the majority of the rabbinic academy *declined* to say that a haver had to live like a priest (since priests avoided corpse-impurity). Unhindered, most scholars concluded that Rabbis and Pharisees were haverim and that they lived like priests.

We may conveniently see how such scholars thought and argued if we consider the relevant parts of the article by I. M. Ta-Shma on 'Niddah' (the menstruant) in the *Encylopaedia Judaica*:

> . . . the people observed many restrictions and minutiae with regard to the prohibition relating to the menstruous woman. In ancient times a menstruous woman was completely segregated, particularly in Erez Israel where the laws of purity were still in vogue from the time when the Temple existed. Excluded from her home, the menstrous woman stayed in a special house known as 'a house for uncleanness' (Nid. 7.4), she was called *galmudah* ('segregrated,' RH 26a), and was not allowed to adorn herself until R. Akiva permitted her to do so, that she might not be repulsive to her husband (Sifra, Mezora, 9:12). No food was eaten with a menstruous woman (Tosef. Shab. 1:14) nor did she attend to her household duties, until the stage was reached in which 'during all the days of her menstruation she is to be segregated' (ARN¹ 1, 4). The origin of this segregation lies in the custom, prevalent in Erez Israel long after the

destruction of the Second Temple, of eating ordinary meals prepared according to the levitical rules originally prescribed for sacred food. This custom did not obtain prevalence in Babylonia where there was *neither any reason for, nor any halakhic possibility of, observing absolute purity*, and where accordingly all these expressions of the menstruous woman's segregation were not practiced.[11]

This passage is typical of much of traditional talmudics because all rabbinic statements are accepted at face value, with no concern for social reality. It is also assumed that all texts agree.[12] In fact, the argument that the menstruant lived in a separate house is countered by the statement that R. Akiba allowed her to adorn herself so that her husband would still find her attractive; if she was expelled from the house, there would be no point in beautifying herself for her husband. In terms of social reality, one may note that it was no more practicable in Palestine than it was in Babylonia to provide menstruants with separate houses and to do without their contribution to the day's labour.

Further, the passages do not say what is claimed. The phrase in Niddah 7.4, 'house of impurity', was understood by its earliest interpreters (T. Niddah 6.15) as the 'women's bathhouse', which is much more likely than 'separate dormitory'. The rule under discussion is that bloodstains found near such a place are taken to be impure. The reason this had to be discussed with regard to bathhouses is that Jewish and Gentile women used the same bathhouse, and if the blood was from a Gentile, it was not impure (since Lev. 15 governs only Jews, not Gentiles). If the Mishnah's phrase, 'house of impurity', referred to separate dormitories where Jewish menstruants stayed, the question of the purity or impurity of blood nearby would not have arisen at all. It would be impure menstrual blood from a Jewess by definition.

Nor does Rosh ha-Shanah 26a say that menstruants lived in separate houses, and certainly not in Palestine (as the author claims). It is a (fictional) story of a traveller who discovers that in other places they call 'this' 'that', as the present-day American discovers that in Britain they call the 'trunk' of a car the 'boot', or someone from Britain discovers that North Americans call 'petrol' 'gas'. In this case, a traveller to Gallia (Galatia or Gaul, in any case, not Palestine[13]) found that they called a 'menstruant' 'segregated' – one is not told from what. Separated from intercourse with her husband is more likely than separated from her house.[14] T. Shabbat 1.14 is interesting. The speaker, R. Simeon b. Eleazar (end of second/beginning of third century) asked why the early sages (*ri'shônîm*) did *not* rule that men could not eat with menstruants, and he concluded that they had no need to do so, since they observed the prohibition. This is, in theory, possible: silence may indicate what is taken for granted. In our particular case, however, we shall see that menstruants did not live apart.

If one is going to argue cases by finding proof texts one should take them all into account. Rabbinic literature is very large, and it is not difficult to find several which say that Rabbis did not eat food in priestly purity – or that doing so did not matter. There are numerous examples,[15] some of which will be mentioned below (D§2.a), but I would not wish to use them as primary evidence for the Pharisees. I mention them here only to indicate that they constitute a supplementary rebuttal of the views we have just been considering.

With this, we depart from most traditional Talmudists. Proof texts which are not even compared with contrary evidence tell us nothing. Since, however, Alon says that menstruants had separate houses, citing also Niddah 7.4,[16] and since Neusner largely agrees (see below), I shall here marshall the evidence which shows that the notion that menstruants went into purdah is not true. We cannot say that they ate at the same table as non-menstruants, since no evidence covers the point; but we can show that full separation was not practised.

Alon viewed Josephus and Philo as *proving* his case that the (*pharisaic*) sages extended the bounds of priestly purity to their own (lay) lives. ('Levitical Cleanness', p. 232). We shall consider the passage from Philo below (pp. 164, 264–67), and here deal only with Josephus. The passage which Alon regarded as decisive is *Antiq.* 3.261f.:

> He [Moses] banished from the city alike those whose bodies were afflicted with leprosy and those with contagious disease [*gonēn hreomenous*]. Women too, when beset by their natural secretions, he secluded until the seventh day, after which they were permitted, as now pure, to return to society [*endēmein*]. A like rule applies to those who have paid the last rites to the dead: after the same number of days they may rejoin their fellows [*endēmein*].

This, Alon thought, showed that the Pharisees had imposed the halakah of priestly purity on all and sundry: menstruants were secluded. At this point Josephus is presenting Num. 5.2–3, which banishes the leper, the person with corpse-impurity and the zav from settled communities. To this list he adds menstruants. He changes the verb, from 'banish' to 'seclude': lepers and zavs are banished, menstruants secluded. It appears that he puts the corpse-impure in the same category as menstruants. Does this passage reflect first-century Palestinian practice? The summaries of the law in *Antiq.* 3 and 4 are often summaries of what is written, not of what was done, while at other times they are highly idealized. Another passage helps clarify

Josephus's view of contemporary practice. In describing the actual temple in
War 5 (not recalling the Mosaic ordinances, as in *Antiq.* 3), he states that
women when menstruating could not enter the temple. The wording is
telling: 'The entire city, on the one hand (*men*), was closed to those with
gonorrhoea or leprosy, while on the other (*de*) the temple was closed to
women during menstruation' (5.227). The *men . . .de* formulation contrasts
the purity maintained in the city with that of the temple. I think that we must
accept *War* 5.227 as representing Jewish practice as Josephus knew it: only
the temple was closed to menstruants, not the city. This does not yet prove
that a menstruant was not relegated to a separate lean-to outside the main
house, or that she was not shut up in a room inside the main house, but it does
indicate that she could walk the streets of Jerusalem – possibly touching
someone! Thus the most extreme form of exclusion, banishment from the
city to a separate encampment, was not inflicted on menstruants.

The question of physical separation from impurity is important, and we
may with profit continue the consideration of Num. 5.2–3, as well as the case
of the menstruant. We previously saw reason to doubt that this passage was
fully in force in the first century (see on the zav in B above, pp.144f.). I wish
now to collect all the evidence on the leper, the zav and the person with corpse
impurity, some of which was given above.

On lepers – expelled according to Num. 5; Lev. 13.46 and *Antiq.* 3, and
'shut up' pending tests according to Lev. 13.4 – we have supporting evidence
from the Mishnah. According to Middoth 2.5 there was, inside the outer wall
of the temple, a Chamber of Lepers – presumably where they were 'shut up'.
Negaim speaks of 'shutting up' lepers, though there are important exceptions
(not a bridegroom and not during a festival (!), Negaim 3.1–3). Thus Num. 5
is supported by Leviticus, Josephus and the Mishnah. I think that shutting up
suspected lepers and expelling them from the city when the case was proved
was common practice.

With regard to the zav, Num. 5 is supported by Josephus in *Antiq.* 3 and
War 5, using the words *gonēn hreomenous* (*Antiq.* 3) and *gonorroios* (*War* 5) –
gonorrhoea or spermatorrhoea, the same term which appears in Num. 5.2 in
the LXX (*gonorryē*). On the other hand, as we noted above, the zav is not shut
up or cast out according to Lev. 15, but is assumed to be living at home. The
Mishnah supposes that a zav associates with other people (e.g. Zabim 3). In
this case a decision is more difficult, because of *War* 5.227. My guess is that
in the first century cases were distinguished: not every emission from the
penis which is not the natural ejaculation of semen indicates a serious
disease, and probably only those with a prolonged or severe case of
spermatorrhoea were expelled. The first chapter of Mishnah Zabim
distinguishes a partial zav from a full zav and depicts a procedure of

continuing inspection of a man who has an emission from his penis. This may have been practised in the first century.

Because of the number of people involved, it is antecedently improbable that people with corpse-impurity were actually expelled from the town or village. People died at home, and they were mourned by the extended family, neighbours, friends and probably even casual acquaintances. Expulsion of the mourners would also be cruel. We might dismiss Num. 5 on these two grounds alone. Since in *Antiq.* 3 Josephus seems to classify the corpse-impure with the menstruant, we may assume that he construed the biblical passage to require only 'seclusion', not 'banishment'. When, however, he describes Jewish funeral customs, he mentions that those 'who pass by' are to join the cortège, and that subsequently the house and its inhabitants must be purified (*Apion* 2.205), but he says nothing of keeping the impure physically separated from others. The Mishnah assumes that people with corpse-impurity live at home. We shall see below that the pharisaic material evidences great interest in tracking down corpse-impurity, but we never read that those who had it were sent away. From Philo we may learn that people were kept outside the temple while being purified of it, but not that they were kept outside the city (*Spec. Laws* 1.261).

When we add *Apion* 2.205 to the Mishnah and to the impracticability of such an expulsion, and further take into account the silence of our sources as to its terribly disruptive effects, we may conclude on this point too that the more humane practice was the custom. The corpse-impure, despite Num. 5, were not expelled from the city, and it is unlikely that they were segregated from other family members.

With regard to menstruants, 'al ehad kamma ve-kamma, 'how much the more!'. Can one imagine the size of the shelters necessary to contain the post-puberty, pre-menopausal female population for one-quarter of its life, or the extra number of square feet which each house would require? Where, inside Jerusalem, would there have been space for the separate houses which Alon and others assign to menstruants? Even if the most modest proposal were true, and menstruants were sequestered in separate areas of their own houses, we should have references to the separate rooms. Only people in our field, which is cursed by a perverse literalism, can write such things as that menstruants could not live at home. They read ancient idealizations and believe them, they do not actually *imagine* what it means.[17] In any case, the contrary evidence is conclusive. In addition to the fact that Lev. 15 supposes that menstruants live at home, and that Josephus in *War* 5 supposes that they were in the city of Jerusalem, we note that the Mishnah assumes that they lived at home. Thus Zabim 4.1 discusses the case of a menstruant sitting on a bed with one who was pure. Many of the discussions of *midras*-impurity (the impurity which an impure person conveys to what he or she sits, lies or leans on; impurity 6a–b in section B above) assume that household objects might have acquired it.

I do not argue that women when impure lived precisely as they did when pure. The Babylonian Talmud finally gets around to discussing the problem of a man's sleeping with his wife during her menstruation, but it is a *question*, not a topic already settled. The view which seems to prevail is that husband and wife should not share the same bed even if they have separate night-clothes, though not all agree. It is noteworthy that the Babylonian sages thought that in Palestine couples *did* share the same bed, but with an apron between them (Shabbat 13a–b//ARNA 2). The point of the entire discussion is that one should avoid the arousal of passion, which might lead to intercourse. We should not rule out any and all precautions against sexual relations, but only the extreme view of learned scholars, who think that menstruants were prevented from touching food and were excluded from the house or regular furniture. I should note here that Alon's translator, Israel Abrahams, rendered his statement that menstruants had separate houses (*batîm meyûhadîm*) as 'separate chambers', making it sound a bit more reasonable.[18] Neusner sounds more reasonable yet: menstruants did not touch food or eat with the men, and they changed beds and chairs rather than houses.[19] It only sounds more reasonable. Let us recall the considerations of time, money and space from above. The small householders who, Neusner has pointed out, are the assumed actors in the Mishnah certainly did not have the time to do the domestic work one-fourth of the month, and probably neither the money nor the space which even Neusner's proposal envisages.[20]

When we add to this the total absence from the Mishnah of the enormous number of discussions that separate furniture would have entailed, we must conclude that Neusner's view is no more likely than that of Ta-Shma or Alon. Arguments from silence, unless properly bolstered, are precarious. Thus I note that we *do* have numerous discussions about midras-impurity, and that menstruants are the prime source of this impurity. Since there are a lot of these passages, and none about the supposed separate rooms or shelters, we must conclude that menstruants lived at home and in their regular quarters.

What, then, is the meaning of *Antiq.* 3.261f., according to which menstruants and the corpse-impure suffered some degree of seclusion? Josephus here probably reflects the rules which he and his kind – the aristocratic priesthood – followed. Josephus and others of his class could of course provide both the space and the staff to make the separation of menstruants possible, and they would certainly have had ways of avoiding contact with the corpse-impure. This probably accounts for his statement in *Antiq.* 3.261f. People who occupied small houses could not have lived in the same way.

Purity was an ideal in ancient Judaism. Physical separation from impurity was probably talked about more than it was practised, and modern scholars think about what they read more than about the size of first-century houses and the hours in a Pharisee's day. Scholars are sometimes even less realistic than were the Rabbis, who knew that they might pick up midras-impurity from something on which a menstruant sat, lay or leaned. Their rules take account of this as probable, though according to modern scholars it would have been impossible, since menstruants had separate quarters. The interplay between theory and reality can be seen in Yadin's discussion of the laws of separation in the Temple Scroll.[21] The Scroll, describing the future Jerusalem, requires three separate areas, built east of the city, for lepers, zavs and men who have nocturnal emissions (11QTemple 46.18). Menstruants and women after childbirth were to be expelled from any city, not just Jerusalem (48.14–16). Yadin contrasts these harsh regulations with the humane view of the Rabbis (whose rules, he writes, were 'then in force'), who excluded menstruants *only* from their houses (quoting Alon, at the point where he relies on Josephus and Niddah 7.4).[22] Where were the menstruants' separate houses in Jerusalem? Yadin did not put the question, I assume because, once he quoted Alon, he stopped thinking like an archaeologist. We have seen that in fact neither Josephus nor Niddah 7.4 refers to extra houses. But what if there were such references in the Mishnah? Should one not take into account the problems of size, space, time and money? In discussing the problem of latrines for the Essenes, which were not to be in the city (11QTemple 46.13–16) or the 'camp' (1QM 7.6f.), Yadin dealt with such issues very realistically, counting cubits, measuring distances, studying references to latrines in a variety of sources, and attempting to locate the 'Gate of the Essenes' in Jerusalem.[23] The same kind of realism will, I think, rule out the possibility of separate quarters for menstruants.

This has taken a lot of space, more space than can be given to each and every sub-topic under the heading Purity Laws as Applied to the Laity's Food. I shall confide to the reader why. We have, in effect, disposed of Alon's article. I shall say a bit more about it, but he claimed that he relied principally on Josephus and Philo, and it was necessary to examine at least one point from Josephus in some detail. No small part of Neusner's overall view has also been undermined, though in his case we shall go through more evidence in order to construct a positive picture of pharisaic practice. I have also wanted to illustrate how the evidence can be sorted. Josephus knew what first-century Palestinian Jews did, at least on average; yet he did not *describe* it in every line he wrote. I attach great weight to his evidence about first-century practice, once I am assured that this is the topic. To reach that point, one must study the issue and all of the passages. Similarly with the Mishnah and

Tosefta. The sentence 'a haver eats ordinary food in purity' does not prove that he did so – especially when the next line states that he did not avoid corpse-impurity.

Besides studying the question and noting conflicting passages, we should ask what the existing material presupposes. I might be persuaded that menstruants and the corpse-impure camped outside the city if a tractate included such a passage as this: 'On their way from the shelter to [the place of] purification, a corpse-impure [person] must not overshadow a menstruant, and a menstruant must [pick] no more grapes [along the path] than she can [consume] before [she reaches] the immersion pool.' (With apologies to Danby.) That would give one pause, but there is nothing of the sort. Instead, the presupposition of rabbinic literature is that menstruants lived at home, slept in their own beds and so forth. We noted that the passages which some take to prove the contrary do not even say what is attributed to them. There is a whimsical romanticism about T. Shabbat 1.14: in the good old days our crowd were really pure. That this degree of purity is idealized in one late passage is an interesting thing to know. But we learn nothing from it about pre-70 practice. Neusner cites no passages, being content with the simple repetition of a traditional view.

§6. Alon's essay (n. 3 above) on the boundaries of purity deserves separate mention because he knew full well that the evidence is not uniform, and he attempted to face up to the fact. His essay often states acutely what the issue is, but it includes confusion of the topic, irrelevant evidence and apparent self-contradictions. Adolf Büchler had long before argued that handwashing was a post-70 development and that the imposition of priestly laws on the laity came after the second revolt.[24] Alon wished to prove that Büchler was wrong, and that the early sages had accepted the purity laws and applied them to the populace (not all of whom obeyed). His final conclusions were very close to Büchler's, though along the way he kept saying that he was proving something stronger, more in line with traditional talmudics. Thus he wrote that the rules which he had discussed *obligated* (*ḥiyyēb*) the impure to avoid the pure.[25] His final conclusions, though, were much more modest: The Pharisees divided on the issue, some not accepting the extension of purity, and in any case the extension is not possible (see the end of Alon's essay). He several times alluded to the practical impossibility of extending purity, a most important point.

I have called it a self-contradiction to say that extending purity was both required and impossible, but that is not quite fair. Putting it this way, however, allows me to make with some force a point which those who use Alon's work should bear in mind. He wanted to prove the early *existence* of this or that halakah. The conclusions, in which he grants that people neither agreed with it nor followed it, are closer to describing actual practice. When he wrote that 'the halakah' on eating ordinary food in purity goes back to pharisaic sages, he claimed no more than that the idea had come into existence and that some people thought it to be a good one. They 'required' it in this sense. Alon was well aware that it was not generally agreed to and could not in fact be followed. Whether it was an early idea or not is another issue, but his arguments in favour of this point should not be cited by those who wish to write social history. Here his modest conclusions about what people did are more to the point. He was interested in the earliest attestation of a given halakah, as many Christian scholars are interested in the sources and origin of dogma. Finding a first-century source for a dogma does not prove that the dogma was generally held, and one should make this sort of distinction in reading Alon.[26]

It is still necessary to pay attention to his work, since he did not establish that the *idea* of Ordinary Food in Purity was widespread and early as successfully as he thought. He was, for one thing, sporadically unclear on what the *topic* is. He sometimes distinguished purity rules, at other times ran them all together, as if all equally were the extension of *priestly* laws to the laity. Here we see the consequence of his incorrect opening assumption, which has been shared by many, that the Bible applies laws of purity only to the priests or only in connection with the temple ('Levitical Cleanness', p. 190). This assumption allowed him to think that acceptance of any purity rule at all proved the desire to live like a priest. I shall illustrate the sporadic muddledness of the topic, and we shall see further inconsistencies in his argument.

Attempting to prove that 'the halakah' which required the extension of priestly laws was early, Alon cited Demai 6.6, on selling olives only to another haver (ET 218; Heb. 166). (This mishnah has to do with the problem of 'gnat-impurity', as I shall show below.) He then continued, 'Similarly' 'the halakah' is proved by a discussion between the Houses of Hillel and Shammai on handwashing at special meals (Berakoth 8.2,3). There is therefore no reason to regard Mark as mistaken, he urged, when he 'expressly testifies' that 'the Associates and many of the people were accustomed to eating their ordinary food in purity' (ET 218f.; Heb. 166).

The subject has been badly confused. Neither rule is a priestly rule applied to laity, though Alon thinks that each shows that 'the halakah' about eating secular food in purity was in force. Food contaminated by gnat-impurity (Lev. 11.32–38), we saw above, is prohibited to all alike; it is not a law that applies only to the temple or the priests. It is like the prohibition of pork, though less fiercely stated. Neither is handwashing a priestly law which has been extended to the laity. It is an innovation. Its origin, purpose and spread will occupy us below. For the sake of argument I shall grant what I think the evidence contradicts: all Pharisees practised it all the time. Let it be so. It is still not a priestly or temple law, but Alon considers it on equal footing with all the *other* (*she`ar*) rules of purity (ET 222; Heb. 168). How do these two rules support the general case? Do they prove that Pharisees avoided corpse-impurity or kept menstruants away from their food, as did the priests? They are irrelevant to the topic. Moreover, after making each proposal Alon largely retracts it. Thus after saying that we should believe Mark's statement on handwashing, he concludes that it was 'an exaggerated generalization' and that 'the halakah' was both uncertain and disputed (ET 221f.; Heb. 168).

For a moment it appears that the issue will be clarified. 'It cannot be inferred from the washing of the hands that all other laws of purity pertaining to unconsecrated foodstuff were firmly established and kept in practice' (ET 222; Heb. 168). His conclusion, however, does not pay attention to the differences among purity rules. He considers that they all constitute something called 'the halakah' and that they bear equally on the question of lay people living like priests – though two of the purity rules which he discusses, gnat-impurity and handwashing, are irrelevant.

Some of Alon's article is in favour of a very general point: that in first-century Judaism there was a positive concern for purity (section 3, ET 225–230; Heb. 169–174). This is both true and important. Unfortunately he took this evidence to prove that lay people observed the laws of purity as scrupulously as priests (ET 228; Heb. 172). He attached great weight to Philo's statement that Jews bathed after being in a room with a corpse (*Spec. Laws* 3.205–206; Alon, at n. 94). Philo is reporting what Moses wrote: 'So careful was the lawgiver . . .' At one point, however, his account is different from the actual Mosaic law: according to Philo one who enters a room where a corpse is must first be purified by bathing and washing the clothes and may not until then touch anything. Then comes the biblically pre-scribed seven days of impurity with additional rites before one can enter the temple. This shifts bathing from the end of the rite (Num. 19.19) to the beginning and gives it an independent status. One might infer that Philo was not just reporting the law, and had not accidently scrambled the passage, but was informing the reader that Diaspora Jews bathed after being in a room in which someone had died. Let us accept this (see ch. IV). The development of new purity regulations in the Diaspora is both interesting and important, and here we have an instance of it. But Philo's additional ablutions are not a priestly law; priests were to avoid corpse-impurity, not perform an extra-biblical washing after incurring it. New purity rules, while interesting for understanding Diaspora Judaism, do not prove what Alon claims – the widespread agreement that lay people should live like priests. And, of course, they do not show that Pharisees had adopted such a programme.[27]

Confusion of topic is most substantial in the discussion of the purity laws of Lev. 11.32–38, 'gnat-impurity'. Alon–like Neusner after him – took these to be purity laws which are parallel to corpse-impurity, as if they were not general prohibitions, but affected only the priests and the temple, so that if a layperson undertook to keep them, he was extending priestly purity. This is an error, one which results in confusion and wrong conclusions. The laws on 'swarming things' in Lev. 11 are, as we saw, generally binding, as are the other food laws in that chapter. The laws of Lev. 11.32–38 are harder to keep than are the laws forbidding pork and shellfish, and one can believe that fewer people heeded them; but they belong to the same category.

As has become clear, these laws are important to Pharisaism. I shall give three examples of such rules here (not necessarily from the pharisaic layer), partly to show what these discussions look like when one meets them in rabbinic material, partly to complete the review of Alon's evidence.

(a) According to Demai 2.3 (cited by Alon, n. 50), a haver will neither sell an 'am ha-'arets foodstuff which is wet or dry nor buy from him foodstuff which is wet. The distinction between *wet* and *dry* points to Lev. 11.34 any foodstuff which is wet, if a dead swarming thing falls on it, is impure and, as the sequel shows, is 'impure to you', the same phrase used of pork etc. in earlier verses. The point of the rabbinic passage is that a haver would buy from an ordinary person only foodstuff which was dry, since if it came to him wet, a dead swarming thing might already have fallen on it. He would not sell foodstuff, whether wet or dry, to someone whom he did not trust, since that person might moisten it and then expose it to dying insects.

(b) Demai 6.6 (Alon, at n. 77) is a Houses dispute: The House of Shammai maintain that a man should sell his olives only to a haver, while the House of Hillel hold that he may also sell them to one who is only trustworthy with regard to tithes. Alon and others suppose this to be an attempt to make ordinary food as pure as priestly, but in fact it is to safeguard it against the dead swarming thing. Olives, before they are ready to be pressed for their oil, ooze. Thus moist, they are susceptible to gnat-impurity. The Houses went to some trouble to be sure that they avoided it.

(c) Alon regarded his strongest rabbinic evidence as coming from T. Makshirin 3.7, 9, 10, 5, 6 (cited ET 210, 213 n. 65, 214 n. 66; referred to as important, p. 226; Heb. 161, 163 nn. 65 and 66, 171). This is 3.5: 'At first the bundles of cucumbers and gourds in Sepphoris were declared impure because they were wiped with a sponge when plucked from the ground. [Subsequently] the people of Sepphoris undertook not to do so' (T. Makshirin 3.5). Cleaning the vegetables with water, intentionally, exposed them to the impurity of Lev. 11.34.

I do not doubt that Alon, if asked, would have said immediately that Lev. 11.34 is the biblical law in question. He claimed that these passages proved that the sages forbade the defilement of common food (ET 226; Heb. 171) – which is perfectly true. But he said this in the context of arguing that *priestly* law was *extended* to the laity. For this, the passages produce no evidence at all. Applying Lev. 11 to a concrete case is not extending the priestly law.

It is worth repeating that Alon's conclusions are much more modest than the points at which he seems to aim in the heart of the essay. I am not sure that the conclusions are correct, but if one went no further one would not be saying much: *some* Pharisees observed *some* priestly food laws *some* of the time – when possible, which was not often. I shall myself argue that they first extended corpse impurity and then tried to avoid contracting it from their new sources, as a kind of gesture towards living like priests. This much, little more, can be shown by good evidence.

D. THE PHARISEES AND PRIESTLY FOOD LAWS ACCORDING TO NEUSNER

§1. The most interesting and important aspect of Neusner's work of the 70s is his effort to stratify rabbinic material. As we noted above, he first went through most of it searching for traditions attributed to named Pharisees or to the Houses of Hillel and Shammai (*Rabbinic Traditions*). Subsequently he went through the Mishnah, assigning almost every passage to a general stratum (pre-revolt, between revolts, after the second revolt). This stratification was based primarily on the logical development of each legal topic. I have only praise for this effort. He did not, of course, study every passage in great detail and come to a nuanced judgment. He did, however, make general chronological divisions which make sense.

Neusner's work in this area is to be contrasted to that of J. N. Epstein, who also stratified rabbinic material. He compiled a fairly short list of sections of the Mishnah which are pre-70 by making a range of observations, of which I give two examples. (1) Kiddushin 1.10 promises that a person who performs 'but a single commandment' will do well, will 'have length of days', and will 'inherit the land'. This is the land of Israel, as in Deut. 6.18. Epstein remarks, 'What a great distance lies between our mishnah and Aboth 5.19', which speaks of 'eating in this world' but 'inheriting' the world to come. The restriction of reward to this world in Kiddushin 1.10 points to an early date.[1]

(2) Epstein dates Bikkurim 3.1–5 early because it refers to carrying first fruits to the temple and even mentions the custom of Agrippa (whom Epstein takes to be Agrippa II).[2] I find some of Epstein's arguments convincing and some not. I am not, for example, persuaded that Sanhedrin 6.1–7.3, the discussion of the four kinds of execution, is early. Epstein thought that it must be, since forty years before the destruction of the temple the power to inflict capital punishment was taken away from the Sanhedrin.[3] He assumed that the discussion of death penalties was practical, and so thought that it must be pre-30. I think it more likely that the discussion is theoretical, and that the Mishnah's definitions of 'stoning', 'burning' and the like never controlled actual practice. The difference between rabbinic theory and real life is pointed to in Sanhedrin 7.3. My purpose here, however, is not to debate such questions point by point.

Epstein paid especial attention to what was stated anonymously (the $s^e tam$, which I shall anglicize 'stam'). In general, he viewed the anonymous layer of each tractate as the earliest form, and he attempted to attribute it to a Rabbi, primarily by finding parallels. Thus, for example, he regarded Kinnim, almost all of which is anonymous, as the 'mishnah' of R. Joshua, since some of it is attributed to R. Joshua elsewhere (e.g. Kinnim 3.3f.; cf. Zebahim 67b).[4] R. Joshua was a Levite, a member of the generation born before the destruction of the temple. According to talmudic tradition, he was at least thirty years old when the temple was destroyed.[5] We shall see below that many of the discussions which Neusner considers pharisaic are to be attributed to R. Joshua and his contemporary, R. Eliezer.[6]

Neusner generally takes the stam to be late, and thus he attributes Kinnim to the period after 140.[7] This eliminates it – and the entire topic, bird offerings – from material which might be considered pharisaic. One of the most serious weaknesses of Neusner's work is his treatment of the stam, and we shall see this at various points in the following pages.

My purpose here is not to referee between Neusner and Epstein, nor to evaluate each of their attributions. I think that both modes of analysis should be undertaken, though not by me. They require a competent Talmudist, but one who is open to Neusner's principles and methods. Perhaps when the personalities of the present day are forgotten, such a person will appear. I have assigned myself a much more modest task: the study of the topics covered by Neusner's passages. The situation as I see it is this: it is Neusner's work which, to the non-Talmudist, seems to give scientific proof for the definition of the Pharisees as a 'pure-food club'. I am persuaded that this is entirely wrong: both the conclusion overall and also Neusner's own account of the story told by his passages. Thus they are the focus of the following analysis. I shall begin by explaining what Neusner did and exemplifying the problems which one encounters, so that readers of this work will have an idea of how tentative or firm conclusions about the Pharisees may be if they are based on these passages.

As I indicated above, Neusner's approach was to accept as pharisaic passages which are attributed to a named Pharisee or to the Houses of Hillel and Shammai.[8] He argued extensively and well that attributions are generally reliable. He has later criticized those who hold this view as fundamentalists.[9] Fundamentalism is indeed a problem in the field, but nevertheless the argument that we may broadly accept attributions is sound. There was no general tendency to retroject legal rulings and to attribute them to the great figures of the past. The most-often-named Rabbi in the Mishnah is R. Judah (b. Ilai), mid-second century, not Hillel, who was considered by the Mishnah's editor and his immediate predecessors to be the founder of the right line of interpretation, nor Akiba, who was considered to be the most acute halakist of the rabbinic movement.

Stories, as distinct from legal rulings, are to be doubted. As Neusner put it, 'history might be falsified, but never law' (*Rabb. Trads.* III, p. 272). The 'never' is too strong, but it points in the right direction. It is especially telling that in some large and important areas of law (see G§1 below) there are few attributions to Pharisees or to the Schools. Thus the conclusion:

> The attributions of laws and disputes to the pre-70 Pharisees are apt in the main to be reliable, for the later rabbis evidently did not assign to pre-70 Pharisees, or to the Houses, disputes or laws on subjects about which the pre-70 Pharisees in fact did not hand on traditions. (*Rabb. Trads.* III, p. 230).

This applies, however, only to themes, not necessarily to details, which were more often altered (ibid.).

This is an extremely important point, and I shall cite three cases which illustrate the fact that there was no programatic effort to retroject legal rulings to earlier sages.

> To render such an alley-entry valid, the School of Shammai say: [It must have] both side-post and cross-beam. And the School of Hillel say: Either side-post or cross-beam . . . In the name of R. Ishmael a disciple stated before R. Akiba: The School of Shammai and the School of Hillel did not dispute about an entry less than four cubits [wide], which is valid if it has either side-post or cross-beam; but about what did they dispute?[10] – about one whose width was from four to ten cubits, which according to the School of Shammai, must have both side-beam and cross-beam, and,

according to the School of Hillel, either side-post or cross-beam. R. Akiba said: They disputed about both cases. (Erubin 1.2)

The issues of less than four cubits and between four and ten cubits had not previously been mentioned, and the insertion of this topic shows infelicitous editing. Also, the reader may be inclined to accept the view of Ishmael's student with regard to what the Houses debated rather than that of Akiba. Whatever the decision, we see a lack of editorial coercion. A disagreement between Akiba and his rival, Ishmael, about what the Houses said is openly published.

The following discussion is similar:

Whatsoever is leavened, flavoured, or mingled with Heave-offering, *Oriah*-fruit, or Diverse Kinds of the Vineyard, is forbidden. The School of Shammai say: It can also convey uncleanness. And the School of Hillel say: It can never convey uncleanness unless it is an egg's bulk in quantity. Dositheus of Kefar Yatmah was one of the disciples of the School of Shammai, and he said: I have heard a tradition from Shammai the Elder who said: It can never convey uncleanness unless it is an egg's bulk in quantity. (Orlah 2.4–5)

Here an early first-century sage is said to recall that Shammai had held the opinion just attributed to Hillel, thus making them agree. Usually the two are presented as holding contrasting views, and a consistent editorial policy would have eliminated Dositheus's comment. In the end we do not know what Shammai said on the topic, and there will always be uncertainty about this and many other details. We see, however, the relative indifference towards attributions and opinions. We cannot imagine, for example, a gospel containing such a comment about a saying of Jesus: 'Jesus said: "The Son of man is lord of the Sabbath". According to Andrew, however, he said "The Son of man always observes the sabbath".' The gospels contain internal inconsistencies, but one must search hard for a direct conflict with regard to who said what (see John 21.22–23).

The next example is more complicated. Yebamoth 15.1–2 has this sequence:

Anonymous statement
Modification by R. Judah
Conclusion by 'the Sages'
Reply by House of Hillel ('we have heard of no such tradition')
Reply by House of Shammai
Conclusion: House of Hillel accepted the position of House of Shammai

This cannot be correct: The Houses of Hillel and Shammai preceded R. Judah, and this passage has them enter a discussion after him. There is, however, a parallel in Eduyoth 1.12. The discussion follows this sequence: House of Shammai (=anonymous opinion of Yebamoth 15.1), House of Hillel (same as above), House of Shammai (same as above), and the same conclusion. It appears that the editor of Yebamoth gave the opinion of the House of Shammai as the stam, and then inserted a later comment by R. Judah. He concluded by picking up the Houses debate and quoting it.

This shows clearly that there were editorial confusions, and consequently the possibility of incorrect attribution. In arguing, with Neusner, that the attributions are in the main reliable we are not saying that they are 100% accurate. In this case a parallel in Eduyoth helps us straighten out an obvious confusion in Yebamoth. We may not always be so lucky. Despite uncertainties at this level, we see that there was no consistent effort to harmonize or to make everything come out neatly. The confusions serve as a partial guarantee on the general reliability of the material: no policy has been imposed on it.

A major issue in Rabbinic Traditions – both Neusner's work of that title and the topic itself – is the overall date and reliability of the Houses material. These passages make up the bulk of 'pharisaic' material – if they are pharisaic rather than post-70. Epstein argued that all the instances in which the House of Hillel is said to reverse its view in favour of that of the other House are really from the mishnah of R. Joshua, to whom we referred above.[11] This argument was based on parallels, instances in which the House of Hillel in one source 'reverses', while it is R. Joshua in another. Thus in Oholoth 5.3–4 the House of Hillel changes its opinion on an issue of corpse-impurity and teaches according to the House of Shammai. In T. Ahilot 5.10–11 this exchange is said to be between R. Joshua and a student of the House of Shammai. Epstein concludes, 'the one who "reversed" was R. Joshua' (p. 60). It is difficult to go through Epstein's examples without agreeing that the passages in which R. Joshua is named as an individual who accepts the House of Shammai's view are 'authentic' and that the statement that the 'House of Hillel' changed is a simplifying editorial effort. This does not, however, prove that the topic, and the disagreement on it, entirely arose post-70. On the contrary, accepting Epstein's argument that in these cases R. Joshua accepted the view of the 'House of Shammai' is perfectly compatible with thinking that the debate arose earlier. Only at the time of R. Joshua did 'the House of Hillel' reverse their view.

There are, however, post-70 traditions among the Houses material. Simply skimming it will reveal instances: thus Maaser Sheni 5.7 and T. Maas. Sh. 3.14, where 'at this time' probably means 'after the destruction of the temple'.[12] Other times, however, the Houses are evidently independent of and prior to Joshua and Eliezer (e.g. T. Arakhin 4.5). (Epstein, of course, had not claimed that they were not.)

Neusner – noting instances in which the Houses were equivalent to Eliezer (= House of Shammai) and Joshua (= House of Hillel) (e.g. *Rabb. Trads.* III, p. 201) – sought a *Sitz im Leben* for the disputes, a time in which the followers of Hillel had not yet gained ascendency over those of Shammai, and he found it in the first Yavnean generation, that is, in the first decades after 70 (ibid. II, p. 4). He also argued, on the whole satisfactorily, that the Houses really existed in pre-70 Jerusalem. The difficult fact that R. Johanan b. Zakkai himself cannot be firmly connected to them Neusner explained by proposing that, since the Houses were apparently quite small, there may have been several pharisaic circles. Johanan himself had not lived long enough to shape the Houses traditions in Yavneh after the destruction of Jerusalem (*Rabb. Trads.* III, pp. 276f.), and thus it was his disciples, Joshua and Eliezer, who are connected with the Houses debates, not R. Johanan himself. The evidence that the Houses existed before 70 is that several Houses disputes are 'verified', cited by a sage in the first post-70 generation (ibid., pp. 199–201). The assumption is that there was no wholesale pseudepigraphy: later Rabbis did not first invent the Houses dispute and then discussions of it by early Yavnean Rabbis.

Uncertainties in detail are almost the rule rather than the exception. Sometimes the stam (anonymous opinion) of the Mishnah is attributed to one of the Houses in the Tosefta.[13] Sometimes what is attributed to a House in one source is attributed to a later Rabbi in another.[14] Parallels will reveal that one source, usually the Tosefta, corrects another, usually the Mishnah, with regard to the Houses. In these cases both cannot be equally correct. A simple example is provided by Betzah 1.3//T. Yom Tov 1.8. According to the Mishnah, the Houses divided on whether or not a ladder could be moved on a festival day[15] in order to reach the dovecote. The Tosefta states that the Houses agreed that the ladder could be moved, but disagreed over whether it could be returned to its previous place.

In all such cases the particular position taken by one of the Houses is a matter of relative unimportance for our study. *We are not seeking 'pharisaic law' in the sense of requiring to know what a majority of Pharisees actually did in disputed cases. If we were, we could not discover it, since most of the Houses material consists of unresolved disagreements.* We wish to know, primarily, *what the topics were.* If we find that the Houses – even if the Houses are really Rabbis Joshua and Eliezer, just after 70 – debated the details of purity in such a way as to presuppose that they accepted the priestly laws for themselves, we shall have to conclude that they did wish to live 'like priests'. If, however, the debates are *whether or not* the purity laws applied to their own food, or if we find that they neither presuppose nor address the issue, we shall come to the opposite conclusion. Which view was held by which House is irrelevant, and the question whether or not the debate took place in the 60s or 80s is not crucial.

The rabbinic debates presuppose a lot, and the presuppositions can be analysed.[16] At a technical level, one notes that sometimes a Pharisee or one of the Houses glosses the stam. Thus in Berakoth 6.5b the stam is, 'If he said [the benediction] over the savoury he is not exempt from saying it over the bread'. This is then glossed by the House of Shammai: 'or over aught that was cooked in the pot'.[17] The House of Shammai *presuppose* that blessings at mealtime were required. Because of the uncertainties, one passage proves little, but evidence can accumulate.

The full study of this matter, again, requires a Talmudist. One would have not only to catalogue the cases in which a Pharisee or a House glosses the stam, but also find all the parallels to the anonymous opinion – which might be attributed in another source. Here there is enough work for a few doctoral theses, at the end of which we would have a collection of information which would be very valuable for defining pharisaic law and its presuppositions.

In this study I shall note only large presuppositions. Sometimes a set of presuppositions will underlie an entire tractate, including its earliest level. In Makhshirin, for example, it is simply presupposed that the words 'water be put' in Lev. 11.38 are to be applied not only to seed but also to food, thus combining vv. 34 and 38. It is further presupposed that 'be put' indicates human intention and includes a natural process which the owner of the foodstuff desired (we saw above the best example, the oozing of olives before they are pressed). Various Pharisees might have disagreed about the application of these principles, but all the surviving discussions share the same assumptions. The assumptions behind the discussions are, for our purposes, more important than the specific decisions which were based on them.

The passages discussed in what follows are those identified as 'pharisaic' in *Rabbinic Traditions*. In the last few pages I have attempted to show two ways in which the selection of passages could be improved: one could make use of Epstein's work, and one could analyse the stam when it is glossed by a Houses discussion. At the conceptual level, a study of Pharisaism should also include analysis of presuppositions behind pharisaic and other early debates. The net effect of such studies would be to expand pharisaic topics and concerns beyond those of Neusner's passages. Some of his data might be eliminated, but much more would be added. Further, the focus of 'Pharisaism' would shift. If one included such topics as Kinnim, bird sacrifices, the temple would loom larger than it does in the material which he selected. Such alterations in the data which are used would modify but not reverse the results of the present study. I shall return to the point in the conclusion.

In what follows I shall disagree with Neusner sharply. I wish all the more to emphasize at the outset that my disagreements are based on his own analytical work, without which the discussion would be impossible.

§2. Neusner made a systematic selection of the evidence, and his work on the Pharisees marks an advance over that of scholars who used any and all rabbinic material. He did not, however, reject the standard scholarly views about purity nor the faults which accompany them. The passages which Finkelstein, Jeremias and others relied on, about the haver eating food in purity (Demai 2.2–3; T. Dem. 2.2–3; 2.20–22), do not make it into Neusner's list of pharisaic passages, but he accepted all the assumptions which scholars have made who have relied on those passages. I shall specify the faults:

(*a*) Neusner – along with other scholars, Alon excepted – did not ask the significance of the fact that by no means all post-70 passages support the view that the Rabbis applied the laws of purity to themselves and their own food. We noted above that the sages did *not* accept the proposal that a haver should avoid corpse-impurity (Demai 2.3), which indicates that not all the priestly rules were followed in the second century – the date of most of the haverim passages. As Alon knew, there are a lot of passages which oppose the notion of eating ordinary food in purity. According to T. Miqva'ot 6.8 'she who discharges semen is pure for ordinary food' (cf. T. Miq. 6.7). According to 'another opinion' in T. Berakot 5.27, 'washing hands does not apply to ordinary food', and according to T. Ber. 5.13 it is optional. Parah 11.4 states that a person who was impure in a way specified by the Bible, and who had immersed himself, but upon whom the sun had not yet set (who was not, therefore, pure by biblical law), could eat not only common food but also second tithe. The next mishnah states that a person who was impure 'according to the words of the scribes' (not the Bible) could eat common food even if he had not yet immersed himself. The last two rulings are the conclusions of 'the Sages' against R. Meir, who flourished in the mid-second century. If the question of eating in purity was being debated from the middle of the second century on, we should conclude that it was not settled before 70 – especially since these debates *are not comments on earlier traditions*.

We are asked to accept as central to Pharisaism, then, a doctrine which is not *presupposed in later material*. Possibly the Rabbis were less strict than the Pharisees, but the fact that the second-century Rabbis did not presuppose what is believed to be the main point of Pharisaism should give one pause. This evidence, to repeat, is what led Alon to conclude that 'the halakah' was not agreed on by all Pharisees and was not generally accepted.

(*b*) Neusner, like many others, did not note the importance of the distinctions which the Houses made between the priests' food and their own with regard to harvesting, handling and processing it. The distinction is often expressed as a concern with the sequence of actions: at what point do we start or stop handling food in purity? Most passages about *handling* in purity deal with the period before the priests' food is separated. The chronological division in rules of handling (before/after the separation of offerings) proves that the Pharisees did not apply to ordinary food the same rules which they applied to the priests' food.

It is hard to believe, but nevertheless it is true, that many discussions of purity when handling food do not pay attention to whose food it is. I think that the explanation is that scholars have not adequately appreciated that the Bible does not require that offerings be handled in purity, and that this itself was an innovation. The fact is, as we shall see, that the Pharisees did not agree among themselves with regard to purity rules when handling the *priests'* food. Had this been seen, people would have been more careful about saying that Pharisees handled their own food in purity.

Alon, for example, granted that most passages about handling food in purity might have been about handling holy food. More precisely, he said that 'in most instances we have no means of deciding with certainty whether the reference is to unconsecrated food prepared in purity or to pure food which is heave-offering, dough-offering, or tithes'.[18] This, I think, is in error; or at least it is in error if one looks only at the Houses disputes. Alon thought of all of rabbinic literature as a whole, and I am happy to grant that, from such a perspective, the issue might look different. We shall see, however, in E§2 below, that it is easy to determine that the Houses applied 'purity' only to the priests' food. Alon did not discuss these passages at all in his essay. Had he done so, he doubtless would have seen the distinction: purity in handling the priests' food; impurity in handling their own.

Neusner looked at the passages but did not see the point. He noted that according to T. Terumot 3.12 the wine vat is rendered impure after the removal of the priests' portion,[19] but he failed to see what this meant: the rest of the wine, drunk by non-priests, was impure. He added the passage to those which proved that lay Pharisees applied purity to their own food.[20]

(*c*) Neusner, like other scholars who have discussed 'eating ordinary food in purity', did not think about it concretely enough to imagine what it would mean. He stated that a menstruant was not allowed to touch food, and that she had to change bed and chair,[21] but he did not ask who then prepared the food, where the separate furniture was kept, or who moved it and put it away after menstruation (since it would render impure anyone who touched it). He also failed to specify which types of impurity were avoided or were removed before eating. But this is a fault which the Pharisees – or, later, the Rabbis – would not have committed. *They* would have specified: 'common food must be eaten in a state of purity except in the following cases: after childbirth, etc.'. There is no such specification in early rabbinic literature. Equally absent are discussions of which funerals to attend. Since the Bible requires the priests to avoid funerals and graveyards, with a few exceptions (Lev. 21.1–3), the Pharisees – had they lived like priests – would have needed to apply this rule to themselves, and this in turn would have led to legal discussions of borderline cases. But there are none. In short, were Pharisaism based on 'secular food in purity' the Pharisees and their successors would have said so, would have clarified what they meant, and would have made exceptions when necessary. None of these conditions is fulfilled.

(*d*) The absence of positive evidence that the Pharisees ate ordinary food in purity is striking. Neusner ignored this absence in an especially remarkable way, since *his own analyses of the tractates* demonstrate it. We have just seen that he thought that the menstruant was not allowed to touch food or use her regular furniture. Yet when he analysed the tractate Niddah (The Menstruant), these supposed extensions of the laws of purity did not appear. He argued that the tractate 'began' before the turn of the first century. In describing its early stage, he stated that its principles originate in scripture and that *therefore they are not* 'conceptions distinctive to [sic!] Pharisaism or ... definitive of, the Pharisaic viewpoint'.[22] This is the bedrock of evidence on the basis of which he concluded that at the heart of Pharisaism lay the concern to eat ordinary food in priestly purity and that therefore Pharisees kept menstruants away from their food. One of the crucial tractates, his own analysis showed, does not have the ideas which in his summaries he claims to be distinctive of Pharisaism.

This is also the case with regard to other relevant tractates. Thus the assumption that the subject is 'food' dictates Neusner's conclusions on immersion pools (Mikwaoth). In the general summaries of what it all means, we find that the question which starts the topic of immersion pools was 'How to attain cleanness for the table?', and that the answer was 'rain', which (when it collected naturally in a pool) brought 'purification for the table'.[23] The table, however, is conspicuous by its absence from Mikwaoth. We read of a bed being immersed (Mikwaoth 7.7, probably from a post-70 layer), and utensils (e.g. 6.2), but not the table. The immersion of the bed does not necessarily imply 'pure food'. The immersion of vessels might have to do with ordinary food, though there is no statement to that effect. Nor are we told that the utensils are to be immersed if touched by a menstruant. The immersion of an utensil might have to do with the purity of tithes and offerings to the temple, or with the possibility that dead gnats or flies had contaminated it.

(*e*) He failed also to note the absence of the corollary rulings which would have been generated by the decision to apply purity to ordinary food. Besides such topics as what to do with the menstruant's furniture and which funerals to attend (c above), and lists of exceptions to the rule (nursing mothers are not to be put out of their own rooms/beds), one would get more discussion of the food itself: why are we, though like priests in our eating standards, allowed to eat the blemished firstlings rejected by the temple? And so on, almost forever.

(*f*) Like Alon and most other scholars, Neusner supposed that biblical purity laws applied only to the priests and the temple, so that accepting *any* purity law showed the desire to live like a priest. It is remarkable that, after describing biblical laws in ch. 1 of *The Idea of Purity in Ancient Judaism*, where it is perfectly clear that there are non-priestly and non-temple purity laws, he wrote this:

> The Pharisees, like the Dead Sea commune, believed that one must keep the purity laws outside of the temple. Other Jews, following the plain sense of Leviticus, supposed that purity laws were to be kept only in the temple. (*Idea of Purity*, p. 65)

(*g*) The most important instance of this wrong supposition is that he joined others in confusing Lev. 11 with the laws of purity which governed only the temple and the priesthood. In what appears to be a basic statement, Neusner claims that this chapter 'clearly implies that what is suitable for the altar is suitable for the table, and what is unclean for the altar makes the Israelite unclean'.[24] This is not so; the logic is faulty. It is true that 'what is suitable for the altar is suitable for the table'. The incorrect part of the statement is the second, that 'what is unclean for the altar makes the Israelite unclean'. That is so only with regard to *types* of animals: a donkey would defile both the altar and the individual who ate it. But many animals which could not be sacrificed could be eaten: for example, a blemished lamb, whose absence from the literature we have just noted. In other words, the suitability of food for an ordinary Israelite was a necessary but by no means sufficient condition for its acceptibility by the priests. Lev. 11 does not equate the altar and the ordinary table: it simply excludes some animals from both. What *positively* made food suitable for the priests was another matter. The full analogy between the altar and the common table which Neusner proposes is neither implied in Leviticus nor specified in pharisaic material.

Having made, on the basis of misreading Lev. 11, a false equation between food for the altar and for the common table, he naturally pressed on and made the parallel equations: people had to be as pure as priests in order to eat;[25] the food had 'to be prepared and consumed in a state of cultic cleanness'. The tables themselves had to be as pure 'as the table of the Lord in the Temple'.[26]

None of this has any support whatsoever. For example, the purity of the altar required the sacrifice of a bull and a goat on the Day of Atonement (Lev. 16.18f.). In pharisaic/rabbinic material there is no replacement purity rite for the table.

Neusner's conclusions about ordinary food and purity are rivalled for lack of nuance and judgment only by Ta-Shma on the menstruant. Neusner set out to provide a critical account in distinction from traditional and fundamentalist Talmudics. He succeeded, in a much larger and more difficult body of literature, in establishing some of the rules of critical judgment which govern biblical studies. By this standard, Alon was less than fully critical. Yet Alon took account of contrary opinions within the literature, and he also thought realistically enough to know that the laws of purity could not be fully applied to ordinary people and their ordinary food. Neusner stratified and organized the material better than previous scholars – and then ignored his own analyses in favour of the conclusions of the most uncritical Talmudists.

This constitutes a minor academic tragedy, but the analytic part of his work remains promising and should be explored.

§3. The most misleading part of Neusner's work is his counting of passages. We have seen that he and others have tended to run purity laws together, as if washing their hands could prove that Pharisees would not eat with menstruants. Neusner goes well beyond this: he considers that almost everything under the sun counts as 'secular food in purity'.

Near the conclusion of *Rabbinic Traditions*, he summarized his results thus:

> Of the 341 individual pericopae alluded to above, no fewer than 229 directly or indirectly pertain to table-fellowship, approximately 67% of the whole. The rest are scattered through all other areas of legal concern, a striking disproportion.[27]

A few pages later he characterized the 67% as covering 'the fitness of food for Pharisaic consumption'.[28] The immediate context of this statement is a summary of the Houses debates, but he intends it to cover pharisaic law in general. This conclusion, if true, might seem definitively to settle the issue of the Pharisees, food and purity.

(*a*) The first thing to be said is that the summary is erroneous and seriously misleading. By no means 67% of the Houses debates (or of the pharisaic laws) have to do with 'table-fellowship', and especially not with secular food in purity. In E§10 below, I shall discuss the three passages which directly deal with the topic (though they do not say that Pharisees fully lived like priests).[29] Using Neusner's total number, this is .8% of the whole, slightly less than 1/100. Neusner, to be sure, wrote 'indirectly'; but this too is inaccurate. The passages which he counted, for the most part, are completely unrelated to what he called 'the sectarian topic' of ordinary food in purity. One might find a half-dozen passages which could be described as indirectly related.

Before considering the table of Houses disputes which accompanies Neusner's statistical conclusion, let us move one step earlier and take the cases of Shammai and pre-Hillelite Pharisees (excluding, that is, Hillel himself, so as to avoid complexities which are irrelevant to the present point). The overall argument in this section of Neusner's work is that the pharisaic laws reflect the party's 'sectarianism'. There were, he stated, two points which made the Pharisees a sect: ordinary food in purity and their different laws of tithing 'and other agricultural taboos'. The second point he regarded as less certain.[30] This means that the weight of the argument that the Pharisees were a sect falls on their eating ordinary food in purity. He then listed the topics of pharisaic debates. To pre-Hillelite Pharisees he attributed principally 'purity rules, Temple rites, agricultural taboos'. He continued, 'Only the marriage-contract stands outside of the sectarian framework' (p. 290). One immediately pauses: the temple rites, which, he showed, are very prominent among the legal traditions attributed to Pharisees before Hillel and Shammai,[31] are not 'sectarian' rules about ordinary food. They include the major controversy over whether or not to lay one's hand on the head of a sacrifice brought on a festival day. Sacrifices are holy food. The agricultural taboos/purity rules include such passages as T. Makshirin 3.4: Joshua b. Perahiah said that wheat from Alexandria is susceptible to purity because the baling machine throws water on it[32] – Lev. 11 one more time. Do *any* of the pre-Hillelite passages deal with purity when eating ordinary food? No, not one. It is not just the marriage contract which is outside the 'sectarian' topic, but all of the debates: every single one.

For Shammai Neusner listed rulings on these topics:

sabbath observance	phylacteries
heave offering	second tithe
uncleanness	ploughing in the seventh year
uncleanness from a bone	observance of Sukkot and Yom
liability of an agent for mis-	Kippur by children
deeds on behalf of another	

He then commented that only the issue of the dishonest agent is 'outside the pattern' (of the 'sectarian' framework).[33] This is simply baffling. Heave offering, second tithe, sabbath, sabbatical year, phylacteries – these have nothing to do with eating food in purity – except, of course, heave offering and second tithe, but these are not *ordinary* food.

What Neusner did is quite simple: after defining 'sectarian' as requiring laws on ordinary food in purity, he changed the topic long enough to count, and then he said that the count bore on the opening definition; but it does not do so. In the end he counted any food or any purity discussion as bearing on the 'sectarian issue', when all but a small handful have no relationship to it. Eating Passover in purity has *no* relation, direct or indirect, to eating ordinary food. Planting more than one crop in the same field bears *neither* directly *nor* indirectly on the purity of food. Misplanting is a transgression; it does not render the food impure.[34] Leaving a 'forgotten sheaf' behind for the poor is not a sectarian food law – not even indirectly. And so on and on through the entire list. Detailed evidence that passages have been inappropriately categorized will be presented after we address the problem of counting to determine importance.

(*b*) Neusner's statement that 67% of the Houses passages bear on secular food eaten in purity is not true, nor is the description of pre-Houses passages. But what if he had accurately described them? In the last chapter in this volume I address more largely the genre of rabbinic halakic discussions. Here I shall say briefly only that the discussions are legal in character and therefore treat in greatest detail the most difficult parts of law. Counting the number of passages on each topic will reveal difficulty, not necessarily significance, since the most difficult parts are seldom the most important. We shall see below that the Pharisees paid great attention to the laws of dead swarming things in Lev. 11, but *no* attention to pork, hares and vultures. The reason is that on the big items there was nothing to debate. The biblical exclusions are absolutely clear, and only more extensive travel could have revealed difficulties (e.g. the classification of the hippopotamus and giraffe). The problems created by gnats and flies required discussion. It would be wrong, however, to conclude that they cared a great deal for the gnat and fly laws, but nothing at all for those on pork and cats. Yet that is the conclusion to which counting leads.

Above I argued that pharisaic silence on secular food in purity, and especially on the corollary laws which such a rule would entail, counts against the notion that they made it a central concern. I now argue that silence on pork and cats proves that they took the laws for granted and did not need to discuss them. Silence points one way in one case, and another in another, because of the nature of the material. It discusses details of application. Major laws which are in the Bible, and about which there are few complications, did not need detailed discussion about how to apply them. But extensions of the law beyond the Bible would generate the very kind of discussions which the Mishnah and the Tosefta offer in abundance on points other than ordinary food in purity. Silence must be construed quite differently in one case than in the other. Grey areas, borderline cases and extensions or amendments of biblical law are precisely the sorts of things discussed extensively by the Pharisees and Rabbis.

Numerous rulings inevitably arise in such cases: we noted above that this does not mean that borderline cases were more important than the Ten Commandments (I.B; see further below).

Neusner's count, which has appeared to so many to settle the question of the central point of Pharisaism, fails in every way. It is wildly inaccurate; if accurate it would not prove what he claimed.

§4. I shall now show in more detail how Neusner mis-categorized passages and consequently misinterpreted the basis of Pharisaism. This essay, however, is not so organized as to answer the question, 'what was most central to Pharisaism?' To do that we should have to analyse what the Pharisees presupposed. Neusner's work provides quite a lot of information about their presuppositions, but a good deal more work needs to be done, work which I hope other people will do. I intend to deal primarily with the topic of secular food in purity, but in order to do that I need to show in detail that Neusner mis-categorized vast tracts of rabbinic discussion. Showing this involves explaining one or more topics which are actually irrelevant to food and purity. This task is, however, to be welcomed, for pursuing it will allow some illustrative material to be introduced on topics about which they thought a great deal: Work, Agriculture and Charity.

(a) If one counts Neusner's pharisaic passages, the largest category is Work. While I do not think that counting settles the question of what was most important, for the sake of this exercise I shall engage in it. Counting is actually quite complicated. Neusner said that he counted pericopes, but one would better count rulings or debates (some pericopes have more than one debate, some debates extend over more than one pericope). Then there is the issue of parallels; Neusner counted a lot of discussions twice. Parallels, however, are not always in perfect agreement. What does one count in the case of a correction or a partial variant? If I really cared about counting, I would have sorted out these problems, devised a decimal system to take care of partial parallels, and presented a statistical table. I decided against it. I counted instead separate rulings or debates in the Houses material in the Mishnah. Taking only the Mishnah excludes most parallels and overlaps. There are, in Neusner's list of Houses passages, a total of two hundred mishnaic debates.

Of these, seven are on work during sabbatical years, nine on work on the sabbath, and twenty-one on work during festival days. These come in the main tractates which deal with work: Shebiith (the seventh year), Shabbath (the sabbath day), Erubin (altering the limitations on walking and carrying on the sabbath) and Betzah (festival days). In other tractates (Maaseroth, Pesahim and Hagigah) there are three more on work in connection with holy days: a total of forty, 20% of the total. This is far and away the largest single topic, and my lists indicate that this would hold good if one carried out a full statistical analysis.

The tractate Betzah deserves special mention. In Neusner's subsequent work on the history of mishnaic law, Betzah is singled out as the only tractate in the division Moed (Appointed Times: recurring holy days) which can be considered pre-70 with regard to 'the fundamental ideational structure, generative conception, or problem';[35] that is, it is a topic which the Pharisees worked through so thoroughly that its direction and general structure were not changed post-70. Surely, then, it was an important pharisaic topic, and Neusner's significant, though neglected, analytical work has shown it to be so.[36]

We recall from I.B above that festival days are like the sabbath, in that work is prohibited, but unlike it, since there is a major exception: work which produces food for that day is permitted. We further recall that the large number of attributed pharisaic debates on this topic results from its complexity, not its importance: festival days get more debates than the sabbath, not because they were more important, but because the topic is complicated. Finally, let us recall the major debate: can hands be laid on a sacrifice on a festival day? One of the sacrifices in dispute was the peace offering. Now let us ask whether or not this topic, which Neusner counted as the 'sectarian' issue of ordinary food in purity, actually falls under that category. It does not. The discussion of peace offerings has to do with *food*, but it is not ordinary food. Nor is the topic, 'What food is suitable for Pharisees to eat?' It is, rather, 'What work may be done on a festival day?'

The general topic of Betzah is work and food. This is the subject set by the biblical texts. Because of the 'food' half of the topic, Neusner included Betzah (and numerous passages about food and work in other tractates) in his count of ordinary food in purity. But these passages are related neither directly nor indirectly to ordinary food and priestly purity, nor even to the vaguer concern which Neusner attributes to the Pharisees, 'table-fellowship'. They were included only because of his unannounced change of topic when making his count.

(*b*) Another large topic is agriculture, especially rules governing planting. The Bible prohibits sowing two kinds of seeds in 'your field' (Lev. 19.19), or in 'your vineyard' (Deut. 22.9). People who planted naturally wanted to know just what this meant. Surely one should not take Lev. 19.19 to mean 'in any two plots owned by you', since that would make each farmer dependent entirely on one crop. It was necessary to define a 'field' so as to allow a reasonable mixture of crops:

If he would lay out his field in plots each bearing a different kind [of crop], the School of Shammai say: [Between each he must leave a space equal to] three furrows of ploughed land. And the school of Hillel say: The width of a Sharon yoke. (Kilaim 2.6)

The editor notes that 'the opinion of the one is not far from the opinion of the other'. Still, it had to be sorted out. Some rule had to be devised in order to meet the problem of Lev. 19.19, and when farmers went out to mark their plots for planting, they had to put the stakes *somewhere*. It was as easy to do it 'right' as 'wrong'.

This topic has to do with food, and many think of it as a purity law. We noted above (pp. 139f.) that technically this is not correct: the purity/impurity terminology does not occur. Leaving this aside, we note that observing the rules about planting does not touch the issues of with whom one eats (table-fellowship) and whether or not ordinary food must be handled and eaten in a state of purity. On the contrary, if Deut. 22.9 is transgressed, the food is no longer ordinary, but is 'sanctified'; that is, it is forfeited to the temple and is to be eaten by the priests! Obeying the law does not keep the food pure: it allows it to be eaten by quite impure non-priests. Planting has financial conse-quences because the ways around Lev. 19.19 require space. But the purity of the person and of the food when it is consumed is not an issue, nor is this a temple or priestly law applied to common life. Priests were not supposed to work the soil.

Numerous other agricultural rulings have to do with charity, such as how much to leave behind after reaping. One charity discussion is directly related to the question of different plots: If plots were sown between rows of olive trees, should one give charity (leave gleanings) from each separate patch of land (Peah 3.1)?

Neusner made an effort to justify the change of topic from 'eating common food in purity and only with others who are pure' to 'any discussion of purity' and 'any discussion which touches on food'. The effort, rather than helping, made things worse. 'And the agricultural laws, just like the purity rules, in the end affected table-fellowship, namely what one might eat.'[37] Confusion mounts: 'table-fellowship' is *with* whom, not *what food*. In any case the rules about planting, charity and work on festival days affect neither.

The shift to 'any discussion about purity' and 'anything related to food' brought a lot of the Mishnah, quite incorrectly, under the headings 'table-fellowship' and 'sectarian pattern', since a great deal of the Mishnah has to do with food. As Neusner has pointed out, the main actors envisaged in much of the Mishnah are small landowners,[38] who were engaged in growing, handling and selling food. The Mishnah also covers household rules, and so it takes up preparing food. Further, it deals with temple issues, and thus with sacrifices (some of which go for food), tithes and offerings – more food. None of this, however, has anything to do with (1) table-fellowship, the issue of who eats with whom (except in the case of holy food), nor (2) the purity of ordinary food nor (3) the purity of people who eat ordinary food.

§5. We have seen rather a lot of things wrong with Neusner's work, sometimes faults shared with many others. Because of the length of the list I shall summarize the principal points of the present section:

> Numerous post-pharisaic passages show that it had not already been decided that laypeople should observe the priestly laws of purity. Even the second-century haverim passages do not maintain that position in detail (D§2.a).

> Most pharisaic passages which discuss handling food in purity have to do with tithes and offerings for the priesthood, not ordinary food (D.§2.b).

> It would be impossible for lay families to eat ordinary food in purity (D§2.c).

> Key tractates (e.g. Niddah and Mikwaoth) do not contain the rules which it is supposed should be central to them (D§2.d).

> We have neither the corpus of corollary rules which would have been required had the Pharisees intended to maintain priestly purity (e.g. exceptions to the rule), nor discussions of why they are allowed to eat food forbidden to the priests (blemished animals) (D§2.c,e).

> The laws of Lev. 11, which are often discussed, are not altar laws which are applied to lay food (D§2.f).

> Neusner's count is erroneous; if accurate it would not prove the case (§3).

> In §4 it was shown in detail that passages which Neusner included in the 'sectarian' issue of the Pharisees' own food almost always deal with quite different subjects, such as Work.

We shall now work our way through the pharisaic discussions of purity to see what they were actually about. Before we plunge in, an apology may be in order. The analysis of rabbinic (including pharisaic) law is difficult, probably the most difficult topic in the study of ancient Judaism. This is so, not because the material is especially difficult as legal discussions go, for it is not, but because any ancient and foreign legal corpus is at first difficult. In order to evaluate competing views about the Pharisees, however, we must deal with concrete issues and the legal debates about them, and I shall present the material in enough detail to allow the reader to assess it as evidence.

E. PHARISAIC PURITY DEBATES

Although purity does not play the role in pharisaic material which Neusner would have us believe, it is important, and the Pharisees were interested in it. Since the primary question is whether or not they imitated *priestly* purity, we shall begin with the form of impurity which priests were supposed to avoid, corpse-impurity. Consideration of this topic and the next (handling the priests' food, §2) will disprove the theory which we are testing. The further topics will lend support, but I wish to press on and give a positive account of pharisaic purity concerns, using the passages which Neusner selected. The selection of passages is not perfect, but I think that it is useful. Since he is the only one who has based a definition of Pharisaism on this material, and since he misdescribed it, a fresh examination is needed.

§1. Corpse-impurity. We shall see that the Pharisees were concerned to define corpse-impurity and to extend it, but the reasons must be carefully assessed. There are several possible motives for their doing so:

1. The extensions could have been unconscious. Laws sometimes mean things to one generation which they did not mean when written.

2. They may have been concerned to define corpse-impurity for biblical reasons: to be sure they did not enter the temple or eat Passover when corpse-impure. A slight extension of biblical law would lead them to avoid handling food for the priesthood when they had corpse-impurity. We shall take up rules about handling the priests' food in §2.

3. It is theoretically possible that they tried to avoid contracting corpse-impurity. Three possible motives come to mind: possibly they wished to be able to enter the temple on short notice; or they wished to imitate the priesthood, at least partially; or they sought a higher than normal degree of purity *for its own sake*. In the absence of an explicit statement of motive, it might prove impossible to distinguish among these. Here I wish to make two points. First, we do not have explicit statements of motive. Scholars often discuss the topic as if the Pharisees or Rabbis quote Exodus 19.6, 'a kingdom of priests', as giving their motive for trying to be pure;[1] but they do not do so. All motives are conjectural on our part; the sources give us none. Second, the third possibility, purity for its own sake, existed and was important. It should not be neglected when one is searching for motives.

4. Possibly they wished to live in seclusion from others and from normal impurity, creating in their own houses a substitute temple, and considering themselves the only true people of God. We shall see that this, the common interpretation, is the one which may be ruled out.

We shall now take up the passages:

(*a*) We notice, first, instances in which corpse-impurity is closely defined, without any obvious intention of going beyond biblical law. Numbers 19.11–22 discusses it in terms of a body lying in a 'tent', because of the narrative convention that the laws were given in the wilderness (e.g. Num. 1.1). Two questions immediately arise: What is a 'corpse'? What is a 'tent'?

The Houses of Hillel and Shammai debated the question of how much of a person's body constituted a 'corpse', a question not directly asked by the Bible, but an obvious one to raise. There are numerous discussions about how large a part of a dead body must be to cause corpse-impurity: Oholoth 2.3; Eduyoth 1.7; T. Shabbat 1.18 (=the stam in Oholoth 16.1); T. Ahilot 3.4 (cf. stam in Oholoth 2.1).

With regard to what counted as a 'tent', they discussed the case of two houses joined by a common roof, disagreeing slightly (Oholoth 11.1). A commoner problem would have been the upper room. Since biblical law was couched in terms of a tent, it naturally did not take into account a two-storey house, and discussion was required. The Pharisees took up the almost metaphysical question of the ability of corpse-impurity to travel. If there was a crack in the hatch between the lower room and the upper, how big would it have to be to allow corpse-impurity to penetrate (T. Ahilot 12.1)? What if, on the hatchway between the lower house and the upper room, there was a pot with a hole in it? Could the impurity go through the pot to the upper room (Oholoth 5.2)? If the pot had no hole, did it protect the upper room and its contents (5.3)? (For impurity in the upper room see also Oholoth 5.4; T. Ahilot 5.11.)

The third biblical topic is 'vessels' or 'utensils' (*kelîm*).[2] Numbers 19.15 states that open vessels which are in the same room as a corpse become impure. This led to the assumption that a stopped-up vessel protected what was in it, but details had to be resolved (e.g. Kelim 9.2; T. Ahilot 15.9; cf. stam Oholoth 15.9). In connection with vessels there was further discussion about the ability of corpse-impurity to travel. What if a vessel had a lid, but a chain attached the lid to the vessel? Could impurity travel along the chain, bypass the lid and enter the vessel (Parah 12.10; T. Parah 12.18)? The academic nature of this enquiry is seen in the remarkable discussion of Oholoth 11.8: Imagine that, within the house wherein lay a corpse, there was (1) a cistern in which there was (2) a candlestick which partially projected above the rim of the cistern, over which (3) stood a basket of olives. Would the corpse-impurity travel from cistern via candlestick to olives? The Houses disagreed (Oholoth 11.8). Posing the question probably helped clarify other problems.

(*b*) The passages just discussed begin with questions set by the biblical text, but they press on to incorporate a post-biblical idea: that impurity travels.[3] We do not know whether or not only Pharisees had it, but it led to major expansions of what was made impure by a corpse. Asking about the spread of corpse-impurity was a natural clarification of biblical law when one had an upper room or when it was doubtful whether or not a lid truly sealed the contents of a vessel. The notion of travelling, however, led to discussions of situations not envisaged in the Bible at all. I shall exemplify this very important extension of corpse-impurity:

1. It could escape through a hole or opening (Oholoth 13.1,4; 15.8; T. Ahilot 14.4).

2. The Houses also discussed the entrances to the room where the corpse lay. According to the anonymous opinion of Oholoth 7.3, all doors and doorways were impure *unless* there was *intention* to take the corpse out through one of them, in which case the other entrances were pure (cf. T. Ahilot 8.7). The Houses disagreed as to whether or not the intention must have preceded death, but in either case we see here a major pharisaic innovation: impurity sometimes depends on human intention.

3. The Pharisees were concerned that people should not walk over ground which contained a corpse, or part of one, inadvertently, and they discussed what grounds need be examined for parts of corpses. Gentiles were suspected of hiding abortions, not burying them properly, and so the Houses considered examining the drains and dunghills around the former residence of a Gentile (Oholoth 18.8; on searching see also T. Ahilot 16.6).

4. This points to a substantial expansion of the rules of corpse-impurity which the Pharisees either made or accepted: anything which a corpse *overshadows* is impure, anything which overshadows a corpse is impure. This non-biblical notion, while not unique to the Pharisees (see pp. 34f.), greatly extends the area of corpse-impurity, especially when combined with the idea that impurity travels along connectives:

> If a baking-oven stood within the house and it had an arched outlet that projected outside, and corpse-bearers overshadowed it [with the corpse], the School of Shammai say: All becomes unclean. The School of Hillel say: The oven becomes unclean but the house remains clean. (Oholoth 5.1)

Similarly it was discussed whether or not a man who leaned out of a window and overshadowed a corpse conveyed impurity to the house (11.4; cf. 11.3,5,6).

Thus far we have seen only a concern for definition: where is corpse-impurity and where not? Some of these discussions seem to me to be entirely academic. In addition to the question of the cistern, candlestick and basket of olives (Oholoth 11.8), we might cite Oholoth 11.4, on the man who leaned out of a window and so overshadowed a corpse. This is a likely enough situation, but the discussion was expanded to the questions of whether or not he was wearing clothing and whether or not he could convey impurity to a man leaning out of a window above him – who could in turn convey impurity to his 'tent'. We see here the typical desire to make definitions so thoroughly that all *conceivable* possibilities are covered, at least in principle.

We also see an expansion of world view. That impurity travels in the way assumed by the Pharisees is a post-biblical idea, but it became central in many pharisaic discussions. Further, the idea of human intention, greatly and correctly emphasized by Neusner, is original to the Pharisees as far as we know. Thus even when they are only *defining* or *clarifying* biblical law, they are operating with some post-biblical categories.

We do not thus far know that Pharisees tried to avoid corpse-impurity. We may be confident that they did not avoid corpse-impurity of the most obvious and biblical kind: that contracted by being in the room with a dead person and caring for the body. They would also not have avoided one of the new sources of corpse-impurity, overshadowing, if the overshadowing came from their accompanying the body of a dead relative or acquaintance to the graveyard. We shall see below that priests and their families mourned in a field next to the graveyard. This implies that others mourned within the graveyard thus incurring corpse-impurity by overshadowing. These impurities are actually *required* by piety. We saw above the passage in which Josephus wrote that people who pass by a funeral cortège are expected to join in mourning (*Apion* 2.205), and there are several talmudic passages which say approximately the same thing (e.g. Ketubot 17a; Berakot 18a). This probably represents the general custom of Palestinian laity, and there is no hint that Pharisees avoided the pious duty of becoming corpse-impure. This means that they did not live like priests, since priests were commanded to avoid corpse-impurity for all but the next of kin (Lev. 21.1–3).

What about the new forms of corpse-impurity, those which come from remote or accidental sources (a corpse overshadows a stove vent and thus renders the house impure)? Probably Pharisees sought to avoid them. We are never told this directly, nor are we given any motives for the avoidance of corpse-impurity. There are, however, some points to be noted: (1) The extremely careful definition of where corpse-impurity is and is not probably encouraged caution. When someone was dying, one should make sure that the vessels were securely stoppered, that there were no undesired holes in the walls and that the eventual door of egress had been designated. One should not have an oven which projected out of the house into an alley or street down which a corpse might be carried. This, at least, we may take to be the point of the concern to define. (2) The simple reading of Num. 19.12 is that it positively commands people to rid themselves of corpse-impurity: 'he shall purify himself with water on the third day and on the seventh day . . .' It is true that the penalty is only for defiling the temple (19.20), but those who looked carefully would find a command to purify themselves after a death. From here it would be an easy step to the view that new sources of corpse-impurity should be avoided. The next points show that at least some people drew both conclusions. (3) In a passage which we encounter several times in this study, Josephus wrote that Tiberias was built over a former graveyard, and he added that this made it 'contrary to the law and tradition of the Jews' (*Antiq.* 18.38). This may have been because of the insult to the dead, but in the context, which refers to seven days' impurity, the statement probably means that Josephus regarded it to be against the law to contract corpse-impurity unnecessarily. (4) In *Antiq.* 3.262 Josephus wrote that the law requires one who remains corpse-impure for more than seven days to sacrifice two lambs – a rule that is not in the Bible. This probably reflects reading Num. 19.12 as a positive commandment which should not be transgressed. Being free of corpse-impurity was considered good, and the Pharisees, along with others, considered purity to be good for its own sake.

We may conclude that, as did others, they sought to avoid unnecessarily contracting corpse-impurity, and that they especially tried to avoid its new sources. It is to be noted that the new sources of the impurity are not connected to the pious requirement to care for the dead; they are either accidental or at one remove from personal contact or both. It is one thing to make sure that your vessels are securely stoppered. It would be quite another to refuse to mourn a married sister or an uncle, which is what the law requires of priests.

Although the material which we have seen does not contain the explicit statement, 'Avoid the corpse-impurity' or 'Throw away the contents of the unstoppered vessel', we may infer them.

(*c*) Pharisees and food in the room with a corpse. This is a difficult topic, and I shall give the principal passage in full.

An earthenware vessel can protect aught [that is within it from contracting uncleanness from a corpse that is under the same roof]. So the School of Hillel. And the School of Shammai say: It can protect only foodstuffs and liquids and [other] earthenware vessels. The School of Hillel said: Why? The School of Shammai said: Because with an *Am-haaretz* it is susceptible to uncleanness, and a vessel that is susceptible to uncleanness cannot interpose [to protect from uncleanness]. The School of Hillel answered: but have ye not pronounced the foodstuffs and liquids therein clean? The School of Shammai said to them: When we pronounced the foodstuffs and liquids therein clean, we pronounced them clean for himself [the ordinary person alone]; but when thou declarest the vessel clean thou declarest it so for thyself as well as for him. The School of Hillel changed their opinion and taught according to the opinion of the School of Shammai. (Eduyoth 1.14)

The Bible states that 'Every open vessel (*kᵉlî*), which has no cover fastened upon it, is unclean' if in a 'tent' with a corpse (Num. 19.15). So why are the Houses debating this particular pot? As the discussion makes clear, the pot belongs to an 'am ha-'arets, and the Pharisees had to assume that his pot was already impure for some other reason (from dead insects or a zav), and thus that it should already have been broken. The passage says that the vessel was *susceptible* to impurity, and 'susceptible' points to fly-impurity (see below, p. 201). Since the Pharisees did not trust the ordinary people to keep utensils free of fly-impurity, they assumed that it was contaminated and thus could not, from their own point of view, interpose to protect things which were in it from corpse-impurity. It could interpose against corpse-impurity for the 'am ha-'arets' food, but the Pharisees thought that his food was already contaminated with fly-impurity (or, less likely, zav-impurity). The Pharisees, the passage presupposes, will not eat the 'am ha-'arets' food – or at least not what is kept in an earthenware vessel – and the passage serves to declare the *vessel* impure. That is: if the Hillelites maintained that *they* could eat food which had been in a pot inside a room with a corpse in an 'am ha-'arets' house, they would be implying that the pot itself was pure – or, rather, would be pure after it had been sprinkled twice with the special mixture of ashes and water. The Shammaites persuaded them that they had to consider the pot impure *on other grounds*; it needed to be broken and not cleansed of corpse-impurity.

There is a related debate: if a sound pot (one without a hole) was over a hatchway which separated a room with a corpse from an upper room, did the pot interpose to prevent corpse-impurity from entering the upper room and contaminating its contents? The Shammaites argued that the pot protected only food, liquids and other earthenware vessels, and the Hillelites finally agreed (Oholoth 5.2–3). The issue is the same: the house and pot belong to an 'am ha-'arets. The Shammaites persuade the Hillelites that this pot (which should already have been broken) protects from corpse-impurity only things which Pharisees are not going to borrow or buy from an 'am ha-'arets anyway. That is, the pot protects them for the

ʾam ha-ʾarets. They do not need to be sprinkled.

With regard to our topic, these debates presuppose that the Pharisees would not eat food which had contracted corpse-impurity. That, however, they saw as the supposition of the biblical law on corpses. Everything in a room with a corpse, except for a closed vessel, is impure and requires sprinkling (Num. 19.14–19), and they read the passage as meaning that a closed vessel protected what was in it. They assumed that the ʾamme haʾarets agreed: they too worried about getting things into closed vessels or into an upper room protected by a vessel when a death was imminent. The Pharisees feared that the ʾamme ha-ʾarets would use a vessel into which a dying fly had fallen. They granted that the ordinary people protected themselves from impurity *by their own lights*, but that on some points they were not reliable, especially with regard to earthenware vessels. We shall see in section F that the Pharisees regarded the ordinary people as being reliable in the handling of holy food.

We also note that the Houses did not suppose that their rules should be imposed on others. They stayed away from the food and earthenware vessels of the ordinary people, but they did not 'decree' that the ordinary people had all sorts of impurities and could not enter the temple.

Finally, all the laws which figure in these passages apply in the Bible to one and all: they are not priestly. It is post-biblical interpretation to say that a closed vessel protects what is in it, so that the contents do not require sprinkling to remove corpse-impurity, but the general law about sprinkling for corpse-impurity applies to all Jews, and the rule about the contents of a closed vessel is a fair inference from the Bible. Similarly the Pharisees' worry about earthenware vessels which belonged to ordinary people had to do with biblical impurities which affect everyone's vessels, not just the priests': being touched by a zav (Lev. 15.12) and being contaminated by a dead swarming thing (Lev. 11.32f.).

(*d*) I shall now try to draw conclusions about Pharisees and corpse-impurity:

1. Pharisees had a special interest in corpse-impurity. Their world view, which included the conception that impurity could travel in ways not envisaged in the Bible, led them to see it as affecting houses and people which overshadowed (or were overshadowed by) a corpse. Foodstuff and vessels in a room above the 'tent' where the corpse lay might contract the impurity.

2. The principal reason for defining the spread of corpse-impurity could have been concern about entering the temple. One should know whether or not one had it to avoid a grave violation.

3. Since they accepted that they should be pure when handling the priests'

food (§2 below), they may have wished to avoid corpse-impurity to protect the priesthood.

4. The special concern for corpse-impurity may have been influenced by the fact that the Houses were located in Jerusalem. Not only might members wish to be able to enter the temple on short notice, they probably also thought that Jerusalem should be kept purer than the outlying areas. The idea of concentric circles of purity is basically biblical,[4] but it was elaborated during the period of the second temple. Palestine is purer than Gentile lands, Jerusalem purer than the rest of Palestine,[5] and the temple purer yet; within the temple were five degrees of purity (Gentiles, Israelite women, ordinary Israelites, priests, the high priest on the Day of Atonement). Corpse-impurity, above all others, was to be kept away from the temple. The idea of concentric circles and the emphasis on corpse-impurity were not peculiar to the Pharisees. It may have been their contribution to try to extend the area in which corpse-impurity was kept to a minimum. We may note an analogous case: the Essenes prohibited sexual relations within Jerusalem (CD 12.1f.; 11QTemple 45.11f.).

5. The evidence does not show that Pharisees accepted the Bible's priestly purity laws for themselves. On the contrary, it proves that they did not do so. We are told that they intended to define a certain door as the one through which a corpse would be carried – not that they would not go in through that or any other door, and not that they would not lean against the outside frame of the door. We do not hear that they left their houses before the death of a relative, that they refused to care for the dead or that they did not attend burials. If such rules existed, they would reveal an actual effort to live like priests. The opportunity for saying so was there, but it was bypassed.

6. Nevertheless the careful concern for definition of corpse-impurity must imply some sort of behaviour. We may say that they tried to avoid accidental and indirect corpse-impurity. If one knew where it had travelled, one would not inadvertently use an impure utensil or eat impure food.

7. There is a better way of combining (5) and (6): *the accidental sources of the impurity which they wished to avoid they had first to create.* This procedure of creation and avoidance is probably important. To avoid the biblical sources of corpse-impurity would have meant not being good citizens and loyal members of the family. The restrictions on priests were scriptural, and so no blame attached to them when they did not come to the funeral of an uncle or brother-in-law. For the lay Pharisees, however, living like priests would have meant excluding themselves voluntarily from normal family and civic life, and they had no wish to do this. Had they done it, it would have brought blame from the community, and we should hear that they were misanthropists (and so on). Instead of avoiding corpse-impurity as defined by the Bible, they

extended it and then avoided some of the extensions. This probably shows that their reasons were pious; that is, they wished to be especially pure.

8. Since the issue is corpse-impurity, above all a priestly and temple law, we may view their careful extension and avoidance as a *minor symbolic gesture towards* 'living like a priest'. They could live partially 'like priests' in their own minds, while not accepting the anti-social aspects of the priestly law. To symbolize that life they chose to make a few small gestures towards living like priests, taking on by no means the full range of prohibitions which governed the priests' lives.

How minor the gesture was should be emphasized. We have seen that modern scholars find it easy to think that small extensions of the purity laws meant that the Pharisees in their own houses lived like priests in the temple. This shows our lack of imagination. The lay Pharisees *knew* what priests' lives were like, and they did not for one minute confuse themselves with priests. Priests could not work the land, while Pharisees[6] could and many did; priests could enter the court of the priests and eat the most holy things, Pharisees could not; priests always, or almost always, immersed before sunset, Pharisees did not; priests wore square beards,[7] Pharisees did not; there were restrictions on priests' marriage partners which did not apply to others – and so on. The entire way of life of the priesthood was different from that of the laity, and lay people who lived in a society where there were functioning priests would never have thought that they lived 'like priests'.

We shall see in the next section, §2, discussions of searching mourners' fields for corpses, so that priests and their families, and people who were to eat Passover, would not contract corpse-impurity. This reveals very concretely that the Pharisees did not put themselves on a par with the priesthood. They did not employ 'amme ha-'arets to search fields to keep pieces of corpse out of their (the Pharisees') way; they were prepared to search on behalf of the priests.

9. I think it most likely that the Pharisees had a desire for purity *for its own sake*. Purity symbolized not just the priesthood, but Godliness.

10. The discussions of pots and food in Eduyoth 1.14 and Oholoth 5.2f. show that the Pharisees did not try to impose all their rules on others. They declared the food pure for the 'am ha-'arets, and that constitutes an admission that people were not *required* to live like Pharisees.

11. The same two passages show that the Pharisees avoided the food and vessels of the ordinary people (see section F).

§2. The Purity of Tithes and Offerings. A lot of the rules which Neusner counted as being about 'secular food in purity' are in fact about holy food – sacrifices, offerings, tithes and the Passover meal. As we saw in III.B, most of these are to be eaten only by people who are pure. Some of the sacrifices and offerings were consumed by the priests inside the temple; others could be taken outside the temple and shared with their families; laypeople were to eat second tithe, Passover and their share of the peace offerings in purity. We may distinguish between the purity of the people eating holy food (a biblical requirement) and purity observed in handling the food before it is eaten (assumed in Isa. 66.20, but not required by biblical law).

Before taking up these two categories, we should note one discussion about the priests' food which involves the public sacrificial service and the handling of meat from an animal which had already been sacrificed. According to the House of Shammai, if the flesh of a Most Holy Thing – which had to be eaten inside the temple – contracted impurity from a secondary source, it should be burnt outside the temple, but inside if the impurity was from a primary source. The House of Hillel took the opposite view (Shekalim 8.5). What rule the priests followed we do not know, but this passage goes together with a small number of others which deal with public rather than private practice. It is noteworthy that the Houses disagree.[8]

(*a*) Debates about eating holy food in purity:

1. The Houses asked, if there is a field near a burial area which is used for mourning, does it need to be examined for corpses to prevent those who eat heave offering from contracting impurity (Oholoth 18.4; T. Ahilot 17.13)? The priests and their families (who ate heave offering) presumably mourned next to the graveyard, and the worry is that some corpses or parts of corpses might be found in that field as well. Here we see a concern to keep the priests and their families – not themselves – from inadvertently contracting corpse-impurity.

2. Food which priests could share with their families included peace offerings, first fruits (of produce) and firstlings (of animals). According to Num. 18 the following rules apply: (1) The 'wave offerings' (the priests' share of peace offerings) are to be eaten by the priests, their sons and daughters, and everyone in the *household* who is *pure* (v 11). (2) The first fruits are also to be eaten by everyone in the *house* who is *pure* (v 13). (3) The firstlings are given to the priests and their sons and daughters, but the text mentions neither purity nor household (vv. 17–19). The omissions in vv. 17–19 drew exegetical attention. A household might include people who were not of priestly descent, and sons and daughters – especially daughters – could not be assumed to be pure. The Houses disagreed about the significance of the different treatment of firstlings. The House of Shammai wished to exclude other members of the priests' house; they were of the opinion that 'only priests are numbered with [those who eat] firstlings'. The House of Hillel permitted firstlings to Israelites (that is, non-priests; T. Bekorot 3.15, which is to be preferred to Bekhoroth 5.2). Exegetically, the House of Shammai

took the view that 'sons and daughters' in the verse on firstlings (Num. 18.19) excluded the other members of the priest's household (who were, however, permitted the first fruits of produce). The House of Hillel understood the passage in Numbers as a whole, at least on this point, and applied 'household' to first fruits and firstlings alike.

They also disagreed as to whether or not a menstruant could eat a firstling (T. Bekorot 3.16), the House of Shammai forbidding and the House of Hillel permitting. In this case, it was the Hillelites who wished to break up the text: Although for peace offerings and first fruits purity is specified, that is not the case for firstlings; but 'daughters' are explicitly permitted to eat firstlings. Thus the Hillelites 'allowed' a menstruant to eat the firstling. The Shammaites thought that purity should cover the whole section. In these passages the Houses do not show consistency of exegetical technique, but consistency of result: the Hillelites would allow the priests' food to be shared more widely than would the Shammaites.

We may again note that priests doubtless did as they wished. If, however, one wanted pharisaic support or advice, he still had a choice.

(*b*) There are many more debates about *handling* holy food. In the pharisaic materials a large assumption is made: food which, by biblical law, is to be eaten in purity must also be handled in purity, beginning at a very early point in its production and supply. This is presupposed, never argued for or about. It is so fundamental to a large number of pharisaic discussions that it must be a very early view. Above I called it an innovation, and so it was, but probably not pharisaic. It may be regarded as 'pietist' in a more general sense.

The point at which purity starts being applied to holy food is important, and so we should first list the sequence of events: planting, cultivating, harvesting, carrying from the fields to the place of preparation, preparation (grinding grain to make meal, pressing olives and grapes to make oil and wine, and so on), setting aside, placing in containers, conveying to the place of consumption. Let us now apply to this list the two small pieces of early evidence on handling the priests' food, both of which have been cited previously. By the time of Isa. 66.20 (whenever that was), it was assumed that food eaten inside the temple should be carried there in pure containers; that is, purity began at a late stage in the sequence, just before it was actually eaten. This, at least, is the most the evidence allows us to say. The next evidence is Judith 11, a passage which is often erroneously taken as proving that the custom of handwashing is early. According to this chapter (*c.* 150–125 BCE) a desperate band decided to *eat* the first fruits and tithes which had *already been sanctified and set aside* for the priests. They did this, even though it was 'not lawful for any of the people so much as to touch these things with their hands' (Judith 11.13). This does not reflect a handwashing rule – as if the first fruits could have been handled by impure people who washed their hands, or as if it would have been all right had they rubbed the holy food with their noses. The point is that ordinary people could not even *touch* the food once it had been sanctified and set apart, much less *eat* it. The food in the story had not yet been taken to the temple or given to priests, who either sometimes or regularly collected it,[9] but it had already been set aside. It is probable that the magic moment which rendered it untouchable had come when it was separated. That is, taking wine as an example, impure people could have planted the vines, pruned them, harvested the grapes, put them into the wine vat, crushed them, and put the wine into jars. Either in the act of filling some jars part of the wine was designated first fruits (or first tithe), or after the jars were filled some of them were set aside. Combining this with Isa. 66.20, we may accept that the jars themselves were pure (they were uncontaminated by dead insects and had not been touched by a zav). Separation sanctified the wine; and, according to Judith, it could thereafter not be touched by an impure person. This implies that the priests and Levites collected it (or that it was conveyed to the temple by specially purified people).[10]

This does not prove that in the second part of the second century BCE (the generally accepted date of Judith) purity was required of the laypeople who harvested and stored the offerings, since we have information only about handling them after they were consecrated. We can see already, however, that the requirement of purity for the priests' food tended to be made at an earlier point in the food chain. Not only must the priest and his family, as the Bible requires, eat first fruits in purity and in a pure place, the offerings must be carried to them by someone who is pure, and carried in pure vessels. Presumably the same requirements applied to lay people's holy food, such as second tithe.

A similar rule is seen in the *Covenant of Damascus*:

Let no man send to the altar a burnt-offering or a grain-offering or frankincense or wood by the hand of any man affected with any of the types of uncleanness, thus empowering him to convey uncleanness to the altar. (CD 11.18–20)

The concern here is the purity of the *altar*, not primarily of the food which the priests ate. This nevertheless shows a parallel development, to require purity at an earlier stage than is required in the Bible. Handling holy food and objects in purity even before they were used seems to have become the general practice among pious groups.

When we pick up the Houses disputes, we see that they assume that the offerings must be handled in purity – though they disagree on most details, including the point at which this begins to be done. Many of the discussions which follow concern 'heave offering', *t'rûmah*, which I shall pause here to explain.[11] This word is used in various ways in the Bible, sometimes as a synonym for first fruits (Num. 15.20), sometimes as a separate offering (e.g. Neh. 10.37f. [ET 10.36f.]; 12.44). In rabbinic literature, the word has two different significations. It sometimes refers to a separate offering – neither tithe nor first fruits. It was small in quantity (one-thirtieth to one-sixtieth of the crop), and it had the great advantage that, unlike first fruits and firstlings, it could be given to the priesthood after the destruction of the temple.[12] Secondly, the word was used generically to mean 'any food which the priests and their families eat'. Thus, for example, the Rabbis called the priests' portion of the tithe 'heave offering of tithe', and they often discussed rules about 'those who eat heave offering', meaning the priests and their families. Since in the mishnaic period heave offering in the restricted sense was still given to the priests, and since the same word was used generically, it is extremely prominent in rabbinic literature. In most cases we shall not need to determine which meaning is intended.

The pharisaic debates are these:

1. What happens if a small amount of impure heave offering falls into a larger amount of pure heave offering (Terumoth 5.4; expanded in T. Terumot 6.4)?

2. Must both grapes and the wine that is produced from them be handled with pure hands until the offerings are separated (Tohoroth 10.4)?

3. Can the wine vat be made impure after first tithe had been removed, or only after second tithe has been removed (T. Terumot 3.12)?

4. Must fenugreek and vetches which are heave offering be handled in purity (Maaser Sheni 2.3–4; Eduyoth 1.8; T. Ma'aser Sheni 2.1)? (These would be used as food only in case of famine, and the Houses debated whether or not they should be dealt with on the assumption that they were foodstuff.)

5. Must jars containing grapes or wine given as heave offering be pure (Maaser Sheni 3.13; T. Ma'aser Sheni 2.18)?

6. How can grapes be gathered if they grow over a grave area (Oholoth 18.1)? (They are to be gathered before heave offering etc. are separated, and thus they should be gathered in purity; see further below.)

7. What circumstances render dough offering impure (Tebul Yom 1.1)?

Similarly the Houses debated the purity of the food eaten by ordinary people on especially holy occasions or for holy reasons – second tithe (consumed by the offerer in Jerusalem in a state of ritual purity), the Passover offering and the like:

8. What if second tithe contracts impurity (Maaser Sheni 3.9; expanded T. Ma'aser Sheni 2.16)?

9. Does a field of mourners (near a graveyard) need to be examined for corpses to prevent those who eat the Passover meal from eating it in impurity (Oholoth 18.4)?

10. May a woman during stage two of childbirth-impurity touch 'Holy Things' (eaten within the temple), eat second tithe (eaten by laypeople in purity), set apart dough offering or handle heave offering (eaten by priests' families outside the temple) (Niddah 10.6–7)? (The answer was 'yes', except for 'Holy Things'. These mishnayot reveal exegetical work on Lev. 12.4, which prohibits the woman from touching 'anything holy', *kol qôdesh*. The Mishnah takes the term to refer to 'Most Holy Things', eaten in the temple. For other holy food there was a lower standard of purity.[13])

(*c*) There are several points to be emphasized.

1. These discussions Neusner counts as dealing with 'secular food in purity', but we see that they have to do only with holy food.

2. The Pharisees agreed that some purity observances should apply to the handling, not just the eating, of holy food. A woman with childbirth-impurity stage two could not touch food eaten inside the temple. The debate about whether or not hands must be pure when putting grapes into the winepress (before heave offering has been separated; Toh. 10.4), reflects an *agreement that when heave offering is separated the hands must be pure*. The only question is whether or not they must be pure at an earlier point. When the discussion is compared to Isa. 66.20 and Judith 11, we see (a) that it is definitely *hands* which are the issue for the Pharisees, and that washing them makes them pure for handling heave offering; (b) that the Pharisees did not agree on just when purity should start. The Shammaites thought that the grapes must be put into the press with pure hands, the Hillelites that the priests' share of the wine must be set apart with pure hands. Both put purity a step or so earlier than Judith 11, which requires purity after the wine has been separated.

3. All the discussions of handling holy food, and of *when* one could be impure in dealing with food, show that it was *not* expected that all food be handled in a state of purity. If Pharisees always handled their own food in purity, there would be no reason to debate *at what point* they should start handling *the priests' food* in purity. Were the widespread view of them true, we would have to imagine them as thinking, 'Though we handle and eat all food in purity, we must still ask whether or not heave offering must be handled in purity.' Not even the Pharisees, who doubtless loved detail and precision, some of it academic, would have conducted such discussions.

Especially noteworthy is the last passage in the list, which *allows* a woman with childbirth-impurity stage two to eat even second tithe and to touch heave offering. This requires the inference that a woman in this state could touch ordinary food. The passage on pure hands when handling heave offering also shows that there was no general requirement to have pure hands when gathering and preparing food.

4. As is usually the case, these passages are debates, many of them unsettled. Sometimes the editor or transmitter of the passage says that the two parties finally agreed (e.g. Terumoth 5.4), but in most of these cases we cannot speak of pharisaic *law*. Even when the Houses are said to have agreed, we may doubt that pre-70 Pharisees agreed. The Houses, we noted, often represent the first generation after the destruction of the temple. While we may accept that they deal with pre-70 topics, and that they reflect differences of opinion before 70, we should nevertheless think that a later editorial comment that the Houses agreed may well refer only to the post-70 Houses. The debates do not tell us how many Pharisees lived in one way or the other, but only what the Houses disagreed about. We may infer that they agreed upon and lived by rules which are presupposed in the debates.

5. We continue to see a special concern for the rules of corpse-impurity, though (as we noted above) the concern is not for themselves when they eat ordinary food, but rather for the priesthood at all times and for themselves before the Passover. Oholoth 18.4 shows how strictly Pharisees wished to avoid bringing corpse-impurity into contact with the temple, the priesthood, or their own food *on those occasions when* it should be eaten in purity – in this case, Passover.

6. Oholoth 18.1, however, makes the point even better, and it also reveals another pharisaic invention:

> How can they gather the grapes in a Grave-area? Men and vessels must be sprinkled the first and the second time; then they gather the grapes and take them out of the Grave-area; others receive the grapes from them and take them to the winepress. If these others touched the grape-gatherers they become unclean. So the School of Hillel. The School of Shammai say: They should hold the sickle with a wrapping of bast, or cut the grapes with a sharp flint, and let them fall into a large olive-basket and bring them to the winepress.

The principal concern in this passage is for the purity of the priesthood. When the grapes are gathered they still include the portions for the priests, and we learn here that the Pharisees wished the priests' food to be kept apart from corpse-impurity from the time of harvesting on. In a graveyard this was a challenge. The grapes must also be pure when they reach the wine vats, since the wine from them would mix with other wine, from which offerings would eventually be taken. In discussing Tohoroth 10.4 (under (*c*) (2) above) we noted that heave offering grapes and wine need be handled with pure hands either when the grapes are put into the press (the Shammites) or when the priests' portion of the wine was separated (the Hillelites). We now see a concern to *harvest* in purity. The difference is the kind of impurity: in harvesting they wished to protect the priests from the most virulent and anti-priestly form of impurity, corpse-impurity (Oholoth 18.1). In Tohoroth 10.4, on handling (non-graveyard) grapes or separating wine with pure hands, they were concerned with the other impurities, probably gnat-impurity in particular.[14] Thus corpse-impurity was avoided from the time of harvesting on, while other impurities became a concern at a later point.

The solution of the House of Hillel to the problem of grapes in a graveyard is ingenious and shows a novelty of conception: the grape-gatherers and their baskets can be *inoculated* against corpse-impurity in advance. 'Sprinkled the first and the second time' refers to the rite of removing corpse-impurity, but here it is 'removed' beforehand. Then the grapes are pure, and so is the wine made from them, provided that the people who carry the grapes to the winepress do not touch the grape-gatherers. It must be doubted that farmers had immediate access to the special water used for corpse-impurity, and it is likely that the Hillelites had in mind sprinkling with ordinary water – another minor gesture.

The House of Shammai's proposal is less inventive: the gatherers should not touch the grapes themselves, but cut them and let them fall directly into the basket. Cutting should be done with flint (stone does not contract corpse-impurity), or with a sickle wrapped with bast. The bast (a fibrous material) probably was thought to serve as a 'vessel' around the sickle which prevented corpse-impurity from passing through the harvester to the sickle and then to the grapes.

(*d*) Conclusion. We see considerable innovation in this section. It was agreed that at an early point in the food chain purity must be observed so that holy food – not ordinary food – would not be contaminated. The disagreements probably show that, when the temple was destroyed, these rules were still developing. They were not so old that there was unanimity about how to keep the priests' food (and their own Passover and second tithe) pure. But that purity should be observed sometime before holy food was eaten was accepted by the Pharisees (and probably by others). In one case the Hillelites displayed a conceptual development: the inoculation against corpse-impurity. This idea, to be sure, seems to have stopped here, and we learn no more of it.

§3. The Purity Laws of Leviticus 11. We shall now look in some detail at the rules about which we have heard so much. I have already indicated that part of Lev. 11 attracted considerable pharisaic interest. The major food prohibitions – not to eat pork, lions, snakes and so on – seem not to have attracted special interest. Most Jews observed them, and the Bible is so clear that little more could be said. We may assume that the Pharisees strictly observed the major food laws of Lev. 11.1–31, despite the fact that the method of counting to determine importance would 'prove' that they were not observed.

(*a*) Pharisaic definitions and presuppositions. What did attract detailed discussion was the difficult section Lev. 11.32–38, which deals with secondary impurity conveyed by the carcasses of 'swarming things' (insects, weasels, crocodiles etc.). We may recall the principal points:

> And anything upon which any of them [namely, the impure swarming things] falls when they are dead shall be unclean, whether it is an article of wood or a garment or a skin or a sack, any vessel [utensil] that is used for any purpose; it must be put into water, and it shall be unclean until the evening; then it shall be clean. (Lev. 11.32)

The chapter continues by stating that a dead 'swarming thing' which falls into a vessel makes its contents impure and that the vessel must be broken or washed (depending on what it is made of); the carcass makes food impure *if* it (the food) gets wet. There are further rules and then these final verses, which became very important for the Pharisees:

> And if any part of their carcass falls upon any seed for sowing that is to be sown, it is clean; but if water *is put* on the seed and any part of their carcass falls on it, it is unclean to you. (Lev. 11.37–38)

There are the normal definitional problems. The weasel is classified as a swarming thing in Lev. 11.29, but there are obvious reasons for classifying it as a wild animal. According to the House of Shammai it should be treated as both: an olive's bulk of the carcass would render impure anyone who carried it (since it is a wild animal), while a lentil's bulk would render impure anyone who touched it (since it is a swarming thing) (Kilaim 8.5). This Mishnah presupposes agreement on the minimum quantity of the carcass of a wild animal or a creeping thing which was required before the laws of Lev. 11.25 (carrying the carcass of an impure animal) and 11.31 (touching the carcass of a swarming thing) came into effect. These quantities are assumed throughout the Mishnah, generally appearing in discussions which appear to be second century (e.g. Shabbath 10.5; Oholoth 13.5,6; Mikwaoth 5.7; see also the stam of Oholoth 1.7; Tohoroth 3.4). This reminds us how incomplete our knowledge of Pharisaism is: were it not for the single attribution of Kilaim 8.5 to the House of Shammai, the olive's bulk / lentil's bulk requirements for carrion- and gnat-impurity might be considered to be a second-century innovation.[15]

Specifying a lentil's bulk of the carcass of swarming things resulted in the elimination of at least a few worries about dead insects. Despite the Bible, a single dead gnat would not render impure a large quantity of food. It would require a dead insect approximately as big as a fly. This new definition justifies a change in the catchword we have used, from 'gnat-impurity' to 'fly-impurity'.

An even more important limitation of the biblical law was devised. According to Lev. 11.34, food is impure 'if water comes upon it', but according to 11.38 seeds on which a dead fly falls become impure 'if water is put' on them. The Pharisees decided that 'is put' should apply both to seeds and food, and they took the passive to mean 'by a human intentionally'. They then further decided that moisture which a human wanted to have on the food, even if it got there without human activity, fell under the rule 'if water is put'. These decisions are not argued for in the surviving literature, but rather taken for granted.

The result was that foodstuff which someone wanted to be moist, or which was intentionally moistened, was *susceptible* to this form of impurity – the impurity of swarming things forbidden to Israel to eat. It will be seen that this was an important legal decision. Intention is within the individual's control, and thus one would know when to take special efforts to protect foodstuff from coming into contact with dead forbidden creatures. Rain and dew would not make food susceptible to fly-impurity, only moisture which the owner or handler of the foodstuff wanted to be there.

We saw in discussing Alon and Neusner that both assumed that applying the laws of Lev. 11.32–38 constituted an *extension* of temple or priestly laws. We also saw that these are neither. Now it must be emphasized that when they are applied they are not *extended* but rather *reduced*. The smallest of the swarming things are stricken from the list: one need not worry about individual gnats, mites, midges, fleas and the like. The problems of dew, rain and accidental moisture are also eliminated: only moisture which one put or wanted on the foodstuff counts.

The rule that intention is decisive is seen, for example, in the discussion of the case of a man who shook a tree in order to bring down fruit, but who also shook loose moisture which fell on the fruit. In this case all agree that the fruit was not thereby made susceptible to fly-impurity (Makhshirin 1.2), since the moisture fell coincidentally. The Houses disagreed, however, about the case of someone who intended to shake the moisture off a tree. What fell during the actual shaking, of course, rendered any fruit which it touched susceptible to impurity; but what about the drops which fell first on to another shrub, and later on to foodstuff? The Houses disagreed about their effect on fruit below them. The question was whether or not intention governed the drops which fell only later (Makhshirin 1.3; cf. 1.4; these mishnayot are paralled in T. Makshirin 1.1–4, with some variations and corrections). Further Houses debates can be seen in Makhshirin 4.4–5 //T. Mak. 2.6; Uktzin 3.6b,8,11.

(*b*) Olives and haverim. Within this category of law, olives were of special interest. We noted above that olives, if left long enough, will become moist of themselves. That condition is desired by a person who wishes to press them and produce olive oil. Since it is desired, the natural secretion of the olives counts as moisture which 'is put' on them. In Tohoroth 9.1 (cf. T. Toh. 10.2) there is a debate which runs from the Houses to Rabban Gamaliel II concerning just when olives become susceptible to fly-impurity, the final opinion being the most lenient: only when the entire lot is ready to be pressed. Further discussions of olives are found in Tohoroth 9.5,7. A special problem was raised by olive-peat – a fuel made from the residue of olives after oil had been extracted. If before it dried entirely it became impure, did it render the stove impure (T. Kelim Baba Qamma 6.18; cf. Kelim 9.6)? The Houses disagreed. Presumably the House of Hillel, which thought not, held that the moisture which was still on the olive-peat was no longer desired to be there, and so did not fall under the rule, 'if water is put'. The House of Shammai presumably noted that earlier the moisture had been desired.

A passage that indirectly connects the Houses to the haverim, Associates, concerns olives:

> The School of Shammai say: A man may sell his olives only to an Associate. The School of Hillel say: Even to one that [only] pays Tithes. Yet the more scrupulous of the School of Hillel used to observe the words of the School of Shammai. (Demai 6.6; partial // T. Ma´aserot 3.13)

A probably later mishnah states that a haver should not sell to an ordinary person either foodstuff which is wet or dry, or buy from him foodstuff that is wet (Demai 2.3). The point in both these mishnayot is that, when selling food, the scrupulous would try to avoid the possibility that the buyer would let it become impure: thus the rule not to sell olives to one who is not scrupulous, and later not to sell such a person any foodstuff: he might let the olives grow moist, or even moisten other foods, and not protect them from dead swarming things. One could buy food which was dry from even the least scrupulous person, since it could not have become impure.

Another passage which includes the problem of the susceptibility of wet foodstuff to impurity makes a direct link between the Houses and the haverim: if someone wants to join the Association, how long is the probation period before he can be trusted with regard to liquids? The Shammaites propose thirty days, the Hillelites twelve months (Bekorot 30b//T. Demai 2.12; see further below under midras-impurity).

(*c*) Utensils. Because of Lev. 11.32, dead swarming things were held to pollute other things besides food: 'Whether it is an article (*k'li*) of wood or a garment or a skin or a sack, any vessel (*k'li*) that is used for any purpose [literally, 'work', *m'la'keh*]'. In accord with this verse, rabbinic discussions use the term kelim, usually translated 'vessels', as a generic for 'articles which are used in work', which are better called 'utensils' (n. 2). The carcasses of swarming things are one of the major sources of impurity for kelim, which are also rendered impure by being in a room with a corpse (Num. 19.15), by being touched by a zav (Lev. 15.12), and by coming into contact with semen (Lev. 15.17, 'every garment and every skin') (see the list, Kelim 1.1). Thus kelim constitute a large and complicated topic.

When we turn to the pharisaic passages about kelim, we note that the principal problems, again, were definitional: What is a keli? If the use to which it is put changes, is it still susceptible to impurity? If it has been damaged, is it considered 'broken' (which would purify it; e.g. Lev. 11.33)? Tubes may be used in work, and so are susceptible to incurring fly-impurity. But if a tube is attached to the head of a staff for decorative purposes, is it still susceptible? The House of Shammai thought that it was susceptible until damaged (since otherwise it could be withdrawn and used for work), while the Hillelites thought that it became insusceptible as soon as its function changed (Kelim 14.2). 'How much damage constitutes destruction?' is discussed by the Houses in Kelim 29.8//T. Kel. Baba Batra 7.4.

According to Kelim 15.1 R. Meir, second century, ruled that a chest which could hold forty *se'ah* of liquid (that is, large enough to be an immersion pool; see §8) was not susceptible to impurity. Apparently this distinction is earlier, since the Houses debated whether the measurement was made on the inside or outside of the chest (Kelim 18.1; one detail corrected in T. Kel. Baba Metsia 8.1).

(*d*) Handwashing. Two very difficult mishnaic passages about handwashing are explained in the Tosefta in such a way as to connect them with the avoidance of fly-impurity. The mishnayot are these:

> The School of Shammai say: They wash the hands and then mix the cup. And the School of Hillel say: They mix the cup and then wash the hands. (Berakoth 8.2)

> The School of Shammai say: A man wipes his hands with a napkin and lays it on the table. And the School of Hillel say: [He lays it] on the cushion. (Berakoth 8.3)

As Alon pointed out, it is very difficult to explain these mishnnayot if one does not follow the Tosefta.[16] According to its interpretation, the problem with

mixing the cup had to do with *liquids*, and liquids point to the purity laws of
Lev. 11.32–38, since it is only fly-impurity which is dependent on moisture.
The Houses seem to have contemplated the following situation: One is
sitting at table. If dead flies have fallen on it since it was last immersed, it has
fly-impurity (Lev. 11.32; on immersing the table, cf. Mikwaoth 7.7). This
impurity can be acquired by the hands and then conveyed to foodstuff via
moisture. How can one mix wine without having the impurity pass from
hands through splashed liquid to food or drink? The answer was that the
hands should be washed. But when?

The Tosefta explains the first debate thus: The Shammaites' concern was
that if one mixed the cup before washing, the contents might splatter on to the
outside of the cup. Touching the moisture with impure hands would cause
the impurity to pass to the cup. For this reason they wished first to wash the
hands and then mix the cup. The Hillelites, however, regarded the outside of
the cup as being impure in any case and wished to wash the hands after
mixing the contents (T. Ber. 5.26). The reason is not given, but it may have
been to remove any splashes of liquid from the hands. If one mixed, washed
and then dried, there would be no external moisture which could serve to
convey impurity to food.

The Tosefta on wiping the hands (after washing them) indicates that the
Shammaites feared that *liquids* on the napkin would come into contact with
impurities on the cushion, while the Hillelites feared that the same liquids
would become impure through contact with the table (T. Ber. 5.27). The
question seems to have been, which is more likely to have had contact with a
lentil's bulk of a swarming thing, the table or the cushion?

It need hardly be added that the concern with hands as special conveyors of
fly-impurity is post-biblical, and handwashing in this context may be a
pharisaic innovation.

(*e*) Conclusion. In discussing biblical purity laws we noted that those of
Lev. 11.32–38 are incomplete, as are many other biblical laws. Kelim which
contract fly-impurity are to be broken or washed, but we are not directly told
what to do with food and seeds which are polluted, nor is it indirectly
indicated what people who touch a dead swarming thing are to do. The
Pharisees accepted the implication not to use the food. That is why there are
restrictions on buying from and selling to the unscrupulous. They also
decided that a person who touches, even indirectly, a dead swarming thing,
whose impurity is mediated by *liquid*, must wash his or her hands. This may
be one of the main points which led the Pharisees to adopt handwashing.

It is necessary to emphasize that these discussions do not show that
Pharisees wanted to keep *priestly* purity laws, as Alon, Neusner and others
have supposed. Leviticus 11 contains laws governing all Israel. It explicitly

includes the topic of insects which fall on food and seeds. The Pharisees reduced the worries about these laws by deciding that a lentil's bulk of carcass was required and that human intention was crucial. This made it possible to know when to protect foodstuff against dying insects and when not.

§4. Midras-impurity. Midras-impurity is the secondary impurity of things on which a person sits, lies or leans if that person is a zav, a zavah, a menstruant, or a woman in stage one of childbirth-impurity. Leviticus 15 states that items which are under such people are impure, and that other people who touch them are impure (e.g. 15.10; these impurities are listed as 6a-b in section B). We saw above that the Mishnah did not think that zavs and menstruants were expelled from their houses. Since they stayed at home, they made rather a lot of things impure, with the result that the impurity would spread to other residents of the house. The purification rite for those who acquire impurity from a bed, chair or saddle is either simply waiting for sunset (Lev. 15.10) or bathing, washing the clothes and waiting for sunset (15.21,27).

(a) Degrees of purity and probability of impurity. There is a lengthy and possibly important passage which ranks people according to the probability of their having midras-impurity. Rivkin, noting that the Pharisees in Hagigah 2.7 are not contrasted with Sadducees, did not include the passage in the pharisaic corpus.[17] Neusner regarded the main part of the passage as early, reflecting views about eating holy food before the idea arose (as he thinks) that Pharisees should eat ordinary food in purity.[18] For the present purposes, we shall accept the passage as pharisaic.

> For Pharisees the clothes of an *Am haaretz* count as suffering *midras*-uncleanness; for them that eat Heave-offering the clothes of Pharisees count as suffering *midras*-uncleanness; for them that eat of Hallowed Things the clothes of them that eat Heave-offering count as suffering *midras*-uncleanness; for them that occupy themselves with the Sin-offering water the clothes of them that eat of Hallowed Things count as suffering *midras*-uncleanness. Joseph b. Joezer was the most pious in the priesthood, yet for them that ate of Hallowed Things his apron counted as suffering *midras*-uncleanness. Johanan b. Gudgada always ate [his common food] in accordance with [the rules governing] the cleanness of Hallowed Things, yet for them that occupied themselves with the Sin-offering water his apron counted as suffering *midras*-uncleanness. (Hagigah 2.7)

We have here a sequence of ascending purity:

'Am ha-'arets / ordinary person	a lay person who was not a Pharisee
Pharisee	lay Pharisees are here meant

Those who eat heave offering	priests when out of the temple and their families
those who eat Holy Things[19]	priests while in the temple
those who handle sin-offering water	the priests who mix the ashes of the red heifer with water, to remove corpse-impurity

According to this passage Pharisees were more careful to avoid sitting or lying on impure chairs and beds than were ordinary people, *but less careful* than priests' families – and still less careful than priests who were on duty, who in turn were less careful than those who handled the water used to remove corpse-impurity.

The point is then illustrated: Joseph (or Jose) b. Joezer was a priest (*c.* 150 BCE); but, presumably when he was not on duty in the temple, he might convey impurity to those who were. Johanan b. Gudgada (a Levite *c.* 100 BCE) was a very rare person: he tried always to eat food as if he were a priest in the temple (those who eat holy things). This passage most distinctly states that Pharisees did not try to achieve the degree of purity of priests while serving in the temple, that even a very pious priest did not maintain this degree of purity when outside the temple, and that there was one noteworthy individual who did try to eat ordinary food in purity.

Neusner, as we noted, coped with Hagigah 2.7 by proposing that its gradations of purity, with Pharisees definitely lower than priests' families, comes from the early history of the party, and that later they undertook to eat all food in the same purity as priests in the temple (moving up two rungs on the ladder).[20] Gradations of purity, however, are seen not only early but also late, and in no instance do the Pharisees (or later the Rabbis) attribute to their own ordinary food the same level of purity as that of Holy Things, nor even of heave offering. Niddah 10.6–7 requires a higher degree of purity for Holy Things than for heave offering and dough offering (see §2. b (10)) and it puts the Pharisees' own holy food (second tithe) into the lower of these two categories. Having made this distinction with regard to the priests' food and second tithe, they can hardly then have claimed that *they themselves*, every day, were as pure as priests *in* the temple, that their tables were as pure as the altar, and that their everyday food was eaten in full purity. Hagigah 2.7 fits Pharisees into a hierarchy, parts of which are seen in the Houses material. Thus it cannot be made to vanish by attributing it to a period before the Pharisees decided to live like priests.

We cannot know that Hagigah 2.7 is a description of how all pre-70 Pharisees lived. But, for what it is worth, it indicates that Pharisees were more scrupulous with regard to one (minor) form of impurity than were other laypeople. We are not directly told that Pharisees intended never to contract midras-impurity, but we may infer the effort to avoid it when possible.

(*b*) Locating midras-impurity. There are several passages attributed to the Houses which define where midras-impurity might be, and which thereby imply that Pharisees sought to avoid it when they could. Some examples:

1. A trough for mixing mortar was, according to the House of Shammai, susceptible to midras-impurity; the House of Hillel disagreed (Kelim 20.2//T. Kel. Baba Metzia 11.3).

2. A sheet, which while a sheet was susceptible to midras-impurity, was no longer susceptible if made into a curtain. The Houses disagreed only about just when it became a curtain (Kelim 20.6).

3. The Houses disagreed as to whether a leather bag or wrapper for garments was susceptible to midras-impurity (Kelim 26.6; cf. T. Kel. Baba Batra 4.9).

4. The Houses debated when scroll-wrappers were susceptible to midras-impurity (Kelim 28.4).

5. They debated whether or not a bride's stool which lost its seat-boards was susceptible to midras-impurity (i.e., was it still a stool? Kelim 22.4a).

6. They debated whether or not a bride's stool which was attached to a trough was considered part of the trough, and so not susceptible, or nevertheless still a stool, and so susceptible (Kelim 22.4b).

There are other Houses debates which touch on midras-impurity, which will be listed under other topics (e.g. Niddah, the menstruant: see Niddah 10.8//T. Niddah 9.19 below).

These discussions and others primarily constitute an effort to determine when one might have contracted midras-impurity. The passages define rather than prohibit. We are not told, 'On no account sit on a chair on which a zav may have sat', but rather, 'this is one place where you might contract midras-impurity (according to the Shammaites)'. Nor are we told, 'if you sit on a zav's chair you may not eat'. No transgression of biblical law is involved in contracting this form of impurity, and nothing follows from it – except what concerns the temple. Thus Pharisees wanted to know when they had it and when not.

(*c*) Avoiding it. That they endeavoured to avoid midras-impurity is implied by Hagigah 2.7 (since the clothes of ordinary people were more likely to convey it than were the clothes of Pharisees). Avoidance is also implied in the three passages which directly support the view of 'ordinary food in purity'. According to T. Shabbat 1.15 the Houses debated whether or not a Pharisee who is a zav may eat with an 'am ha-'arets who is a zav. Once the Pharisee is impure, why not? The passage presupposes that ordinarily a Pharisee would not eat with an 'am ha-'arets, probably because of midras-impurity, which the garment of the 'am ha-'arets was assumed to have. Other purity questions are possible, but midras-impurity is the most likely. Bekorot 30b//T. Demai 2.12, as we noted above, is the one passage which links the Pharisees to the haverim directly. The question is, when a person wishes to join the Association, how long is the probation period? According to the House of Shammai, it is thirty days for liquids, twelve months for garments. The House of Hillel hold that it is twelve months in both cases. The question about liquids may be reworded this way: After a person says that he wishes to observe the laws of Lev. 11.32–38 (as interpreted by the Pharisees), how long will it be before he uses up all the liquids which may already be contaminated, *or* how long will it be before he learns all the rules? The second item, garments, are subject to midras-impurity. The assumption here is that people immerse their clothes, bed and chair only once in twelve months.

We may take it, then, that Pharisees wished to avoid midras-impurity when possible, and that this desire limited their associations.

(*d*) Conclusion. In this category we see again an interest which is in part academic and which is conceptually interesting: when an item changes function it also changes its susceptibility to impurity. A sheet is made impure if (for example) a zav lies on it. But if the sheet is altered and is used as a curtain, it is not susceptible to impurity from that source (though corpse-impurity is a different matter). I call this 'academic' because there was another obvious way of purifying a sheet: immersing it. Thus this rule is not primarily practical, designed to save expense by reusing impure sheets, but academic in that it defines susceptibility to impurity by function.

The question of motive is difficult. Direct contact with midras-impurity would keep one from entering the temple (so Lev. 15). But it was transmitted in full strength only once: if a zav sat on a chair, the chair had midras-impurity, and this impurity was conveyed to someone else who sat on the same chair, and to his garments. But the second person passed it on in a weakened form. Through how many stages each impurity could be transmitted is an exceptionally difficult topic, and one on which the early material is not plentiful. I do not pretend to know what Pharisees thought they could not do if they contracted second-hand midras-impurity from an 'am ha-'arets. (That is: the 'am ha-'arets sat on a menstruant's chair, and then the Pharisee touched his garment.) According to the anonymous mishnah Zabim 5.6 (attributed by Epstein to R. Joshua;[21] thus fairly early), a man who touches a zav renders heave offering impure at third remove. If the Pharisees operated by this principle, they would have sought to avoid sitting on things which had been sat on by people who had touched a zav, so that they could handle food from which the offerings had not yet been separated. It does not seem to me to be certain that they accepted this rule. A woman in stage two of childbirth-impurity – thus with second-grade impurity – could eat second tithe and set apart dough offering (Niddah 10.6f., discussed above). This inclines me to doubt that the Pharisees thought that midras-impurity rendered heave offering impure at third remove.

If, however, they did think that, we have a motive for the avoidance of midras-impurity. They wished to be able to handle the priests' food.

We should nevertheless grant that they may have avoided midras-impurity as much as possible for the sake of their own food. If they did this, they applied to their own food some aspects of the laws which governed priests.

§5. Sex. Two states of impurity prohibit sexual relations: menstruation and childbirth-impurity stage one. Menstruation is determined partly by self-inspection and partly by counting days (seven from the first sign of blood), but this is an area of life where there is a lot of irregularity, and thus there are interesting legal questions.

(*a*) Uncertainty. There is one exceptionally important disagreement between Hillel and Shammai (not the later Houses): According to Shammai a woman is deemed impure from the time when she notes a flow of menstrual blood, while according to Hillel she is deemed impure on any days when she did not use a test-rag if the next time she used one a flow was noted (Eduyoth 1.1; Niddah 1.1). Thus, if a woman tested for menstruation on Monday and found no blood; did not test on Tuesday, but did have intercourse; and tested on Wednesday and found blood, Shammai was of the view that she was to be deemed pure on Tuesday. Hillel judged that she should be deemed a menstruant on Tuesday, and thus the couple would owe sin offerings for involuntary transgression. 'The Sages' decided on a different rule from either of these.

(*b*) Assumptions. The next passage reveals the acceptance of one convention and one interpretation which the Pharisees did not regard as additional rules of their own, but as binding exegesis of the written law.

The 'interpretation' is that immersion is required of a woman who bleeds. We noted that this is not stated in the Bible,[22] and that the reason probably is that, at the time of Leviticus, women never entered the temple. The Pharisees, and probably Jews in general, assumed that the bathing laws which in Lev. 15 are applied to men should be applied to women as well. This may well have been so taken for granted in the first century that it was not identified as 'interpretation'. In the pharisaic discussions it is assumed, never argued for or about.

The convention is connected to the menstrual period, which the Bible specifies as lasting seven days, no matter how many days the flow actually lasts (Lev. 15.19).[23] According to the Pharisees, after the seven-day menstrual period there are eleven days during which blood is not considered menstrual. This period is stated by the stam of Niddah 4.7, but the Houses disputes below also presuppose it. The importance of the convention of eleven days will be apparent: for eleven days one is free from expecting menstruation, and thus free from thinking that a sign of blood signals the beginning of seven days of sexual abstinence. Repeated bleeding during the eleven-day period makes a woman a zavah (Lev. 15.25, 'a discharge of blood for many days, not at the time of her impurity'). It appears from T. Niddah 9.19 that the Houses agreed that 'many days' means 'two days if consecutive',[24] and it is probable that they required three discharges if on non-consecutive days (cf. the discussion of the zav, Zabim 1.1–4). One sign of blood during the eleven-day period was meaningless; it was neither 'discharge' nor menstruation. Because of the 'two consecutive day' rule, however, it followed that a woman who showed blood within the eleven-day period should not have intercourse but should wait to see what happened the next day. Until then she had to be deemed impure (so the stam of Niddah 4.7, a rule accepted by the Houses). After the eleventh day blood would indicate the onset of menstruation, and the woman would be impure for seven days.

This convention attracted attention to the status of blood *on* the eleventh day. Could there be a non-menstrual 'discharge' which started on the eleventh day, since from the twelfth day menstruation might begin? If a woman showed blood on the eleventh day, could she immerse and have sexual relations after sunset, on the grounds that the blood could not be either menstruation or the beginning of a discharge?

The passages in which these assumptions are revealed are a bit complicated:

> They [the Houses] agree that if she saw blood *within* the eleven-day period and immersed that same evening and then had intercourse, they both render impure what they lie on and sit on, and they owe an offering. (Niddah 10.8c)[25]

cf.: The House of Shammai said to the House of Hillel: Do you not agree that, since in the case of a woman who sees blood *within* the eleven-day period and who immerses that same evening and then has intercourse, she renders impure what she lies and sits on and owes a sacrifice – (T. Niddah 9.19b)

therefore also does not the woman who sees blood *on* the eleventh day owe a sacrifice? The House of Hillel say to them: No; For if you say, with regard to a woman who sees blood *within* the eleven day period, that the next day is added to it to establish *zibah*, you must say, with regard to one who sees blood *on* the eleventh day, that the next day is not added to it to establish *zibah*. The House of Shammai said to them: If this is the case, she does not render impure what she sits on and lies on. The House of Hillel said: Though we expand the impurity of what is lain and sat on (in a stringent way), we shall limit the requirement to bring a sacrifice (in a lenient way). (T. Niddah 9.19c)

cf.: If she saw blood *on* the eleventh day and immersed herself at nightfall and then had connexion, the School of Shammai say: [Both] convey uncleanness to what they lie upon or sit upon, and they are liable to an offering. And the School of Hillel say: They are not liable to an offering. (Niddah 10.8a)

According to Niddah 10.8c and T. Niddah 9.19b the Houses agreed that a woman who saw blood within the eleven-day period had to wait a day before immersing and having intercourse. This is the 'two- consecutive-day' rule. If it was not observed, the Pharisees thought that sexual relations required a sacrifice; that is, sex in this circumstance was treated as equivalent to inadvertent intercourse with a menstruant. The requirement of a sacrifice shows that, in their view, both the eleven-day rule and the two-consecutive-day rule are binding interpretations of the law. We are not told, however, which law had been transgressed – a point to which we shall return.

A woman who showed blood *on* the eleventh day could not be a menstruant, according to the pharisaic convention. But similarly she could not be a zavah, since that requires blood on two consecutive days. Blood on the twelfth day would make her a menstruant, and so the period of two consecutive days could not begin on the eleventh day. Following this logic, the Hillelites thought that bleeding on the eleventh day could make a woman neither a menstruant nor a zavah, and intercourse after immersion (they assumed that immersion is required) was legal. Legality is proved by the rule that the couple did not owe a sacrifice. Put another way: In the sequence – blood on the eleventh day, immersion, intercourse after sunset – there was no transgression of biblical law (T. Niddah 9.19c; Niddah 10.8a). Although there was no transgression, the Hillelites thought that all was not quite as it should be. Their general rule was that a woman who bled *any time* during the eleven-day period should wait a day before having intercourse, since blood on the next day would make her a zavah. Even though blood on the next day would not, in this particular case, make her a zavah (but rather a menstruant), still, to be strict, the couple should have waited until a pure day had passed. Thus in the sequence sketched just above, there was no transgression of biblical law, and so no sacrifice; nevertheless the couple had not been scrupulous enough, and they conveyed impurity to what they lay and sat on – midras-impurity. The Hillelites here show a conception of an *intermediate state* of impurity. As their answer in T. Niddah 9.19c makes clear, they were prepared to expand the rules of midras-impurity, but not the law on sin offerings, on the basis of 'scribal' authority.

The Shammaites apparently thought that a woman who saw blood on the eleventh day was strictly governed by the rules which applied if she saw it on the ninth or fifth: she had to wait a full day, and so she should not immerse and have intercourse. If she did, both she and her husband conveyed midras-impurity and owed sacrifices.[26]

The Houses debated one further possibility with regard to blood on the eleventh day: A woman sees blood on the eleventh day and waits until the twelfth day. Seeing no blood then either, she immerses and has intercourse. Afterwards, but still on the twelfth day, blood again appears. The Shammaites' view was that both woman and man convey uncleanness to what they lie upon or sit upon, but they are not liable to an offering. 'And the School of Hillel say: Such a one is gluttonous [yet is not culpable]' (Niddah 10.8b). The couple had waited through part of a pure day and thus, in the eyes of the Shammaites, were half-guilty, while the Hillelites merely frowned disapprovingly. We see here again a view of an intermediate stage of impurity, this time held by the Shammaites.

Let us now consider a bit more closely what the Houses consider 'law' and what not. The specification of eleven days they regard as a binding rider on the law of menstruation: blood during the eleven days after completion of a menstrual period is not menstrual blood. They also consider binding the two-consecutive-day rule for establishing zivah: a woman who sees blood on two consecutive days during the eleven-day period is a zavah. Both these views simply define the phrases of Lev. 15.25: 'a discharge of blood for many days' means 'two if consecutive'; 'not at the time of her impurity' means 'during the non-menstrual eleven-day period'. The Houses then press ahead, however, to the opinion that, if a woman shows blood during the eleven days, she and her husband cannot have intercourse until they know what will happen next. They must wait a day, and intercourse without waiting is a *transgression* which requires a sin offering. The Houses agree on this if the first sign of blood is on days one to ten, and we now leave aside their debates about the eleventh day.

What law has been broken? Not the prohibition of intercourse during menstruation, since the blood cannot have been menstrual. Not the implied prohibition of intercourse during a state of zivah. Zivah requires a wait of seven days of purity before sacrifices are brought (Lev. 15.29), but in the rabbinic discussions both parties are 'fined' a sin offering for the act of intercourse before it is established whether or not the woman was a zavah. Thus the Pharisees have created, and regard as binding, a new legal category; intercourse with a woman who is potentially a zavah; and they equate it with inadvertent intercourse with a menstruant.

Unfortunately we cannot know who agreed or disagreed with them. In two passages, non-pharisaic pietists complain that the priests convey menstrual impurity to the altar (Ps. Sol. 8.12; CD 5.6f.). These charges are not eye-witness testimony to blood on the priests' clothing when they enter the temple, but rather are based on legal disputes about when intercourse is permitted. We know from this only that there were disagreements, but not who held what position.

(c) Relaxations of the law. The Houses modified the prohibition of intercourse with a menstruant for the sake of weddings. If at the time of marriage the wife had not previously menstruated, they agreed that any blood which appeared should be considered to have come from the rupturing of the hymen, not from menstruation. The House of Shammai limited the period during which blood was deemed to be from the wound to four days; the House of Hillel left the period open. If the wife was old enough to menstruate, and her period was due at the time of the marriage, the House of Shammai allowed one night's intercourse anyway, the House of Hillel four nights. If her period had already started before the wedding, the House of Shammai allowed only 'the coition of obligation', while the House of Hillel allowed the whole night (Niddah 10.1).

(d) Testing for blood. According to the stam of Niddah 2.1, after sexual relations two test-rags should be used, one for him and one for her. The Pharisees apparently agreed, for the Houses divided on the issue of whether two rags are needed for each act or for each night (Niddah 2.4). They also debated other questions with regard to the purity or impurity of blood from women (Niddah 2.6; 4.3// (with some differences) T. Niddah 5.5–6).

§6. Zavim and Zavot: miscellany. We have already seen a good deal of the woman with a 'discharge' or 'flux', a zavah. Just above we learned that the Pharisees assumed that intercourse with her is forbidden (Niddah 10.8; T. Niddah 9.19). This is not a biblical prohibition, but has been taken over from the prohibition of sexual relations with a menstruant, or it has been inferred because the zavah renders others impure – or both.[27] Both male and female zavs (zavim and zavot, respectively) figure in the rules of midras-impurity, since they are both sources of it. There are only a few more points about zavs to consider, and we shall do so briefly.

In discussing biblical law, we proposed that people probably did not regard every male who had an unexpected emission from his penis as suffering from gonorrhoea, and we noted that the Pharisees distinguished a full from a partial zav. The Houses debated the question of the status of a man who had one unexpected emission. The House of Shammai held that he is like a woman 'who watches day against day' after a show of blood within the eleven-day period: i.e., he is deemed impure until one full day passes. The Hillelites maintained that he is like a man who had a nocturnal emission: he is purified by bathing and sunset (Zabim 1.1; T. Zav. 1.1). The opening paragraphs in the tractates in both the Mishnah and Tosefta include several other discussions of what makes a man a full zav (Houses: Zabim 1.1–2; T. Zav. 1.1–8). Here we find again an intermediate state of impurity: a partial zav conveys midras-impurity but is not required to bring a sacrifice (required of a zav in Lev. 15.14–15).

§7. Utensils: miscellany. Kelim are subject to impurity from several sources (above, Midras-impurity). There are two further points to be noted. First, the Pharisees again developed or accepted a conception of an intermediate state: the 'half-utensil' (e.g. T. Kelim Baba Qamma 2.1). The other is that the Houses discussed the purity or impurity of vessels if left with someone else or in public (T. Tohoroth 8.10). We shall discuss the second point under the heading 'Exclusiveism'.

Most discussions about utensils are definitional and were illustrated under Midras-impurity: is X a keli? when does change of function or damage alter its status? Further passages are Kelim 11.3; T. Kel. Baba Qamma 2.1; T. Kel. Baba Metzia 3.8; 4.5; 4.16; 11.7; T. Kel. Baba Batra 5.7–8.

§8. Immersion Pools. The Bible prescribes bathing for several impurities (e.g. intercourse), and we have just seen that it was extended to other cases (e.g. menstruation) by the Pharisees and probably others. With the construction of the large Court of the Women, it was an obvious step to say that women, after impurity because of menstruation or some other flow of blood, should bathe, just as did men who touched their beds. There was another obvious development: to define 'bathing'.

(*a*) Definitions and presuppositions. People generally accepted the idea that the bathing which is commanded in the Bible should be done in a special pool. Complete immersion was required by the Essenes, as is shown by CD 10.11–13 and the existence of several pools at Qumran. With regard to the rest of the population, archaeology has revealed numerous pools large enough to allow complete immersion.[28] They have survived because they were entirely or partially cut into bedrock,[29] and often all that has been lost is the roof over those partially cut into the bedrock. A pool which was used for religious reasons – what is usually called 'ritual purity' – is called a *miqveh*, plural *miqva'ôt*.[30]

Though no biblical passage defines the 'bathing' required by Lev. 15, there was a partial exegetical basis for the use of special pools which were quite large. Leviticus 15.16 states that a man who has a nocturnal emission shall bathe 'his whole body' (cf. 'bathe his body', 15.13; 22.6), and this verse probably led to the view that removal of impurity required that one bathe one's whole body at the same time; that is, immerse. Leviticus 11.36 states that 'a spring or a cistern holding water shall be pure' even if a dead swarming thing falls into it. 'Cistern holding water' is in Hebrew *bôr miqveh-mayim*, from which the rabbinic term miqveh for an immersion pool was derived. From the passage people deduced that running water (a spring) is pure and that a pool of standing water is pure, *so* pure that they cannot be rendered impure even by a dead swarming thing. It was then a fairly easy step to say that the impurities of Lev. 15 had to be removed by such water. This exegesis seems to have been accepted throughout Palestine in the first century.

A spring is readily identifiable, but thus far we have not defined a pure pool. It had to be large enough to allow 'the whole body' to be bathed. Was special water required? Since the verse in Leviticus mentions a 'spring', one might think that the pool had to be filled with spring water. Another verse probably helped add a source from which suitable water could come. Leviticus 15.13 states that a zav, at the end of his affliction, must bathe in 'living' or 'running' water. This, together with the word 'spring' in Lev. 11, seems to have led to the view that pure water is 'natural', either it is running by itself, or it has collected by itself.

The Pharisees, as we shall see, concluded that purification required a pool of water which collected naturally and which was large enough for immersion. The volume was put at 40 *se'ah*. Estimates of this quantity range from 250 litres to 1,000 litres; we may conveniently think of 500 litres, approximately 110 Imperial gallons, 125 US gallons.[31] Many of the pools, however, are much larger than this. One at Qumran would hold 9,000 litres (*c.* 2,000 Imperial gallons, 2,250 US), but larger ones were quite common.[32]

What we do not know is how non-Pharisees defined pure or valid water. All agreed, however, on pools large enough for full immersion.

Miqva'ot constitute the only physical evidence which is distributed widely enough to permit the study of 'unity and diversity' in first-century Palestine, and they permit us to study immersion more closely than is possible with any other regular practice. Thus we shall look at them in a bit more detail.

The study of these pools is a new industry which is rapidly growing. A lot of miqva'ot had been found before 1963–1964 but not identified as such.

Scholars considered but on the whole rejected the possibility that the pools at Qumran were for religious purification.[33] The first miqveh which was universally accepted as such was found in the 1963–1964 excavation season on Matsada,[34] Herod's fortress near the Dead Sea which was used as a last refuge by some of the Sicarii (often incorrectly called 'Zealots') after the fall of Jerusalem in CE. 70. The reason this miqveh was not disputed is that it fits rabbinic description precisely. The pools at Qumran, and some of the other immersion pools already found at other sites, do not agree with rabbinic halakah; and scholars, clinging to the view that the Pharisees and then the Rabbis dictated what everyone in Palestine did and thought, did not see them for what they were. They were often called simply 'stepped pools'. Among archaeologists, there are still 'maximalists' and 'minimalists' – respectively, those who take all stepped pools to be miqva'ot (to remove impurities) and those who require a pool to be built as the Rabbis decreed before calling it a 'miqveh'. I side with the maximalists, whose leading spokesman is Ronny Reich. That the 'stepped pools' are miqva'ot becomes clear when they are compared to other facilities which used water.

In Palestine there are six principal types of water installation which were dug or built for residential purposes.[35] (1) Cisterns. Cisterns, which were very widely used to collect and store rainwater, are readily identified: they are enormous chambers cut into the rock, with very small entrances. It is usually impossible to walk down into cisterns, but in cases where this can be done (e.g. the cistern on the top of Matsada) the steps occupy a very small percentage of the excavated area. Water was stored in cisterns in many parts of Palestine, and it is impossible to mistake a cistern for anything else. Similarly, since almost everybody dug cisterns, it is not reasonable to think that other types of pool were cisterns, since all other pools would have been less efficient for water storage. (2) Bathtubs. These are fairly short and shallow. A bathtub is usually long enough for a person to sit down and stretch out the legs, or stretch them out partially, but not to lie down entirely. Water was probably poured over the bather. If the tub was filled, the water would come up to the abdomen or chest. Immersion would not be possible. (3) Immersion pools. An immersion pool is deep relative to its surface area (unlike a bathtub), but there is nevertheless a lot of surface area (unlike a cistern). One of the miqva'ot at the Herodium, to take a fairly average example, is 3.6 metres by 2.0 metres on the surface and 2.0 metres deep (in round figures, 12 ft × 7 ft × 7 ft deep).[36] Other miqva'ot are closer to three metres (c. 10 feet) deep. Steps occupy a fair percentage of the total space (contrast cisterns), and they go all the way to the bottom, but the person who immersed would go down the steps only as far as necessary.

The extra depth allowed solids to sink and kept the water relatively clean.[37] Since these pools are usually close to a cistern, they themselves cannot have been cisterns. They also are not bathtubs, which are much easier to have (since they are smaller), which require much less water, and which are a good deal more comfortable. The water for a bathtub can be heated and changed; that in an immersion pool cannot be heated and can be changed only with difficulty, since there are no heating facilities[38] and there is no drainage plug. These pools are, thus, miqva'ot, used to remove the impurities of Lev. 15. (4) Sometimes there is a further pool, often of similar size, but without steps, beside the miqveh. The miqveh just described has a companion pool, which is 3.5 metres × 1.4 by 2.7 deep. These adjacent pools are very important, as will be explained below. Relatively few miqva'ot have twin unstepped pools beside them. (5) Bathhouses. These exist in the Hasmonean and Herodian palaces, and there were probably some public bathhouses in the first century.[39] Jewish bathhouses included miqva'ot and often bathtubs. They were distinguished by also having caldaria (hot rooms) or (in at least one case) a heated pool. There is no possibility of confusing one function with another. The heated pool in the Hasmonean bathhouse in Jericho is in the same complex as a bathtub and a miqveh. The heated pool is much smaller than a miqveh: 1.8 metres × .9 × 1.4 deep, c. 6 ft × 3 × 4½ deep. As Netzer points out, this is the only 'immersion' pool 'in which one could descend to the bottom without fear of drowning'.[40] One could immerse in it by bending over, though it may have functioned as a hot tub, for relaxation and pleasure. The size, however, drives home how remarkable and distinctive are the miqva'ot. They allow immersion even when, in a long dry spell, the level falls substantially. Their *raison d'être* is immersion and nothing else. (6) There were swimming pools at Jericho (built by the Hasmoneans, used and beautified by Herod), Matsada and the Herodium (though to call the last a swimming pool is to belittle it).[41] They are very large in area and open to the sky, and they cannot be confused with cisterns, miqva'ot or bathtubs.

Thus each type of water installation is distinctive. The unheated stepped pools, 2 metres (7 feet) or so deep, without drains at the bottom, were miqva'ot (whether approved by Pharisees or not).

Once one identifies stepped pools as miqva'ot, they can be found more-or-less everywhere. They are in both the wealthy Upper City (West Jerusalem) and the poorer Lower City (south of the temple wall); they are in all of Herod's palaces; they are in Sepphoris, on Matsada, in Gamla, at Qumran and elsewhere (above, n. 28). Not infrequently the steps are divided or partitioned, so that one could go in one way and out another; sometimes there are two sets of steps. In miqva'ot used by numerous people, this could have been a form of crowd control, but partitioned steps were also used in private miqva'ot, and probably they served to separate the impure, on the way in, from the pure, on the way out.[42]

Several people in Israel took a great deal of trouble to show and explain miqva'ot to me (see the Preface). Despite this coaching, I cannot pretend to be an archaeologist, and my views are those of an amateur. I shall, however, offer an amateur's description. Miqva'ot are of basically three types:

1. They are sometimes built below the level of a spring and fed by an aquaduct. This is the case in the Hasmonean and Herodian palaces at Jericho. The abundant springs made Jericho a very prosperous place during the second temple period. The rulers used the area as a winter resort, and there are remains of several palaces. In such a place, where there was a source of water above the miqveh, the supply, sanitation and purity of the water were straightforward. A channel provided a flow of fresh, 'living' water which flushed the miqveh and prevented stagnation and slime. These pools were seldom, if ever, emptied, and they contain a lot of sediment.[43]

2. Some miqva'ot are beside an unstepped pool.[44] They have been found at Jericho, Jerusalem, Matsada (built by the Sicarii), Sepphoris and elsewhere.[45] In some cases one can still see a lead or clay pipe at the top which connects the two pools. This type of miqveh is explained by the stam of Mikwaoth 6.8:

> They may render Immersion-pools clean [by mingling the drawn water in] a higher pool [with undrawn water] from a lower pool, or [the drawn water in] a distant pool [with undrawn water] from a pool that is near by. Thus a man may bring a pipe of earthenware or lead . . .

The people who built such pools had a 'pharisaic' conception of pure or valid water: it had to be undrawn, that is, not carried by a human. The water was valid if it collected naturally from rain, or if it flowed naturally from a spring. *Or*, as we now learn, drawn water could be put into contact with undrawn water, and the drawn water was thus purified. This explains the second pool, for which we may use the later Hebrew name, *'ôtsar*, 'treasury' or, in this case, 'storage pool'. When it rained, both pools were filled. The miqveh was used until it became desirable to change the water or add to it. Drawn water was then put into the stepped pool, and the pipe at the top was briefly opened. This brought the old, undrawn water of the 'otsar into contact with the new, drawn water in the miqveh, and the latter was purified. The earliest known example of such a pool is found at the Hasmonean palace at Jericho. Though the pool was connected to a spring by a water channel, nevertheless they used a second pool and a pipe. Netzer proposes that the second pool served to purify the water of the miqveh in case the flow from the spring was interrupted (e.g. by damage to the aquaduct).

We should note that this 'pharisaic' construction marks some of the earliest pools known. We cannot yet know whether the miqveh/'otsar combinations at Jericho were built during a time when the Pharisees were in favour with the Hasmonean ruler, or whether the theory of purifying the water by contact was widespread. There were also, however, single miqva'ot in Hasmonean Jericho. We shall return to this below.

3. There are numerous single miqva'ot which have neither an 'otsar nor a source of running water. These are found in some of Herod's palaces, in Jerusalem, especially the Upper City, Sepphoris and elsewhere. There are three possibilities about the water in such pools: (*a*) it was not changed except when it rained, and stagnation was mitigated only by adding drawn water to it; (*b*) it was changed by hand and refilled with drawn water; (*c*) it was emptied by hand and refilled with water from a cistern on the roof of the house. Since these pools are found in the houses of aristocrats and the king, who knew about bathing and bathtubs, it is difficult to think that the water was not changed. Thus it was probably changed by hand (that is, by the hands of servants); we may eliminate (*a*). (*c*) is hard to evaluate, since roofs of houses have not survived. Eric Meyers, who has drawn this possibility to my attention, also tells me that at Sepphoris he has found ceramic pipes which could carry water from a rooftop cistern to the miqveh. The Pharisees, however, would still consider this water to be 'drawn' (see Mikwaoth 4.5). As far as I have been able to determine the numerous single miqva'ot in the Upper City did not have pipes running into them from above, and for these the most likely possibility is (*b*): emptied by servants and refilled by drawing and carrying water.

The first two types (miqva'ot supplied with spring water and miqva'ot connected to 'otsarot) are unquestionably valid by the rules of the Pharisees. Though the mishnah about connecting two pools, given above, cannot be dated pre-70, it is nevertheless shown by archaeology to explain a system which was used as early as the days of the Hasmoneans. We may, then, take this mishnah to define an immersion pool which the Pharisees would accept. They objected to using drawn water for miqva'ot.

That pools fed by a spring would be accepted is clear from pharisaic debates in rabbinic literature about how much drawn water could be used to top up a pool without rendering it invalid.[46] An interesting passage has Hillel argue that 1 hin (=3 qavs or 12 logs) of drawn water made the immersion pool invalid, while according to Shammai 9 qavs had this effect.

This is not much: 3 qavs = 3.6 litres, less than 1 gallon; 9 qavs = 10.8 litres, *c.* 2½ gallons. Since a miqveh held thousands of litres, a tiny percentage of drawn water was being discussed. Earlier, Shemaiah and Abtalion had held that 3 logs (=.9 litres) made the pool invalid (Eduyoth 1.3).[47] This was the rule that ultimately prevailed. Similarly the Houses discussed how much rain was required to make an invalid pool pure again (Mikwaoth 1.5; cf. T. Miqva'ot 1.7,10). All these debates reveal the view that drawn water may invalidate a miqveh.

The existence of the third type of pool shows that the aristocracy and possibly others did not accept the entirety of this reasoning. The idea of a 'pool' they agreed with, and this might have been pre-pharisaic.[48] They also thought that the pool should be large enough for immersion. They probably would prefer running water if they could get it, but often they could not. There are no springs higher than the Upper City, and there is no spring higher than Sepphoris (to name only two places where single pools without running water have been found). In these cases, they stored large quantities of water in cisterns (as did everybody), and doubtless they sometimes renewed the miqveh with drawn water.

I think that the case of non-pharisaic practice can be proved by Herod. He clearly had advisers, and he accepted their opinions – for example, in having priests trained as masons to build the inner court of the temple and the sanctuary itself. He also built miqva'ot. Herod knew about Roman or Hellenistic baths, as well as about immersion pools, and he incorporated the latter in the former. As Reich has pointed out, in Herod's baths the miqveh serves as the frigidarium (cold bath) in the Roman system.[49] In Herod's baths, however, from the tepidarium or from the vestibule one could enter *either* the frigidarium/miqveh *or* the caldarium (hot room).[50] This was not typical of Roman baths. Herod's arrangement allowed him (and his immediate household) either to use the miqveh or to go into the hot room.[51]

In Jericho, as I noted above, there is no question of the validity of the water, since abundant spring water was channelled through the area used for living and recreation. Thus the absence of 'otsarot in the Herodian bathhouses in Jericho tells us little. On the top of Matsada, however, the possibility of flushing the miqveh with new water would occur very seldom. There is no spring, and rain rarely falls on the mountain itself. The water is gathered from Wadis when there is rain in the hills above. Here the miqva'ot built by Herod – both his own and the large public bathhouse – do not have the second pool with a pipe.

Herod was a strict enough Jew to train priests as masons, not to put his image on coins, not to decorate his palaces with images of birds, beasts and people,[52] and to have immersion pools wherever he lived. He did not, however, follow the pharisaic prescription. One cannot think that this was personal idiosyncracy. Rather, his advisers, presumably priests, did not follow it. One then notes that, with very few exceptions, the pharisaic second pool is not found in the houses of the aristocrats, many of whom were also priests, in the Upper City. Which pools near the entrance to Herod's temple served the public is not clear – or at least, not clear to me – but some of them are not build according to pharisaic standards.[53] It is possible that two Hasmonean pools can be identified just outside the wall of the pre-Herodian temple (in an area subsequently incorporated into the Court of the Gentiles by Herod).[54] It appears that these pools were not 'pharisaic'. Thus three bits of evidence – Herod's miqva'ot, the aristocratic/priestly miqva'ot in the Upper City, and some of the public miqva'ot near the temple – indicate that priestly/aristocratic circles did not accept the pharisaic second pool.

Not many archaeologists will agree with my analysis. Some will maintain that many pools were pharisaic even though we cannot now see it, and that non-pharisaic pools were not for purification. The study of miqva'ot is still in its youth; in most cases final archaeological reports have not yet been published. When full technical details are available, things may be clearer. Meanwhile, there is resistance to the idea that there were non-pharisaic pools – just as, for a long time, people doubted the identification of the pools at Qumran.

Those who think that the halakah of the Rabbis was always in force can offer two responses to the problem posed by different building standards. Ehud Netzer, contemplating the fact that at Jericho there are both twin pools and single pools, proposed that 'under ordinary conditions' – that is, when the aqueduct was bringing fresh spring water to the bathhouse – the single pools could serve as miqva'ot, but that when the flow of water was interrupted 'the absence of a storage pool made it impossible to use them for ritual purposes'.[55] This is the 'non-pharisaic pools were not miqva'ot' view. It does very well for Jericho, where most of the time (we may suppose) the water flowed, and where in any case there were always one or two miqva'ot with 'otsarot for the priests to use, so that they could eat (the Hasmoneans were priests). It does not, however, meet the problem posed by the fifty or so single miqva'ot in the Upper City, where there was never a supply of spring water. Here Netzer's early suggestion, that such pools were not used for purification, has been disproved by subsequent evidence.[56]

The principal talmudic response is that there is no problem. The aristocratic and Herodian pools are also valid, because, once a pool holds the requisite quantity of rainwater, and provided that the rainwater goes in first, any amount of drawn water can be added without rendering the pool invalid. This assumption is seen, for example, in Mikwaoth 3.1 and 4.4. The discussions between Shemaiah and Abtalion, and Hillel and Shammai, about how much drawn water can be added, according to this view, mean 'how much can be added to the pool *before* 40 se'ah of rainwater have run into it?', not 'how much drawn water can be used to top up the pool?' By attributing this view to the Pharisees, one can argue that they would have validated any large pool, provided that they could be sure that rainwater went in first.

> Once it possesses the minimum quantity of 40 *se'ah* of valid water even though 'someone draws water in a jug and throws it into the *mikveh* all day long, all the water is valid'.[57]

On this view, the aristocratic miqva'ot were originally filled with rain water, and then repeatedly topped up with drawn water, the water not being changed except during the rainy seasons. This would meet mishnaic requirements.

We have seen that the anonymous mishnah on connecting two pools (Mikwaoth 6.8), though it cannot be dated pre-70, nevertheless reflects pre-70 conditions: there were such pools. Do, then, Mikwaoth 3.1 (R. Joshua) and 4.4 (anonymous) explain the single miqva'ot? Were the miqva'ot with neither spring nor 'otsar just as valid in the Pharisees' eyes as the other two types?

This seems to me unlikely. I think it more probable that something was at stake in the difference between miqva'ot with and without 'otsarot. Considering all the pools as equally 'pharisaic' leaves some questions unanswered.

1. It does not explain why there were two methods of building, one requiring twice as much labour as the other, if both were satisfactory in the eyes of the same authorities, the Pharisees. The amount of labour required to excavate several cubic metres of bedrock means that those who dug second pools were strongly motivated.

2. It does not explain why single pools are found especially in aristocratic areas but double pools seldom, while the relatively few double pools are mostly in the poorer Lower City.[58] Could the aristocrats not afford to have double pools dug? Were they less concerned with sanitation? It is to be remembered that the main advantage of the double pool is that the miqveh could be emptied (or partially emptied) and refilled with drawn water, then purified by contact with the water in the 'otsar. By pharisaic rules, single pools could be cleaned only at a time of heavy rainfall. By these rules, then, the aristocrats were the least sanitary. This is true even if one accepts as pharisaic the view that *any* quantity of drawn water could be added to the top, as long as the original 40 se'ah of rainwater remained. As long as the old water remained deep enough to be above the head, it would become increasingly

unsanitary. The only way to get the sludge out of the bottom of the pool, and to add enough new water to make the pool clear, would be to take out a lot of the old water, down to knee level.

3. The proposal that all pools met the pietist requirements also does not explain why the Sicarii – or at least some of them – dug new double pools on Matsada. The Sicarii made some alterations in Herod's public bathhouse, though whether they used its miqveh, or only its other facilities, cannot be known. But they also dug two new sets of double pools. Herod's ample pools were more likely invalid (in their view) than inadequate in size. The new pools are quite small.[59]

4. As a semi-argument I mention a curious fact. In Jericho, one of the Hasmonean sets of two pools, between which there was a channel, was reused in the Herodian period, but the channel was blocked up. At the Herodium, the unstepped pool beside the miqveh (in the set discussed above) was filled with rubble (broken pottery) of the Herodian period, apparently while the miqveh itself was still in use.[60] These pools are only straws in the wind, but they help us see that people disagreed about miqva'ot. Some may have objected to linked pools as strongly as others objected to drawn water.

I begin at a different point from the talmudist. He as a rule starts with 'the halakah', finished and complete, codified by Maimonides, and finds earlier evidence for it. The evidence may be fragmentary and may even be surprising, perhaps apparently contradictory, but whatever the evidence is, it fits somehow or other, and it proves the halakah's existence. We noted this above when discussing Alon (III.C). Early evidence which disagrees completely with 'the halakah', but which is on the same subject, he saw as proving the halakah's early existence. On miqva'ot, the modern talmudist has Maimonides, who said that any amount of drawn water may be added, as long as originally there were 40 se'ah of rainwater. Some mishnayot presuppose this view, showing it to be much earlier than Maimonides, and it 'explains' the aristocratic pools. They simply did not clean their pools out, despite having the servants to do the work, but kept topping up the stagnant, grotty water.

This seems to me most unlikely, for the reasons given above, but also because I start at a different place. The Bible says nothing about pools of x size, nor does it require immersion. Given the differences which we know existed within second temple Judaism, I am amazed that in the first century so many Jews in Palestine agreed (1) that there should be pools; (2) that they should be large enough to allow immersion. Hasmoneans, Essenes, Pharisees, Herod, ordinary people, the aristocrats (including the aristocratic priesthood) – all agreed. And in all probability immersion before entering the temple was *enforced*: thus the pools near the entrance. This is an unexpected, almost a fantastic degree of uniformity, once one recognizes that immersion pools are not required by the Bible.

It asks too much to demand that everybody *also* agreed to the rule of 40 se 'ah of rainwater and 3 logs of drawn water (Mikwaoth 4.4). This is against the simplest construal of the evidence – which is that some people had single pools and changed the water whenever they wished, without worrying about 'drawing' it; while others had double pools and, when they changed the water, validated the new water by bringing the water of the second pool into contact with it. They cleaned the entire system out, if at all, during heavy rains.

That not everyone accepted the pharisaic prohibition of drawn water is also supported by rabbinic evidence. Reich has pointed out the importance of the rabbinic view that a person is impure ('renders heave offering unfit') who puts his head and the greater part of his body into drawn water, as is the person upon whom three logs of drawn water fall.[61] These rules are attributed to the House of Shammai in Shabbat 13b, where they are said to be among the 'eighteen decrees' which the Shammaites forced the Hillelites to accept (see Shabbath 1.4). They also appear as the stam of Zabim 5.12, which Epstein attributes to R. Joshua, and this supports their attribution to the period of the Houses.[62] These rules oppose two practices: immersing in drawn water and bathing after immersion by having clean, drawn water poured over the bather. The mere existence of these passages proves that not everyone accepted the Pharisees' views, and the first decree shows that somewhere, sometime, someone immersed in drawn water. We may assume that the passage is directed against more than one person. Therefore the decree which is attributed to the Shammaites opposes the practice of some group which did not accept the pharisaic definition of valid water.

One cannot accidentally immerse in drawn water. To accomplish it, a large pool must be filled by human effort – a lot of human effort. If one used a jug which would hold twenty litres (five gallons), one would have to fill and empty the vessel 500 times to move 10,000 litres (2,500 gallons). Even partially emptying and refilling a miqveh by hand would be very heavy work. Such a labour-intensive method of filling miqva'ot probably indicates that the other group could afford servants.[63]

The aristocrats of the Upper City are the best candidates for the role. It is unlikely that a non-pharisaic practice of this sort sprang up only after 70. We are best advised to accept the passage as late pharisaic rather than early rabbinic, and to see it as directed against the aristocrats – whom we now know to have had single miqva'ot.

It is striking that the prohibition of drawn water is said to be an enactment which originated with the House of Shammai, since the Pharisees had earlier ruled out the use of drawn water (Eduyoth 1.3, Shemaiah and Abtalion). Why would they now 'decree' that those who used it were impure? As I have frequently pointed out, the Pharisees generally tolerated the practice of others. They had defined valid water for their own immersion pools, but they had not tried to keep others from using different types of pool. The Shammaites (still following Shabbat 13b) now declared that a person who immerses in drawn water renders heave offering unfit. If accepted, this would primarily affect priests and their families, who ate heave offering, and secondarily people who handled it *en route* to them. Transgressing the Shammaites' rule was not, in their own eyes, a 'sin', and those who used drawn water were not excluded from 'Israel'. The Pharisees distinguished their traditions from the law, and said merely that those whom they opposed rendered heave offering unfit.

The second rule, that one on whom drawn water falls also renders heave offering unfit, is against bathing after immersion. Reich points out that this rule affects people who use a public bathhouse: they should immerse afterwards, not before. But it is equally against those who sit in a bathtub and have a servant pour warm, clean water over them after they immerse in the cold pool. Now we note that in many of the aristocratic houses in the Upper City there is a bathtub near the miqveh, as part of a bathing complex. Even though the water in the miqveh may have been changed more then twice a year, it would still have been stagnant. People who could afford it, and who cared about such things, bathed after immersing.

On numerous grounds, I think it likely that the aristocrats did not accept the pharisaic prescriptions about valid pools. This will be resisted by those who think that everyone accepted what the Pharisees said. Shabbat 13b/ Zabim 5.12, however, opposes current practice and proves non-compliance with pharisaic/rabbinic definitions. Those who nevertheless disagree with me about changing the water in the miqva'ot will, I think, agree that the aristocrats had bathtubs near their immersion pools so that they could bathe after immersing. One of the decrees attributed to the Shammaites opposes this practice, and it formulates the opposition in terms of rendering heave offering unfit for priestly consumption. Thus the poor aristocrats were declared impure by the pharisaic council when it was dominated by the Shammaites on at least one ground. We might as well grant that they were attacked on two grounds, and that they had used drawn water in their miqva'ot to keep them fresher than the seasonal rains in Palestine would permit under pharisaic rules.

One notes that, if the temple was still functioning at the time of the Shammaites' decree, the aristocrats kept on using their pools, bathing afterwards, and entering the temple, unhindered by it. The Upper City, in fact, was intimately connected with the temple. Some of its residents were priests, as may be concluded from the large number of stone tables and vessels found in the houses.[64] Some houses had more than one miqveh, which would imply frequent immersion; priests and their families immersed daily so that they could eat in purity (III.B). One of the residents bore the name of a high priestly family, Kathros. Because many stone weights were found in the house, Avigad suggests that he may have been a purveyor of incense to the temple.[65] It is these people who, like Herod, ignored the pharisaic preference for two pools, and who carried on running things as they wished.

Is there a *Sitz im Leben* for the decrees that people are impure if they immerse 'the head and the greater part of the body' in drawn water, and if they have three logs of drawn water fall on them? The 'eighteen decrees' – which cannot be precisely counted – have produced a lot of speculation both early and late. They are said to have been passed in the upper room of Hananiah b. Hezekiah b. Garon 'on that day' when the Shammaites forced the Hillelites to vote as they ordered. We saw above (pp. 87f.) that the tradition about 'that day' became increasingly violent and that it cannot be taken at face value. On the other hand, the decrees about immersing and bathing require an occasion on which a group of Pharisees or Rabbis tried to impose their view on others. One of the common explanations of the 'eighteen decrees' provides a suitable occasion. Most of the decrees are restrictive, and some can be seen as anti-Gentile. Some scholars, in view of this general characteristic and the attribution of the decrees to the period of Hananiah b. Hezekiah b. Garon (said to have been the head of the house of Shammai in the generation before the revolt[66]), conclude that the decrees belong to the period just before the outbreak of war.[67] A time of crisis often leads to severe measures, and the Shammaites felt that the aristocratic priests were not strict enough. One then notes that it was a Hillelite, Simeon b. Gamaliel, who cooperated with the Sadducean high priest Ananus and others in the coalition government (the *koinon*) early in the revolt.[68] He doubtless thought that Ananus could immerse as he wished and still eat heave offering.

I should distinguish between a general proposal, about which I feel fairly confident, and a more precise but speculative suggestion. General: The miqveh + 'otsar system was probably devised by the Pharisees, though naturally some non-members accepted it. Such systems were installed by at least one Hasmonean under pharisaic influence. From the time of Herod on, the Pharisees lost influence in high places. They acquired a realistic estimate of their ability to control religious observance, and they exercised prudence and tolerance. With regard to immersion, they continued to debate the precise definition of valid water among themselves (Eduyoth 1.3), but they all disapproved of the custom of the aristocrats – only one pool and a good bath after using it. The aristocrats, Herod and anyone else could and did make miqva'ot to suit themselves, and the Pharisees accepted the situation. At an unknown date, however, some Pharisees or Rabbis passed a decree that drawn water renders the bather impure.

Speculative: The decree may have been passed by the Shammaites against Hillelite objections (probably without threat of violence), and it may have been triggered by the time of crisis just before the revolt broke out. The Hillelites never fully agreed, and it was they who forged the closest links with the Sadducees and other aristocrats in the early years of the war.

In any case, the decree was not effective, and the aristocratic priests carried on sacrificing, eating heave offering, and bathing as they wished.

(b) Miscellany. The Houses debated other aspects of water which purifies, such as whether a rain-stream purifies vessels (Mikwaoth 5.6). It is especially interesting that they debated an issue of intention with regard to purifying vessels. If someone put vessels of any kind whatsoever under the water-spout which fed rainwater into the immersion pool, the House of Shammai argued that the pool was rendered invalid. The reasoning was that the water had been temporarily contained in a vessel on the way to the pool, and thus it counted as 'carried'. The House of Hillel, however, argued that vessels left under the spout accidentally did not affect the water in the pool. Here as elsewhere, intention was required. According to R. Jose, the debate remained in his day where the Houses had left it: that is, some followed one practice, some another (Mikwaoth 4.1; partial in // T. Shabbat 1.19).

In one case the Shammaites are said to have performed a physical act to try to enforce their view. In Jerusalem there was a trough hewn out of the living rock which had in it a hole as large as the spout of a water skin. Many thought that the hole meant that the trough was usable: since it could not hold water, it was not a vessel, and water which flowed through it was 'living', not 'drawn'. According to the tale of R. Judah b. Bathyra, the House of Shammai disagreed that the hole was adequate and held that the trough was a vessel and that the water was thus 'drawn'. 'The School of Shammai sent and broke it down, for [they] say: [It is still to be accounted a vessel] until the greater part of it is broken down' (Mikwaoth 4.5).

The story also points to the fact that all kinds of things might be immersed, not just people. The Bible discusses washing garments and utensils (e.g. Lev. 11.32; 15.8). The Houses debated rules about the immersion of utensils (T. Miqva'ot 5.2) and even water (Mikwaoth 10.6). We noted above the anonymous discussion of immersing a bed (Mikwaoth 7.7; cf. Kelim 18.9), which the laws of Lev. 15 could be seen as requiring (since a zav and others render impure what they lie on). Beds could be taken apart, and the miqva'ot, with a surface area of (for example) 2 metres × 3.6 metres (7 ft × 12 ft), could easily accommodate a mattress.

§9. Handwashing. The Mishnah does not contain very many pharisaic passages about handwashing, but there are enough to prove that Pharisees practised it. Handwashing was greatly elaborated by the Rabbis, and this easily leads one to consider it a major aspect of Pharisaism. It appears to be assumed, and thus agreed on by all, *from the time of Hillel and Shammai*, and we may take it in that sense and after that time to be important. The elaboration of rules about it, however, plays nothing like the role in the pharisaic corpus that it does in rabbinic literature generally.

Handwashing, we recall (I.D), is not a biblical requirement. Priests were required to wash (*rahats*) their hands and feet before sacrificing (Ex. 30.18–21; 40.31), and a zav should rinse (*shataf*) his hands before touching anyone (Lev. 15.11). Otherwise the Bible does not command handwashing. The Pharisees and Rabbis, as we shall see below, were well aware of this.

(*a*) Origin. There are a lot of potential sources for the introduction of handwashing as a purity practice. Within Jewish literature handwashing signifies innocence, as in Deut. 21.6–7, where the elders of the city nearest to the body of a man who was found slain wash their hands; handwashing and innocence are also connected in Psa. 26.6 and 73.13. The phrase 'clean hands' indicates innocence or uprightness (Psa. 24.4), and guilt of various kinds is sometimes thought of as clinging to the hands (Ezek. 23.37; Job 16.17; 31.7). The development of handwashing as a rite was doubtless facilitated by such passages, and possibly they help explain its origin.

Handwashing is attested in the Diaspora from a fairly early date, but in connection with prayer, not food. We shall see below the possibility that pagan influence accounts for Diaspora practice (pp. 262f.). The widespread custom of handwashing may have influenced Palestinian Judaism, but it is not possible to explain the pharisaic rules on the basis of Diaspora practice.

We have seen that 'bathing' or 'washing' (*rahats*) had been defined in Palestine as 'immersing', and this may have been an incentive towards handwashing. Since immersion is often not practicable, there may have been a natural desire to find some washing rite which could readily be performed.

(*b*) Hands and heave offering. We saw above (p. 197) that the Houses debated when to wash hands in connection with producing wine, whether before putting the grapes in the press (the Shammaites) or only when actually separating the priests' portion of the wine (Tohoroth 10.4). According to Tohoroth 9.5 the hands should be washed before crushing olives from the oil of which an offering would be made. It is not certain that this is pharisaic, but it concludes a discussion of olives which is attributed to the Houses, and it agrees with the Shammaites' requirement to wash hands before putting grapes into the winepress.

The impurity which was removed by handwashing was probably fly-impurity. Tohoroth 10.4 connects handwashing, grapes, wine production and heave offering. The farmer desired the grapes to be soft and juicy before putting them in the wine vat, and so they were susceptible to fly-impurity. It may be that the Pharisees thought that hands should be washed before handling anything which would eventually become food for the priests (or their own holy food), though they disagreed about the point at which this should be done. This is supported by a discussion in Shabbat 13b–14b, according to which it was Shammai and Hillel who originally decreed that (unwashed) hands are impure and render heave offering unfit for the priesthood. In a presumably post-pharisaic passage, Bikkurim 2.1, handwashing for all heave offering and first fruits is required.[69] The evidence is not completely clear, but it is possible that the Pharisees moved from requiring handwashing before handling *moist* holy food to requiring it before handling any such food.

It should be emphasized that there is no evidence that they required handwashing before handling their own ordinary food.

Handwashing before handling the priests' food is a double extension of purity rules. (1) We recall that the Bible does not command that the priests' food be handled in purity during harvesting and processing, only that they eat it in purity. (2) Handwashing is not a biblical purification. There is a weak attempt in the Babylonian Talmud to ground exegetically some of the rules about handling heave offering (Shabbat 14b, top), but even there most seem to have recognized that handwashing was simply 'decreed'. In terms of our discussion in ch. II, it is a *tradition*, not an *interpretation* of the Bible – even a clever one. Furthermore, it seems to come fairly late in the pharisaic movement. If the later Rabbis thought that Hillel and Shammai decreed it, it means that they, at least, could identify no earlier traditions; and neither can we.

(*c*) Handwashing and sabbath. We saw above (pp. 203f.) that handwashing in Berakoth 8.2f. is interpreted in the Tosefta (T. Berakot 5.25–28) in such a way as to connect it with fly-impurity. The problem is moisture on the hands or cup, and fly-impurity on the table, which can be conveyed to other things via moisture. We should now note that the setting of these passages is the sabbath or festival meal (although Neusner and Alon both discuss them as if they apply to all meals[70]). One of the topics is the sequence of washing the hands and mixing the cup (of wine with water), and the Tosefta explicitly points out that the wine is brought in only after the holy day – festival or sabbath – has begun (T. Ber. 5.25).

The likely line of development was from washing hands before handling the priests' food to washing hands before their own special meals on sabbaths and festivals. Leviticus 23 lists the following under the heading 'holy convocations, my appointed feasts': sabbath, Passover, the festival of Weeks (Shebuoth or Pentecost), the festival of Booths (Sukkot). Possibly the priestly author intended 'holy convocations . . .' in 23.2 to be an early warning of the following topic, and thought that only the pilgrimage festivals, which follow the second statement of the theme in 23.4, are to be called 'appointed feasts'. Whatever the original intention, as the text stands sabbaths (23.3) come after 'holy convocations, my appointed feasts' in 23.2. It appears that sabbath and festival meals were days when, among the Pharisees, special rules applied, one of which was handwashing.

The handwashing disagreements are these: before or after mixing the cup; before or after sweeping the room (Berakoth 8.2,4 // T. Ber. 5.26–28); where the napkin should go after it dried the hands (Berakoth 8.3). The disagreements on sequence may reflect the fact that handwashing was not a long-held and deep-rooted practice. Agreement ran no further than handwashing on holy days.

Other passages, of uncertain date, discuss handwashing in the context of communal meals (T. Ber. 4.8; 5.6) – which again would have been the sabbath and festival meals, or times when a peace offering had been sacrificed. That Pharisees ate in groups on the sabbath is made likely by the discussions in Erubin about how legally to carry a vessel from one house to another. Post-70 passages do not, however, show uniformity. According to T. Ber. 5.13 washing before a meal is optional, afterwards compulsory; T. Ber. 5.27 presents an alternative version to one of the Houses disputes: 'One does not wash hands for ordinary food.' These support the view that handwashing before meals was fairly late and not central.

Thus far we see handwashing for two purposes: handling heave offering and avoiding impurity at sabbath and festival meals. Both these, it appears, are connected, at least originally, with fly-impurity. This is reasonable. Hands not infrequently swat insects, especially in warm climates, and it is hands which touch tables etc. on which dead insects have fallen.

(*d*) Handwashing and scripture. Pharisees thought that sacred books rendered the hands impure, and they discussed whether or not Ecclesiastes has this effect; that is, whether or not it is scripture (Eduyoth 5.3; Yadaim 3.5). The origin of this idea is unknown, but the general phenomenon is attested elsewhere. The person who burns the red heifer was thereby made impure (Num. 19.6–7). The ashes of the red heifer were used to remove corpse-impurity, and coming into contact with such a potent source of purity by a kind of reverse logic resulted in impurity. That seems to have been the case with books regarded as scriptural: since they were *so* holy they rendered the hands impure. We are not told, however, what the hands could not do because of scripture-impurity.[71]

(*e*) Handwashing and prayer. Some people practised handwashing or other ablutions in connection with morning prayer,[72] but apparently the Pharisees were not among them. Alon pointed out that the rabbinic evidence in favour of washing before praying in the morning is late.[73] He also called attention to this interesting passage:

> The Morning Bathers say, 'We bring a charge against you, O Pharisees, for pronouncing the Divine Name in the morning without prior immersion'. The Pharisees answer, 'We charge you, O Morning Bathers, with uttering the Name from a body containing impurity'.[74]

This shows quite clearly that there were pietists who were not Pharisees, and who were concerned with developing new purity practices.

§10. Ordinary food in purity. I shall now pull together the passages which indicate that Pharisees observed special laws of purity in connection with ordinary food. Not all of these bear on the question of eating secular food while following rules which governed only the priests, but it will be useful to have them all in mind.

(*a*) They paid elaborate attention to the biblical laws of gnat-impurity, modifying them so that they would be more readily observable (ruling that intention governed moisture; enlarging the quantity of the carcass of swarming things to the size of a lentil, which led to the new designation 'fly-impurity'). They observed these in a way which surely marked them out. Especially noteworthy is the prohibition of selling olives to an ordinary person (Demai 6.6). According to R. Simeon b. Gamaliel II, the Houses refused to sell the ordinary person other bulk foodstuff which might become wet and thus susceptible to fly-impurity (T. Ma'aserot 3.13). In the discussions of whether or not an 'am ha-'rets' earthenware vessels protect their contents from corpse-impurity, the Houses presuppose that his vessels are impure, probably because of fly-impurity (Eduyoth 1.14; Oholoth 5.3).

It may well be that the ordinary people did not observe the laws of gnat- or fly-impurity at all: that they left moist olives and grapes lying out before turning them into oil and wine, that they did not always put a stopper in their vessels which contained liquids, and so on. The priests, the Pharisees and other pietists may have been alone in heeding Lev. 11.32–38. These verses contain purity laws which affect food. Does keeping them prove that the Pharisees lived like priests? No, because according to the Bible they govern everyone all the time, not just priests, and not just holy food. The concern to keep them simply proves scrupulous observance of the law, not imitation of the priesthood.

Further, we saw that even with regard to fly-impurity, which they tried to avoid on their own account, they were stricter with regard to the priests' food.

Though they would doubtless try to strain a fly out of one of their own liquids before it drowned, Hillel and Shammai 'decreed' handwashing in connection with heave offering (though the Houses disagreed about the point in the food chain at which hands should be washed). If, as I have suggested, handwashing in connection with heave offering was primarily to remove fly-impurity, we must conclude that with regard to this impurity, which was a major concern, they applied a higher standard to the priests' food than to their own.

(*b*) From the time of Hillel and Shammai the Pharisees practised handwashing in connection with sabbath and festival meals. This again is not a priestly law applied to their own food. It is not a law at all, as they knew quite well. The appropriate heading is 'self-identity'.

(*c*) Corpse-impurity was a major concern. First of all, the Pharisees extended the biblical law by deciding that they would keep the priests' food from ever contracting corpse-impurity. We saw the extraordinary discussion of how to do this when grapes overhung a graveyard (Oholoth 18.1, above, p. 198).

Secondly, by introducing (or accepting) the conception of 'overshadowing' they vastly expanded the domain of corpse-impurity and then tried to avoid becoming impure according to the new rules. This included not using ovens which had been overshadowed by a corpse. It is quite possible that the extension of corpse-impurity was not an original contribution by the Pharisees, but rather that it was older and wider. In this case, their concern to avoid the new forms of corpse-impurity could be seen as springing simply from the desire to be pure: they accepted a *common* extension, defined it and then avoided the impurity. If, however, we link the extension and avoidance of corpse-impurity together – what they avoided they had first to create – we could see here a 'minor gesture' towards imitation of the priesthood. Failing to attend an uncle's funeral, or the funeral of one's married sister, would be imitating the priesthood. They did not do this. *Thus they did not live like priests.* 'Minor gesture' is as far as we can go.

They avoided food which had been contaminated with corpse-impurity, and it appears that the ordinary people did so as well (Eduyoth 1.14; Oholoth 5.3). This was probably self-evident interpretation of the law: It follows from Num. 19 that food in the room with a corpse was impure; it appears to have been generally understood that people avoided impure food, though this is not directly commanded in the Bible.

(*d*) The Pharisees probably tried to avoid midras-impurity. According to Hagigah 2.7 they did this better than did ordinary people, less well than priests when not on duty and their families. One discussion about food probably has to do with midras-impurity: A Pharisee who is a zav may (House of Hillel) or may not (House of Shammai) eat with an 'am ha-'arets who is a zav (T. Shabbat 1.15). While zavim, of course, both were equally impure. The presupposition of the debate is that ordinarily a Pharisee would not eat with an 'am ha-'arets. The topic, eating with a zav, points towards midras-impurity. It will be recalled that this is a very light impurity, acquired by touching certain things which had been in contact with an impure person, removed by bathing and the setting of the sun.

The Pharisees apparently made some efforts to keep this impurity away from their own food, and this distinguished them from the ordinary people. We should consider here the only passage which directly connects Pharisees and haverim, T. Demai 2.12//Bekorot 30b.[75] The question is, How long is the probation period for one who wishes to join the Association? The topics are liquids and garments: how long will it be before the person's liquids and garments are pure? or, How long before the person can learn how to deal with them correctly? Garments are subject to midras-impurity, and the plain implication is that the Houses avoid it.

This impurity, which is listed as 6a-b in the section on biblical purity laws above, applies in the Bible only to priests, the temple and holy food. For a lay person to avoid midras-impurity would be to live like a priest. The Pharisees *tried* to avoid midras-impurity; shall we conclude that they lived like priests? The only way truly to have done this would have been to expel their wives during menstruation and for the first week or two after childbirth (depending on the sex of the child). If they had intercourse after sunset, they would have had to immerse before eating or *handling* their own food. That is, they could not work the land before immersion. These are, approximately, the rules that the priests observed, or should have observed when they ate first fruits or their portion of the peace offering at home. We have no evidence about what the priests actually did. Some were quite poor and would have found it very hard to keep this law – hard to find the extra space, the extra furniture and the extra food (their wives had to eat something).

The Pharisees probably did immerse their beds, chairs and garments more often than did other people. Yet this does not mean that they ate only when they were free of midras-impurity. I return to the case of the menstruant. She renders her bed impure, and it renders anyone who touches it impure. If Pharisees did not sleep with their wives when menstruating, we would have a collection of rules on separate furniture and its handling, or on the shelters where menstruants stayed. We do not have them; therefore they slept together. In this case, did the Pharisees immerse as soon as they arose? No, that would have made them 'morning bathers', which they were not.

The evidence is against the notion that the Pharisees actually avoided midras-impurity. Their trying to avoid it when possible may be called, again, a minor gesture towards living like priests. Hagigah 2.7 seems to place them exactly: less careful than priests' families.

That they did not actually live like priests is proved not only by the fact that lay families, especially farmers, could not do so, but also by other points noted above. Unlike priests, they ate blemished animals. Unlike priests, they attended funerals. And they handled the priests' food with a degree of purity which they did not apply to their own.

How important were these rules to the Pharisees? Purity was certainly important to them, and protecting the priesthood and the temple from impurity was a very substantial concern. The purity of their own food seems to have been of less importance. One does not find the zeal to avoid midras-impurity which marks the discussions of keeping corpse-impurity and other impurities away from the priests and their food (searching the mourners' fields, handling heave offering with washed hands, and so on). The importance of the purity of their own food, however, may go far beyond the number of discussions which survive. We may connect this with the question, What did they do about it? The first answer is that we do not know. But let us guess. To avoid midras-impurity they may well have immersed beds, chairs, garments and vessels periodically – possibly monthly. This is far more likely than that the Pharisees expelled their wives during menstruation and after childbirth. Between immersions, however, there would be periods when the bed, chair and other furniture were impure.

If they established some sort of routine – and purity must be observed by routine, one cannot worry about it at each moment – the routine could have been essential to their behaviour, while occupying relatively little of their time and energy (see further below) and generating few laws.

Let us pause to consider how to balance two considerations. Perhaps, if we see anything at all which indicates concern to live like a priest, we should assume it to be the tip of an iceberg. In this case the 'tip' is the evidence that they avoided some forms of corpse-impurity and, when possible, midras-impurity; and the few passages which tie these to their own food. The other consideration is that the distinctions about *handling* food fix on holy food, especially heave offering. The only possible reason for having special rules about heave offering is that they did not handle their own food with the same degree of purity. The firmer evidence is surely the latter. We are now at the decisive point, and so I shall recall some of the passages:

> Must hands be washed before putting grapes in the wine vat, or *only* when separating heave offering (Tohoroth 10.4)?

> Can the wine vat be made impure after first tithe has been removed, or *only* after second tithe (T. Terumot 3.12)?

Must fenugreek and vetches which are heave offering be handled in purity (Maaser Sheni 2.3–4 and parr.)?

Must jars containing grapes or wine which will be given as heave offering be pure (Maaser Sheni 3.13)?

Which holy food may a woman with stage two of childbirth-impurity touch (Niddah 10.6–7)?

There are others under §2.b above, but these will do. Perhaps I should add one from §2.a: the Hillelites' view that Gentiles and menstruants may eat firstlings (T. Bekorot 3.16; Bekhoroth 5.2). I think that it is not possible to look at these passages, to accept them as pharisaic, and to conclude that the Pharisees handled and ate their own food in purity.

Let me rephrase the point of hesitation: since Pharisees did not observe the purity laws of the priesthood with regard to their own food, *why did they have so many rules about corpse-impurity and midras-impurity?* I propose, To make minor gestures towards extra purity.

I call them *minor* gestures in comparison with what they are thought to have done: expelled their wives, done all the domestic work one week in four, and so on. The word 'minor', however, probably misleads us with regard to their own intention. It sounds as if they made the comparison which I have made, and found their own efforts trivial. This is most unlikely.

We cannot assign precise motives, but I think that we can safely assign a general one: to be pure, because purity is good. We have more than once come upon this point, and we shall see it in some detail in the section on purity in the Diaspora. The Pharisees, being ancients, did not have the modern problem with externals, and they did not think that practising externals proves the absence of internals. They thought that the two went together. 'Clean hands and pure heart'; 'sound mind in sound body'. These are the counsels of two of the parents of the modern West, Israel and Greece.[76]

Let me return to the question of time spent. They could not have spent the time on priestly purity which Neusner and many others would have us think. They had other things to do than keep priestly laws. Like others, they worked from dawn to dusk. They had in addition to do extra chores, such as keeping their liquids, vessels and moist olives and grapes covered. And they had to *study*. The legal discussions attributed to Pharisees never take study as their topic, and thus mechanical counting failed to reveal to Neusner that it is a main theme. It is the basis of the entirety of the material, and every discussion rests on it. But since the rules which are the result of study do not actually use the word ('we know x because we have studied it'), he concluded that this was not an important aspect of Pharisaism.[77]

One of the things that we know about the Pharisees from non-rabbinic sources is that they mastered the law and its interpretation. According to Josephus they were the most 'precise' interpreters of the law (*War* 2.162; *Life* 191; cf. *War* 1.108–109; Acts 26.5; 22.3). Even more telling is the following incidental remark: When Josephus was attempting to organize the defence of Galilee at the time of the first revolt, the Pharisee Simeon b. Gamaliel challenged his competence and persuaded the common revolutionary council (*koinon*), of which he was a member, to send an investigating committee. The question, of course, was how well Josephus knew the laws and traditions – not whether or not he had studied Roman military tactics. There were four members of the committee. One was of a high-priestly family, one was an ordinary priest and a Pharisee, and two were lay Pharisees, 'from the lower ranks' (*dēmotikoi*). They were all 'of equal education' (*Life* 196–197). The lower-class Pharisees knew the law, just as did the upper-class priest.

In terms of hours spent, study probably consumed more time than anything else, except their normal occupations. Study of the law and of their extra-biblical traditions, along with belief in life after death,[78] were the two main marks of the Pharisees – not tithes and purity. Their achievement of a special degree of purity – higher than that of the ordinary person, lower than that of priests' families – was doubtless an important characteristic, perhaps the third most important.

F. EXCLUSIVISM

One of the most common views of the Pharisees is that they were sectarian in the sense of exclusivist: they associated only with themselves and they considered all others to be outside the people of God.[1] What is the evidence of pharisaic purity rules, which would have to bear much of the weight of that hypothesis? We should also consider here briefly their tithing rules, which are often thought to have helped make them a separate society. We shall see that there is no evidence for full sectarianism, and the concerns which were peculiar to them were just enough to give them the feeling of group solidarity and distinction, not to make them isolated from the rest of Israel.

§1. We take first the question of tithes. Tithes were surveyed in I.F, and in ch. IV we shall examine all the sources of priestly revenue, in order to determine which parts the Pharisees were most zealous for. Here we need note only two points:

(*a*) Although the existence of the category 'doubtful-if-tithed produce' shows that the Pharisees were enthusiastic about tithing, if necessary tithing what they bought as well as what they sold, they were not actually fanatical. The most substantial pharisaic discussion in the Mishnah about tithing is this:

> *Demai*-produce may be given to the poor and to billeted troops to eat. Rabban Gamaliel used to give *demai*-produce to his labourers to eat. The School of Shammai say: Almoners should give what has been tithed to them that do not give tithe and what is untithed to them that do give tithe; thus all will eat of what is duly tithed. But the Sages say: Almoners may collect food and distribute it regardless [of the rules of *demai*-produce], and let him that is minded to tithe it [according to the rules of *demai*-produce] tithe it. (Demai 3.1)

This passage reveals what I regard as a characteristic pharisaic trait: distinguishing between what is in the Bible and what not. The Bible does not say that people who buy food and doubt that it has been tithed must tithe it. The Bible commands *the farmer* to tithe or (if one consumes one's tithe) to redeem it by paying its equivalent plus one-fifth to the temple (Lev. 27.30–31). To do more, to tithe food which one buys, is going beyond the law, and the Pharisees were here as elsewhere happy to go beyond it. But there were limits. The House of Shammai wanted charity organized so as to ensure that all food, whether bought or given away, was tithed. 'The Sages' (standing in for the Hillelites?) disagreed and left it to the individual. Further, Rabban Gamaliel II himself, son of the great Pharisee Simeon b. Gamaliel, gave doubtful-if-tithed food to his workmen. At most we may assume that Pharisees made sure that food which they bought, ate and sold was tithed, if necessary tithing it again (possibly only partially, see below). They seem not to have patrolled the land, insisting that all food in the country be treated in the way they treated it.

The Hillelites' position in T. Ma'aser Sheni 3.15 also shows moderate enthusiasm. When one receives demai-produce, one should reserve and not eat *only* the 'heave offering of the tithe', that is, the priests' tenth of the Levites' tenth. The buyer of the produce could eat the rest of first tithe – the Levites' 9/100ths.

(*b*) First tithe could be directly collected by the priests and Levites (pp. 46f. above). This must have reduced the quantity of possibly untithed produce on the market. Demai 6.6 implies that there were more tithers than haverim, and this is almost certainly correct.

Did the tithing rules result in a limit on the people with whom Pharisees did business? It seems that insistence on tithing excluded fewer than were excluded by the insistence on the laws of fly-impurity and midras-impurity.[2] The people were more likely to pay the priests' portion of tithe than to watch where they sat, immerse their clothes, and cover their moist olives. They were reluctant (on average) to pay the Levitical portion of first tithe, but not all Pharisees zealously paid it from demai-produce, and thus the issue of the Levites' 9/100 did not always interfere with trade.

Yet the very existence of the category, demai-produce, shows both that there were some non-tithers and that Pharisees conducted business with them anyway. I do not think that strictness with regard to tithing made the Pharisees extremely exclusivist in business. We see here *some* separation, but by no means full social and commercial separation from non-pharisaic Jews. We now consider the effect of purity laws.

§2. Purity and exclusivism.

(*a*) Handwashing had to do with the Pharisees' own special meals, with what they did after handling scripture, and with offerings for the priests. None of these affected their ordinary dealings with other people.

(*b*) They seem to have trusted the ordinary people with regard to the most important points of the laws concerning the purity of food. This is explicit in a 'Beforetime' passage, a category not included by Neusner, but one which may be considered to represent the same generation as the Houses passages.[3]

> Beforetime they used to say: They may exchange Second Tithe [money in Jerusalem] for the produce of an Am-haaretz. Then they changed this and said: Also for money of his. (Tebul Yom 4.5)

The situation envisaged is that the Pharisee has sold his produce at home and brought the money to Jerusalem to buy replacement second tithe produce, and the vendor whom he finds is an 'am ha-'arets. The Pharisees were willing to buy from the 'am ha-'arets, which shows that they trusted him to have kept his second tithe produce pure. A later passage indicates that the Rabbis trusted the ordinary people with regard to priestly purity: vessels left with an 'am ha-'arets who knows that they belong to a priestly family will not become impure with corpse-impurity (though they should be considered to have acquired midras-impurity) (Tohoroth 8.2; on the assumption of midras-impurity, cf. Hagigah 2.7, discussed above). Another presumably later passage states that with regard to heave offering most people are trustworthy 'at the seasons of wine-presses and olive-vats'; that is, when separating heave offering was directly in mind. Other points of trustworthiness are also listed (Hagigah 3.4–5).

(*c*) The only purity law which is said to affect the purchasing and selling of ordinary food is the prohibition of selling olives (Demai 6.6). Even if this is expanded to include selling other produce in bulk (T. Ma'aserot 3.13), or even selling any food and buying food that is wet (Demai 2.3, perhaps post-pharisaic), we see that there was no total ban on trading. In particular,

Pharisees could buy dry food (e.g. grain) from ordinary people with no worries about purity.

The evidence on food thus far, then, is of a good deal of care, and some restrictions on trade with others, but not a complete ban. Under the headings of purity and tithes we have seen a desire to be stricter than most people, and in that way to have their own position marked out as 'separate'. Yet they regarded the ordinary people as more-or-less trustworthy with regard to the major biblical laws. Second tithe food could be bought from ordinary people, and so could dry food. This is a far cry from the rules of the Essenes, who, according to Josephus, would starve if expelled, rather than break their vows to eat only the pure food of the community (*War* 2.143). The Pharisees' trading limitations were caused by their attempt to enforce *biblical* laws which were supposed to be incumbent on all Israel, not their own traditions, and not priestly laws which they wished applied to the laity in general. Trading restrictions were caused by devotion to the laws concerning tithing and wet food.

(*d*) The Pharisees were willing to work beside and with others. The question about the potential midras-impurity of a mixing trough (Kelim 20.2) indicates that they wished to know whether or not they *might have* picked up midras-impurity by leaning against a trough, against which a zav had already leant. They did not pass a rule that they could not work with ordinary people. The consequence of knowing that they had midras-impurity would have been immersion and washing their clothing.

(*e*) It is important to recall that the Houses, and in fact Hillel and Shammai themselves, disagreed about very important rules of purity, including the amount of drawn water which could be used in an immersion pool (Eduyoth 1.3), whether or not vessels could be rinsed in water as it ran into an immersion pool (Mikwaoth 4.1), and whether or not menstrual impurity should be assumed for the days between a negative and a positive test (Eduyoth 1.1//Niddah 1.1; above, p. 209). Logically, the stricter party in each of these cases should have assumed the other to be impure all the time. The House of Shammai should have assumed that followers of the House of Hillel routinely added too much drawn water to their immersion pools and regularly washed vessels in the water which ran to the immersion pool. Either of these would render the entire pool invalid, and thus the House of Hillel should have been shunned by the other party as impure. Similarly the House of Hillel should have suspected members of the House of Shammai of regularly being impure from menstrual blood. In fact this did not happen. A later Mishnah comments on the fact: despite such important disagreements about pure and impure, 'neither scrupled to use aught that pertained to the others in matters concerned with cleanness' (Yebamoth 1.4). This tolerance was probably based on their knowledge that on these topics they were elaborating the law, and they knew what was biblical and what not. A further point will support this probability.

(*f*) Although the Pharisees disagreed among themselves about such things as immersion pools, they disagreed more with the Sadducean chief priests. It is also probable that the Pharisees did not trust the Sadducees to observe the right days of menstrual impurity (cf. the later mishnah Niddah 4.2) – just as the Hillelites could suspect the Shammaites. Yet, despite these disagreements with the group which governed the temple and its purity, the Pharisees – unlike the Qumran sect – worshipped there and brought sacrifices, obviously assuming that its rules of purity did not transgress *biblical* law in such a way as to render the temple cult invalid.

(*g*) Exclusivism: conclusion. Discussions of the Pharisees as excluding the ordinary people from the social and religious life of Judaism, and as condemning them as sinners,[4] suppose that the Pharisees controlled Judaism as a religion.[5] 'Exclusivism', then, is a charge that they, the dominant group, kept others away from the privileges and comforts of their religion. The present discussion is based on the assumption that the Pharisees could control their own commercial dealings and their own group meals (on sabbaths and festivals), but very little else. They probably did not eat with the ordinary people, and trade with them was also under restraints. It was not a question of the Pharisees' excluding the common people from religion and society; only the priests could have done that. The question was, could they limit business and social contact with them, so that they (the Pharisees) could have their own identity. It appears that they both could and did, and that they did it without causing too much offence. They seem to have had a very appreciable public following and to have been admired and respected.

The Pharisees did not cut themselves off entirely from the common people. As I have several times proposed, they knew that they went beyond the Bible, and they did not equate their own rules – about many of which they disagreed among themselves – with the binding will of God (see ch. II). They thought that those who obeyed the principal biblical injunctions, and who kept its major purity laws, were members of the people of God. This included both the ordinary people and those who followed a different interpretation of the law – the Sadducees. The Pharisees had the feeling of being stricter and holier than most, but not that of being the only true Israel.

§3. This means that they maintained their own self-identity but did not constitute a *sect*. Neusner's definition of sectarianism is this: a group of people who interpreted and obeyed laws 'in a way different from other groups or from society at large', or who observed laws which were peculiar to them.[6] This definition is too general to be helpful: it applies to all groups. If we are going to make distinctions, we should reserve the word 'sect' for a group which was to an appreciable degree *cut off* from mainline society. It should *reject* some important part of the rest of society, or it should *create* an alternative structure. Neusner frequently compared the Pharisees to the Dead Sea Sect, finding basic agreements and minor differences.[7] But the differences are large and clear, and they show that one was a sect and the other not.

The Dead Sea sect – not the group represented by the *Covenant of Damascus* – rejected central parts of common Judaism: the temple and its sacrifices under the present regime. It had an alternative structure. It was a complete society, made up of priests, Levites and Israelites. Its priests, the Zadokites, were the true high priests, and the leading priests in Jerusalem were usurpers. Its covenant contained things which were 'hidden' from the rest of Israel; it had access to more of the Mosaic revelation than did others. It had its own plan for the temple building, a partially different set of feasts, and – of great importance – a different calendar.[8]

These points led to or resulted from complete separation. None of them can be paralleled among the Pharisees. The latter had leaders, but not an alternative priesthood. They had their own interpretations of the law, as well as further traditions, but they did not claim that they had more of the Mosaic law than did the Sadducees or the common people (see ch. II), and their differences of interpretation did not lead to a socio-political split. They accepted the temple, they championed the rights of the current priesthood, they brought their sacrifices, and they kept holy days when everyone else did. How people can look at these facts, which cannot be disputed, and conclude that the Pharisees were a sect like the Dead Sea group I find puzzling. Some vocabulary should be found to allow us to make reasonable distinctions among groups.

It should be said that by 'people' I mean lots of people, by no means only Neusner. Alan Segal, for example, regards the Pharisees as a sect and even makes the claim that they always ate together so as to keep pure (possibly confusing sabbath and festival meals with everyday meals).[9] Others, however, now begin to recognize that the Pharisees were not sectarian in the way the Dead Sea covenanters were.[10] If one insists on calling them a sect, however, one should offer a different word for the Dead Sea group. Would schismatics do? The distinction between sect and party seems to me perfectly adequate: the Pharisees and Sadducees were parties; the group of CD were a party, though more extremist than the Pharisees (CD accepts the temple and the sacrifices); the Qumran community was a sect.[11]

While not a sect, the Pharisees were also not 'ordinary people', 'amme ha-'arets. They were certainly conscious of being different. They did mark boundaries: others had midras-impurity more often than they did; others were less conscious of corpse-impurity, both extending it less and avoiding it less;

others probably did not observe special rituals at sabbath and festival meals, or at least not the same ones the Pharisees kept; others kept apart from the priests' food only the most obvious impurities (corpse- not midras-impurity); others did not start handling the priests' food in purity as early in the food chain as they (the Pharisees) did; others were less willing to support the Levites, and some were even less willing to support the priests. On the other hand, the boundaries were permeable. Pharisees would work beside others, knowing that they might catch midras-impurity; they walked in the same crowded streets[12]; they went to the same bath houses[13]; they bought and sold with other people, though avoiding some items. They even bought from other people when they knew that it would cost them a percentage of the goods (at least a tithe of the tithe).

§4. Sectarianism in the Judaism of the second temple period usually implies soteriological exclusivism: Only our group will be saved in the world to come, or will be vindicated in the final war between good and evil. The pharisaic traditions to which we have access are legal discussions, not soteriological. We cannot infer from them, however, soteriological exclusiveness. The Pharisees seem not to have thought that their own rules of behaviour, when they went beyond the Bible, were strictly *required*. This implies that they did not think of others as heinous transgressors.

G. CONCLUSION

§1. This many pages on purity may seem to imply that the Pharisees were interested in it above all else and that they were, if not a 'pure food club', at least a 'purity club'. A full and evenhanded treatment of Neusner's passages – that is, the rabbinic legal passages which are attributed to Pharisees or to the Houses – would result in many pages about Work, a large number under the heading 'Non-purity aspects of tithes, sacrifices and offerings', a good number on 'Festivals' and 'Private worship', several on 'Agriculture', 'Charity', 'Civil law' and 'Family law' (especially if vows are included), and a few on 'Food' (food itself, not its purity). Purity has generally been taken as defining the Pharisees, and I think that their purity practices have been misdescribed and misinterpreted. On the other hand, purity really was important to them. Thus all these pages. I hope that the reader will not infer from the page count what I wish to deny: that Pharisaism was essentially a purity movement. It is not true, despite Neusner, that a 'Mishnah' before 70 would have been only about making meals.[1] The purity of their own food was not their major concern.

I shall say more fully what this essay is *not*.

(*a*) I have not made a new and critical selection of passages. As I see it, such a task would involve the following (in addition to taking into account Rivkin's and Neusner's passages): (1) Studying the efforts of other scholars, particularly J. N. Epstein, to stratify the material. In chs 2–4 of his *Introductions to Tannaitic Literature*, he dealt with 'The First Mishnah', 'Remnants of Early Mishnaic Collections' and 'Intermediate Mishnahs' (the 'Mishnahs' of R. Joshua and R. Eliezer, who are frequently the sources of Neusner's Houses passages). (2) Attempting to attribute the stam (anonymous opinion), especially when it seems to be presupposed by a Houses debate (again, see the work of Epstein). (3) Querying more closely the date of Neusner's passages. Some of the Houses debates are clearly post-70, and they may not always take up pre-70 topics.

I think that Neusner's selection of passages marks an advance, since he applied *a* method of stratifying the material to the study of the Pharisees. Rivkin also used a select number of passages as his foundation stones (those in which $p^c r\hat{u}sh\hat{i}m$ are opposite $ts^c d\hat{u}q\hat{i}m$), but his test seems to me to be too restrictive. Most other scholars who have published books about the Pharisees, however, have gathered material from rabbinic literature generally, especially including the second-century haverim passages. Some principle of selectivity is better than none, but the field still awaits a comprehensive study of which rabbinic passages count as 'pharisaic'.

It is not true that the only passages which might contain information about the Pharisees are those which can definitely be dated before 70. Archaeology shows that purifying water in a miqveh by connecting it with another pool is much earlier than the earliest literary evidence. It also reveals that stone vessels were not subject to impurity and that making them was a substantial industry. Literature does not even hint at the second fact, and it points somewhat weakly to the first. Similarly a description of Pharisaism which is limited to passages which are demonstrably early is bound to be imperfect.

On the other hand, scholarship before Rivkin and Neusner sinned on the other side. I am old enough to remember how it used to be. The entirety of rabbinic literature was taken to be 'Pharisaism'. Christian scholars especially thought of the Talmuds and Midrashim, running down to the eighth century or so, as forming the 'background' of the New Testament, and they used them as such: that is the point of Billerbeck's commentary, which has been and still is used by people who want to write about the 'Jewish background'. But many Jewish scholars worked on the same assumptions, and others were only marginally different. This had a semi-academic basis: people thought very generally about 'tradition', and they regarded ancient Jews as hanging on to inherited material. An early tradition might crop up anywhere. The theory 'might crop up anywhere' often justified choosing whatever struck one's fancy. This view, that all rabbinic literature is 'traditional', and that many or most traditions are old, dominates the older literature. To mention a completely innocuous example: H. St John Thackeray, in translating Josephus, often referred in the notes to 'early tradition' or 'tradition', by which he meant the wide range of rabbinic parallels or contrasts which were adduced by Julien Weill, the French translator.[2] Talmudic scholars sometimes refer to the entire vast body of rabbinic literature as 'tradition'.[3]

Neusner has done more than any other individual to change this entire way of thinking. As I wrote above, it is not that he has a clear programme and is consistently working it out. He continues to publish things whose fundamentalism would embarrass the most conservative talmudists. He has nevertheless called the question of date to everyone's attention, and this is all to the good. The burden of proof in Jewish studies very badly needed to be shifted from those who doubt antiquity to those who assert it, at least long enough to make clear how much unconscious retrojection there has been.

The model for historical research, however, should not be that of the courtroom, in which there are only two possibilities, and in which one side must bear the burden of proof – early until proved late, *or* the reverse. That is too crude for the information gained from our discipline. I am hopeful that a new generation of scholars will continue the search for the Pharisees, and in doing so will carefully *sift* and *weigh* the extremely difficult evidence.

(*b*) As the opening paragraph of this section indicates, I have not discussed all of Neusner's passages, but have concentrated on purity. It cannot be emphasized too strongly that, despite its length, this essay is not a full and well-balanced description of 'pharisaic legal topics'. And, to repeat what was said above, it is not designed to answer the question, 'What is the essence or centre of Pharisaism?' I offered above a very general answer – study and application of the law – but much more could be said.

(*c*) Nor does this essay respond directly to the question, What role in pre-70 Palestinian society did the Pharisees play? Neusner proposed that, from the time of Hillel on, they basically dropped out.[4] Although the essay does not take up most of the relevant passages, and the question deserves more study, I shall venture the opinion that this is not quite right. It is true that most of the passages in Neusner's study have to do with things which are in the individual's control, and this includes some public actions. Hands were or were not laid on a sacrificial animal's head in public, but evidently the individual could decide whether or not to do it. Few of the debates about the temple, sacrifices and civil law raise the issue of public control or influence, or the desire for it; but, still, there are a few. Neusner counted only two 'matters of civil law and torts'. There are by my count several more than that, but I agree that one does not find the body of civil law which one would expect if the Pharisees had their own courts and had to pass judgment on numerous issues, or if they disagreed with common law as enforced by the magistrates.[5] The common notion, that they governed Palestine indirectly, told the priests what to do, and served as *the* legal experts for the populace on all and sundry issues is not supported by the legal corpus. To this extent I agree with him. This does not, however, prove the opposite, that they dropped out, cared for society not at all, and entered their own little world in which their houses became make-believe temples.

In section C we noted that Rivkin proposed that the Pharisees made rules on all subjects equally, in contrast to Neusner's view that they fixed on their own food, and that our study would modify both opinions. It has modified Neusner's in a fairly radical way. The previous paragraph points towards a modification of Rivkin's, though only in summary fashion. Public issues, especially civil and criminal law, account for very little of the material. The report about the Shammaites breaking down a water trough to keep it from being used is unusual and serves to emphasize how little the pharisaic debates would affect public policy and behaviour.[6]

While this study does not demonstrate the case, I think that the Pharisees of the post-Herod period will fall between the two extremes of running everything and dropping out. This is one of the most important topics for further research.

§2. Summary of results:

(*a*) The Pharisees had a positive concern for purity: it was better to be pure than not. They were not alone. The same was true of a lot of Jews and of a lot of pagans. Even Paul was concerned with his own brand of purity.[7] Such words as 'purity' (*hagneia*), 'holy' or 'sanctified' (*hagios*), 'without blemish' (*amomos*), 'cleanse' or 'purify' (*katharizo*), along with many others, were widely used in the ancient world, and used in a favourable way. Often they were used metaphorically – morally 'without blemish' – but their positive use in a metaphorical sense reveals that the words did not carry negative overtones.[8] 'Ritual purity', as I remarked at the outset, now has to many people an unfavourable connotation, and it is thought that what is wrong with the Pharisees is that they favoured it. But this would only mean that what is wrong with them is that they lived in the ancient world – where most people favoured it. Most Christian scholars, I realize, think that it was precisely 'ritual' which Jesus and Paul attacked. Since the major point of the Jewish law which is treated negatively in both the synoptic gospels and Paul is the sabbath, the assumption that they attacked 'ritual' implies that rest on the sabbath should be considered 'ritual'. It was instead commemorative (of God's rest) and ethical (not only men, but also women, servants, animals and the land itself were allowed to rest).

The Pharisees' concern to be pure went beyond the requirements of the law – as did that of others. Many people avoided 'overshadowing' corpses, lots of Jews would not use Gentile oil (not prohibited by the Bible), and Jews in the Diaspora imitated pagans, who dipped, sprinkled and washed.[9] People thought that purity was a good thing, and they tried to avoid impurity, even though it had no practical consequence. There were many who wanted to be able to 'distinguish between the holy and the common' (Ezek. 22.26; CD 12.20; Sukkah 5.5). The Pharisees fully participated in this spirit. They differed from others in many particulars, they defined certain impurities very carefully, they probably extended corpse-impurity more than did most, and they may have tried harder than did most to avoid the new sources of this impurity. The desire to be pure, however, they shared with the populace in general.

(b) The two purity laws to which they gave most attention were corpse-impurity and fly-impurity. The former they greatly extended, but did not expect others to accept; the latter they reduced but tried to enforce or, at least, encourage.

1. Corpse-impurity was extended by two post-biblical theories: that it travels and can escape a 'tent' through holes; that corpses convey impurity by 'overshadowing' (or by being overshadowed). The Pharisees knew that they had developed corpse-impurity well beyond its biblical definition. They tried to avoid contracting it from its new sources, but they did not try to avoid contracting it from its main sources, the corpse itself and the room where it lay. Moreover, they seem not to have agitated for everyone to accept their views. If the vent of one of their ovens was overshadowed by a corpse, they may have broken the oven. We do not hear that they decreed that corpses could not be carried in such a way as to overshadow vents which projected into the street, nor that, when someone else's vent was overshadowed, they dashed into the house and broke the oven.

This striking combination of extension and avoidance results in a minor symbolic gesture towards living 'like a priest'. They did not keep the actual priestly law, to avoid corpse-impurity except for the next-of-kin.

2. Non-priestly Pharisees may have been the only laypeople to try to keep the laws of Lev. 11.32–38. Despite their scrupulousness, clearly revealed in this set of rules, they like others allowed a lot of biblical laws to fall into disuse. They completely ignored most aspects of Num. 5.2–3, which require the exile of zavs and those with corpse-impurity along with lepers. We can say 'completely ignored' not only because we have no discussions of Num. 5.2–3, but also because the discussions about zavs and the corpse-impure presuppose that they live at home. Probably most people ignored in the very same way the laws about gnat-impurity. The biblical laws, in fact, cannot be

kept as they stand: one would have to cover fruit and olive trees every time it rained, break down one's oven every time a gnat or midge was overcome by the heat – and so on. The Pharisees decided to keep this set of laws, and to do so they made them observable. They ruled, first, that a single gnat would not render anything impure: impurity required an insect as large as a lentil, and I have suggested that a fly is the size that they settled on. Secondly, they decided that moisture which came on to foodstuff accidentally, or against one's will did not count.

Having made these laws observable, they not only tried to keep them, but to *discourage* others from transgressing them. The restrictions on buying would keep only themselves pure: they would not buy olives from an 'am ha- 'arets, because they did not wish to risk bringing into their own houses food which had fly-impurity. But the restrictions on selling, which cover foodstuff both wet and dry, represent an active wish to get others to conform to their views. Fly- impurity is paralleled in this respect with some pharisaic sabbath practices. The Shammaites would not give to others, even Gentiles, work which would require them to break the sabbath (Shabbath 1.7–9). They wished to encourage everyone to keep it.

The extensions of corpse-impurity are entirely post-biblical, and they were recognized as such, not being justified by clever exegesis; and the Pharisees made no effort to enforce them. In contrast, one of the main modifications of Lev. 11.32–38 is exegetical: the passive 'if water *is put*' of 11.38 is applied to the entire biblical section. The Pharisees could regard this modification not as tradition, but as *true interpretation*. They held the modified laws to be biblical, and they wanted them kept generally, not just by themselves as identity markers.

(*c*) Most of the other purity topics reveal 'tidying-up'. Women should bathe after menstruation and childbirth-impurity stage one. This brings them approximately into line with the rules governing men. Zavim and zavot cannot have intercourse; this corresponds to the rule for menstruation. Menstruation cannot begin until the twelfth day after the end of the previous seven-day menstrual period; this convention tells one when to apply the laws of Lev. 15.19–24 and when those of 15.25–30.

Even the decision to handle the priests' food in purity may be in part extrapolation from the Bible. I have several times called attention to Isa. 66.20, which refers to bringing cereal offerings in pure vessels. Further, the woman with childbirth-impurity stage two is forbidden by Lev. 12.4 to touch 'anything holy' (*kol qôdesh*). Whether because of these passages or not, the Pharisees and others concluded that some purity rules should apply to the handling of some holy food. The Pharisees thought that corpse-impurity must be kept away from all of the priests' food from a very early point in the food chain (though they disagreed on the precise point and on how this was done). They thought that even the´amme ha-´arets would protect priests' vessels from corpse-impurity. The Pharisees would go further and protect them from midras-impurity as well.

All the rules on sex are 'tidying-up', since the Bible itself forbids sex with a menstruant. Deciding just what this means, and applying the prohibition to like cases (sex with a zavah) required some attention, but the biblical base is clear.

Immersion pools, and the definition of valid water, constitute an extreme case of clarifying the Bible. The basic notion that one must define 'bathing' – both the activity and the water used – shows a concern to specify precisely what is required by biblical law. That 'bathing' means 'immersion' is a bit of a leap (one taken by others as well), though it has as its basis the verse which requires a man who has a nocturnal emission to bathe his whole body (Lev. 15.16). That valid water must not be 'drawn', and that it purifies invalid water by contact, are definite innovations, though again there was a partial biblical base. It is noteworthy that the Pharisees disagreed on how much drawn water was acceptable, and that they used the temple even though its immersion pools may not have conformed to their definitions. Precisely at the point of innovation they became more tolerant of others.

(d) Handwashing is also an innovation. The practice as such did not originate with the Pharisees, but they made their own use of it. What is remarkable – given the role it plays in descriptions of the Pharisees – is the evidence that it was 'decreed' by Hillel and Shammai for the first time, and that it was practised only with regard to the priests' food, their own holy food, and their meals on sabbaths and festival days.

(e) The Pharisees' purity rules cut them off to some degree from the ´am ha-´arets. While the latter might keep the priests' vessels free of corpse- impurity, they would have felt no such obligation towards lay Pharisees, and in any case they were not wholly trustworthy about midras-impurity and fly-impurity. Pharisees therefore would not eat with ordinary people, and their trade with them was restricted.

(f) The Pharisees did not, however, live like priests. The desire to reduce their exposure to corpse-impurity and midras-impurity may be taken as token or symbolic gestures towards that as an ideal. In any case they and others held the ideal of being *pure for its own sake*, and this may be a better way of categorizing their special concerns.

While the conclusions of this study must be put forward with some tentativeness, the evidence on priestly purity is so uniform that here we may have greater confidence. There is absolutely *no* evidence that the Pharisees really tried to live like priests. This would have generated discussions of what funerals to attend and of the disposal of blemished animals – for example. The best evidence, however, is the very extensive body of material dealing with handling holy food (holy in the broad sense: both that eaten inside the temple and that eaten outside). These passages cannot be harmonized with the theory that the Pharisees handled all food in purity. One would have to eliminate this entire large category, and the stratification of the material is not *that* tentative. The statement that they lived like priests in the temple, and that their tables were kept as pure as the altar, are such gross overstatements that they are completely misleading.

(*g*) We have seen throughout that they thought in some cases but not all that their views should be obligatory on other people. I shall list here all the points which I have noted in the study of purity.

1. They kept certain impurities away from their own food, but they would 'allow' the ordinary people to eat some food which they themselves would reject (Eduyoth 1.14).

2. On the other hand, they applied stricter rules to the priests' food than to their own. There is no indication that they tried to keep ordinary people from giving food to the priesthood, and thus they seem to have regarded their own rules about handling heave offering as optional. In any case, they disagreed among themselves.

3. They distinguished themselves from other people by their handling of demai-produce; there is no hint that they campaigned to impose on the general populace their policy of going beyond the call of duty. The House of Shammai proposed a mini-campaign to make sure that charitable contributions were tithed, but a leader of the same generation (Gamaliel II) observed much less rigorous rules.

4. They did not attempt to enforce their views about undrawn water on others. There is one story about the Shammaites to this effect, but greater weight must be given to the facts that the Pharisees continued to use the temple even though the Sadducean chief priests did not accept their views about valid water, and that they tolerated one another, even though they disagreed about how much drawn water could be used in an immersion pool.

5. Although they regarded the clothes of the 'amme ha-'arets as more likely than theirs to have midras-impurity, there are no decrees 'forbidding' the ordinary people to enter the temple.

6. They regarded as binding the rule that, during the first eleven days after a menstrual period, a show of blood on two consecutive days made a woman a zavah, and that she could not have intercourse while she waited for the second day to pass.

7. Similarly they held that intercourse with a zavah (and presumably with a zav) was forbidden.

8. We saw under (*b*) above that they regarded their extensions of corpse-

impurity as affecting only themselves, but held their views of fly-impurity to be binding interpretation.

A study of other pharisaic rules would have revealed the same range. Some sabbath interpretations they saw as optional (eruvin), others as binding. Presumably they would have liked it if more people emulated them. But on practices which they knew to be unbiblical, they did not think that theirs was the only view and that those who did not agree were transgressing the revealed word of God. According to Betzah 2.6 (a post-pharisaic passage), Rabban Gamaliel II recalled that his father, the Pharisee Simeon b. Gamaliel, 'applied the stringent ruling to [Pharisees] but the lenient ruling to Israel'. This seems to have been true in those cases in which they were able to distinguish their own customs from exegesis of the Bible.

This supports the distinction which I proposed in ch. II between their *traditions* and their *interpretations*. Few of the passages in that chapter can be dated to the pharisaic layer; but the Rabbis' view that people who were impure only according to 'the words of the scribes' were not truly impure, and could enter the temple, seems to stand in continuity with the Pharisees.

(*h*) Finally, we return to the old question of the Pharisees and the haverim. I have previously resisted the simple equation of the two, and I am still inclined to do so, but perhaps less strongly than before. Most of the haverim passages are second-century; and since the rules were still being debated, it is hard to accept that the Pharisees *were* haverim and had worked out comprehensive guidelines for the Association. On the other hand, there are three passages which draw the Pharisees and the haverim together. One is the distinction of 'our' food from that of the ʿam ha-ʾarets (Eduyoth 1.14). Since ordinarily the haverim are contrasted with the ʿam ha-ʾarets, here there is a parallel between the Pharisees and the haverim. The second is the statement that olives should be sold only to a haver (Demai 6.6). This seems to mean that the haverim, like the Pharisees, could be trusted to keep dying insects off of moist olives. This is a very strong point of agreement. The third is the discussion of whether or not a Pharisee who is a zav can eat with an ordinary person who is a zav. This implies that ordinarily Pharisees did not eat with ʿamme ha-ʾarets, and this again parallels the Pharisee with the haverim. This exhausts my wisdom on the topic. In the early material the haverim are mentioned once. Does this support the view that 'haverim' is just another word for 'Pharisees', or that they were a different group with some similarities?

§3. Presuppositions. What the Pharisees presupposed that is not in the Bible is a large and important topic, and it deserves a more detailed study than I am competent to make. Neusner has produced quite a lot of evidence about what is presupposed in the tractates of the Mishnah. Here I wish only to pull together the points which we have come across.

(*a*) Corpse impurity can travel through holes etc.

(*b*) Corpses render impure by overshadowing (or by being overshadowed).

(*c*) Holy food should be handled in purity, and this should begin before it has been separated (an advance on the presupposition of Judith 11.13). Corpse-impurity should be kept away from the priests' food from the time of harvest on; and, to prevent contamination of moist heave offering, hands should be washed at some point after harvest and before delivery – the precise point being a matter of debate.

(*d*) What is consumed within the temple requires greater purity than holy food eaten outside the temple (heave offering, first fruits, Passover, second tithe). This is said explicitly in the presumably later mishnah Hagigah 3.1, but it is presupposed in the pharisaic materials. Hagigah 2.7 reveals still more grades of purity.

(*e*) Minute quantities of carrion and the carcasses of swarming things do not render impure. The minimum for impurity is an olive's bulk for carrion, a lentil's bulk for swarming things.

(*f*) The biblical command to bathe to remove certain purities requires special pools and special water. 'Bathing' means 'immersing'.

(*g*) An immersion pool should hold 40 se'ah of water, enough to allow immersion of the whole body at the same time.

(*h*) Anything which could hold that much is not susceptible to impurity.

(*i*) Drawn water is not valid for purification.

(*j*) Valid water renders invalid water usable by contact.

(*k*) When an item changes function it changes its susceptibility to impurity.

(*l*) There are eleven days during which a woman's blood is not considered menstrual.

(*m*) Women immerse after menstruation and stage one of childbirth-impurity.

(*n*) There are intermediate stages of impurity. People who are not zavs by biblical law, and who therefore do not owe a sacrifice, may nevertheless convey midras-impurity. A person whose purification requires immersion and sunset, and who has immersed, is partially pure (the tevul yom).

(*o*) Intercourse with a zavah transgresses the law and requires a sacrifice. This is an interesting case, since the Pharisees seem not to have regarded this as an extra-biblical tradition. They presumably read Lev. 15 in this way.

(*p*) There are 'half-utensils'.

(*q*) A person who acquires foodstuff which may not have been tithed should separate from it all or part of the required offerings or tithes.

I do not have any grand conclusions to draw from this list. We may, however, briefly relate it to the previous list of what they considered binding and not. Which of their *presuppositions* did they regard as optional? In the topics which we have considered, the rules of demai-produce and some of the extensions of corpse-impurity are most obviously traditions which they knew were not biblical. The disagreements about handling holy food in purity probably reflect consciousness that they were going beyond the Bible. It seems to have been commonly agreed that some rules of purity should apply to the handling of the priests' food, and even the ordinary people seem to have accepted a few such rules, but it was also recognized that biblical commandments did not cover the topic.

The Pharisees thought that all and sundry should observe their interpretation of the laws of Lev. 11.32–38 (swarming things), and like everyone else they thought that 'bathe' in the Bible means 'immerse'. In other cases it is hard to be sure. They presumably realized that the zavah and the menstruant are not required by Lev. 15 to bathe, but they may not have realized that the Bible does not prohibit the zav or zavah from having intercourse. Possibly I am wrong about what they realized or did not realize about the relationship between their customs and the written law. I am convinced in general that both categories existed: some developments of biblical law were unconscious, some highly self-conscious.

§4. Some people who have heard me lecture on the details of pharisaic law have thought that I was proving what I previously denied, that Pharisees were 'legalists'. Prior to the present work I have not discussed the religion of the Pharisees as such, limiting myself rather to bodies of literature.[10] I wish, nevertheless, to reply to this point. The Pharisees were extremely interested in all aspects of the law, and they studied and applied it in great detail, taking pains in some cases to go beyond it, in others to make it easier to observe. If that were what 'legalism' meant, they were legalists. That is not, however, the meaning of the word as it is normally used. It refers, instead, to interior attitude and to a soteriology: legalists *care more* about legal trivia, especially *exterior rites*, than about important matters of the spirit; they are *self-righteous*, regarding their precise performance of minor requirements as making them better than others; they consider that their performance constitutes a *claim upon God* and will force him to save them because of their *merit*, not his grace.

Since these matters are internal, they are the appropriate targets for polemic. One person can always charge another with insincerity and hypocrisy; the issue is difficult to put to the test. Watching Paul's strenuous endeavours to convert Gentiles and defend himself, an opponent could say that he hoped by his efforts to force God to accept him: it was all a desperate attempt at self-justification. The undoubted *efforts* of the Pharisees and of Paul do not prove motive. It is my own view that, when people profess pious aims – they do what they do because God commanded it, and they wish to respond to his grace by obeying his will – we should give them the benefit of the doubt and take their word for it. This should especially be done when judging ancient groups. Conceivably an ancient individual could be proved to be hypocritical, but we cannot investigate an entire group, except generally. Only if the basis of Pharisaism as an -*ism* could be shown to be legalistic and hypocritical should we judge Pharisees to be guilty on those counts.

Let me give an example of how religious polemic works and of how the polemicist fixes on interior attitude: Replying to twelve articles by Swabian peasants in 1525, Luther noted their professed willingness to be better instructed by those learned in scripture.

> If that is their serious and sincere meaning – and it would not be right for me to interpret it otherwise, because in these articles they come out boldly into the open, and show no desire to shun the light – then there is good reason to hope that things will be well. . . . But if this offer of theirs is only pretense and show (and without doubt there are some of that kind of people among them; for it is not possible that so great a crowd should all be true Christians and have good intentions, but a large part of them must be using the good intentions of the rest for their own selfish purposes and seeking their own advantage). . . .[11]

Here Luther starts with the principle which I just proposed for judging the Pharisees – we have no right to do other than to take them at their word. He then proceeds to say what everyone will agree, that not all members of a large crowd are sincere. Finally, however, he proposes that 'a large part of them' are taking advantage of the good intentions of others. This is one of the numerous ways which Christian scholars have developed for denigrating the Pharisees: in response to the evidence that first-century Judaism in general rested on belief in the grace of God, they start by proposing that some were unworthy and self-righteous. Soon we are back where we started: Judaism is a religion of self-righteousness. I propose that we assess the -*ism* on the basis of its own principles: let its representatives describe their motives.

This, however, is easier said than done. The nature of the surviving literature means that we do not have direct professions of piety from the Pharisees. We do not have their private prayers. We may be sure, however, that they said the Shema' twice a day ('when you lie down and when you rise up', Deut. 6.7), and that they prayed at the same time. The Mishnah expects prayer three times a day (Berakoth 4.1), and we are safe in thinking that the Pharisees prayed at least twice. If they prayed a third time, it was probably in public – that is, in their place of work – as is implied by Matt. 6.5. That they prayed *only in order to make a show* is polemic – aimed, appropriately, at what is hidden, their motive. Josephus said that the prayers twice each day were thanksgiving (*Antiq.* 4.212f.). I think that we should accept this; they prayed to thank and praise God. Luke offers us a prayer by a self-righteous Pharisee, which many Christians regard as representative (Luke 18.10–12). It would be better to assess their piety on the basis of the Shema´ (love God with heart, soul, mind and strength) and the Eighteen Benedictions. We do not, of course, have access to a standard form of prayer from the pre-70 period, and in fact there was no set text. Nevertheless, the surviving Eighteen Benedictions probably reflect the main themes of the daily pre-70 prayers. I offer one prayer, from a collection found in the Cairo Genizah:

> We thank thee, Our God and God of our fathers,
> For all of the goodness, the lovingkindness, and the mercies
> With which thou has requited us, and our fathers before us.
> For when we say, 'our foot slips', Thy mercy, O Lord, holds us up.
> Blessed art thou, O Lord, to whom it is good to give thanks.[12]

If one will compare such a prayer as this with the 'thanksgiving' psalms from Qumran, and add Josephus' statement that the daily prayers were for thanksgiving, one will, I think, have a good idea of the motives which the Pharisees daily professed.

The Pharisees tithed meticulously. Were they trying to obligate God to save them because of their merit? Presumably they paid first fruits just as carefully, and in this case we can know what they said when they handed over the first and best of their produce to the priest. This is the Avowal, said at the Feast of Weeks when presenting the first fruits:

> A wandering Aramean was my father, and he went down into Egypt. . . . And the Egyptians treated us harshly . . . Then we cried to the Lord the God of our fathers, and the Lord heard our voice. . . . And he brought us into this place and gave us this land, a land flowing with milk and honey. And behold, now I bring the first of the fruit of the ground, which thou, O Lord, hast given me. (Deut. 26.5–10)

Why suppose that they said this every year and meant not a word of it? that what they really meant was, 'now you owe me one'?

Perhaps Josephus may be allowed to speak for them all. At the sacrifices Jews do not ask God for blessings, 'for he has given them spontaneously and put them at the disposal of all, but for capacity to receive, and, having received, to keep them' (*Apion* 2.197). In giving thanks, and in obeying the scriptural instructions to put the commandments on their doors and arms, they proclaim 'the greatest of the benefits they have received from God', thus showing to all 'the loving care with which God surrounds them' (*Antiq.* 4.212–213). Josephus learned this theology from someone, probably his priestly teachers.[13] The Pharisees were surely equally conscious of God's grace.

IV

Purity, Food and Offerings in the Greek-Speaking Diaspora

A. INTRODUCTION: THE DIASPORA AND JERUSALEM

It has often been thought that the details of observance of the law in the Diaspora were settled by decrees sent by Palestinian sages.[1] A common view is that the Sanhedrin or *Bet Din*, the supposed court in Jerusalem which dictated interpretation and practice, came to decisions and imposed them on Jews everywhere. Some even say that, when the topic was 'religious', a Pharisee served as president, since the Sadducees did not care much about the law, and the Pharisees were the acknowledged experts.[2] Pharisees told everyone in Palestine what to do, and they extended their role and their rule to the Diaspora.

The result of this view has been that evidence of religious practice in the Diaspora has often been understood in light of Pharisaic views – and Pharisaic views have been found in Rabbinic literature running all the way to the middle ages. We saw above that Alon fitted some of Philo's statements on purity into 'the halakhah' of the Palestinian sages;[3] as we shall discover, Philo's practices were quite different.

While some assume Pharisaic dominance throughout the world, others equally dogmatically assert that there was so much diversity that we should not speak of Judaism, but rather of Judaism*s*, a different *-ism* for each social group.[4] Akiba, Josephus and Bar Kokhba, Neusner informs us, 'would scarcely have understood one another', much less have known that they were members of the same religion.[5] On this view, Philo would have seemed like a man from outer space to his Palestinian contemporaries.

There is no doubt that Judaism in the first century was quite diverse, but there were also unifying factors.[6] Akiba and Bar Kokhba understood each other perfectly well, and they knew that they both belonged to Judaism, though probably they did not agree on all points. Earlier, Hillel and Philo could probably have figured each other out, but Philo would not have changed his purity practices just because Hillel said so. The question of Unity and Diversity in Judaism is a large one, and dogma does not shed much light on it. It has been less thoroughly addressed than has Unity and Diversity in early Christianity, and there as well more work needs to be done. Here I wish to make a contribution to understanding a few individual points of *praxis* in the Diaspora.

'The Diaspora' is short for 'the Greek-speaking Diaspora of approximately 100 BCE to CE 100': the Diaspora reflected in the writings of Philo, Josephus,[7] many of the books of the New Testament, some of the Apocryphal or Deutero-canonical works, and a large number of the 'Old Testament Pseudepigrapha'. On a map, one may draw a curving line from Alexandria to Rome, skipping only Palestine. Rome, for our purposes, counts as 'Greek-speaking', because of the large number of Greek documents sent to it or emanating from it (Paul's letter, I Clement, Ignatius' letter, the works of Justin Martyr, to name the most prominent). The chronological boundaries will have to be construed flexibly, since not all the evidence can be precisely dated, and sometimes earlier evidence (e.g., *The Letter of Aristeas*) can be quite valuable for our themes.

The topics are the interrelated ones of purity, food and offerings; and these lead us also to consider Jewish separatism. In another essay I have dealt with separatism in some detail, and here I shall only touch on it.[8] The opening assumption of this chapter is that Diaspora Jews were capable of reading and interpreting the Bible, and that they did not sit, patiently waiting for the Houses of Hillel and Shammai to send them their disagreements, so that they would know at least two ways of resolving a given issue. The romantic ideal of the opening paragraph is, in my view, wrong in all its parts. I do not intend here to argue extensively against it, for the question of Who ran what? is a large one and must be approached from a lot of different directions. Here I shall assume substantial Diaspora independence, though two prefatory discussions will be useful in setting the stage for consideration of the three legal topics. The discussion of the topics will be seen to confirm the opening assumption.

In saying that I doubt that the *Bet Din* made legal rules and sent them throughout the world, I do not wish to deny that some Jerusalem authorities communicated with Diaspora communities on some matters. S. Safrai refers to the statements in Acts 9.1, 14, 21 as supporting the view that the Nasi (president or patriarch) and the Sanhedrin sent envoys to the Diaspora as early as the days of Paul.[9] The texts specify, however, not the rabbinic sage or sages, but the high priest or chief priests. Safrai also cites II Macc. 1.10, 18 and 2.14f. The letter which opens II Maccabees is best seen (with Goldstein) as partly authentic (1.1–10a) and partly a forgery (most of 1.10b–2.18).[10] We need not debate details here, but we may accept that Jerusalem authorities (that is, the high priests) wrote to the Diaspora about the kind of major events mentioned in the letter, the re-purification of the temple and the institution in the month Chislev of a new festival. This is what we could expect. There was such a thing as Judaism (no plural), and there were common interests. That the temple was purified, and that there would be a new festival to commemorate the occasion, were major and noteworthy items. This does not prove that later the Hillelites and Shammaites wrote letters to Diaspora Jews pointing out that they disagreed whether, at the sabbath meal, one should wash his hands before or after mixing the cup. One of the numerous things wrong with the view that the academy of sages sent decrees around the world is that the evidence of early Rabbinic literature itself points to disagreements and variety of practice. On relatively few points was there such uniformity that Jerusalem could dictate Diaspora practice: practice in Jerusalem itself was not tightly controlled.

Pilgrims to Jerusalem would have carried news back and forth, and this offers another way in which Jerusalem could have influenced the Diaspora. Yet there is little evidence that this happened, and on one point we must be surprised at its paucity. We now know that more-or-less everyone in Palestine agreed that 'wash' or 'bathe' in Lev. 15 means 'immerse your entire body' (III.F.§8 above). Diaspora pilgrims would have experienced the joy of immersing in the dark and not very sanitary pools before entering the temple. Palestinian Jews, however, used miqva'ot not only before entering the temple, but to remove domestic impurities as well (e.g. semen-impurity and menstrual impurity), as is shown by the presence of immersion pools far away from the temple. One would think that many pilgrims would have returned to the Diaspora and dug deep pools. Yet there is, as far as I know, only one reference to immersion pools in the Diaspora – though Philo, as we shall see, discusses ablutions several times.[11]

In principle, I quite agree that, on major matters, the clearly expressed view of Jerusalem (spoken by the high priest, not the supposed Pharisaic Nasi) would have been taken most seriously in the Diaspora. There were means of communication, and for major items these were probably used. Yet Diaspora practice, where we can test it, seems not to have been dependent on rules from Jerusalem – much less on rules originating from the Pharisees there.

B. PURITY

Recently James D. G. Dunn proposed that Pharisees exerted pressure on Antiochene Jews, or at least on James, who applied pressure to Christian Jews in Antioch, to observe laws of purity more strictly, and that this was one of the factors which led to the breach of relations between Jewish and Gentile Christians there (Gal. 2.11–14).[1] For example, he cites Hagigah 2.7, which gives a list of ascending degrees of impurity: ordinary people, Pharisees, priests when not on duty and their families, priests when on duty, and the priests who prepare the water of purification (for removing corpse impurity).[2] He then states that

> Once the concept of differing degrees of purity within the temple ritual [mistakenly taking the first three groups to be involved in the temple ritual] was translated into rules governing everyday table-fellowship it inevitably meant that different degrees of association were possible – he who lived at a stricter level of purity could not eat with one who observed a less strict discipline.[3]

Dunn supposes that the list in Hagigah 2.7 is a pharisaic law and that this law was applied to secular food. He then supposes that these distinctions in levels of purity would have been observed in Antioch. It is to be noted that the passage is not a law, but rather an observation about the scrupulousness of certain groups with regard to one of the most minor impurities, midras-impurity.[4] There is no reason to extend this non-law to Jewish practice in Antioch. The grades of purity, while not limited to the question of *serving* in the temple, have to do with the temple and holy food. Priests' families were more likely to be free of midras-impurity than were lay Pharisees, since priests' families ate first fruits (outside the temple). There is no implication that Jews in the Diaspora, who did not supply food for the temple,[5] needed to be graded on this scale, or were persuaded by Pharisees to try to avoid midras-impurity.

I cite this only as an example of the way in which mistaken assumptions dominate the discussion of Diaspora purity. Dunn wishes to transfer pharisaic discussions to the Diaspora. Let us instead ask what the evidence is of purity practices there.

§1. Undefined ablutions. There is a good deal of evidence which indicates that Diaspora Jews washed for religious purposes, though often we cannot say when or for what specific reasons. The connection of places of worship and the sea probably indicates that washing was connected with prayer or reading the scripture.

(a) According to Josephus, the decree of Halicarnassus on the rights of Jews in that city, following Julius Caesar's favourable decrees about them (c. 47 BCE; cited in *Antiq.* 14.190–216),[6] included the following stipulation:

[They] may build places of prayer near the sea, in accordance with their native custom (*to patrion ethos*). (*Antiq.* 14.258)

The meaning of 'build places of prayer near the sea' (*tas proseuchas poieisthai pros tēi thalattēi*) has often been debated. It could be translated 'offer prayers beside the sea'. This has been argued by W. Schrage and Shaye Cohen, among others, though Martin Hengel prefers the traditional view, that synagogues are in mind.[7] The plural makes 'offer prayers' more likely, since it would be a bit surprising for the Jews to be given the right to build two or more synagogues beside the sea at Halicarnassus. On the other hand, the evidence which follows immediately shows that synagogues were sometimes built beside the sea. In either case, the connection of the sea with prayer or a house of prayer is notable and probably points towards some kind of washing in connection with prayer and worship.

(b) According to Acts 16.13, Paul and his companion went to a river near Philippi expecting to find there a synagogue.

(c) Several Diaspora synagogues were built near the sea.[8]

(d) At least one Diaspora synagogue, at Priene, contained a large basin, presumably for ablutions.[9] There was a fountain in the forecourt of the synagogue at Sardis, which some think was used for handwashing.[10] These synagogues are later than the first century, and we cannot be certain that they represent first-century practice.

(e) In the romance *Joseph and Aseneth*, during her conversion to Judaism Aseneth, at the command of the angel, washes her hands and face 'with living water' (*Jos. and Asen.* 14.12,15). This was probably only to remove the ashes (see 14.3), though a later passage seems to indicate that living water might be able to effect some kind of transformation (18.8–10). None of this, however, points to a customary rite.

I shall add here two passages about ablutions from the apocrypha. Though they do not purport to reflect Diaspora practice, they do show that literature which circulated in the Greek-speaking Jewish world depicted washing before prayer or the sabbath as customary.

(f) II Macc. 12.38 relates that Judas and his army purified themselves (*hagnisthentes*) before the sabbath 'according to custom' (*ethismos*). 'Purification' probably involved the use of water.

(g) Judith bathed (*ebaptizetō*) in a spring each night and then prayed (Judith 12.7–8).

From this material I draw only one short, general conclusion: many Diaspora Jews associated some sort of washing with prayer, attendance at synagogue or both. What did they do in the sea? Immersion and handwashing are both possible. The next evidence points towards the latter.

§2. Handwashing. We have previously noted that evidence of handwashing is found in the Diaspora earlier than in Palestine. Here I shall give the two passages in full.

(a) *Letter of Aristeas*, c. 150 BCE, Alexandria:[11]

At the first hour of the day they attended the court daily, and after offering salutations to the king, retired to their own quarters. Following the custom (*ethos*) of all the Jews, they washed their hands in the sea in the course of their prayers to God, and then proceeded to the reading and explication of each point. I asked this question: 'What is their purpose in washing their hands while saying their prayers?' They explained that it is evidence that they have done no evil, for all activity takes place by means of the hands. (*Arist.* 304–306; cf. Josephus, *Antiq.* 12.206)

It is striking that washing the hands in the sea while praying is called 'the custom of all the Jews', but it is unfortunately not quite clear what this means. It would have been physically impossible for all Jews to reach the sea every morning, and the next passage to be considered refers to saying the morning prayers in bed. More likely, the custom referred to was simply handwashing while praying, not necessarily in the sea. Or perhaps we should take the passage in an even less precise sense, as indicating an *occasional* custom, perhaps practised on the Sabbath, of washing the hands in the sea during morning prayers. This would explain the evidence that synagogues were often near water. It may be that handwashing at home during prayer was generally practised. We may at least take handwashing while praying as the author's ideal.

The *Letter of Aristeas* was written too early to have been influenced by Pharisaism, and in any case the connection between washing and *prayer* is not pharisaic, though it is made later in the rabbinic movement.[12]

(b) According to the third *Sibyline Oracle* (160–50 BCE)[13] pious Jews

... at dawn ... lift up holy arms toward heaven, from their beds, always sanctifying their flesh [variant: hands] with water (*Sib. Or.* 3.591–593).

(c) It is just worth mentioning that Philo may provide evidence of handwashing as a common activity (please note the qualification). The verb in *Arist.* 305 is *aponiptesthai*, which is often used of washing the hands in pagan literature (so Liddell and Scott). Mark uses *aniptois* for unwashed hands (7.2) and *nipsontai* for the act of washing them (7.3). In the Pseudepigrapha which survive in Greek *niptein* refers to washing the feet, the hands and feet, or (as in *Jos. and Asen.*) the hands and face.[14] The same is true of the New Testament (Matt. 6.17; John 13). *Niptein* and its cognates, in other words, refer to washing part of a person. It was not used to mean 'bathe'. Philo will soon be the object of a fuller study, and we shall see that he distinguished quite carefully between 'bathe' and 'sprinkle', and also that he used both words metaphorically. Here I wish to note that he often used *ekniptesthai* metaphorically as well (wash off the soul etc.): e.g. *Change of Names* 49; 124; *Cherubim* 95; *The Worse Attacks the Better* 170; *Who is the Heir?* 113; *Unchangeableness of God* 9; *Dreams* 2.25; *Spec. Laws* 1.281. While he never mentions the rite of handwashing, the metaphorical use of a cognate of *niptein* may indicate that he and others practised it. Possibly *ekniptesthai* is used just for the sake of variety. I am inclined to think, however, that, like other terms cited below, the metaphor reflects an actual religious practice. It gains force if it refers to something which his readers actually did, and handwashing is a possibility, followed by footwashing and washing the face.

With or without the support of Philo's metaphor, it seems to me that we must accept as common the practice in the Diaspora of some form of washing, probably handwashing in connection with prayers, and especially in connection with the synagogue service. The sea seems to have been the preferred 'basin',[15] though at least some would use a basin in the synagogue itself or possibly in their own homes. Probably ablutions before observing the sabbath were common. The evidence is not quite dense enough to allow us to say that handwashing each day during prayer was *generally practised*, though it may well have been. At the very least, it was a sign of special devotion.

Handwashing is connected with food in Mark 7.3f., which is a parenthetical explanation to the readers:

> For the Pharisees, and all the Jews, do not eat unless they wash their hands, observing the tradition of the elders; and when they come from the market place, they do not eat unless they purify themselves; and there are many other traditions which they observe, the washing of cups and pots and vessels of bronze.

To wash utensils and vessels made of things other than earthenware is in accord with biblical law governing certain impurities (e.g. Lev. 11.32; 15.12). Handwashing, however, we have thus far seen in only two contexts: the Pharisees washed hands before handling the priests' food and before their own holy meals; Jews in the Diaspora washed hands (or performed other ablutions) in connection with worship. The passage just quoted from Mark expands handwashing considerably: before all meals and after returning from the market. To know how to evaluate Mark's evidence, we should first have to know who he was and where he lived. My own view is that he was a Gentile and that his information about Judaism was that of an observer. I think that he was wrong about the Pharisees: their debates about handwashing before sabbath and festival meals seem to exclude the possibility that they washed hands before every meal. Mark presumably generalized about Jewish practice on the basis of partial information, and I take his report to mean that some Jews who were known to him (that is, some Diaspora Jews) washed their hands more often than they prayed.

With regard to the source of handwashing, in discussing the Pharisees I suggested three possibilities (III.E§9): (1) Possibly it developed as a substitute for full bathing (which in Palestine was understood as immersion). (2) It may have been introduced under the influence of pagan practice, where hands were washed before sacrificing and praying. (3) Perhaps it derived from the numerous biblical references to the hands as the instrument of evil and defilement. Washing the hands to symbolize innocence or repentance is a fairly obvious thing to do, especially at the time of prayer, and the symbolism is made explicit in the passage from *Aristeas*. In particular we may note the phrase 'clean hands and pure heart' in Ps. 24.4, which requires this state of those who go up to the temple. Since in the Diaspora private and synagogal prayer had to substitute entirely for the temple service, handwashing may have been adopted on the basis of the Psalm.

I think that the third possibility must be at least a partial explanation of ablutions in the Diaspora. Just as in Palestine there were rites of purification before entering the temple, so in the Diaspora there were ablutions in connection with private or communal worship.

I wish here, however, to call attention to the second possibility, pagan practice, which Diaspora Jews would often have seen. I believe that it was an important source for rites of purification in the western Diaspora.

Pagans routinely washed their hands, or at least dipped the right hand, when entering a temple and before praying or sacrificing.[16] Homer attributes the practice to Priam:

> [He] bade the housewife that attended pour over his hands water undefiled; and the handmaid drew nigh bearing in her hands alike basin [*chernips*] and ewer. Then, when he had washed his hands, he took the cup from his wife and then made prayer . . . (*Iliad* 24.302–306)

The Delphic oracle permitted the sacrifice of animals 'which willingly nod[ded] at the washing of hands'.[17] Lucian, ridiculing religion, wrote that

. . . no man shall approach the holy ground with unclean hands. Yet there stands the priest himself, wallowing in gore. . . . (*On Sacrifices* 13)

Ginouvès explains that when entering a temple the hand was sometimes only dipped. Pagans attached great importance

to appearing in a state of bodily purity in the sanctuary of the god: at the entrance of the sanctuary, [the worshipper] would find a basin on a high pedestal, or a similar receptacle, of metal or earthenware, supported by a tripod, where he could scoop up some water, to sprinkle himself – a symbol of complete purification – or simply dip his right hand.[18]

My guess is that we have here the major source of handwashing among Diaspora Jews, and pagan influence on purity practices will be confirmed when we study Philo's terminology in the next sub-section. One need not think that Jews consciously imitated pagan practice, and they themselves may well have thought of handwashing as being virtually prescribed by Ps. 24.4. Like others who adopt foreign practices, they probably explained what they borrowed in light of their own sacred traditions.

§3. Philo: washing to remove corpse-impurity and semen-impurity.

(*a*) Philo several times refers to corpse-impurity and its removal. It is difficult to know when he intends only to be describing biblical law, or what was actually done at the temple (where he had been as a pilgrim, *Providence* 2.64), and when he is referring to his own practice in Alexandria and, presumably, that of other Jews there. We shall take the passages in order of significance and detail.

1. In *Dreams* 1.209–212 Philo reports that those who would sacrifice must first be sprinkled[19] with a mixture of ashes and water. This is simply a report of the ritual for removing corpse-impurity which is required by Num. 19. Philo assumes here and elsewhere – doubtless correctly – that all pilgrims underwent the seven-day rite before being allowed into the temple. Since Philo discusses the 'ashy-sprinkled' person so often, it will be useful to explain the symbolic value which he attaches to the rite: The mixture of ashes and water reminds the worshipper of the two elements of which humanity is made. This induces humility before God.

2. In *Spec. Laws* 3.89 Philo emphasizes that even those who have committed no sin cannot enter the temple until they have bathed (*apolouson-tai*) and been sprinkled (*perirranamenoi*).

3. A fuller account of the rite is found in *Spec. Laws* 1.256–266: both soul and body must be purified before sacrificing. The body is purified 'by sprinklings and ablutions' (1.258), as Colson (LCL) translated two words which require a bit of attention. The Greek is *dia loutrōn kai perirrantēriōn*. A

loutron is either a bath, a bathing-place or the water for washing. The plural can be used for 'water',[20] and so *dia loutrōn* could be either 'by water' or 'by baths'. A *perirrantērion* is primarily a basin,[21] though Liddell and Scott offer also the meaning 'whisk', referring to the utensil used in ritual sprinkling. The act of sprinkling, as a noun, is *perirransis*; the verb is *perirrainein* (and cognates). Because of its ending, the noun *perirrantērion*, which is what Philo uses here and elsewhere, cannot be the activity 'sprinkling'. Colson's translation, 'sprinklings and ablutions', very reasonably balances the terms and gives good sense. Philo could easily have balanced them himself, by using *loutēr* or *loutērion* with *perirrantērion* (since a *loutērion* is also a basin), or by using *perirransis* with *loutron*, both referring to the activity (sprinkling and washing). A strict rendering of what he actually wrote would be that purification is achieved 'by [making use of] water [*loutroi*] and basins/whisks [*perirrantēria*]', or 'by washings and [by making use of] basins/whisks'. In an attempt to provide more accuracy than smoothness, I shall translate this phrase 'by washing and [sprinkling from] basins'.

It would be nice if we could visualize the activity. I suspect that Philo has in mind one action – sponging or sprinkling oneself from a basin. We shall see below that this is distinguished from 'bathing'.

Perirrantēria were standard features in Greek society. According to Ginouvès, they were basins on pedestals or tripods which were often used for sprinkling. They stood, among other places, at the boundaries of the market (the *agora*); 'outside the *perirrantēria*' meant 'outside the agora, which was bounded by basins'. 'Inside the *perirrantēria*' could mean 'inside the sanctuary', since they also stood at the entrance to temples.[22] The term conveys a primarily religious meaning, which is appropriate to Philo's topic.

After a second introductory comment that the worshipper, before sacrificing, is purified 'by washing and [sprinkling from] basins', Philo then describes the rite more precisely: The law is not content to require only one sprinkling or bathing, but bids the worshipper stay outside the sanctuary for seven days, being sprinkled on the third and seventh day, and then to bathe. Only after all these preparations does it allow sacrifice (1.261). That branches of hyssop are used for sprinkling is mentioned in 1.262. This description is completely in accord with Num. 19.

4. The fullest treatment, and the one which raises the question of rites in the Diaspora, is *Spec. Laws* 3.205–206. I shall quote it in full according to Colson's translation.

> . . . even those who have touched the corpse of one who has met a natural death must remain unclean until they have been purified by aspersions and ablutions (*perirranamenoi kai apolousamenoi*). Indeed (*mentoi*) he did not

permit even the fully cleansed to enter the temple within seven days and ordered them to purge themselves (*aphagnizesthai*) on the third and seventh. Further too, those who enter a house in which anyone has died are ordered not to touch anything until they have bathed themselves (*apolousōntai*) and also washed the clothes which they were wearing.

Colson's view, which seems to me correct, is that the initial 'aspersions and ablutions', which we may more literally render 'sprinkling and bathing', purify, but are still inadequate for entrance into the temple, which requires 'purging' on the third and seventh day. I think that it is just possible to take 'sprinkling and bathing' to be part of a general introduction, as if Philo wrote, 'the law requires sprinkling and bathing: specifically, before entering the temple, one must purge . . .' The normal force of *mentoi*, however, is to make a contrast with what has preceded, yielding a meaning which we may paraphrase thus: 'those who touch a corpse must remain impure until they have sprinkled and bathed themselves; yet even so, though already perfectly pure, Moses forbids them to enter the temple until they purge . . .'

If this second construal (which agrees with Colson) is correct, Philo has a domestic rite of sprinkling and bathing which is not connected with entering the temple, but which purifies a person who touches a corpse for all other purposes.

A second peculiarity of the passage is that, when he turns to those who are in the house with a corpse, but who do not touch the body, he requires bathing and washing the clothes, and he does not mention the temple. The Bible requires the same seven day 'purging' as for a person who touches a corpse (LXX Num. 9.19, *aphagnisthesetai*), as well as bathing and washing the clothes, and the entire rite is connected to entering the temple.

This is a bit complicated, and so I shall first present a chart and then summarize the peculiarities of Philo's description. For the sake of comparison, I shall include passage (3) above.

Num.19	*Spec. Laws* 1.261	*Spec. Laws* 3.205–206
[11]if one touches corpse	before sacrificing, worshipper is purified *loutrois kai perirrantēriois* – not sprinkled only once, or bathed and then allowed immediately into the sanctuary, but rather	if one touches corpse, impure until purified by being sprinkled (*perirranamenoi*) and bathing (*apolousamenoi*); yet cannot enter temple for 7 days, until
[12]be purified (*hagnisthēsetai*) on the 3rd and 7th days; if not purged (*aphagnisthē*) on 3rd and 7th days not pure and [13]defiles tabernacle.		purged (*aphagnizesthai*) on the 3rd and 7th days
[14]everyone in house with corpse		those in house with a corpse not

impure 7 days		to touch anything until
[17-19]for [all] the impure take ashes and water, sprinkle (*perirranei*) on 3rd and 7th days; on the 7th be purged (*aphagnisthēsetai*), wash clothes and bathe (*lousetai*);	is sprinkled (*perirrainesthai*) on the 3rd and 7th days, bathes (*lousamenos*) and then	bathe (*apolousōntai*) and wash clothes
[20]otherwise defiles sanctuary.	enters	

Numbers 19 repeats the seven-day rite, stating it briefly as a requirement for the person who *touches* a dead body, and giving it in fuller detail after mentioning people and things which are in the 'tent' with the corpse. In the one passage where Philo distinguishes those who touch from those who are in the same house, he gives the seven-day rite only once, for those who touch the corpse. And, as we noted above, he distinguishes the seven-day rite, required to enter the temple, from 'sprinkling and bathing', which come first. A third difference is that he says that people in the house with a corpse are 'not to touch anything' until they have bathed and washed their clothes. According to Numbers, such people render impure what they touch.

The net result of these differences from Num. 19 is that sprinkling, bathing and washing the clothes are no longer connected exclusively with entrance to the temple, nor with the purifying purging by means of the mixture of ashes and water which was available only at the temple. For those who touch a corpse, Philo distinguishes 'sprinkling and bathing', which make one 'very pure', from 'being purged' on the third and seventh days. For those in the house with a corpse, he mentions neither the seven-day rite nor entry to the temple, but instead prohibits 'touching anything' until they bathe and wash their clothes.

It is likely that in Philo's circle people sprinkled and bathed at home after the funeral, and counted this as 'purifying', even though they knew that entrance to the temple required further rites.

The two philonic passages which are summarized in the chart have different topics, and the distinction supports this proposal. *Spec. Laws* 1.261 starts at the temple: a discussion of first-fruits and other offerings leads up to the question of who sacrifices. Philo then gives the main parts of the biblical rite: seven days, sprinkling on the third and seventh day, bathing – in the biblical sequence. Going to the temple is the topic, and he reports what actually happened when one went there.

The subject of 3.204–206 is the sanctity of life: Moses so guarded against murder that even touching a corpse leads to sprinklings and bathing. This purifies one, except for entering the temple. Here Philo gives a domestic rite, prior to and independent of the temple ritual, observable in all cases of death – which is the topic.

That there was a domestic rite, and that some Jews practised sprinkling and bathing after corpse-impurity, and in fact as a kind of cure-all rite of purification, quite apart from making pilgrimage to the temple, is rendered more probable by the next passages.

(*b*) After sexual relations neither party can touch anything (*tinos psauein*) until they have 'made use of water and [sprinklinng from] basins' (*loutrois kai perirrantēriois chrēsthai*) (*Spec. Laws* 3.63). There are two differences from Lev. 15.16–18: Philo adds '[sprinkling from] basins'; the Bible has only *lousontai hydati*, 'bathe with water', and he adds 'not touch anything'. Leviticus is surprisingly relaxed about what impure people touch. One has to be pure to enter the temple, and priests and their families must be pure when eating holy food, and it is explicitly said that a woman with childbirth-impurity stage two[23] cannot touch anything holy (Lev. 12.4); but saying that people with semen-impurity cannot touch things until they are purified goes beyond the written law. (And it is not pharisaic!) The statement shows that Philo thought that sprinkling should immediately follow each act of sexual congress.

(*c*) Before receiving the law at Mount Sinai, the people abstained from sexual relations and other pleasures, 'purified themselves with washing and [sprinkling from] basins' (*loutrois* and *perirrantēriois*) for three days, and washed their clothes (*Decalogue* 45). This looks like an all-purpose rite, expanded in comparison with Ex. 19.10–15, according to which they abstained from sex and washed their clothes.

(*d*) These words – washing and sprinkling-basins – are often used by Philo in a metaphorical sense. The mind of the worshipper is made fair 'by making use of washing and [sprinkling from] basins' (*loutrois kai perirrantēriois chrēsamenon*) (*Spec. Laws* 1.191). There are similar phrases, used of the mind or soul, in *Change of Names* 124; *Planter* 116 and elsewhere.

When Philo wanted to say 'bathe', he could do so perfectly well. For this he used *louein* or *apolouein*. The LXX, for the Hebrew *rahats*, 'bathe' or 'wash', ordinarily used *louein*: twelve times in Lev. 15 alone, and the same verb appears in Num. 19.7, 8, 19. Philo, we have seen, used *apolouein* for bathing before the seven-day rite (*Spec. Laws* 3.205) and for those who were in a house with a corpse (3.206), and *louein* as the conclusion of the seven-day rite in the short description in 1.261. In summarizing Lev. 22.4–6 (on the priest who has an emission), he used, as does the LXX, *louein* (*Spec. Laws* 1.119). From this I infer that by *loutroi* and *perirrantērioi*, 'washing and [sprinkling from] basins', he meant something other than bathing.

In defining these two words, I had recourse to pagan usage, and particularly to Ginouvès' study of lustration in the Greek world. We should, however, ask about the possible biblical background: would reading the Bible lead to the view that 'washing by [the use of] sprinkling-basins' should be a general means of purification?

Loutron is not a common word in the Bible. It is found in Song Sol. 4.2; 6.5 [6] (of the place for washing sheep) and in Ben Sira 31.25 (ET 34.25) for washing after touching a corpse, but not elsewhere. Neither is sprinkling a frequent biblical requirement, except for the blood of sacrificial animals and sometimes oil. Water is sprinkled in purifying the leper or the leprous house (Lev. 14.7,51 [*perirrainein*]); the Levites are sprinkled with water (Num. 8.7); and the corpse-impure are sprinkled with the mixture of ashes and water (Num.19). That is all, as far as the law goes. In one passage, Ezek. 36.25, sprinkling (*hrainein*) is used as a general term for purification: 'I shall sprinkle clean water upon you, and you shall be clean from all your uncleannesses, and from all your idols I will cleanse you'. Did Philo draw from this passage in Ezekiel the idea that sprinkling was an all-purpose rite of purification? And did he take 'ablutions' from Ben Sira's use of *loutron* and then combine it with Ezekiel's sprinkling?

This is possible, but most unlikely. He knew, as did Palestinian Jews, that, with the few exceptions just mentioned, the Bible favours washing all over – bathing, interpreted in Palestine as immersing. The reader of the Bible, whether in Hebrew or Greek, would never come up with the idea that one should splash water on oneself out of a basin standing on a pedestal. We have seen, however, that there was another source for *loutroi* and *perirrantērioi*: pagan religion. Strikingly, Philo was aware of it. In *Spec. Laws* 1.262 he contrasts the Mosaic requirements with those of other religions:

> In almost all other cases men use unmixed water for the sprinkling. By most people it is taken from the sea, by others from the rivers, and by others it is drawn in ewers from the wells. But Moses first provided ashes . . .

This is a *men . . .de* construction, contrasting others with Moses. More literally, the passage runs, 'On the one hand almost all others . . . on the other hand Moses'. The 'almost all others' are pagans, and they are sprinkled (*perirrainontai*). Ablutions are also attributed to pagans in *Cherubim* 90–96. Other nations have festal assemblies, and they 'cleanse their bodies with washings and purifications' (*loutrois kai katharsiois aporryptontai*), though they do not wash their souls (95). Philo criticizes those who enter 'the temple*s*' after bathing and making fair their bodies (*lousamenos phaidrynētai to sōma*) but not their souls, which need to be 'subjected to sprinkling-basins and cleansing purifications' (*perirrantēriois kai katharsiois hagneutikois chrēsamenon, Unchangeableness of God* 7–8). These again are pagans, as the plural 'temples' indicates.

I propose the following explanations of these data:

1. Jews in Alexandria, or at least some of them, purified themselves after contact with a corpse by washing and/or sprinkling water from a basin (*perirrantērion*), and they performed the same rite after sexual relations. The commandments not to touch anything when one is corpse- or semen-impure (*Spec. Laws* 3.206; 3.63), which are not in the Bible, lend support to the idea that these rites were practised in Alexandria. Had Philo written that the impure could not touch anything *holy*, one would think that he had picked up this prohibition from Lev. 12.4 and supposed that in Palestine, where one was often within reach of holy food, all the impure had to be careful not to touch it. But saying that a person should not touch *anything* makes it sound like an everyday rite, one that is not specifically Palestinian. After sex, he thought, people should immediately get up and purify themselves by using a basin which stood on a pedestal at a convenient height.

It appears that not only Philo thought this. Justin Martyr attributes to Trypho the statement that the requirement to wash after sexual intercourse was among the laws which Jews could still keep after the destruction of the temple (*Dialogue with Trypho* 46). The Bible does not, strictly speaking, require washing after sexual relations: it states that semen renders those whom it touches impure, and that the impure cannot enter the temple. Here as elsewhere, however, Jews regarded purity as something positively to be desired, and they thus regarded remaining impure as wrong. For this reason, they washed after contacting semen.

2. Alexandrian Jews may also have washed or sprinkled from a basin before attending synagogue: this may be the significance of Philo's addition of this rite to Ex. 19, which recounts the preparations for receiving the law. Perhaps Jews in his day sprinkled before entering the synagogue, where the law was read. (Compare pp. 259f. above.)

3. It is possible, even probable, that water was used for purifications in ways not explicitly stated by Philo. The Alexandrian Jews, for example, may well have extended the requirement of washing to menstruants, as did the Pharisees (above, pp. 209–11), on analogy with the laws governing other impure people. 'Washing and [sprinkling from] basins' may have served as a general rite of purification to remove all and sundry impurities, whether explicitly mentioned in the Bible or not. The metaphorical use of these terms indicates that lustrations were actually practised, since otherwise the metaphors lose their bite.

4. If Jews who sprinkled and washed wanted biblical support for their practice, they could cite Ezekiel and possibly Ben Sira (assuming that it was regarded as biblical).

5. They were probably influenced by pagan rites, which made use of ablutions and sprinklings. In terms of purifications, Philo distinguished Jews from pagans by pointing out the superiority of using ashes in addition to water. Apart from this, the only difference was that pagans did not purify their hearts. Jews did not, I assume, consciously adopt pagan customs. Social influence is more subtle than that.

6. Pagan influence probably extended to their use of the sea as the preferred basin. We noted above considerable evidence for washing in the sea (*Aristeas*, the location of synagogues). Now we may connect this with Philo's description of the pagan preference: most people take lustral water from the sea (*Spec. Laws* 1.262).

§4. Purity: conclusion. In discussing Alon's view of the purity of ordinary food, with much of which I disagreed, I pointed out that one of his arguments was the general one that purity was positively valued in first-century Judaism.[24] This is both right and important. It was so valued that people in the Diaspora came up with non-biblical purity laws.

By biblical law, all Diaspora Jews were impure all the time: everyone had to be assumed to have corpse-impurity, which could be removed only at the temple. Childbirth-impurity also required sacrifices (Lev. 12.6–8), as did leprosy and discharge (Lev. 14.10 and often; 15.14,29). Purification could be attained only by pilgrimage, and would necessarily last for only a short time. Nevertheless, Philo, if I have construed him correctly, thought that people who carried out a non-biblical domestic rite after corpse-impurity were *really* pure, in spite of not being allowed to enter the temple.

One might have thought that, since Diaspora Jews could not be pure enough to enter the temple, they would not have worried about impurity one way or the other: if corpse-impure already, why wash after intercourse? Why wash the hands while praying? But, we have seen, they did. They were not legalists. A legalist presumably would take refuge behind the legal situation and do nothing. That, at least, is what Jeremias and others accuse the Pharisees of doing: using casuistry to evade obedience of the spirit of the law.[23] The Diaspora Jews, like the Pharisees, wished to do what the law required, as best they could, and more. Did doing more prove that they were piling up a treasury of merits by doing works of supererogation? Diaspora literature is as silent on the topic as is early rabbinic.[26] Doing more meant entering into the spirit of the law, going after what it was driving at (to put it colloquially). Palestinian Jews went in the same direction. Many of them, we saw above, wanted to avoid or cleanse themselves of impurity even when, by biblical law, it had no practical consequence. Those who lived over the old graveyard in Tiberias were no more corpse-impure than those who went to funerals once or twice a year. Nevertheless, some people objected to living there.

They wanted to be 'pure', even if not according to the law, because purity was part of godliness. They wanted to be pure just as they wanted to be honest, truthful and kind. We now make a great distinction between 'inner' and 'outer', and those of us who are Protestants, or heirs of the Protestant tradition, distrust external forms. It should be remembered that, to ancient Jews, 'love the neighbour' and 'love the stranger' were not vague commandments about the feelings in one's heart, but were quite specific. 'Love' meant 'Use just weights and measures'; 'Do not reap your field to the border, but leave some for the poor'; 'Neither steal, deal falsely nor lie'; 'Do not withhold wages which you owe'; 'Do not take advantage of the blind or deaf'; 'Do not be biased in judgment'; 'Do not slander' – and so on, through the verses of Lev. 19 and many others. The biblical legislators seem to have known a great secret of human psychology: act in a desirable way, and your feelings will take care of themselves. One may experiment: sit in a dark room, act scared and observe how the feeling of scaredness begins. Do charitable deeds: see if you do not start feeling more kindly towards others.

And so the Diaspora Jews – those who left records – wanted to be pure, body and soul. Purity of heart and purity of body, despite the previous paragraph, *can* be separated, and Philo charged that with pagans this was the case. This was, in appreciable measure, unjustified polemic. But when it came to his own faith and practice he saw clearly: purify the body; go to the temple and spend seven days outside; think while you are there; consider the ashes and water with which you are sprinkled. If you do this, you will hear 'the voice of the [two] elements themselves' saying. 'We are the substance of which your body consists'. This is who you are. Now think whence the substances come and whither they go. You are a creature of God; think what it means (*Spec. Laws* 1.266).

Philo, of course, was an allegorizer of unusual talent. Yet I venture the thought that most people who went through the rites asked, Why? What do they teach? There were other teachers besides Philo who thought in this way, as Pseudo-Aristeas on washing the hands or on the food laws will show. That author could also allegorize.[27] But whether teaching was sophisticated allegory or not, it was common in the ancient world to ascribe symbolic meaning to outward actions. No thoughtful Jew wished to separate purity of body from purity of soul and mind. And most synagogues must have had a thoughtful member or two.

C. FOOD

There is less to be said about food laws in the Diaspora, because the biblical prohibitions are clear and comprehensive and there was little room to debate them. As far as I have noted, the Diaspora evidence has not been conveniently collected, and I shall make at least a start. We shall see that there are some points of interest and a couple of puzzles.

§1. **Prohibited foods.** We shall first recall some basic points from III.B. Food laws may be called purity laws, since forbidden creatures are characterized as 'impure' (Lev. 11.1–30; Deut. 14.3–21). They are also, however, called 'abominations' (Lev. 11.10–13, 20, 41–41). This is an emotive word, doubtless chosen to foster abhorrence, and the language seems to have been effective. Refusing to eat certain foods, of which pork and shellfish are best known, has always been a strong mark of Jewish identity. The martyrological literature sometimes features coercive measures to make Jews eat pork (e.g. IV Macc. 5–6).

The food laws rule out many forms of red meat, allowing only the easily domesticated animals (sheep, goats and cattle) and a few which are undomesticated (wild sheep and goats, deer, antelopes and the like; Deut. 14.4–5). Sea creatures with fins and scales are allowed, not shellfish and molluscs. Birds of prey are forbidden, but pigeons, doves and other domestic fowl are allowed. Insects and other 'swarming things' (weasels, rodents, lizards, crocodiles and so on) are forbidden, except for insects 'which have legs above their feet, with which to leap on the earth' (Lev. 11.21). This permits, locusts, crickets and grasshoppers.

The possible reasons for these selections have exercised much better minds than mine, with no definitive solutions coming forward,[1] and I shall propose no general explanation. The prohibition of all beasts of prey and of most animals and birds which cannot be domesticated, as well as those used for transportation and farming, is striking. That is the net result of the requirement that pure animals chew the cud and part the hoof. The law of hoof and cud excludes, among domestic animals, those that work (camels, horses and donkeys) – plus swine. These laws favour domestication in three ways: herds and flocks are encouraged, since they provide edible meat; agriculture is encouraged, since most work-animals (save oxen) cannot be eaten; spending time hunting is discouraged (how effectively depends on the population of deer, wild sheep and goats). With this socio-economic clue and one further comment I shall retire from the field. The prohibition of pork is contrary to the socio-economic explanation, since swine are easily domesti-cated and cheaply fed. They do well on the whey of sheep's milk. One must suppose that some strong motive underlies their exclusion. But it is not possible to provide a single convincing explanation of the prohibition of pork, since we do not know when and under what circumstances it arose. For example: swine are not suitable for nomads, and when the nomadic ancestors of the biblical legislators settled down, they may have regarded swine as symbolic of their previously-settled enemies. This and numerous other hypothetical possibilities cannot be assessed unless we can fix the origin of the prohibition.

Meat is subject to one other prohibition: the blood and fat must not be consumed. The blood may be poured or sprinkled upon the altar or poured upon the ground, but it may not be eaten. This is repeated again and again: eat neither fat nor blood (Lev. 3.17); eat no blood at all, the penalty is 'cutting off' (7.26f.); neither Israelites nor resident aliens may eat blood (17.10–13); the warning of 'cutting-off' is repeated in 17.14.

These basic prohibitions did not change in the Diaspora. The list of permitted meats, however, was subject to local variation. In the LXX the ten permitted animals of Deut. 14.4–5 include the buffalo (that is, the water buffalo of Egypt) and the giraffe, while the mountain sheep and roebuck of the Hebrew list drop out.[2] The LXX list is repeated by Philo (*Spec. Laws* 4.105). With regard to fowl, he adds cranes and geese, neither one mentioned in the LXX, but locally available (4.117). When it comes to the prohibitions, however, Philo gives no alterations, but repeats the list of prohibited creatures and of blood and fat (*Spec. Laws* 4.100–118). A lot of space is taken up offering reasons for the exclusions. With pork in mind, he explains that the richest and most succulent meat is forbidden in order to discourage gluttony (*Spec. Laws* 4.100).

As we shall see just below, Diaspora Jews generally kept these laws. In addition there was a prohibition about wine which appears only once in the Bible, where it is implied rather than explicitly stated: Jews should not drink Gentile wine. According to Daniel, Nebuchadnezzar, the king of Babylon, brought leading, handsome and intelligent Jewish youths to his own palace and ordered that they be given the best of everything while learning the language and lore of their conquerors. The best of everything included his own food and wine. Daniel asked not to be forced 'to defile himself', and he and three friends ate vegetables and drank water (Dan. 1.1–16). Gentile wine is not prohibited in the legal books, since the topic does not arise, but Daniel serves as a biblical basis for not drinking it. The difficulty which it raised is straightforward: in ancient cultures people poured libations to their gods whenever they drank wine.[3]

Several passages in Josephus show that many or most Jews preferred not to use Gentile oil. It is hard to know just what was wrong with it. Oil, the olives from which it was made and the vessels in which it was kept were subject to gnat-impurity, and that could have led to avoiding it. In one passage Josephus states that the Jewish inhabitants of Caesarea Philippi had no *pure* oil, which makes one think that a purity law was at stake.[4] Liquids are especially subject to impurity, and there were two principal liquids used as food: wine and oil.[5]

Admonitions neither to eat Gentile meat nor drink Gentile wine are frequent in Jewish literature. The 'admonitions' are often not direct, but appear in the descriptions of heros and heroines, of whom Daniel was the archetype. There is evidence that some Jews wished to avoid Gentile food entirely. I count all the following passages – many of which are exemplary legends – as 'Diaspora', since they circulated and have survived in Greek. The place of composition is sometimes uncertain. In any case the question is what to do about food when in the company of Gentiles, especially those in a position of superiority.

Seven brothers and their mother were tortured and executed on the orders of Antiochus IV rather than eat pork (II Macc. 7).

Antiochus IV ordered some Jews to eat pork and food sacrificed to idols. At least one, Eleazar, refused, and he was tortured and killed (IV Macc. 5.1–6.30).

When Judith decided to ingratiate herself with Nebuchadnezzar's general, Holofernes, so that she could kill him, she took along *everything* which she needed to eat: her own wine, oil, grain, fruit and bread (Judith 10.5). She declined other food and ate only her own until, on the fourth day, she could carry out her mission (12.2, 9f., 19; 13.8).

When Tobit was taken captive to Nineveh, his kinfolk ate Gentile food, but he did not (Tob. 1.10f.).

In an expansion of Esther 4.17, Esther reminds God in prayer that she had not eaten food from Haman's table nor graced the royal drinking party (*symposion*) with her presence nor drunk the wine of libations (Esth. 14.17 in the RSV translation of the Apocrypha; Esth. 4.17x in Rahlf's enumeration).

The Egyptian Jews kept separate from Gentiles 'with respect to foods', and this, along with their separateness in worship, led to hostility against them (III Macc. 3.4–7).

The Jews of Syria tried to avoid use of local oil and preferred that of Palestine (Josephus, *War* 2.591). According to *Life* 74, the Jewish inhabitants of Caesarea Philippi regarded Grecian oil as not in accord with their ordinances (*nomima*). Earlier Seleucus Nicator had granted Jews who settled in new cities outside of Palestine extra money so that they could import their own oil rather than use that of foreigners (*Antiq.* 12.120).

The treatment of food in *Joseph and Aseneth* requires a few more words. The topic is Joseph's marriage to Aseneth,[6] and the author claims that this daughter of an Egyptian priest converted to Judaism before Joseph would consider her as a suitable partner (conversion is not implied in Gen. 41.45). Part of the author's evangelistic concern is to persuade Jews not only to require conversion before intermarriage, but also not to eat *with* Gentiles. When Joseph visited the house of Aseneth's family, he ate at his own table (*Jos. and Asen.* 7.1). He refused to kiss Aseneth because her mouth blessed idols and she 'ate from their [the idols'] table bread of strangulation and drank from their libation a cup . . .' (8.5). Happily, she converted, the marriage could take place, and a feast was prepared at her house (18.5). The couple were joined by her parents, and they all 'ate and drank and celebrated' (20.8).

This is a 'hard-line' work, opposing some forms of social intercourse between Jew and Gentile, and clearly holding Gentile food in abhorrence (8.5). Yet Jewish food is not mentioned, only what Aseneth customarily ate. When Joseph sat at his own table, we do not learn what he dined on or how it was supplied. Aseneth's pagan family put on the wedding banquet, but the problem of organizing Jewish food is not mentioned. This time, apparently, we are to understand that they all sat together, though only Aseneth had converted. She is not separated from her own family, and apparently they have become suitable dining-companions for Joseph because one member of the family converted.

One cannot press a romantic tale too hard on its details, especially when there are substantial variations among the manuscripts, as there are in this case. This granted, it is still striking that the exclusivism of the early part of the romance is not maintained through the story of the feast. The author doubtless favoured conversion prior to intermarriage, but he also believed in cordial relations between Jews and pagans in Egypt. Before Joseph met Aseneth, he was on good terms with her father, who is praised, and who praises him (e.g. 1.3; 3.3). The author may have thought that Joseph and Aseneth should sit at a separate table at their wedding feast, and that they should have food prepared separately from that of the others, but it would be too anti-social to say so. Joseph's initial refusal to kiss Aseneth expresses the full Jewish horror of Gentile meat and wine, but the author offers no practical help on how to avoid Gentile food while not breaking off social relations, except the separate table of 7.1. Did Joseph travel with a kitchen tent?

The *Letter of Aristeas* is clearer. The author is a bit reluctant to discuss the details of 'meats and drink and beasts' which are impure (*Arist.* 128), arguing that all people have such lists[7] and that the point of the Mosaic legislation is to separate Jews from idolatry. 'Meat and drink and clothes' are not their concerns, but rather 'the sovereignty of God'. The purity laws have the same function (128–142). Gentiles should 'not take the contemptible view that Moses enacted this legislation because of an excessive preoccupation with mice and weasels or suchlike creatures' (144). As a concession Pseudo-Aristeas explains two examples. The forbidden birds either are carnivorous, or they dominate other birds by strength, taking food at the expense of the permitted birds (among which he, like Philo, includes geese). Some forbidden birds will seize lambs and defile human corpses. By permitting the eating of peaceful birds, Moses indicated that people should 'not achieve anything by brute force, nor lord it over others . . .' (145–149). The second example is the cloven hoof, which symbolizes 'setting apart each of our actions for good' (150, elaborated in what follows). There are further justifications of why some creatures are forbidden (to 166).

A main feature of *Aristeas* is the description of the relationship between the Jewish translators and Ptolemy, who (according to this romance, which was widely accepted) commissioned the translation of the Hebrew scriptures into Greek. They regularly dined together, and the king ate food prepared in accord with Jewish requirements (181).

§2. Summary. Thus far we have seen four major points:

(*a*) There is a sizable body of literature which favours keeping the food laws, and there was no dispute over living creatures which the Bible prohibits. The list of permitted creatures could expand as Jews encountered new animals and birds which conformed in characteristics to those permitted in the Bible.

(*b*) Some Jews expanded the categories of food which they would not consume. Many avoided Gentile oil. Some (as in Judith) would have Jews eat only their own food.

(*c*) Most of the literature is paraenetic or hortatory. The descriptions of martyrdom, the stories of the heroines Judith and Esther, the romance about Joseph – all are exemplary and are designed to urge that others live up to the ideal. This probably points towards the fear that the food laws were not being kept as strictly as many wished.

(*d*) We have noted a problem: how to socialize with Gentiles while keeping the food laws. We may now take up (*c*) and (*d*).

§3. Practical issues:

Ad §2.c.: Can we determine how well Jews in the Diaspora actually kept the food laws – meaning now not the extension to cover oil, but the prohibition of most animals and blood and fat, and the implied prohibition of Gentile wine? It should first be said that not all Jews always obeyed them. The evidence for this is quite straightforward: sometimes it was almost impossible to do so. A decree of Sardis directed 'the market-officials of the city' to see to it that 'suitable food' for the Jews was available (*Antiq.* 14.259–261). Dolabella, legate of Asia, complained in a letter to Ephesus that Jews could not obtain their 'ancestral food' (14.226). The permission to 'manage their own produce', granted by the Roman proconsul in a letter to Miletus, probably means that Jews should be allowed to organize their own food supply (*Antiq.* 14.245).[8] These passages imply that, at some times and in some places, Jews did not have suitable food and drink. This would also have been the case when they travelled, except when they reached a city where they could be put up by other Jews. They could respond to this situation by eating vegetables and drinking water, and that is the point of some of the passages listed above. But we must assume that some transgressed.

While we assume some transgression when Jews could not obtain their own meat and wine, we should otherwise assume general obedience. There are two arguments in favour of it. One is the well-known effectiveness of social pressure. Not all Jews in the Diaspora lived in a distinct 'quarter', but many did, and major transgression would have been noted. The best evidence is that pagans criticized and ridiculed Jews because of their food laws. The curiosity that they would not eat pork, probably the favourite red meat in the ancient world, was especially striking, though some critics also mentioned hare.[9] That Diaspora Jews avoided pork is almost as certain as that they observed the sabbath (for which there is overwhelming attestation from all sources, including Julius Caesar's remission of tribute in the sabbatical year and the general acceptance by Gentiles that Jews could not bear arms because of the sabbath law).[10]

The supply of food in Hellenistic cities was the responsibility of the city council, which appointed market managers (the *agoranomoi*; in Latin, the *aediles*),[11] though a Roman legate could intervene with the council (e.g. Dolabella's letter to Ephesus, above). The principal concern of the city fathers and officials was the grain supply.[12] Meat, as in Rome, may often have been left to private enterprise.[13] It required little managerial time, since it was a fairly minor part of the market and was supplied locally. Meat could be freshly butchered, or it could be smoked or salted,[14] but still it had to be produced nearby.

Jews might object to meat which appeared in the public market for one or more of three reasons: it might be pork, it might have blood in it, or it might be from an animal sacrificed to a pagan god.[15] Jews could avoid the first difficulty without any trouble. Pork was popular and common in the Gentile world,[16] but it is readily identifiable, and Jews could and did refuse to eat it. Lamb and kid were probably less abundant than pork, since the adult animals have more uses, but still there were sheep and goats throughout the Mediterranean, and Jews need not have gone entirely without red meat because of a lack of suitable animals. In classical Greece, the only animals which were offered for sale in the market were those which could be sacrificed, and these in turn were primarily the domestic animals: cattle, sheep, goats and pigs.[17] According to Marcel Detienne, not only were sacrificial and edible animals the same, there was an 'absolute coincidence of meat-eating and sacrificial practice'; 'all comestible meat must result from a sacrificial killing'.[18] The comment that Jews would not eat hare (at n. 9 above), however, shows that these rules were not followed throughout the Graeco-Roman world in the first century. Meat from animals which were not sacrificed was available in various cities in the Roman Empire. Despite this diversity, Gentiles did eat meat from sheep and goats, and so Jews could find meat from pure animals.

Though New Testament scholars seem to assume that pagan meat was from animals 'improperly killed' from the Jewish point of view,[19] the method of slaughtering need not have been much of a difficulty. On the whole, pagan sacrificial technique was like Jewish: the animal bled to death. In some cases the victim's head was drawn back (*aueruō*), and the carotid artery was opened with a stab. In other cases the throat was slit (*entemnō*). Most of the blood was drained and thrown on the altar.[20] Jean-Louis Durand gives a detailed description of a sacrifice in which the throat was cut, and he notes that, after the animal was slaughtered and before it was butchered, there was still some blood in the carcass. This, however, was soon eliminated. The animal was eviscerated, the joints were separated, and then the meat was boned. This removed any remaining blood, even though evisceration and dismemberment began with the carcass lying on its back, rather than hung up in the Jewish manner.[21] Eating blood was not forbidden, though as a rule the liquid blood went to the altar, to the ground, or to the priest as blood-pudding.[22] The nobler viscera were considered to be condensed blood, and these were eaten by the priest or by other major participants in the rite.[23]

Greek sacrificial technique did not prohibit cutting the trachea (or windpipe), and if it was cut the animal might strangle on its own blood. The Rabbis regarded this as objectionable, though they did not completely prohibit cutting the trachea part of the way through, and there were disagreements about how much of the windpipe and gullet (esophagus) could be cut (Hullin 1.2; 2.1; 3.1). There are two clues which indicate that some Jews considered that Gentile slaughtering resulted in 'strangulation'. In *Jos. and Asen.* Joseph complains that Aseneth has eaten 'bread of strangulation', (*arton agchones*, 8.5; cf. 21.14), which might mean 'meat from an animal which strangled on its own blood', though meat is not usually called 'bread'. The 'apostolic decree' supports the view that some Jews suspected that Gentiles ate meat from 'strangled' animals (Acts 15.20, 29; 21.25).[24]

Wherever the rules of classical Greece were followed, then, meat from suitable animals (especially sheep and goats) could be found, and the meat would be free of blood. The animal, however, would have been sacrificed to a pagan deity,[25] and at least some Jews would have thought that it had strangled on its own blood.

But, we have seen, the rules of classical Greece did not obtain throughout the Mediterranean in the first century. 'Secular' meat was available, and the slaughtering technique was the same as for sacrifices. The *mageiros* became a butcher and cook, but he started out as an official in pagan cults.[26] In Greece there was only one mode of slaughtering,[27] and it is likely that most Mediterranean butchers observed the same technique. This would mean that, at least some of the time in some cities, meat could be bought in the market which was from suitable animals, which had no blood, and which had not been offered to an idol. Further, pagan meat, if not sold immediately after slaughter, like Jewish, was salted.[28] This both preserved it and absorbed any remaining blood.

A reasonable Jewish citizenry in a city with reasonable merchants – willing to slaughter 'correctly', but without sacrificing – could have found acceptable meat. Yet, we have seen, there were objections to Gentile meat, and in some cities Jews lodged protests because suitable food was not available. There seem to be two possible explanations. Perhaps merchants would not cooperate and would not supply meat which was acceptable to Jews. This, the human dimension, was, I think, more likely to have been the actual problem in the first century than were differences in slaughtering. The complaints in the two passages mentioned above (a letter from Dolabella to Ephesus; a decree of the Sardis council requiring the market managers to supply Jews with suitable food) indicate that the problem could be remedied. Pagans could be required to make available food which Jews would eat.

The second possibility is that, because of ignorance, general suspicion, or the long-standing association of meat with sacrifice, Jews were reluctant to eat Gentile food, especially meat, just because it was Gentile. The objection, that is, may not have been technical – 'it has blood in it' – but vague and traditional – 'our family has never eaten Gentile meat'.

My guess is that both the possible explanations are true, one covering some cases and one others. Some Jews would eat Gentile meat if they could receive the right assurances about it, others simply would not eat it because it was Gentile.

How much of a problem was meat offered to idols? As Barrett recognized, this is difficult to assess. New Testament scholars, quite naturally, start with Paul. He appears to envisage three possibilities: that his converts might partake of 'the table of demons' (I Cor. 10.21), presumably by eating at a temple; that in the market they might buy food which had been dedicated to a pagan god ('eat whatever is sold in the market . . .', 10.25); that they might dine with a pagan who would offer them such food ('if one of the unbelievers invites you . . . eat whatever is set before you', 10.27). It is understandable, then, that scholars have generally thought that 'the greater part of the meat sold in the shops was "offered to idols"' or that 'much though not all . . . of the food offered for sale in ancient towns had, in whole or part, passed through sacred rites in heathen religious establishments'.[29] The last comment, which is from Barrett's commentary on I Corinthians, is less nuanced than his earlier discussion in 'Things Sacrificed to Idols'. There he noted that in 1934 Cadbury had cautioned against overestimating the percentage of meat which had been offered to idols, pointing out, among other things, that a shop in Pompeii had 'entire skeletons of sheep'.[30] Had the animals been slaughtered in a temple, the priests would have kept some (usually, as in the Jewish peace offering, the right leg).[31] Barrett added two points: a reference from Plutarch which implies that 'secular' meat was available, and the general consideration that little red meat was eaten in any case.[32]

Despite all this, it may nevertheless be that in most Mediterranean cities 'meat offered to idols' was more plentiful than non-sacrificial meat in the market. Sometimes there would have been very little non-sacrificial meat. As Barrett noted, along with many others, meat was a fairly rare food in the Mediterranean, and the diet was mostly grain, legumes and dairy products, plus fish. Pompeii was not an average city, but served as a resort for the wealthy, and other cities may have been less well supplied.[33] The truth is that we cannot know how much meat was available in any given place, and we certainly cannot generalize across the whole Roman empire. The meat supply of a city depends on what is raised in the hinterland, and this is governed in part by topography. Supply is also seasonal. In Spring, for example, more male lambs and kids come of age than are needed for breeding, and so many of them can be sacrificed or slaughtered. That Passover comes in the Spring is not a coincidence.

We can, however, make one safe generalization. Pagans and Jews alike preferred to have an animal do double duty: one sacrificed it and then ate it.

This points towards relative scarcity of meat. Many Palestinian Jews may well have eaten little meat except the Passover lamb and their portion of peace offerings, usually made at the pilgrimage festivals and bought with second tithe money.[34] Similarly many Gentiles may have eaten little meat except what was sacrificed. 'The round of festivals was continuous, and pagan occasions were woven thickly into the fabric of the Greek city's year, especially during the period of the Roman empire.'[35] At festivals there were sacrifices, and these may have supplied much of the meat in the ordinary person's diet. While we cannot know what percentage of the total meat available in a Graeco-Roman city was from sacrificial animals, it appears from I Corinthians that it *could* constitute a substantial problem, especially for Gentile converts, who were accustomed to eating it.

What attitude towards it did Jews take? Many doubtless abhorred sacrificial meat, and this attitude can be seen in *Joseph and Aseneth*[36] and IV Macc. 5.2. Otherwise meat offered to idols does not appear (as far as I have noted) in the surviving literature.[37] Jews could readily avoid it, as they could avoid pork, and doubtless most of them did so.

We should consider, however, the possibility of another attitude among some Diaspora Jews. Let us recall the exhortatory character of the literature, which is aimed at keeping Jews from eating Gentile meat and drinking Gentile wine, and sometimes at keeping them away from Gentile food altogether. This implies that some were not as strict as the most zealous Rabbi (as Barrett seems to imply they were, in citing Abodah Zarah as revealing the stance of Diaspora Jews).[38] One of Paul's responses as he wrestled with the problem of meat offered to idols was, When a guest, do not raise the question, but do not eat the meat if its origin is pointed out (I Cor. 10.27–29). This may well have been a common Jewish attitude when dining with pagan friends. Barrett thinks that this is Paul's most *un*Jewish attitude.[39] My own guess is that it too has a home somewhere in Judaism.

This is not the place to rehearse the evidence, but it should be borne in mind that many Jews wanted to fit into the common culture, as long as doing so did not involve blatant idolatry. Some Jews participated in the main socializing aspects of Gentile city life – theatres, gymnasia and civil government. 'These activities included at least passive contact with idolatry, and they show willingness to overlook formal, civic idolatry in order to participate in the broader civilization.'[40] Such Jews may have taken the very attitude towards food which Paul recommended in I Cor. 10.27–29, and for very similar reasons: they did not want to be completely cut off in a ghetto. Not all Jews were fanatical. We cannot quantify, but we may suppose that Jewish attitudes towards pagan meat varied.

I am proposing that some Jews regarded the minor, formal idolatry involved in eating sacrificial meat as less serious than transgressing either of two prohibitions which are among the strongest in the Bible: do not eat pork, shellfish, donkey etc.; do not consume blood. If they did not examine their hosts on the origin of food which they were served, their attitude towards meat would correspond, more or less, to their attitude towards games (*agōnes*). 'Someone may be sacrificing something to an idol or giving homage to a hero; personally, I am paying no attention.' Many Jews, to be sure, were much stricter. But some participated in common Gentile activities as long as they could avoid major, blatant transgression.

Ad §2.d. This brings us to the question of how Jews and Gentiles managed to see one another socially if this involved eating together – as it often did. One answer was to eat Jewish food. We do not hear that vessels in which pork had been cooked were a problem, and it seems to have been only the actual food that constituted a difficulty. The king in *Aristeas* had Jewish food prepared, presumably in the regular kitchen. All a Gentile would have to do to entertain a Jewish friend would be to buy meat and wine from a suitable source. It was not necessary to have a separate set of Jewish dishes and utensils.[41]

The second answer may be given by Paul, as we just noted: do not enquire. Transgressions committed inadvertently are light, and it is probable that many people did not worry about them too much, and this would have allowed a considerable range of social intercourse.

The third possibility is given in the exemplary literature: bring your own food and wine, or eat vegetables and drink water.

Despite these obvious solutions, the Jewish food laws did restrict socialization. Apollonius Molon, first century BCE, called the Jews atheists and misanthropes and accused them of being unwilling to associate with others.[42] According to Diodorus Siculus, of about the same period as Apollonius, Jews would not share the table with other people.[43] Such statements as these are not calm, unbiased social description (as Christian scholars sometimes take them to be[44]), but are aspects of exaggerated or completely fabricated charges which were often on a level with the later accusation that Christians were cannibals. Nevertheless, in matters of food and drink some social reality does stand behind the malicious accusations that Jews were misanthropes. III Macc. 3.4–7, cited above, states that Jews were separate with regard to worship and food, and there are similar remarks in other Jewish literature. Many Jews and Gentiles accepted the food laws as imposing a barrier and did not sit down to work out how they could be accommodated while allowing social intercourse.

Elsewhere I have described more fully how thoughtful Jews regarded their partial separatism from others.[45] We saw it above in discussing the *Letter of Aristeas*: the point of the food laws was to prevent idolatry. The author added that by bad relationships people become perverted (*Arist.* 130). Had the Jews fully assimilated, they would have accepted idolatry. By remaining apart they not only kept their own lives free of it, they stood up for monotheism in the pagan world, possibly serving thereby as a light to the Gentiles. As bad companions lead to perversion, good lead to improvement (ibid.) Jews welcomed association with those who respected their laws (such as the king in *Aristeas*), and especially with those who wished to share their worship of the one God, even when they did not fully convert.

It remains only to be added that Graeco-Roman society posed the same general problems to Christians. After the first generation, relatively few Christians worried about the food laws; but the issues of idolatry, participation in civic festivals and games, and socializing with pagans were the same, and many Christians withdrew from all such activities.[46]

D. OFFERINGS FROM THE DIASPORA

This section started life as an essay on an event in the early history of the Christian movement which is both very important and a bit puzzling. The church in Antioch was mixed, and it was the custom for Jews and Gentiles to eat together, presumably when commemorating Jesus' last supper. Peter visited the Christian community in Antioch and at first joined the common meal. James, Jesus' brother, however, sent a message to him, as a result of which Peter withdrew and would eat only with other Jews. Paul attacked him for being hypocritical (Gal. 2.11–14). What has never been clear in this incident is what the problem was from the point of view of strict Jewish practice. Why did James object to Peter's eating with Gentiles?

The simplest explanation has always seemed to me to be that they were eating Gentile meat and drinking Gentile wine (section C above). James Dunn has argued, however, that the community in Antioch probably was not transgressing the law in any major or obvious way,[1] and he has a good point. Paul shows himself squeamish over 'meat offered to idols' in I Cor. 8, 10; and in Rom. 14 he shows respect for those whose consciences do not permit the eating of meat – presumably Gentile meat. He might have tolerated Peter's withdrawal if it was caused by transgression of a major Jewish law. Thus it is possible that the offence at Antioch was not anything as blatant as the consumption of pork which had been sacrificed to an idol.

I hasten to add that we cannot be sure. Arguments from what Paul's response to a given situation 'would have been' will not lead to certainty. In the surviving literature he treats circumcision both as rejection of Christ and as indifferent (Gal. 5.1–4; 6.15; I Cor. 7.19). His attitude depended on circumstances. Thus it is possible that on some occasions he thought that Jewish scruples over food were quite acceptable (Rom. 14), while on another that Jews *should* transgress the law. We cannot exclude the possibility that in Antioch a substantial Jewish food law was being ignored, that Peter withdrew from blatant disobedience, and that Paul thought that he should have transgressed. I think it worthwhile, however, to consider the circumstances which Dunn suggests: the mixed church in Antioch was not breaking a major Jewish law.

If not, we must go in search of a new explanation of the problem with joint meals. Dunn suggested that Jews in Antioch were under pressure from Palestinian Pharisees, who campaigned for strict practice, and who wished to enforce two views, both at home and abroad: (1) that Jews not associate with Gentiles because Gentiles were impure; (2) that Diaspora Jewish food should be tithed.[2] I think that these suggestions are entirely wrong, though they agree in part with views of other noted scholars.

It is certainly true, and it was adequately demonstrated by Alon,[3] that some Jews considered Gentiles as such to be impure with a special form of impurity. But this had as its source the view that Gentiles were not subject to the laws of Lev. 12, 15 and Num. 19, which made most Jews impure most of the time. Could Gentiles then enter the temple? No, they had their own kind of impurity which could be removed only by conversion. The Houses of Hillel and Shammai disagreed on how serious it was compared to Jewish impurities. Did it last a day, like semen-impurity, or a week, like corpse-impurity (Pesahim 8.1)? This was a topic which had to be settled before proselytes could enter the temple or eat Passover, but it did not affect daily life in the Diaspora. If Diaspora Jews refused to sit beside people who were impure, they would have had to become hermits, and in fact could not have associated with one another or even with themselves.[4]

I think that there is a good deal to be said in favour of the view that James feared that Peter's efforts to convert Judaeans to belief in Jesus as Messiah would be hindered if he were known to associate *too much* with Gentiles, not because of a technical ruling about their degree of impurity, but on the general grounds that too much association might bring him into contact with idolatry in some way or other.[5] I shall not, however, elaborate on this possibility now, but rather turn to Dunn's second proposal, that the food had not been tithed. This leads us into some interesting questions about the practice of Diaspora Jews, interesting enough to deserve study, quite apart from the issue which led to the dispute at Antioch.

It is not difficult to dispose of the evidence which Dunn cited to support his view, but I soon discovered both that other scholars, such as C. K. Barrett and S. Safrai, had also proposed that Diaspora Jews tithed, and that it is difficult to uncover just what they sent to the temple and what it should be called. The substantial question is what triggered the study which follows. Gifts from the Diaspora are important because they reveal loyalty to the temple – or, if they were not abundant, lack of it – and thus they bear on the question of unity and diversity. And, besides, there is sheer curiosity: what did Diaspora Jews do?

§1. Proposals that Diaspora Jews tithed. We shall first take up Dunn's evidence. He does not cite many passages from the Mishnah and Tosefta about tithing, and it is surprising that he omitted references to tithing from Syria and paying Poor Tithe from Ammon and other places. These passages, some of which are noted by Safrai, are interesting, but I shall reserve discussion of them until I give a comprehensive sketch of rabbinic views about support of the priesthood below, in §6. For the present we need only note that Dunn considered enough rabbinic passages to know that, in proposing that Pharisees urged Diaspora Jews to tithe, he went against the overall view of the Mishnah.[6] On other points in the essay he accepted rabbinic literature without question as representing the Pharisees. For example, he used as evidence for pre-70 pharisaic views Aboth 3.3, attributed to R. Simeon b. Yohai, a second-century Rabbi,[7] the tractate Abodah Zarah, in which Jacob Neusner found no pharisaic passages;[8] Makkoth 2.3, a discussion attributed to four second-century Rabbis (which further does not say what Dunn claims); and Eliyahu Rabba 10, a text from the eighteenth century.[9] What evidence in favour of tithing in the Diaspora leads him to break his rule of supposing that post-70 rabbinic law governed Jews everywhere in the 40s and 50s, especially Pharisees?

He cites four passages. (1) He claims that Tobit 1.6–8 shows that tithes were 'scrupulously observed from a home in Nineveh', not noting that these verses refer to the time when Tobit was 'in [his] own country, in the land of Israel' (1.4), before he was taken to Nineveh (1.10). The reading of just a few more verses would have put the matter right. (2) Dunn supposes that when the Jews of Miletus were given permission to 'manage their produce' they were allowed to tithe (*Antiq.* 14.245). 'Manage produce' is not likely to mean 'tithe'. This passage, like those on tithes from Syria, will be more fully discussed below (§4). (3, 4) He states that Philo refers to tithing on the part of Jews in Rome (*Embassy* 156) and Alexandria (*Spec. Laws* 1.153). The word in these passages, however, is not *dekatai*, tithes, but *aparchai*, literally 'first fruits'. The meaning of *aparchai* is flexible, and Philo's usage is complicated. We shall consider both fully below. In §4 we shall see that *Embassy* 156 refers to the temple tax and *Spec. Laws* 1.153 to first fruits; there is no possibility that either passage refers to tithes. In short, Dunn has no evidence at all for tithing in the Diaspora. This is not surprising, since none exists.

The arbitrariness involved in selecting evidence deserves note. Dunn accepts post-135 rabbinic passages as evidence that pre-70 Jews, led by Pharisees, shunned contact with Gentiles,[10] yet he does not accept post-135 passages as evidence that pre-70 Pharisees did not expect tithes from the Diaspora. Consideration of the nature of the two issues would lead to the reverse position. Evidence of hostility to Gentiles which comes from the period after two bloody wars should not be retrojected to the period before them. With regard to tithes, the Rabbis were extremely enthusiastic, since the priesthood was thereby preserved. There is no reason to think that second-century Rabbis reduced the area from which they wanted tithes to come. If pre-70 Pharisees favoured tithing from the Diaspora, we cannot explain the second-century rabbinic view that tithes came only from Palestine.

According to Safrai, pilgrims from the Diaspora brought heave offerings (t‘rûmôt), tithes and firstlings. The carrying of grain, grapes, olives, wine, oil and animals from, say, Ephesus to Jerusalem would have been a remarkable feat for pilgrims. It is not surprising that later he speaks of their bringing 'redemption-money' in lieu of 'dues and tithes'. He noted that the practice of sending tithes from the Diaspora to the temple was unknown to the Tannaim and to Josephus. His explanation of this was that the custom had lapsed by the first century and was referred to only in very old traditions. In apparent contradiction to this view, he also proposed that Philo knew about it and that even after the destruction of the temple Egyptian Jews brought 'dues and tithes' to Israel.[11] The theory of a forgotten halakah allows him to bypass the problem that Josephus and the early rabbinic literature show that the Diaspora did not pay tithes, while utilizing some late rabbinic passages in favour of tithes. This will all eventually become clear, though I shall again defer consideration of most of the rabbinic passages, especially those about the Poor Tithe from Ammon etc. Besides these, Safrai cites two passages which we have already noted and which will be considered below (Antiq. 14.245, 'manage produce'; Spec. Laws 1.152, aparchai), as well as Aboth de R. Nathan A ch. 20 and p. Hallah 60a.[12] In this preliminary section we shall deal with the last two rabbinic passages.

I shall quote the first passage, ARNA 20 (end) in full, as well as Safrai's comment, so that the reader may see the difference in genre:

'They made me keeper of the vineyards, but mine own vineyard have I not kept' (Song Sol. 1.6): Said the Holy One, blessed be He: 'Who had caused me to show favor to the Gentiles? Only Israel!' For so long as the Gentiles enjoy tranquillity, the people of Israel are afflicted, cast off, driven about.

Another interpretation of 'They made me keeper of the vineyards, but mine own vineyard have I not kept'. The verse refers to Israel at the time they were exiled to Babylon. Up rose the prophets in their midst and urged them: 'Set aside heave offerings and tithes!'

They answered: 'This very exile from our land has been visited upon us only because we did not set aside heave offerings and tithes. And now you tell us to set aside heave offerings and tithes!'[13]

Safrai regards this passage as providing a clue to something that really happened:

... whether because of a 'prophetic ruling' or a 'commandment of the Sages' or other reasons of Halakah, or because of a lasting tradition of an ancient halakah preceding or contradicting our Mishnah [Kiddushin 1.9], it was the practice in many parts of the Diaspora to set aside dues, tithes, firstlings and other priestly gifts. This was probably not done to the same extent or with the same strictness as in the Land of Israel, but it did take place among the Jews of the Diaspora. Thus we read in a homiletical commentary: '"They made me keeper of the vineyards" . . .'[14]

In terms of date, the passage itself is anonymous, but ARN as a whole is a commentary on the mishnaic tractate Aboth and can be no earlier than the third century CE.[15] In terms of content, it says that, during the Babylonian exile, when there was no temple, and Jerusalem was desolate, the people declined to support the priests in Babylon, saying that they had not tithed even in Palestine. In terms of genre, this is a homily; like most, it is one of several possible homilies on a biblical passage. A homiletical flourish about a period eight hundred years earlier, which says that Jews in Babylonia did not tithe to support the exiled priests, much less send contributions to the destroyed temple and the deserted city, does not prove that Diaspora Jews sent tithes to Jerusalem in the days of the second temple.

Safrai thinks that one can derive from such passages direct information about what people did: 'it was the practice', 'it did take place'. The principal fault, in my view, is reading ancient literature in such a flat way. I commented above on the perverse literalism which plagues us, Jewish and Christian scholars alike (III.C at n. 17). It leads New Testament scholars to read Paul's charges in Rom. 1 and 2 and state that he is giving a concise but completely factual account of Gentile and Jewish behaviour. They see no hyperbole: he, after all, wrote holy scripture, and what is holy about it is that it consists of flat narration of facts. Rabbinic literature is frequently treated in the very same way.

It is possible to infer social reality from a homily when the homily can be given a definite setting. Conceivably the passage just quoted could mean 'Give more to your local synagogue, the one here at Chorazin in the year (CE) 257'. Safrai's reading of it as historical description of what Jews did during the Babylonian exile and later, it seems to me, puts it in the wrong genre.

From the second passage, p. Hallah 60a, Safrai cites the sentence, 'Our teachers in the land of exile set aside priestly dues and tithes'.[16] The full statement is this: 'R. Yohanan said, "Our teachers separated heave offering and tithes in exile until *ha-rôbîn* came and cancelled them."' This is certainly a curious passage. R. Yohanan was a third century Palestinian Amora. To whom did he refer as 'our teachers'? Presumably not pre-70 Jews of the Diaspora. And who were 'the young men' (*ha-rôbîn*) who cancelled the practice? These are usually taken to be the sons of R. Hiyyah, that is, contemporaries of R. Yohanan.[17] This would mean that R. Yohanan's immediate teachers, in the second or early third centuries CE, separated tithes when in exile, and that this was stopped by his contemporaries. While I cannot explain what the passage means, there is no reason to take it as an ancient tradition which had bypassed the Tannaim and which proves that Diaspora Jews brought tithes to the temple while it still stood. It does not even say that. Possibly it reflects the separation of tithes in the Diaspora to support local priests, or the meaning could be the same as Bekorot 53a, which refers to *separating* tithe of cattle (treated as second tithe), but doing so as a pious symbol. This passage interprets Bekhoroth 9.1 as meaning that in the Diaspora the cattle were consecrated and kept until they became blemished, at which time they became available for secular use. Whatever the meaning of p. Hallah 60a, however, it sheds no light on pre-70 Diaspora gifts to the temple.

Safrai also cites non-literary evidence, which will turn out to be important. According to ostraca from Edfu and a papyrus from Arsinoë, after the revolt Rome required from Jews a tax over and above the temple tax, called *aparchai*. He takes this to show that before the destruction of the temple, Jews sent 'first fruits, dues or tithes' to Jerusalem in addition to the temple tax.[18] We find here both more evidence that Diaspora Jews contributed what they called *aparchai* to the temple and the terminological looseness of Safrai's discussion. It will turn out that the terms matter.

Thus far, we have seen references in Philo, Josephus and the papyri to *aparchai*, usually translated 'first fruits'. Is it possible that the problem in Antioch was not that tithes had not been deducted, but that first fruits had not been sent, and that this failure meant that the food should not be eaten by Jews? The answer is 'No', but that is not self-evident. It is here that we come to the actual problem of practice in the Greek-speaking Diaspora: to what does *aparchai* refer, and how common was it to send *aparchai*? The meaning of the different words for offerings is sometimes complicated, and as we have seen even scholars sometimes use the terms loosely (reading *aparchai*, which literally means 'first fruits', and translating it 'tithes').

At various points in this volume we have come upon the problem of tithes and other offerings, and I wish now to give a full review of the sources of income for the temple and the priesthood according to the Hebrew Bible (§2); the LXX where relevant (§3); Greek-writing Jewish authors (§4); fragmentary evidence recovered by archaeology (§5); the Pharisees and Rabbis (§6). We shall also consider the question of who was enthusiastic about the payment of tithes and other offerings (§7) and the view of common Judaism, based on the Bible, of the geographical regions from which each source of income could be derived (§8). In §9 I shall summarize the status of food in the Diaspora from which offerings had not been separated, and offer conclusions in §10. The fact that Safrai could say that Diaspora Jews paid tithes indicates that a fairly full review is needed.

§2. Support of the temple according to the Hebrew Bible. I shall give a list of the temple's income according to the Hebrew Bible as it now stands, not an historical analysis of when each source of income was added. We saw above (I.F) that first-century Jews, who read the Bible as a whole, were forced to conflate various laws which in fact came from different periods of Israel's history. According to the Bible, then, the temple, the priests and the Levites were supported in the following ways:[19]

(*a*) Sacrifices and offerings were brought to the temple as sin offerings, guilt offerings and peace offerings. From these sources the priests got meat, hides and cereals. None of this concerns the present issue, and so it is not necessary to be more precise. It is important for understanding later developments, however, to recognize that sacrifices provided the priests with a lot of food while they were on duty (one twenty-fourth of the time), and that when sacrifices ceased pressure was put on the other sources of revenue. No one knew that the destruction of the temple in CE 70 would be permanent, and so the priesthood had to be preserved. This helps explain the rabbinic emphasis on tithing, which did not depend on the existence of the temple.

(*b*) Jews throughout the world sent the temple tax of one-half shekel or two drachmas. This paid for the temple's 'overhead', especially the daily whole-burnt offerings (see the list of things which the tax provided, Neh. 10.34 [ET v. 33]).[20]

(*c*) The priests and their families were partially supported by first fruits and firstlings (see n. 19). The first fruits of produce (agricultural food, but also sheep shearings and the like) need be no more than a token amount. Firstlings were the first-born of each animal species, either the animal itself (sheep, goats and cattle) or financial compensation (for the first-born of animals prohibited as food). The first-born son was also to be redeemed by money. The principal words and passages are these: *re'shît*, 'first fruits' (Lev. 23.10; Num. 15.20f.; 18.12; Deut. 26.2; Neh. 10.38 [ET v. 37]; 12.44); *bikkûrîm*, 'first produce' (Lev. 23.17,20; Num. 18.13; Neh. 10.36 [ET v. 35]); *b'kôrôt*, 'firstlings' (Num. 18.15; Neh. 10.37 [ET v. 36]).

(*d*) According to the Pharisees and later the Rabbis, there was a further agricultural offering which fed the priesthood, called *t'rûmah*, 'heave offering'. In the Pentateuch *t'rûmah* is not (as far as I have noted) a separate offering. In Num. 15.20, for example, it is used as a synonym for first fruits (*re'shît*), and sometimes it is simply a general term for 'offering' (e.g. Lev. 7.32,34). It is listed separately in Nehemiah, however, and there it does seem to be a term for a distinct offering (e.g. Neh. 10.38 [ET v. 37]; 12.44; see n. 19). Rabbinic literature of all strata takes it for granted that *t'rûmah* is distinct (see below). On the basis of Nehemiah I count it as 'biblical'.[21]

(*e*) One-tenth of all produce and of all animals (not just one-tenth of the increase) was to be given to the Levites, who in turn paid one-tenth to the priesthood. This may be called 'first' or Levitical tithe.[22] The priests' portion of first tithe – the 'tithe of the tithe' (Num. 18.26) – often went by other names in later literature. It was called 'heave offering of tithe' by the Rabbis, and sometimes 'first fruits of tithe' by Philo (*Spec. Laws* 1.157; *Change of Names* 2).[23] The *distinction* between first fruits and first tithe cannot be missed (e.g. Neh. 10.35–38 [Heb. vv. 36–39]; Num. 18.12–32; noted by Philo, *Spec. Laws* 1.151–157).

It may be useful to remind English-speakers that 'tithe' means 'tenth'. It is an antiquated form which has been retained only in the special meaning of the gift of a tenth for religious purposes, and the contemporary English-speaker does not necessarily understand the etymological meaning of the word. The Hebrew and Greek words, *ma'aser* and *dekatē*, however, were not obsolete, but quite clearly said 'tenth' to people who used them. Thus it was less likely in the ancient world than it is in the modern English-speaking world to use the term 'tithe' for offerings in general, or for any offering other than the one-tenth required by various passages in the Bible.

(*f*) Anyone who wished could make a freewill-offering (*n'dabôt*: Lev. 7.16; 23.38 and elsewhere).

(*g*) Property of any sort could be vowed or dedicated to the temple (*n'darîm*: the same passages).

§3. The LXX (see the note on how books of the LXX are cited, above p. 58).

(*a*) 'Tithe' (*dekatē*, *epidekaton*) is used in the LXX, with very few exceptions, where the corresponding word appears in Hebrew: e.g. Lev. 27.30–32; Num. 18.21–24; Deut. 14.22; Neh. 10.37f. [Heb vv 38f.]; 12.44. In the key passages 'tithe' is clearly distinguished from 'first fruits' (Num. 18; Neh. 10, 12). The distinction is also clear in Tob. 1.6; Judith 11.13.

(*b*) When the Hebrew distinguishes the 'first' offerings as either *bikkûrîm*, 'first produce', or *bᵉkôrôt*, 'firstlings', the Septuagint faithfully follows: *prōtogennēma* in Lev. 23.17,19; Num. 18.13; Neh. 10.35 (and also Tob. 1.6); *prōtotokos* in Num. 18.15,17; Neh. 10.35f.

(*c*) The fun begins when we turn to translations of *reʾshît*, the Hebrew generic term for 'first', and *tᵉrûmah*, the word often translated 'heave offering'. For both terms, the Greek reader usually found *aparchē*, a word which we saw above, and one which requires attention.

In the pagan world, *aparchē* and *aparchomai* could refer to the first part of a sacrifice or to a gift of first fruits (in agreement with etymology), but the terms could also be used for an offering in general.[24] Moulton and Milligan found in the sub-literary texts the meanings 'legacy-duty' and 'a personal "gift" to the goddess' (in a Magnesian inscription).[25] The LXX shows approximately this same range of meaning.

In the LXX, as we saw, tithes (*dekatai*) are always clear and distinct, but the meaning of *aparchai* is not nearly so obvious as the Greek *prōtogennēma* or *prōtotokos*, or as the Hebrew *reʾshît*, *bikkûrîm* and *bᵉkôrôth*. This would have been true even if *aparchē* had been used only to translate *reʾshît*, since the Greek word, to native speakers, had a wide range of meaning. Clarity was not enhanced by the decision of the translators to use *aparchē* to translate both *reʾshît* and *tᵉrûmah*.[26] It translates the former, for example, in Num. 15.20, the latter in Lev. 22.12. The wide use of *aparchē* can also be seen in the translation of various lists of offerings: One of the crucial verses for our topic, Neh. 10.38 (ET v. 37), for example, where the Hebrew reads 'the first fruits of your meal and your *tᵉrûmah*', in the LXX reads 'the first fruits of your grain' only. In Neh. 12.44 *tᵉrûmôt*, *reʾshît* and *maʿasᵉrôt* (heave offering, first fruits and tithes) become in Greek only *aparchai* and *dekatai* (first fruits and tithes). In Deut. 12.6 for the Hebrew 'tithes and *tᵉrûmah*' the Greek has only *aparchai*. We must suppose that the translators of the LXX did not regard *tᵉrûmah* as a separate offering which required its own Greek equivalent, and the result is that the meaning of *aparchē* was broadened beyond 'first fruits'.

Thus far we see that *aparchē* in the Diaspora would have been taken as a very general agricultural offering. Its meaning expanded still more in LXX Exodus, where it was used for the offering of gold, silver and other precious stuff to build the tabernacle (Ex. 35.5, translating *tᵉrûmah*; 39.1 [Heb. and ET 38.24], where it is used for *tᵉnûpah*).[27] The result of this is that *aparchē*, which already had a broad meaning in Greek, might appear to the Greek reader to mean almost anything but 'tithe'.

§4. We shall now examine more particularly the usage of three Jewish authors who wrote in Greek during the time of the second temple.

(a) Both Josephus and Philo summarize the biblical legislation which provided income for priests and Levites, and on the whole they repeat the terminology of the LXX. In the lists which follow, I give the items in Philo's sequence.

Philo, *Spec. Laws* 1.132–157		Josephus, *Antiq.* 4.68–75	
aparchē of dough	132f.	some (of the first) cakes	71
aparchē of other produce	134	aparchai of produce to priests	70
prōtotoka ('firstlings')	135f.	firstlings (*to gennēthen prōton*)	
		of edible animals	70
		1½ shekels for other firstlings	71
money for first-born sons	137–40	5 shekels for first-born (*prō-*	
		totokos) son	71
aparchē of produce and animals[28]	141		
meat from sacrifices	145	food from sacrifices for sins	75
meat from other animals[29]	147	meat from slaughtered animals[29]	74
hides	151		
aparchai are given to priests via			
the temple	152		
not everyone gives aparchai	153–155		
tithes (*dekatai*) to Levites	156	tithe (*dekatē*) to Levites	68
Levites' tithe to priests (give		Levites' tithe to priests	69
tithes as first fruits)	157		
		aparchai of sheep-shearings	71
		Nazirites' hair	72
		korban dedications	73

We may note also the summary of main items in *Antiq.* 4.241–242:

first fruits of produce (both *prōton genomenon* and *prōteleia*)   241
dekatai for Levites and banquets[30]   242

These lists make clear that the distinctions among gifts to the temple which we found in the Bible were apparent to first-century readers. It is especially striking that Josephus, though he knew Nehemiah in Hebrew, has no term which could represent heave offering as a distinct item. Presumably the reason is that in *Antiq.* 4 he is summarizing the Mosaic legislation and does not take Nehemiah into account. Or possibly, writing in Greek, he simply gives the categories which can be seen in the LXX – where, as we have noted, heave offering is not a distinct category.

The lists above do not tell us what Jews in the Diaspora sent to the temple. These are only summaries of biblical legislation, which did not take into account a non-resident Israelite citizenry.

(b) The other source of income for the temple (as distinct from the care and feeding of the priests and Levites) was the temple tax. This is taken note of by Pseudo-Aristeas, Josephus and Philo.

1. *Arist.* 34, 40 and 42 refer to 100 talents of silver 'for sacrifices and other [requirements]' (// Josephus, *Antiq.* 12.50).

Pseudo-Aristeas depicts this money as one of a large number of gifts from Ptolemy. As such, it is not, strictly speaking, the temple tax, which was to be paid by Jews. Its purpose, however, is the same as that of the temple tax: the official or public offerings and general expenses. My guess is that the author intended this to be a precedent which would allow Egyptian Jews of his own time to send the temple tax. Ancient governments controlled the export of money, and (as we shall immediately see) during the Roman period it was a point of Jewish privilege that Diaspora Jews could pay the tax. There is, as far as I know, no direct information about the rights of Jews in Ptolemaic Egypt to pay the tax.

2. The 'sacred money' (*ta hiera chrēmata* or simply *ta hiera*) which Augustus allowed Diaspora Jews to send to Jerusalem is to be identified as the temple tax (*Antiq.* 16.163, 166, 169).

3. *Aparchai* means the temple tax in *Antiq.* 16.172 (quoting a letter from the proconsul to Ephesus).

That these references in *Antiq.* 16 are to the temple tax, rather than to miscellaneous contributions, follows from their official character.[31] The decree of Augustus begins by re-affirming the rights which Julius Caesar gave the Jews (16.162), and it is probable that he had permitted the temple tax to be collected and sent to Jerusalem, though the decrees which Josephus cites in *Antiq.* 14 do not directly say so.[32] At any rate, the two-drachma or half-shekel tax was the sum which, Jews argued, the Bible directly requires every male Jew to pay. Payment of the tax, conversely, identified people as Jewish. Official permission to send the money was needed, since the sum from each province or geographical region would be quite large. Unless the Jews had permission 'from the top', city councils or Roman administrators might stop the outflow of funds. Subsequent history also shows that the money which was covered by Rome's decree was primarily the temple tax: it was this very tax of two drachmas which Vespasian diverted to another purpose after the failure of the first revolt; therefore the temple tax was the tax which Rome officially knew about and sanctioned. If Rome previously had permitted Jews throughout the empire to send tithes to Jerusalem, Vespasian would have appropriated more than two drachmas. When the 'Jewish Tax', paid to Rome, replaced the temple tax, the total amount was in any case increased, since all Jews, not just adult males, had to pay it, and Vespasian would have probably welcomed a chance to charge Jews a tenth of their income.[33]

4. Josephus refers to the delivery of *to didrachmon*, 'the two-drachma [coin]' from Babylon in *Antiq.* 18.312f.

5. Philo often used *aparchai*, in the plural, to refer to the temple tax (thus without question *Embassy* 156f.; 291; 311–316; probably 216; certainly *Spec. Laws* 1.77–78).

Embassy 156f., 291 and 311–316, like the passages in *Antiq.* 16, refer to Augustus's permission to Jews to collect money. In 312 it is evident that this money is the temple tax, since its purpose is said to be to pay for the sacrifices – that is, the daily public sacrifices. *Spec. Laws* 1.77f. is clearer yet. Here the *aparchai* are said to be payable by every male beginning at age twenty and to be for 'ransom', *lutra*, as in LXX Ex. 30.12. Since *aparchai* elsewhere in the *Embassy* refers to the temple tax, it is probable that we should understand the term in *Embassy* 216 in the same way.

Here we begin to see the consequences of the fact that *aparchē/ai* had a wide range of meaning. There was no single Hebrew or Greek word for 'temple tax', and thus a variety of terms could be used, including especially 'first fruits'. It will be recalled that Dunn thought that one of these passages, *Embassy* 156, referred to tithes.

(*c*) The same three authors – Pseudo-Aristeas, Josephus and Philo – indicate that Jews also sent further gifts to the temple. We should note what terms they used and what the terms imply.

1. In *Arist.* 40 = *Antiq.* 12.50, in addition to the 100 talents 'for the sacrifices', there are further gifts, called *aparchai* of *anathēmata*.

Though these gifts are said to be sent by the king, I again assume that the purpose and terminology reflect Jewish practice as it was in Egypt, or as Pseudo-Aristeas wished it to be. The term *anathēmata*, which is used for *herem* in Lev. 27.28, means 'something devoted [to the temple]'. The usual meaning in Greek is 'votive offerings' – statues, plaques and monuments which are set up in a holy area, often with an inscription.[34] In the present case, the author of *Aristeas* has in mind vessels, goblets, a table and the like (*Arist.* 33, 42). Probably *aparchai* has its most general meaning, 'offerings', so that the phrase *aparchai anathēmatōn* means 'gifts of valuable objects which are dedicated to the temple'.

2. According to *Arist.* 157f., God 'has ordained every time and place for a continual reminder of the supreme God and upholder (of all).

Accordingly in the matter of meats and drinks he commands men to offer first fruits [*aparksamenous*] and to consume them there and then straightaway.'

In the translation in *OTP* II, R. J. H. Shutt notes at 'consume' that the text is corrupt, but, he adds, 'the meaning is clear' (p. 23 n.2). Even assuming that one accepts from Eusebius the reading *sygchrēsthai*, ('makes use of', thus 'consume'), rather than *sygchōrēsai* ('come together'), as well as 'offer first fruits' (which is also in doubt), it is still not clear what is intended.[35] If the author is thinking of biblical legislation, the meaning is straightforward: the passage refers to firstlings and first fruits of produce, but does not reflect Diaspora practice. The phrase 'every time and place', however, seems to include the Diaspora. In this case, it could mean one of two things: One is that Jews should set aside some of their foodstuff as *dedicated* to God, even though not sent to the temple – along the lines of Bekorot 53a. Secondly, the author might intend that Jews should set aside some money in lieu of foodstuff and later send it to the temple.

3. In the passage in which Josephus describes gifts from Babylonian Jews, he mentions *anathēmata* in addition to the temple tax (*Antiq.* 18.312f.). The references in the same passage to a 'treasury' or 'bank' (*tamieion*) and 'monies' (*chrēmata*) indicate in this case that the word refers to cash.[36]

4. and 5. In *Spec. Laws* 1.153f. and *Moses* 1.254 Philo *may* use *aparchai* to refer to contributions from the Diaspora over and above the temple tax.

We saw above that in *Spec. Laws* 1 Philo discusses the sources of the priests' income according to the Bible. Relying on the terminology of the LXX, he describes the biblical *aparchai*, 'first fruits', in *Spec. Laws* 1.141,152).[37] In most of the discussion there is no reason to think that he has in view offerings from the Diaspora, since he is explaining biblical legislation. In 1.153f., however, he complains that 'we' do not always give first fruits and that consequently the priests are not as prosperous as they should be. 'We' may very well include the Diaspora, rather than being an accusation of Jews in Palestine. If so, *aparchai* does not mean 'tithes' (as Dunn proposed), since they are taken up in 1.156f. under the distinct term, *deketai*. Because of the context, it is also unlikely that Philo has here switched to the temple tax (though *aparchai* can bear that meaning). Thus this may be a reference to miscellaneous gifts from the Diaspora over and above the temple tax.

The second passage similarly seems to be an instance in which Philo digresses from the biblical account in such a way as to reveal Diaspora practice. In narrating the story of Moses, he describes how the Israelites gave the spoil of their conquests to God. He continues, 'For, just as every pious person gives first fruits of the year's produce, whatever he reaps from his own possessions, so too the whole nation set apart the kingdom which they took at the outset . . . as the first fruits of their settlement' (*Moses* 1.254).[38] It is possible that 'every pious person gives first fruits' (*aparchetai*, the present tense of the verb) is a generalization about biblical law. Alternatively, it is conceivable that the phrase refers to the donation of the temple tax. It seems most likely, however, that Philo thought of all pious Jews of his own time and place as setting aside the first fruits of their income as a separate gift to the temple, over and above the two-drachma tax. It is to be noted that in this passage *aparchetai* cannot refer to tithes, since the emphasis is on giving what was taken *first* (*euthus*, 'at the outset') – not a tenth of everything taken.

(*d*) Philo twice uses *aparchē/ai* to refer to biblical legislation regarding tithes. According to *Spec. Laws* 2.120, the Levites were supported by *aparchai*. Since the only income of the Levites according to biblical law was the tithes, Philo here stretches *aparchai* to mean 'tithes'. In *Change of Names* 191 he states that the Levites give the priests 'first fruit of first fruit' (*aparchēs aparchē*), which he then correctly explains as a tithe of (first) tithe.

Thus we see that Philo could use *aparchē/ai* to refer to the temple tax or the biblical tithes given to the Levites, as well as to the biblical offering of first fruits, but that he could also employ the term to refer to gifts from Jews in general, apparently not just from those who lived in Palestine. In these two passages (*Spec. Laws* 1.153f.; *Moses* 1.254) the meaning of *aparch-* cannot be 'tithe' and is probably not 'temple tax'. It is, as far as I have noted, the only term in Philo which may refer to gifts from the Diaspora over and above the temple tax. These two passages seem to support the possibility that Diaspora Jews sent to Jerusalem gifts which were called *aparchai*, but which were neither the temple tax nor tithes.

(*e*) We now turn to a passage in Josephus which was noted above and which requires further treatment. Safrai and Dunn take *Antiq.* 14.245f. to refer to tithes. This is a letter to Miletus from the Roman proconsul[39] ordering that the Jews be allowed to observe the sabbath, perform their 'ancestral rites' and 'manage their produce' (*karpos*) in accordance with their custom (*ethos*). 'Manage' or 'handle' (*metacheirizesthai*) does not easily mean 'sell 10% of the produce and send the money to Jerusalem'. If the produce itself were sent, 'handle' might be appropriate; but sending crops is most unlikely. Probably not many Jews in Miletus were farmers; but even if they were, only a few crops could be tithed – e.g. grain or fruit which could be dried. Sending anything else to Jerusalem would be pointless, since the food would spoil *en route*. All other passages refer to money or objects made of precious metals. Jews, we have seen, needed permission to send money out of their home province, but in granting this right no one would use the term 'handle produce'. Thus this passage does not refer to anything sent to Jerusalem – neither foodstuff nor money. The order to the magistrates and council of Miletus much more likely means that they should allow the Jews to control their own food supply (above, p. 277). The Jews' right to have appropriate food is granted in the decree of Sardis in this same collection of decrees (14.261), and this is the most likely meaning of 14.245.[40]

We may now summarize the few bits of evidence which may reveal that Diaspora Jews sent miscellaneous gifts called *aparchai* or *anathēmata*.

1. The only passage which unambiguously mentions gifts which Jews sent to the temple, over and above the temple tax, is *Antiq.* 18.312, where *anathēmata* refers to money sent from Babylon, not from the Greek-speaking Diaspora. It is possible, of course, that Josephus's description of the collection and conveyance of money reflects the practice of the western as well as the eastern Diaspora.

2. The passage in *Arist.* 40 (// *Antiq.* 12.50) about *aparchai* of *anathēmata* probably reveals that Egyptian Jews sent gifts which they called by such terms. In the narrative context, however, the donor is Ptolemy.

3. In *Moses* 1.254 and *Spec. Laws* 1.153f., Philo probably refers to miscellaneous contributions from the Diaspora as *aparchai*. In neither text, however, is this certain. He might have in mind biblical legislation as it refers to Palestinian Jews (*Spec. Laws* 1.153f.), or he might be using *aparchai* to mean the temple tax (*Moses* 1.254) – as he does in other cases. In neither passage, however, can the meaning be 'tithes'.

4. I regard *Arist.* 157f. as too uncertain to support any conclusions.

§5. Evidence revealed by archaeology. When Safrai pointed to Egyptian ostraca and papyri, he put his finger on crucial evidence.[41] There are numerous receipts for the 'Jewish Tax', imposed on all Jews by Vespasian and continued by his successors,[42] which replaced the two-drachma temple tax. In Egypt, the charge for the two-drachma tax was eight Egyptian drachmas, plus two obols for handling and conversion of the money. The receipts for years 2 and 4 of Vespasian's reign are for that sum. Thereafter, however, the rule is that Jews paid eight drachmas for the Jewish tax, two obols for handling, and one drachma for *aparchai*, apparently in the plural.[43] Thus ostracon no. 168:

... son of Nikias: in respect of the two-drachma tax on the Jews for the 5th year of Vespasian, 8 drachmai 2 obols; in respect of the *aparchai*, 1 drachma.

Or no. 180:

> Paid by Akyntas Kaikillias freedman of Sarra, in respect of the two-drachma tax on the Jews for the second year of Titus Caesar, 4 drachmai 1 obol [i.e., half]; in respect of the *aparchai*, 3 obols [i.e. half of one Egyptian drachma].

Commenting on these receipts, Tcherikover correctly noted that the Greek *aparchai* is wider in meaning than the Hebrew *bikkûrîm*, which some had suggested as its Hebrew equivalent.[44] Smallwood, who based her understanding of the term on one of Philo's three meanings (*aparchai* = temple tax), found *aparchai* in these receipts puzzling, since clearly the word refers to money in addition to the 'Jewish Tax'.[45]

The papyrus from Arsinoë mentioned by Safrai lists fifteen people, of both sexes and all ages, and levies a total charge of 125 drachmas for the tax (15 × 8 drachmai 2 obols), plus 15 drachmas for the *aparchai*.[46]

While certainty cannot be attained, it appears that it took the Romans a few years to discover that many Jews had sent to Jerusalem, in addition to the temple tax, a small voluntary contribution, which they called *aparchai*. In Egypt, at least, the Roman administrators decided to quantify this further contribution as one-eighth of the basic tax and then to add it to the 'Jewish tax'. One Egyptian drachma is a very small sum. If the temple tax was equivalent to two days' pay for day-labourers,[47] the additional *aparchai* was one-fourth of a single day's wage. This is a long way from being a tithe.

The most likely reconstruction of Diaspora practice, based on combining the evidence from literature, ostraca and papyri, is that many Diaspora Jews sent supplementary gifts to the temple when they remitted the temple tax. Wealthy individuals may have sent or brought substantial gifts, but Jews in general made a small contribution. It is possible that little of this supplementary donation reached the temple. It may have been required for the transportation of the tax itself. Jews who gave it, however, could have felt that they were responding to the biblical passages which require *aparchai*. It would have been impossible, on the basis of the LXX, to know just what *aparchai* should be, but the general spirit of biblical legislation about 'first fruits' (whatever terms were used) is that of a token contribution, given to thank God for his much greater bounty (see the Avowal in Deut. 26.5–11). Diaspora Jews could not have thought that they were actually fulfilling Deut. 26, which requires a trip to the temple, but they may have wanted to keep the spirit of the law.

By no means everyone pitched in (taking *Spec. Laws* 1.153 to refer to the Diaspora), but the imposition of the extra tax early in Vespasian's reign seems to show that previously many Jews had made offerings of 'first fruits'.

The Diaspora Jews, left entirely to their own devices, without Pharisees whizzing around the Mediterranean telling them what to do, read the Bible and did what they thought was appropriate. If the passages in *Aristeas* refer to

Diaspora practice, as seems likely, the custom of sending supplementary gifts began too early to be the result of pharisaic influence.[48] One may read all the decrees and letters in *Antiq.* 14 and 16, giving rights to Jews in the Diaspora, without finding a single pharisaic peculiarity. Diaspora Jews too loved the law and wanted to obey it, and they did not depend on Pharisees to tell them to do so.

We have not established that the problem in Antioch which led Peter and Paul to fall out had to do with first fruits, but it is likely that some Diaspora Jews made contributions which they called by that name.[49]

§6. Offerings in rabbinic literature. The Rabbis, of course, made lots of distinctions, basically following Nehemiah. They offer us a tractate on *t'rûmah*, 'heave offering', as a separate item[50] and elaborate its difference from other offerings, while 'first fruits' are divided into three tractates – firstlings (of animals, Bekhoroth), first fruits (of agriculture, Bikkurim), and dough-offering as first fruits of the dough (Hallah).[51] None of these, perhaps not quite needless to say, is confused with 'tithes'. While the full depiction of these offerings is rabbinic rather than pharisaic, there are enough passages attributed to the Houses of Hillel and Shammai to show that the Pharisees accepted these divisions. We shall take the offerings and tithes one-by-one, emphasizing what geographical region they came from in the rabbinic view.

(*a*) First fruits, including firstlings and dough offering, were defined as in the Bible: first fruits of produce had no prescribed quantity (Bikkurim 2.3), and the same would have been true of the dough offering. Firstlings, of course, were prescribed: one could not give only part of a first-born animal. All these 'firsts' had to be brought to the temple, and the giver had to be present to make Avowal before a priest (Bikkurim 2.2,4; Deut. 26.1–11). Thus they lapsed with the destruction of the temple. They could be given only from Palestine (Bikkurim 3.2); supplementary gifts from beyond Palestine were not equivalent to first fruits (3.11).

(*b*) Heave offering the Rabbis understood to be a very small percentage of agricultural produce – from one-thirtieth (the House of Shammai) to one-sixtieth (Terumoth 4.3). They were of the view that it was not necessary for heave offering to be brought to the temple, and thus it survived the temple's destruction (Bikkurim 2.2). The Rabbis thought that it, like the tithe, should be given from 'Syria', which, in their idealized world, truly belonged to Israel (below, pp. 301–303), but need not be given from other lands (T. Terumot 2.9f.; Terumoth 1.5).[52]

(*c*) Pharisaic/rabbinic views about tithing were summarized in I.F. Here we need to note only two points: the relative importance of tithes and the geographical regions from which they could be given.

1. One sees in both pharisaic and rabbinic material a distinct pecking order: some offerings were holier and more important than others. First in sanctity were Holy Things, eaten by priests within the temple itself (e.g. Hagigah 3.1); these we leave aside. Next came first fruits and heave offering. The Rabbis regarded intentional consumption of these by a lay person as a capital offence, while unintentional consumption meant that the offering should be repaid, plus one-fifth (Bikkurim 2.1//Hallah 1.9; Terumoth 6.1; differently Terumoth 7.1). Tithe was less important, though the priests' portion was more important than the Levites'. It was not regarded as an offence to eat first tithe if the priests' portion had already been removed (Berakoth 7.1).[53] The Hillelites themselves were more rigorous about 'heave offering of tithe' than about the Levites' portion (T. Ma'aser Sheni 3.15).[54]

The Pharisees and Rabbis, then, emphasized the full Levitical tithe, partially because that is what people were in danger of omitting. The elaboration of the rules of demai-produce after 70 shows that they wished to see provision made not only for the priests but also the Levites; first tithe was the only source of legal income for the Levites. Heave offering, however, was if anything emphasized more.[55] It will be recalled that heave offering and tithe could be given with or without the temple, and this helps account for the space devoted to them in the Mishnah.

2. The Rabbis limited tithes to food grown or consumed in Palestine (e.g. Demai 1.3; T. Demai 1.4, 9–11). That is, they thought that Palestinian purchasers of certain imported food should treat it as demai-produce and pay tithe on it (Demai 2.1). They thought that 'Syria' was included in the land of Israel for the purpose of both first fruits and tithes (Hallah 4.7; Maaseroth 5.5; Oholoth 18.7). Referring to first fruits, Hallah 4.11 states that 'he who owns [land] in Syria is as one that owns [land] in the outskirts of Jerusalem'. According to Yadaim 4.3 some Rabbis in the late first century thought that Ammon and Moab should pay Poor Tithe in the seventh year: that is, in the year in which no tithes were given in Palestine, these areas should help support the poor. This was argued by R. Tarfon (first generation after 70), whose view prevailed. It was then reported to R. Eliezer, who replied:

> Go and tell them, Be not anxious by reason of your voting, for I have received a tradition from Rabban Johanan b. Zakkai, who heard it from his teacher, and his teacher from his teacher, as a *Halakah* given to Moses from Sinai, that Ammon and Moab should give Poorman's Tithe in the Seventh Year.

This is one of the famous 'Mosaic' halakot which were known to only one individual (see ch. II).

Part of R. Tarfon's argument was that 'they' – the Elders, as the sequel makes clear – had imposed Poor Tithe on Egypt, and so it should be similarly imposed on Ammon and Moab. Safrai takes it to be a simple fact that 'Egyptian Jews sent the Poorman's Tithe to the Land of Israel as well as the gifts for the priests and levites',[56] and this is one of the passages which 'proves' that Diaspora Jews tithed.

It is not intrinsically unreasonable to think that, in sabbatical years, Diaspora Jews dug deeper into their pockets and sent extra sums to Palestine. I think that Yadaim 4.3, however, is actually a piece of rabbinic romanticizing. Rabbis may have 'decreed' that Poor Tithe be paid from Ammon and Moab, and earlier 'Elders' may have 'imposed' Poor Tithe on Egyptian Jews, but this does not prove that these decrees and impositions were accepted. In fact, if Egyptian Jews paid Poor Tithe, one would have expected Philo to mention it. This case, however, need not be decided. The discussions of Poor Tithe in the sabbatical year prove that, even in the rabbinic view, Ammon, Moab and Egypt did *not* pay first tithe to the Levites and the priests (contrary to Safrai). The Rabbis thought that first tithe and the seventh year applied to the same foodstuff: what was grown in the Land of Israel, what was grown on land in 'Syria' which was owned by Jews, and some things which were imported (e.g. Hallah 2.2; 4.7). Ammon, Moab and Egypt could send Poor Tithe in the sabbatical year precisely because they were not subject to the laws of the seventh year and of first tithe. Thus Yadaim 4.3 is irrelevant for the question of first tithe. All we learn is that, if Jews in those lands sent extra gifts in the sabbatical year, some Rabbis would call them 'Poor Tithe' rather than 'additions to first fruits which are not like first fruits' (Bikkurim 3.11).

What about tithes and first fruits from 'Syria'? There is more than one definition of the land which was subject to tithes and the sabbatical year. Some passages accept the most exaggerated description of the extent of the Davidic/Solomonic empire (I Kings 4.24), and these 'require' obedience to the laws of tithes, first fruits or the seventh year in a very large area, including the land north and northeast of Palestine which had been (supposedly) subject to Solomon. This did not include the Phoenician coast in the vicinity of Antioch. The line turns northeast, inland, at Chezib (biblical Achzib, south of Tyre, about 200 miles or 320 km south of Antioch), and runs east to the Euphrates and north to the Amanah (see e.g. T. Ahilot 18.14; Hallah 4.8; T. Terumot 2.10; Shebiith 6.1; and elsewhere).[57] In other passages, however, some of which are quoted in an inscription found in the synagogue at Rehob, the area subject to tithes is smaller. According to J. Sussmann's summary, commencing at the southwest corner the line runs northward from Ascalon to ʾAkko [Ptolemais], northeast to Caesarea Philippi, south-eastward to Bostra, southward to Rekem de Gaia (Petra), and finally westward, back to Ascalon.[58]

The inscription is dated after the completion of the Palestinian Talmud, that is, after the fourth century CE. Two of the passages which are the source of the inscription, T. Shevi'it 4.11 and Sifre Deuteronomy 51, are, presumably, tannaitic – i.e., before c. CE 220.

A possibly pharisaic passage, Demai 1.3, may provide us with direct evidence on the geographical boundaries of tithing according to the pre-70 Pharisees. This mishnah, which lists exemptions from the rules of demai-produce, in effect lists exemptions from tithing. The list includes 'the country beyond Chezib', the northernmost point of Palestine, and this puts all of rabbinic Syria outside the region from which tithes come.[59]

For the sake of argument, however, let us take as 'pharisaic' the various passages which apply tithing to 'Syria', either a very large Syria (based on I Kings 4.24) or a smaller one (the Rehob inscription and its sources). We do not learn from either group of passages who actually did what while the second temple still stood. As in the case of Poor Tithe, we see a range of opinion about what gifts from certain geographical areas should be called. During the first century neither the Pharisees nor the Rabbis could enforce tithing rules, either in Palestine or beyond it. That is why they had the category of demai-produce: they had to buy things which perhaps had not been tithed. At a maximum, we learn something about what a Pharisee or Rabbi might have said if consulted by someone who farmed land across the border. The sage would have to establish whether the land was owned or let, and then he would have to place it on his mental map (drawn maps were extremely scarce). Different sages may have had different 'maps'. He could then advise the farmer that he *should* tithe, or that he *could not* tithe. In the latter case, he would be telling the farmer that donations from him ought not to be titled 'tithes'. The farmer, in any case, could give what he wished.

The standard caution that rabbinic passages are often theoretical (or fanciful) should be repeated and, in this case, emphasized. According to one of the passages which requires Jews who own land in Syria to tithe, the land remains subject to tithes even if it is sold to a Gentile – once Jewish, always Jewish (T. Terumot 2.11). No proof text is quoted, but the Rabbi who thought this up may have been engaging in creative exegesis of such a verse as 'every place on which the sole of your foot treads shall be yours' (Deut. 11.24; cf. Sifre Deut. 51). Not every rabbinic passage describes what people actually did (as we have seen throughout). I venture the opinion that all the passages about tithing from Syria or from Greater Israel are fanciful, though I would not wish entirely to exclude the possibility that some Jews in these territories would have done what Palestinian sages advised. What we would like to know, with regard to pre-70 practice, is what the high priests advised. We shall return to this below.

§7. Enthusiasm for tithes and offerings. Pursuing the question posed by Dunn, we now ask who would have been zealous about gifts to the temple and to the priests and Levites. Certainly the Pharisees were. They believed in upholding the biblical law. As will any group which studies law, they made distinctions, in this case degrees of sanctity. We need to have these before us again, and I repeat them in descending order: (1) Holy Things, eaten within the temple; (2) heave offering and first fruits, eaten by priests and their families outside the temple; (3) the priests' share of first tithe, 'heave offering of tithe', eaten by priests and their families outside the temple; (4) the Levites' share of the tithe, eaten by Levites and their families anywhere.

The lengths to which Pharisees would go in pursuit of getting all this food to the temple and its staff, and keeping it pure on their behalf, depended in part on its degree of sanctity, in part on the reliability of the populace to contribute it. The offerings of Holy Things they did not have to encourage; people brought sacrifices. They could bring them from anywhere, and the pilgrims who thronged Jerusalem for the pilgrimage festivals doubtless offered lots of sacrifices,[60] One has the impression from rabbinic literature that gifts of first fruits were not problematic because people freely gave them. The Rabbis told stories about people trying to give first fruits from outside Palestine and being refused, though they were permitted from 'Syria' (Hallah 4.11).[61] Heave offering, they thought, was permitted to be given by anyone (Terumoth 3.9) from anywhere (1.5), but it was obligatory only from produce grown in Israel. Since they discussed only foodstuff as heave offering, not monetary substitutions for it, we may think that the Rabbis did not expect it from elsewhere. When 'Syria' or other land outside Israel is mentioned in connection with heave offering (Terumoth 1.5; T. Terumot 2.9f.), the reference is casual, simply exemplifying another point (someone who owns land in Palestine and 'Syria' may not give heave offering from the Syrian produce in place of heave offering from Palestine). There are no 'decrees' about 'imposing' heave offering on other countries. Reasoning back from rabbinic literature, we may suppose that Pharisees did not travel to encourage heave offerings from their Syria.

Approximately the same may be said of tithes as of heave offering, except that at different times various rabbis tried carefully to define the geographical limits for tithes. Within those boundaries, they would have welcomed tithes, but again they do not discuss the problems of transportation or converting the produce into cash, so that one has the impression that they did not wage campaigns for tithes from 'Syria' or 'Greater Israel'.

In fact, travelling and writing letters in order to encourage donations from outside Israel clearly did not fall within the rabbinic purview. We may safely deny it to the Pharisees. There is, first, the evidence of only moderate enthusiasm on tithes which is attributed to the House of Hillel and Rabban Gamaliel II (i.e., to the first generation after 70) in passages referred to above (p. 236). As we saw, the Pharisees did not regard eating the Levites' portion of first tithe to be an offence, and the Hillelites did not accept the rule that they had to pay full tithe on demai-produce. Secondly, there is the inference from the rabbinic attitude: if the post-70 Rabbis, who worried about the support of the priests and Levites when the temple was destroyed, nevertheless did not look abroad for food (except during the seventh year), how much less would the Pharisees have done this in the days of the temple's prosperity.

Thirdly, there is evidence that the Pharisees generally trusted the ordinary people of Israel to pay the most important and sacred dues. Scholars often think that the Pharisees regarded the ordinary people as outcasts or 'sinners' because they would not tithe. It turns out, however, that the only part of the clergy's income which the Pharisees thought that the common people shirked was the Levites' portion of first tithe – and the Pharisees did not think that it was a transgression for a layperson to eat the Levites' share. I shall briefly recall some passages which demonstrate rabbinic trust of the common people (see above, pp. 236f.).

The Hillelites' decision to donate only the priests' portion of tithe from demai-produce (T. Ma'aser Sheni 3.15) means that they assumed that the 'amme ha-'arets took out heave offering and first fruits themselves, which were more sacred, and which the Hillelites would have run no risk of consuming. The Judaeans were considered trustworthy with regard to heave offering 'at the seasons of winepresses and olive vats' (Hagigah 3.4); more people were trustworthy with regard to tithes than purity (Demai 6.6). The common people were also reliable to handle holy food correctly. In addition to Tohoroth 8.2 and Tebul Yom 4.5, cited above, we may add Demai 1.3, which may be pharisaic:[62] the 'amme ha-'arets could be assumed to have handled correctly dough offering, produce while it still contained heave offering, and the residue of meal offerings (as well as second tithe, which they ate themselves).

There seem to be two explanations of this situation. The priestly portions were, for one thing, small amounts (one-thirtieth to one-sixtieth for heave offering, one-hundredth as 'heave offering of tithe'; while the temple stood, token contributions for first fruits; the gift of firstlings was probably the most substantial tax for small farmers). The Levites' portion, both before and after the temple was destroyed, was nine-hundredths of the produce, and it was this large amount which the common people tended to be untrustworthy about. Secondly, the priesthood seems to have been highly revered by the ordinary people. This is seen throughout biblical and post-biblical Jewish history, though the view that the people gave the Pharisees their loyalty obscures the role and importance of the priests.[63]

Besides the Pharisees, there were others who 'believed in' all of these offerings, and who may have been even more enthusiastic. The priests and Levites favoured full payment of all tithes and offerings. After the destruction they did not change their minds: they were interested parties and sought continuation of tithes and presumably of the rabbinic heave offering. With regard to the pre-70 period, Josephus wrote that two priests who went with him to assess the situation in Galilee collected the tithes and returned home (*Life* 29–63). A passage in the Tosefta depicts priests and Levites as standing by the threshing-floor waiting for what is due them, and even squabbling over the produce (T. Peah 4.3). According to T. Menahot 13.21 Abba Saul b. Batnit and Abba Jose b. Johanan (post-70) cried Woe! on the houses of the high priests for beating them. This may show that the priesthood continued to enforce its claims.

The view that it was only Pharisees (and later Rabbis) who emphasized tithing results from the strange literalism which runs through both New Testament and Judaic scholarship. We do not have texts from priests and Levites as such (except for Josephus), and what scholars have to read is rabbinic literature. They find there that tithing was upheld. Often they fail to note the rabbinic distinctions and nuances – but, worse, they suppose that no one else cared about it. I propose that the priests and the Levites cared a good deal, without regard to party membership. And the same of course applies to all the other sacrifices and offerings. The Pharisees and Rabbis were largely laypeople, and they believed in full observance of the law as they interpreted it. They urged others not to shirk, and after 70 the Rabbis supported the claim of the priests and Levites to full tithes and heave offering. They were not, however, the only people who encouraged obeying the biblical law on these points.

§8. The views of priests, Levites and ordinary people. In all probability no Palestinian Jews thought that Diaspora Jews owed tithes or first fruits. The justification for bringing everyone into happy harmony is that the biblical position is quite straightforward. Tithes were to be given from 'the land', which to a first-century reader meant not 'any soil', but the land of Israel (Lev. 27.30); Num. 18.21 specifies every tithe 'in Israel', and Nehemiah states that first fruits, heave offering and tithes should be carried to the temple (by the givers), though tithes could also be collected by the Levites

(Neh. 10.35–38, Heb. v. 36–39). First fruits are to be taken of 'all that is in their land', obviously Israel (Num. 18.13). According to Deut. 26.1–4 the giver of first fruits must present them to a priest at the temple and make an avowal. This contrasts with the treatment of tithes in 26.12, which are not brought to the temple.

Those who read these passages in Hebrew – both Pharisees and non-pharisaic priests – naturally drew the conclusions which, we have seen, were held by the Rabbis: first fruits have to be brought to the temple, and thus could not be brought after 70; tithes could still be collected without regard to the temple; both first fruits and tithes had to be from the Land of Israel. The Rabbis differed from Nehemiah on one point. Nehemiah 10.37 (Heb. v. 38) states that the first fruits of dough (or coarse grain) and *t'rûmah* must be brought to the temple, but the Rabbis did not think this of heave offering. I do not know whether this was an exegetical decision or a case of benign neglect of the passage, so as to support the priesthood after 70.

Clever exegesis, of course, could have found a way around the evident connection between these gifts and the land of Israel. Our detailed examination of a mass of literature, which altogether spans five hundred and fifty years or more (from *Aristeas* to the inscription at Rehob), shows that this was not done. In the case of the Rabbis in particular, silence with regard to the plain sense of the Bible means consent. We have seen that some of them exerted their wits a bit in order to enlarge the 'Israel' from which tithes came and in order to include 'Syria'. That is the limit of their inventiveness on this topic. The second- to fourth-century discussions of Syria and Greater Israel are, in some ways, the best evidence that Pharisees did not expect tithes from Antioch and its hinterland – or from Egypt, Asia Minor, Greece or the rest of the Diaspora. If the Pharisees had already multiplied the geographical areas which were supposed to tithe, the rabbinic discussions would have reflected that decision in some way or other.

When we add this evidence to that of the Greek-speaking writers and the evidence of Egyptian receipts for the Jewish Tax, we may conclude with perfect confidence that the only *expected* or *required* offering from the Diaspora was the temple tax, though some people may have given more, calling their gifts *aparchai* or *anathēmata*. The priests may have called such donations *n'dabôt*, 'freewill offerings'. It is noteworthy that Josephus does not use *ekousios*, the principal Greek term for freewill offerings.[64] This indirectly supports the view that the meaning of *aparchē* was expanded in Greek-speaking Judaism: there must have been voluntary gifts, and they must have been called something.

§9. The status of food in the Diaspora. What is the consequence of our discussion thus far for the status of food in the Diaspora? Was anything wrong with it if some part of it had not been sent to the temple (or sold for money to send to the temple)? No, nothing at all. No one thought that it was not to be eaten unless contributions had been taken from it. No Diaspora food belonged to the priests. We learn of priests in the Diaspora,[65] and it would have been eminently reasonable for them to claim support from Jews in their own communities, but there is no evidence to this effect (unless it is provided by p. Hallah 60a, above, p. 288).

Just as neither Pharisees nor priests thought that Diaspora Jews *owed* agricultural dues, there is no hint that Diaspora Jews felt *obligated* to pay anything other than the temple tax. Our three Greek-writing authors (Pseudo-Aristeas, Philo and Josephus) dealt long and lovingly with contributions to the temple. Nowhere is there a word about obligation, except payment of the temple tax.

And there would have been were it true. Information about the obligation of the Diaspora to send produce (or money in lieu of it) would have come either from the Greek-language sources or from rabbinic literature. (1) Both Philo and Josephus spend some time on the rights which Diaspora Jews had in the empire. They were allowed to assemble, while other groups were forbidden, and they were allowed to send the temple tax.[66] Had it been Jewish law that Diaspora Jews should pay a further tax, we would have learned of the request – which probably would have been turned down as being outrageous. No provincial official, and no city council, would want Jewish residents to send 10% of their earnings each year to Palestine. Two days' wage was bad enough. Had the Jews requested of Julius or Augustus Caesar the right to tithe, and had it been granted, there would have been local resistance. In fact, however, it was neither requested nor granted. (2) If the food of the Diaspora had been, in the views of the Pharisees, subject to levy by the Temple, the Rabbis would have mentioned it (as argued above). They *did* discuss, as we have seen, longed-for offerings from Syria, Ammon and Moab. And they also discussed the differences among the offerings – which were due before the destruction, which after, and so forth. Here were two splendid opportunities for the Rabbis to discuss the grand old days, when the Pharisees forced Diaspora Jews to pay tithes and first fruits, and laid them under the ban if they would not. They passed them up, knowing that biblical law, accepted by themselves and the Pharisees before them, was that the agricultural dues were required only from Palestine.

§10. Conclusions.

(*a*) Since Dunn discussed tithes in connection with the dispute between Peter and Paul in Antioch, we may consider the situation there briefly. The problem was not whether or not tithes or offerings had been separated from the food eaten by the members of the church. Could there, however, have been a campaign for *voluntary* contributions from the Diaspora which James took exceptionally seriously? The evidence is against it. We must apply here again the observation that, after 70, when main sources of priestly revenue had ceased, the Rabbis still did not look abroad for food for the priests. Dunn did not, to be sure, argue the case on the basis of priestly need, but on the supposedly heightened national tension which put a premium on loyalty to the law. As the revolt drew nearer, he thought, the standard expectation that all Jews everywhere should tithe would have been intensified.[67] One must doubt the theory of a steady escalation of fervour in the decades before 66. Apart from this, however, his notion of the standard expectation is in error.

(*b*) The question raised by Dunn, in effect, 'What views were there about gifts to the temple in the Diaspora?', had not previously, as far as I know, been sorted out. I have tried to do this. While we have learned nothing positive about the Antioch debate between Peter and Paul, we have had a chance to study a small bit of a neglected area: which parts of biblical law applied to the Diaspora? We have seen a high level of consciousness of the differences between 'the Land' and other lands but also evidence of good will and generosity towards the temple on the part of Diaspora Jews, which implies a recognition that all Jews were part of one community – though some could participate more fully than others.

V

Jacob Neusner and the Philosophy of the Mishnah

After *Rabbinic Traditions about the Pharisees before 70*, Jacob Neusner began an analysis of the Mishnah which had several aspects. I judge the most important to be the effort to discover chronological layers, and ch. III above is a partial response to some of the results of that work. Here I wish to take up a second aspect of his programme: the attempt to describe the 'philosophy' of the Mishnah. I shall give principal attention to *Judaism: The Evidence of the Mishnah* (1981), which summarizes the argument of the forty-three volumes which constitute his *History of Mishnaic Law*.[1] I shall also address some of the aspects of a trilogy published between 1983 and 1985, which carries forward the work on the Mishnah. The trilogy's overall title is *The Foundations of Judaism: Method, Teleology, Doctrine*; individual volumes are *Midrash in Context: Exegesis in Formative Judaism* (1983); *Messiah in Context: Israel's History and Destiny in Formative Judaism* (1984); *Torah: From Scroll to Symbol in Formative Judaism* (1985).

There have been relatively few substantial attempts to assess critically this vast body of publications. This is to be regretted. Neusner's own comment on responses to his efforts to stratify the material is that the theological climate in 'Jewish institutions of Jewish learning' meant that his work would not receive 'an enthusiastic welcome'. 'In fact', he added, 'it got none'.[2] 'None' is an exaggeration,[3] but only a slight one. The consequence is that many scholars in other fields – especially New Testament – have picked up from his work a general spirit of scepticism about dates (above, pp. 112f.), but have done so in a vacuum, unaided by critical evaluation. His view of the overall message of the Mishnah has generally been dismissed or accepted – again, with little critical probing.[4] He has also produced a vast number of translations, to which there are only a few critical responses,[5] as well as books aimed at almost every educational level. There are comments to be made at each point of his publishing enterprise.[6] Here we shall take up just one: the meaning and message of the Mishnah.

§1. Summary of *Judaism: The Evidence of the Mishnah*. In the Introduction we meet most of the problems which will concern us below. Neusner is here engaged in the difficult task of simultaneously asserting and denying the basic theses of years of work. It is probably the difficulty of doing this which is responsible for the unusual lapses from his ordinary standard of clear prose. In all his work one has to contend with jargon and endless repetition, but the Introduction abounds in such sentences as these:

> Consequently, if I could locate a saying within the known, established pattern of the logical unfolding of a problem, I was on solid ground in maintaining that a saying lacking a name in fact fits into the thought of a given stage in the unfolding of the logical exposition of a tractate's problem. (p. 19)

Thus we learn that determining a statement's place allows one to determine its place. Or this:

> In the end, therefore, I simply must state at the outset that the facts upon which my picture of the history of the ideas of the Mishnah is based may be explained in ways other than that way composed by the picture which I present in this book. (pp. 21f.)

He intends to say that an alternative explanation is possible. We shall see later that he does not actually think so, and this perhaps accounts for the extraordinary sentence.

By the time one finishes this tortuous Introduction, one is prepared for a difficult, tortuous book. There are some terrible sentences lying ahead:

> The evidence and its condition at the several layers into which it is here sliced up are what must govern the description of the evidence and the organization of an account of its condition in the principal stages of its formation. (p. 45)

Neusner never frees himself from tautology, but for the most part what follows is surprisingly easy. He drops the effort to retract his dominant hypothesis and asserts it straightforwardly and clearly: *the Mishnah exhaustively presents the metaphysical world view of a social group.*

Chapter 1 sketches a part of the major hypothesis: other literature reveals other world views. IV Ezra and II Baruch speak for the majority of Jews, those who thought historically and who hoped for a coming redemption. This is 'utterly unrelated' to the message of the Mishnah (p. 37). The Mishnah is similarly to be distinguished from gnosticism. It has its own 'world of meaning' (p. 43), which Neusner states on p. 27: 'The Mishnah's framers' deepest yearning is not for historical change but for ahistorical stasis.'

We meet here another assertion fundamental to the overall argument: 'The Mishnah may be shown to be a kind of philosophy' (p. 44). This misapprehension of the genre of the work is fatal to *Judaism* and the books that follow it. We shall spend appreciable space exploring the issue and its ramifications. Here we note Neusner's admission that this cannot be discovered by reading what the Mishnah says: 'It may be demonstrated to be a response to a common set of concerns for creation and revelation and redemption. But it does not speak of these things . . .' (p. 44). This admission contradicts one of the major methodological proposals of all of his work: that the Mishnah tells us explicitly and exhaustively what 'it wants' us to know (§3.a below).

Chapters 2, 3 and 4 divide the material chronologically: the state of each topic in each of the three periods: before the first war (66–73), between the wars, and after the second war (132–135). Neusner proposes that the early laws stem from a group which neither controlled nor wished to control any areas of life outside the domestic sphere. Some of his subsequent analysis refutes this view. The identity of the originating group, however, is a secondary issue in the book. Principal interest attaches to the description of the world view of the final document (see §4 below).

Chapter 5 is far away the best and most helpful part of the book. It is an analysis of the degree to which the tractates of the Mishnah spring from scripture. The introduction is misleading, as it attacks straw men, and the conclusions drawn from what is missing from the Mishnah are wrong. As is the case throughout, the genre of the Mishnah is ignored, and far-reaching conclusions have as their support the mistake about genre and the argument from silence. But the analysis itself is extremely illuminating. Especially telling is the examination of the Divisions of Holy Things and Purities (pp. 204–217), where we discover at the foundation of the topic items which Neusner elsewhere denies to the originating group. This will be laid out in §3.

Chapter 6 is the conclusion of the work. Here we read, once more, of the view which Neusner attributes to the document as a whole, and we see emphasized the exclusiveness of that world view: it opposes others. More interestingly, Neusner proposes that three groups have contributed to the Mishnah: priests and laymen who wanted to live in the secular world as if they were priests in the temple; scribes; small householders. Here he finally grapples with the problem of genre – or, rather, refuses to grapple with it. He at least mentions it. He proposes that the philosophers of the Mishnah, intending to convey a metaphysical or ontological world view, wrote it up in another guise. The apparent genre is legal discussion about everyday activities, but the true genre of the Mishnah is that of the detective puzzle: rather like E. A. Poe's 'The Gold Bug', the work contains a hidden message. That message, Neusner points out, is as unrelated to the text of the Mishnah as it is to all other Jewish literature.

The appendices are a mixed lot, but some are worthwhile. Various of Neusner's students contributed discussions of the tractates in the Division of Agriculture, and these are very useful. Appendix 4, which gives scriptural verses important in the Mishnah, is a valuable contribution, and Appendix 5 is a topical outline of the Mishnah, a very nice thing to have, even though the outline is occasionally misleading. The principal error is forcing logical and harmonious patterns on unruly and sometimes poorly organized material. Nevertheless, one can learn a lot by studying it.

§2. World view and genre: the basic hypothesis. The principal thrust of the book is towards establishing a series of equations: the Mishnah = an entire world view = the framers' collective mind = a social group or groups. The first three equations are consistently maintained. The fourth one, the assertion that a group actually once held the world view, is both affirmed and denied. The word 'exhausts' here plays a role: either the Mishnah 'exhaustively' presents the world view of a group or it does not. Both positions are put forward. This contradictory and therefore difficult discussion about the group behind the Mishnah, and what else they may have thought, will occupy us in §4.

We turn just now to the world view which the Mishnah reflects. Whether or not it speaks for a group, it does, according to Neusner, present a *total* world view. It 'exhaustively express[es] a complete system – the fit of the world view and way of life – fantasized by its framers' (p. 24). The key word in the Mishnah's world view is stasis: 'what the Mishnah really wants is for nothing to happen. . . . The one thing the Mishnah does not want to tell us about is change, how things come to be what they are' (p. 235). What is important is not the linear line of history, but the vertical line which connects the altar, or the hearth and table which substitute for it, with heaven. 'The Mishnah's framers' deepest yearning is not for historical change but for ahistorical stasis' (p. 27).

What counts as evidence for this world view? There are three major arguments.

1. The topics of the Mishnah cover aspects of life which are repeated and, in fact, perennial. The Division of Appointed Times deals with the occasions when 'sacred time intervenes and effects the perfection formed of the union of heaven and earth, of Temple . . . and Israel. . . . It is not a return to a

perfect time but a recovery of perfect being.' Thus the Division is ahistorical at its core (p. 132). The 'agendum' of the Division is not historical time, but what is 'cultic and ahistorical' (p. 136). The Division of Women similarly is concerned only with the restitution of order in cases of 'anomaly, changes or disorder' (p. 143). The Division of Damages is concerned 'to maintain perfect stasis' by insisting on 'an essential equality of exchange' (p. 144). And so through the other Divisions.

2. What is not in the Mishnah is at least as important as what is. Appointed Times do not include 'something which happened to Israel' (p. 136). 'The whole corpus of prophecy and history is neglected by the Mishnah' (p. 169). Neusner assumes that the Rabbis opposed or rejected what they omitted.

> When the philosophers confronted the sizable heritage of Israel and made the choice to ignore most of what had been done since the time of the formation of the Mosaic codes . . ., they made a stunning comment. . . . Their judgment was that nothing of worth had happened from the time of Moses to their own day. (pp. 170f.)

We see here part of the argument that the Mishnah is not only ahistorical but anti-historical, and that it represents a social group which renounced history.[7]

3. The very language of the Mishnah proves its essentially ahistorical thrust: it is written in the present tense. This is suitable to 'the sequence of completed statements and static problems. All the action lies within. . . .' (p. 326).

The arguments from topics covered and not covered are very interesting and are instructive for academic argument in general, and I shall return to them in §3. It must first be said, however, that the effort to construct a metaphysical world view out of the Mishnah founders on a very simple but completely fatal error: a mistake about genre.[8]

Neusner proposes that the authors were *philosophers* and *intended* to construct a metaphysical and anti-historical world view. The curious notion that the Mishnah is metaphysics and that the authors were philosophers crops up early and is repeated page after page throughout: 'The Mishnah may be shown to be a kind of philosophy. It is not poetry' (p. 44). He reverses the second statement elsewhere,[9] but, either way, it gives no substance to the first. There are other choices – including the right one. Neusner, however, ignores them. He makes the fundamental assumption that the contents of the Mishnah tell us *all that the authors want to say* 'about their view of the world as they see it or as they want to see it' (p. 15). The tractates tell us 'what people wish to know about those ideas.' (Note 'ideas'.) The only thing 'people want to know' about sources of impurity is 'rules for their definition and application' (p. 156). 'From knowing what people want to know about a given topic, it is a small step to ask what they think important' (p. 125). What they think important is what is in the Mishnah. *Since they wrote down in this one work everything which they thought was important, we can reconstruct their world view by itemizing the topics* (p. 125). 'What the system as a whole wishes to declare is fully expressed' (p. 230).

This echoes one of the major themes of earlier works. Speaking of the mishnaic Rabbis, he has claimed that the six orders of the Mishnah constitute 'the most important things' which the rabbis of the late first and second centuries could specify. 'What they put in they think essential, and what they omit they do not think important.' How Neusner knows this we are not told, but he is confident of it. The Rabbis cannot have attached much importance to 'the great issues of theology', such as sin and atonement, suffering and penitence, divine power and divine grace, since there are no tractates on such topics.[10] Topics are everything. What is not a topic is opposed; things that are topics, when added together, are a world view.

This would be an extraordinary position to take were the Mishnah actually a *Summa*. Almost everyone knows that even philosophers do not put into their books everything which they think important. All the more is this true of a collection of legal debates and opinions – which is what the Mishnah is.[11]

Since he assumes that the Mishnah is metaphysical philosophy, Neusner marvels at the things which are not there and which would be there if it were ordinary metaphysics. Then he has to propose that it is a curious and very fragile metaphysics. But the things which are not there, which cause him to write in exclamations of discovery, are not there because they are not subject to legal discussion.

Once one recognizes what the Mishnah is, all of its aspects which Neusner finds 'stunning' become self-evident. The Division of Appointed Times deals with sacred moments, not history: but how many laws governing Sunday opening in the Western world give a history of the observance of the 'Sabbath'? The Mishnah gives scant attention to things which happen only once (*Messiah*, p. 38): but law codes seldom do; they thrive on what is repeated. 'Woman as mother' is not discussed: but until recently the law stayed aloof from suitable and unsuitable motherhood. The civil law favours fair exchange, and thus a static world: but not many laws favour theft, fraud and unfair exchange.

Neusner makes a good deal of the fact that the Mishnah is written in the present tense (p. 236) and that it makes use of only a 'few formal patterns of syntax' (p. 244). The present tense shows that the Mishnah cares nothing for history, but only for 'static problems' (p. 236), while the limited syntax points to 'the conception that the norms are axiomatic for, and expose the logic of, all situations in general, but pertain to none in particular'. All this goes to show that 'what is concrete and material is secondary' (p. 246). Thus the formulas and present tense point towards a semi-Platonic world view, and they prove that the Mishnah's apparent topics are not its real subject matter.

In fact, of course, he has simply stumbled upon characteristics of grammar and syntax which are frequent in legal and semi-legal writing. David Daube years ago wrote on the legal force of the present tense in laws,[12] and it may be discerned if one will only pick up a tax form or a highway code. These are also characterized by a limited syntactical range. I offer a paragraph from p. 7 of the 1988 instructions for tax form 1040, which is required of all US citizens and residents. This is one of the rules governing tax returns by married couples:

> If you file a separate return, you each report only your own income, exemptions, deductions, and credits, and you are responsible for the tax due on your own return. However, if you live in a community property state, special rules apply.

Here we see the present tense and one of the repeated syntactical constructions. Full analysis of the instructions would reveal a small number of other formulations besides 'if you . . . you . . .', but not a large number. The same formulations appear no matter what the content. Neusner's comment that 'the formal aspects of the Mishnaic rhetoric are empty of content' (p. 244) would apply perfectly.

Laws characteristically do not give historical preambles and eschatological conclusions. Prophecy is entirely missing. I offer some short selections from the British Highway Code:

> Motorways are dual-carriageway roads. . . . Slow-moving vehicles, agricultural vehicles and some carriages used by invalids are . . . prohibited. It is an offence to pick up or set down a passenger or a hitch-hiker on any part of a motorway including a slip road.

> On carriageways with three or more lanes the normal 'Keep to the left' rule still applies.

Here we see again the present tense, and, further, the exclusive focus on the present. We are not told, 'Once upon a time Britain had no Motorways, until the great minister . . . arose, who built the M1, at which time there was only one. And now we look forward to the time when all Britain will be paved and, besides Motorways, there will be only slip roads.' The present situation is described, and rules are given in the present tense. There is no history, there is no eschatology.

It is true that there often are historical preambles to laws in the Bible, but their absence from the Mishnah does not prove that the Rabbis consciously rejected history along with historical preambles. One need not look to modern codes to find laws without an explicit historical setting. It suffices to begin with Leviticus 1.1. Here we see many of the phenomena which Neusner finds so remarkable when he meets them in the Mishnah. Leviticus has a fictional address by God to Moses, which sometimes requires the future tense ('When you come into the land which I give you, the land shall keep a sabbath to the Lord', Lev. 25.2), but most of the laws are 'timeless'. Does this mean that the priestly authors had an entirely different world view from that of their contemporaries? That does not follow.

Neusner proposes that the 'philosophers' of the Mishnah opposed the larger group of Israelites who twice went to war with Rome. How does he know this? History, and especially salvation in history, are not in the Mishnah. It would have been more insightful to note simply that they are excluded by the genre.

At the conclusion of the book, when Neusner finally discusses genre, he does not face it as a problem but attempts to finesse it. Mistaking a collection of legal discussions for a work of metaphysics, and supposing that this collection of discussions contains everything thought by the authors to be important, are major errors. The attempt to maintain this position, while granting that the Mishnah is what it is, produces double talk. It turns out that the Mishnah was written in a *secret* and demanding *code* which can be penetrated only by a remarkably sensitive genius.

The Mishnah, Neusner writes, is 'a sustained philosophical treatise in the guise of an episodic exercise in ad hoc problem solving' (p. 261). The philosophers intended 'to talk abstractly about what they deemed urgent', but they mysteriously chose to use 'the concrete language and syntax of other sorts of minds'.

The framers of the Mishnah shaped its topics 'into hidden discourse on an encompassing philosophical-physical problem of their own choosing' (p. 262). The Mishnah has 'a dense program of philosophical convictions', and it takes positions on 'a vast range of perennial issues of the mind'. Yet it 'is little more than a mass of specific problems, a morass of concrete details. . . .' 'Through the medium of the law the Mishnah says what it wants to say to its age and about its world' (p. 271). The Mishnah is philosophy, but not 'in an accessible form'. Its actual topics are 'odd' (p. 264).

These other minds whose formulas the Mishnah's philosophers used, and whose discussions of legal cases they employed to express their semi-Platonic philosophy, were scribes who addressed small householders (pp. 235, 241, 250–256). The cases which they ostensibly discuss are trite and even ridiculous. 'In concrete form, the issues are close to comic.' The real meaning, of course, is not comic: if one converts these trivial discussions – or, using alchemy, transmutes their dross to gold – it is seen that 'in abstract form the answers speak of nothing of workaday meaning' (p. 262).

The authors of the Mishnah, then, wrote in code, but they did not intend to conceal. The work is demanding, and 'it [has a] quite precise expectation', namely, that it be decoded. This work, apparently directed to small householders, in fact was intended to address 'a sophisticated and engaged sociointellectual context within the Israelite world'. True, it does not say that it addresses such an audience. It was written to be read by one whose mind can impose 'wholeness' 'upon discrete cases in the case of the routine declarative sentence, and upon discrete phrases in the case of the apocopated one.' This requires 'high sophistication and profound sensitivity' on the part of its interpreter (p. 247). The reader must be able to perceive 'the subtle and unarticulated message of the medium of syntax and grammar' (p. 247). Platonism is disguised in 'grossly material costume' (p. 273), but the profundity behind comic triviality can be 'grasped and understood by people of mind' (p. 246). The first such reader, we are to understand, has now appeared.

It is evident that Neusner wants the Mishnah to be more profound than it is. We often read that his findings are 'stunning', a word which becomes all too common in the trilogy. Minor laws are called 'profound' (e.g. pp. 157, 164), and he discovers with awe that a human must mix the ashes of the red heifer with water. This shows that 'man is the key figure in the preparation of purification water' (p. 162); such observations lay the foundation for his conclusion about the centrality of human intention and action – as if law codes customarily govern things like the accidental mixing of ashes and water. Generically, law presupposes human action.

The mistake about the Mishnah's genre, then, has several aspects. Thinking that its authors intended to express an entire world view, Neusner assumes that they denied whatever they did not include. Then he offers a positive account of their world view, and in doing this he misinterprets some of the Mishnah's stylistic features, such as the present tense and repeated formulas. These are characteristic of its true genre – legal discussion – but he tries to derive metaphysics from them. The result is the remarkable proposal that the Rabbis wrote in code: they wrote about everyday matters, but intended to convey a philosophical message about Timelessness. The mistake about genre leads Neusner further and further astray: not only does he fail to say what the Mishnah is, he bases his positive description on stylistic elements which should be explained in another way, and finally he offers a fantastic solution to the dilemma in which he has put himself.

Thereby falls the grand design. Yet there is rather a lot left. Two aspects of the argumentation are especially worth considering. These are (1) the argument that what a document means is what is on the surface, and its counter, that its meaning is not expressed but must be inferred; and (2) that what is not there speaks louder than what is.

§3. The argumentation.

(a) What it says and what it means. Neusner has for years claimed for himself the methodological virtue of 'radical nominalism' (p. 23), a virtue captured by the slogan 'what we cannot show we do not know'.[13] That is, he claims to attribute to a group or an individual only what can be proved, and to do so in its own terms and categories. Others are castigated for having conceptual schemes which are not 'concentric with the evidence' (or which are 'assymetrical to the evidence', p. 89), and for saying things which the document itself does not 'wish to know', while he stays just with what the document says.

Further, he claims to interpret what the document *explicitly* says. 'The one thing any student of the Mishnah knows is that its framers are pitiless in giving detail, in saying everything they wish, and in holding back – so far as we can tell – nothing we might need to know to plumb their meaning' (*Messiah*, p. 25). 'To what may be implicit I confess myself blind and deaf . . .' (*Messiah*, p. 23). That his interpretation follows just what is said, and goes no further, is repeatedly claimed in *Judaism*. The authors of the Mishnah 'clearly propose to tell us about their view of the world' (*Judaism*, p. 15); 'the mere outline of a tractate . . . reveals very clearly right on the surface, the blatant outline of precisely what the framers of that tractate deemed critical about the topic under discussion' (p. 125); 'what the system as a whole wishes to declare is fully expressed' (p. 230); and so it goes, for page after page.

The reader will immediately see that Neusner does not in fact follow his proclaimed method. The metaphysical world view which he perceives in the Mishnah is certainly not *in* it; the entire argument about the encoded message is based on the view that the Mishnah does not explicitly say what 'it wishes' to communicate. Thus in addition to saying that he interprets only what is explicitly present, he must also say that he has discovered what the Mishnah means but does not mention. The Mishnah is a philosophy about 'creation and revelation and redemption', 'but it does not speak of these things' (p. 44). In contrast to the claim that the meaning of the Mishnah lies 'on the surface', he often proposes that it can be found only in 'the deep structure of [a] tractate' (e.g. pp. 160; 278). The admission that the work does not say what he takes it to mean becomes a major theme of the last chapter. This is its fullest expression:

The Mishnah's deepest convictions about what lies beyond confusion and conflict are never spelled out; they lie in the preliminary, unstated exercise prior to the commencement of a sustained exercise of inquiry, a tractate. They are the things we know before we take up that exercise and study that tractate.

To this is added an even more telling footnote: 'Since the Mishnah rarely bothers to spell out what we know, it makes studying a tractate rather difficult' (p. 269).

The entire discussion about the Mishnah's code is an admission that Neusner is not interpreting what is there. There is not much of an attempt to harmonize the theory that he interprets only what is there, 'blatantly' present on the surface, and the counter theory, that he finds meaning not in what is said, but in the deep structure and in the presuppositions which lie behind the text. It may be that this is intended to be such an effort: 'The Mishnah's mode of discourse rarely wishes to announce what it proposes to say' (*Judaism*, p. 245). Since he had earlier written that the authors 'clearly proposed to tell us about their view of the world', perhaps we should think that what lies on the surface is 'what the Mishnah proposes to say', but that this bears small relationship to what it 'wishes to announce'. But, no, I suppose not. We cannot think that Neusner believes that there is a distinction between 'what it proposes to say' and 'what it announces that it will say' – though he does offer it on p. 245.

The truth is that Neusner, like everybody else, attempts to glean from a text information which is not there in so many words. The only curiosity is that he claims not to do this, but just to say what is there. He uses this claim to disarm the reader, and he brandishes it against others as a weapon, but all that exists is the claim. Here indeed we have words which do not say what the author really does. Against other reconstructions of Judaism which include the Mishnah, he can argue that if there is no tractate on a topic it cannot be central to the Mishnah (see above at n. 10). The Mishnah has no tractate on the destruction of the temple, therefore the concern for salvation in history cannot have been important for its authors (p. 31). When it comes to his own proposals, however, this argument does not apply. There is no division or tractate on The Priesthood, but nevertheless only priests could have posed the questions of the Mishnah, and priestly concerns are central to it (pp. 224, 233). There is no tractate on Making Pure Meals, but nevertheless the first layer of the Mishnah has to do entirely with pure meals (pp. 59, 91). The truth is that he has no objection to finding ideas behind the Mishnah. The question is whether he has found the right ones.

There is another flaw in his claim to interpret just what is there: he simply declines to mention much that is there. Theology disappears entirely.[14] Tamid 7.4 expresses the hope for 'the day that shall be all Sabbath and rest in the life everlasting', but this passage and others merit no mention as part of the Judaism for which the Mishnah is the whole evidence. The songs and prayers of Tamid 7.4 do not even manage to get into the topical outline of the tractate (p. 370). Not only does Neusner's Mishnah not include passages which discuss the world to come, it is against the very idea: his 'framers' of the Mishnah opposed the idea that anything would happen in the future. So it is with other theological concepts. No small part of the Mishnah has to do with atonement, but atonement is a theological idea, and so it is not included in discussions of the world view of the Mishnah. The tractate Yoma (on the Day of Atonement) is mentioned only once, and all that is said of it is that it is told in narrative style (p. 249).

Now we may pose the question: does the semi-Platonic world view lie behind the Mishnah? Though this world view is not *in* the Mishnah, and though other things are, is it nevertheless presupposed? We may put the question with clarity, not being plagued by the pretence that nothing can be known about what is presupposed. The answer to the question is that Neusner has not even begun to establish that his proposed world view lies behind the Mishnah. He has not begun to do this, since he declined to read the Mishnah as law. He has violated the first principle of interpretation: to interpret a text according to what it is, not according to a set of questions and answers which are not in it. He could have gone with the evidence and asked what legal principles lie behind detailed points, wherein they differ from the biblical codes, and finally what the differences imply about overall viewpoint. Instead he puts forward the view that the authors *intended* to write philosophy, that they modestly chose to hide it in the guise of detailed legal discussions, and that it requires a reader of remarkable perception to decode the secret message.

The presuppositions behind a law code should not be difficult to sort out. Laws *are* based on assumptions and values which are not directly articulated within the corpus of law itself – though they may be clearly stated elsewhere, or in the reasonings offered when opinions are handed down. These assumptions and values, however, will be discovered by analysing what is *directly* presupposed, not by postulating a single, all-embracing and exclusive world view peculiar to and exhaustive of the collective mind of a small group. Neusner, in fact, had at his disposal a set of just such observations about what is directly presupposed.[15] They run directly contrary to his main conclusions, however, and so are ignored.

First of all, we note that he very acutely observes some changes from the biblical view of the altar and the cult. In discussing Zebahim (Animal Sacrifices), he points out that the authors do not think that the altar has the 'power of sanctification *ex opere operato*', and that here they disagree with the author of the story about Nadab and Abihu (Lev. 10.1–3). He correctly concludes: 'Someone before the beginning of the tractate's intellectual history has reached a conclusion taken for granted later on among the framers of the tractate's program of inquiry' (p. 206). Similarly in discussing the Tevul Yom (a person who has been immersed, but who will not be completely pure until the sun sets), he notes that 'in the dim past of the tractate is the conception, which scripture certainly does not know, that the person is unclean in a diminished sense of uncleanness' (p. 213). In discussing the Sabbath laws of the earliest layer of the Mishnah, he points out that it is both 'self-evident and demonstrable' that

> long before the destruction of the Temple the Sabbath constituted a fully exposed set of observances and rites, [and thus] it is clear that in the Mishnah we have only those matters subject to the attention of the sages. We do not have a full repertoire of laws generally kept by the people, nor are we apt to have before us all the ideas of the Mishnah's progenitors on the subject of the Sabbath. What we do have is evidence or ideas selected, from what is surely a much larger corpus, for sustained examination. (p. 89)

It is indeed self-evident, and here we have the germ of a good book.

In all three cases we see that there are assumptions which are not argued for and which are, therefore, simply presupposed.[16] In the examples from Zebahim and Tevul Yom these unargued assumptions are different from those of the Bible. Silence in such cases points to ideas which are taken for granted.

These observations, however, play no role in Neusner's overall description of the philosophy behind the Mishnah, and certainly not of his characterization of the group or groups which stand at its origin. He has often said that the group found at the earliest stratum of the Mishnah was concerned only with *domestic* purity and other laws which govern the eating of *secular* food. Here he has two assumptions with regard to the *cult* which were presupposed in the earliest stratum, and he grants that the originating group must have had a lot of Sabbath laws that did not need to be discussed. Yet these presuppositions, conflicting as they do with his oft-repeated theories, cannot be given prominence, nor even be allowed a place in the Introduction or Conclusion.

Had Neusner noted the theological ideas which are in the Mishnah, he could have asked about the presuppositions behind them as well. The requirement of atonement and the promise of the world to come presuppose a covenantal conception: Israel as a whole and individual Israelites begin 'in' and they remain in the group destined for the world to come if they atone for transgressions. One would then also note that every sin can be atoned for, including taking the name of God in vain, for which the Bible itself says there is no atonement (Ex. 20.7; Deut. 5.11). Consideration of this point would have led him to see the conception of God's mercy which is presupposed in the Mishnah. But all this lies outside the world view which he has created, and it goes unmentioned.[17]

Thus he left out of the Mishnah's world view things which can be shown to have been presupposed. But is the world view which he attributes to the Mishnah there at all? He produces virtually no evidence. He does not show that the proposed world view accounts for the concrete laws. There is no consistent line of inference backwards from the laws, from 'the legal discussion is X', to 'the assumed legal principle is Y', to 'Y is a value which correlates with other inferences at the same level', to 'inferences at the level of Y are consonant with world view Z'. Missing are the middle two steps. He simply says that 'legal discussion X proves world view Z', when legal discussion X could come from almost any world view. Laws regulating marriage and restricting divorce do not require a world view which denies change. Neusner, however, says that they do (pp. 142f.), and this sort of statement makes up most of the argument of the book. One could just as well argue that, since Jesus prohibited divorce entirely (Matt. 5.31–32; 19.1–12 and parr.), he wanted there to be no change and opposed the idea that the kingdom of God would come.

Neusner's proposed world view is actually based not on the contents of the Mishnah and inferences backwards from them, but on what, according to him, is not there: prophecy, history and eschatology.[18] This requires us now to turn to the argument from silence.

(b) E silentio. Various arguments from silence occupy such a major place in Neusner's work that they deserve special reflection. I shall enumerate arguments from silence and comment briefly.

1. Silence may indicate areas which are common and taken for granted. This is a perfectly reasonable use of silence, provided of course that one can show what is taken for granted. I listed above three examples in which Neusner effectively shows what is presupposed. His work would be much better if he made more frequent use of this form of analysis and if he allowed its results to influence his conclusions.

2. Silence, he proposes, may show that authors wrote in code. They 'propose to say' one thing, but do not 'wish to announce it', and so do not mention it. This suggestion is without academic merit.

3. One conclusion to be drawn from silence Neusner unfortunately never notes and seems not to know. What is not there may be absent simply because it does not fit the genre. This in fact accounts for rather a lot of the things which are not in the Mishnah.[19]

4. This leads us to Neusner's major use of the argument from silence: silence equals dissent; more, it shows direct opposition. The world view attributed to the Mishnah depends heavily on the assumption that its authors opposed everything which is not in it. This erroneous but basic assumption goes hand in glove with the mistake about genre: the authors of the Mishnah intended to express (in code) a world view, 100% complete, and thus opposed whatever is not there. The Mishnah does not discuss the two wars and therefore opposed the view – redemption in history – which led to them. They wrote about Time (actually, Appointed Times) but did not mention the meaning of history or the world to come, and therefore opposed the idea that Israel's history held meaning and that anything would happen in the future. So Neusner.

Silence may, of course, result from dissent. One suspects that this explains why so few talmudists discuss Neusner's work. Is he then correct that the mishnaic Rabbis opposed those who thought that the history and future of Israel were important, but chose not to argue against them? Not on the present showing. The genre mistake is too fundamental. One would have to introduce further evidence – which, as we shall see, Neusner argues against doing – and study the authors as people who lived in a given community at a certain time. There is no particular reason for the Mishnah to discuss the history of Israel or its future. History and future are not governed by law, and law is essentially timeless – or, rather, is usually presented as if it were so. The law may change tomorrow, but today's law does not say, 'until the future, at which time . . .' (except in a few special circumstances).

In assessing the view that the lawyers of the Mishnah opposed whatever is not discussed, we may return to the analogy with modern laws and their 'framers'. The authors of tax law and the highway code are not necessarily opposed to the study of history and preparation for the future. Nor need we deny to them the pressing concerns of the society around them. One will find little in law about patriotism. Concrete acts may be forbidden and punished by law – such as defacing the flag, evading the draft, and betraying secrets to the enemy. But the law will not devote a tractate, much less a division, to the topic Patriotism. This does not mean that lawyers and legislators are unpatriotic. Passing laws which govern what is Regular does not keep the law-givers from responding to the Irregular and Disorderly in ways not envisaged by the law. Lawyers can one day insist on the timeless principles of the tax law and the next day march off to war, without putting a single word about war in the tax code. World views, in fact, are not very often exclusive. Most of us carry two or three around with us all the time.

We cannot, to be sure, entirely rule out the possibility that the authors of the Mishnah were opposed to wars of liberation. Pacifism has often been ascribed to the Pharisees, for example, who had something to do with the early stage of what became the Mishnah.[20] I do not think that the collateral evidence about Pharisaic pacifism is very good: Josephus wished to repress information which would make the Romans think that important groups in Israel hoped for political liberation. Thus Josephus's silence about political insurgency by the Pharisees may be his own bias, and absence of the national aspiration from the Mishnah may be the result of the selectivity of the genre. But in order to get at this question, which is an interesting and important one, one would have to stop attributing to a social group a world view which is constructed by observing what is not in a work of one genre.

This brings us to a more fundamental flaw than any we have yet discussed, since it is related to them all: the identification of social groups which held the world view attributed to the Mishnah.

§4. Social groups, world view and bodies of literature.

(a) We recall the basic hypothesis: the Mishnah is the full and perfect representation of the world view of a small collection of social groups, who constituted a minority within Israel. Other people faced the issues of the first two centuries CE by going to war and searching for power. The Mishnah's philosophers opposed this solution and sought redemption in stasis (p. 171; cf. p. 118).

Neusner attempts to define who these people were. Behind the Mishnah were the priests and other temple 'castes and professions', who alone would have made such a choice (p. 224). More particularly, the final form of the Mishnah reflects the interests of three groups: priests and laymen who thought like priests, scribes, and small householders. This is a very interesting part of his work, and there are numerous good observations, such as the list-producing proclivity of scribes. Yet there are three major flaws in the proposal.

1. In discussing groups and their literary products, Neusner confuses structuralism with social history. We saw that he finds the Mishnah's world view in its 'deep structure' (*Judaism*, p. 111), and in this vein he personifies it: 'it wants to know', 'it pretends', 'it wishes to claim' (pp. 159f., 189). This then becomes 'what *people* want to know' (p. 156, my emphasis). Methodologically, this is an impossible leap. Documents are not people. In real life, people think things and are interested in things which they do not write in every document they create.

2. The second flaw, alluded to above, is that Neusner both affirms and denies that the Mishnah presents the world view of a group.

... what makes up a world view and way of life are the people who see, or are supposed to see, the world in one particular way and expected to live in accord with a way of living congruent with that singular world view. (p. 236)

The Mishnah presents a system, distinctive, whole, fully interacting in all its parts, capable of making a coherent statement. True, that statement expresses the view-points of diverse social groups. But it is one statement, made to a single world in behalf of a single world. (p. 237)

These statements from the conclusion are both predicted and contradicted in the Introduction. First he entertains the possibility that the creators of the Mishnah may have had some of the thoughts now found in other bodies of literature, such as the Talmuds, the Targums, the Tosefta, the Midrashim, and the liturgy (pp. 2–4). In the same pages, however, he states that each body of literature represents a different 'Judaism' and speaks for a different group:

We also do not know how or when the writings of the one group, those of the people behind the Mishnah, came to form part of a single kind of Judaism, and to intersect and fuse with the writings of another, for instance people behind the Targums, the synagogue liturgy . . . (pp. 3f.)

He then adds that he is not certain that the groups were entirely separate.

In the rest of the work he simply supposes that the world view of the Mishnah was held by a group, since it is not only a world view, but also a way of life (p. 166). He concludes by denying that this group could have held any of the thoughts in other bodies of literature: the Mishnah is the 'whole evidence' for its form of Judaism (p. 237).

The same confusion and self-contradiction run through the Introduction to *Messiah*. Neusner claims that 'each system of Judaism' – which includes (1) world view, (2) way of life and (3) 'mode of bonding people into the social group' – 'worked out its Judaism in its own way' (*Messiah*, p. 6). Those who held to 'the Messiah myth' had made a 'sole and exclusive choice' (ibid.). They are contrasted with the sages of the Mishnah, who 'cared not at all' for the world beyond Israel and had 'no interest in the history of Israel' (p. 9). He says that things were not actually that simple, but that he will treat them as if they were (p. 7). But he does not just treat them as if they were, he argues that each body of literature represents a different group. Only the Talmuds melded the diverse 'Judaisms' into one (e.g. *Messiah*, pp. xxiii, 14f.).

Behind this confusion of reiterated statements and counter statements there are three clear points. One is that the thrust of all Neusner's work is towards claiming that Judaism was so fragmented in the first and second centuries that one must speak of 'Judaisms', which had messages which were 'utterly unrelated' to one other (*Judaism*, p. 37).

Secondly, in summarizing and programmatic essays which he reproduces in vast numbers, he unhesitatingly equates each Jewish 'system' with a 'world view', a 'way of life' and 'a circumscribed social group'.[21] It appears that he really holds the most simplistic form of the various views which he asserts in the books being considered here.

The third clear point is that all the other evidence which might tell us something about the mishnaic Rabbis is assigned to other groups. He opens, we saw, by saying that there might be other evidence, but he proceeds to deny it. George Foot Moore used the Midrashim, and thus he used material which 'derives from circles which cannot be deemed at all concentric with the social and intellectual group behind the Mishnah' (p. 7). Not only do II Baruch and IV Ezra speak for a distinct group, so do the halakic Midrashim (p. 7; *Messiah*, p. 5 n.), Aboth (*Messiah*, p. 42), the liturgy (ibid., p. 38), and the Targums other than Onqelos (ibid., p. xvii.).

The claim to have a nuanced view, while writing as if he makes simple equations between each literary compilation and a distinctive group (e.g. *Messiah*, p. 7) probably shows that Neusner has heard criticisms. But the nuance is only claimed and never informs the argument, and his conclusions completely deny the possibility that the thought of any given group might be reflected in more than one literary product.

3. The arbitrary limitation of evidence requires further comment. Were one to attribute any other material to the mishnaic Rabbis, the world view which Neusner assigns them would disappear. The people who worked on the Aramaic Targums were interested in more aspects of the Bible than static ritual. Most striking, however, is Neusner's treatment of Aboth and the liturgy. These have provided other scholars with crucial evidence for understanding the Rabbis, and so I shall say a few more words about how Neusner handles them.

Before the publication of *Judaism*, Neusner had been seriously criticized for refusing to take the liturgy into account,[22] and this may explain why he now mentions it. On pp. 3f. he attributes it to another group, while granting that he cannot be certain. It is, however, excluded from the world view which he attributes to the group behind the Mishnah. In order to see how the liturgy would change this world view, one does not need to suppose that the mishnaic Rabbis wrote it, nor that we have precisely what they used. One need only suppose that they said prayers which contained a good number of the main themes of the Eighteen Benedictions. One could make no selection of these themes which did not include redemption in history, hope for the future, belief in repentance and atonement and numerous other things, all attributed by Neusner to 'another group'.

He cannot deny that the Rabbis knew prayers which were at least similar to the Eighteen Benedictions, and so he tries to finesse the problem. The Mishnah was concerned only to standardize 'the principal outlines of worship', and its sages intended 'not to create liturgy but to legislate about it' (p. 86). This is part of his view that they 'cared for nothing but rules' – as if they made rules for things to which they were utterly indifferent. Once he grants that they made rules about prayers, he must grant that the prayers existed, which means that people, including the rule-makers, said them. Had the mishnaic Rabbis really opposed the world view of the Eighteen Benedictions, they should have offered an alternative collection of prayers. But they did not, and Neusner accepts the fact that they said 'blessings for various gifts of nature' (p. 86; 'nature' is presumably Neusner's translation of 'God'). Having granted the case of his critics, that the framers of the Mishnah shared a common liturgy with others, he then drops it and excludes its concern from their world.

He turns to Aboth in the trilogy and simply eliminates it.[23] Many of the names in Aboth are also in the other tractates of the Mishnah, but in Aboth, he claims, they are pseudonyms. He does not even consider the tractate to be part of the Mishnah, but rather to have been written fifty years after the Mishnah was completed. What is the evidence? 'Since the latest named authorities of Abot derive from the period a generation or two after Judah the Patriarch, . . . who flourished at about 200 CE, we may date Abot at about 250 CE.' (*Torah*, p. 6). The other tractates of the Mishnah are not dated by the last names in them, and Neusner along with everyone else finds layers of material. Why not take the saying of Rabban Gamaliel III in Aboth 2 2 as simply a late insertion? We encounter dogma. In Aboth, all names other than the last are the result of pseudepigraphical activity.

Neusner's other defence of the exclusion of Aboth is even weaker. The sayings 'do not square with anything stated by the same sages anywhere else in the Mishnah' (*Torah*, p. 32). Here we meet the flat rejection of other evidence: they did not say anything other than Neusner attributes to them, because it is *different*. Therefore they could not have. A Rabbi could think only one sort of thing.

Actually, the Rabbis and others (according to Neusner) were more limited than that. Akiba, Josephus, Bar Kokhba and the Teacher of Righteousness 'would scarcely have understood one another, let alone have known they all evidenced the same -ism' (*Judaism*, p. 22). Had they comprehended one another, there would have been mutual rejection: the Jews responsible for different bodies of literature would not have 'accepted one another as part of the same social group and cultic community' (p. 8).

This is evidently untrue. Josephus understood the heirs of the Teacher of Righteousness, the revolutionaries of his own day and the predecessors of R. Akiba. Akiba and Bar Kokhba surely understood each other. It appears that Akiba was executed after the Bar Kokhba revolt, and doubtless he knew why.[24] With regard to membership in the same group and cultic community: the Qumran sect, it is true, withdrew from the temple; but, prior to 70, no one else did. And the Qumranians understood the Sadducees, Pharisees and others perfectly well. They attacked their interpretations of the law, and they offered their own, which cover the expected topics of common Judaism: who were the true chief priests? what is the correct calendar? what are the right ways of observing the law? Further, during the first revolt, Essenes fought along with other Jews (*War* 2.152f., 567). They all shared a common -ism, a fact which is seen most clearly in their debates about how best to define it.[25]

(*b*) The characteristics of the originating group. Neusner focuses on describing social groups at two chronological moments: the origination of mishnaic material before 70 and the coalescence of three groups during the final period of the Mishnah's development (140–200). His conclusions about the originating group did not change between 1971 and 1981; and, sadly, they have not often been analysed or criticized. As we noted in ch. III, by the time of writing *Judaism* he sometimes (not always[26]) hesitated to call this group 'the Pharisees', since he had come to realize that his description of the original group does not coincide with other evidence about the Pharisees. His view about the earliest layer of the Mishnah, however, did not change:

> the beginnings of the Mishnaic system lie . . . among lay people pretending to be priests by eating their food at home as if they were priests in the temple, and also among priests with so intense a sense for cultic cleanness that they do the same. (p. 226)

Neusner says that he hesitates whether or not to call the group a sect, and concludes that 'sect' is too specific and that 'group' is the better term (p. 71). This follows his calling the group a 'sect' (pp. 69f.), and subsequently he continues to do so (e.g. 119). As so often, he seems to show that he has heard criticism, and he responds by saying that he retracts or modifies his view, but he does not actually make the modification.[27]

I shall not discuss the evidence that counts against this definition of the group responsible for the earliest layer of the Mishnah. The argument is essentially the same as ch. III above, though the definition of the evidence changes. Instead of choosing passages which are attributed to a Pharisee or the Houses, Neusner looks instead at the logically earliest layer of each tractate. As we noted above, Betzah turns out to be early, and we again read that it has to do with meals, and thus with eating together, and thus with laypeople eating in priestly purity, when in fact it discusses work. We saw above that his own analyses of the presuppositions of the earliest layer count against his definition of the originating group (at n. 15). Neusner's list of early tractates is an interesting one,[28] but in this essay I wish to leave it without further discussion and turn to the groups which were responsible for the final Mishnah.

(c) The final coalescence. As we saw above, Neusner proposes that in the Mishnah as a completed document one can see the evidence of three groups: priests and laymen who thought like priests; scribes; small householders (pp. 232–256). The priests supply concern with holiness and the scribes supply formal rhetoric, list-making and categorizing. The householders are the subject of the material. 'The building block of Mishnaic discourse, the circumstance addressed whenever the issues of concrete society and material transactions are taken up, is the householder and his context' (p. 235).

This is well observed. Kings, soldiers and bankers are not to the fore. 'Normality' is the word of the independent but not wealthy householder. Discussions of buying foodstuff may point towards small tradesmen, but most of the time we have the impression of being in the hands of scribes who make rules about farmers. There are, however, criticisms to be made here as well.

1. On p. 240 he gives a list of tractates in three columns, one for each social group: 'Tractates of principal concern to priests: temple and cult'; 'Tractates of principal concern to Scribes: courts and documents'; 'Tractates of principal concern to householders: home and farm'. While I like the effort to make such distinctions, I fear that many of the tractates are in the wrong column. Under the first (topics of concern to priests), for example, we find Demai (food which may not have been tithed) and Terumoth (heave offering) as the first two items. These tractates, however, do not discuss their topics from the priests' point of view. Priests did not ask themselves, 'When we buy food which may not have been tithed, which of the gifts to the Levites and priests must we deduct before we can eat the remainder?' That is a layperson's question, and it is the question of Demai. Similarly with Terumoth, one asks 'How do we handle food before heave offering is separated?' and similar questions. These, again, are topics for the laity. The priests did not harvest and separate heave offering, they received it and ate it. And, of course, the laymen who debated such topics were not treating themselves like priests. They distinguished their food from that of the priests. One could similarly query the categorization of most tractates on the first list.

The tendency to misdescribe and miscategorize the material, either to force it to deal with purity or to find in it profound philosophy, especially marks his treatment of the Division of Women (Nashim), much of which he places in the last period of the Mishnah's growth. He states that the laws deal not with 'women in general', but with 'what is important about women to the framers of the Mishnah' (p. 138). This turns out to be the 'two crucial stages in the transfer of women and of property from one domain to another' (p. 138); that is, marriage and its dissolution. This, which is what one should expect of legal discussion, suddenly becomes purity: 'The regulation of the transfer of women is the Mishnah's way of effecting the sanctification of what, for the moment, disturbs and disorders the orderly world' (p. 141). '. . . the goal and purpose of the Mishnah's Division of Women are to bring under control and force into stasis all of the wild and unruly potentialities of sexuality' (p. 143).

Purity ('sanctification'), stasis and the control of sexuality are not there. They are, as so often, simply claimed rather than shown to be present. What is there is apparent: legal discussions about the parts of life which laws govern. Neusner has not found 'what interested the framers of the Division of Women': possibly they really were interested in wild and unruly sexuality; possibly it would have alarmed them. Who knows? What they discussed were the topics of law which involve women.

2. As he did in *Rabb. Trads.*, in *Judaism* and the volumes which it summarizes, Neusner equates centrality with frequency, when in fact, in this genre of material, one should make the reverse assumption: only dubious points are subject to lengthy debate, and what is central is what is taken for granted.[29] I am no more surprised that the Mishnah does not have a tractate on The Covenant than I am that the tax code does not have a long chapter on Patriotism. This argument is presented in more detail above, pp. 14–16; 171f., where it is also noted that Neusner's work provides information about what is taken for granted. The problem is that he did not see its importance, and sometimes even denied it.

The most remarkable development of this misunderstanding is that, when he discusses the amount of space spent on 'gray areas', he does not see that they imply important black and white areas, but thinks instead that the Rabbis attached importance to Grayness.

> Gray areas . . . fill up nearly every chapter of the Mishnah. But underneath the surface is an inquiry of profound and far-reaching range. It is into the metaphysical or philosophical issues of how things join together and how they do not, of synthesis and analysis, of fusion and union, connection, division, and disintegration. What we have [here] is a sustained philosophical treatise in the guise of an episodic exercise in ad hoc problem solving. (p. 262)

Just here, where he could have inquired after the legal principles on which arguments over details are based, he chose again to deny the genre of the work and to assert that it is philosophy in code.

§5. Conclusion. What do we have at the end of it all? As I have several times indicated, I regard his analytical work as insightful and helpful, if not yet definitive (see ch. III). His constructive account of the philosophy of the Mishnah, however, rests on a mistake about genre, misdescribed evidence, omission of relevant material, false use of the argument from silence, and the confusion of structuralism with social history.

Neusner regards the 'singular' view of the final framers of the Mishnah as very fragile. It fell 'to pieces nearly as soon as it [came] together' (p. 237). The Mishnah, which is 'the whole evidence' for this world view, united 'for a fleeting moment' 'social elements quite unlike one another, indeed not even capable of serving as analogies for one another' (p. 237). This 'fleeting moment', however, like a later 'brief, shining moment' fortunately was written down; written down, to be sure, in 'another guise', until the arrival of its decoder.

In fact, the world view which Neusner attributes to the Mishnah can be found neither in it nor behind it. The real Rabbis not only made rules about when the Eighteen Benedictions should be said, they prayed them; and when they prayed them they asked God to restore Jerusalem and to have mercy on his people Israel. They discussed problems created when different laws overlapped not because of an abstract philosophical interest in Overlapness,[30] but because they wanted to obey all the commandments. They shared both piety and an interest in sorting out the law with other Jews. Many of their legal concerns will be found in any literature which deals with Jewish law (e.g. 1QS, 11QTemple and Jubilees), though naturally there are some differences in detail and in topics covered. Common piety is difficult to discover in the Mishnah, since it is not the subject of legal debate (compare pp. 253f. above). Careful study of the material, however, can disclose many of its aspects, as Neusner himself periodically grants.[31] A true account of the world view of the mishnaic Rabbis will make them part of common Judaism, rather than a fleeting denial of it.

Notes

I The Synoptic Jesus and the Law

A. INTRODUCTION

1. On 'ideal' scenes, see Rudolf Bultmann, *History of the Synoptic Tradition*, rev. ET 1968, p. 39. Bultmann's intuition that synoptic sayings are often earlier than their settings may not be correct; but if it is correct, it still results in uncertainty, since a saying without a context is usually ambiguous. Dismissing Bultmann's scissors-and-paste approach, however, does not lead to the conclusion that entire passages are now to be considered 'authentic'. On the contrary, those who will not attempt to probe behind the passages as we have them must be more uncertain of their historical reliability than Bultmann was. See on this Sanders and Davies, *Studying the Synoptic Gospels*, 1989, chs 8, 20–22.

2. It is touched on occasionally below. See 'Pharisees, role and influence of' in the Index.

3. Eduard Schweizer, *Jesus*, ET 1971, p. 32.

4. Geza Vermes, *Jesus the Jew*, 1973, p. 35.

5. Josephus was a Jewish priest, born in CE 37. He fought against Rome in the Jewish revolt which began in 66, surrendered, and lived to be its historian (*The Jewish War*). He subsequently wrote *The Jewish Antiquities*, *The Life*, and *Against Apion*.

6. Geza Vermes, *Jesus the Jew*; Martin Hengel, *The Charismatic Leader and His Followers*, ET 1981; Gerd Theissen, *The First Followers of Jesus*, ET 1978.

7. *Jesus and Judaism*, 1985, ch. 8.

8. This question is raised by Neusner; see p. 133 below.

9. 'To transgress the law in matters either small or great is of equal seriousness, for in either case the law is equally despised' (IV Macc. 5.20f.); cf. Aboth 4.2.

B. SABBATH

1. Most conveniently, see Molly Whittaker, *Jews and Christians: Graeco-Roman Views*, 1984, pp. 63–73. The full texts of passages from pagan literature are in Menahem Stern, *Greek and Latin Authors on Jews and Judaism*, 3 vols, 1976–1984. In *Dialogue with Trypho* 46, Justin Martyr has Trypho the Jew say that the commandments which can still be kept in the post-70 period are sabbath, circumcision, months, and some of the laws about washing. It is curious that this list omits food, but otherwise it is what one would expect.

2. The prosbul was a legal device for securing the repayment of loans in the sabbath year. It was necessary, because otherwise moneylenders would hesitate to make loans in the sixth year of the seven-year cycle, since debts could not be collected in the seventh year (Neh. 10.31 [Heb. v. 32]). The prosbul is attributed to Hillel in Sifre Deut. 113; cf. Shebiith 10.3–4, where the wording is less likely. That the prosbul (whether because

Hillel proposed it or not) was actually used is clear in a text from the Judaean desert. In a document dated the second year of Nero (13 Oct. 55–12 Oct. 56), a borrower promises to repay a loan, plus interest of one-fifth, 'even if it is a year of rest' (*Discoveries in the Judaean Desert* II, pp. 100–104, no. 18).

3. On rules about defecation, see Yigael Yadin, *The Temple Scroll*, ET 1983, I, pp. 294–304.

4. Vermes, *The Dead Sea Scrolls. Qumran in Perspective*, 1977, pp. 101–102; CD 11.13–14 and elsewhere.

5. There were debates about precisely what had to be constructed: e.g. Erubin 1.2.

6. See Neusner, *Rabb. Trads.* I, pp. 379f.

7. According to T. Hagigah 2.10, the Shammaites laid hands on the head of a peace offering on the day before the festival day.

8. For the assumption, see the gemara on Pesahim 6.3 (Pesahim 69b–70b). The earliest *direct* comment which I have found to the effect that individuals did not bring sacrifices on the sabbath is Rashi's (eleventh century), cited by Liebermann in discussing T. Hagigah 2.10: Saul Lieberman, *Tosefta Ki-Fshutah* V, 1962, p. 1301.

9. For example, Pesahim 6.1.

10. As we shall see below (p. 133), in more recent works Neusner hesitates to call the originating group of the rabbinic movement 'the Pharisees', but by whatever name they go, he still attributes to them a lack of concern with broader society. Thus, for example, in *Messiah in Context*, 1984, he wrote that 'priest and sage cared not at all' for 'the world out there beyond Israel', and that these two groups had 'no interest in the history of Israel and its meaning' (p. 9). Pharisees are subsequently called 'priest[s] manqué' (p. 13), and this statement attributes the supposed priestly/scribal world view to them. This section is reprinted, with minor alterations, in *Judaism in the beginning of Christianity*, 1984; the quotations are found on pp. 38, 42.

11. 'Since . . . long before the destruction of the Temple the Sabbath constituted a fully exposed set of observances and rites, it is clear that in the Mishnah we have only those matters subject to the attention of sages', Neusner, *Judaism: The Evidence of the Mishnah*, 1981, p. 89. Unfortunately, this perception, which would have dramatically changed his work of the 1970s and the early 80s, is usually missing; rather, it is usually denied. His usual position is that the Mishnah (for example) 'fully express[es]' what it 'wishes to declare' (p. 230), or that 'the mere outline of a tractate' 'reveals very clearly, right on the surface, . . . precisely what the framers of that tractate deemed critical about the topic under discussion' (p. 125). See more fully the final chapter of this volume.

12. Compare Neusner on the absence of a history of Israel from the Mishnah: the authors 'made a stunning comment'. 'Their judgment was that nothing of worth had happened from the time of Moses to their own day' (*Judaism*, pp. 170f.).

13. For example, Alan Segal, *Rebecca's Children*, 1986, p. 35.

14. For the question of whether or not only Pharisees thought that corpse-impurity was contracted by 'overshadowing' a corpse, see below pp. 34f.

15. On local government, see Martin Goodman, *State and Society in Roman Galilee, A.D. 132–212*, 1983, pp. 157–165.

16. Trans. Chaim Rabin, *The Zadokite Documents*, 1958.

17. That the Pharisees did not try to force others to accept their own rules, when they went beyond the Bible, was noted above. This will be seen at point after point. See 'Coercion' and 'Tolerance' in the index.

C. FOOD

1. According to Philo the Therapeutae in Egypt (or some of them) were very abstemious and ate only bread flavoured with salt and sometimes hyssop (*The Contemplative Life* 34–37). There may have been other ascetic groups. I do not intend here to deal with asceticism, but rather with the interpretation and observance of the biblical food laws.

2. The main sources of priestly income are canvassed below, ch. IV.D§2 (biblical law), and IV.D§6 (rabbinic views).

3. I assume that the Levites' portion of the tithe was not stored at the temple, but was given to them where they lived. See further the discussion of tithes in section F below.

4. Josephus states that there were 20,000 priests (*Apion* 2.108), probably intending to include Levites. On numbers, cf. Joachim Jeremias, *Jerusalem in the Time of Jesus*, ET 1969, pp. 198–204.

5. In the LCL ed., ad loc. This obviously inadequate explanation has often been accepted.

6. On this topic see further ch. IV below.

7. On the uncertainty involved in revising and re-setting sayings, see *Jesus and Judaism*, pp. 132–136; *Studying the Synoptic Gospels*, chs 20–21.

8. See A. B. Du Toit, 'Hyperbolical Contrasts: A Neglected Aspect of Paul's Style', *A South African Perspective on the New Testament*, ed. J. H. Petzer and P. J. Martin, 1986, pp. 178–186.

D. PURITY

1. On the food laws as purity laws, see C above.

2. Cf. Justin Martyr, *Dialogue with Trypho* 46.

3. A wide range of dates has been proposed for *Aristeas*; see G. W. E. Nickelsburg in *Jewish Writings of the Second Temple Period* (CRINT II.2), 1984, pp. 77f.; R. J. H. Shutt in *OTP* II, 1985, pp. 8f.). Shutt prefers *c.* 170 BCE (*OTP* II, pp. 9f.). The period 150–100 BCE has often been suggested, and these dates would also make *Aristeas* earlier than any Palestinian evidence on handwashing. The third *Sibylline Oracle* is dated by John Collins to the period 163–45 BCE (*OTP* I, pp. 354f.), which is earlier than the date at which Pharisees accepted handwashing (the time of Hillel and Shammai; see pp. 227–29 below).

4. George Nickelsburg hesitates between ascribing Judith to the Persian or Hasmonean period, but is inclined to put the final form of the work in the latter, not long after the time of Judas Maccabaeus – that is, before 150 BCE (*Jewish Literature between the Bible and the Mishnah*, 1981, pp. 108f.). Josephus's first reference to the Pharisees is in his account of the Hasmonean Jonathan, who died in 143 BCE, but the first narrative which attributes any action to them is from early in the reign of John Hyrcanus, 134–104 (*Antiq.* 13.171; 13.288f.).

5. See III.E§2.c.2; III.E§3.d.; III.E§9.

6. See Yigael Yadin, *Masada. Herod's Fortress and the Zealots' Last Stand*, ET 1966, pp. 166f.; Nahman Avigad, *Discovering Jerusalem*, ET 1983, pp. 139, 142.

7. See Avigad, n. 6 above.

8. Benjamin Mazar, 'Herodian Jerusalem in the Light of the Excavations South and South-West of the Temple Mount', *IEJ* 28, 1978, p. 236.

9. Sanhedrin 11.3 appears to point in the opposite direction; see the discussion II.C§1.k below.

10. These cases are discussed in ch. III, where full evidence is given.

11. See *J & J*, pp. 188–198, which argues the case against Jeremias and others.

12. Elisha Qimron and John Strugnell, 'An Unpublished Halakhic Letter from Qumran', *Biblical Archaeology Today*, ed. Joseph Aviram and others, 1985, pp. 400–407, here pp. 403f. The editors think that the letter comes from an early date. It is to be noted that early in his reign John Hyrcanus (134–104 BCE) broke with the Pharisees; their views were again in force during the reign of Salome Alexandra (76–67 BCE). See *Antiq.* 13.288–296; 13.408.

13. Vermes, *Perspective*, p. 94.

14. On identification of immersion pools, see pp. 215–17 below.

15. 11QTemple 45.11–12; cf. Yadin, *The Temple Scroll*, pp. 171–173.

16. See section J below.

17. Gedalyahu Alon, 'The Bounds of the Laws of Levitical Cleanness', *Jews, Judaism and the Classical World*, ET 1977, p. 201. Alon grants that washing the hands for prayer is 'taught in the Talmud only by Amoraim' (i.e. after CE 220). His argument that 'the halakah' is early depends on the *Letter of Aristeas* and *Sib. Or.* 3. See below, III.C.

18. Sepphoris, under the leadership of lay aristocrats, was loyal to Rome in the first revolt (*Life* 30–36). That it contained priestly aristocrats is only a guess, but it is the most likely place for the more prosperous non-Judaean priests to have lived.

19. Josephus wrote that Tiberias was settled by 'a promiscuous rabble' (*Antiq.* 18.36–38). It should not be inferred, however, that the settlers had no regard for the Jewish law. They opposed the plan of Gaius (Caligula) to set up a statue in the temple (*Antiq.* 18.269–272). At the time of the revolt, though Sepphoris was pro-Roman, Tiberias was not, and after the Roman conquest of Galilee many Tiberians went to Jerusalem to continue the fight (*Life* 345–353).

20. That Jesus wished to break down Judaism's purity barriers is the main thesis of Marcus Borg, *Conflict, Holiness and Politics in the Teaching of Jesus*, 1984; cf. now *Jesus: A New Vision*, 1987. Borg's Jesus should have led the Tiberians in a march on the temple.

E. OFFERINGS

1. On this topic, see H. W. Wolfson, *Philo*, 2 vols, 1947, II, pp. 237–252.

F. TITHES

1. Deut. 14.22f. requires that Israelites tithe grain, wine, oil and firstlings. This probably should be read as if it said 'tithe grain, wine and oil and give the firstlings of the flock and herd'; i.e., give one animal of each species, not give one-tenth of the animals born each year. The second reading is, however, possible.

2. Even though Leviticus and Numbers may be later than Deuteronomy, it is doubtful that the idea of a 10% tax is entirely a post-exilic creation. Thus Deuteronomy may represent an attempt to reform the tax system.

3. 'First fruits', *aparchai*, in *Antiq.* 4.70 is a generic which covers both crops and animals. See the discussion of the Hebrew terminology below, IV.D, n. 19.

4. First-century Jews reconciled Lev. 7.31f. and Deut. 18.3 by interpreting the passage in Deuteronomy as applying to animals slaughtered at home. See *Antiq.* 4.74; Hullin 10.1; Philo, *Spec. Laws* 1.147.

5. Zebahim 5.8: it is second tithe, eaten in Jerusalem by 'anyone'; Hagigah 1.4: the tithe of animals may be used as a peace offering (also consumed by the person who brought it);

Menahoth 7.5: tithe of cattle may be used as a thank offering (a sub-category of the peace offering).

6. The history of the tithe of animals is a puzzle. As I have indicated above, Lev. 27.32 seems to require that a tenth of all animals owned be paid 'to the Lord'. This requirement, however, follows the requirement of 10% of produce (27.30), and the tax on animals may have been read in light of the tax on produce, that is, as 10% of the annual increase. Jub. 32.15 requires that 'the whole tithe of oxen and sheep' be given to the priests. Whether this means 10% of the increase or of animals owned is not certain. What is clearest is that neither Josephus nor the Mishnah expects the tithe of animals to be given to the priests or Levites. I am indebted to Chaim Milikowsky for assistance on this point. Perhaps light will be shed on the tithe of animals when the full text of 4QMMT is made available. According to the editors, it deals with this question: Qimron and Strugnell, 'An Unpublished Halakhic Letter from Qumran', p. 401.

7. Josephus notes that Rome forgave Judaea's taxes in the sabbatical year (*Antiq.* 14.202), and it follows that tithes could not have been collected in that year.

8. On the Pharisees' and Rabbis' view that common people were 'trustworthy' with regard to second tithe, see below, p. 237.

9. I take it that passages which indicate that tithes were collected locally can be reconciled with those which say that they were to be taken to Jerusalem: individuals *could* take them, but usually paid them locally; the temple organized transportation to Jerusalem, whence they were distributed. Cf. Mark Wischnitzer, 'Tithe', *Enc. Jud.* 15, col. 1156–1162, here 1161.

10. On the Pharisaic ranking of gifts to the temple, and on their view of what the common people could be counted on to pay, see below, III.F and IV.D.

G. TEMPLE TAX

1. Alternatively, the passage in Exodus can be viewed as a post-exilic insertion, later than Nehemiah, which assumes an annual tax and raises it from one-third to one-half shekel. So Schürer/Vermes/Millar, *HJP* II, p. 271.

2. On whether or not this sum represents the temple tax, see further below, p. 293.

3. See Schürer/Vermes/Millar, *HJP* II, pp. 272–273; III, pp. 54, 58, 122–123.

4. Mary Smallwood cites C. Wessely as estimating that in first-century Egypt the value of the temple tax 'was the equivalent of four or five days' wages for a day-labourer', but she notes that he cited no evidence for the estimate. See *The Jews under Roman Rule*, 1981, p. 374 and n. 64.

5. On a legal confiscation of some of the temple tax, see Cicero, *Pro Flacco* 28.66–69 and Stern's comments (Stern, *Greek and Latin Authors* I, pp. 196–201). Cicero refers to approximately 100 Roman pounds of gold at Apamea, 20 pounds at Laodicea, and 100 at Adramyttium.

6. David Daube, 'Temple Tax', *Jesus, the Gospels, and the Church*, ed. E. P. Sanders, 1987, pp. 121–134.

H. OATHS AND VOWS

1. So M. H. Pope, 'Oaths', *IDB* 3, pp. 575–577, here 576f.

2. L. I. Rabinowitz, 'Vows and vowing', *Enc. Jud.* 16, cols. 227f., here 227.

3. There are two known inscriptions, one on an ossuary, discussed below, another on a stone vessel. The vessel has on it, besides the word *korban*, the outline of two birds. It doubtless contained an offering for the temple. See A. I. Baumgarten, '*Korban* and the

Pharisaic Paradosis', *Ancient Studies in Memory of Elias Bickerman. The Journal of the Ancient Near Eastern Society* 16–17, 1984–1985, pp. 5–17, here p. 7.

4. *Anathēmata* for gifts which were vowed to the temple continued in use (e.g. *Antiq.* 18.312f.; 12.50 // *Arist.* 40). This is the translation of *ḥerem* in Lev. 27.28 and elsewhere.

5. On these, see 1QS 5.8; 1QH 14.17; CD 15.5f.,8–12; 16.1–5.

6. So also Baumgarten, '*Korban*', p. 9.

7. Saul Lieberman, *Greek in Jewish Palestine*, 2nd. ed., 1965, pp. 138f.

8. Lieberman, pp. 115–143, esp. 136, 138f.

9. See the material from the *Covenant of Damascus*, Philo and Josephus in Baumgarten, '*Korban*', pp. 9f. The story about Antipas, cited above, implies that he was ignorant of the view reflected in *Antiq.* 5.169.

10. Baumgarten, '*Korban*', p. 7, citing an ossuary text printed by Joseph Fitzmyer and D. J. Harrington, *A Manual of Palestinian Aramaic Texts*, 1978, no. 69.

11. Baumgarten, pp. 10–12.

12. On accepting Matt. 23 as accurately representing legal practices of the Pharisees, cf. above, on whitewashing tombs and washing the outside of cups. On the setting of Matt. 23, see Kenneth Newport, *The Sources and* Sitz im Leben *of Matthew 23*, DPhil. thesis, Oxford University, 1988. For the present point see also Lieberman, *Greek in Jewish Palestine*, p. 134.

I. BLASPHEMY

1. Following the LXX and some modern scholars, I take *vayyiqqōb* in Lev. 24.11 to be from *naqab*, 'specify', rather than from *qabab*, 'curse'. Both yield the same form, but *naqab* is used in 24.16. See further the discussion of Philo and the Mishnah below.

2. The usage of the LXX is summarized by Herman Beyer, '*Blasphēmeō ktl.*', *TDNT* I, pp. 621f., partially incorrectly. He misreads both Ezek. 35.12 and II Macc. 15.24.

3. H. A. Wolfson, *Philo* II, pp. 121f.

4. *Spec. Laws* 1.53; *Moses* 2.205; Josephus, *Antiq.* 4.207; *Apion* 2.237.

5. *Moses* 2.115; cf. 2.132: cited by Wolfson, *Philo* II, p. 121 n. 59.

6. Lev. 24.11 reads *va-yiqqōb . . . 'et ha-shem va-yᵉqallēl*. The Mishnah renders *qillēl*, 'curse', by another word which means 'curse', *giddēp*, and it uses the participle *ha-mᵉgaddēp* to mean 'the blasphemer'. The Rabbis understood *va-yiqqōb* to be from *naqab*, 'specify', and rendered it by *pirēsh*, 'make explicit'. Thus, in the rabbinic view, to be guilty one must curse God, using his proper Name. The interpretation of the LXX is the same. Wolfson (*Philo* II, p. 121) incorrectly wrote that the Mishnah translated *naqab* 'curse'.

7. This was recognized by Joachim Jeremias, *The Proclamation of Jesus*, ET 1971, p. 11.

8. Günther Bornkamm, *Jesus of Nazareth*, ET 1960, p. 81.

9. E. Schweizer, *Jesus*, p. 14.

10. Joachim Jeremias, *The Proclamation of Jesus*, p. 118 and n. 1.

11. Norman Perrin, *Rediscovering the Teaching of Jesus*, 1967, p. 139.

12. Vincent Taylor, *The Gospel According to St. Mark*, 1959, p. 196.

13. Rudolf Bultmann, *The History of the Synoptic Tradition*, pp. 14–16; on 'ideal' scenes, pp. 39–41.

14. Martin Hengel, *Studies in the Gospel of Mark*, ET 1985, pp. 37f.

15. D. R. Catchpole, 'The Answer of Jesus to Caiaphas', *NTS* 17, 1971, pp. 213–226, quotation from p. 226; *The Trial of Jesus*, 1971, p. 196.

16. I have never been fully persuaded that Luke's account is independent of Mark's, though the separation of the two questions about 'titles' – which presumably Luke would have held together had he been composing freely – does give me pause. Often Luke's

passion narrative is thought to be dependent on a non-Markan source which also lay behind John. This too has attractive features, one of which is that John's account of private interrogation is intrinsically more plausible than the synoptic account of a Sanhedrin trial. Similarly one could argue in favour of the priority of Matthew's version of Jesus' answer to the high priest; why would the evangelist have rejected Mark's 'I am'? I think that the literary problems of the passion narratives deserve the attention they have received, and I leave them aside with some regret.

17. Cf. Taylor, *St. Mark*, pp. 569f.

18. See, for example, Deut. 14.1; in Deut. 32.6f. God is Israel's father.

19. Ethelbert Stauffer, *Jesus and his Story*, ET 1960, pp. 102, 142–159.

20. Ibid., p.102.

21. See the Discussion in Morna D. Hooker, *The Son of Man in Mark*, 1967, pp. 172f. and n. 5.

22. Sanders, *J & J*, ch. 11.

23. Many scholars recognize that the charge about the temple is historically accurate. Taylor, *St. Mark*, p. 566, is representative.

24. Cf. G. D. Kilpatrick, *The Trial of Jesus*, 1953; Catchpole, *Trial*, pp. 131f.; Hooker, *Son of Man*, p. 172.

J. WORSHIP AT HOME AND SYNAGOGUE

1. For the beginnings of the Christian Sunday, see I Cor. 16.2; Acts 20.7; Rev. 1.10.

2. According to Tamid 5.1 the passages said by the priests were the ten commandments; the Shema'; Deut. 11.13–21; Num. 15.37–41.

3. Danby incorrectly has 'enter [the Temple] to eat of their Heave-offering'. Heave offering was not eaten in the temple, but rather by the priests annd their families outside the temple. It was to be eaten in purity, and thus it had to be eaten after sunset (see e.g. Lev. 15.18). For the definition of heave offering, see pp. 290, 299 below. For 'entering their houses' in Berakoth 1.1, see Albeck's note *ad loc.*

4. See *Paul and Palestinian Judaism*, pp. 114, 168 and n. 104, 179, 341, 364.

5. One may compare 'do not kill' with the implied positive commandment, 'help people live'. These are weighed quite differently in law.

6. See the discussion in *Paul and Palestinian Judaism*, pp. 112–114; *Paul, the Law and the Jewish People*, p. 115 n. 8.

7. One might have expected *tôtapôt*, 'bands', which appears in Deut. 6.8, translated by the RSV 'frontlets'; cf. Deut. 11.18; Ex. 13.16.

8. This etymology is accepted in Schürer/Vermes/Millar, *HJP* II, p. 480.

9. A mezuzah parchment found in Qumran cave 8 contains Deut. 10.12–11.21; curiously, not the Shema'. Traditional Jewish practice has been to put into the tefillin the four passages in which the wearing of 'these words' on the hand and forehead is commanded (Ex. 13.1–10; 13.11–16; Deut. 6.4–9; 11.13–21). These passages appear on a tefilla' text in two pieces found in the Judaean desert: *DJD* II, 1961, pp. 80–85, and in one found in Qumran cave 8: *DJD* III, 1962, pp. 149–161. According to J. T. Milik, the maximum choice of passages included in tefillin and mezuzot in Qumran was Ex. 12.43–13.16; Deut. 5.1–6.9 (the ten commandments plus the Shema'); Deut. 10.12–11.21 (*DJD* VI, 1977, p. 38), but there was a lot of variation. It is noteworthy that the passages are strongly convenantal. For a summary of passages which were used, see Schürer/Vermes/Millar, *HJP* II, pp. 479f. and notes. See further K. G. Kuhn, 'Phylakterien aus Höhle 4. von Qumran', *Abhandlungen der Heidelberger Akademie der Wissenschaften*, 1957.

10. The Eighteen Benedictions are the prayers said by many Jews of the rabbinic period in connection with saying the Shema'. They focus on repentance, forgiveness, thanksgiving for the election, and the hope of redemption. On these and other 'statutory prayers', see Joseph Heinemann, *Prayer in the Talmud*, ET 1977.

11. For further passages, see *Paul and Palestinian Judaism*, p. 232 nn. 106, 107.

12. *DJD* VII, 1982, pp. 105–136.

13. See T. Berakot 2.4 on saying the Shema' in the synagogue (anonymous); 3.5 on praying the Eighteen Benedictions 'with the congregation' (whether in a synagogue or not; R. Akiba, second century).

14. Lee Levine, 'The Second Temple Synagogue' in Levine (ed.), *The Synagogue in Late Antiquity*, 1987, pp. 20–22. 'Of Pharisees and Sadducees we know nothing in this regard' – that is, set communal prayers (p. 20).

15. Sean Freyne, however, regards the synagogues in Galilee as being the 'recognised place[s] of prayer for the pious Jew', *Galilee, Jesus and the Gospels*, 1988, p. 43; cf. p. 202.

16. The biblical requirement was that the last lamb was sacrificed at twilight (literally 'between the two evenings', Ex. 29.39; Num. 28.4; translated by the RSV simply 'evening' but literally by the JB). The Mishnah's specification of the eighth and a half hour is, if anything, too early. The day was reckoned as lasting for twelve hours; the length of an hour fluctuated with the seasons. Thus according to the Mishnah the evening sacrifice was slaughtered *c*. 3.30 and offered at 4.30. This leaves at least two hours for the closing activities: recitation, prayers, incense, banking of fire etc.

17. Since the temple tax paid for the daily whole-burnt sacrifices, and since Ex. 30.12,16 connect the tax with 'atonement', the natural implication is that the whole-burnt sacrifices atoned. The LXX, however, translates the Hebrew 'thank offering' as a 'praise offering' (e.g. Lev. 7.12). This left Philo without an offering of thanksgiving (*eucharistia*), which may explain why he interpreted the daily offerings as thank offerings.

18. On prayer in Philo, see Wolfson, *Philo* II, pp. 237–252.

19. See e.g. Fragments 18 and 29–32 line 4 (*DJD* VII, pp. 110, 113). That the prayers are said in the evening, not at night, is clear in 3.6 and Fragments 29–32 line 12 (p. 113).

20. The mishnaic word for 'afternoon' is *minḥah*, the basic meaning of which is 'offering'; Ezra 9.5 refers to the *minḥat ha-'ereb*, the evening offering, and this probably explains the rabbinic use of *minḥah* to mean 'afternoon'.

21. In T. Berakot 3.1–3, however, there are suggestions about how to relate all three daily prayers to the temple timetable.

22. Lawrence Schiffman maintains that prayer twice a day was 'normative' in some circles and that the times were primarily determined by the temple service ('The Dead Sea Scrolls and the Early History of Jewish Liturgy', in Levine (ed.), *The Synagogue in Late Antiquity*, pp. 37–40). Josephus and the Houses dispute (Berakoth 1.3) make me think that some Jews who prayed twice a day did so at the time of the Shema', not the time of the afternoon whole-burnt offering.

23. See e.g. Billerbeck, *Kommentar* I, pp. 397–399, on Matt. 6.5.

24. There is a large recent literature on synagogues, and it is a topic where progress is being made. See, for example, Martin Hengel, 'Proseuche und Synagoge: Jüdische Gemeinde, Gotteshaus und Gottesdienst in der Diaspora und in Palästina', *Tradition und Glaube*, ed. G. Jeremias and others, 1971, pp. 157–184 (also in Gutmann 1975); J. Gutmann (ed.), *The Synagogue: Studies in Origins, Archaeology and Architecture*, 1975; Gutmann (ed.), *Ancient Synagogues: The State of Research*, 1981; Lee I. Levine (ed.), *Ancient Synagogues Revealed*, 1981; Levine, ed., *The Synagogue in Late Antiquity*, 1987; J. Gwyn Griffiths, 'Egypt and the Rise of the Synagogue', *JTS* 38, 1987, pp. 1–15; Lester L.

Grabbe, 'Synagogues in Pre-70 Palestine: a Re-assessment', *JTS* 39, 1988, pp. 401–410.

25. I cannot here debate in detail the issue of the spread of synagogues and their relative prominence in Jewish religious life. I assume that after 70 they took on roles which had belonged to the temple before 70, and also that before 70 the importance and scope of synagogal activities expanded as one moved away from Jerusalem. With regard to the period before 70, I accept the arguments of people whom I regard as judicious maximalists: those who see the synagogues as being very important, but who are careful not to retroject post-70 information into the pre-70 period. For a model essay along these lines, see Levine, 'The Second Temple Synagogue: The Formative Years', in Levine (ed.), *The Synagogue in Late Antiquity*, pp. 7–31. In the same volume, Shaye Cohen argues, on the basis of pagan and Christian references, that the synogogue was not institutionally prominent before the third century, and he proposes that archaeological evidence supports this view ('Pagan and Christian Evidence on the Ancient Synagogue', pp. 159–181, esp. 161). Certainly synagogues became extremely prominent in the third century, and one cannot attribute to the first century grandiose structures like the later synagogue at Sardis. Nevertheless, I think that virtually every Jewish community had a synagogue, that the 'synagogue' or 'house of prayer' was a building, and that most Jews went to a synagogue once a week.

26. The meaning of *tas proseuchas poieisthai pros tēi thalattēi* in *Antiq.* 14.258 has been often debated. It could be translated not 'build places of prayer beside the sea' but 'offer prayers beside the sea'; this has been argued most recently by Cohen ('Pagan and Christian Evidence', p. 165 and n. 20). This is the likeliest translation of the phrase (see below, p. 259), but for the present point this does not matter. The decree refers to sacred rites, festivals and gatherings, and Jews had to hold these *somewhere*; if this clause is not permission to build buildings, it implies that one or more already existed. In the next paragraph the decree of Sardis grants the Jews a 'place' for their prayers (14.260). There is also good evidence that many synagogues in the Diaspora were by the sea. See ch. IV.B below at n. 8.

27. See Lee I. Levine in Levine (ed.), *Ancient Synagogues Revealed*, p. 1 (summarizing subsequent essays); in *The Synagogue in Late Antiquity*, p. 10.

28. The Theodotus inscription has been often published. See, for example, Adolf Deissmann, *Light from the Ancient East*, ET repr. 1965, pp. 439–441. Kee (see n. 29) argues that the inscription comes from the second half of the second century C.E. or even later (pp. 7f.). This is almost impossible, since it must have come from a time (1) when some priestly families were wealthy; (2) when wealthy priests thought it worthwhile to add quarters and bathing facilities for Greek-speaking Jewish pilgrims; (3) when both of these conditions obtained in Jerusalem. To justify a second-century date Kee will need to revise the history of Aelia Capitolina (as the Romans re-named Jerusalem) very substantially. The article by Safrai to which he refers hardly proves the case. Cf. Kee's remarks on the evidence used by Talmudists in writing about the synagogue (pp. 1–3).

29. After the present work was in the press, an article by Howard Kee appeared which is remarkably ill-informed and often incoherent, and which may create a great deal of confusion ('The Transformation of the Synagogue after 70 C.E.', *NTS* 36, 1990, pp. 1–24). Kee argues that there were no first-century synagogues in Palestine. At points he appears to mean only that they were called *proseuchai* (the most common term in Greek), or that they had no distinctive and characteristic architectural features, but the general thrust is that gatherings of Jews were held in houses and that there were no special buildings called 'synagogues'. He first dismisses the discussions of synagogues in Josephus as not referring to Jerusalem (p. 2) – which is perfectly correct, but then he drops them

entirely, as if they do not refer to anything. He dismisses Philo because he usually used the word *proseuchē*, and Kee further claims, completely erroneously, that by *Synagōgē* Philo referred to the community rather than to a meeting place (p. 5). Josephus's discussion of the large synagogue at Tiberias (*Life* 277 – 279) is also dismissed because he called it a *proseuchē*. (p.6) Kee then writes that 'the absence of references to these Jewish meeting places as synagogues in the period before 70 CE is consistent' (p. 7) – thereby omitting Josephus's and Philo's references to synagogues at Caesarea and elsewhere (see below). He redates the Theodotus inscription, thus eliminating epigraphical evidence for pre-70 synagogues (n. 28 above). He further claims that the synagogues at Gamala (Gamla) and Magdala 'turn out to be nothing more than private houses' (p. 8). Alternatively, 'synagogues' were simply 'space set aside in public buildings'. He then points to the lack of 'distinctive architectural features of a place of worship or for study of Torah' (p. 9).

This is so confused that it is difficult to reply, but I shall try. (1) The pre-70 synagogue at Gamla is nothing like a private house. I do not mean that it had a Gothic spire: all that is left is the floor and part of the wall. It is one large room, with rows of benches around the sides. Connected to it, with a window looking into the main room, is a very small room, which might hold eight or ten people at a pinch. Private houses look quite different. Nor is the building an enormous public edifice within which some space was set aside as 'the synagogue'; there is just the one room, with a few rows of seats, and a very small additional room. Similar remarks apply to the synagogue at Matsada. (Magdala is irrelevant because it is not pre-70, but the synagogue there is not like a private house.) (2) The *proseuchē* at Tiberias would hold more than 600 people, and was thus larger than *most* private houses. When there, Josephus prayed 'in the regular way' (see above). (3) The difference in name simply shows that these public buildings, used for worship and instruction, as well as for other meetings, could be designated by more than one word in Greek. In one passage Philo calls the buildings which 'on the seventh day' stood 'open in every city' *didaskaleia*, 'schools' (*Spec. Laws* 2.62). This is not evidence for the existence of three separate institutions; it reveals, rather, that people who wrote in Greek could use various descriptive titles. The most frequent term – *proseuchē*, 'prayer' – points towards worship more clearly than does the less-frequent term 'synagogue', and this does not help Kee's underlying thesis, which is that there were no special buildings for worship and study of the law. (4) The synagogue (called by that term) at Caesarea was used by the Jews on the sabbath for worship or study: at any rate, for 'religious' purposes. That is why the pagans defiled it. Josephus writes that on the sabbath, when the Jews assembled at the synagogue, they found that the place had been 'desecrated' (*memiasmenos*). The building seems to have been used *only* on the sabbath, since the desecration was not discovered until then. It was thus neither a private house nor a public building in common use. (5) Philo explicitly calls *synagōgai* 'sacred places' (*hieroi τοποι*), where people sat in rows (*Every-Good Man* 81). (6) Kee misuses comments by archaeologists in arguing that there were *no* 'distinctive architectural features'. When archaeologists make such remarks, they refer to such features as a niche for a torah-scroll, a particular orientation (either towards Jerusalem or facing east, like the temple), or a particular floor-plan ('basilica'), and the like. They do not mean that the floor plans are like those of private houses, and no one who glances at one will think so – just as no one who actually reads the discussions by Philo and Josephus of study and worship in the synagogue/house of prayer will think that these buildings did not exist. I especially recommend the reading of *Life* 276–303 (public meetings and prayer in the *proseuchē*); *War* 2.285–290 (description of a synagogue in Caesarea; cited by Kee as *Wars* 2.14–4.5); *Spec. Laws* 2.62f.; *Every Good Man* 81.

30. I think that it is quite likely that Josephus had read Philo's *Hypothetica*, though the possibility of their using a common source cannot be ruled out. For the present point, however, I count them as independent witnesses. Josephus's summary of the Mosaic law in *Antiq.* 4 was not substantially derived from Philo, and the non-biblical laws which he attributes to Moses cannot all have been taken from the *Hypothetica*.

31. On these and other passages, see Cohen (n. 25), pp. 165f. I do not share his view that each synagogue served *only* the functions which are mentioned in connection with it.

32. Synagogues democratized worship 'by taking it out of priestly hands' (Levine, *Synagogue in Late Antiquity*, p. 7). A. T. Kraabel states that 'everything we know about Diaspora synagogue organization indicates that it was led by laymen from the outset' (in ibid., p. 54). This overlooks *Hypothetica* 7.12–13. See also the next note.

33. A person who was a 'priest and teacher of wisdom' is mentioned in an inscription found at the Sardis synagogue (fourth century CE). The context is lost, but this is nevertheless a small bit of evidence that priests retained their identities and teaching role. See Hanfmann, 'The Ninth Campaign at Sardis (1966)', *BASOR* 187, October 1967, p. 38.

34. There is a survey of some of the major terms for 'important men' in Josephus by William Buehler, *The Pre-Herodian Civil War and Social Debate*, 1974. The analysis could be improved, and it would be helpful were the survey extended, but it is quite a useful start.

35. Goodman, *State and Society in Roman Galilee*, e.g. pp. 33f.

36. For this list of pharisaic activities, see Shmuel Safrai, 'Oral Tora', *The Literature of the Sages* I, 1987, pp. 35–119, here p. 37. He proposes that 'oral tora' governed all these activities, and he attributes all oral tora to the Pharisees or their successors (p. 35). The earliest layer of rabbinic literature, as Neusner has pointed out, presupposes that most of those to whom its rules apply were small householders, often owners of farms.

37. The questions 'Who ran what?' and 'Who did what?' will be a major theme of my forthcoming *Judaism 63 BCE–CE 66*, and here I make no effort to substantiate this paragraph in detail.

38. I am indebted to Loveday Alexander for this point.

39. Levine is doubtful that synagogue worship before 70 was influenced in detail by the temple service. See *Synagogue in Late Antiquity*, p. 22 and the reference to Heinemann.

40. Cf. J. Weingreen, *From Bible to Mishna*, 1976, ch. 6. These aspects of temple worship were relatively late developments. For prayer, see Isa.56.7; Sirach 50.17; for singing, Sirach 50.18. For prayer at the sacrifices, see also *Apion* 2.196; Philo, *Providence* 2.69. Some scholars trace the development of synagogal worship back to the Babylonian exile, in which case influence could have run from synagogue to temple. The Babylonian origin of synagogues seems to me, however, to be unlikely. For debates over origins, see the literature in n. 24 above.

K. FASTING

1. M. D. Herr, 'Fasting and Fast Days', *Enc. Jud.* 6, cols. 1189–1195, here 1189.

2. It is possible that all these fasts commemorated different events connected with the first destruction of the temple: Herr, col. 1191.

3. Vermes, *Jesus the Jew*, pp. 69–72.

4. Goodman, *State and Society in Roman Galilee*, p. 100.

L. CONFLICT OVER THE LAW

1. As noted more than once, the Essenes were a party with more than one wing. Some lived near the shore of the Dead Sea and are represented by the *Community Rule* (1QS) and numerous other documents. Others lived in towns and villages and are represented by the *Covenant of Damascus* (CD). It seems to me that Josephus' description (*War* 2.119–161) is not a bad effort. Some points correspond to 1QS and some to CD; for some there is no parallel.

2. Jonathan Goldstein, *I Maccabees*, The Anchor Bible 41, 1976, p. 66.

3. Yadin, *The Temple Scroll*, p. 85, citing with approval Shmaryahu Talmon.

4. See Geza Vermes, *Perspective*, pp. 150–154.

5. Elisha Qimron and John Strugnell, 'An Unpublished Halakhic Letter from Qumran'. Qimron has only recently become associated with editing the document.

6. I leave aside here the period of interruption in the settlement at Qumran, the favourable treatment of the Essenes by Herod, the implication of the name 'Essene' for one of the gates in Jerusalem, and other interesting points which show slightly shifting relationships between the Essenes and other Jews.

7. See, for example, Schürer/Vermes/Millar, *HJP* I, pp. 221–224. There are three reasons for taking the leaders of the revolt against Jannaeus to be Pharisees: the Pharisees are said to have been among those who were hostile to Hyrcanus I *and his sons*, one of whom was Jannaeus (*Antiq.* 13.288); on his deathbed Jannaeus counselled Salome Alexandra to avoid his difficulties and to make peace with the Pharisees (*Antiq.* 13.400–404); when the Pharisees gained power under Salome Alexandra, they retaliated against those who had advised Jannaeus to crucify 800 men (*Antiq.* 13.410). These passages, one pointing forwards to hostility against Jannaeus and two backwards, all implicate the Pharisees.

8. Neusner, *From Politics to Piety*, 1973 and elsewhere.

9. That the teachers who got the eagle torn down were Pharisees is inference; Josephus does not say so (see *War* 1.648–650; *Antiq.* 17.149–157). That Pharisees were involved in the insurrection of CE 6 is stated in *Antiq.* 18.4, 23–25.

10. On these, see pp. 224–27.

11. Quoted from Neusner, *Rabbinic Traditions About the Pharisees Before 70*, 1971, II, p. 125.

12. See *Rabb. Trads.* III, pp. 266–268; II, pp. 123, 125; I, p. 320.

M. CONCLUSIONS

1. In a recent article James Dunn attributes to me the view that on the law Jesus was 'very close to the Pharisees'. What I wrote was that 'Jesus and his diciples were obviously not *haberim*', which made them members of the majority (*J & J*, pp. 265f.; cf. 210), and that he was opposed by the 'normally pious', including Pharisees and others (pp. 288f.). I do not think that Jesus was especially close to the Pharisees. I did suggest, however, that Jesus on the whole observed the law, and Dunn's discussion perhaps results from the assumption that only Pharisees were observant – which is against all the evidence. (James D. G. Dunn, 'Pharisees, Sinners, and Jesus', *The Social World of Formative Christianity and Judaism*, ed. Jacob Neusner and others, 1988, pp. 264–289, here 275f.)

2. See section A above.

3. See section A above.

4. David Daube, *The New Testament and Rabbinic Judaism*, 1956, pp. 55–62; W. D. Davies, *The Setting of the Sermon on the Mount*, 1964, pp. 101–103.

5. Cf. Daube (n. 4), pp. 55f.

6. See I.D n. 12 above.

7. Daube, p. 60.

8. See my discussion in *J & J*, pp. 302f. On the Jesus who cried Woe! on the temple, see Josephus, *War* 6.300–309; on the golden eagle, *War* 1.648–650; *Antiq.* 17.149–167.

II Did the Pharisees have Oral Law?

A. INTRODUCTION

1. In recent years this debate has centred around Birger Gerhardsson's *Memory and Manuscript*, 1961. See e.g. Jacob Neusner, *Rabb. Trads.* III, pp. 143–179. This is also part of the focus of Peter Schäfer's 'Das "Dogma" von der mündlichen Torah im rabbinischen Judentum', *Studien zur Geschichte und Theologie des rabbinischen Judentums*, 1978, pp. 153–197. His principal concern was to determine the historical stages of the growth of the 'dogma'.

2. M. D. Herr, 'Oral Law', *Enc. Jud.* 12, cols. 1439–1442, here 1439f.

3. See Ephraim E. Urbach, *The Sages*, ET 1975, pp. 186–188.

4. Shmuel Safrai, 'Oral Tora', *The Literature of the Sages*, Part 1 (CRINT II.3.1), 1987, pp. 35–119.

5. I have collected most of these in section E.2.c of 'Law (Judaism, NT Period)', *Anchor Bible Dictionary*, forthcoming.

6. Safrai, 'Oral Tora', pp. 40f.

7. Safrai, p. 48.

8. See also pp. 36f., especially the list of things which they governed on p. 37, which includes synagogues, courts and the temple.

9. Safrai, p. 54.

10. Safrai, in effect, eliminates rules which are different from pharisaic/rabbinic rules, by saying that they are from 'the earlier halakah': all rules are pharisaic, including those which are anti-pharisaic, which (he proposes) were once taught by some Pharisee or other (see pp. 40f. and n. 30).

11. Herr, col. 1442; Safrai, p. 41; Urbach, p. 293.

12. See Safrai, p. 41.

13. Schäfer, 'Das "Dogma" von der mündlichen Torah', pp. 189–191.

14. Herr, 'Oral Law', col. 1441.

15. Schürer/Vermes/Millar, *HJP* II, pp. 340f. This section is on 'Torah Scholarship', and in the next section we learn that all 'Torah scholars' were Pharisees. Thus Pharisees governed for the whole period 175 BCE to CE 135. These pages are taken over from the original Schürer (ET 1885, II.1, pp. 332f.). Vermes's own view is more nuanced; see *The Dead Sea Scrolls. Qumran in Perspective*, 1977, pp. 119f.

16. Morton Smith, 'Palestinian Judaism in the First Century', repr. in H. A. Fischel (ed.), *Essays in Greco-Roman and Related Talmudic Literature*, 1977, pp. 183–197, esp. 190–197. Others have accepted this view; see Jacob Neusner, e.g. *From Politics to Piety*, 1973; Shaye J. D. Cohen, *Josephus in Galilee and Rome*, 1979; Sanders, *J & J*, pp. 309–317; Martin Goodman, *The Ruling Class of Judaea*, 1987. That Pharisees did not control Galilee is clearly implied in Goodman's earlier work, *State and Society in Roman Galilee*, esp. pp. 78, 93.

17. *Antiq.* 13.296; 13.408–411; *War* 1.110f.

18. This may be implied by *Antiq.* 13.296. *War* 1.110, however, seems to put the rise of the Pharisees later. The legal debates in 4QMMT may be, in part, against the Pharisees, in which case the letter was written at a time when pharisaic practice was in force. Unfortunately, the letter cannot be dated, but the editors suggest that it may come from a fairly early period in the sect's history. See Qimron and Strugnell, 'An Unpublished Halakhic Letter', pp. 400f. (date), p. 402 (some points are against pharisaic interpretation).

19. Hyrcanus' brother, Aristobulus II, opposed both Hyrcanus and the Pharisees; thus Hyrcanus may have allied himself with the Pharisees. See *Antiq.* 13.411–415; *War* 1.113f. One of the accounts of Hyrcanus' attempt to try Herod gives a Pharisee a prominent role: *Antiq.* 14.168–176.

20. After the death of Salome Alexandra, her two sons, Hyrcanus and Aristobulus, contested for leadership. Within four years of the Queen's death, Pompey conquered Jerusalem (63 BCE). Antipater became Hyrcanus's advisor, and soon his sons, including Herod, came to the fore.

21. The Pharisees refused Herod's demand for a loyalty oath (*Antiq.* 17.42; cf. 15.370f.), and some of them were convicted of participating in a conspiracy against him (*Antiq.* 17.43f.). I use 'nuisance value' of them because of *Antiq.* 13.288: 'So great is their influence with the masses that even when they speak against a king or high priest, they immediately gain credence.' It is recognized on all hands that this description does not belong where Josephus puts it, the reign of Hyrcanus I, since he was both high priest and king; 'high priest *or* king' is anachronistic. The statement probably comes from Nicolaus of Damascus' history, in which case it was Nicolaus' retrojection of the situation as he knew it in the time of Herod (see e.g. Daniel Schwartz, 'Josephus and Nicolaus on the Pharisees', *JSJ* 14, 1983, pp. 157–171). Since neither the Pharisees nor anyone else posed much of a threat to Herod, and the populace did not revolt against him, Nicolaus is probably here only grumbling that the Pharisees could make a nuisance of themselves.

22. Safrai, p. 37; see the list of activities above, I.J. at n. 36.

23. Cf also *Antiq.* 13.288 (n. 21 above); 13.298; 18.15.

24. For examples, see *J & J*, pp. 312–317. This point lies at the heart of Smith's original observation: 'the influence of the Pharisees with the people, which Josephus reports, is not demonstrated by the history he records' ('Palestinian Judaism', p. 193).

25. Schürer/Vermes/Millar, *HJP* II, p. 340.

26. E.g. *Antiq.* 17.41–45; see note 21 above.

27. We recall that the community of the *Covenant of Damascus* brought sacrifices.

28. See Safrai, p. 54.

29. 11QTemple appears to allow fourth-generation resident aliens to enter the outer court (the text requires some restoration). See Yadin's discussion of 11QTemple 40.6, *The Temple Scroll* II, p. 170; I, pp. 247f., 251.

30. On the date of 11QTemple, see Yadin, *Temple Scroll* I, pp. 386–390. The provisions for women and long-standing resident aliens in the Temple Scroll have some exegetical basis. See Yadin's references, II, p. 170. These passages do not, however, provide the basis for a Court of the Gentiles open to all comers.

31. See above, I.B.

32. See above pp. 99f. While I cannot accept the proposal of Urbach and others that Josephus's statement does not relate to the biblical text, but rather contrasts 'oral' and 'written' interpretations, there is no reason to doubt that the Sadducees wrote down their interpretations and opinions (thus the rabbinic reference to the 'Book of Decrees'; for

references, see n. 11 above). It seems to me quite possible that priests taught and were taught from handbooks which conflated the biblical laws and arranged them to accord with current interpretation. I wonder, in short, if Josephus's classification of the law in *Antiq.* 4.199–301 is entirely original. Note that Moses consigned his books 'to the priests' (*Antiq.* 4.304; Deut. 31.9), and it was primarily priests who had to know the law.

33. See A. I. Baumgarten, 'The Pharisaic *Paradosis*', *Harvard Theological Review* 80, 1987, pp. 63–77.

34. *War* 2.165; *Antiq.* 18.16; Mark 2.18 and parrs.; Acts 23.8.

B. PHARISAIC TRADITIONS AND ORAL LAW

1. Wilhelm Bacher, *Tradition und Tradenten in den Schulen Palästinas und Babyloniens*, 1914, p. 41; Shäfer, 'Das "Dogma" von der mündlichen Torah'.

2. Urbach, *The Sages*, pp. 292f.

3. W. D. Davies, *Jewish and Christian Studies*, 1984, p. 8 = 'Law in First Century Judaism', *IDB*, 1962, p. 91.

4. Mayer I. Gruber has noted that this terminological problem is well known. See his interesting essay, 'The Mishnah as Oral Torah: A Reconsideration', *JSJ* 15, 1984, pp. 112–122. The paper was read at the SBL in 1979.

5. Ellis Rivkin, *What Crucified Jesus?*, 1984, pp. 86–87.

6. Rivkin, *A Hidden Revolution*, 1968, e.g. p. 183.

7. E.g. 'From Scripture to Mishnah. The Origins of Tractate Niddah', *JJS* 29, 1978, pp. 135–148, here 147; *Judaism: The Evidence of the Mishnah*, 1981, p. xiv.

8. 'Jacob Neusner's Mishnah', *Midstream*, May 1984, pp. 27–28.

9. Neusner, *Torah. From Scroll to Symbol in Formative Judaism*, 1985, pp. 144–145.

10. In *Formative Judaism: Religious, Historical and Literary Studies*, third series, *Torah, Pharisees, and Rabbis*, essays I and III prefigure *Torah*. The contradictory quotations are from essay II, pp. 15, 27.

11. Neusner, *The Mishnah before 70*, 1987, pp. 132–139.

12. Neusner, *The Oral Torah*, 1986, pp. viii–ix, 64f. He calls these various possibilities 'two positions', but enumerates them as 'first', 'second' and 'third', with two further alternatives.

13. Neusner, *Scriptures of the Oral Torah*, 1987, p. 1.

14. J. L. Houlden, in *TLS* April 5, 1985, p. 391.

15. *Judaism in the beginning of Christianity*, 1984, pp. 95f.

16. *Messiah in Context*, 1984, pp. 123, 132; cf. *Torah*, pp. 7f., 108. For academic discussion, see Moshe David Herr, 'Mekhilta of R. Ishmael', *Enc. Jud.* 11, cols. 1267–1269; for ARN see Judah Goldin, 'Avot de-Rabbi Nathan', *Enc. Jud.* 3, cols 984f. In *Messiah* and *Torah*, Neusner relied on articles by Herr (whose name he consistently misspelled) for the dates of the midrashim, but he misconstrued the articles. Herr proposed the end of the fourth century as the date of the final redaction of the Mekilta; Neusner took it as the date of the entire contents, which is quite a different matter.

17. Urbach, *The Sages*, p. 290.

18. *Torah*, pp. 24f.

19. Perhaps in part by typographical error: his reference (p. 25) to Parah 11.4,11 is probably a mistake for Parah 11.4[–6; Tohoroth 4.7],11.

C. RABBINIC PASSAGES

1. There was considerable debate as to whether or not the biblical purity laws applied to Gentiles. This is a sub-topic of the general question, How much of the Mosaic law, if any, applies to Gentiles?

2. That is, it is implied by Deut. 6.8. Gruber takes this to be a non-biblical rule ('The Mishnah as Oral Torah', p. 117).

3. Cf. Sanhedrin 11.2, 'the torah goes forth'; above, p. 114.

4. Page 88.

5. On handwashing and scripture, see III.E§9.e.

6. The rabbinic formula is 'halakah to Moses by (or from) Sinai', which Bacher explained as short for 'halakah [given] to Moses by [God on] Sinai': *Tradition und Tradenten*, p. 33 n. 2.

7. The Pharisees who are listed in sets of two in Aboth 1.4–12.

8. George Foot Moore, *Judaism in the First Centuries of the Christian Era*, 1927, vol. I, p. 256. Similarly Schäfer, 'Das "Dogma" von der mündlichen Torah', pp. 161f.

9. See II.A at n. 33.

10. I am dependent on the passages collected by Bacher, 'Satzung vom Sinai. Halakhah Le-Moshe MiSinai', *Studies in Jewish Literature*, ed. David Philipson and others, 1913, pp. 56–70; *Tradition und Tradenten*, pp. 33–46.

D. CONCLUSIONS AND SUMMARY

1. So F. H. Colson *Philo*, vol. 8 (LCL), p. 435.

2. See above, I.D at n. 12.

III Did the Pharisees Eat Ordinary Food in Purity?

A. INTRODUCTION

1. For scholars from Finkelstein to Neusner, see below, C. State of the Question. Numerous scholars accept the view of those just named, and I make no effort to catalogue them. For my earlier discussions, see *Paul and Palestinian Judaism*, pp. 154–155; *J & J*, pp. 187–188.

2. Gedalyahu Alon, 'The Bounds of the Laws of Levitical Cleanness' (C. n. 3 below), p. 222 n. 85.

3. See the masterly study by A. Büchler, *Studies in Sin and Atonement in the Rabbinic Literature of the First Century*, 1939 (repr. 1967), which deals also with biblical usage.

B. BIBLICAL PURITY LAWS

1. The Hebrew day started at sunset. Semen-impurity requires bathing and the setting of the sun. Thus, to be pure after intercourse or other ejaculation, one must bathe and wait for the next sunset.

2. On heave offering, see IV.D§2, §6.

3. According to Josephus (*Antiq.* 20.181, 206f.), the ordinary priests starved when the tithes were stolen by servants of a chief priest. See above, I.C. Perhaps we should take the stories as indicating that the priests did not generally 'wink' at the rules. The story about

two priests in Rome who lived on figs and nuts (*Life* 14) points in the same direction.

4. See above, p. 10.

5. On conflation of the biblical tithing laws, see I.F.

6. I use 'first fruits' generically to refer to any of the numerous 'firsts' which were given to the priesthood – the first of the grain, of the meal after grinding, of the dough, of sheeps' wool, of animals, and so on (for a list see e.g. Neh. 10.35–37 [Heb. 10.36–38]). In Num. 18, 'first fruits', both *re'shît* and *bikkûrîm*, refer to produce (18.12f.), as distinct from the 'firstlings' or 'first-born', *bekôrôt*, of animals (18.15,17). See more fully below, IV.D, n. 19.

7. See below, pp. 194f. The passage says that it is not lawful to touch first fruits 'with their hands', and some people infer from this that handwashing was already being practised. That seems not to be the point. The emphasis lies on people imparting impurity by touch, and touching is usually done with the hands.

8. There is a very valuable discussion of the use of 'purity' in Old Testament scholarship to mean 'what is external and non-ethical' in Mary Douglas, *Purity and Danger*, 1966, pp. 25–27.

9. The descriptions in Lev. 13 make it clear that the biblical 'leprosy' is not limited to what is now considered clinical leprosy.

10. Deut. 23.12–14 [Heb. vv. 13–15] implies that excrement is impure: it must be kept outside the 'camp', which is 'holy', and also kept away from God's sight. According to Josephus, the Essenes kept that rule, and also washed after defecation, which shows that they regarded it as an impurity (*War* 2.148f.). 1QS 7.15 provides that a person who 'draw[s] out his left hand to gesticulate with it shall do penance for ten days'. It may be that the left hand was used after defecating. Sifra, however, takes Lev. 5.3 to refer forward: 'human impurity' refers to corpse-impurity; the word 'impurity' is repeated in order to include zavs, menstruants and women after childbirth (Sifra Vayyiqra'd'Hobah pereq 12.8 (to Lev. 5.3). Some modern commentators understand the passage to refer to the impurities named in Lev. 11–15 (e.g. R. K. Harrison, *Leviticus*, 1980, p. 69). See further I.B at n. 3 above.

11. Throughout this discussion of biblical laws, I shall translate *raḥats* 'bathe', though it may also mean 'wash'. In the first century it was taken to mean 'immerse'.

12. The evidence on whether or not a zav – a man with spermatorrhoea – was excluded from the community in the first century is mixed. See further below, pp. 158f.

13. The laws of exclusion in Num. 5.2–3 are discussed in C.

14. This large statement can be justified only by a full study. In *Judaism 63 BCE–CE 66: Practice and Belief*, forthcoming, I argue that first-century practice can best be determined by seeking instances in which Leviticus, Nehemiah, and I and II Chronicles – or any one of them – is supported by Josephus, Philo or another first-century source, including the earliest layer of rabbinic literature. In case of conflict between, say, Leviticus, Nehemiah and Josephus on the one hand, and Deuteronomy and the Mishnah on the other, it is probable that standard practice followed the former. An example of this sort of comparison can be seen on pp. 157–62 below, where I discuss which impure people were expelled from inhabited areas.

15. This does not complete the critical assessment of the exclusions from civil life required by Num. 5.2–3; see further 157–62 below. It may be noted here, however, that some of the laws governing purity, the sacrifices and the temple were, in the first century, dead letters. I shall not necessarily mention all of them, but one, Lev. 17.3–5, is discussed below.

16. There is a large literature on the principles behind the biblical purity laws, of which the single most interesting work is Mary Douglas's *Purity and Danger*, 1966. In ch. 3 she proposed that what is *whole* is pure, and that thus things are pure which fit perfectly into a definable category. The purity laws rule out what is anomalous or ambiguous. Holiness was

thus extended: it 'was given a physical expression in every encounter with the animal kingdom and at every meal' (p. 57). This is a very helpful explanation, and it has been widely accepted, in whole or in part. I think that it is correct to say, however, that scholars now do not think that Douglas fully explained the biblical purity laws. This is an overall impression gained from attending a lengthy session on The Pig at the 1988 meeting of the Society of Biblical Literature and the American Academy of Religion. I shall offer partial explanations of some of the purity laws below, §4, and in IV.C.

17. See n. 15 on the treatment in this essay of laws which were dead letters.

18. In the story of Judith, the heroine bathes every morning and then prays (Judith 12.7f.). According to T. Yadaim 2.20, however, the Pharisees do not bathe before morning prayers, unlike 'the morning bathers'. T. Berakot 2.12f. discusses the immersion of a zav before saying the Shemaʿ. This implies that ordinarily people did not immerse each morning.

C. SECONDARY LITERATURE: THE STATE OF THE QUESTION

1. Louis Finkelstein, *The Pharisees* I, p. 77.

2. Joachim Jeremias, *Jerusalem in the Time of Jesus*, ET 1969, pp. 251,266 (=*Jerusalem zur Zeit Jesu*, 1962, with author's revisions to 1967).

3. Gedalyahu Alon, 'The Bounds of Levitical Cleanness', *Jews, Judaism and the Classical World*, ET 1977, pp. 209–211, 215 (='Tehuman shel Halakot Taharah', *Mehqarim be-Toldot Yisra'el* I, 1967, pp. 160–161, 164).

4. Schürer/Vermes/Millar, *HJP* II, §26. Pages 398–400, on the complete separation of the Pharisees from the ʿamme ha-ʾarets, and the supposed pharisaic equation of themselves and 'the true community of Israel', are essentially taken over from the old Schürer (see II.2, ET 1885, pp. 19–25).

5. Ellis Rivkin, 'Defining the Pharisees: the Tannaitic Sources', *HUCA* 40–41, 1969–70, pp. 205–249. See also *A Hidden Revolution*, 1978.

6. H. Strack and P. Billerbeck, *Kommentar zum Neuen Testament aus Talmud und Midrasch*, 4 vols, 1924 and subsequent years, IV.1, pp. 334–339.

7. We shall discuss tithes briefly in section F below; see also I.F above.

8. Rivkin did not try to date the passages containing the word *pᵉrûshîm*, but an attempt to do so confirms his results.

9. See A. n. 1.

10. See p. 202, on Demai 2.3 and 6.6.

11. *Enc. Jud.* 12, cols. 1141–1148, quotation from 1145, italics mine.

12. This is not to say that all Talmudists have drawn the same conclusions as Ta-Shma. Finkelstein (*The Pharisees* I, pp. 26–28; 74–77), for example, argued that only Jerusalemites kept the laws of purity, and that the Pharisees wanted to apply purity to food all the way back to the farmer, but he did not say in detail what this meant, nor did he discuss the implications for the menstruant.

13. See Adolphe Neubauer, *La Géographie du Talmud*, Paris 1868, pp. 317, 413. As a third possible 'Gallia', Neubauer mentions an island near Numidia.

14. So also Neubauer, ibid., p. 306 n. 3.

15. As Alon was perfectly aware. The existence of contrary texts led him to modest conclusions (see below).

16. Alon, 'Halakot Taharah', p. 172; see p. 160 below.

17. Societies can be organized so as to provide separate housing for women all the time because of menstruation, or for the period of menstruation, and anthropologists know of

such customs. Among the Huli, a people of highland Papua New Guinea, men and women do not live together because of the danger of menstrual blood, and it is considered dangerous for a man if a woman steps over his legs, food or weapons. Some Nigerian tribes also separate menstruants physically. With regard to Jewish Palestine, the argument is that such arrangements would have left some sign in the sources. Either we would read of a special room, a lean-to against each house, or separate encampments; and there would have to be collateral laws: a non-menstruant may not step over the threshold . . . and the like.

18. Alon, 'Levitical Cleanness', p. 228; 'Halakot Taharah', p. 172; Alon cites an article by Epstein which I have not seen.

19. Jacob Neusner, *A History of the Mishnaic Law of Women*, 5 vols., 1979–80, V, p. 189; cf. *Rabb. Trads.* III, p. 295.

20. Some may suppose that the housework was not a problem, since people lived in extended families, and the non-menstruant women could do the work. This is not likely: (1) women who live together often menstruate at the same time; (2) there is no evidence that people lived in extended families. Daughters married near puberty. Rabbinic law does not discuss houses run by grandmothers and the like. On the non-evidence for households of extended families, see Goodman, *State and Society*, p. 36.

21. See the very helpful chart in Yadin, *Temple Scroll* I, pp. 282–285, and the discussion, pp. 285–307.

22. Yadin, *Temple Scroll* I, p. 307.

23. Yadin, *Temple Scroll* I, pp. 294–304.

24. A. Büchler, *Der galiläische 'Am-Ha'ares des zweiten Jahrhunderts*, 1906; repr. 1968.

25. 'Levitical Cleanness', p. 228; Heb., p. 172.

26. This comment applies to several of Alon's essays. In 'Association with Gentiles' I discuss this aspect of his work more fully.

27. Ch. IV in this volume discusses the issues of this paragraph, including the positive desire for purity.

D. THE PHARISEES AND PRIESTLY FOOD LAWS ACCORDING TO NEUSNER

1. J. N. Epstein, *Mevo'ot le-Sifrut ha-Tanna'im* (*Introductions to Tannaitic Literature*), 1957, p. 53.

2. Epstein, ibid., p. 44.

3. Ibid., p. 56. The reference to 'forty years before the destruction of the temple' comes from Sanhedrin 41a.

4. Ibid. p. 62.

5. Ibid. p. 59; *Enc. Jud.* 10, col. 279.

6. For other examples of Epstein's work, see Baruch M. Bokser, 'The Achievement of Jacob N. Epstein', *The Modern Study of the Mishnah*, ed. Jacob Neusner, 1973, pp. 13–55.

7. *Judaism*, p. 151.

8. On the question of whether or not the earliest layer of the Mishnah is pharisaic, according to Neusner's current view, see p. 133 above.

9. Neusner, *Reading and Believing*, 1986. See my review in *Journal of Religion* 68, 1988, pp. 333–336.

10. This formula, 'they did not dispute about. . . ; about what did they dispute?', is quite common in the discussions of the Houses' traditions, especially in the Tosefta.

11. Epstein, *Introductions*, e.g. p. 60.

12. So both Danby and Albeck, ad loc.

13. See e.g. Tebul Yom 2.5//T. Tev. Y. 2.2; Oholoth 2.1//T. Ahil. 3.4; Oholoth 15.9//T. Ahil. 15.9.

14. E.g. Kelim 20.6//T. Kel. B. M. 11.8. Cf. Neusner, *Rabb. Trads.* II, p. 86.

15. Work on festival days is discussed in I.B above.

16. Neusner's *History of the Mishnaic Law* is full of useful observations about what is presupposed. Thus he wrote, 'Let us now turn to the presuppositions of the Houses and Yavneans, those points agreed upon by all parties, or, of still greater probative value, taken for granted by all parties without the need of articulate agreement at all' (*A History of the Mishnaic Law of Purities* V, p. 222. In searching for the 'philosophy' of the Mishnah, he proposed that a form of Platonism was presupposed though completely unarticulated. In ch. V in this volume, I shall argue that the philosophy is wrongly ascribed to the Mishnah. The direct presuppositions of legal debates, however, can be proved beyond dispute. The entire topic of what the Pharisees and Rabbis presupposed has been clouded by his subsequent claim that he finds no presuppositions at all, but interprets only what lies on the surface. See e.g. 'The Theological Enemies of Religious Studies. Theology and Secularism in the Trivialization and Personalization of Religion in the West', *Religion* 18, 1988, pp. 21–35, here 26f.; below, pp. 318f.

17. A few other examples: T. Terumot 3.14; Mikwaoth 1.4–5; Kelim 14.2; Makhshirin 5.9.

18. Alon, 'Levitical Cleanness', p. 205.

19. *Rabb. Trads.* II, p. 87.

20. *Rabb. Trads.* III, p. 292 (listed as T. Terumot 3.2).

21. 'Women cannot have sat on the same chairs or beds or prepared meals in the way in which they did when they were not menstruating', *Women* V, p. 189; cf. *Rabb. Trads.* III, p. 295.

22. *Purities* XXII, p. 90.

23. Ibid., p. 87.

24. Ibid., p. 77.

25. Ibid., p. 78.

26. Ibid., pp. 75f.

27. Neusner, *Rabb. Trads.* III, p. 297.

28. *Rabb. Trads.* III, p. 304.

29. Hagigah 2.7 (which puts pharisaic purity below priestly); T. Shabbat 1.15; T. Demai 2.12//Bekorot 30b.

30. *Rabb. Trads.* III, p. 288. What is 'less certain' is that the tithing rules were different from the rest of society, which is required for the definition of a 'sect'. On tithes, however, we may be sure that the Pharisees disagreed with the aristocratic priesthood. See I.F. above.

31. E.g. *Rabb. Trads.* I, p. 64; cf. III, p. 307.

32. So Neusner, *Rabb. Trads.* III, p. 82, following Jastrow.

33. *Rabb. Trads.* III, p. 290.

34. By biblical law, misplanting makes the food 'sanctified', holy; see below, §4.b.

35. *Appointed Times* V, p. 199; cf. pp. 154, 161.

36. Betzah joins a small number of basically pre-70 tractates: Yebamoth from the division Nashim (Women); Oholoth, Niddah, Zabim, Kelim, Mikwaoth and Parah from Tohoroth (Purities); none from either Qodashim (Holy Things) of Nezikin (Damages: civil and criminal law). (I here leave aside Zeraim (Agriculture), which has been analysed

by Neusner's students, in order to concentrate on his own work.) On the division Purities, see *Purities* XXII, pp. 88–94; 132–136. The conclusions are found also in *The Mishnah Before 70*, 1987. For Yebamoth, see *Women* V. pp. 187f.; for Betzah, see *Appointed Times* V, pp. 199–200. It should be emphasized that the selection of these tractates is based on analysis of when the 'generative ideas' and basic structures of the tractates arose. Neusner does not think that only they contain pre-70 materials, not that all the material in them is pre-70. On the contrary, many were greatly developed later.

37. *Rabb. Trads.* III, p. 288.

38. Neusner actually says 'householders' (*Judaism*, p. 235; cf. p. 166), but that they were householders who for the most part owned and farmed land is clear.

E. PHARISAIC PURITY DEBATES

1. E.g. Neusner, *From Politics to Piety*, p. 83.

2. In Num. 19 *kʰli* means 'vessel', since the issue is whether or not it is open. Often, however, especially in rabbinic discussion, the word means 'utensil'.

3. For the Pharisees, this was true of corpse-impurity, but not of other impurities. Pure water, they held, was contagious (§8, on immersion pools). In the Bible neither purity nor impurity travels, though some impurities can be conveyed by touching (Lev. 15). Lev. 6.18, 27 (Heb. 6.11, 20) is sometimes taken to say that whoever touches the cereal offering or sin offering *becomes* holy: so the RSV at 6.18. But the meaning is that everything which touches the offering is 'sanctified' in the sense of 'forfeited to the temple'.

4. The Holy of Holies was always distinguished from the rest of the temple. 'Concentric circles' is not accurate, since the temple walls were oblong. The term, however, conveys the right idea.

5. That Jerusalem was holier than the rest of the country is clear, for example, in *Antiq.* 12.146 ('Nor shall anyone bring into the city . . .'), and in the story of the Roman standards which Pilate brought in (*War* 2.169–174).

6. Throughout this passage, 'lay Pharisees' are meant. Some, of course, were priests.

7. Lev. 21.5: priests 'shall not shave off the edges of their beards'. It would not surprise me if some priests, especially the aristocrats, desiring to look like other aristocrats (who, in turn, looked like Julius Caesar or Augustus: clean-shaven, short haircut), shaved. The Bible does not require priests to have beards, only not to cut the edges, and some may have seized upon this exegetical possibility.

8. For a discussion about the flesh of Hallowed Things, see Tebul Yom 2.5, attributed to the Houses in T. Tevul Yom 2.2.

9. How offerings and tithes reached individual priests and Levites is a difficult question. See I.F, n. 9 and further G. Alon, 'On Philo's Halakha', *Jews, Judaism and the Classical World*, pp. 89–137. The passage in Judith seems to presuppose that priests collected the first fruits. That at least sometimes priests and Levites collected is proved by Josephus, *Life* 63; T. Peah 4.3.

10. In an interesting article Solomon Spiro proposed that the haverim were a lay group who kept special purity laws precisely so that they could be the purveyors of the priests' food: 'Who was the *Haber*? A New Approach to an Ancient Institution', *JSJ* 11, 1980, pp. 186–216.

11. The fullest explanation of heave offering and its relationship to other offerings will be found in IV.D.

12. See Bikkurim 2.1–5; Terumoth 4.3.

13. The Bible uses both 'Most Holy Things', eaten by the priests in the temple (Lev. 6.16f.; Num. 18.9), and also 'Holy Things', referring to any of the gifts and offerings which the priests ate, whether in the temple or at home with their families (Lev. 22.1–16). The Rabbis sometimes distinguished the 'Most Holy Things' (things eaten in the temple, plus the whole-burnt offering) from the 'Minor Holy Things' (eaten by priests and families outside the temple, or by laypeople, after having been brought to the temple: peace offerings, Passover lamb, etc.): see Zebahim 5.4–8; 10.6 (5.5 lists Most Holy Things, though the term is lacking). They did not, however, always distinguish holy food by these terms. In Niddah 10.6–7 'Holy Things' refers to 'Most Holy', and the 'Minor Holy Things' are listed rather than designated by this term.

14. The present passages do not reveal the connection between handwashing and gnat-impurity, but it will become clear in §9 below.

15. Neusner (*Rabb. Trads.* II, p. 71) does not discuss the date of the distinction which is presupposed in Kilaim 8.5. If he discusses the question in *History of Mishnaic Law*, I have not found it. On these minima as 'riders' to the biblical law, see above, pp. 116, 124, 127.

16. Alon, 'The Bounds of the Laws of Levitical Cleanness', p. 218.

17. Rivkin, 'Defining the Pharisees'.

18. Neusner, *Rabb. Trads.* I, pp. 63f.

19. With the meaning 'Most Holy Things': see note 13 above.

20. *Rabb. Trads.* I, p. 64.

21. Epstein, *Introductions*, p. 64.

22. Above, p. 143.

23. Some people say that Jewish tradition requires sexual abstinence during the days of bleeding, however many, and then seven more days for purification before sexual relations can be resumed. Thus e.g. Léonie Archer, 'The Role of Jewish Women in the Religion, Ritual and Cult of Graeco-Roman Palestine', *Images of Women in Antiquity*, 1983, pp. 273–87, here 281–283. This is true neither of the Bible nor of early rabbinic literature. Only during the Amoraic period in Babylonia does one encounter the expectation of seven days free of menstrual blood before intercourse can be resumed (Niddah 66a; Shabbat 13b).

24. In rabbinic parlance, a woman with a flow of blood within the eleven-day period 'watches' or 'guards' 'day against day'; that is, she waits for a second occurrence of blood, tests for it the next day, and in the meantime does not have intercourse: Pesahim 8.5; Horayoth 1.3; Niddah 4.7; Zabim 1.1. In the last passage the phrase is attribute to the Shammaites.

25. My translation, which departs from Danby at two points. Danby has 'if she suffered a flux' for 'if she saw blood'. 'Flux', however, usually refers to the discharge of a zav or zavah, to mean an emission which is neither semen nor menstruation. In this passage the Hebrew literally is 'the woman who sees', that is, 'in the case of a woman who sees blood'; and the problem is knowing what the blood signifies. The second point is that for 'within the eleven day period' Danby has 'during the eleventh day'. This case, however, must be distinguished from 10.8a,b, which deal with blood *on* the eleventh day.

26. Neusner (*Rabb. Trads.* II, pp. 306f.) confused this issue with that of blood on the day or two days after the end of the seven-day menstrual period. Cf. the discussion in Niddah 72a, where the English translation in the Soncino Talmud largely supports my interpretation against both Danby and Neusner. See also the notes by Albeck in his edition of the Mishnah, which in part support the view taken here.

27. The stam of T. Zavim 1.9 states that a zav may not have intercourse, but it does not give the reason.

28. It is premature to try to count them, and in any case not all the known pools were in use at the same time. About 50 have been found in West Jerusalem and about 20 in Jericho. There are numerous pools near the entrance to the temple and more in the residential area below and southwest of the temple mount. I count a total of 7 on Matsada (2 built by its last defenders), and there are several in Sepphoris. These are, as far as I know, the largest concentrations thus far discovered. Several more place names will appear below, and Hanan Eshel has kindly supplied me with references to pools at five different locations which are not cited here at all. The estimate of 50 in West Jerusalem I owe to Ronny Reich. The number at Jericho is from Ehud Netzer, 'Ancient Ritual Baths (*Miqvaot*) in Jericho', *The Jerusalem Cathedra* 2, ed. Lee I. Levine, 1982, pp. 106–119, here p. 106.

29. For examples of each type, see Ronny Reich, 'A *Miqweh* at 'Isawiya near Jerusalem', *IEJ* 34, 1984, pp. 220–223 and Plate 28.

30. This is the rabbinic term. The Dead Sea Sect may well have had its own word (cf. *mishpatim* where the Rabbis would use halakot), but, as we shall see, miqveh was derived from the Bible, and I shall use it throughout.

31. For the range 250–1,000 litres, see David Kotlar, 'Mikveh', *Enc. Jud.* 11, cols. 1534–1544, here 1536; in choosing 500 litres as an appropriate round number, I follow Netzer, 'Ritual Baths in Jericho', p. 107. Nahman Avigad chose 750 litres, which shows how uncertain the quantity is (*Discovering Jerusalem*, ET 1983, p. 139).

32. Bryant G. Wood, 'To Dip or Sprinkle? The Qumran Cisterns in Perspective', *BASOR* 256, 1984, pp. 45–61. See further n. 36 below.

33. On this history, and for solid arguments that many Qumran pools were immersion pools, see Wood, 'To Dip or Sprinkle?'. He shows that Qumran had enough water, over and above the amount needed for the necessities of life, to use the pools for immersion.

34. Yigael Yadin, 'The excavation at Masada – 1963/64, Preliminary Report', *IEJ* 15, 1965, pp. 55f.

35. I leave aside public pools, aquaducts and the like.

36. Ehud Netzer, *Greater Herodium. Qedem* 13, 1981, p. 47. If full, this miqveh would hold 14.4 cubic metres of water, 14,400 litres; 3,170 Imperial gallons; 3,800 US.

37. So Netzer, 'Ritual Baths in Jericho', pp. 108, 117.

38. For one heated pool, see (5) below. Eric Meyers informs me that one miqveh at Meiron has a warmer and that this also may be true of one at Jericho.

39. Reich remarks that 'not a single public hot bath-house (excluding the palatial ones) dating to the Second Temple Period has been found to date in any contemporary Jewish settlement' ('The Hot Bath-House (balneum), the Miqweh and the Jewish Community in the Second Temple Period', *JJS* 39, 1988, pp. 102–107, here p. 103). There are, however, second-century rabbinic references to bathhouses, and I therefore think it likely that a few such facilities existed in the first century (see Goodman, *State and Society*, pp. 44f., 61, 83f.).

40. Netzer, 'Ritual Baths in Jericho', pp. 113f.

41. The pool at the Herodium was large enough for small boats and had in its centre a 'folly' or pavilion for entertainment. On Herod's swimming and recreational pools, see Netzer, *Herodium*, pp. 10–30, summary pp. 28–30, with references to literature on the other sites.

42. See Reich, 'Mishnah Sheqalim 8:2 and the Archaeological Evidence', *Jerusalem in the Second Temple Period*, ed. A. Oppenheimer and others, 1980, pp. 225–256 (Hebrew); 'A *Miqweh* at 'Isawiya'; 'Four Notes on Jerusalem', *IEJ* 37, 1987, pp. 158–167, here p. 161.

43. Netzer, 'Ritual Baths in Jericho', p. 108.

44. There are also twin or paired miqva'ot, two stepped pools side-by-side. In this simplified classification, I consider them as two miqva'ot without companion pools.

45. Pictures of the miqveh at Sepphoris can be conveniently seen in *BA* 49.1, March 1986, p. 17.

46. On whether or not 'top up' is correct, see below.

47. I have taken the litre equivalents from Eliezer Sternberg and Haim Hermann Cohn, 'Weights and Measures', *Enc. Jud.* 16, cols. 376–392, here cols. 380, 387f.

48. We do not know just how or when the use of pools originated. Were it not for Qumran, one might argue that the entire development was pharisaic, since the Pharisees influenced some of the Hasmoneans, and the earliest evidence is Hasmonean. The Qumran sectarians, however, had the same general idea, and one hesitates to say that the Essenes derived the notion of immersion pools from the Pharisees. Miqva'ot were used at Qumran over a long period: one miqveh, for example, was damaged by an earthquake and not repaired, others being used instead. We do not know how to date the earliest Qumran miqveh. If, however, the Essene view was independent of the Pharisees, as seems probable, then the general idea of immersion pools may well have been pre-pharisaic. Too little is known of pre-Hasmonean practice to allow us to exclude the use of pools in the Greek period.

49. Reich, 'The Hot Bath-House, the Miqweh and the Jewish Community', p. 106.

50. Netzer, *Herodium*, p. 49.

51. See David B. Small, 'Late Hellenistic Baths in Palestine', *BASOR* 266, 1987, pp. 59–74, here pp. 65–68. Note also the sequence, dressing rooms-frigidarium-tepidarium-caldarium, in a bath complex at En-Gedi built between CE 76 and 135: B. Mazar and I. Dunayevsky, 'En-Gedi. Fourth and Fifth Seasons of Excavations Preliminary Report', *IEJ* 17, 1967, pp. 133–143, here p. 143. (This bath was built on top of an earlier miqveh.)

52. See e.g. Netzer, *Herodium*, p. 43.

53. The existence of pools in this area was noted by Benjamin Mazar, 'Herodian Jerusalem in the Light of the Excavations South and South-West of the Temple Mount', *IEJ* 28, 1978, pp. 230–237, here p. 236.

54. Reich, 'Two Possible *Miqva'ot* on the Temple Mount', *IEJ* 39, 1989, pp. 63–65. The line of the Hasmonean temple wall is not certain.

55. Netzer, 'Ritual Baths in Jericho', p. 114.

56. Unfortunately I did not have the opportunity of discussing this question with Professor Netzer. Eric Meyers informs me, however, that he has now changed his opinion.

57. Kotlar, 'Mikveh', col. 1537, quoting Maimonides.

58. Physical exploration of pools in the Lower City is not presently possible, but some miqveh + 'otsar combinations can be seen. Meir Ben-Dov informs me that the triple system (including a cistern) was the rule.

59. I am not proposing that the Sicarii were Pharisees, though some of them may have been. It is likely that different pietists held similar halakic views.

60. For the first case, I rely on tutored observation. For the second, see Netzer, *Herodium*, pp. 47f.

61. Reich, 'The Hot Bath-House', pp. 104f.

62. Epstein, *Introductions*, p. 64.

63. Reservoirs built on roofs or high ground would also supply a miqveh with water which the Pharisees would count as 'drawn', since it would have been contained in a 'vessel'. This would be a less labour-intensive way of immersing in drawn water, but there

is thus far insufficient evidence for such reservoirs. A reservoir which would flush a miqveh several times between rains would have to be extremely large and thus extremely heavy.

64. Almost everyone – ancient and modern alike – agrees that stone utensils and tables were not susceptible to impurity, though I do not know the reasoning. For the assumption, see e.g. Parah 3.2; Kelim 22.10 (a bathhouse bench). Stones used to make ovens presented special problems: Kelim 5.11; 6.2–4. My guess is that there is an exegetical basis: the major passages on the impurity of utensils do not mention stone, but only earthenware, wood, leather etc.: Lev. 11.32; 15.12. Num. 19.15, 'every open vessel' which is in a room with a corpse becomes impure, was apparently circumvented in some way. For a general description of stone objects, see Meir Ben-Dov, *In the Shadow of the Temple*, ET 1985, pp. 157–160. On the use of lathes to produce large stone vessels, see Shimon Gibson, 'The Stone Vessel Industry at Hizma', *IEJ* 33, 1983, pp. 176–188.

65. See Avigad, *Discovering Jerusalem*, ch. 3 for a general account of finds in the Upper City which relate to the period of the second temple; for Bar Kathros, see pp. 129–131; on stone vessels and tables in general, pp. 165–183.

66. Wilhelm Bacher, *Die Agada der Tannaiten* I, 1903, p. 19.

67. Zeitlin, for example, made a precise proposal: CE 65, after the flight of Cestius. See Solomon Zeitlin, *The Rise and Fall of the Judaean State* II, 1969, e.g. pp. 358f.

68. *Life* 189–192.

69. In Bikkurim 2.1 the verb is 'wash' (*raḥats*); cf. the distinction between 'rinse' (*nôṭᵉlin*) and 'immerse' (*maṭbilin*) in Hagigah 2.5.

70. Alon, 'The Bounds of the Laws of Levitical Cleanness', pp. 218f.; Neusner, e.g. *Rabb. Trads.* II, p. 162.

71. The common ground between what is sacred and what is *im*pure – both being treated as matters of taboo – has long fascinated scholars, and I am here cutting short an interesting and complicated discussion. See, for example, Douglas, *Purity and Danger*, chs 1 and 10.

72. *Arist.* 305f; *Sib. Or.* 3.591–593; p. 30 above.

73. Alon, 'The Bounds of the Laws of Levitical Cleanness', p. 201. Alon grants that washing the hands for prayer is 'taught in the Talmud only by Amoraim' (i.e. after CE 220). His argument that 'the halakah' is early depends on the *Letter of Aristeas* and *Sib. Or.* 3.

74. T. Yadaim 2.20, cited following the translation in Alon, 'Levitical Cleanness', p. 196 (where 1.20 is a typographical error for 2.20).

75. The passage is omitted from Neusner's summary list in *Rabb. Trads.* III, pp. 291–294. In the main discussion Neusner follows Lieberman in preferring the version in Bekorot 30b (*Rabb. Trads.* II, pp. 246f.).

76. Ancients knew that it was possible to have the externals without the corresponding internals, but it is a modern tendency to suppose that observance of the former implies absence of the latter.

77. *Rabb. Trads.* III, pp. 296f.

78. E.g. *War* 2.163; Acts 23.6. Belief in life after death was not peculiar to the Pharisees, and it is more likely that all except the Sadducees held some form of this belief (see *Paul and Palestinian Judaism*, pp. 151 n. 19; 354 n. 18; 388 n. 4). Despite this, such a belief was *characteristic* of Pharisees.

F. EXCLUSIVISM

1. See III.C§1 above; for 'outside the people of God', see e.g. Jeremias, *Jerusalem in the Time of Jesus*, p. 259: Pharisees thought of themselves as 'the true Israel'.

2. This agrees with the view of Raba in discussing the passage about a pharisaic zav eating with an 'am ha-'arets who was a zav: 'The majority of the 'amme ha-arez do render tithes, but [we fear] lest he associate with him and he provide him with unclean food in the days of his purity' (Shabbat 13a).

3. According to J. N. Epstein, *Introductions*, pp. 63f. and n. 36, these passages are the halaka of R. Joshua, probably repeating Houses debates.

4. Joachim Jeremias and others; see the discussion in *J & J*, pp. 188–198.

5. The Pharisees were the 'new ruling class', Jeremias, *Jerusalem in the Time of Jesus*, p. 267. Jeremias's view is clearer in *The Proclamation of Jesus*, ET 1971, pp. 108–113, where he says that 'according to the convictions of the time' the ignorance and behaviour of the ordinary people, the 'amme ha-'arets, stood in the way of their salvation (p. 112). 'The convictions of the time', in his view, were dictated by Pharisees. This emerges partially from the fact that he uses the rabbinic term for the ordinary people when he (incorrectly) says that they were excluded from salvation, partially from the fact that a few pages later, when he elaborates on the point, he cites (mistranslated and misunderstood) rabbinic passages as proving that it was the Pharisees who refused all association with the 'amme ha-'arets on the grounds that they were sinners (pp. 118f.). Every aspect of this discussion is in error. The Rabbis did not exclude the ordinary people from salvation; Demai 2.3 does not refer to Pharisees; the Pharisees did not control 'the convictions of the time'.

6. *Rabb. Trads.* III, p. 288.

7. E.g. *Purities* XXII, pp. 3; 100: central for both groups was observance of priestly law at home, especially at table; 'Mishnah begins in a sect not unlike . . . Qumran' (p. 8). See further pp. 37–49.

8. Own system of atonement: 1QS 8.4; alternative and complete society: 2.19–22; Zadokites the true high priests: 5.2; only they knew full contents of the covenant: 5.8–12; different plan for temple and different calendar: 11QTemple.

9. Alan Segal, *Rebecca's Children*, pp. 52, 58, 117. 'The Pharisees had to live near each other, forming small clubs . . ., whose members ate together in order to ensure that none of them ate food which was unsuitable' (p. 125).

10. E.g. Shaye Cohen, *From the Maccabees to the Mishnah*, 1987, pp. 116–119, 162.

11. See *Paul and Palestinian Judaism*, pp. 267, 425f. for the general point; 156f., 373f., 383–385, 405f., 408f., 314, 425 on the 'sectarianism' of different bodies of literature.

12. A mid-second century mishnah (R. Meir and R. Jose b. Halafta) says that during festivals those who were pure walked in the middle of the street, those who were impure to the side; the rest of the year it was reversed (Shekalim 8.1). I am inclined to see this as a nostalgic fantasy, though it is not as extreme as Parah 3.2 (which must be read to be appreciated).

13. I infer this partly from silence (there are no discussions of separate bath houses for Pharisees) and partly from later texts: the Rabbis, somewhat cautiously, used public bath houses, including those used by Gentiles. See e.g. T. Miqva'ot 6.3–4; T. Tohorot 8.11. Cf. III.E n. 39.

G. CONCLUSION

1. *Judaism*, p. 59.

2. E.g. *Josephus*, LCL vol. IV, p. 510.

3. Alon, 'The Bounds of the Laws of Levitical Cleanness', p. 227: 'the removal of the menstruant . . . is also taught by tradition' (*ha-masoret*, Heb., p. 172).

4. Neusner, *From Politics to Piety*, pp. 80–83; *Rabb. Trads.* III, pp. 305f.

5. Neusner, *Rabb. Trads.* II, p. 296: the discussions 'do not leave the impression that Pharisees bore heavy responsibilities in the administration of justice.'

6. This would not be greatly changed if one included Tamid as pharisaic; it is descriptive, and we do not know that the Sadducees would have disagreed very often. On Tamid, see Epstein, *Introductions*, pp. 27–31.

7. Michael Newton, *The Concept of Purity at Qumran and in the Letters of Paul*, 1985.

8. Some examples from Paul: I Cor. 6.11; II Cor. 7.1; Phil. 2.15; I Thess. 3.13; 5.23; for *hagneia*, I Tim. 4.12; 5.2.

9. On oil, see *War* 2.590–592; *Life* 74; *Antiq.* 12.120; for dipping and sprinkling in the pagan world, see the next chapter.

10. See *Paul and Palestinian Judaism*, p. 62. In *J & J* I ventured some remarks about the Pharisees' influence or lack of it, but I did not describe their religious values.

11. Quoted from Hans Hillerbrand, *The Protestant Reformation. The Documentary History of Western Civilization*, 1968, p. 68.

12. Petition seventeen in a text of the Eighteen Benedictions found in the Cairo Genizah. See Joseph Heinemann, *Prayer in the Talmud*, ET 1977, pp. 26–29.

13. Tessa Rajak assumes that priests had no interest in teaching the law and that Josephus was taught by Pharisees (*Josephus*, 1983, pp. 19–33). Both points, I think, are incorrect, though for the present purpose the question is irrelevant. On priests as continuing their traditional educational activities, see recently S. N. Mason, 'Priesthood in Josephus and the "Pharisaic Revolution"', *JBL* 107, 1988, pp. 657–661.

IV Purity, Food and Offerings in the Greek-Speaking Diaspora

A. INTRODUCTION

1. See e.g. Safrai and Dunn, both cited below.

2. Thus, for example, Ze'ev W. Falk, *Introduction to Jewish Law of the Second Commonwealth* I, 1972, pp. 55f.; S. Safrai, 'Jewish Self-Government', *The Jewish People in the First Century* (CRINT 1.1), 1974, pp. 388f.

3. Above, p. 157. See Alon, 'Levitical Cleanness', p. 232.

4. E.g. Jacob Neusner, ed., *Judaisms and their Messiahs*; 'Parsing the Rabbinic Canon with the History of an Idea. The Messiah', *Formative Judaism: Religious, Historical and Literary Studies* III, 1983, pp. 173–198, esp. 173.

5. Neusner, *Judaism*, p. 22.

6. Some scholars have attributed to me the view that one form of Judaism was 'normative' in the second temple period (e.g. James H. Charlesworth, reviewing *Jesus and Judaism* in *JAAR* 55, 1987, p. 623; *Jesus within Judaism*, 1988, p. 238). What I argued, and would still maintain, is that, despite diversity on many points, there was a common, underlying feature, found in most of the surviving literature from the period 200 BCE–CE

200: belief in election by God's grace and the requirement to observe the law. See 'The Covenant as a Soteriological Category and the Nature of Salvation in Palestinian and Hellenistic Judaism', *Jews, Greeks and Christians*, ed. Robert Hamerton-Kelly and Robin Scroggs, 1976, pp. 39–44; *Paul and Palestinian Judaism*, pp. 419–428. Both these summarizing conclusions emphasize diversity on very important points, such as the questions of who constitutes Israel and of the nature of salvation. Belief in election and law, however, was common. This has now been accepted by, among others, Jacob Neusner. Thus, for example, *Major Trends in Formative Judaism* III, pp. 31f.: my term 'convenantal nomism' gives 'the gist of Israel's piety in the first century'.

7. Josephus is perhaps not a primary witness to distinctive practices in the Diaspora, and sometimes we do not know whether his descriptions of Jewish law apply to the Diaspora. There are, however, some bits of hard evidence about the Diaspora in Josephus, as we shall see.

8. 'Jewish Association with Gentiles and Galatians 2:11–14', *The Conversation Continues. Essays on Paul and John Presented to J. Louis Martyn*, ed. Robert Fortna and Beverly Gaventa, 1990.

9. S. Safrai, 'Relations between the Diaspora and the Land of Israel', *The Jewish People in the First Century* (CRINT 1.1), pp. 205f.

10. Jonathan A. Goldstein, *II Maccabees* (AB 41A), 1983, pp. 157–167.

11. In Justin's *Dialogue with Trypho*, Justin accuses the Jews of digging pits or cisterns (*lakkoi*) which purify only the body (*Dial.* 14.1). Subsequently, Trypho gives as a core commandment washing after touching anything prohibited by Moses and after sexual relations (*Dial.* 46.2). The verb is *baptizesthai*, which possibly but not necessarily means immersion. That the whole body should be washed is indicated in *Sib. Or.* 4.165, but the author has in mind rivers rather than cisterns.

B. PURITY

1. James D. G. Dunn, 'The Incident at Antioch (Gal. 2:11–18), *JSNT* 18, 1983, pp. 3–57. I discuss several aspects of his paper in 'Jewish Association with Gentiles'.

2. On this passage, see above, pp. 205–7.

3. Dunn, p. 17.

4. Midras-impurity is the secondary impurity which comes from touching something on which a menstruant or a person with a discharge lay or sat. See above, III.E§4.

5. This is the argument of section D below.

6. On these and other decrees and letters in Josephus, see below IV.D, n. 39. If Josephus places Caesar's decrees at the correct point in his career, they were made before the war against Scipio and Cato (*Antiq.* 14.185).

7. W. Schrage, '*Synagōgē*', *TDNT* VII, p. 815 n. 100; Cohen, 'Pagan and Christian Evidence', p. 165 and n. 20. Martin Hengel, 'Proseuche und Synagoge', *Tradition und Glaube*, p. 176.

8. Delos, Aegina and Miletus are mentioned by E. L. Sukenik, *Ancient Synagogues in Palestine and Greece*, 1934. See further Martin Hengel, 'Die Synagogeninschrift von Stobi', *ZNW* 57, 1966, pp. 145–183, here p. 167 and n. 76a; Hengel, 'Proseuche und Synagoge', *Tradition und Glaube*, p. 176; W. Schrage, '*Synagōgē*', *TDNT* VII, p. 814 n. 99.

9. A. T. Kraabel, 'The Diaspora Synagogue: Archaeological and Epigraphic Evidence since Sukenik', *ANRW* II.19.1, 1979, pp. 477–510, here 490; G. Foerster, 'A Survey of Ancient Diaspora Synagogues', in Lee I. Levine, ed., *Ancient Synagogues*

Revealed, 1981, pp. 164–171, here 166. Possibly Delos should be added. See Levine, *The Synagogue in Late Antiquity*, p. 11.

10. Andrew R. Seager, 'The Building', in the section 'The Synagogue and the Jewish Community', *Sardis from Prehistoric to Roman Times*, by George M. A. Hanfmann, 1983, p. 169. The krater may have been a public fountain, with a door to the synagogue to allow use. See Hanfmann, 'The Ninth Campaign at Sardis' (1966), *BASOR* 186, April 1967, pp. 17–52, and 187, October 1967, pp. 9–62, here 187, p. 18; cf. the reconstruction, p. 60. A photograph can be seen in Seager, 'The Synagogue at Sardis', *Ancient Synagogues Revealed*, ed. Levine, p. 183. According to Hengel ('Synagogeninschrift', p. 167), 'oftmals befand sich dann im Vorhof eine Brunnenanlage für rituelle Waschungen'.

11. See the translation and introduction by R. J. H. Shutt in *OTP* II, pp. 7–11. Scholarly views on dating range quite widely (I.D, n.3), but Shutt argues that *c.* 170 BCE is most likely.

12. On bathing before morning prayers, see above, p. 150.

13. So J. J. Collins in *OTP* I, p. 356.

14. Especially in the Testament of Abraham: e.g. T. Ab. A 3.7,9; 6.6. See Albert-Marie Denis, *Concordance grecque des Pseudépigraphes d'Ancien Testament*.

15. One may compare here rabbinic comments on bodies of water which serve as miqva'ot: Mikwaoth 1.1–8.

16. See Walter Burkert, *Greek Religion*, ET 1985, p. 77.

17. Quoted from Burkert, *Greek Religion*, p. 56.

18. René Ginouvès, *Balaneutikè*, 1962, pp. 309f. I owe the passages from Homer and Lucian to Ginouvès, who cites numerous others as well.

19. Colson and Whittaker, (LCL edition of Philo's works, vol. 5, pp. 409–11) take *perirranesthai* as middle, 'sprinkle oneself'. In view of Num. 19, I take it as a passive.

20. Liddell and Scott cite Xenophon, *Cyropaedia* 7.5.59, *en loutrois*, 'while bathing'.

21. Ginouvès, pp. 299–310.

22. Liddell and Scott interpret *perirranteria agoras* as 'the parts of the market-place sprinkled with lustral water', but it is better to follow Ginouvès' special study.

23. Childbirth-impurity stage one lasts for one week (for a boy) or two weeks (for a girl). Thereafter comes stage two, which lasts thirty-three or sixty-six days, and which concludes with sacrifices: Lev. 12.1–5.

24. Above, pp. 164f.

25. Joachim Jeremias, *The Proclamation of Jesus*, pp. 146f.: the Pharisees evaded the main requirements of the law while fulfilling the 'regulations for purity with the utmost scrupulosity'; they used casuistry to avoid facing the seriousness of sin.

26. An old charge against Jews in general and Pharisees in particular is that they believed in works of supererogation and a treasury of merits: e.g. Jeremias, ibid., p. 147. For others who proposed this, see *Paul and Palestinian Judaism*, pp. 37, 39, 45, 47–49, 102. I pointed out that Moore and Sjöberg had argued that this view is not correctly attributed to the early Rabbis (pp. 47,57), and I added my own argument that passages on *zekut* do not refer to stored-up merits which can be transferred at the judgment (pp. 183–188).

27. See on the food laws, *Arist.* 128–142, discussed below.

C. FOOD

1. See III.B, n. 16.

2. Here I assume that the translators have done their work correctly. R. H. Colson notes that the English equivalents of the Greek list 'must be regarded as uncertain' (LCL, *Philo* VIII, p. 70, on *Spec. Laws* 4.105). The addition of the giraffe in the LXX and Philo, however,

is clear. The RSV's translation of the eighth animal in the list, *dishon*, as 'ibex' is generally regarded as incorrect: 'antelope' is to be preferred. The RSV used 'antelope' for the ninth animal, the *t*'*ŏ*, the meaning of which is doubtful. I have been aided by *Fauna and Flora of the Bible*, in the UBS Helps for Translators series, 2nd ed., 1980.

3. Walter Burkert, *Greek Religion*, pp. 70–73.

4. *Life* 74. Oil, like milk and honey, could be given as an offering to the dead, but it is doubtful that Jews assumed that some of each batch of oil had been so offered. See Karl Meuli, 'Griechische Opferbraüche', *Gesammelte Schriften*, pp. 907–1012, here p. 915. On oil, see further the summary of passages below. In an essay which will appear in the *Festschrift* for Geza Vermes, Martin Goodman proposes that rejection of Gentile oil was based on 'pervasive religious instinct' rather than interpretation of a specific law.

5. Milk is so perishable in hot climates that it does not figure in discussions of storing, selling and buying foodstuff.

6. In Hebrew (Gen. 41.45) the woman's name is spelled 'As^cnath (with *a* as the final vowel), but in Greek it was transliterated Aseneth.

7. *Arist.* 128 says that humanity 'as a whole shows a certain amount of concern for the parts of their legislation concerning meats and drink and beasts considered to be unclean'. We shall see below the theory in classical Greece that only domestic animals should be eaten, but this leaves out of account the fact that in Greece as elsewhere some people hunted. Whether or not some animals were completely avoided is not clear. In Egypt, however (where *Aristeas* was written), there were food laws. Examples of other peoples' lists of forbidden foods may be seen in Stern, *Greek and Latin Authors on Jews and Judaism*: see 'pig' in the index.

8. On this passage, see below, pp. 296f.

9. Pagan comments on Jewish food laws are conveniently collected by Molly Whittaker, *Jews and Christians: Graeco-Roman Views*, Cambridge 1984, pp. 73–80. The only animal besides the pig which is mentioned is the hare. For the text (from Plutarch's *Questiones Convivales*), see Stern, *Greek and Latin Authors* I, p. 552; ET 556.

10. Above, p. 8.

11. Titles and offices were much more complicated. One may see the entries for these two words in the standard encyclopaedias and dictionaries, as well as such studies as those by K. Köster and Herz, cited in the next two notes.

12. On this see Kurt Köster, *Die Lebensmittelversorgung der altgriechischen Polis*, 1939.

13. In Rome, the supply of meat came under official control only in the middle years of Septimius Severus (emperor 193–211): Peter Herz, *Studien zur römischen Wirtschaftsgesetzgebung. Die Lebensmittelversorgung. Historia* Einzelschriften 55, 1988, pp. 162–169.

14. Herz, p. 162 and n. 65.

15. Cf. C. K. Barrett, 'Things Sacrificed to Idols', *Essays on Paul*, 1982 (orig. publ. 1965), pp. 40–59, here p. 41: Jews would object to meat if it was either offered to idols or improperly slaughtered. In *The First Epistle to the Corinthians*, 1968, p. 188, he wrote that food sacrificed to idols was unacceptable for three reasons: it was tainted with idolatry; tithes had not been paid; proper slaughtering could not be assumed. The second of these was not an issue (see D below).

16. Herz (n. 13 above) states that in Rome pork was the main meat, though there was also beef.

17. Greek sacrificial practice varied widely, because of the diversity of cults and cult sites. According to Pausanias, the Colophonians and Spartans sometimes sacrificed

puppies (*Description of Greece* 3.14.9f.). The worship of Artemis Laphria in Patrae included burning wild animals alive, which Pausanias says was unique (7.18.8–13). Other exceptions to the general rule could be cited.

18. See Marcel Detienne, 'Culinary Practices and the Spirit of Sacrifice', pp. 3, 5, 11; Jean-Pierre Vernant, 'At Man's Table: Hesiod's Foundation Myth of Sacrifice', pp. 24f., both in Detienne and Vernant (eds), *The Cuisine of Sacrifice Among the Greeks*, ET 1989.

19. Barrett, 'Things Sacrificed', p. 42; *The First Epistle to the Corinthians*, p. 188. Hans Conzelmann wrote that 'of course the Jew is only allowed to partake of animals that have been ritually slaughtered', though he did not think it worthwhile to cite evidence (*I Corinthians*, ET 1975, p. 139).

20. See Walter Burkert, *Greek Religion*, p. 56; *Homo Necans*, ET 1983, p. 5; Ludwig Ziehen, 'Sphagia', *Paulys Real-Encyclopädie*, Zweite Reihe, sechster Halbband, cols. 1669–1679, here 1670f.

21. Jean-Louis Durand, 'Greek Animals: Toward a Topology of Edible Bodies', in Detienne and Vernant, *The Cuisine*, pp. 90–92, 101; cf. Vernant, 'At Man's Table', p. 41.

22. Meuli, 'Griechische Opferbraüche', p. 945.

23. Durand, 'Greek Animals', p. 99.

24. The Greeks accused the Scythians of actually strangling animals with a noose, but it is doubtful that *Jos. and Asen.* and Acts refer to 'strangulation' in this sense. On the Scythians, see François Hartog, 'Self-cooking Beef and the Drinks of Ares', in Detienne and Vernant, *The Cuisine*, pp. 173, 175. 'And from what is strangled' in Acts is missing in some manuscripts.

25. Many sacrificed animals were eaten on the spot (Burkert, *Greek Religion*, p. 57: 'It is not infrequently prescribed that no meat must be taken away: all must be consumed without remainder in the sanctuary'), but some were sold in the market (Detienne, 'Culinary Practices', p. 11).

26. Kurt Latte, 'Mageiros', *Paulys Real-Encyclopädie* 14.1, cols. 393–395; Detienne, 'Culinary Practices', p. 11; Vernant, 'At Man's Table', pp. 25f.

27. Detienne, 'Culinary Practices', p. 11.

28. On pagan meat, see n. 14; I infer that Jews salted meat from Ezek. 43.24, which says that priests should salt whole-burnt offerings. This is confirmed by Zebahim 6.5. The priests (Ezekiel was a priest) in this and in other respects treated offerings as food for God, and this implies that meat was generally salted. On the use of salt in the temple, see also Lev. 2.13; Ezra 6.9; Middoth 5.3.

29. Kirsopp Lake, *The Earlier Epistles of St. Paul*, 1911, p. 198; C. K. Barrett, *The First Epistle to the Corinthians*, p. 188.

30. H. J. Cadbury, 'The Macellum of Corinth', *JBL* 53, 1934, pp. 134–141.

31. Meuli, 'Opferbraüche', pp. 941–947. On the distribution of choice pieces, see also Detienne, 'Culinary Practices', p. 13; Durand, 'Greek Animals', p. 105.

32. Barrett, 'Things Sacrificed', p. 48.

33. Barrett, ('Things Sacrificed', p. 48) considers the question whether or not meat was considered a desirable luxury. Trimalchio's banquet in Petronius's *Satyricon* (e.g. 36, 40, 47, 49) strongly suggests that it was.

34. Spending second tithe money on peace offerings had several advantages: it (1) helped Jews meet their obligation to spend second tithe money in Jerusalem; (2) provided food while they fulfilled their obligation to attend the festival; (3) gave some food to the priesthood and some to the altar; (4) allowed them to have a banquet. Note also Lev. 17.3–5, which assumes that it is reasonable for people to bring to the temple all animals which they slaughter.

35. Tessa Rajak, 'Jews and Christians as Groups in a Pagan World', *'To See Ourselves as Others See Us': Christians, Jews, 'Others' in Late Antiquity*, ed. J. Neusner and E. Frerichs, 1985, pp. 248–262, here p. 251.

36. *Jos. and Asen.* 8.5; 10.13; 11.9, 16; 12.5.

37. *Pseudo-Phocylides* 31 'is missing in all the important manuscripts. It is probably a Christian interpolation. . . .': P. W. van der Horst, in *OTP* II, p. 575 ad loc.

38. Barrett, 'Things Sacrificed', p. 49.

39. 'Things Sacrificed', p. 49.

40. See Rajak, 'Jews and Christians as Groups in a Pagan World'. The quotation is from my 'Jewish Association with Gentiles'.

41. The problem of mixing meat and dairy products, because of the thrice repeated commandment not to seethe a kid in its mother's milk, is referred to in a Houses debate, Hullin 8.1 (fowl and cheese; see I.C). Even there, however, the question of separate dishes does not arise. The exception is the case of Jewish priests in Rome, who avoided all cooked foods, perhaps because they objected to the cooking vessels (above, p. 26).

42. Atheists and misanthropes: quoted by Josephus, *Apion* 2.148; would not associate: *Apion* 2.258.

43. Jews 'alone of all nations avoided dealings with any other people'; their ancestors 'had been driven out of all Egypt as men who were impious . . .'; 'they would not share the table with any other race'. Diodorus Siculus, *Bibliotheca historica* 34–35.1.1–2, text and translation in Stern, *Greek and Latin Authors on Jews and Judaism* I, pp. 181–183. Stern translates 'share the table' as 'break bread'.

44. E.g. Philip Esler, *Community and Gospel in Luke–Acts*, pp. 78–80.

45. 'Jewish Association with Gentiles'.

46. Nonna, Gregory Nazianzen's mother, '"never once grasped the hand or kissed the lips of any heathen woman"' (Peter Brown, *The Body and Society*, 1988, p. 286, quoting Gregory, *Oratio* 18.10). John Chrysostom 'made no secret of the fact that he wished the theater, the hippodrome, even the busy agora, to fall silent forever' (p. 313).

D. OFFERINGS

1. James D. G. Dunn, 'The Incident at Antioch', *JSNT* 18, 1983, pp. 3–57, here esp. p. 15.

2. Dunn, p. 16. For Dunn's further suggestion about purity, see IV.B above.

3. Gedalyahu Alon, 'The Levitical Uncleanness of Gentiles', *Jews, Judaism and the Classical World*, pp. 146–189.

4. The view that impurity prevented association, and especially association with Gentiles, is very old, has been refuted more than once, is completely in error, and yet is constantly repeated by Christian scholars. See, for example, A. Büchler's reply to Emil Schürer, 'The Levitical Impurity of the Gentile in Palestine before the year 70', *JQR* 17, 1926–27, pp. 1–81. See further Alon's essay (previous note) and mine (next note).

5. This is one of the main arguments of my 'Jewish Association with Gentiles', Martyn Festschrift.

6. Dunn, p. 15.

7. Dunn, p. 12.

8. 'I found no available materials in the Division of Damages for the period before the wars', Jacob Neusner, *Judaism*, p. 62. Abodah Zarah is in Nezikin, 'Damages'. See further *A History of the Mishnaic Law of Damages*, part V, *The Mishnaic System of Damages*, 1982, p. 151: the earliest materials in Abodah Zarah are Yavnean.

9. Dunn, p. 18.

10. Dunn, p. 18, citing mishnaic passages on the impurity of Gentiles. See n. 4 above.

11. Safrai, 'Relations', pp. 201f.

12. Safrai, 'Relations', pp. 199–203.

13. *The Fathers According to Rabbi Nathan*, ET Judah Goldin, 1956, p. 97.

14. Safrai, 'Relations', pp. 200f.

15. More precisely, ARN is a commentary on an earlier form of Aboth than the one now in the Mishnah; the third century date, however, still stands. See Goldin, 'Avot de-Rabbi Nathan', *Enc. Jud.* 3, cols. 984f.

16. 'Relations', p. 201.

17. Following Jastrow: see *Dictionary s.vv. rôbe`/rôbeh; tûrgmana`*.

18. Safrai, p. 202.

19. One may compare the discussion in Schürer/Vermes/Millar *HJP* II, pp. 257–270, which is fundamentally the same as the original Schürer. There are a few differences between that discussion and this one. It is not necessary for the present purpose to debate the issues, but I shall mention two points for those who wish to investigate the question more closely. (1) Schürer takes *re`shît* to be the 'best' rather than 'first', and sees *bikkûrîm*, 'first produce' as being a different and separate offering from the time of its introduction. He then equates *re`shît* with *t`rûmah* (on the basis of Neh. 10.38). My presentation takes *re`shît* to be the early form of 'first fruits' and *bikkûrîm* and *bekôrôt* to be later terms which both specify and enlarge the general category of 'first'. *Re`shît* I understand as being maintained in later literature in specific contexts, such as *re`shît* of dough (Neh. 10.38; Num. 15.20; for a different special use see Lev. 23.10). Thus I read Num. 18.12–13 not as two different, partially overlapping offerings, but as covering between them all agricultural 'firsts': *re`shît* of wine, oil and grain; *bikkûrîm* of (everything else) that grows from the soil. Schürer/Vermes/Millar, *HJP*, treat *re`shît* in Num 18.12 as *t`rûmah* (p. 263 n. 20). The first-century reader, however, must have often understood *re`shît* as a generic for 'firsts', or as a synonym for *bikkûrîm*, because of Deut. 26. That they connected it with *t`rûmah* seems to me unlikely. The last term clearly refers to a separate offering, as far as I see, only in Nehemiah. (2) Schürer accepts the Mishnah's view that *bikkûrîm* were paid on only the 'seven kinds' of Deut. 8.8. I find no biblical support for this, and suspect that it may be a pharisaic/rabbinic reduction.

20. That Jews actually paid the temple tax is adequately proved by Rome's redirection of it after the first revolt. For the tax and the later *fiscus Judaicus*, see E. Mary Smallwood, *The Jews under Roman Rule*, Leiden, 1981, e.g. pp. 124–127, 515–516.

21. Whether or not the aristocratic priesthood and the other non-pharisaic Jews regarded *t`rûmah* as a separate offering, rather than as a general word for 'offering' or as a synonym for 'first fruits', is an interesting question, though it cannot be pursued here. It was in their interests to accept it, and I shall assume that they did so.

22. See I.F above. We noted that in the first century the tithe of all cattle owned was interpreted in other ways, and that this payment, which would have been a capital tax, was not collected. Schürer/Vermes/Millar (*HJP* II, p. 259) suggest that the tithe of cattle may have been collected at the time of the Chronicler, though perhaps even then it was only an ideal.

23. The rabbinic term probably comes from Num. 18.26–29 ('*t`rûmah* of the Lord, a tithe of the tithe', v. 26), Philo's from Num. 18.30 LXX ('when you remove the *aparchē* from the tithe . . .').

24. Liddell and Scott s.v. *aparchē*.

25. Moulton and Milligan, *Vocabulary of the Greek Testament*, s.v. *aparchē*.

26. While *t'rûmah* is sometimes translated by a general word for 'offering', such as *eisphora* (Ex. 30.13–15), it is often rendered by *aparchē*.

27. The Hebrew terms are very difficult to translate in these passages, and the Hebrew reader would be hard-pressed to make them fit into a scheme derived by conflating Leviticus, Numbers and Nehemiah – the scheme used by the Rabbis. They are, respectively, 'heave-offering' (or 'lifted-up-offering') and 'wave-offering'. The latter usually refers to the 'breast that is waved' before the Lord (from the peace-offering; Lev. 7.30).

28. We need not try to straighten out the overlap between 1.134 and 1.141, except to note that Schürer/Vermes/Millar treat 1.134 as *t'rûmah* (II, p. 263 n. 20).

29. Philo, Josephus and the Mishnah agree that some of the meat of animals slaughtered away from the altar should be given to the priests: I.F, n. 4.

30. These are, respectively, 'first tithe' (for Levites) and 'second tithe' (for banquets – that is, money which is to be spent in Jerusalem). Josephus's third tithe, Poor Tithe, is mentioned in 4.240.

31. On accepting Josephus's quotations of documents, see below, n. 39.

32. *Antiq.* 14.214f. refers to the right to 'contribute money to common meals and sacred rites', and to assemble and 'collect money', but this possibly relates only to money for local meals and the like. Dolabella's letter to Ephesus affirms the Jews' right to 'make offerings for their sacrifices' (14.227), but again this might cover only local gatherings and meals.

33. On the 'Jewish Tax', see Smallwood, *The Jews Under Roman Rule*, pp. 371–378 and elsewhere (see the index).

34. See e.g. *War* 2.413; 4.181,649; 5.562; *Apion* 1.11; *Antiq.* 7.44f. and often. In *Antiq.* 9.254 *anathēmata* are distinguished from money.

35. See the text and apparatus by H. St J. Thackeray, p. 578 in H. B. Swete, *An Introduction to the Old Testament in Greek*, revised by R. R. Ottley, 1902.

36. Josephus also uses *anathēmata* to refer to offerings in general: *War* 6.335 and probably *Antiq.* 18.19 (sent to the temple by Essenes).

37. Philo frequently discusses the biblical legislation regarding first fruits. See e.g. *Spec. Laws* 1.117, 120, 126, 128, 129, 183, 255, 279; *Spec. Laws* 2.41, 162, 168, 171 – and often.

38. Following the LXX, Philo read Num. 21.1–3 as saying that the Israelites 'devoted' the Canaanite kingdom to the Lord. The Hebrew probably refers to its destruction.

39. I accept the quotations of documents in Josephus as being generally authentic, as do most scholars. See, for example, Smallwood, *The Jews under Roman Rule*, pp. 558–560. Horst Moehring has pointed to the difficulties which ancient authors had in finding or verifying the actual texts of decrees, and his study encourages caution. See 'The Acta *Pro Judaeis* in the *Antiquities* of Flavius Josephus', in J. Neusner, ed., *Christianity, Judaism and other Graeco-Roman Cults: Studies for Morton Smith at Sixty*, part 3, 1975, pp. 125–158. In this discussion, I accept *tous karpous metacheirizesthai* as the term actually used in the letter quoted by Josephus. This is partly for lack of any option; but it may be defended on the grounds that Josephus knew, at least approximately, who sent goods and money where, and that he would have employed appropriate terms if he was paraphrasing rather than quoting.

40. In his discussion of *Antiq.* 14.245 Safrai curiously states that the 'edict equates the produce [i.e., for the tithes] with the payments which fulfilled sacred duties, that is, the half-shekel, with whose transfer to Jerusalem the permission was essentially concerned' (p. 202). The letter in question mentions neither the temple tax nor sending money to

Jerusalem. Safrai appears to be arguing that the right to handle produce refers to tithes, and that tithing thus had the same status in Roman eyes as did the temple tax: it was allowed.

41. I am indebted to W. E. H. Cockle and Peter Parsons for advice on some aspects of this material.

42. On the later history of the 'Jewish Tax', see Schürer/Vermes/Millar, *HJP* II, p. 272 and notes.

43. Peter Parsons informs me that the reading *aparchai* in papyrus 168, cited just below, which is usually taken to prove the use of the plural, is not entirely secure. *Aparch*() would be safer, but for convenience I shall continue the custom of using the plural.

44. Victor A. Tcherikover and Alexander Fuks, *Corpus Papyrorum Judaicarum*, 3 vols, II, section IX (basically completed by Tcherikover before his death). For his comment, see p. 115 n. 1. The ostraca which imply total payment of nine drachmas plus two obols are nos. 167–180, 183, 186, 210, 213. Those which specify only eight drachmas in Vespasian's first years are nos. 162–166. The extra drachma was not, however, always charged in later years: see nos. 205, 208.

45. Smallwood, *Jews under Roman Rule*, p. 374 n. 63.

46. Tcherikover and Fuks, *Corpus Papyrorum Judaicarum* II, section X (by Fuks), no. 421.

47. I.G above.

48. See I.D, n. 3.

49. Two inscriptions on Delos, referring to Samaritans, speak of 'Israelites who pay first fruits to . . . Gerizim' (*hoi aparchomenoi*). We do not, however, know to what this refers. See Schürer/Vermes/Millar/Goodman, *HJP* III.1, p. 71.

50. We recall that *t'rûmah* is used in rabbinic literature chiefly of this separate offering, but sometimes it is used of the priestly portion of the Levitical tithe, and other times it is used to designate any food which may be eaten by priests outside the temple.

51. See the distinctions in Bikkurim 2.1–5 and Hullin 11.1–2. As explained in n. 19, I treat 'firsts' as a general category with several sub-divisions.

52. As Lieberman explained, the Mishnah's rule that heave offering cannot be given from outside the land in lieu of heave offering from Palestine, and vice versa, does not mean that heave offering *should* be given from outside the land. Rather, the sentence exemplifies the previous rule, that heave offering from what is exempt cannot replace heave offering from what is liable. See Saul Liberman, *Tosefta Ki-Fshutah, Zera'im* I, 1955, pp. 313.

53. Cf. the anonymous mishnah Baba Metzia 4.8, which does not require that an added fifth be paid by someone who consumes the Levites' portion of first tithe.

54. On this ranking of offerings, see also Terumoth 3.7; Hagigah 2.7.

55. This is based on accepting Neusner's stratification of passages in *Rabbinic Traditions about the Pharisees* and *History of the Mishnaic Law*.

56. 'Relations', p. 202.

57. See the discussion by Adolphe Neubauer, *La Géographie du Talmud*, Paris, 1868, pp. 5–10. The rabbinic idea of land counted as 'Syria' depends on I Kings 4.24 rather than on the more modest proportions implied by II Sam. 24 (Joab's census) and other passages. It is incorrect to say that the Rabbis considered Syria to be part of Palestine because of a common border and a large Jewish population (so Isaiah Gafni, 'Syria', *Enc. Jud.* 15, col. 639). On this basis they would have included the Phoenecian coast – and Egypt. They were students of the Bible, not of ethnographic distribution.

58. J. Sussman, 'The Inscription in the Synagogue at Rehob', *Ancient Synagogues Revealed*, ed. Levine, pp. 146–153, quotation from 149.

59. The argument in favour of the pharisaic origin of the passage is this: At the conclusion of the list, the Houses of Hillel and Shammai are said to disagree about sweet or spiced oil (i.e. they disagree about whether or not it counts as food; it was used for anointing). Neusner takes the Houses tradition to include only the sweet oil, not the rest of the mishnah (see Neusner, *Rabb. Trads.* II, p. 63; III, p. 219, where T. Demai 1.3 is an error; T. Demai 1.26 is meant, or else p. Demai 1.3). While this is a possible division of the text, it is also possible that the Houses agreed on the list of exemptions, with the sole exception of spiced oil. Alternatively, the Houses debate on spiced oil is a gloss on an earlier list. On either view a statement which limits tithing to Palestine is pharisaic.

60. According to *Antiq.* 3.317–319 even some Gentiles tried to bring sacrifices.

61. According to Bikkurim 3.11, one could *add* produce which was not from Palestine to first fruits.

62. See n. 59.

63. I must again refer forward, to *Judaism 63 BCE – CE 66*, forthcoming.

64. See Lev. 7.16; 22.23; 23.38; Num. 15.3; 29.39; Deut. 12.6; 12.17. In all but the last passage the Greek term for freewill offering is *ekousios*.

65. Philo, *Hypothetica* 7.13 (they taught on the sabbath); Josephus, *Apion* 1.32 (they kept their genealogies). They are mentioned on inscriptions at Sardis and Dura: A. Thomas Kraabel, 'Social Systems of Six Diaspora Synagogues', *Ancient Synagogues. The State of Research*, ed. Joseph Gutmann. Brown Judaic Studies 22, 1981, p. 84.

66. See e.g. *Antiq.* 14.215; 16.163–71; *Embassy* 156.

67. Dunn, pp. 10f.

V Jacob Neusner and the Philosophy of the Mishnah

1. See III.C above. It is unnecessary to give a full bibliography here. Some of the volumes are referred to in ch. III, and full publication details may be seen in the bibliography to *Judaism*.

2. Jacob Neusner, *The Mishnah before 70*, 1987, p. xi. Cf. Yaakov Elman, 'The Judaism of the Mishna: What Evidence?', *Judaica Book News* 12, 1982, p. 17.

3. See, for example, the reviews by Cohen, Petuchowski and Maccoby, cited below.

4. It has been dismissed by not being discussed, and usually accepted by scholars in other fields. See e.g. William A. Clebsch, review of *Judaism: The Evidence of the Mishnah*, *Religious Studies Review* 9, April 1983, pp. 105–108. Elman (review, p. 18) regards Neusner as 'most successful in his attempt to characterize [the Mishnah's] world-view as a whole'.

5. An exception is Lieberman's review of Neusner's translation of the Palestinian Talmud: Saul Lieberman, 'A Tragedy or a Comedy?' *Journal of the American Oriental Society* 104, 1984, pp. 315–319.

6. On Neusner's undergraduate textbooks, see my review of *Judaism in the beginning of Christianity*, *Theology* 88, 1985, pp. 392f.

7. In *Messiah* there is a modification of the terminology. He states that the Mishnah appears to be ahistorical and anti-historical, but that the authors actually had a different concept of history (p. 41). This turns out to be only a terminological distinction. He still proposes that, for the mishnaic Rabbis, events play virtually no role and that they did not hope for redemption in history (e.g. p. 20).

8. Cf. Hyam Maccoby, 'Jacob Neusner's Mishnah', *Midstream* May 1984, p. 26; Shaye J. D. Cohen, 'Jacob Neusner, Mishnah, and Counter-Rabbinics. A Review Essay', *Conservative Judaism* 37, 1983, p. 55.

9. The Mishnah is 'a book of great poetry', Jacob Neusner, 'The Mishnah and the Smudgepots', *Midstream*, June/July 1986, p. 46.

10. Jacob Neusner, 'The Talmud as Anthropology', Annual Samuel Friedland Lecture, The Jewish Theological Seminary of America, New York, 1979, pp. 15, 25, 31f.

11. There has been a learned debate on the genre of the Mishnah, the question being whether or not it is a legal *code*. The question may be raised because many of the discussions do not reach conclusions. I shall avoid this debate. It is safe to say 'collection of legal discussions'. For a delineation of the problem, see David Weiss Halivni, 'The Reception Accorded to Rabbi Judah's Mishnah', *Jewish and Christian Self-Definition II: Aspects of Judaism in the Graeco-Roman Period*, ed. E. P. Sanders and others (1981), pp. 379f. n. 3. Weiss Halivni is of the view that the Mishnah was meant to be a code, but a limited one.

12. David Daube, 'Haustafeln', *The New Testament and Rabbinic Judaism*, pp. 90–97. Daube notes that the present participle is the most frequent verbal form in early rabbinic law, and he proposes that it 'reflects the Rabbinic view of the secondary, derivative, less absolute nature of post-Biblical rules' (p. 91). While the participle in the Mishnah has a range of meanings, the main idea is that whatever is right is done, provided only that it is known to be right. He offers modern analogies, such as 'a boy gets up when an elderly person looks for a seat' or 'on ne fume pas ici'. The present participle occurs even in Greek in the Haustafel of I Peter. Daube proposes that there 'it expresses not a command addressed to a specific person on a specific occasion, but a rule' ('Participle and Imperative in I Peter', in E. G. Selwyn, *The First Epistle of St. Peter*, 1947, p. 470).

13. Neusner's response in the symposium article, 'The Mishnah: Methods of Interpretation', *Midstream*, October 1986, pp. 38–42, here p. 42.

14. Cf. Jakob J. Petuchowski, review of *Judaism: The Evidence of the Mishnah*, *Religious Studies Review* 9, April 1983, p. 112; Cohen, review, pp. 50, 56–57, 59. 'That the rabbis who produced the Mishnah were in no way inspired by biblical ideals of justice or compassion, or by concepts of covenant, grace, salvation, free will or love, is about the most unlikely hypothesis ever constructed . . .' (Maccoby, 'Authenticating the authoritative', *TLS*, August 13 1982, p. 887).

15. See above, III.D, n. 16.

16. Cohen produces other examples: review, p. 53.

17. See my argument in *Paul and Palestinian Judaism*, e.g. pp. 71, 177–179, 235f.; Neusner's criticism: 'The Use of the Later Rabbinic Evidence for the Study of Paul', *Approaches to Ancient Judaism* II, ed. William Scott Green (*BJS* 9, 1980), p. 55; my reply: 'Puzzling Out Rabbinic Judaism', ibid., pp. 70–75.

18. Petuchowski (review in *RSR*, pp. 110–111) correctly points out that Neusner overlooks aspects of history and prophecy which are in the Mishnah. For the sake of the argument I leave this point aside.

19. Cf. Maccoby, 'Jacob Neusner's Mishnah', p. 26.

20. E.g. Louis Finkelstein, *The Pharisees*, pp. 347–350. Neusner argued that the Pharisees withdrew from politics at the time of Herod and Hillel: *From Politics to Piety*.

21. E.g. Jacob Neusner, 'Parsing the Rabbinic Canon', p. 173.

22. On Neusner's omission of the evidence of the liturgy: Sanders, 'Puzzling Out Rabbinic Judaism', p. 72 (1980); 'A Response to Jacob Neusner's "Mishnah and

Messiah",' pp. 5–9 (SBL, December, 1983); Hyam Maccoby, 'Jacob Neusner's Mishnah', *Midstream*, May 1984, p. 26 (citing 'Puzzling Out'); Alan Segal, 'Covenant in Rabbinic Writings', *Studies in Religion/Sciences Religieuses* 14, 1985, pp. 53–62; Elman, review, p. 24.

23. Cf. Maccoby, 'Jacob Neusner's Mishnah', p. 27; Cohen, review, p. 57; Petuchowski, review, p. 113.

24. A rigorous examination of passages about Akiba's relationship to Bar Kokhba and his death reveals that he probably did approve of the rebellion as a messianic war and that he was imprisoned and executed in connection with the revolt. See the fundamental work by Peter Schäfer, 'Rabbi Aqiva und Bar Kokhba', *Studien zur Geschichte und Theologie des rabbinischen Judentums*, Leiden 1978, pp. 65–121; *Der Bar Kokhba-Aufstand*, Tübingen, 1981; 'Rabbi Aqiva and Bar Kokhba', *Approaches to Ancient Judaism* II, ed. William Scott Green, pp. 113–130.

25. There is another Neusner on this point, as on most. Sometimes he argues that there was such a thing as common Judaism and cites the correct evidence for it. 'To state matters simply, the life of Israel in its land in the first century found structure and meaning in the covenant between God and Israel as contained in the Torah. . . . The piety of Israel, defined by the Torah, in concrete ways served to carry out the requirements of the covenant. This holy life under the Torah has been properly called "covenantal nomism", a phrase introduced by E. P. Sanders to state in two words *the complete and encompassing* holy way of life and *world view of Israel* in its land in the first century'. 'All the radical claims of holiness-sects, such as Pharisees and Essenes, of professions such as the scribes, and of followers of messiahs, each in its particular manner, gave expression to an aspect or emphasis of the *common piety* of the nation. Priest, scribe, messiah – all stood upon the same continuum of faith and culture with the rest of Israel'. ('"Covenantal Nomism". The Piety of Judaism in the First Century', *Major Trends in Formative Judaism* III, 1985, pp. 9–34, quotations from 31f., 33, my italics.) The essay emphasizes the Shema´ and the Eighteen Benedictions. My criticisms are directed against the Neusner of the books under review. These are among his most influential writings, and the essays in which he states the opposite position are less well known. Cf. above, pp. 110–113.

26. A person who ate ordinary food in priestly purity is still called 'the Pharisee' in *Messiah*, p. 13.

27. On the difference between a 'sect' (cultic break) and a 'party' (difference of opinion, but no break), see *Paul and Palestinian Judaism*, pp. 267 and nn. 74, 425f., 156f., 373f., 383–385.

28. See above, III.D, n. 36.

29. Maccoby, 'Jacob Neusner's Mishnah', p. 26; Elman, Review, p. 24.

30. In *A Religion of Pots and Pans*, 1988, Neusner repeats the assertion that discussion of the details of everyday life reflects philosophical interest in 'enduring issues of mind', such as the Nature of Mixtures (p. 91). I have not been able to see four volumes titled *The Philosophical Mishnah*, but I assume that they maintain the same view.

31. See n. 25 above.

Bibliography

1. EDITIONS AND TRANSLATIONS CITED OR QUOTED

Apocrypha and Pseudipigrapha

The Letter of Aristeas, ed. H. St J. Thackeray, in H. B. Swete, *An Introduction to the Old Testament in Greek*, revised by R. R. Ottley, Cambridge 1902, repr. New York 1968.

Die Oracula Sibyllina, ed. Joh. Geffcken, *Die griechischen christlichen Schriftsteller der ersten drei Jahrhunderte*, Leipzig 1902.

Other Greek texts: pp. 815–925 in Albert-Marie Denis, *Concordance*: see Bibliography 2.

The Old Testament Pseudepigrapha, vol. I *Apocalyptic Literature & Testaments*, vol. II *Expansions of the 'Old Testament'*, etc., ed. James H. Charlesworth, New York 1983, 1985. (Cited as *OTP* I & II.)

The Dead Sea Scrolls

Discoveries in the Judaean Desert II: Les grottes de Murabba'ât, ed. P. Benoit, J. T. Milik and R. de Vaux, Oxford 1961.

Discoveries in the Judaean Desert III: Les 'Petites Grottes' de Qumrân, ed. M. Baillet, J. T. Milik and R. de Vaux, Oxford 1962.

Discoveries in the Judaean Desert VI: Qumran Grotte 4, vol. II, ed. R. de Vaux and J. T. Milik, Oxford 1977.

Discoveries in the Judaean Desert VII: Qumrân Grotte 4, vol. III, ed. Maurice Baillet, Oxford 1982.

The Temple Scroll, ed. Yigael Yadin, 3 vols. + supplementary plates, English ed., Jerusalem 1983.

The Zadokite Documents, ed. Chaim Rabin, 2nd ed., Oxford 1958.

The Dead Sea Scrolls in English, tr. Geza Vermes, 3rd, revised and augmented ed., Harmondsworth 1987.

Rabbinic Literature

Sishah Sidre Mishnah (*The Six Orders of the Mishnah*), ed. Chanoch Albeck, 6 vols., Jerusalem and Tel Aviv 1958–1959.

The Tosefta According to Codex Vienna etc., ed. Saul Lieberman, 4 vols. (the first three orders), New York 1955–1973.

Tosephta, ed. M. S. Zuckermandel, 1875, repr. Jerusalem 1963.

Talmud Yerushalmi, Krotoshin edition, 1866, repr. Jerusalem 1969.

The Mishnah, tr. Herbert Danby, Oxford 1933.
The Tosefta, tr. Jacob Neusner and others, 6 vols., New York 1977–1986.
The Babylonian Talmud, Soncino ed., general ed. I Epstein, 35 vols., London 1935–52, repr. in 18 vols., London 1961.
The Fathers According to Rabbi Nathan, tr. Judah Goldin, New Haven 1955.

Other Jewish Literature and Texts

Corpus Papyrorum Judaicarum, 3 vols., ed. Victor A. Tcherikover and Alexander Fuks, Cambridge, Mass. and Jerusalem 1957, 1960 and 1964.
Josephus, ed. and tr. H. St J. Thackeray (vols. 1–5), Ralph Marcus (vols. 5–8) and Louis Feldman (vols. 9–10), LCL, London and Cambridge, Mass. 1926–1965.
Philo, ed. and tr. F. H. Colson (vols. 1–10) and G. H. Whitaker (vols. 1–5), LCL, London and Cambridge, Mass. 1929–1943.

Early Christian Literature

Justin Martyr, *Dialogue with Trypho*, ed. Georges Archambault, *Textes et documents pour l'étude hist. du christianisme*, 2 vols., Paris 1909.
Justin Martyr, *Dialogue with Trypho*, ET in *The Ante-Nicene Fathers* I, ed. Alexander Roberts and James Donaldson, American repr. ed. A. Cleveland Coxe; repr. Grand Rapids n.d., pp. 194–270.

2. REFERENCE WORKS

Denis, Albert-Marie, *Concordance grecque des Pseudépigraphes d'Ancien Testament*, Leuven and Leiden 1987.
Encyclopaedia Judaica, 16 vols., ed. in chief Cecil Roth, corrected ed., Jerusalem n.d.; vol. 17, Supplement, 1982.
Hatch, Edwin and Henry A. Redpath, *A Concordance to the Septuagint*, 2 vols., Oxford 1897, repr. 1954.
The Interpreter's Dictionary of the Bible, 4 vols., gen. ed. G. A. Buttrick, Nashville 1962; Supplementary Volume, gen. ed. Keith Crim, 1976.
Jastrow, Marcus, *A Dictionary of the Targumim, the Talmud Babli and Yerushalmi, and the Midrashic Literature*, Philadelphia 1903, repr. New York 1950.
Kasovsky, C. Y., *'Otsar Leshon ha-Mishnah*, rev. ed., 4 vols., Tel Aviv 1967.
Kasowski, C. J. (the same as above), *'Otsar Leshon ha-Tosefta*, 6 vols., Jerusalem 1932–1961.
Kittel, Gerhard and Gerhard Friedrich, eds., *Theological Dictionary of the New Testament*, 9 vols., ET ed. G. W. Bromiley, Grand Rapids 1964–1974.
Liddell, Henry George and Robert Scott, *A Greek-English Lexicon*, revised and augmented by Henry Stuart Jones, 9th ed., Oxford 1940.
Lisowsky, Gerhard, *Konkordanz aum hebräischen alten Testament*, Stuttgart 1958.
Moulton, James Hope and George Milligan, *The Vocabulary of the Greek Testament*. Illustrated from the Papyri and other non-literary Sources, London 1930.
Moulton, W. F. and A. S. Geden, *A Concordance to the Greek Testament*, 5th ed. revised by H. K. Moulton, Edinburgh 1978.
Pauly-Wissowa, *Realencyclopädie der klassischen Altertumswissenschaft*.
Rengstorf, Karl Heinrich, *A Complete Concordance to Flavius Josephus*, Leiden 1973–1983.

3. GENERAL

Alon, Gedalyahu, *Jews, Judaism and the Classical World*, ET Jerusalem 1977.
— *Mehqarim be-Toldot Yisra'el* I, Tel Aviv 1967.
Archer, Léonie J. 'The Role of Jewish Women in the Religion, Ritual and Cult of Graeco-Roman Palestine', *Images of Women in Antiquity*, ed. Averil Cameron and Amélie Kuhrt, London 1983, pp. 273–287.
Avigad, Nahman, *Discovering Jerusalem*, ET Nashville 1983.
Bacher, Wilhelm, *Die Agada der Tannaiten* I, Berlin 1903, repr. 1965.
— 'Satzung vom Sinai. Halakhah Le-Mosheh MiSinai', *Studies in Jewish Literature in Honor of Kaufmann Kohler*, ed. David Philipson and others, Berlin 1913, pp. 56–70.
— *Tradition und Tradenten in den Schulen Palästinas und Babyloniens*, Leipzig 1914, repr. 1966.
Barrett, C. K., *The First Epistle to the Corinthians*, New York and London 1968.
— *Essays on Paul*, London 1982.
Baumgarten, Albert I., '*Korban* and the Pharisaic *Paradosis*', *Ancient Studies in Memory of Elias Bickerman. The Journal of the Ancient Near Eastern Society* 16–17, 1984–1985, pp. 5–17.
— 'The Pharisaic *Paradosis*', *Harvard Theological Review* 80, 1987, pp. 63–77.
Ben-Dov, Meir, *In the Shadow of the Temple*, ET New York 1985.
Beyer, Hermann, '*Blasphemeo ktl.*', *TDNT* I, pp. 621–625.
Billerbeck, Paul: *See* Strack.
Bokser, Baruch M., 'The Achievement of Jacob N. Epstein', *The Modern Study of the Mishnah*, ed. Jacob Neusner, S. P.-B. 23, Leiden 1973, pp. 13–55.
Borg, Marcus, *Conflict, Holiness and Politics in the Teaching of Jesus*, New York and Toronto 1984.
— *Jesus: A New Vision*, San Francisco 1987.
Bornkamm, Günther, *Jesus of Nazareth*, ET London and New York 1960.
Brown, Peter, *The Body and Society*, New York and London 1988.
Büchler, A., *Der galiläische 'Am-Ha'ares des zweiten Jahrhunderts*, Vienna 1906, repr. 1968.
— 'The Levitical Impurity of the Gentile in Palestine before the year 70', *JQR* 17, 1926–27, pp. 1–81.
— *Studies in Sin and Atonement in the Rabbinic Literature of the First Century*, London 1929, repr. 1967.
Buehler, William, *The Pre-Herodian Civil War and Social Debate*, Basel 1974.
Bultmann, Rudolf, *History of the Synoptic Tradition*, rev. ET Oxford 1968.
Burkert, Walter, *Greek Religion*, ET Oxford 1985.
— *Homo Necans: The Anthropology of Ancient Greek Sacrificial Ritual and Myth*, ET Berkeley & Los Angeles 1983.
Cadbury, H. J., 'The Macellum of Corinth', *JBL* 53, 1934, pp. 134–141.
Catchpole, D. R., 'The Answer of Jesus to Caiaphas', *NTS* 17, 1971, pp. 213–226.
— *The Trial of Jesus*, S. P.-B. 18, Leiden 1971.
Charlesworth, James H., *Jesus within Judaism*, New York and London 1988.
— Review of Sanders, *Jesus and Judaism*, *JAAR* 55, 1987, p. 622–624.
Clebsch, William A., Review of Neusner, *Judaism: The Evidence of the Mishnah*, *RSR* 9, April 1983, pp. 105–108.

Cohen, Shaye J. D., *From the Maccabees to the Mishnah*, Philadelphia 1987.
— 'Jacob Neusner, Mishnah, and Counter-Rabbinics. A Review Essay', *Conservative Judaism* 37, 1983, pp. 48–63.
— *Josephus in Galilee and Rome*, Columbia Studies in the Classical Tradition 8, Leiden 1979.
— 'Pagan and Christian Evidence on the Ancient Synagogue', *The Synagogue in Late Antiquity*, ed. Levine, pp. 159–181.
Collins, J. J., 'Sibylline Oracles', *OTP* I, pp. 317–472.
Conzelmann, Hans, *A Commentary on the First Epistle to the Corinthians*, Hermeneia, ET Philadelphia 1975.
Daube, David, 'Temple Tax', *Jesus, the Gospels, and the Church*. Essays in Honor of William R. Farmer, ed. E. P. Sanders, Macon 1987, pp. 121–134.
— 'Participle and Imperative in I Peter', in E. G. Selwyn, *The First Epistle of St. Peter*, London 1947, pp. 467–488.
— *The New Testament and Rabbinic Judaism*, London 1956, repr. 1973.
Davies, W. D., *Jewish and Christian Studies*, Philadelphia 1984.
— *The Setting of the Sermon on the Mount*, Cambridge 1964.
Deissmann, Adolf, *Light from the Ancient East*, ET London 1910, repr. 1965.
Detienne, Marcel, 'Culinary Practices and the Spirit of Sacrifice', *The Cuisine of Sacrifice*, ed. Detienne and Vernant, pp. 1–20.
Detienne, Marcel and Jean-Paul Vernant, eds., *The Cuisine of Sacrifice Among the Greeks*, ET Chicago 1989.
Douglas, Mary, *Purity and Danger. An Analysis of the Concepts of Pollution and Taboo*, London 1966, repr. 1984.
Dunn, James D. G., 'The Incident at Antioch (Gal. 2:11–18), *JSNT* 18, 1983, pp. 3–57.
— 'Pharisees, Sinners, and Jesus', *The Social World of Formative Christianity and Judaism*, ed. Jacob Neusner and others, Philadelphia 1988, pp. 264–289.
Durand, Jean-Louis, 'Greek Animals: Toward a Topology of Edible Bodies', in Detienne and Vernant, *The Cuisine of Sacrifice*, pp. 87–118.
Elman, Yaakov, 'The Judaism of the Mishna: What Evidence?', *Judaica Book News* 12, 1982, pp. 17–25.
Epstein, J. N., *Mevo'ot le-Sifrut ha-Tanna'im (Introductions to Tannaitic Literature)*, Jerusalem 1957.
Esler, Philip Francis, *Community and gospel in Luke–Acts. The social and political motivations of Lucan theology*, SNTSMS 57, Cambridge 1987.
Falk, Ze'ev W., *Introduction to Jewish Law of the Second Commonwealth* I, Leiden 1972.
Fauna and Flora of the Bible, UBS Helps for Translators, 2nd ed., 1980.
Finkelstein, Louis, *The Pharisees. The Sociological Background of their Faith*, 2 vols, 3rd ed. with suppl., Philadelphia 1962.
Fitzmyer, Joseph and D. J. Harrington, *A Manual of Palestinian Aramaic Texts, 2nd Century BC – 2nd Century AD*, Rome 1978.
Foerster, G. 'A Survey of Ancient Diaspora Synagogues', *Ancient Synagogues Revealed*, ed. Levine, pp. 164–171.
Frerichs, Ernest S., William Scott Green and Jacob Neusner (eds), *Judaisms and their Messiahs at the Turn of the Christian Era*, Cambridge 1987.
Freyne, Sean, *Galilee, Jesus and the Gospels*. Literary Approaches and Historical Investigations, Dublin 1988.
Gafni, Isaiah, 'Syria', *Enc. Jud.* 15, cols. 636–639.

Gerhardsson, Birger, *Memory and Manuscript*, 2nd ed., ET Uppsala 1964.

Gibson, Shimon, 'The Stone Vessel Industry at Hizma', *IEJ* 33, 1983, pp. 176–188.

Ginouvès, René, *Balaneutikè. Recherches sur le bain dans l'antiquité grecque*. Bibliothèque des Écoles Françaises d'Athènes et de Rome 200, Paris 1962.

Goldin, Judah, 'Avot de-Rabbi Nathan', *Enc. Jud.* 3, cols. 984f.

Goldstein, Jonathan A., *I Maccabees*, AB 41, New York 1976.

— *II Maccabees*, AB 41A, New York 1983.

Goodman, Martin, 'Kosher Olive Oil in Antiquity', forthcoming.

— *The Ruling Class of Judaea*, Cambridge 1987.

— *State and Society in Roman Galilee, A.D. 132–212*, Totowa, NJ 1983.

Grabbe, Lester L., 'Synagogues in Pre-70 Palestine: a Re-assessment', *JTS* 39, 1988, pp. 401–410.

Green, William Scott (ed.), *Approaches to Ancient Judaism* II, BJS 9, Chico 1980.

Griffiths, J. Gwyn, 'Egypt and the Rise of the Synagogue', *JTS* 38, 1987, pp. 1–15.

Gruber, Mayer I., 'The Mishnah as Oral Torah: A Reconsideration', *JSJ* 15, 1984, pp. 112–122.

Gutmann, Joseph (ed.), *Ancient Synagogues: The State of Research*, BJS 22, Atlanta 1981.

— (ed.), *The Synagogue: Studies in Origins, Archaeology and Architecture*, New York 1975.

Halivni, David Weiss, 'The Reception Accorded to Rabbi Judah's Mishnah', *Jewish and Christian Self-Definition II: Aspects of Judaism in the Graeco-Roman Period*, ed. E. P. Sanders and others, London and Philadelphia 1981, pp. 204–212.

Hanfmann, George M. A., 'The Ninth Campaign at Sardis (1966)', *BASOR* 186, April 1967, pp. 17–52, and *BASOR* 187, October 1967, pp. 9–62.

— *Sardis from Prehistoric to Roman Times*. Results of the Archaeological Exploration of Sardis 1958–1975, Cambridge, Mass. 1983.

Harrison, R. K., *Leviticus: An Introduction and Commentary*, Tyndale OT Commentaries, Leicester 1980.

Hartog, François, 'Self-cooking Beef and the Drinks of Ares', *The Cuisine of Sacrifice*, ed. Detienne and Vernant, pp. 170–182.

Heinemann, Joseph, *Prayer in the Talmud: Forms and Patterns*, Studia Judaica 9, ET Berlin and New York 1977.

Hengel, Martin, *The Charismatic Leader and His Followers*, ET Edinburgh and Philadelphia 1981.

— 'Proseuche und Synagoge: Jüdische Gemeinde, Gotteshaus und Gottesdienst in der Diaspora und in Palästina', *Tradition und Glaube. Das frühe Christentum in seiner Umwelt*. Festgabe für Karl Georg Kuhn, ed. G. Jeremias, H. W. Kuhn and Hartmut Stegemann, Göttingen 1971, pp. 157–184. Also in Gutmann 1975.

— *Studies in the Gospel of Mark*, ET London and Philadelphia 1985.

— 'Die Synagogeninschrift von Stobi', *ZNW* 57, 1966, pp. 145–183.

Herr, Moshe David, 'Fasting and Fast Days', *Enc. Jud.* 6, cols. 1189–1195.

— 'Mekhilta of R. Ishmael', *Enc. Jud.* 11, cols. 1267–1269.

— 'Oral Law', *Enc. Jud.* 12, cols. 1439–1442.

Herz, Peter, *Studien zur römischen Wirtschaftsgesetzgebung: Die Lebensmittelversorgung*. Historia Einzelschriften 55, Stuttgart 1988.

Hillerbrand, Hans, *The Protestant Reformation*, The Documentary History of Western Civilization, London 1968.

Hooker, Morna D., *The Son of Man in Mark*, Montreal and London 1967.

van der Horst, P. W., 'Pseudo-Phocylides', *OTP* II, pp. 565–582.

Houlden, J. L., Review of Neusner, *Judaism in the beginning of Christianity*, *TLS* April 5, 1985, p. 391.

Jeremias, Joachim, *Jerusalem in the Time of Jesus*, ET London 1969.

— *The Proclamation of Jesus*, ET London 1971.

Kee, Howard Clark, 'The Transformation of the Synagogue after 70 CE', *NTS* 36, 1990, pp. 1–24.

Kilpatrick, G. D., *The Trial of Jesus*, Oxford 1953.

Köster, Kurt, *Die Lebensmittelversorgung der altgriechischen Polis*, Berlin 1939.

Kotlar, David, 'Mikveh', *Enc. Jud.* 11, cols. 1534–1544.

Kraabel, A. Thomas, 'The Diaspora Synagogue: Archaeological and Epigraphic Evidence since Sukenik', *ANRW* II.19.1, 1979, pp. 477–510.

— 'Social Systems of Six Diaspora Synagogues', *Ancient Synagogues*, ed. Gutmann, pp. 79–91.

— 'Unity and Diversity among Diaspora Synagogues', in *The Synagogue in Late Antiquity*, ed. Levine, pp. 49–60.

Kuhn, K. G., 'Phylakterien aus Höhle 4 von Qumran', *Abhandlungen der Heidelberger Akademie der Wissenschaften, Philosophisch-Historische Klasse*, 1. Abhandlung, Heidelberg 1957.

Lake, Kirsopp, *The Earlier Epistles of St. Paul*, London 1911.

Latte, Kurt, 'Mageiros', *Pauly-Wissowa* 14.1, cols. 393–395.

Levine, Lee I. (ed.), *Ancient Synagogues Revealed*, Jerusalem 1981.

— (ed.), *The Jerusalem Cathedra*. Studies in the History, Archaeology, Geography and Ethnography of the Land of Israel, vol. 2, Jerusalem and Detroit, 1982.

— 'The Second Temple Synagogue: The Formative Years', in *The Synagogue in Late Antiquity*, ed. Levine, pp. 7–31.

— (ed.), *The Synagogue in Late Antiquity*, Philadelphia, ASOR, 1987.

Lieberman, Saul, *Greek in Jewish Palestine*, 2nd ed., New York 1965.

— *Tosefta Ki-Fshutah* 9 vols., New York 1955–1973.

— 'A Tragedy or a Comedy?', *JAOS* 104, 1984, pp. 315–319.

Maccoby, Hyam, 'Authenticating the authoritative', *TLS*, August 13 1982, p. 887.

— 'Jacob Neusner's Mishnah', *Midstream*, May 1984.

Mason, S. N., 'Priesthood in Josephus and the "Pharisaic Revolution"', *JBL* 107, 1988, pp. 657–661.

Mazar, Benjamin, 'Herodian Jerusalem in the Light of the Excavations South and South-West of the Temple Mount', *IEJ* 28, 1978, pp. 230–237.

Mazar, Benjamin and I. Dunayevsky, 'En-Gedi. Fourth and Fifth Seasons of Excavations – Preliminary Report', *IEJ* 17, 1967, pp. 133–143.

Meuli, Karl, *Gesammelte Schriften*, 2 vols., ed. Thomas Gelzer, Basel and Stuttgart, 1975.

Meyers, Eric M., Ehud Netzer and Carol L. Meyers, 'Sepphoris, "Ornament of Galilee"', *BA* 49, March 1986, pp. 4–19.

Moehring, Horst, 'The Acta *Pro Judaeis* in the *Antiquities* of Flavius Josephus', *Christianity, Judaism and other Graeco-Roman Cults*. Studies for Morton Smith at Sixty, ed. Jacob Neusner, part 3, Leiden 1975, pp. 125–158.

Moore, George Foot, *Judaism in the First Centuries of the Christian Era*, 3 vols., Cambridge, Mass. 1927–1930.

Netzer, Ehud, 'Ancient Ritual Baths (*Miqvaot*) in Jericho', *The Jerusalem Cathedra* 2, ed. Levine, pp. 106–119.

— *Greater Herodium. Qedem* 13, Jerusalem 1981.

Neubauer, Adolphe, *La Géographie du Talmud*, Paris 1868.

Neusner, Jacob, '"Covenantal Nomism". The Piety of Judaism in the First Century', *Major Trends in Formative Judaism*, 3rd series, *The Three Stages in the Formation of Judaism*, BJS 99, Chico 1985, pp. 9–34.

— *Formative Judaism: Religious, Historical and Literary Studies*, 3rd series, *Torah, Pharisees, and Rabbis*, BJS 47, Chico 1983.

— *From Politics to Piety: The Emergence of Pharisaic Judaism*, Englewood Cliffs 1973.

— 'From Scripture to Mishnah. The Origins of Tractate Niddah', *JJS* 29, 1978, pp. 135–148.

— *A History of the Mishnaic Law of Appointed Times*, 5 vols., Leiden 1981–1982.

— *A History of the Mishnaic Law of Damages*, 5 vols., Leiden 1982.

— *A History of the Mishnaic Law of Purities*, 22 vols., Leiden 1974–1977.

— *A History of the Mishnaic Law of Women*, 5 vols., Leiden 1979–80.

— *The Idea of Purity in Ancient Judaism*, with a critique and commentary by Mary Douglas, SJLA 1, Leiden 1973.

— *Judaism: The Evidence of the Mishnah*, Chicago 1981. Cited as *Judaisim*.

—— (ed.), *Judaisms and their Messiahs*: see Frerichs.

— *Judaism in the beginning of Christianity*, Philadelphia and London 1984.

— *Messiah in Context: Israel's History and Destiny in Formative Judaism*, Philadelphia 1984.

— *Midrash in Context: Exegesis in Formative Judaism*, Philadelphia 1983.

— 'The Mishnah and the Smudgepots', *Midstream*, June/July 1986, pp. 40–46.

— *The Mishnah before 70*, BJS 51, Atlanta 1987.

— *The Oral Torah: The Sacred Books of Judaism*. An Introduction, San Francisco 1986.

— 'Parsing the Rabbinic Canon with the History of an Idea: The Messiah', *Formative Judaism*, 3rd series, pp. 173–198.

— *Rabbinic Traditions About the Pharisees Before 70*, 3 vols., Leiden 1971.

— *Reading and Believing*, BJS 113, Atlanta 1986.

— *Scriptures of the Oral Torah: Sanctification and Salvation in the Sacred Books of Judaism*, San Francisco 1987.

— 'The Talmud as Anthropology', Annual Samuel Friedland Lecture, The Jewish Theological Seminary of America, New York 1979.

— 'The Theological Enemies of Religious Studies. Theology and Secularism in the Trivialization and Personalization of Religion in the West', *Religion* 18, 1988, pp. 21–35.

— *Torah: From Scroll to Symbol in Formative Judaism*, Philadelphia 1985. Cited as *Torah*.

— 'The Use of the Later Rabbinic Evidence for the Study of Paul', *Approaches to Ancient Judaism* II, ed. Green, pp. 43–63.

Newport, Kenneth, *The Sources and Sitz im Leben of Matthew 23*, D. Phil. thesis, Oxford University, 1988.

Newton, Michael, *The Concept of Purity at Qumran and in the Letters of Paul*, SNTSMS 53, Cambridge 1985.

Nickelsburg, G. W. E., 'Stories of Biblical and Early Post-Biblical Times', *Jewish Writings of the Second Temple Period* (CRINT II.2), ed. Michael E. Stone, Assen and Philadelphia 1984.

— *Jewish Literature between the Bible and the Mishnah*, Philadelphia and London 1981.

Noth, Martin, *Leviticus. A Commentary*, ET London 1965.

Perrin, Norman, *Rediscovering the Teaching of Jesus*, London and New York 1967.

Petuchowski, Jakob J., Review of Neusner, *Judaism: The Evidence of the Mishnah*, *RSR* 9, April 1983, pp. 108–13f.

Pohlenz, Max, *Die Stoa: Geschichte einer geistigen Bewegung*, 2 vols., 2nd ed., Göttingen 1959.

Pope, M. H., 'Oaths', *IDB* 3, pp. 575–577.

Qimron, Elisha and John Strugnell, 'An Unpublished Halakhic Letter from Qumran', *Biblical Archaeology Today*, ed. Joseph Aviram and others 1985, pp. 400–407.

Rabinowitz, L. I., 'Vows and vowing', *Enc. Jud.* 16, cols. 227f.

Rajak, Tessa, 'Jews and Christians as Groups in a Pagan World', *'To See Ourselves as Others See Us': Christians, Jews, 'Others' in Late Antiquity*, ed. J. Neusner and F. Frerichs, Chico 1985, pp. 248–262.

— *Josephus: The Historian and His Society*, London 1983.

Reich, Ronny, 'Four Notes on Jerusalem', *IEJ* 37, 1987, pp. 158–167.

— 'The Hot Bath-House (*balneum*), the Miqweh and the Jewish Community in the Second Temple Period', *JJS* 39, 1988, pp. 102–107.

— 'A *Miqweh* at 'Isawiya near Jerusalem', *IEJ* 34, 1984, pp. 220–223 and Plate 28.

— 'Mishnah Sheqalim 8:2 and the Archaeological Evidence', *Jerusalem in the Second Temple Period*, ed. A. Oppenheimer and others, Jerusalem 1980, pp. 225–256 (Hebrew).

— 'Two Possible *Miqwa'ot* on the Temple Mount', *IEJ* 39, 1989, pp. 63–65.

Rivkin, Ellis, 'Defining the Pharisees: the Tannaitic Sources', *HUCA* 40–41, 1969–70, pp. 205–249.

— *A Hidden Revolution*, Nashville 1968.

— *What Crucified Jesus?*, Nashville 1984 and London 1986.

Safrai, Shmuel, 'Jewish Self-government', *The Jewish People in the First Century* (CRINT I.1), ed. Safrai and Stern, Assen 1974, pp. 377–419.

— 'Oral Tora', *The Literature of the Sages*, part 1 (CRINT II.3.1), ed. Safrai, Assen and Philadelphia 1987, pp. 35–119.

— 'Relations between the Diaspora and the Land of Israel', *The Jewish People in the First Century* (CRINT I.1), pp. 184–215.

Sanders, E. P., 'The Covenant as a Soteriological Category and the Nature of Salvation in Palestinian and Hellenistic Judaism', *Jews, Greeks and Christians: Religious Cultures in Late Antiquity*. Essays in Honor of William David Davies, ed. Robert Hamerton-Kelly and Robin Scroggs, SJLA 21, Leiden 1976, pp. 11–44.

— *Jesus and Judaism*, London and Philadelphia 1985.

— 'Jewish Association with Gentiles and Galatians 2:11–14', *The Conversation Continues*. Essays on Paul and John Presented to J. Louis Martyn, ed. Robert Fortna and Beverly Gaventa, Nashville 1990.

— 'Law (Judaism, NT Period)', *Anchor Bible Dictionary*, forthcoming.

— *Paul, the Law and the Jewish People*, Philadelphia 1983 and London 1985.

— *Paul and Palestinian Judaism*, London and Philadelphia 1977.

— 'Puzzling Out Rabbinic Judaism', *Approaches to Ancient Judaism* II, ed. Green, pp. 65–79.

— Review of Neusner, *Judaism in the Beginnings of Christianity*, *Theology* 88, 1985, pp. 392f.

— Review of Neusner, *Reading and Believing*, *Journal of Religion* 68, 1988, pp. 333–336.

Sanders, E. P. and Margaret Davies, *Studying the Synoptic Gospels*, London and Philadelphia 1989.

Schäfer, Peter, *Der Bar Kokhba-Aufstand*, Tübingen 1981.

— 'Rabbi Aqiva and Bar Kokhba', *Approaches to Ancient Judaism* II, ed. Green, pp. 113–130.

— *Studien zur Geschichte und Theologie des rabbinischen Judentums*, Arbeiten zur Geschichte des antiken Judentums und des Urchristentums 15, Leiden 1978.

Schiffman, Lawrence H. 'The Dead Sea Scrolls and the Early History of Jewish Liturgy', in *The Synagogue in Late Antiquity*, ed. Levine, pp. 7–31.

Schrage, Wolfgang, '*Synagōgē*', *TDNT* VII, pp. 798–841.

Schürer, Emil, *A History of the Jewish People in the Time of Jesus Christ*, 3 vols. in 5 parts, ET Edinburgh 1885–1891.

— *The History of the Jewish people in the age of Jesus Christ*, New English version revised and edited by Geza Vermes, Fergus Millar and Martin Goodman (vol. III only), 3 vols. in 4 parts, Edinburgh 1973–1987. (Cited as Schürer/Vermes/Millar, *HJP*, or Schürer/Vermes/Millar/Goodman, *HJP*.)

Schwartz, Daniel, 'Josephus and Nicolaus on the Pharisees', *JSJ* 14, 1983, pp. 157–171.

Schweizer, Eduard, *Jesus*, ET London 1971.

Seager, Andrew R., 'The Building', in the section 'The Synagogue and the Jewish Community', in Hanfmann, *Sardis from Prehistoric to Roman Times*, pp. 168–78.

— 'The Synagogue at Sardis', *Ancient Synagogues Revealed*, ed. Levine, pp. 178–184.

Segal, Alan, 'Covenant in Rabbinic Writings', *Studies in Religion/Sciences Religieuses* 14, 1985, pp. 53–62.

— *Rebecca's Children· Judaism and Christianity in the Roman World*, Cambridge, Mass. 1986.

Shutt, R. J. H., 'Letter of Aristeas', *OTP* II, pp. 7–34.

Small, David B., 'Late Hellenistic Baths in Palestine', *BASOR* 266, 1987, pp. 59–74.

Smallwood, Mary, *The Jews under Roman Rule from Pompey to Diocletian. A study in political relations*, SJLA 10, Leiden 1976, repr. 1981.

Smith, Morton, 'Palestinian Judaism in the First Century', repr. in *Essays in Greco-Roman and Related Talmudic Literature*, ed. H. A. Fischel, New York 1977, pp. 183–197.

Spiro, Solomon, 'Who was the *Haber*? A New Approach to an Ancient Institution', *JSJ* 11, 1980, pp. 186–216.

Stauffer, Ethelbert, *Jesus and his Story*, ET London 1960.

Stern, Menahem, *Greek and Latin Authors on Jews and Judaism*, 3 vols., Jerusalem 1976–1984.

Sternberg, Eliezer and Haim Hermann Cohn, 'Weights and Measures', *Enc. Jud.* 16, cols. 376–392.

Strack, Hermann and Paul Billerbeck, *Kommentar zum Neuen Testament aus Talmud und Midrasch*, 4 vols. in 5 parts, 1924–1928.

Sukenik, E. L., *Ancient Synagogues in Palestine and Greece*, London 1934.

Sussmann, J., 'The Inscription in the Synagogue at Rehob', *Ancient Synagogues Revealed*, ed. Levine, pp. 146–153.

Ta-Shma, I. M., 'Niddah', *Enc. Jud.* 12, cols. 1141–1148.

Taylor, Vincent, *The Gospel According to St. Mark*, London 1959.

Theissen, Gerd, *The First Followers of Jesus: A Sociological Analysis of the Earliest Christianity*, ET London 1978 (=*Sociology of Early Palestinian Christianity*, Philadelphia 1978).

Du Toit, A. B., 'Hyperbolical Contrasts: A Neglected Aspect of Paul's Style', *A South African Perspective on the New Testament*. Essays . . . presented to Bruce Manning Metzger, ed. J. H. Petzer and P. J. Martin, Leiden 1986, pp. 178– 186.

Urbach, Ephraim E., *The Sages: Their Concepts and Beliefs*, ET Jerusalem 1975.

Vermes, Geza, *Jesus the Jew*, London 1973 and New York 1974.

— *The Dead Sea Scrolls: Qumran in Perspective*, London 1977.

Vernant, Jean-Pierre, 'At Man's Table: Hesiod's Foundation Myth of Sacrifice', *The Cuisine of Sacrifice*, ed. Detienne and Vernant, pp. 21–86.

Whittaker, Molly, *Jews and Christians: Graeco-Roman Views*, Cambridge 1984.

Weingreen, J., *From Bible to Mishna: The continuity of tradition*, Manchester 1976.

Wischnitzer, Mark, 'Tithe', *Enc. Jud.* 15, cols. 1156–1162.

Wood, Bryant G., 'To Dip or Sprinkle? The Qumran Cisterns in Perspective', *BASOR* 256, 1984, pp. 45–61.

Wolfson, H. A., *Philo: Foundations of Religious Philosophy in Judaism, Christianity, and Islam*, 2 vols., revised ed., Cambridge, Mass. 1962.

Yadin, Yigael, 'The excavation at Masada – 1963/64, Preliminary Report', *IEJ* 15, 1965, nos. 1–2.

— *Masada: Herod's Fortress and the Zealots' Last Stand*, ET Jerusalem 1966.

Zeitlin, Solomon, *The Rise and Fall of the Judaean State*, vol. II, *37 BCE – 66 CE*, 2nd ed., Philadelphia 1969.

Ziehen, Ludwig, 'Sphagia', *Pauly-Wissowa*, Zweite Reihe, sechster Halbband, 1929, cols. 1669–1679.

Index of Passages

BIBLE

OLD TESTAMENT

NEW TESTAMENT

APOCRYPHA AND PSEUDEPIGRAPHA

JOSEPHUS

PHILO

RABBINIC LITERATURE

MISHNAH

TOSEFTA

BABYLONIAN TALMUD

PALESTINIAN TALMUD

OTHER RABBINIC LITERATURE

ESSENE LITERATURE

OTHER ANCIENT SOURCES

Index of Names

Index of Subjects

Ablutions, Diaspora, 258–72; pagan, 262–63, 268, 270; *see also* Purity: Handwashing, Immersion; Sea

Aboth, date of, 113; as pseudonymous, 327

'Amme ha-'arets/ordinary people, 16, 33, 35, 36, 47, 106, 128, 152, 154, 188–190, 207–8, 231, 232–33, 237–39, 240–42, 247, 248, 250, 358 n. 2; trustworthiness of, 238–39, 248, 304

Analogy, arguments from, 11, 20–22, 90

Antioch, dispute in, 283–84, 307–308

'Antitheses', 93–94

Aparchē(ai), 285, 288–90, 291, 292–99, 306; *see also* First fruits

Aristeas, Letter of, date of, 335 n. 3

Aristocrats, aristocracy, 31, 40, 45, 79–80, 102, 160; immersion pools, 219–27; hair styles, 353 n. 7

Asceticism, 335 n. 1

Basins (for purification), 259 and n. 10 (361), 263–64, 267–68, 269–70

Beer, 145–46

Blasphemy, in OT, 57; LXX, 58; Josephus, 58–59; Philo, 59–60; Mishnah, 60; Essenes, 60; Synoptic gospels, 60–65, 92

Calendar, 85, 103–4, 358 n. 8

Charity, 71, 182, 237, 242

Civil and family law, 14, 244–45

Coercion (and lack thereof), 12, 22–23 and n. 17 (334), 35–36, 40, 88, 108, 190, 192, 237, 246; *see also* Tolerance

Conflict/disagreement, and death, 3, 86–87, 94; over law, 4, 9, 12, 22–23, 32, 35–36, 37, 40–41, 55–56, 84–89, 94–96, 213, 224–27, 230, 239–40

Confusion, 111, 162–65, 182, 324, 325, 331, 341–43 n. 29

Counting, 14–16, 177–81, 200, 235; *see also* Importance

Courts: *see* Punishment

Diaspora, Jewish, relation to Palestine, 256–57, 283–308

Divorce, 3, 5, 91, 94, 98

Eighteen Benedictions, 72 and n. 10 (340), 254, 331; *see also* Liturgy; Prayer

Eighteen Decrees, 87–88, 224–27

Elders, 79

'Êrûb, eruv, 9, 22, 106–107, 123

Essenes,
  Origin of, 84
  Branches of, 15–16, 26, 53, 344 n. 1
  And other Jews, 84–85 and n. 6 (344), 328; sect, in contrast to Pharisees, 241; sect, but belonged to 'Judaism', 328; and Gentiles, 26